About the Authors of *Management Information Systems: A Contemporary Perspective*

Kenneth C. Laudon is Professor of Information Systems at New York University's Graduate School of Business. He holds a B.A. in Economics from Stanford and a Ph.D. from Columbia University. His books include *Computers and Bureaucratic Reform, Communications Technology and Participation*, and *Dossier Society*. Professor Laudon has also authored numerous articles in professional journals concerned with the organizational and social impacts of computerized information systems. Professor Laudon has testified as an expert before the United States Congress. He has been a consultant to the Office of Technology Assessment, the Office of the President, several executive branch agencies, and many Congressional Committees. Professor Laudon also acts as a consultant on systems planning and strategy to several Fortune 500 firms.

Professor Laudon's current research is on the planning and management of very large scale information systems for the 1990s. This research is funded by the National Science Foundation.

Ken Laudon's principal hobby is sailing in New England.

Jane Price Laudon is a management consultant in the information systems area and a professional writer. She specializes in systems analysis and design, data administration, data management, system controls, EDP auditing, and software evaluation.

Jane received her Ph.D from Columbia University. She has taught at Columbia University and the New York University Graduate School of Business. The author of three books, she maintains a lifelong interest in Oriental languages and civilizations.

The Laudons have two daughters, Erica and Elisabeth.

Management Information Systems: A Contemporary Perspective, is the first book the Laudons have written together. This book reflects a deep understanding of MIS research and teaching as well as practical experience designing and building real world systems.

MACMILLAN SERIES IN INFORMATION SYSTEMS

Henry C. Lucas Jr.
New York University
Consulting Editor

MANAGEMENT INFORMATION SYSTEMS

A Contemporary Perspective

Kenneth C. Laudon

New York University

Jane Price Laudon

Azimuth Corporation

Macmillan Publishing Company

New York

Collier Macmillan Publishers

London

Macmillan Publishing Company
866 Third Avenue, New York, New York 10022

Collier Macmillan Canada, Inc.

Library of Congress Cataloging-in-Publication Data

Laudon, Kenneth C.
  Management information systems.

  Includes index.
  1. Management information systems.   I. Laudon, Jane
Price.   II. Title.
T58.6.L376   1988   658.4'038   87-11163
ISBN 0-02-368100-4

Printing: 5 6 7 8   Year: 9 0 1 2 3 4 5 6 7

ISBN   0-02-368100-4

Dedicated to **Erica and Elisabeth**

Preface

This book is based on the premise that professional managers in both the private and public sectors cannot afford to ignore information systems. Information systems have become so vital to the management, organization, operation, and products of large organizations that they are too important to be left to technicians. A few years ago, this statement was not true.

Briefly, it is difficult—if not impossible—to manage a modern organization without at least some grounding in the fundamentals of what information systems are and how they affect the organization and its employees.

Accordingly, this book has been written for nontechnical undergraduate and MBA students in finance, accounting, management, and the liberal arts who will find a knowledge of information systems vital for their professional success. This book may also serve as a first course for students who subsequently major in information systems at either the undergraduate or graduate level.

The book reflects major trends in the systems and organizations of the late 1980s. Three related trends are apparent. The development of powerful microprocessors and telecommunications networks means that we can now put what used to be called a mainframe computer on every desk. Second, these changes in technical capacity have brought about a change in the role and conception of information from that of a nuisance to that of a strategic resource. Third, changes in technical capacity and the role of information are bringing about changes in the role of management and in organizational structure.

One result of these changes is that the work of organizations depends increasingly on what its information systems are capable of doing. Increasing market share, becoming the low-cost producer, developing new products, and/or increasing employee productivity depend more and more on the kinds and quality of information systems in the organization.

A second result of the new role of information systems is that managers are not only expected to use systems but are also expected to:

- Participate in the design of systems.
- Manage the procurement of systems.

- Devise controls over systems.
- Critique existing systems and suggest alternatives.
- Choose among alternative telecommunications options.
- Manage and control the influence of systems on employees and customers.
- Allocate resources to competing system alternatives.
- Suggest new uses for systems.

These new management responsibilities require a deeper understanding of systems than ever before.

Although this book is addressed primarily to private organizations, public sector managers are no less susceptible to these trends and changes in management and organization.

This book was intended as a second-generation book to reflect these new underlying realities. Four major new thrusts in this book distinguish it from previous works:

- The organizational and management foundations of information systems.
- The strategic role of information resources.
- The use of systems analysis and design techniques to build systems.
- The management of information resources.

These thrusts can be identified easily by examining the Table of Contents. Part I is concerned with the organizational foundations of systems and their emerging strategic role. Part II provides a traditional technical foundation for understanding computers and information systems. Part III emphasizes systems analysis and design. Part IV is devoted to management of the information resource.

Key topics include the following:

- The strategic role of systems.
- Tools and techniques for analysis and design.
- Alternatives to traditional analysis and design.
- Artificial intelligence applications.
- Managing information resources.
- Causes of systems success and failure.
- Management of microcomputing.
- Management of telecommunications.

This book makes a large stylistic departure from previous works. Each chapter begins with a small case study describing a systems development at a major firm or organization that is appropriate to the chapter. Throughout each chapter, we have included many short vignettes drawn from the real systems world to illustrate concepts. At the end of each chapter, we have provided a small case study drawn once again from the real world of systems applications. Finally, at the end of each part of the book, there is a major case study.

In all, there are 40 short case studies, 5 major case studies, and over 70 vignettes drawn from industry sources. These examples describe how well-known, major American corporations are using information systems.

The purpose of these case studies is to dramatize the realism and importance of the issues discussed. The world of information systems is exciting and dynamic. The cases and vignetttes help to explain the material, heighten interest, and provide practical examples. These cases are also useful as in-class discussion material. Students and instructors alike should find the reading insightful and at times provocative.

The emphasis on realism and practical examples reflects in part the unique backgrounds of the authors as practitioners. Kenneth Laudon, in addition to teaching and writing academic books and articles, has had 15 years of experience as a consultant in the planning and implementation of very large information systems in both the public and private sectors. Jane Laudon is a management consultant in the systems area with 10 years of experience in planning, designing, and implementing systems.

Resources

This book was developed over 6 years from MBA and financial executive courses taught at the Graduate School of Business, New York University. For many students, this was their only course in systems. For many others, this introductory course became the first course of their major.

We have found microcomputers to be an excellent way of illustrating the concepts of the course. Included in the support package for the text is a series of optional management software cases called **Solve it!**. **Solve it!** consists of management cases (diskette and workbook) that can be solved using any personal computer spreadsheet or database software. Three different sets of **Solve it!** cases are available: spreadsheet cases, database cases, and combination cases. The **Solve it!** cases are drawn from real-world management problems, ranging from Main Street small businesses to Wall Street banking firms. The emphasis is on student discovery of how to use computer software to solve management problems in organization, coordination, analysis, and decision making. The cases also reinforce key concepts in the text concerning files, databases, microcomputers, and systems analysis and design.

The systems analysis and design exercises concluding Chapters 11 and 12 can be hand drawn. Many of the illustrations were drawn using a microcomputer-based product: Flowcharting from Patton and Patton Software, San Jose, California. Students in our classes find this software inexpensive and very useful for system and organization diagrams.

Book Outline

The four parts of the book are designed to be relatively independent of each other. Each instructor may choose to emphasize different parts.

Part I provides an extensive introduction to real-world systems and focuses on how systems fit into the larger literature on organizations and management. These chapters are important for understanding the larger environment in which systems operate. Chapter 4 in particular illustrates how systems must adjust to an environment of competition and organizational politics. Chapter 5 describes how systems must be built in order to serve management interests and decision-making behavior.

Part II provides a background in computer hardware and software. Increasingly, students come to class with much of this knowledge from previous courses. For such students, Chapters 6 and 7 may be skipped. Students are less well prepared in database concepts (Chapter 8), and most students find this material helpful in understanding microcomputer database software. Chapter 9 describes telecommunications systems, an area familiar to few students. Chapter 10 describes the implications of microcomputing and the difficulties of managing microcomputers.

Part III, the largest section of the book, focuses on systems analysis and design—the art of building systems. Increasingly, in our own courses, we find students very interested in how to build systems. Moreover, in the professional literature, systems analysis and design is an area of immense change due to the introduction of powerful microcomputers, fourth-generation languages, decision support systems, and computer-aided design tools. In this part the students can put to work the material on the strategic role of systems, organization, and management learned in Part I.

Example systems analysis and design exercises are included at the end of Chapter 11. In general, we find that students are most interested in building systems for organizations that they can easily contact and identify. University systems—from the registrar and bursar to the career development office—provide excellent, if sometimes unwilling, examples.

Part IV concludes the book with a focus on how to manage

information resources (Chapter 20) and information systems (Chapter 21) successfully. Both of these chapters reopen the question of how systems fit into organizations—a question raised initially in Part I. Most students find these discussions very exciting because they provide a broad overview of how information systems relate to organizational design, strategy, and operations.

Chapter Outline

We have made every effort to ensure that each chapter is lively, informative, and sometimes provocative of further thought and debate. Each chapter contains the following:

- A detailed outline at the beginning to provide an overview.
- An opening case study to establish the theme and importance of the chapter.
- A list of learning objectives at the beginning.
- A chapter summary that identifies significant themes and topics.
- A list of key terms that the student can use to review concepts.
- A number of review questions that students can use to test their comprehension of the material.
- A set of discussion questions that can be used for class or study group discussion or as research topics.
- A case study at the end of each chapter that illustrates important themes.
- A list of references at the end of each chapter for further research on topics.

Major Case Studies

At the end of each part, there are major case studies that describe important system developments at well-known firms and organizations: the Social Security Administration, the Chrysler Corporation, and the Ocean Spray Corporation. These major case studies integrate the major themes of each section. These cases can be used for class discussion or term projects.

Acknowledgments

The production of any book involves many silent partners and valuable contributions from a number of persons. We would like to thank in particular our editors at Macmillan for encouragement, insight, and strong support for the duration of this project. Ron Stefanski, who guided most of the project, provided close support during our learning process and sustained our enthusiasm during the writing. William Oldsey and Charles Stewart lent their expertise and support to the final stages of the project. Special thanks to Jack Repchek for his encouragement.

Many of the critical ideas in the book were developed over a number of years in conversations with colleagues at many universities and comments from students at NYU. Special thanks go to Ken Kraemer, Rob Kling, John King, and Nick Vitalari at the University of California (Irvine); Lynne Markus (UCLA); Helmet Krcmar (CUNY); James B. Rule (State University of New York Stony Brook); and Alan F. Westin (Columbia University).

Laura Spadafino and Edward Cahill read early drafts of the entire manuscript with the eye of real-world practitioners.

The NYU Graduate School of Business and the Information Systems Department provided a very special learning environment, one in which we and others could rethink the MIS field. Special thanks to Henry C. Lucas (editor of this series), Margrethe Olson, Jon Turner, Ted Stohr, and Jack Baroudi. Vasant Dhar provided critical remarks on Chapter 17, and Bill Sasso and Barry Floyd helped shape some of the ideas in Chapters 12 and 13.

K.C.L.
J.P.L.

Contents

PART THREE: Building Information Systems: Contemporary Tools, Techniques and Approaches 337

PART FOUR: Managing Information System Resources 639

PART ONE

Organizational Foundations of Information Systems

Contemporary information systems are both technical and social in nature. Managers must understand the relationship between information systems and the structure, functions, and politics of organizations. Information systems must be responsive to management interests and decision-making processes as well. Part One places information systems in the context of organizations and highlights their strategic role.

Chapter 1 introduces the concept of an information system and illustrates the role that information systems play in organizations. There are many different kinds of information systems and they support different organizational levels and functions. Because information systems involve both technical and behavioral challenges, there are many relevant perspectives.

Chapter 2 provides realistic examples of the five major types of information systems in organizations: Transaction Processing Systems; Management Information Systems; Office Automation Systems; Decision Support Systems; and Executive Support Systems. These various systems serve different purposes and different audiences in the organization.

Chapter 3 highlights the strategic role that can be played by information systems in organizations today. Strategic information systems have transformed organizations' products and services; relationships with customers and suppliers; and internal operations. Leading U.S. corporations have used information technology for competitive

1

advantage. To use information systems strategically, organizations may have to undergo extensive change.

Chapter 4 explores the relationship between organizations and information systems. Information systems are intimately tied to organizational structure, culture, political processes, management, and work. Organizations build information systems for a variety of reasons: sometimes to gain new efficiencies, other times to preserve market share or to match a competitor.

Chapter 5 examines how systems can support management decision making. An important first step is to understand how managers actually make decisions. As it turns out, this is not a simple matter. The chapter compares individual and organizational models of decision making and shows how information systems should be designed to support managerial decision making and work.

Part One Case Study: "Chrysler Corporation System Strategy: Technology Plus Management Theory Equals Formidable Automation Strategy". This case illustrates how information systems can be used effectively for strategic advantage. One key part of the answer is that organizations must change in order to match technology to the nature of the problem. Chrysler's investment in automation and new information systems has fueled its accomplishments in product development and manufacturing strategy.

CHAPTER 1

Introduction to Information Systems

■ OUTLINE

(Continued on next page)

"We don't just deliver packages. We deliver information with them for customer peace of mind," says Harry Dalton, the managing director of systems engineering and design for Federal Express. Federal Express ships more overnight packages, while charging more per package, than any other overnight delivery service. It has outpaced its rivals in a highly competitive area by using information systems to ease customers' fears that packages will be late or lost.

Federal Express uses a series of integrated systems to deliver packages on time while tracking them at every point along the route to their final destination. Regional order-taking centers automatically transmit customer pickup information to local dispatching centers, which in turn radio this information to 9000 Federal Express couriers. Inside each Federal Express truck, a small computer tracks packages and keeps drivers informed of their delivery schedules and locations. The truck computer is connected to Federal Express's main computers through an FM radio telecommunications link. Couriers have been known to arrive while the customer is still making the shipping arrangements with the company. Each package airbill contains a bar code that is scanned at several points in transit. The scanned data are fed via telecommunications links to a central computer, where it can be accessed for customer inquiries about a package's progress. Federal Express can sort its packages automatically and can prepare bills on computer terminals without using any paper.

Adapted from "Redefining an Industry through Integrated Automation," *Infosystems*, May 1985.

Federal Express illustrates the new role that information systems have come to play in organizations and industries. Aside from keeping track of orders and bills, information systems today play a strategic role in business by defining new products and services, maintaining a competitive edge, and providing new opportunities for management control.

In this chapter the student will learn:
- How to define an information system.
- The difference between computer literacy and systems literacy.
- Why managers at all levels must understand information systems.
- The different kinds of information systems.
- The major trends in information systems.

- The major conceptual approaches to information systems.
- The major challenges to building effective information systems in organizations.

1.1 Introduction

What is an Information System?

An *information system* can be defined as a set of procedures that collect (or retrieve), process, store, and disseminate information to support decision making and control (see Figure 1.1). In this book we are concerned exclusively with *formal, organizational, computer-based information systems (CBIS)*. Each of these terms will now be discussed.

Formal Systems

Formal systems rest on accepted and relatively fixed definitions of data and of procedures for collecting, storing, processing, disseminating, and using these data. The CBIS we describe here are structured—that is, they operate in conformity with predefined rules that are relatively fixed and not easily changed.

Informal information systems (such as office gossip networks), by contrast, rest on implicit agreements and unstated norms of behavior. These systems have open definitions of goals, opportunistic methods of data collection, and virtually unlimited channels of distribution and use. They are essential for the life of an organization, but they are beyond the scope of this text.

Computer-Based Information Systems (CBIS)

Most organizations have formal organizational information systems based entirely on paper-and-pencil technology. These *manual systems* serve important needs, but they are not the subject of this text.

We are concerned here with computer-based information systems (CBIS). From now on, when we use the term *information systems*

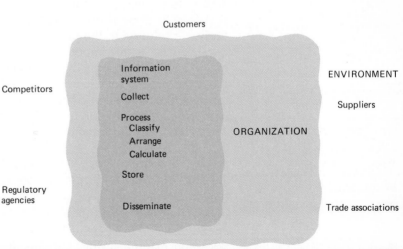

FIGURE 1.1
Basic operations of an information system. The basic operations of information systems are to collect, process, store, and disseminate information in an organization. Information may be collected from inside the organization or from the external environment and may be distributed to insiders and outsiders.

we will be referring to formal organizational systems that rely on computer technology—both hardware and software.

Organizations

A major theme of this text is that information systems are a part of organizations. Organizations are composed of different levels and specialties, which in turn produce different interests, often conflict, and certainly differences in perspective.

Information systems described in this book come out of this organizational cauldron of differing perspectives, conflicts, compromises, and agreements that are a natural part of all organizations.

There is no formula to be followed ritually when analyzing an organizational problem or an information system solution. To understand and build information systems, students must first understand the structure, function, and politics of organizations. Then they must understand the capabilities and opportunities provided by contemporary information technology.

The Difference Between Computers and Information Systems

A sharp distinction must be drawn between a computer and a computer program, on the one hand, and an information system on the other. Electronic computers and related software programs are the technical foundation, the tools and materials, of modern information systems. Computers provide the equipment for storing and processing information. Computer programs, or software, are sets of operating instructions that direct and control computer processing. Knowing how they work is important in designing solutions to organizational problems. But the *raison d'etre* of computers and computer programs comes from the information system of which computers are just a part.

Housing provides an appropriate analogy. Houses are built with hammers, nails, and wood, but these do not make a house. The architecture, design, setting, landscaping, and all of the decisions that lead to these features are part of the house and are crucial in finding a solution to the problem of putting a roof over one's head.

Likewise with computers and programs: They are the hammer, nails, and lumber of CBIS. Understanding information systems, however, requires one to understand the problems they are designed to solve, the architectural and design solutions, and the organizational processes that lead to these solutions. Computer literacy must be augmented with information system literacy.

Different Kinds of Systems

Because there are different interests, specialties, and levels in an organization, there are different kinds of systems. Figure 1.2 illustrates one way to depict the kinds of systems found in an organization. Here the organization is divided into strategic, managerial, and operational levels, and further divided into specializations such as sales and manufacturing. Systems are built to serve these different organizational interests (Anthony, 1965).

EXECUTIVE
SUPPORT SYSTEMS
(ESS)

DECISION
SUPPORT SYSTEMS
(DSS)

MANAGEMENT
INFORMATION SYSTEMS
(MIS)

OFFICE
AUTOMATION SYSTEMS
(OAS)

TRANSACTION
PROCESSING SYSTEMS
(TPS)

5-year sales trend forecasting	5-year operating plan	5-year budget forecasting	Profit planning	Manpower planning

Strategic-Level Systems

Sales management	Inventory control	Annual budgeting	Capital investment analysis	Relocation analysis
Sales region analysis	Production scheduling	Cost analysis	Pricing/profitability analysis	Contract cost analysis

Management Control-Level Systems

	Machine control	Payroll	Auditing	Compensation
Order tracking	Plant scheduling	Accounts payable	Tax reporting	Training & development
Order processing	Material movement control	Accounts receivable	Cash management	Employee recordkeeping

Operational-Level Systems

SALES   MANUFACTURING   ACCOUNTING   FINANCE   PERSONNEL

FIGURE 1.2
The hierarchy of information systems. Organizations and information systems can be divided into managerial, operational, and strategic levels. Information systems are built to serve each of these levels. Organizations also contain specialized subunits or divisions. In large organizations, each division has its own information systems.

Chapter 2 provides real-world examples of the major kinds of systems. It consists of a general overview of systems at the three different levels of an organization.

Operational-level systems keep track of the elementary activities and transactions of the organization, such as sales, receipts, cash deposits, payroll, credit decisions, and the flow of materials in a factory. Systems serving this level of the organization are typically called *transaction processing systems* (TPS). The principal purpose of systems at this level is to answer routine questions and to track the flow of transactions through the organization. How many parts are in inventory? What happened to Mr. Williams's payment? What is the size of the payroll this month?

To answer these kinds of questions, information generally must be easily available, current, and accurate. Examples of TPS include system to record bank deposits from automatic teller machines or one that tracks the number of hours worked each day by employees on a factory floor.

Profit Planning at Xerox

The Xerox Corporation has been performing profit planning using the Interactive Financial Planning System (IFPS), special computer modeling software. For each of its products, Xerox develops a sales forecast and an annual profit model by country. The model includes administrative and distribution costs, estimated currency fluctuations in each country, and anticipated profit margins. The model is supported by about 3500 data files.

Adapted from Jan Snyders, "Planning by the Numbers," *Infosystems*, August 1986.

Management-level systems are designed to serve the monitoring, controlling, decision-making, and administrative activities of an organization. *Management information systems* (*MIS*) focus on daily, weekly, and monthly summaries of transactions that are useful for monitoring and controlling operational-level activities (Gorry and Morton, 1971). The principal question addressed by such systems is: Are things working well? Today's output will be compared with that of a month or a year ago. There is less need for instant information, but periodic reports are required. An example is a relocation control system that reports on the total moving, house-hunting, and home financing costs for employees in all company divisions, noting wherever actual costs exceeded budgets.

Decision support systems (*DSS*) are customized systems that support nonroutine decision making (Keen and Morton, 1978). They tend to focus on less structured decisions for which information requirements are not always clear, especially "what if" questions: What would be the impact on production schedules if we doubled sales in the month of December? What would happen to our return on investment if a factory schedule was delayed for six months? Answers to these questions frequently require new data from outside the organization, as well as data from inside that cannot be drawn from existing operational-level systems. An example is a financial planning system such as that used by the Xerox Corporation for profit planning.

Office automation systems (*OAS*), such as the automated office system to be described, serve management and support clerical activities with facilities for word processing, document reproduction, and electronic messaging.

An Automated Office System

The automated office system at the Lincoln National Life Insurance Company provides word processing, electronic mail, decision support, records management, and end-user programming to 2300 users with 1600 terminals. An outstanding feature is its integrated voice and electronic mail service. Messages typed by users into Lincoln's computer system can be converted to voice and heard over a telephone. Listings of both typed and voice messages can be displayed on computer terminal screens. To reach users without terminals, Lincoln maintains links to MCI Mail, a nationwide electronic mail service. Fully 80% of Lincoln's executives have their own terminals and use them directly for electronic mail. Lincoln credits its office automation system with increasing productivity by 15%.

Adapted from, "Making Office Systems Pay Off," *EDP Analyzer*, February 1985.

Strategic-level systems address strategic issues and long-term trends, both in the firm and in the external environment, that are of interest to senior management. The principal concern is to match changes in the external environment with existing organizational capability. What will employment levels be in five years? What are the long-term industry cost trends, and where do we fit in? What products should we be making in five years?

The kind of information found in most transaction and management systems may not be sufficient to answer these questions. Special senior management systems called *executive support systems* (*ESS*) have been created to organize and present data from many sources. Examples include the integrated boardroom graphics display system that charts the movement of 40 key corporate indicators for Gould, Inc., a large electronics firm, or the Motorola Corporation's visual information system, which we will now describe.

The next chapter will discuss TPS, MIS, DSS, OAS, and ESS in detail, using specific examples of important applications.

Systems can also be differentiated by functional specialty. Major organizational functions, such as sales, marketing, accounting, manufacturing, planning, and personnel, are each served by their own information systems.

In large organizations, subfunctions of each of these major functions also have their own information systems. For example, the

Executive Visual
Information Systems

At the Motorola Corporation in Schaumberg, Illinois, chief executive, operating, and financial officers, along with general managers, have direct on-line access to 200 charts of corporatewide financial, personnel, and marketing data. These executives can select from a menu of custom-tailored charts based on the most current data through terminals in their offices connected to a mainframe computer. Each user can perform "what if?" analyses to answer questions such as "What if we increase our plan by 10%?" and see the results immediately in graph form. The system responds to requests for more detail by linking any chart with any other chart. Because managers can interpret these charts more easily, productivity at meetings has been enhanced. No one argues any longer about the meaning of the charts. They argue about the trends.

Adapted from "Decision Support Graphics Draw a Better Bottom Line," *Business Computer Systems*, August 1985.

manufacturing function might have systems for inventory management, process control, plant maintenance, computer-aided engineering, and material requirements planning.

In a typical organization, operational, management, and strategic-level systems exist for each functional area. For example, the sales function generally has a sales system on the operational level to record daily sales figures and process sales orders. A management-level system tracks monthly sales figures by sales territory and reports on territories where sales exceed or fall below anticipated levels. A system to forecast sales trends over a five-year period serves the strategic level.

Finally, different organizations have different information systems for the same functional areas. Because no two organizations have exactly the same objectives, structure, or interests, information systems must be custom made to fit the unique characteristics of each. There is no such thing as a universal information system that can fit all organizations, even in such standard areas as payroll or accounts receivable. Every organization does the job somewhat differently.

1.2 Why Study Information Systems?

In the 1950s and much of the 1960s, there was little need for this textbook or course. Managers generally did not need to know much about how information was processed in their organizations, and the technology involved was minimal. Information itself was not considered as important then as it is now. In most organizations, it was viewed as an unfortunate, costly by-product of doing business.

Today few managers can afford to ignore how information is handled by their organization. Why is this so?

The Changing Role of Information Systems in Organizations

The first information systems of the 1950s were TPS. These were followed by management-level systems in the 1970s and strategic-level systems in the 1980s. Because early systems addressed largely technical operational issues, managers could afford to delegate authority and concern to lower-level technical workers.

But because today's systems directly affect how managers decide, how senior managers plan, and in many cases what products and services are produced (and how), responsibility for information systems cannot be delegated to technical decision makers. Information systems today play a strategic role in the life of the firm. Chapter 3 describes this new role in greater detail.

One way to illustrate the new relationship between organizations and information systems is shown in Figure 1.3. There is a growing interdependence between business strategy, rules, and procedures, on the one hand, and information systems software, hardware, data, and telecommunications on the other. A change in any of these components often implies changes in other components. This relationship becomes critical when planning for the future. What a business would like to do in five years is often dependent on what its systems will be able to do.

A second change in the importance of systems results from the growing complexity and scope of system projects and applications. Building systems today involves a much larger part of the organization than it did in the past (see Figure 1.4).

Whereas early systems involved largely technical changes that affected few people, contemporary systems bring about managerial changes (who has what information about whom, when, and how often) and institutional "core" changes (what products and services are produced, under what conditions, and by whom).

A payroll system of the 1950s involved the treasurer's office, a few part-time programmers, a single program, a single machine, and a few clerks. This kind of change was largely technical. In contrast, today's integrated human resource system (which includes a payroll component) may involve all major corporate divisions, the Human Resources Department, dozens of full-time programmers, a flock of

FIGURE 1.3

The growing relation between organizations and IS. In contemporary systems there is a growing interdependence between organizational strategy, rules, and procedures, on the one hand, and the organization's information systems, on the other hand. Changes in strategy, rules, and procedures increasingly require changes in software, hardware, databases, and telecommunications. Existing systems can act as a constraint on organizations. What the organization would like to do is in many respects dependent on what its systems will permit it to do.

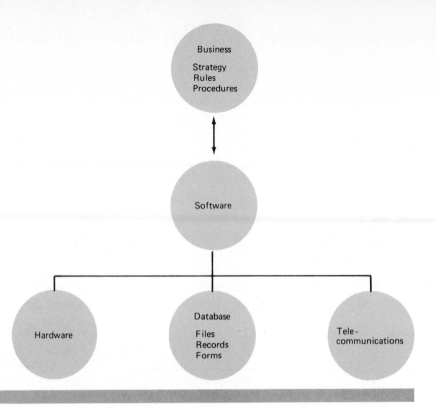

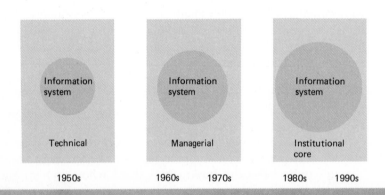

FIGURE 1.4

The changing role of information systems. Over time, information systems have come to play a larger role in the life of organizations. Early systems brought about largely technical changes that were relatively easy to accomplish. Later systems affected managerial control and behavior, and increasingly raised broad institutional questions concerning products, markets, suppliers, and customers.

external consultants, multiple machine and telecommunications environments, and perhaps hundreds of end users in the organization who use payroll data to make benefit, pension, and a host of other calculations. The data, instead of being located in and controlled by the treasurer, are now available to hundreds of employees via desktop terminals, each of which is as powerful as a mainframe computer of the 1960s.

This contemporary system involves both managerial and institutional changes, which are described in Chapter 4 and elsewhere.

The Changing Nature of Information Technology

One reason why systems play a larger role in organizations, and why they affect more people, is the growing power and declining cost of information technology—the microprocessors and peripheral devices that make up the core of information systems.

While the details are covered in later chapters, here it is sufficient to note that it is now possible to put a mainframe computer—which once took up much of an entire floor in the 1960s—on every desktop in an organization of the 1990s.

Part of this new hardware power has been used to make powerful, easy-to-use software available to complete novices. In a few hours, unskilled employees can be taught word processing, project scheduling, spread sheet preparation, and telecommunications packages on a microcomputer, skills that once belonged exclusively to professional programmers. Now it is conceivable that everyone in an organization may be using a computer simultaneously in some way during the work day.

In addition, it is now possible for end users to design their own applications and simple systems without the help of professional programmers.

A good manager cannot afford to ignore the fact that many of his or her employees are using information technology much of the time. Is this use productive? Could it be made more productive? Where are the major bottlenecks? How can we measure the benefits of investing in the technology? Where should professional help be sought, and where can end users design their own solutions?

The Changing Character of Applications

Both the changing role of systems and the new technology have brought about new kinds of systems and applications. Whereas in the past massive systems were built to provide *generic* information on sales, inventory, production, finance, and marketing, it is now feasible and desirable to create custom-made, specialized applications that serve just one or a few people or groups in the organization. Whether they are microcomputer-based spread sheet applications, or collaborative group computing applications, or decision support systems for middle management, the new kinds of applications require direct, close interaction between technical support personnel,

Beyond the Chalkboard: Electronic Tools for Collaboration

Most work in organizations is a result of group efforts. Fully 30–70% of office workers' time is spent in meetings. Paradoxically, most computer systems aim at improving individual work. Group work is left with the chalkboard.

To develop group computing tools, the Xerox Corporation is experimenting with a group computing environment at the Xerox Palo Alto Research Center called *Colab*. Colab focuses on problem solving in face-to-face meetings. It consists of six microcomputer work stations connected by a local area network, a large electronic blackboard or screen, and a stand-up keyboard for a group leader or participant.

Colab is supported by software designed to help groups by facilitating brainstorming, organizing, evaluating, and the presentation of ideas. Unlike manual chalkboards, arguments and notes can be stored for future use and reference, the writing is always legible, and users never run out of chalk.

Adapted from "Beyond the Chalkboard: Computer Support for Collaboration and Problem Solving in Meetings," Communications of the ACM, January 1987.

managers who will use the system, and senior management support. An example of the new kinds of applications is Xerox Corporation's Colab.

One class of new applications—called *expert systems* and described in Chapter 17—require technical experts called *knowledge engineers* to capture the knowledge of skilled workers and managers in computer software. These kinds of systems exemplify the close cooperation and understanding required of both managers and software experts.

The Need to Plan the Information Architecture of an Organization

It is not enough for managers to be computer literate. Systems today require an understanding of major islands or constellations of technologies: data processing systems, telecommunications, and office technologies (see the articles by McKenney and McFarlan, 1982; McFarlan, et al., 1983a, 1983b). Increasingly, these heretofore separate islands of technology must be closely coordinated. Managers today must know how to track, plan, and manage the many islands of technology in a way best suited to their organization. This *systems knowledge* is important.

But in addition, managers must know how to recognize organizational problems and find a systems solution. For this, knowledge of the organization is required.

Together, systems knowledge and organizational understanding shape the information architecture of the organization. *Information architecture* can be defined as the particular *form* that information technology takes in an organization to achieve selected goals or *functions*. Managers increasingly play the critical role in defining information architecture. There is no one else to do the job.

Some typical questions regarding information architecture that today's managers should be able to address are the following: Should the corporate payroll data and function be distributed to each corporate remote site, or should it be centralized at headquarters? Should the organization purchase stand-alone microcomputers or build a more powerful centralized mainframe environment within an integrated telecommunications framework? Should the organization build its own data communications utility to link remote sites or rely on external providers like the telephone company?

While there is no one right answer to these questions, a manager today should at least have the knowledge to deal with them.

1.3 Contemporary Approaches to Information Systems

The study of information systems is multidisciplinary, and no single theory or perspective dominates the field. Figure 1.5 illustrates the major disciplines that contribute problems and solutions to the

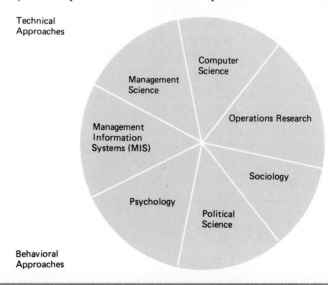

FIGURE 1.5
Contemporary approaches to information systems.

literature. In general, the field can be divided into technical and behavioral approaches. Information systems are sociotechnical systems; they are composed of machines, devices, and "hard" physical technology. In addition, information systems require substantial social, organizational, and intellectual investments to make them work properly.

Technical Approach

Technical approaches to information systems dominated the field in its early years. Computer science is concerned with establishing theories of computability, methods of computation, and methods of efficient data storage and access. Management science emphasizes the development of normative models of decision making and management practice. Operations research focuses on mathematical techniques for optimizing selected parameters of organizations such as transportation costs, inventory control, and transaction costs.

Interested students should examine the following journals for examples of literature in these fields: *Communications of the Association of Computing Machinery (CACM)*, *Management Science*, and *Operations Research*. Articles from these journals are excerpted and referenced throughout the text.

A relatively new field of study, management information systems (MIS) arose in the 1960s and focused exclusively on computer-based information systems aimed at managers (Davis and Olsen, 1985). The MIS discipline, and the first academic departments, emerged in business schools in the United States. Much of the work of MIS is technical, combining the theoretical work of computer science, management science, and operations research with a practical orientation toward building systems and applications. The leading journals in this field are *MIS Quarterly* and the *Journal of Management Information Systems*.

The technical approach to information systems emphasizes mathematically based, normative models to study information systems, as well as the physical technology and formal capabilities of these systems.

Behavioral Approach

A growing part of the information systems field is concerned with behavioral problems and issues. MIS is concerned largely with behavioral problems of system utilization, implementation, and creative design that cannot be expressed with normative models. Other behavioral disciplines also play a role. Sociologists focus on the social, group, and organizational impacts and uses of systems. Political science deals with the political impacts and uses of information. Psychology is concerned with individual response to system realities and cognitive models of human reasoning.

The leading journals in these areas are the *American Sociological Review*, *Administrative Science Quarterly*, *American Political Science*

Review, and the *Journal of Psychology*. In addition, the information systems journals described previously contain many behavioral articles, as do business journals such as the *Harvard Business Review* and the *Sloan Management Review*.

The behavioral approach does not ignore technology. Indeed, information systems technology is often the stimulus for a behavioral problem or issue. But the focus in this literature is generally not on technical solutions, but rather on changes in attitudes, management and organization policy, and behavior (Kling and Dutton, 1982).

Approach of This Text: Sociotechnical Systems

Our experience as academics and practioners leads us to believe that no single perspective effectively captures the reality of information systems. Problems with systems—and their solutions—are rarely all technical or all behavioral. Our best advice to students is to understand the perspective of disciplines other than their own. Indeed, the challenge and excitement of the information systems field is that it requires an appreciation and tolerance of many different approaches.

A sociotechnical systems perspective helps to avoid a purely technological approach to information systems. For instance, the fact that information technology is rapidly declining in cost and growing in power does not necessarily or easily translate into productivity enhancement or bottom-line profits.

In this book, we stress the need to optimize the performance of the system as a whole—both the technical and behavioral components. This means that technology must be changed and designed in such a way as to fit organizational and individual needs. At times, the technology may have to be "de-optimized" to accomplish this fit.

The Economics of Office Work

Information technology involves a much larger investment than merely the work station on a desk. Extensive and costly resources are needed to make it productive. The most costly support elements are organizational. The critical point is not whether a byte of memory costs $0.001 or $0.00001; it is whether management can use the technology to extract economic benefit. Increasing productivity, raising profits, reducing costs, increasing responsiveness to clients and customers—these are the criteria by which to judge investments in information technology.

Adapted from Strassman, 1985.

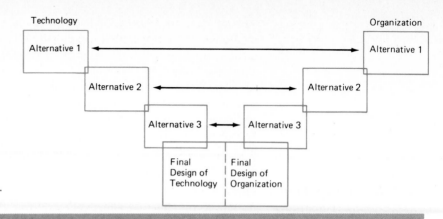

Organizations and individuals must also be changed through training, learning, and planned organizational change in order to allow the technology to operate and prosper. Figure 1.6 illustrates this process of mutual adjustment in a sociotechnical system.

1.4 The Challenge of Information Systems

A senior executive in charge of a $275 million software redevelopment project in the Social Security Administration, which was three years behind schedule, lamented that "senior management just did not understand the difficulty of re-writing over 10 million lines of programming code" (Westin and Laudon, forthcoming).

One important message of this text is that despite, or perhaps because of, the rapid development of computer technology, there is nothing easy or mechanical about building workable information systems. Building, operating, and maintaining information systems are challenging for a number of reasons. We will now discuss seven challenges that students should be aware of. Partial solutions have been developed for each of these challenges. Try to suggest some of them.

Some Important Information Cannot Be Put into a System

Much essential information in an organization is inherently not systematic and therefore cannot be captured and put into a machine. Ideas for new products, the opinions of other managers, plans of competitors, or the intentions of large entities such as nations and societies are examples. Thus, the decision of OPEC countries in the mid-1970s to drastically raise the price of oil, which had far-reaching implications for most organizations in industrial societies and seriously disturbed the econometric models of Western economies, could not be predicted or put into a machine.

The views of key engineering personnel at Morton Thiokol, manufacturers of the space shuttle "Challenger's" solid rocket boosters, although well known throughout the organization, were never part of any formal information system. Views and perspectives contrary to accepted organizational wisdom are frequently not a part of formal information systems.

Information Requires a Context

Much of the information that can be mechanized or automated is often not particularly interesting or important from a managerial perspective. The daily or hourly output of a specific machine on a factory floor can be captured and automated relatively easily, but its significance is quite low (unless it can be related to some other body of information).

The value of information depends on analysis, interpretation, explanation, and finally, understanding. Information requires a context. This context is supplied by the user's stock or core of knowledge. This point is best illustrated by looking at national intelligence failures.

A few weeks before the Japanese attack on Pearl Harbor on December 7, 1941, the following events occurred: The Japanese navy changed all ship and shore call signs and introduced alternating call signs for stations, making it almost impossible for the American navy to locate Japanese ships. The Flag Officers Code used by the Japanese to transmit administrative and operational messages was changed in a manner that resisted decoding. Nevertheless, American intelligence officers established that an entirely new air-naval operations group now existed and was being trained in aerial and sea bombardment. Most of the major Japanese battleships (carriers, destroyers, and submarines) completely disappeared from radio and visual intelligence sightings for the first time in memory. Ongoing decryption of Japanese diplomatic coded communications between Tokyo and Washington indicated that the Japanese were preparing a final ultimatum for American decision makers on a take-it-or-leave-it basis, with December 8, 1941, as the absolutely last date for acceptance, after which "events would take an automatic course." Diplomatic radio messages intercepted by the Americans directed local Japanese observers in Hawaii to utilize a new grid system for describing Pearl Harbor fleet movements and the location of major battle vessels, and to report all movements on a daily basis (Farago, 1967).

Although all of this information was known several days before the attack on December 7, 1941, no organization or person could supply a convincing interpretation of it. A common argument of skilled intelligence analysts is that most of the "real intelligence failures in United States have not been failures in the collection of information but failures in interpretation and analysis of data" (Turner, 1985).

Information without context, by which we mean the absence of analysis, interpretation, or explanation, is thus of little value. Moreover, human beings and organizations develop the context within which information is valuable. Machines, information systems, and related technology can provide only the information.

The Value of Information Decays with Time

The value of information changes rapidly over time. Useful information has a sharp exponential decay function at least from the perspective of management control. The knowledge that a particular product has a defective component is extremely valuable in the early production runs, when changes in subcomponents and assemblies can still be made, as opposed to a year later, after an entire year's production of defective products. Information that is a year or more old may have historical value, may be important for statistical analysis and strategic planning, but is useless from the vantage point of management control. Thus, information must be timely, and timeliness is a significant part of the value of information—the ability to act on it.

Changing Environments, Changing Information Requirements

Information systems exist in a dynamic and changing environment. Organizations do not stand still; they constantly change. For example, several million dollars and several man-years of effort may be needed just to define the information requirements for a new marketing system. Meanwhile, the company may have been merged with an entirely different company and the whole study may be made obsolete because of a new product mix. External organizations also force changes in internal information systems. A state or locality may pass a law requiring all refreshment containers to be returned to the manufacturer and may also raise sales taxes by two cents on each six-pack of refreshments. This will force changes in sales, marketing, inventory, and production information systems.

Complying with the requirements of national legislation frequently entails the creation of entirely new information systems. For instance, when Congress passed the Toxic Waste and Substances Control Act in 1980, thousands of organizations had to develop tracking systems to trace the movement of toxic substances into and out of their production processes. More recently, the Post Office changed the zip code designation from five to nine digits. This, in turn, required corporations to alter their supplier, customer, personnel, and benefit information files. In many instances, simple modifications could not be made and entire new file structures had to be developed.

Information requirements are never static. Information systems built to fit one set of requirements are continually being outdated by changes in the environment.

According to an information industry adage, "systems are never built; they are always being built." Information systems are not mechanistic. Rather, they are like organisms; they are born, grow, become obsolete, and are replaced.

Rapidly Changing Technology

Another challenge provided by information systems is the fact that computer technology is rapidly changing. Costs have been falling sharply, while capacity has increased exponentially. (These changes are described in Chapter 6.) Consequently, systems are often technically obsolete shortly after they are installed. To amortize the costs of expensive hardware and information systems, systems are often used long after more advanced technology has appeared.

A Shortage of Good People

A shortage of skilled programmers and systems analysts in the past decade has resulted in rapid increases in systems personnel costs coupled with a high level of turnover of systems staff (in some organizations, 30–40% of the information systems personnel leave every year). As the demand for computer applications has risen, the shortage of personnel has created a two- to four-year backlog in many information systems departments.

The "Apollo Mentality"

Very few people comprehend the effort required to develop truly effective, efficient, and powerful information systems. Given the success of computers and information systems technology in some highly visible applications—such as the airline reservation systems, credit card and banking systems, and even the space program—both the general public and organizational managers have come to have high expectations about the effectiveness of information systems and the speed with which they can be built. A common attitude is that if we can have an airlines reservation system or put a man on the moon, then we can certainly develop an integrated, on-line inventory database system for a large conglomerate within a year and on a moderate budget.

Many managers do not realize that the Apollo space project and the airline reservation systems required hundreds or even thousands of man-years to develop at a cost that far exceeds the limited data processing budgets of most large organizations today. Of course, most information systems are not that elaborate and could be developed more easily, as many large- and small-scale systems have been. But whatever the magnitude of the project, information system builders must have appropriate skills and sensitivities, as well as the knowledge that their task may be complex. One objective of this text is to discuss all of the organizational and technical considerations that must be taken into account.

1.5 Summary

The purpose of a CBIS is to collect, store, and disseminate information from an organization's environment and internal operations for the purpose of supporting organizational functions and decision making. To be useful, a CBIS must faithfully reflect the organization's requirements for information. It must fit the needs of the specific organizational level and the business function that it is intended to support.

Organizations can be divided into three levels. The *operational* level is concerned with the efficiency of specific tasks and the control of specific production processes. The *management control* level is primarily concerned with planning, controlling, and monitoring operational activities and the use of organizational resources. The *strategic* level is concerned with setting long-term organizational objectives and determining how resources and activities will be controlled. Each of these organizational levels thus has different interests and concerns about information.

TPS serve operational levels of the organization. OAS, MIS, and DSS serve management levels. ESS serve strategic levels of the organization.

Information, and information systems, play a much more important role in organizations today than in the past. The kinds of systems built today are more important for the overall performance of the organization; technologies have become more powerful and more difficult to implement; new applications require intense interaction between professional technical experts and general management. In general, there is a much greater need to plan for the overall information architecture of the organization.

There are both technical and behavioral approaches to information systems. Both perspectives can be combined into a sociotechnical approach to systems.

Building information systems that can effectively meet organizational requirements is a challenging endeavor. Much essential information cannot be captured by formal information systems. Information requirements and the value of information change with time, spurred by rapid changes in computer technology and in the external environment. When building an information system it is important to consider a broad array of organizational and technical factors.

Key Words

Information system
CBIS
Formal systems
Informal systems

Manual systems
Information architecture
Operational-level system
Management-level system

Strategic-level system
Transaction processing system (TPS)
Management information system (MIS)

Office Automation System (OAS)
Decision Support System (DSS)
Executive Support System (ESS)

Review Questions

1. Distinguish between a computer, a computer program, and an information system.
2. What is the relationship between an information system, the organization, and the organizational environment?
3. Identify and describe the three levels of decision making in the hierarchy of organizational activities.
4. Why is information from an external source critical to strategic planning?
5. Define and compare operational-level, management-level, and strategic-level information systems. What categories of information systems serve each level?
6. Why should managers study information systems?
7. What is the relationship between an organization and its information systems? How is this relationship changing over time?
8. What do we mean by the information architecture of the organization?
9. Distinguish between a behavioral and a technical approach to information systems in terms of the questions asked and the answers provided.
10. What major disciplines contribute to an understanding of information systems?
11. Why is building, operating, and maintaining an information system a challenging endeavor?

Discussion Questions

1. Some people argue that the creation of CBIS is fundamentally a social process. Hence, a person who is an expert in information technology may not be suited to design a CBIS. Discuss and comment.
2. It is argued that there is no such thing as a universal information system that can fit all organizations. That is, information systems must be custom-fit to a specific organization. Discuss and comment.
3. A company implemented a highly integrated information system (i.e., a total system). As a result, any transaction entered into the system would immediately affect all related functional subsystems at all levels of activity. Discuss some problems that might arise in this system. What advantages does it offer?

A Manufacturing Resources Planning System Serves Many Purposes

The U.S. chemical industry is highly competitive and tightly controlled. Multi-Chem, a multinational chemical and pharmaceutical manufacturing firm with three U.S. divisions, tries to maintain a competitive edge by maximizing its efficiency in the manufacturing process. One strategy is to have all of its divisions adopt an integrated manufacturing resource planning system (MRP).

The steps involved in turning raw materials into finished chemical products are relatively simple. However, almost anyone in marketing, production, finance, product development, or management can affect the production schedule. A single change in schedule for one product at one plant may cause a "ripple effect" on products, intermediates, and raw materials at another plant. Stresses placed on processes by conflicting business and production demands can result in costly inefficiencies—excess inventory on the one hand and failure to meet customer demands on the other. Production schedules and plans must be continually adjusted to meet the changing business environment.

Like other manufacturers, Multi-Chem tries to minimize these inefficiencies by using a production plan and master schedule to tie all of the manufacturing activities together. The production plan establishes monthly rates of production and is developed to meet the sales plan. The master schedule converts the monthly production rates into a weekly schedule and plans the necessary material and capacity based on anticipated customer demand. A final production schedule, reflecting the availability of material and plant capacity, responds to actual customer orders. The daily production schedule tracks production and shipments on a daily basis to ensure that both production and business plans are met.

Multi-Chem's MRP system helps to meet these planning needs by providing a scheduling system to show what is required by a particular process and when. The system plans all levels of a product from raw materials through finished goods and tracks information to ensure that tasks can be completed quickly and profitably. The MRP system shows today's balance for every product, intermediate, and raw material it tracks. It can project what the balance will be on any future date, given expected sales, shipments, production, and purchases. It can recommend changes in shipping or manufacturing schedules based on its calculation of shortfalls and excesses.

The system is used at many locations by employees whose positions range from inventory clerks to production planners to divisional managers. Some of these users need exact, detailed answers at once. Others expect to see an overall picture once a quarter. The following examples are illustrative:

- Multi-Chem's agricultural chemical products are manufactured at plants in Illinois and Alabama, and about 15 by outside processors under contract. A vendor has shipped defective bottles to an outside processor that produces Ag Chem No. 1. The inventory control clerk in the Contract Manufacturing Department knows that Ag Chem No. 1 is also produced at the Alabama plant. He wants to find out if some bottles can be transferred to the outside processor (in Memphis) without too much impact on the Alabama plant's schedule.
- The director of production is preparing for the quarterly planning meetings with his counterpart in world headquarters. He needs to know the net inventories of Ag Chem No. 5, together with export and marketing plans for the next five quarters.

- Marketing has changed plans for Ag Chem No. 7 (made at the Alabama plant), causing an increased demand for Ag Chem No. 11 (made at the Illinois plant). This change, in turn, may affect the schedule for HCN (an intermediate product made at the Illinois plant). The Illinois plant needs to know how to adjust HCN production. It may also need to rework the schedules for raw materials and labor.

The MRP system runs on the central mainframe computer at Multi-Chem's U.S. corporate headquarters. A network of terminals with telecommunications links to the central computer ties in divisional headquarters, plant sites, and departments. Inquiries such as that of the inventory clerk for the number of bottles on hand can be serviced directly on-line through these terminals. However, the requests for information in the other two examples require much more complex totaling, analysis, and manipulation of data. Computer jobs to provide the answers must be batched together and run later or overnight.

Since the MRP system was installed, Multi-Chem has reported inventory reductions of up to $2 million, with annual savings of $240,000 in inventory carrying costs and a 98% inventory accuracy.

Case Study Questions

1. The MRP is used by people in many functions who need different kinds of information. What organizational levels does it serve? What kinds of organizational functions and decisions does it support? You may find it helpful to put your answers in table form.

Organizational Level	Function	Decision

2. How large a role does this MRP system play in Multi-Chem? Discuss.
3. The builders of the MRP system have stated, "If the only function of MRP to track bottles, a much simpler system could have been developed." Discuss.

References

Anthony, R.N. *Planning and Control Systems: A Framework for Analysis.* Cambridge, Mass.: Harvard University Press, 1965.

Davis, Gordon B., and Margrethe H. Olson. *Management Information Systems: Conceptual Foundations, Structure, and Development*, 2nd ed. New York: McGraw-Hill, 1985.

Farago, Ladislas. *The Broken Seal.* New York: Random House, 1967.

Gorry, G.A., and Morton, M.S. "Framework for Management Information Systems," *Sloan Management Review* 13, No. 1, (Fall, 1971).

Keen, P.G.W., and Morton, M.S. *Decision Support Systems: An Organizational Perspective*. Reading, Mass.: Addison-Wesley, 1978.

Kling, Rob, and Dutton, William H. "The Computer Package: Dynamic Complexity," in *Computers and Politics*, edited by James Danziger, William Dutton, Rob Kling, and Kenneth Kraemer. New York: Columbia University Press, 1982.

McFarlan, F. Warren, McKenney, James L., and Pyburn, Philip. "The Information Archipelago—Plotting A Course," *Harvard Business Review*, (January–February 1983a).

McFarlan, F. Warren, McKenney, James L., and Pyburn, Philip. "Governing the New World," *Harvard Business Review*, (July–August 1983b).

McKenney, James L., and McFarlan, F. Warren. "The Information Archipelago—Maps and Bridges," *Harvard Business Review*, (September–October 1982).

Strassman, Paul. *The Information Payoff—The Transformation of Work in the Electronic Age*. New York: Free Press, 1985.

Tornatsky, Louis G., Eveland, J.D., Boylan, Myles G., Hetzner, W.A., Johnson, E.C., Roitman, D., and Schneider, J. *The Process of Technological Innovation: Reviewing the Literature*. Washington, D.C.: National Science Foundation, 1983.

Turner, Stansfield. *Secrecy and Democracy: The CIA in Transition*. New York: Houghton Mifflin, 1985.

Westin, Alan F., and Laudon, Kenneth C. *A Theory of Information Systems and Organizations: Social Security Administration, 1935–1990*. Forthcoming.

CHAPTER 2

Examples of Information Systems

OUTLINE

In his book *Zen and the Art of Motorcycle Maintenance*, Robert M. Pirsig described the existential pleasures of motorcycle touring and other life-consuming activites. Repairing motorcycles may be an art. But surely so is finding the parts. The Yamaha Motor Corporation, one of the world's largest motorcycle manufacturers, must keep track of more than 80,000 parts in two warehouses at Cudahy, Wisconsin, and Atlanta, Georgia. Dealers need parts quickly (they, of course, do not want to stock 80,000 parts themselves). Customers need their bikes repaired rapidly and want speedy action on warranty claims. Management needs to know which bikes are breaking down, how much warranty repairs are costing, and which parts are in short supply, as well as answers to numerous *unstructured* and *unspecifiable questions*.

Yamaha developed an industry-leading, on-line transaction processing system (TPS) to handle the job. Each dealer is given a data terminal connected by a dial-up telephone modem to Yamaha's two IBM 4341 mainframe computers in Atlanta. These computers, in turn, are connected to 12 Memorex 3652 double-density on-line disk drives with a total storage capacity of 15 gigabytes (15 billion characters of information including numbers and letters).

The system works as follows: When a part is needed, a dealer dials up the central Yamaha computer on a toll-free line. The dealer is prompted by a menu to select the correct parts. Parts are ordered by entering a 12-digit number. At the end of the order, the dealer receives (on his or her own printer) a shipping/packing list that states where each part will come from, back-ordered parts, retail and dealer value, and preferred freight route.

If the part is not in stock or is no longer being made, the dealer can send an inquiry to all other 1500 dealers to check their stock. The system can announce model changes and perform other "broadcast" and bulletin board functions. The system also processes warranty claims. Dealers record who bought each unit and subsequently enter warranty claims. Dealers are now paid for warranty work within 15 days, as opposed to the 45 days it took without a system.

Each week, the order entry system just described down-loads on a batch basis certain critical information to a management information system (MIS), which produces routine reports. The MIS operates a user-friendly on-line interface language (FOCUS) that permits managers to create ad hoc reports, ask novel questions, and support decisions in other ways.

(Adapted from *Infosystems*, January 1985, p. 99.)

In a nutshell, Yamaha's order entry system illustrates the major features of modern information systems:

- On-line access to large amounts of information
- Remote inquiry and job entry using telecommunications links
- Multiple functions of a single system
- Using different types of processing for different purposes
- Multiple levels of users in the organization
- Integration of functions and users into a single system

In this chapter the student will learn:
- The major types of information systems in organizations.
- How information systems work from a functional standpoint.
- Some of the tools used to describe systems.
- The relationship between the various information systems.

2.1 Introduction

It is important to remember that an information system is distinct from the technology on which it operates. (We will explain the technology of systems in later chapters.) Many of the advances in information processing in the last decade have resulted from innovative and powerful *systems design* and *rationalization of procedures*, not just better technology.

Yamaha's parts tracking system, for example, is effective not just because it uses state-of-the art computer technology but also because its design allows Yamaha to operate more efficiently. Yamaha, or any organization, and its procedures must be rationally structured to achieve this result. Before Yamaha could automate its information about parts, it had to have standard codes and descriptions for every part that was used by all of its dealers and warehouses. It also had to have a shipping network and formal procedures for placing and shipping parts orders from dealers. Without a certain amount of rationalization in Yamaha's organization, the on-line computer technology would have been useless.

The types of information systems discussed in this chapter are presented from a functional rather than a technical standpoint. They illustrate how systems work, what kinds of information they contain, who uses the result, and various system designs.

2.2 Tools Used to Describe Systems

Systems are described using a special vocabulary and a special set of graphic symbols. Following are some of the vocabulary and symbols that will help students understand system functions and design. (Additional symbols are presented in chapters devoted to technology, systems analysis, and design.)

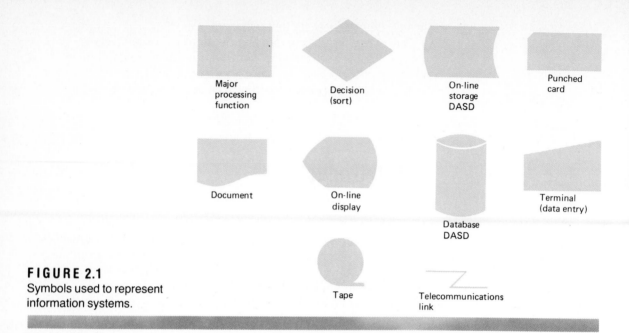

FIGURE 2.1
Symbols used to represent information systems.

Symbols Used to Describe Systems

Figure 2.1 shows the major graphic symbols used in this text to describe systems. Five kinds of devices are important in most system descriptions:

Device	Example
Input	Terminal
	Microcomputer
	Keypunch machine
Processing	Mainframe, minicomputer, microcomputer
Secondary storage	Punched card
	Tape
	Disk
Telecommunications	Modem
	Telephone
Output	Terminal
	Printer

Figure 2.2 shows how these devices make up a system.

Information Storage

In Figure 2.1, five of the symbols refer to different ways of storing information: on-line storage (usually a storage disk), punched card, tape, database, and document. The student no doubt already understands what a tape, punched card, and document are, but *on-line* and *database* may be new words.

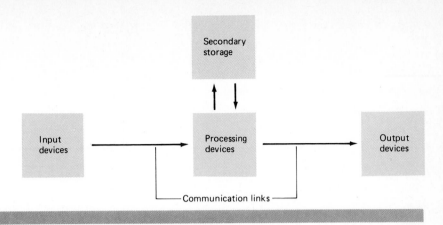

FIGURE 2.2
Major devices in a system.

On-line storage refers to a file of information (like a file on "students" or "courses") that the computer and the user can access immediately. The computer, in other words, is directly connected to the file. A *database* is simply (for now) a collection of on-line files to which the user can gain access. The technology of these and other storage devices is described in later chapters.

Tape storage of data is inexpensive and reliable. Computer tape stores data much like audiotape and videotape store pictures and music, namely, in sequential order using magnetic impressions on a thin film. Disk storage involves using magnetic impressions on a thin steel disk. The advantage here is that the information does not need to be in sequential order and the user can gain access to any piece of information immediately (without reading through all of the other records). The technology is described in later chapters.

Batch and On-Line Processing

An important distinction in the following discussion is that between the two major types of information processing: batch and on-line processing.

Batch processing involves accumulating and storing transactions until the time when it is efficient or necessary, because of some reporting cycle, to process them. This was the only method of processing until the early 1960s and is still common today. *On-line processing*, which is now common, involves entering transactions and processing them immediately.

Which kind of processing one should use depends on which business process the system supports. If periodic or occasional reports or output are required, as in payroll or end-of-the-year reports, batch processing is most efficient. If immediate information and processing are needed, as in the Yamaha order entry system previously discussed, on-line processing is essential.

Figures 2.3A and 2.3B illustrate batch and on-line processing. Generally, batch systems use tape as a storage medium, whereas

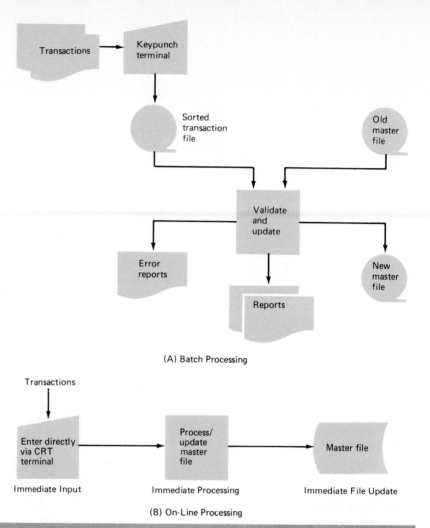

(A) Batch Processing

(B) On-Line Processing

Transactions → Keypunch terminal → Sorted transaction file

Old master file

Validate and update

Error reports

Reports

New master file

Transactions

Enter directly via CRT terminal — Immediate Input

Process/ update master file — Immediate Processing

Master file — Immediate File Update

FIGURE 2.3
Different kinds of processing.
(A) In batch processing, transactions are processed in batches on a regular basis, such as daily, weekly, or monthly. Information in the system will therefore not always be up-to-date at any given moment. A typical batch processing job is payroll preparation. (B) In on-line processing, transactions are processed immediately. Information in the system is always up-to-date and current. A typical on-line application is an airline reservation system.

on-line processing systems use disk storage, which permits immediate access to specific items of information (e.g., a part). In batch systems, transactions are accumulated in a transaction file. Periodically, this file is used to update a master file, which contains relatively permanent information on entities. (An example is a payroll master file, which is updated with time card transactions.) This processing creates a new master file. In on-line processing, transactions are keyed into the system immediately and the system responds immediately. The master file is updated continually.

With this basic vocabulary and set of symbols, we can now describe the major types of systems found in the contemporary organization and how they relate to one another.

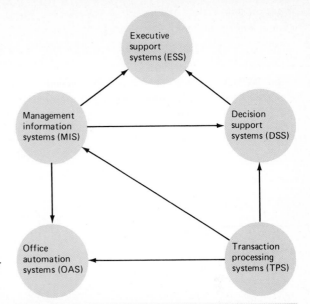

FIGURE 2.4

Types of systems. The different types of systems are related to each other. TPS is a major producer of information for other systems. These other systems both consume information and produce information for other systems. Often these different types of systems are only loosely coupled in most organizations.

2.3 Overview of Systems in the Organization

There is no single system that controls all aspects of computing in an organization. Organizations have many information systems serving different organizational levels and functions. These systems can have a variety of relationships with each other, as illustrated in Figure 2.4.

Five Major Types of Systems

As mentioned in Chapter 1, there are five major types of systems: transaction processing systems, office automation systems, management information systems, decision support systems, and executive support systems. (The features of these systems are summarized in Table 2.1).

At the most elementary level are the *transaction processing systems* (*TPS*). A TPS is a computerized system that performs and records the daily routine transactions necessary to the conduct of the business. Examples are sales order entry, hotel reservation systems, client information (for public agencies), payroll, employee recordkeeping, and shipping. TPS serve the operational level of the organization.

Tasks, resources, and goals at the organization's operational level are predefined and highly structured. The decision to grant credit to a customer, for instance, is made by a lower-level supervisor according to predefined criteria. The decision, in that sense, has been "programmed." All that must be determined is whether the customer meets the criteria.

TABLE 2.1

Characteristics of Information Processing Systems

Type of CBIS	Information Inputs	Processing	Information Outputs	Users
ESS	Aggregate data; external, internal	Graphics; simulations; interactive	Projections; responses to queries	Senior managers
DSS	Low-volume data; analytic models	Interactive; simulations; analysis	Special reports; decision analyses; responses to queries	Professionals; staff managers
MIS	Summary transaction data; high-volume data; simple models	Routine reports; simple models; low-level analysis	Summary and exception reports	Middle managers
OAS	Office documents; schedules	Word processing, storage, retrieval	Documents; schedules; graphics; mail	Clerks; managers
TPS	Transactions; events	Sorting, listing, merging, updating;	Detailed reports; lists; summaries	Operations personnel; supervisors

Two features of TPS are noteworthy. First, TPS span the boundary between the organization and its environment. They connect customers to the firm's warehouse, factory, and management. If TPS do not work well, the organization fails either to receive inputs from the environment (orders) or to deliver outputs (assembled goods). Second, TPS are major producers of information for other systems to be described. Because TPS track relations with the environment, they are the only place where managers can obtain both up-to-the-minute assessments of organizational performance and long-term records of past performance.

Obviously, TPS are extremely important for the modern organization. In the 1960s it was estimated that organizations could survive for a day without functioning computer systems. In the 1980s, as the story of the Bank of New York, in "Banking System Nightmare" shows, TPS failure for a few hours can lead to organizational failure.

Office automation systems (OAS) are computerized devices and systems devoted to document and message processing. Included are word processing, document storage, graphics, reproduction, facsimile transmission, and electronic mail systems. OAS support both clerical and managerial functions, spanning the operational and management levels.

Banking System Nightmare

On November 21, 1985, the Bank of New York's government security system failed, disrupting the entire government securities market and rattling financial center nerves. The bank's government securities clearance system failed because programmers had established an arbitrary limit of 32,000 issues traded per day. On November 20 that limit was exceeded and the computer's central processing unit did not know what to do with the overload.

The system crashed. Suddenly, while the bank could no longer deliver securities to buyers, it was nonetheless purchasing securities from sellers. This caused a shortfall of $22 billion in a few hours, which the bank had to borrow from the Federal Reserve System (the largest borrowing in history). This, in turn, lowered the federal funds interest rate from 8.04 to 7.41% (because of a surplus of cash in the system). The one-day borrowing cost the Bank of New York about $5 million.

The Federal Reserve System's chairman was critical of the Bank's decision to continue doing business once its system went down. He has long suggested that banks develop backup systems and urged a penalty interest rate for banks that borrow to cover their own computer system failures. Congressmen criticized the Bank of New York for continuing to operate even though the bank did not know for sure if it could fix its problem.

Adapted from "DP Nightmare Hits N.Y. Bank," *Computerworld*, December 2, 1985.

Until a few years ago, OAS were normally not included in a textbook such as this one. They were considered separate, largely clerical systems. This is no longer true. OAS today support clerical, managerial, and professional workers. Often the same device (a microcomputer) that supports an office function (e.g., correspondence) also functions as a professional work station, employing analytical models. Office systems increasingly are tied into the organization's other systems.

Management information systems (*MIS*) provide managers with reports and, in some cases, on-line access to the organization's current performance and historical records. MIS primarily serve the functions of planning, controlling, and decision making at the management level. Generally, they condense information obtained from TPS and present it to management in the form of routine summary and exception reports. MIS have highly limited analytical capabilities; they simply use models to present data. Typically, they are oriented almost exclusively to internal, not environmental or external, events. An example is an accounts receivable subsystem that totals the outstanding balances overdue each month.

Some researchers treat MIS as a broad concept including all of the information systems that support the functional areas of the organization (Davis, 1985). However, we prefer to use computer-based information system (*CBIS*) as the umbrella term for all information systems and to consider *management information systems* as those specifically dedicated to management-level functions.

Decision support systems (*DSS*) are devoted to supporting management decisions that are semistructured, unique or rapidly changing, and not easily specified far in advance. They differ from MIS in several ways. DSS have more advanced analytical capabilities that permit the user to employ several different models to analyze information. These systems draw on internal information from TPS and MIS, and they often bring in information from external sources (e.g., current prices of financial futures supplied by another company). DSS tend to be more interactive, providing users with easy access to data and analytical models through user-friendly computer instructions. An example is an ocean ship tracking system that calculates a ship's optimal speed and direction based on current weather, availability of port facilities, and current location.

Executive support systems (*ESS*) are a new category of systems that support decision making by senior management. They serve the strategic level of the organization. ESS address unstructured decisions and involve a generalized computing and communications environment rather than any fixed application or specific capability. ESS are oriented toward external events, although they do draw summarized information from internal MIS and DSS. Although they have limited analytical capabilities, ESS employ the most advanced graphics software and can deliver graphs and data from many sources immediately to a senior executive's office or a boardroom.

ESS represent less a solution to a specific question than a generalized computing and telecommunications capacity that can be applied to many situations. Compared to DSS, ESS tend to make less use of analytical models; instead, they deliver information to managers on a demand and highly interactive basis in a more open-ended manner.

Figure 2.5 depicts the roles played by each of the major types of information systems in the organization.

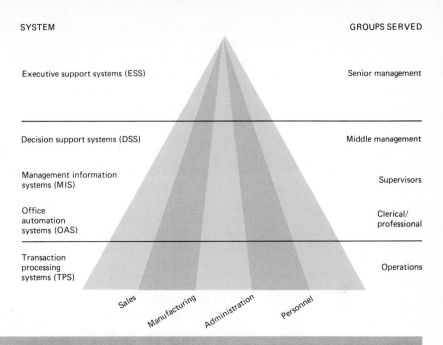

SYSTEM

GROUPS SERVED

Executive support systems (ESS)

Senior management

Decision support systems (DSS)

Middle management

Management information systems (MIS)

Supervisors

Office automation systems (OAS)

Clerical/ professional

Transaction processing systems (TPS)

Operations

Sales   Manufacturing   Administration   Personnel

FIGURE 2.5
Types of information processing systems. Information systems serve different levels and groups within the organization.

The Future: Strategic Role of Systems

Strategic-level systems have been growing in influence and number. One of the most exciting trends has been the growth of strategic information systems that give organizations a competitive advantage. They include not only systems that support upper-management planning but also systems that create new products and services, open new markets, improve the delivery of services, and reduce costs. Information systems are now recognized as playing a strategic role in an organization's survival and prosperity. The strategic uses of information and information systems has become so important that the next chapter is devoted entirely to this issue.

Relationship of Systems to One Another: Integration

Do organizations have a single MIS that serves the entire organization and coordinates all of the special systems previously outlined? Would it not be best to have such a single, total system to ensure that information can flow where it is needed, that it is uniform, and that all new systems are coordinated? Can the concept of MIS subordinate all other systems?

This *total systems* view, although occasionally supported by writers in the field (along with references to *systems theory*), is rapidly becoming outdated. In fact, no organization builds systems this way, and it would be foolish to try. The total systems view assumes that some specialist exists somewhere who can understand "the total information needs" of the organization (Ackoff, 1967). But the activities of a Sears, a General Motors, or even a small manufacturer are so diverse that many different specialists are needed to build different systems serving different purposes.

A more contemporary view is that systems should be integrated with one another—that is, they should provide for the systematic flow of information among different systems. This so-called integrated approach has merits. But integration costs money, and it would be foolish to build bridges among systems simply for the sake of building bridges.

In the real world, managers provide the level of integration needed to operate the business. Connections among systems evolve over time. Most systems are built in isolation from other systems (unless some business reason suggests a different approach). Organizations do not build all systems at once (the resources required would be enormous, the management problems insurmountable). With the development of new hardware and software, especially database management systems and private telecommunications systems, building bridges among systems is becoming less expensive and more reliable.

A penalty is paid for this evolutionary approach to systems. Systems are often not as integrated as they sometimes need to be.

Pulling Things Together at GM

Roger B. Smith, chairman of General Motors, complained in a recent speech "that most large companies were being managed by systems in their infancy. The result often was companies with uncoordinated systems, resembling little more than a collection of empires built by department heads who were fiercely loyal to their own particular functions."

GM, in a move toward a future "paperless" company where all business is conducted over electronic networks, recently bought EDS, Inc., for $2.55 billion. GM operates 80 sites in 26 states, plus overseas divisions. One billion dollars a year is spent on data processing for a hodgepodge of uncoordinated systems developed over the last thirty years. GM believes it has 17 different computer aided design/computer aided manufacturing (CAD/CAM) systems and 65 different word processing systems, and recently discovered 50 telecommunications networks in the company.

Adapted from "A Banner Year for Auto Sales," *The New York Times*, September 10, 1985 and "Survival of the Fattest," *The Economist*, October 12, 1985.

Occasionally, a massive effort is required to develop new data processing and telecommunications systems that can integrate systems. Thus, General Motors recently purchased one of the largest system contractors in the country, Electronic Data Systems (EDS), to develop a seamless, interconnected set of systems.

Obviously, GM needs more integrated systems to compete with imports. EDS will slowly move to centralize, coordinate, and control system evolution. This action, in turn, will lead to more layers of management approval for systems and more bureaucracy. Eventually, centralization will reach the saturation point. Central controls will be nibbled away, and more freedom will be granted to GM's operating divisions to develop needed systems more rapidly.

In short, decisions to integrate systems, to centralize control, are like the tides—they ebb and flow in accordance with business conditions and values. There is no "one right level" of integration or centralization (King, 1984).

2.4 Examples of Information Systems

This section describes the five major types of systems by giving concrete examples of real-world systems that utilize the graphic symbols and vocabulary developed in the first part of the chapter.

System type	Marketing systems	Production systems	Financial systems	Personnel systems	Other types (e.g., university)
Major functions	Sales management Market research Promotion Pricing New products	Scheduling Purchasing Shipping/receiving Engineering Operations	Budget General ledger Billing Cost accounting	Personnel records Benefits Payroll Labor relations Training	Admissions Grade records Course records Alumni
Major application systems	Sales order information system Market research system Pricing system	Materials resource planning systems Purchase order control systems Engineering systems Quality control systems	General ledger Accounts receivable/payable Budget Funds management systems	Payroll Employee records Benefit systems Career path systems Personnel planning systems	Registration system Student transcript system Curriculum class control system Alumni benefactor system

FIGURE 2.6
Typical TPS systems. There are four categories of TPS, as well as other systems that are unique to specific industries. TPS reflect the major business functions found in most organizations: marketing, production, finance, and personnel. Within each of these major functions are subfunctions. For each of these subfunctions (e.g., sales management) there is a major application system.

Transactions Processing Systems

All organizations have five kinds of TPS, even if they are manual or based on the memory of the owner. These five kinds of TPS are marketing, production, financial, personnel, and industry specific (a grab bag of systems unique to a particular industry). Figure 2.6 describes these systems in terms of their major functions and application systems.

Figures 2.7 and 2.8 depict an accounts receivable system and a payroll system developed by the authors for a medium-sized consumer products distributor in New Jersey. The company has over 12,000 customers in the Northeast and a labor force of 205. The system was installed on an IBM System 36 minicomputer.

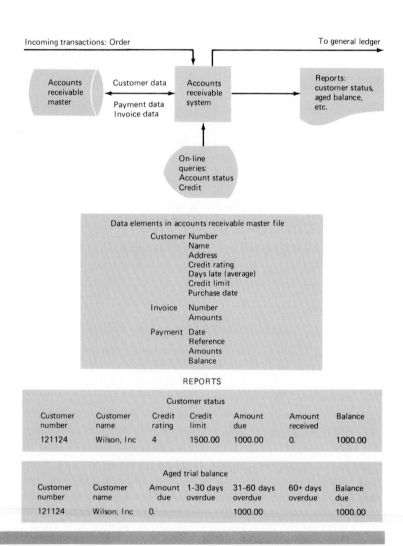

FIGURE 2.7
An accounts receivable schematic.

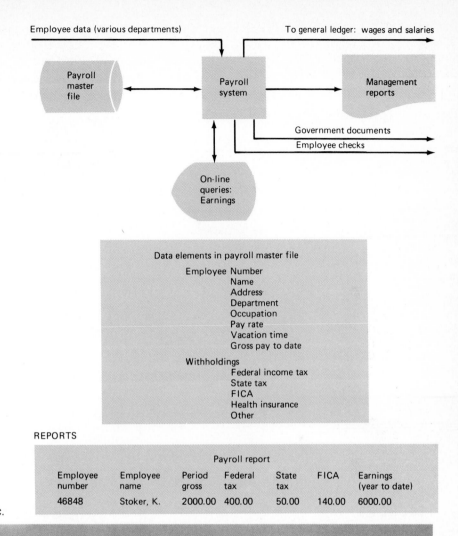

FIGURE 2.8
A payroll system schematic.

The master file in each of the systems is composed of discrete pieces of information (such as a name, address, or customer number) called *data elements*. Data are keyed into the system and the data elements are updated. The elements on the master file are combined in different ways to make up reports of interest to management. Typical reports are shown. Other reports can be composed of any combination of existing data elements.

Office Automation Systems

The ideal OAS would allow for the seamless creation, storage, and communication of documents, voice and written messages, images, and data from any point in the firm to any other point. A more modest goal—still far away—would provide for this capability within a single division or even a single large office. The truth is that

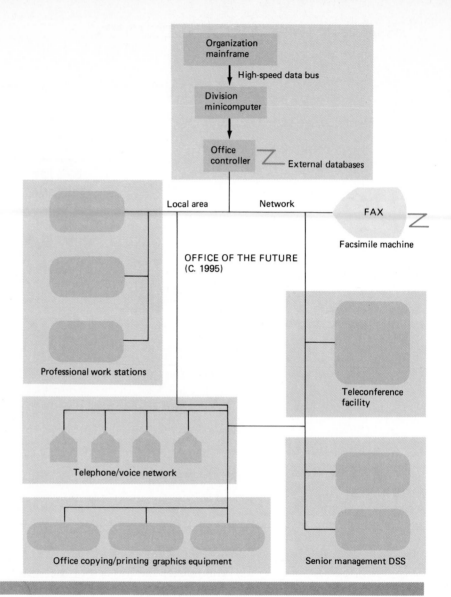

FIGURE 2.9
Office automation: The ideal.
A totally integrated voice/
digital/video office of the
future.

today it is still virtually impossible to create a document on a personal desktop computer, send it to a copying machine electronically for duplication or transparency creation, and then send it to other office workers for their information. Instead of such integrated capabilities, we have many separate automated devices but few means of connecting them.

Figure 2.9 shows an office automation ideal: a fully integrated voice/digital office system that can coordinate the document, image, data, and voice needs of different kinds of office workers, as well as

Manufacturers Hanover Trust's Worldwide Telecommunications Net

Manufacturers Hanover Trust (MHT) had developed prototype office automation systems on a piecemeal basis throughout the 1970s. It quickly became apparent that as an international, multidivisional bank, MHT needed to connect offices in New York and Hong Kong, and to connect different bank division offices both domestically and internationally. Automating one office at a time, one division at a time, would not lead to this broader capability.

MHT decided that it needed a worldwide telecommunications network that could connect different office systems, be available to all employees with either terminals or stand-alone microcomputers, handle corporate data transfers as well as documents, and potentially expand to handle video conferences. In 1982 MHT began operating GEONET—a worldwide telecommunications network that connects local and foreign offices, and within the national U.S. market ties together offices that otherwise have incompatible office systems.

Adapted from "Manufacturers Hanover Corporation—World Wide Network," Harvard Business School Case Study, 1984.

tie into corporate telecommunication and data facilities. The dotted lines indicate that at present most OAS today involve devices that are not linked to one another. One organization that comes close to the ideal is Manufacturers Hanover Trust, a large New York bank.

The development of fully transparent communications networks—sometimes called *integrated services digital networks*—will extend into the 1990s. The evolution of telecommunications systems means that systems do not have to be compatible from the beginning. Incompatible systems can be plugged into a single communications network and, through telecommunications computers permitted to "talk" with one another. (These systems are discussed in Chapter 9.)

Unfortunately, most of the products now available do not allow terminals and equipment from different manufacturers to be connected together. For instance, no product now available can connect an IBM PC to a Xerox machine. Even IBM's powerful office communication system, the Distributed Office Support System (DISOSS), which can connect many IBM products, cannot connect powerful work stations made by Xerox (or many other manufacturers) with

IBM mainframes and even fails to connect some IBM products to one another (Morris, 1985).

It should be clear that most organizations have not developed a single, organizationwide OAS. Nevertheless, many interesting bits and pieces of the future automated office are now on the shelf. Let's look at two: digital image processing and video teleconferencing.

Digital Image Processing

One of the largest impediments to automating offices is finding a way to digitize paper documents that must be preserved as images. For instance, many documents—from marriage licenses, to birth certificates, to contracts of all kinds—require a signature and the preservation of that signature for a long period. Moreover, many basic documents, like purchase orders, invoices, approval sheets, remittance advice, and others, are still stored manually in filing cabinets. Ragan Information Systems of New Jersey has developed a digital means of getting rid of paper filing systems for ATT's accounts payable department.

Images require a very large number of bits to store properly and hence overwhelm data storage devices. Systems like those described previously will become even more powerful when optical disk storage technology is further developed (see Chapter 6).

Getting Rid of Filing Cabinets

ATT Technologies in Kearny, New Jersey, operates a completely automated electronic document image filing and retrieval system. The paperless document system is supplied by Ragan Information Systems (North Arlington, New Jersey). The system processes over 1000 accounts receivable documents per day, saves 500 square feet of file space, permitted 20 less staff, reduced the filing backlog by 95%, and eliminated misfiled and out-of-file conditions.

So called paperless office systems, ATT found, usually relied on manually microfilming documents (microfiche) that reduced paper files but did not automate input, storage, or retrieval of documents. These older systems stored the location of a film box, or microfiche card, but from there it was all manual labor. The Ragan storage and retrieval module stores 1.2 million page images in digital form. Up to 128 modules can be on-line in a single system. The system retrieves a document in 10 seconds, on average.

Adapted from "The Art of Filing," *Infosystems*, January 1985.

The American Video Teleconferencing Corporation (AVTC) has created a hardware/software package that permits inexpensive teleconferencing using existing spare capacity on IBM mainframes and IBM's System Network Architecture (SNA) data network. Most corporations with IBM mainframes and remote time-shared terminals have an SNA network—an in-house digital communications network that ties IBM terminals and mainframes together. The SNA system is rarely utilized fully. The AVTC INFORUM (TM) teleconference system uses the SNA network to transmit still conference images and personal computer graphics from one electronic conference center to another. The cost is approximately $65,000 per facility.

Adapted from AVTC literature.

Video Teleconferencing

Business people have known for years that video conferencing could help bring ideas and people together from remote locations. It could reduce business travel and costs but, most important, could cut down on lost executive time involved in going to and from distant meetings. The problem has been the high cost of installing complex video conference facilities and the lack of off-the-shelf technology that could integrate video images with data and voice transmission. Short of establishing their own television broadcasting system, even large businesses were stymied. A new product—like the one described above—that uses existing built-in computer telecommunication facilities might solve this bottle neck.

Management Information Systems

Most contemporary organizations contain three kinds of MIS. Sometimes this term is used for any computer application. But we mean something quite specific here. The three different types of MIS are strategic business unit MIS, which support a single division or business unit; coordinating MIS; and policy/planning MIS. Figure 2.10 shows where each of these MIS fit into the organization. Table 2.2 describes the characteristics of typical MIS systems.

Unlike MIS are *reporting systems* that summarize the activities recorded in TPS. MIS serve managers interested in weekly, monthly, and yearly results—not in day-to-day activities (Gorry, 1971).

Unlike DSS (to be described subsequently), MIS address structured questions that are known well in advance, are generally not flexible, and have little analytical capability. For instance, one cannot

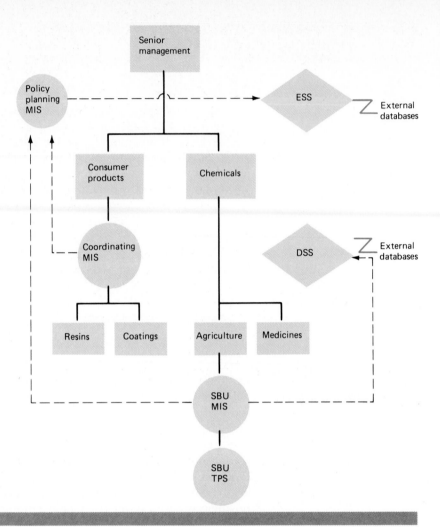

FIGURE 2.10
The three different kinds of management support systems: management information systems (MIS), decision support systems (DSS), and executive support systems (ESS).

instruct an MIS to "take the monthly sales figures by zip code and correlate with the Bureau of the Census estimates of income by zip code." First, a typical MIS contains only corporate internal data, not external data like the Census figures. Second, most MIS have little or no analytical capability—like regression analysis. Third, the data on sales by zip code would not be available unless a user had informed the designer several years earlier that this arrangement of data might be useful. MIS are developed over many years by professional staff working in a formal environment.

What can an MIS do? Figure 2.11 shows a strategic business unit (SBU) reporting system for a fortune 500 consumer products company. The company is organized by product line—SBUs—that act as profit centers. All SBUs have a common MIS system. Information

TABLE 2.2
Characteristics of MIS

1. They support structured and semistructured decisions at the operational and management control levels. However, they are also useful for planning purposes of senior management staff.

2. They are generally reporting and control oriented. They are designed to report on existing operations and therefore to help provide day-to-day control of operations.

3. They rely on existing corporate data and data flows.

4. They have little analytical capability.

5. They are generally past and present (not future) oriented.

6. They are relatively inflexible.

7. They have an internal rather than an external orientation.

8. Information requirements are known and stable.

9. They require a lengthy analysis and design process (on the order of one to two years).

from the TPS systems is downloaded once a week into a number of MIS files. These files can be accessed using user-friendly software that managers themselves can learn to use to structure their reports and queries.

Note that this arrangement of batch reports from the TPS to the MIS permits the TPS to operate without interference from management requests for information. However, the MIS system permits on-line access to managers with a user-friendly software called FOCUS.

This system has many uses. For example, suppose that a patent is about to expire and the controller wants to monitor price movement and customer activity on the product, since competitors will soon be producing it and will most likely cut prices. Or a sales director plans to visit a major customer for negotiations on price and volume discounts. He needs to know if the prices charged to this customer this year are keeping pace with cost increases. Is the customer buying as much as last year? Figure 2.12 shows how the director of sales uses the system to get answers.

The SBU system is one of a new class of advanced MIS systems. It is integrated with multiple TPS files and accepts on-line query languages that managers can use to structure their own reports.

Many older MIS do not have these features. They generally report from separate files, and managers themselves must put the results together (often manually). They typically do not permit on-line access with user-friendly languages. Instead, many MIS

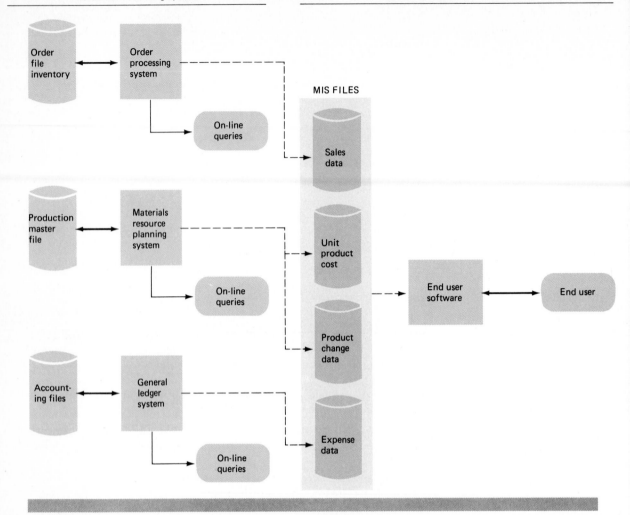

FIGURE 2.11

Strategic business unit reporting system (SBU/MIS). Most MIS systems obtain their data from the organization's TPS. In this case, three TPS systems supply summarized transaction data at the end of the week to the SBU/MIS reporting system. Users gain access to the organizational data through the MIS, using special software easily understood by nonsystem managers. This user-friendly software permits managers to structure—within limits—their own reports without the assistance of system experts or a Data Processing Department. This is one element of end-user computing discussed in later chapters.

MIS HARDWARE/SOFTWARE   SYSTEM DIALOGUE

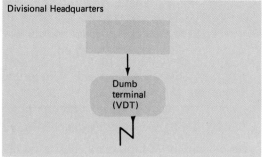

Divisional Headquarters

Dumb
terminal
(VDT)

How much has my customer
bought so far and what is the
profit margin?

Put this request on the network.
Send this request via our leased
line to corporate headquarters.

Corporate Headquarters

Telecom-
munications
monitor
(VTAM)

This is a batch request. Time-
Sharing Option (TSO) will handle
this request.

Time-sharing
system (TSO)

This request calls for FOCUS.

Mainframe
operating
system

Start up FOCUS (a user interface
language).

Application
language
(FOCUS)

Select customer records, average
margin from January to December
1986. Print by product and date
and profit margin.

Database
manager
(FOCUS)

Access MIS FOCUS files and
produce report.

Sales
data
file

Unit
product
cost

Product
change
file

Expense
data
file

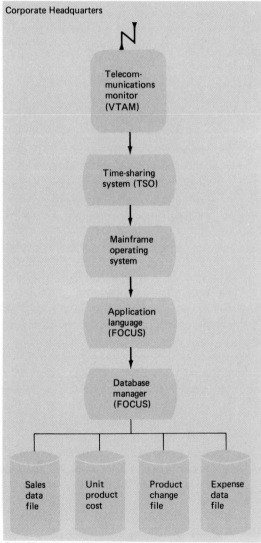

FIGURE 2.12
How the user interacts with
the MIS.

deliver reports periodically to a manager's desk, with little opportunity for the manager to structure them. In many MIS, the manager who requested the report has taken another job. The manager who receives the report may not even know its purpose.

Decision Support Systems

Any system that supports a decision is a DSS. True, but systems support decisions in vastly different ways, and there is a class of systems that supports decisions in a unique way (at least when compared to the past). Contemporary DSS differ from MIS and TPS systems because they focus on the following:

- Flexibility, adaptability, and a quick response
- User initiation and control
- Operating with little professional data professional involvement
- Providing support for unstructured decisions and problems
- Top management decision making

Computer Tracks Chemical Clouds

Union Carbide and other companies have begun to install a DSS made by Safer Emergency Systems, Inc., that predicts the movement of toxic chemical clouds that may leak from chemical plants. The system was installed after the tragic release of methyl isocyanate from a Union Carbide plant in Bhopal, India, on December 3, 1984, which killed at least 2000 people—the largest industrial accident in history.

The results of the DSS will be used to alert fire fighters and local residents. The system predicts cloud movement based on type of chemical, time of leak, type of equipment involved, wind, and temperature. Chemical engineers used to perform these calculations in hours, but the system does it in seconds.

On Sunday August 11, 1985, the DSS was given a trial run in Institute, West Virginia, when a Union Carbide plant leaked aldicarb oxime, causing 135 injuries. Unfortunately, the computer was not programmed to predict the behavior of aldicarb oxime, and the system was of little use. Hundreds of chemicals are made at the plant, and programming for each one costs about $500. So far, only 10 chemicals have been installed on the system. A Union Carbide spokesman noted, "We must make some sort of judgment."

Adapted from "Carbide Computer Could Not Track Gas That Escaped," *New York Times*, August 14, 1985.

Computer Battles Forest Fires

The Forest Service (Bureau of Land Management, Department of the Interior) uses a DSS called the *Initial Attack Management System* to direct fire-fighting efforts for large forest fires. The system uses the type of fuel, moisture, angle of slope, ambient temperature, and wind speed and direction to predict the course of forest fires. The system predicts fire, speed, direction, temperature, length of flames, and length of time required to contain the fire. In a 27,000-acre fire near Helena, Montana, the system successfully predicted that a fire would burn itself out and that a new eight-mile fire line was not necessary. This saved $670,000 in labor and materials.

Adapted from "Computer Helps Battle Forest Fires," *New York Times*, August 1, 1985.

DSS are quick-hit, interactive, model oriented, and action oriented, whereas MIS systems are ponderous, batch oriented, and data oriented (Sprague, 1982; Keen, 1985).

DSS have to be responsive enough to run several times a day in order to correspond to changing conditions like those shown in the two following examples, which help predict the movement of toxic chemical clouds and support fire fighters.

DSS have a different clientele from MIS. DSS tend to be custom built for higher levels of management or, in some cases, for the vast army of "knowledge workers"—managers, analysts, clerks—whose primary job is handling information and making decisions.

The difference between DSS and other systems and the ideal configuration of DSS systems are described in Figure 2.13. Clearly, by design, DSS have more analytical power; they are explicitly built with a variety of models to analyze data. The database is important as well, but the emphasis is on analysis. Second, DSS, by design, are more user oriented; they explicitly include user-friendly software. This follows both from their purpose (to inform personal decision making by key actors) and from the method of design (see Chapter 16). Third, these systems are interactive; the user can change assumptions and draw in new data.

An interesting, small, but powerful DSS is the voyage estimating system of a subsidiary of a large American vertically integrated metals company that exists primarily to carry bulk cargoes of coal, oil, ores, and finished products for its parent company. It owns some vessels, charters others, and bids for shipping contracts in the open market to carry general cargo.

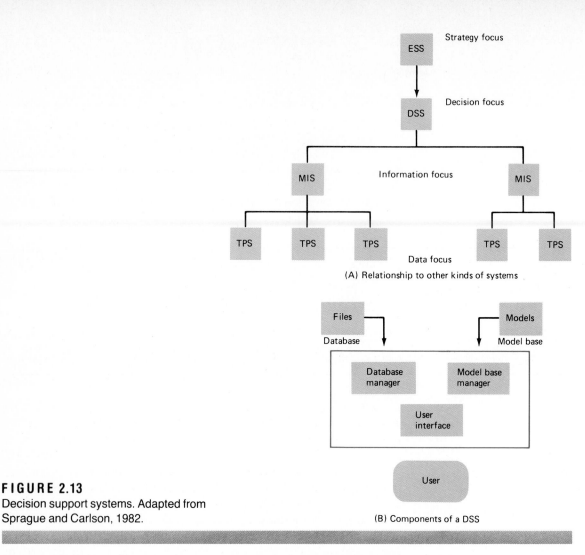

FIGURE 2.13
Decision support systems. Adapted from
Sprague and Carlson, 1982.

A voyage estimating system calculates financial and technical voyage details. Financial calculations include ship/time costs (fuel, labor, capital), freight rates for various types of cargo, port expenses, and so on. Technical details include myriad factors such as ship cargo capacity (deadweight tons, tons per inch immersion, etc.), speed, port distances, fuel and water consumption, and loading patterns (location of cargo for different ports).

An existing system to calculate only operating costs, freight rates, and profit was run on the company mainframe. The reports could not be understood by the managers because of the wealth of technical details they contained; only one person in the MIS department could run the program; and it took several weeks to make

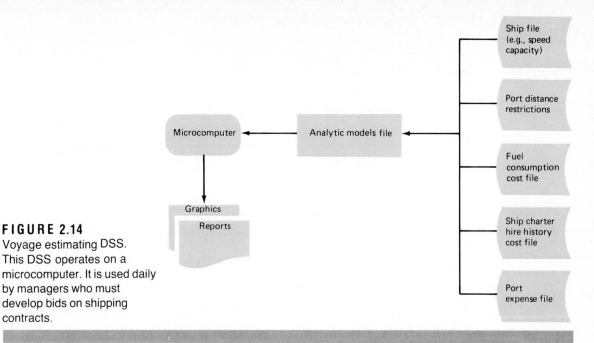

FIGURE 2.14
Voyage estimating DSS.
This DSS operates on a
microcomputer. It is used daily
by managers who must
develop bids on shipping
contracts.

changes in assumptions (cost of fuel, speed). Morever, the system could not answer questions such as: Given a customer delivery schedule and an offered freight rate, which vessel should be assigned at what rate to maximize profits? What is the optimum speed at which a particular vessel can optimize its profit and still meet its delivery schedule? What is the optimal loading pattern for a ship bound for the U.S. West Coast from Malaysia?

Senior and middle management wanted a more interactive system that they could control and run themselves, with as many changes in data and models as they needed and with little interference from data processing professionals. They also needed information immediately to respond to bidding opportunities.

Figure 2.14 illustrates the DSS built for this company. The system operates on a large microcomputer, utilizes a friendly menu-driven user interface, is totally under management control, and required about 60 man-days to build.

Executive Support Systems

Executive support systems (ESS) are the newest addition to the family of systems found in large organizations. Unlike DSS, they represent a generalized computing, telecommunications, and display capability that can be focused and applied to many specific problems. The audience is senior management. The questions ESS must assist in

Putting Corporate Data at Executives' Fingertips

A recent survey by MIT's Center for Information Systems Research found that more than half of the Fortune 500 companies are developing executive information systems in one form or another. Typically, an ESS is a terminal or microcomputer that provides access to personal, corporate, and external databases. They are tailored to the executives' personal needs with easy-to-use, menu-driven software.

Sears, Roebuck and Company has developed its executive support system, as has General Motors. These systems provide instant access to the previous day's operating results. The U.S. Army has developed a system for senior officers that has 1400 charts that are automatically updated each time the data change.

Adapted from "Executive Support Systems Put Corporate Data Base at Top Managers' Fingertips With Touch of a Button" and "Analyze Needs For Executive Systems," in *Computerworld*, March 25, 1985.

answering include: What business should we be in? What are the competitors doing? What new acquisitions would protect us from cyclical business swings? Which units should we sell to raise cash for acquisitions? What is the impact on earnings of proposed changes in the investment tax credit? (Rockart, 1982; Keen, 1985).

Why were these systems not developed years ago? One of the reasons is that senior executives associated keyboard terminals with clerical work. More significantly, the technology was not available. The data flows were often not established because traditional MIS departments did not think in terms of presenting data to senior managers. Equipment was expensive, especially for color graphics terminals and plotters. And, most importantly, user-friendly software simply did not exist before the development of microcomputers.

In Chapter 1 we described several corporate reporting systems directed to senior management at Motorola and Gould, Inc., that utilized predefined tables and graphs to chart a firm's performance, and that permitted interactive linking of charts, changes in assumptions, and other options. Here we will illustrate a less structured executive information system designed for the governor of Massachusetts—more of a personal executive support system.

A Governor's Executive Support System

Technology Systems, Inc., of Lexington, Massachusetts, is marketing an executive information system for senior executives. The system was developed originally for the governor of Massachusetts and has since been marketed to other governors, mayors, and private firms. Written for the Wang VS 100 minicomputer, the system was designed to automate the governor's major tasks: correspondence, scheduling, tracking requests, constituent developments, job applications, and appointees. The system can perform global searches across all files and merge information from any of the files. The result, according to users, is a much better organized office and improved ability to answer the question "what have you done for us?"

Adapted from "Software Running For Office," *Computerworld*, December 23, 1985.

Executive support systems like the one just described have little to do with the operational data of the firm or with analytic models. Instead, they focus more on personal support of senior executives, whose styles differ considerably. Even senior executives with a given style face radically changing environments and questions. Systems must be built that can adapt to these new conditions. ESS are one response to this challenge.

2.5 Summary

There are five major types of information systems in contemporary organizations: (1) transaction processing systems, (2) office automation systems, (3) management information systems, (4) decision support systems, and (5) executive support systems. These various systems are designed for different purposes and different audiences.

Transaction processing systems (TPS) serve the operational level of the organization. They perform and record the daily routine transactions that are necessary to conduct business. They also produce information for the other systems. Many organizations today would come to a standstill if their TPS failed for a day or even a few hours. Examples are systems for order processing, airline reservations, and payroll.

Office automation systems (OAS) support clerical, managerial, and professional workers at the operational and management control levels. They consist of facilities for word processing, document storage, facsimile transmission, and electronic mail. OAS are increasingly tied into other systems in the organization.

Management information systems (MIS) provide the management control level with reports and access to the organization's current performance and historical records. Most MIS reports condense information from TPS and are not highly analytical.

Decision support systems (DSS) support management decisions when these decisions are semistructured, unique, rapidly changing, and not specified easily in advance. They have more advanced analytical models than MIS and often draw on information from external as well as internal sources.

Executive support systems (ESS) support the strategic level by providing a generalized computing and communications environment to assist senior management's decision making. They have limited analytical capabilities but can draw on sophisticated graphics software and many sources of internal and external information.

The different systems in an organization are only loosely integrated. Developing links among systems is costly, but so is the lack of sufficient links.

Key Words

Rationalization of procedures
Secondary storage
Input device
Output device
Batch processing
On-line processing
Direct access file
Master file

Transaction file
Transaction processing system (TPS)
Office automation system (OAS)
Digital image
Management information system (MIS)
Decision support system (DSS)
Executive support system (ESS)
Integration of systems

Review Questions

1. What are five characteristics of contemporary information systems?
2. What do we mean by rationalization of procedures? Why is this essential for building CBIS?
3. List five different ways of storing information.
4. What is the difference betweeen batch and on-line processing? Can you diagram the difference?
5. List the five major types of systems in organizations.
6. What are the five major categories of TPS in business organizations? What functions do they perform? Give examples of each.
7. Describe the components and functions of an idea OAS. Why has this ideal been difficult to achieve?

8. What are the characteristics of MIS? How do MIS differ from TPS? From DSS?
9. What are the characteristics of DSS? How do they differ from ESS?
10. Why are ESS a relatively new phenomenon?
11. How are the five major types of systems in organizations related to each other?

Discussion Questions

1. Discuss the major factors that may prevent an organization from building a totally integrated information system that combines all five types into a single design effort.
2. One of the problems with office automation is that different manufacturers make incompatible equipment. Discuss possible solutions to this problem.
3. Most senior executives do not like to spend a lot of time learning how to use computers, and most do not spend much time looking at reports and numbers. What are the implications of this situation for ESS?

CASE STUDY

Electronic Paper Flow

Blue Cross and Blue Shield of Virginia provides medical and health insurance coverage for 2.2 million people, making it one of the 10 largest Blue Cross and Blue Shield insurance organizations in the country. The company processes about 14 million claims per year for its Blue Cross, Blue Shield, Major Medical, and Comprehensive hospital insurance plans. More than 2000 written inquiries per day from physicians, subscribers, hospitals, and the organization's internal departments must also be handled.

Inquiries consist of requests on claim status and queries about special situations. A research group found that this Blue Cross and Blue Shield organization had accumulated a backlog of 20,000 unanswered inquiries, well above the national standards set by the Blue Cross and Blue Shield Association. Blue Cross and Blue Shield of Virginia was taking an average of 35–40 days to respond to inquiries and was using manual log books to report on their status and location. Status questions about an inquiry required physical searches for hard copy in several locations, and the documents that were behind schedule frequently got lost in the paper shuffle.

To solve these problems, the organization installed PaperFlo, a paper-tracking system from Infocel, Inc., of Rockville, Maryland. The PaperFlo system uses reading wands attached to a series of notebook-sized computer terminals that are linked to an AT&T 3B2 computer.

A self-sticking bar code label is glued to all incoming documents concerning claim status inquiries. The labeled documents are sorted into batches according to insurance plan and origin. By passing the reading wand over the bar code, the inquires are then entered into the PaperFlo system. Additional information such as patient name, contract number, and insurance provider number is keyed into the system from the work stations.

The sorting helps to maintain an inventory on a daily, weekly, and monthly basis, providing information on the nature of each inquiry. The status of the inquiry can be updated by passing the reading wand over the bar code label and keying in the appropriate changes. A control area can then determine when a document was sent to another area, the overall age of the document, and whether inquiries are duplicates. The wand and a few keystrokes delete inquiries that have been resolved.

By automating paper flow, Blue Cross and Blue Shield of Virginia reduced its cycle time to a 3% backlog over 14 days, surpassing the national standard. The system has cut the amount of time required to count each inquiry and has improved customer service. The organization can respond rapidly to phone queries because the system quickly reports on the status of claims being processed. It can also give priority to special requests.

Among PaperFlo's reports is a summary of work loads at each work station that shows total inquiries processed by each work station user. Its findings can be used to estimate the number of workers required during peak seasons and to monitor staff schedules and performance. Blue Cross and Blue Shield of Virginia is planning to tie this system to an on-line system that will provide a uniform format for checking inquiries through the entire organization. Its management notes that the PaperFlo system has created an awareness of inventory management and organizational structure that has helped it outpace other organizations.

Adapted from "System Lets Insurer Track Paper Flow," *Information Week*, July 28, 1986.

Case Study Questions

1. Which characteristics of contemporary information systems does this system illustrate?
2. Prepare a graphic diagram of this system, using the tools for describing systems introduced in this chapter.
3. Which of the major kinds of systems does this system illustrate? What functions does it perform? What organizational levels does it serve?
4. How does this system illustrate the point made earlier in this chapter that many information processing advances have resulted from innovative systems design and rationalization of procedures?

References

Ackoff, R.L. "Management Misinformation System." *Management Science*, Vol. 14, No. 4 (December 1967), pp. B140–B156.

Davis, Gordon B., and Olson, Margrethe H. *Management Information Systems: Conceptual Foundations, Structure, and Development*, 2nd ed. New York: McGraw-Hill, 1985.

Gorry, G.A., and Scott-Morton, M.S. "A Framework for Management Information Systems," *Sloan Management Review*, Vol. 13, No. 1 (1971), pp. 55–70.

Keen, Peter. "A Walk Through Decision Support," *Computerworld*, (January 14, 1985).

King, John. "Centralized vs. Decentralized Computing: Organizational Considerations and Management Options," *Computing Surveys* (Oct. 1984).

Morris, Paul. "What's All This Talk About IBM's DISOSS," *Software News* (February 1985).

Rockart, John F., and Treacy, Michael E. "The CEO Goes On-Line," *Harvard Business Review* (January–February 1982).

Sprague, Ralph H., Jr., and Carlson, Eric D. *Building Effective Decision Support Systems* Englewood. Cliffs, N.J.: Prentice-Hall, 1982.

CHAPTER 3

The Strategic Role of Information in Organizations and Management

- Leveraging Technology
- Breaking Down Organizational Boundaries
- Prerequisite: Organizational Change
- What Managers Can Do

3.6 Summary

In a tough, fragmented market, Metpath, Inc., the nation's largest provider of medical laboratory analyses for private physicians, faced stiff competition from local companies. The technology for laboratory analysis of patient specimens was widely available. Metpath lost its technological edge, customers lacked loyalty, and the competition was discounting heavily. But the company felt that it could keep its customers if it could provide better service and provide additional services in one package. Metpath installed computer terminals in doctors' offices, linking them to its laboratory computers. For a small fee, doctors receive test results as soon as they are determined—not days later.

Far from being just an ordinary order entry system, Metpath's system differentiates its product from that of its competitors, builds barriers against new rivals, and can be used for further product enhancements. Metpath keeps track of patient records and helps in diagnosis, in billing, and even in tracing allergies to drugs. In the future, doctors will use the Metpath system to test for drug interactions before writing prescriptions. Metpath has developed a *strategic system*.

Adapted from Computerworld, May 20, 1985.

Metpath, Inc. is just one of several examples of the strategic role of information systems you will learn about in this chapter.

In this chapter the student will learn:
- How the conception of information has changed in organizations.
- How organizations use information technology to develop new products and services, new relationships with customers and suppliers, and new ways of operating internally.
- How to use information technology to gain a competitive advantage.
- How strategic systems affect industries and organizations.

3.1 Introduction

In the last few decades, there has been a revolution in how organizations look at information and in the information systems that collect, store, and disseminate it. Today, leading companies and organizations are using information technology as a competitive tool to develop new products and services, forge new relationships with suppliers, edge out competitors, and radically change their internal operations and organizations. Government organizations at all levels are using information technology to define new relationships between citizens and the state and among nations.

What Does Strategic Mean?

Strategic systems are those that change the goals, products, services, or environmental relationships of organizations. Systems that have these effects literally change the business of organizations. Merrill Lynch, Pierce, Fenner, and Smith for instance, used information systems to change from the stock brokerage business to the financial services business. Metpath, Inc., in the preceding example, is using information systems to change its business from laboratory testing to integrated physician services.

Information Technology as Organizational Change Agent

In the previous chapter, we emphasized that information systems are designed to serve the various needs of the organization. In this supportive role, information systems sustain the existing organization, the existing products, and the existing procedures of the business.

Information systems continue to play this role, but they are also increasingly being used to change the organization, including its products and internal procedures. In this new role, technology and systems "drive" organizations into new behavior patterns. As we will see, organizations must often change their internal organization to take advantage of the new information systems technology. Using information systems strategically may require new managers, a new work force, and a much closer relationship with customers and suppliers.

3.2 Changing Conceptions of Information and Information Systems

Behind the growing strategic uses of information systems is a changing conception of information. Information is now considered a resource, much like capital and labor. This was not always the case.

Information as a Paper Dragon

In the past, information was often considered a necessary evil associated with the bureaucracy of designing, manufacturing, and distributing a product or service. Information was a "paper dragon" that could potentially strangle the firm and prevent it from doing its real work (see Table 3.1). Information systems of the 1950s focused on reducing the cost of routine paper processing. The first information systems were just semiautomatic check processing, issuing, and

TABLE 3.1
Changing Conceptions
of Information

Conception of Information	Information Systems	Purpose
Necessary evil (1950s) Bureaucratic requirement A paper dragon	Corresponding information systems of this period were called *electronic accounting machines* (*EAM*)	Speed accounting and paper processing
General-purpose support (1960s–1970s)	Management information systems (MIS) Information factory	Speed general reporting requirements
Customized management control (1970s–1980s)	Decision support systems (DSS) Executive support systems (ESS)	Improve and customize decision making
Strategic resource Competitive advantage Strategic weapon (1980s–1990s)	Strategic systems	Promote survival and prosperity of the organization

canceling machines—so-called electronic accounting machines (EAM). The purpose of these machines was to reduce the cost of paper processing, especially in accounting. The term *electronic data processing* (*EDP*) dates from this period.

Information for General Support

By the 1960s, the conception of information had changed. It was recognized that information could provide general support for an organization. The information systems of the 1960s and 1970s were frequently called *management information systems* (*MIS*) and were thought of as an information factory churning out reports on weekly production, monthly financial information flows, inventory, accounts receivable, accounts payable, and the like. This view of information systems was supported by the development of general-purpose computing equipment—hardware that could support many functions rather than simply canceling checks.

Information for Management

The conception of information changed once again in the 1970s and early 1980s. Information—and the systems that collected, stored, and processed it—were seen as providing fine-tuned, special-purpose, customized management control over the organization. The information systems of this period were called *decision support systems* (*DSS*) and *executive support systems* (*ESS*). Their purpose was to improve and speed up the decision-making process of specific managers and executives in a broad range of problems.

In the last decade, most organizations have established good, workable information systems to support daily administrative tasks and specific managerial decisions.

Information as a Strategic Resource

In the mid-1980s, the conception of information is beginning to change once again. Information is now seen as a strategic resource, a potential source of competitive advantage, or a strategic weapon to defeat and frustrate the competition. These changing conceptions of information reflect advances in strategic planning and theory (Porter, 1985a). As a resource, information can be managed. This fact has led to the development of an entire new field called *information resources management* (which is discussed in Chapter 20). This concept is behind the Paperwork Reduction Act of 1980, which requires federal government agencies to develop an information resource officer. The kinds of systems being built to support this concept of information are called *strategic systems*, and their purpose is to ensure the survival and prosperity of the organization in the near future.

3.3 Examples of the Strategic Role of Information Systems

Information systems play a strategic role in the organization in five major ways (see Figure 3.1). Here we describe the way some large corporations have used strategic information systems.

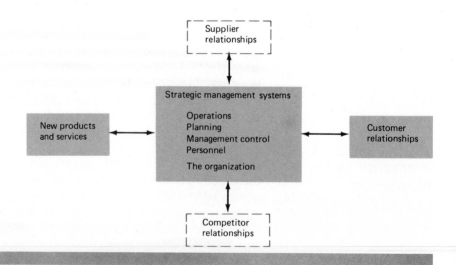

FIGURE 3.1
The strategic role of information systems.

Information Systems Products and Services

Financial institutions have led the way in the use of information systems to create new products and services. Thus, *Citibank*, the nation's largest bank, developed automatic teller machines (ATM) and bank debit cards in 1977. Seeking to tap the largest retail depository market in the United States, Citibank installed its ATM machines throughout the New York metropolitan area, everywhere a depositor might find the time to use them to deposit or withdraw money. Citibank operates 635 ATMs, more than any other single bank. Being a leader in this area permitted Citibank to become the largest bank in the United States in the last 10 years. Citibank ATMs have been so successful that Citibank's competitors, large and small, have been forced to counterstrike with a technological effort of their own called the *New York Cash Exchange* (NYCE). While others respond, Citibank is moving ahead to extend its strategic advantage as described in the following vignettes.

Merrill Lynch, the nation's largest retail brokerage firm, in 1978 developed a new financial product called a *Cash Management Account*, which permitted customers to transfer money freely from stocks to bonds to money market funds and to write checks against these funds cost free. Such flexibility in a single financial product brought Merrill Lynch into the banking industry and broadened its retail market appeal. It also forced other leading brokerage firms to offer a similar service and large banking institutions to counterstrike with their own flexible cash management systems. Citibank responded by developing an electronic home banking system called *Pronto*, which permits persons with home computers to manage funds held by Citibank, to switch funds among a variety of accounts, and to pay bills.

New York Cash Exchange

Some of the largest New York banks have joined together in a three state network, allowing millions of customers to use automated teller machines of any member bank. By the end of the year the New York Cash Exchange (NYCE) will serve 3.5 million customers with 1000 teller machines. Notable by its absence is Citibank, which already operates 635 teller machines. Citibank's retail strategy depends heavily on its ATM machines, and the NYCE poses a competitive challenge to Citibank, which refused to join.

Adapted from "Big New York Banks Link Teller Machines," *The New York Times*, March 7, 1985.

Citibank Strikes Back and Leaps Forward

Citicorp announced major new services to its retail customers. The first to install automatic teller machines, Citibank is pushing hard into home banking, image processing, and customer activated service terminals (CAS). The new customer terminals provide what ATM's can't: check clearing information and other data available only by a visit to the bank. The new machines will be placed alongside exisitng ATMs. To save on the costs of check processing, Citi is moving fast into electronic imaging, which will permit sorting and processing of check documents electronically.

Adapted from "Citicorp Seen as Pacesetter," *MIS Week*, December 19, 1984.

To gain a competitive edge, financial service companies are spending millions of dollars to create information systems that are faster and more flexible than those of their competitors. For instance, *Fidelity Brokerage Services, Inc.*, recently spent $8 million on a system that allows brokers to use desktop terminals to execute stock trades more quickly and less expensively than they could with most competitors, who have to buy their services from outside computing companies (*Business Week*, August 22, 1983). The Group, Life and Health Division of the *Massachusetts Mutual Insurance Company* recently developed its new Magnet Information System. This is a $20 million system that permits customers to pay for insurance in a new way: they deposit money in an interest-bearing account, and the system automatically deducts the payment for insurance each month, permitting them to earn interest on their money longer than in the past. Massachusetts Mutual believes that the company will make a $6 million profit this year compared with losses in several previous years (*Business Week*, August 22, 1983).

While the preceding examples all involve the development and use of *information systems*, there are, of course, a host of products, some relatively invisible to the consumer, that rely on computer components and chips: variable-speed motors, numerically controlled machine tools, industrial control devices, home burglary alarms, and audio laser disks (compact disks) for home stereo listening. These products are different from the ATMs, credit cards, cash management systems, and new payment systems previously described because they are the result of computerized information systems. This distinction between an information system and its strategic utilization, as opposed to products that incorporate computer components, is important.

Strategic Sales and Marketing Systems

While new information system *products and services* are highly visible, less visible but equally powerful are a new array of sales and marketing techniques based on information systems. Crucial to these techniques is the conception of existing information as a resource that can be "mined" by the organization to increase profitability and market penetration. A second feature of these systems is the development of techniques that differentiate products and services from those of competitors. Among the more important large corporations that have developed these systems are *Sears, J.C. Penney, American Hospital Supply, Owens-Corning, Southern Ohio Steel,* and *Management Science of America.*

Sears Roebuck and Company is using a variety of information systems as the backbone of its strategy to become the leader not only in American retailing but also in consumer financial services. Starting with a computerized information database on its 40 million retail customers—the largest retail customer base in the United States—Sears collects, stores, and continually mines its database to reach such targeted groups as appliance buyers, tool buyers, gardening enthusiasts, and mothers-to-be. Sears uses the same data to provide sales leads to other subsidiaries such as Allstate Insurance, brokerage house Dean Witter Reynolds (recently bought out by Sears and now a department within major Sears retail stores), and real estate brokers Coldwell-Banker.

For instance, when a customer buys a washer-dryer from Sears, either on credit or for cash, Sears mails a postcard advertising an annual maintenance contract. If the contract is not purchased, Sears maintains a record of who purchased the machine, using the information the customer supplies on the written guarantee. Each year, Sears sends out an annual maintenance contract renewal form to keep its maintenance business humming. At the same time, Sears routinely sends out notices to customers who purchased washer-dryers about special sales and products for such machines such as soap and replacement parts. Likewise with electric hand tools: Purchasers routinely receive fliers on sales and products put out by Sears.

Sears also uses its customer information database to track the purchases made by credit customers. This information is then used to target direct mail inserts that accompany the monthly credit card bill. In addition, information obtained on the initial credit application, as well as the history of credit purchases, can be used by the Sears marketing staff to target specific subgroups such as males between the ages of 40 and 50 who have a family and live in affluent zip code areas. This information can then be used to target life insurance, brokerage services, and real estate offers (*Business Week*, August 22, 1983).

Not to be outdone, Sears's chief rival, the *J.C. Penney Company*, a retailer with a base of approximately 20 million customers, has initiated a successful technology-based counterstrike. Penney established its own life insurance company (paralleling Sears's Allstate Insurance) and uses information gathered on its credit card applications and information purchased from the Department of Motor Vehicles of various states to target prospective insurance customers.

One of the earliest examples of a strategic sales and marketing system is provided by the *American Hospital Supply Corporation (AHSC)*. AHSC is the largest supplier of medical equipment and supplies to American hospitals. In the 1970s it developed a strategic plan to become a full-line supplier for hospitals, a one-stop source for all hospital needs. This effort required an inventory of more than 30,000 items. Maintaining a huge inventory is very costly. However, it is also costly not to have items in stock; hospitals switch to competitors.

Faced with this dilemma, AHSC placed its own terminals in the hospitals that were tied to AHSC computers by a leased-lined network (discussed in Chapter 11). When customers want to place an order, rather than call a salesperson or send a purchase order, they simply use an AHSC computer terminal to obtain access to the full catalog. The system generates shipping, billing, invoicing, and inventory information for AHSC. The hospital terminals provide customers with an estimated delivery date. The system was installed in 1978, and the company's sales have grown at a 17% compound annual rate. Reduced inventory requirements and lower sales costs have given AHSC a profit margin four times the industry average (Canning, 1984).

An example of a different use of information as a sales and marketing tool is provided by the *Owens-Corning Fiberglass Corporation*, the largest producer of home insulation in the United States. To stimulate sales, Owens-Corning had to make homeowners, especially those who were building new homes, as well as builders and contractors, aware of the advantages of energy-efficient homes and design techniques. Owens developed a substantial database on the energy efficiency of a wide variety of new and old home designs as part of its research effort to develop new insulation materials. It also developed a computer program that uses this information to come up with energy efficiency ratings for new designs and estimates of energy savings for changes in older homes. The company offered free evaluations to builders, contractors, and architects for their home designs if they agreed to buy all of their insulation from Owens and to meet Owens's energy standards. Owens advertised heavily in builders' and contractors' journals and began a direct marketing campaign to homeowners. By offering this unique service, Owens solidified its position as the leading supplier of fiberglass insulation (*Business Week*, August 22, 1983).

In heavy industries such as metals and construction, a powerful determinant of profit or loss is the speed with which inventory can be delivered to a job and used, storage and delivery costs reduced, and construction crews kept busy with sufficient materials.

To help solve these problems, a unique customer-oriented system was developed by *Southwestern Ohio Steel, Inc., (SOS)*. SOS is one of the 10 largest steel service centers in the United States, with annual sales of about $80 million. In 1982 management began to review the entire role of data processing in the firm and the strategic direction of the metals fabrication and distribution industry. More and more customers were demanding just-in-time delivery of steel to reduce their steel inventories and cost. Customers also demanded that the inventory be available when they needed it, so that their construction crews could be kept busy.

SOS top management wanted to know how their existing data processing functions could help solve this problem and expand their customer base even though the steel industry was facing stagnation. SOS's existing information systems were used for the routine accounting purposes typical of the MIS systems of the 1960s and 1970s. Eventually, SOS management identified three "critical success" systems: (1) a buying and inventory management system that would tell management what items customers were buying and what the daily levels of inventory were, (2) a marketing information system that would analyze and project specific customer needs, and (3) a production scheduling system that would minimize both inventories at SOS and delivery times to customers.

After two years of study, experimentation, and prototyping, SOS can now provide immediate access to the customer order status on the telephone, so that customers know precisely when to expect delivery. SOS has experienced a significant increase in the number of sales calls per salesperson because more useful information is available and customers have come to rely on it; it has increased its production efficiency by carefully analyzing customers' buying habits and producing goods in larger batches; and it has obtained more accurate inventory control and management of its slower-moving items. These systems have given SOS a competitive advantage as customers increasingly ask for just-in-time delivery (Canning, 1984).

The SOS system is not simply an information system. It also includes a significant telecommunications component; customers can call a manufacturer's information system. Strategic information systems are often based on the exploitation of new telecommunications technology.

One additional example of a telecommunications-oriented strategic sales and marketing system is provided by *Management Science of America (MSA)*—one of the leading independent suppliers of application software in the United States, with gross revenues of $139 million. After explosive growth in the 1970s, MSA was having difficulty meeting the maintenance needs of customers who had purchased its software. These customers needed expert advice on how to install, modify, debug, and operate MSA software. With its existing telephone installation, MSA was losing customer calls and could not determine who at MSA could best service a call. Moreover, the cost of customer service was rising rapidly. To solve this problem, MSA asked AT&T to develop a nationwide "HELP" number. This permits MSA clients anywhere in the United States and Canada to call one number whenever problems or questions arise. A unique call-routing system directs specific problems to the people at MSA who can best solve them. As a result, MSA clients receive prompt and convenient technical assistance. In addition, by tracking which customers purchased specific software products, AT&T and MSA developed a telemarketing program so that the MSA sales staff could routinely call their customers to inquire if they needed other products and if they were aware of upgrades to the software they had purchased from MSA. The internal call-routing system was also expanded to include teleconferencing, which permitted technicians, sales staff, and buyers throughout the country to conduct meetings without leaving their offices (Porter, 1985b). (Telecommunications and teleconferencing are discussed in Chapter 11.)

Strategic Information Systems Affecting Suppliers

The sales marketing systems just outlined are concerned primarily with the changing relationships between producers and customers. Other strategic systems are aimed at suppliers. These systems are designed to maximize the firm's purchasing power by having suppliers interact with its information system to satisfy its precise business needs.

An example of a strategic, supply-oriented system is that of a large retailer that has linked its materials ordering system electronically to a supplier's order entry system. If, for example, the retailer wants to order 100 sofas for a given region of the country, it simply enters this order into its information system, which automatically checks the order entry system of its primary sofa suppliers. The supplier with the lowest costs and the fastest delivery time is then given the order.

This system is similar to the just-in-time delivery systems developed in Japan and now being installed in the American automobile industry. In these systems, automobile manufacturers enter the quantity and delivery schedules of specific automobile components into their own information systems. Then these requirements are automatically entered into a supplier's order entry information system. The supplier must respond with an agreement to deliver the materials at the time specified. Thus, automobile companies can reduce the cost of inventory, the space required for manufacturing, and the construction time.

These information systems also provide benefits for suppliers. Suppliers can continually monitor product requirements, factory scheduling, and commitments of their customers against their own schedule to ensure that enough inventory will be available. If suppliers are unwilling to go along with this system, they may lose business to other suppliers who are willing to meet these demands.

Perhaps the earliest and most powerful example of a marketing and strategically oriented supply system is the airlines reservation system. About two-thirds of all airline tickets issued in the United States are sold by travel agents using computerized reservation systems. In the late 1960s, using the then advanced third-generation computers, American Airlines developed its SABRE system and United Airlines developed its Apollo system (*Business Week*, May 23, 1983).

Currently, 65% of U.S. travel agencies have terminals connected to one or both of these reservation systems. Since the mid-1970s, American and United have spent more than $500 million on them. While these systems provide unparalleled convenience to airline travelers, as well as to travel agents who must book flights, they also confer considerable market power on the two airlines. For instance, United has begun to include in its contracts with travel agents provisions that prevent them from using any other airlines system if they want to keep Apollo. This is an example of how a strategically

Using Systems to Lock Out Competition

Medium size air carriers are protesting unfair treatment by United Airlines Apollo system and American Airlines Sabre system. Travel agents decide which airline in a multi-airline ticket will receive the revenues. Continental Airlines estimates that manipulating this process causes non-ticketing airlines to lose 350 million dollars in interest a year. Braniff Airlines claims it was driven out of business this way. Testifying before Congress, several airline presidents charged that the reservation systems operated by American and United were listing their flights first, and taking business away.

Adapted from "Do Airlines Play Fair with Their Computers?" *Business Week*, May 23, 1983, and "Airlines Dispute Computer Systems' Fairness," *The New York Times*, March 21, 1985.

oriented supply system gives a supplier a market advantage over a distributor and a customer.

The airline reservation systems operated by United and American can also be used unfairly, and illegally, as a competitive weapon against other airlines. For instance, United and American flights can be listed first on the computer screen, or other airlines can be unlisted or listed mistakenly.

Here public policy—either through the courts or the legislature—has acted to set limits on the uses of information technology to preserve fairness and competition.

Strategic Internal Management Systems

The systems previously described change the strategic relationship between an organization and its markets, customers, and suppliers. Other strategically oriented information systems focus on internal operations, management control, planning, and personnel. These systems are also strategic because they have a critical impact on the survival and prosperity of the firm. The following examples describe the use of information that is used much more dynamically and intensively than as a mere management support tool.

The Wizard system developed by *Avis*, the car rental company, is an example of a strategic internal MIS designed to improve the firm's overall productivity. This system keeps track of the location, costs, and performance of Avis's car rental fleet. This capability, in turn, has permitted Avis to bargain more effectively with its suppliers on the basis of hard data. It has also given Avis an advantage over Hertz, National, and other car rental firms by optimizing the distribution of its car rental fleet to ensure that cars are available where there is a demand for them (Janulaitis, 1984).

The importance of a strategic MIS in improving the operational productivity of a firm is even more apparent in the purchase by *General Motors (GM)* of the *Electronic Data Systems Corporation (EDS)*. GM, the country's second largest industrial corporation, earned more than $3.7 billion on sales of $74.5 billion in 1983. It is the nation's largest automobile manufacturer and employs approximately 700,000 people. EDS earned $71 million on revenues of $786 million in 1983 and employs 14,000 people. GM has always been at the leading edge of information processing, communications, and factory automation (Chabrow, 1985).

Paradoxically, because it is one of the world's largest corporations, GM has developed information systems with no coherent or consistent plan.

The chairman of GM, Roger B. Smith, has declared that his company is in a worldwide technology race to decide which car makers will survive. GM is unable to slash wages to the Japanese level and hopes to use computers to cut the number of hours needed to build cars. In order to attain this advantage, GM must improve its overall productivity. It has chosen to do this by improving its information processing productivity and radically increasing the pace at which information technology is brought into the firm.

GM executives dream of an integrated data processing, office and a factory system in which a seamless network will tend to every aspect of production. Theirs is the vision of a totally integrated operational system in which the parts needed to build cars will be automatically ordered, a sales order entry system will determine the level of factory production, and the sales system will automatically trigger a notification to the financing division of GM (General Motors Acceptance Corporation) to supply a customer with financing.

In order to fulfill this dream, GM purchased EDS for $2.5 billion. EDS was given the job of pulling together all of the computer-based operations at GM from factory automation systems to office automation and communication networks. This has never been done. GM itself does not know the size of its total data processing or information systems budget. The best estimate is approximately $1 billion per year, which is expected to rise in the next five years to nearly $2 billion as GM increases its reliance on information systems.

As GM's in-house integration contractor, EDS does not have an easy task. GM currently employs more than 50 telecommunication networks, 17 different OAS, and more than 15 computer-aided design/computer-aided manufacturing (CAD/CAM) systems. The job of EDS is to reduce the number of vendors, to standardize the data and telecommunications throughout GM, and to link together sales, manufacturing, design, and suppliers into a single seamless web.

The *Grayson Manufacturing Company* provides another example of the development of a strategic management planning system. Grayson, a textile firm with annual sales of about $500 million, is a pioneer in the use of information and information systems. Grayson manufactures towels, bath mats, drapes, and tablecloths. It also sells cloth at intermediate stages in the production process, with production handled at three cloth mills. Grayson, like many other firms, had developed a variety of information systems during the 1970s to support day-to-day operations and management decision making. However, in the 1980s, it became clear that these information systems were not directly linked to the corporation's strategic plans and did not serve those plans well. Grayson then began build an information system uniquely suited to strategic planning (Millar, 1984).

Grayson's strategic plan called for the company.to be the dominant supplier of textile products to the most profitable market segments of the domestic textile market. It also wanted to provide a high-quality work environment for its employees. After identifying the factors in the environment, the industry, and the company that were needed to fulfill these strategic goals, Grayson developed a set of indicators to measure its progress toward its strategic goals.

The resulting information system was called the "Information for Motivation Reporting System." This system permits managers working at a terminal to see, at any given moment, how well the firm is performing against its targeted critical success factors. The system produces reports on a routine basis that can be used in management meetings, highlighting the disparities between the strategic plan and actual performance. This way, Grayson hopes to increase management control over long-term factors in the industry and to ensure that it attains its strategic goals.

An example of internal system that focuses on cost reduction is that of the farm equipment maker *Deere & Company*. As a manufacturer of heavy farm and industrial earth-moving equipment, Deere leads its competitors by being a lower-cost producer. Crucial to its success has been the development of a strategic management control system designed to catalog and inventory the parts needed for Deere's equipment. Deere produces and inventories over 300,000 parts, ranging from tiny screws to hydraulic pumps, and because of its information systems, it has been able to produce "families" of parts more efficiently. The same system enables engineers to design new equipment more quickly and inexpensively. For instance, an engineer who needs a washer or a bolt of a specific thickness and size can search through the database for these parts. Designers can search through the same database to make sure that they design equipment for which Deere already makes parts or has parts in inventory. Thus, neither the engineers nor the designers force the purchase of new parts and equipment. Between 1981 and 1982, Deere shaved an estimated $9 million off the cost of new parts and processes in two of its plants (*Business Week*, August 22, 1983).

A final example of a strategic MIS is provided by a large multinational chemical and pharmaceutical concern with headquarters in the United States. Over the last five years, the personnel department noticed that turnover, especially among younger workers, was rapidly increasing. In the scientific and information systems areas, more than 20% of the employees were leaving after less than two years. Alarmed by these developments, the firm's Human Resources Department conducted a series of exit interviews and surveys.

They discovered that younger employees were leaving in part because the firm did not provide a flexible benefits package. Many of these workers were either single or childless, and their spouses also worked. The human resource information system that provided the medical, insurance, and savings plan benefits for employees, dated from the 1950s and could not respond to employees' varied demands for different kinds of benefits. For instance, young married employees who worked were not interested in receiving medical benefits that were duplicated by their spouse's company. In this instance, an expensive medical plan brought no benefits to workers; competitors were offering these employees more salary and greater contributions to savings plans. Also, young unmarried employees were less interested in generous pension benefits than in the higher salaries that competitors were offering. What was needed was a flexible benefits package, that would allow employees to choose precisely those benefits that they found most useful. Currently, the firm is installing a modern human resources benefit information system that permits employees to make these kinds of tradeoffs when selecting benefits.

3.4 Strategic Implications of Information Systems

Gaining the Competitive Edge

With these examples in mind, it should be clear that in the 1980s information systems can have strategic implications for vital internal organizational features (operations, planning, management control, and human resources) and can alter critical balances with external environmental factors such as new products and services, customers, and suppliers. Together, these internal and external strategic changes affect the competitive advantages that firms have over other firms (Ives and Learmonth, 1984). The systems previously described offer three competitive advantages for the firms that employ them: short-term gains from being the market innovator, the ability to lock in customers and suppliers, and the ability to change the basis of competition (see Figure 3.2).

Short-Term Advantages

By providing a unique product or service that cannot be easily duplicated, or by utilizing a vast information resource that is not available to others, firms can raise the market entry costs for potential competitors. These strategic products, services, and information systems can prevent the competition from responding in kind. For instance, the American Hospital Supply Corporation's system cannot be easily replicated by its competitors; customers cannot be easily convinced to install two, three, or four terminals in their ordering rooms. Partly for this reason, AHSC has been sued several times by competitors for restraint of trade.

On the other hand, raising market entry costs is probably not the most important competitive advantage conferred by information

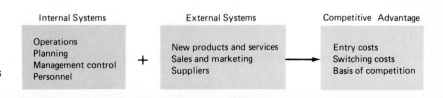

FIGURE 3.2
Strategic information systems and competitive advantage.

systems. Technological advantages can be relatively short-term. Citibank, for instance, which developed the first ATMs in the New York metropolitan area, gained an advantage that lasted for perhaps five years. But as the example of the NYCE showed, other banks, large and small, banded together to develop their own integrated cash-dispensing and transaction-handling remote terminals. A similar situation occurred with the Cash Management Account of Merrill-Lynch. Other brokerage services almost immediately developed competing services. In certain situations such as the airline reservation systems of United and American airlines , the cost of developing similar systems is so large that other airlines are discouraged, especially when they can appear on the American and United systems as "co-hosts," permitting them equal advantage with American and United (McFarlan, 1984).

In general, strategic information systems provide significant, although generally temporary, market advantages, principally by raising the entry costs of competitors. These short-term advantages can, however, be repeated, so that a firm that gains an advantage for five years can utilize the time and the additional resources that leadership brings to ensure that it maintains a technological advantage for the next five years, and so on. Firms can thus build on their initial success and develop a stream of innovative applications if they have the information systems staff and if they understand the strategic importance of information. For instance, a company can parlay a series of innovations into a valuable market image of it as a consistent leader at the cutting edge of technology. This image alone can help maintain the firm's market position.

Locking in Customers and Suppliers

A second competitive advantage conferred by strategic information systems is their ability to lock in customers and suppliers. Strategic information systems can make the costs of switching from one product to a competing product prohibitively high for customers. Electronic home banking is a good example. Once customers key in all of the required digital information on their bills, department stores, checks, and so forth into a single electronic banking system, they find it very difficult to switch to another bank. The banks themselves encourage this situation by developing systems that are incompatible with each another. By making it difficult for customers to switch, the banks, in turn, can directly market a variety of banking services ranging from instant credit, to stocks, to cash management accounts and the like to a captive audience.

American Hospital Supply's inventory, ordering, and control system also provides an example of a situation in which the participating hospitals are unwilling to switch to another supplier because of the system's convenience and low cost.

Changing the Competitive Game	Strategic systems confer a competitive advantage in a third way: by rapidly changing the basis of competition. The strategic information systems previously outlined can propel a manufacturer into an unassailable position as the low-cost, high-quality producer in its field (such as GM or Deere & Company). In other cases, the basis of competition can be changed entirely from cost competition to product differentiation. Thus, besides competing on a cost basis for customers, the airlines are fighting to get their on-line reservation systems into travel agency offices in order to influence purchase decisions. Airlines that can offer convenience, low price, and quick interconnections among a variety of airlines to complete a trip tend to win out. Product differentiation is also the key ingredient to competition in the financial services market. Here strategic information systems provide a competitive edge to those organizations that can utilize information technology to provide a vast array of diverse, integrated financial products.

3.5 Issues for Managers and Organizations

What are some of the implications of the previous examples? How can managers find strategic systems? Clearly, the role of information systems and information has changed from being merely supportive to being strategic. The future belongs to those firms that can effectively use information systems to gain a competitive advantage.

Dangers: Not All Strategic Systems Make Money	The competitive advantages conferred by strategic systems do not necessarily last long enough to ensure long-term profits. Competitors can retaliate and copy strategic systems. Moreover, these systems are often expensive; costs saved by some systems are expended immediately to maintain the system. The long-term impact of strategic systems on the financial community is uncertain, as reported in a survey of two hundred banks by Touche Ross & Co.

A cautious management must be able to translate systems expenditures into medium-term (five years), bottom-line benefits. On the other hand, some strategic systems as we have defined them may be required to stay in the industry. Much like capital expenditures, certain strategic systems have become a common industry practice. |
| ***Leveraging Technology*** | The strategic information systems previously described leverage technology and technology impacts. Until recently, information systems played a relatively minor role in the production, distribution, and sale of products and services. Vast increases in the productivity of information processing made relatively little difference in the |

Technology Yields Small Gains

No group of banks has emerged with a competitive advantage despite the enormous expenditures on systems. The Big Eight accounting firm Touche Ross & Co., in a survey of 200 banks worldwide, recently found that technology costs were higher than anticipated without yielding any long-term competitive advantage. Even Citibank N.A., considered an industry leader in technology and the first to gain market share with automatic teller machines, (ATMs), has found its costs rising in step with its new revenues. No bank is growing significantly and keeping costs down, the study found. Customers are making more frequent, smaller transactions at the ATMs. Fewer tellers are employed, but many high-priced systems specialists have replaced them.

Senior executives were disappointed that computerization did not lead to bottom-line benefits. Many executives believe that they allowed themselves to be driven by the new technology but failed to demand increased returns from its use. Computers have made banking more efficient, but the banks have not been able to get people to pay for it.

Touche Ross also found that bank expenditures on technology will increase sharply in the next decade. But new systems will be more directly related to marketing plans and bottom-line profits.

Adapted from "Technology Yields Banks Slim Return on Investment," *Computerworld*, May 6, 1986.

firm's productivity or bottom-line balance sheet. Now, however, as the operations of an organization have come to depend heavily on information systems, and as these systems penetrate the organization, increases in the productivity of information processing have dramatic implications for the overall productivity of the corporation. This leveraging effect is important when we consider recommendations for management.

Breaking Down Organizational Boundaries

In each of the examples cited previously, there is some blurring of organizational boundaries, both external and internal. This is especially true of telecommunications-based strategic systems (Cash and Konsynski, 1985). Suppliers and customers must become intimately linked. Within organizations, design, sales, and manufacturing departments must work together much more closely. This goal is not easy to accomplish and has frequently been resisted by middle and even senior managers. In fact, the greatest drawback in managing information as a strategic tool may be resistance to change—both the changes that are imposed on an organization and those that employees experience as their jobs are reshaped. Even the identities of employees must change. One is no longer simply a member of the production department or a salesperson. These tasks become increasingly integrated through a single information network. Strategic information systems thus change the loyalties of individuals.

Prerequisite: Organizational Change

Adopting the systems described in this chapter generally involves some kind of organizational change. How much organizational change occurs depends on the specific circumstances. Clearly, however, there is a connection between the strategy of an organization and its internal structure. As companies move to make information systems part of the overall corporate strategy, their internal structure must also change to reflect these new developments. This may involve reducing the staff and increasing the use of the plant. In some cases, it may involve developing an entirely new organizational structure. For instance, GM, in order to develop a comprehensive strategic information system strategy, had to purchase EDS. And to produce a new low-cost, high-technology, Japanese-competitive car (the Saturn), GM also created an entirely new automotive division—a new factory, a new sales force, a new design team, and so forth—to utilize the new technologies. Not all strategic information systems require such massive change, but clearly, many do (*The New York Times*, December 7, 1984).

What Managers Can Do

Some of the major issues facing managers concern how the organization can build information systems of strategic importance. Clearly, information systems are too important to be left entirely to a small technical group in the corporation. Senior managers must initiate the search for opportunities to develop them. Clearly, some industries are far ahead of others in their use of information technology. Some of those that are far behind may be so for a good reason: The technology may not be appropriate. Other industries have simply failed to keep up with the times and thus offer considerable opportunities for vast and rapid changes. Some of the important questions for managers to ask themselves are the following:

- How is the industry currently using information and communication technology? Which organizations are the leaders in the application of information systems technology? What does the future look like?

- What is the direction and nature of technological change within the industry? Where is the momentum and change coming from?
- Are significant strategic opportunities to be gained by introducing information systems technology into the industry? What kinds of systems are applicable to the industry: new products and services, supplier systems, sales and marketing systems?

Once the nature of information systems technology in the industry is understood, managers should turn to their organization and ask other important questions:

- Is the organization behind or ahead of the industry in its application of information systems?
- What is the current business strategic plan, and how does that plan mesh with the current strategy for information services?
- Have the information technologies currently in use provided significant payoffs to the business? Do they largely support the business or drain its resources?
- Would a significant increase in the budget for information services result in a strategic breakthrough for the organization?

Once these issues have been considered, managers can gain a keener insight into whether their firm is ready for strategic information systems.

3.6 Summary

The role of information and information systems has changed dramatically in the last 20 years. Originally designed to speed the processing of paper, information systems enlarged their function to general management support, and then to customized and specific decision support tools. Increasingly, information systems are playing an even more central role in the firm—a strategic role.

Strategic systems are those that lead to the creation of new products and services and to changes in sales, in marketing, in relationships to suppliers, and in internal operations.

Information systems become strategic in several ways. Systems can provide a temporary barrier to market entry by raising the costs of entry; they can lock in customers and suppliers by raising the cost of switching; and they can change the nature of the business by introducing new, related products.

While strategic systems are alluring, several cautions are in order. Not all strategic systems make a profit; they can be expensive and risky to build; and they often require organizational change.

Key Words

Electronic accounting machines
Electronic data processing
Automatic teller machines
Strategic sales system

Product differentiation
Market entry costs
Organizational boundaries

Review Questions

1. Identify four different conceptions of information in organizations.
2. Can you link these conceptions of information with specific types of information systems?
3. How can a strategic information system interface with external and internal environments?
4. What gives Citibank and Merrill Lynch a competitive edge over other financial institutions?
5. How can a firm increase its overall operational productivity through the use of information systems?
6. How can managers find strategic applications in their firm?
7. Why can't competitors easily copy Metpath and American Hospital Supply?
8. How does Sears use credit information in a strategic way?
9. What is meant by *leveraging technology*?

Discussion Questions

1. If firm A pursues a business strategy of being the lowest-cost producer and firm B pursues a strategy of product differentiation, what kinds of information systems would you recommend to their managements? Comment and discuss in functional terms (e.g., product design, marketing, production, administration).
2. Citing declining enrollments and higher personnel and administrative costs, your college president has asked you to suggest how information systems could help the college compete against rival schools. What are your recommendations?

CASE STUDY

American Airlines SABRE Is on the Cutting Edge

In the late 1960s American Airlines developed a rudimentary airlines reservation system called Semi-Automated Business Research Environment, or SABRE. Today SABRE is the world's largest travel agency reservation system. It is the most widely known strategic use of information technology.

SABRE is installed in 11,000 travel agencies and enables agents to serve their customers with airline, hotel, car, and other reservations.

SABRE emerged as a powerful asset for American in the mid-1970s. Robert Crandall (then head of marketing and now CEO) and Max Hopper (head of data processing) were the key managers behind SABRE. In the 1970s, a group of travel agencies banded together to consider building their own reservation system. The major airlines opposed this move and formed a group to build an airline system. Disagreements among the airlines forced American and United to start building their own systems in 1975.

American won the race. In 1976 they started shipping SABRE terminals to travel agencies. This $350 million investment did not become profitable until 1983. Few airlines were willing to take such a chance; most have joined SABRE. Pan Am recently abandoned its system—PANAMAC.

SABRE has continually expanded, offering travel agents and corporate customers more integrated services. It serves as the basis for travel agent office automation; theater tickets, limousines, insurance, and a host of travel-related services can now be purchased or rented through the system.

SABRE accounts for 5% of the gross revenue of the AMR Corporation (American's parent company) but earns more than 15% of its profits.

The biggest threat is that other systems may emerge, based on new, less expensive technology, that could undermine SABRE. For instance, using a home personal computer, individuals can gain access to the Official Airlines Guide and make their own reservations. To forestall this move, SABRE is giving access to individuals in a system called *Easy SABRE*. Corporate users have also been added. But to keep the travel agents happy, SABRE allows corporate travel agents to see only the schedules and services. Reservations are still made through travel agents, preserving their commissions.

Other threats are court suits and legislation based on allegations that American uses its system unfairly to push its own flights rather than those of competitors who fly to the same destination. After a congressional investigation, the Civil Aeronautics Board in 1984 forced American to remove any bias in the display of flights on SABRE screens. Eleven other airlines have joined an antitrust suit against both American and United (which operates a competing system).

SABRE uses five mainframe computers: 3 IBM model 3090s and 2 model 3083s. Hundreds of IBM 3380 disk drives store information on airlines, hotels, and other services. The system handles up to 1200 transactions per second at peak times from 50,000 on-line terminals and personal computers. A total of 400 programmers work on SABRE full time.

Given this experience with large, high-volume systems, American's CEO, Robert Crandall, foresees the need to spend as much as $1 billion in the next few years as American Airlines increasingly expands its business into data processing and telecommunications.

Adapted from "SABRE Gives the Edge to American Airlines," *Information Week*, May 26, 1986, and "American's Crandall Proves DP Profit Potential," *Computerworld*, June 9, 1986.

Case Study Questions

1. Do you think American Airlines has achieved a sustainable strategic advantage? Why or why not?

2. What kinds of additional services or products do you think SABRE could be used for?

3. What impact do you think SABRE will have on the airline industry?

References

Business Week, May 23, 1983. "Do Airlines Play Fair with Their Computers?"

Business Week, August 22, 1983. "Business Is Turning Data Into a Potent Strategic Weapon."

Canning, Richard G. "Information Systems: New Strategic Role," *EDP Analyzer* (January 1984).

Cash, J.I., and McLeod, P.L. "Introducing IS Technology in Strategically Dependent Companies," *Journal of Management Information Systems* (Spring 1985).

Cash, J.I., and Konsynski, Benn R. 'IS Redraws Competitive Boundaries,"*Harvard Business Review* (March–April 1985).

Chabrow, Eric R. "GM Shifts Gears on Information Systems," *Information Week* (January 14, 1985).

Ives, Blake, and Learmonth, Gerald P. "The Information System as a Competitive Weapon," *Communications of the ACM* (December 1984).

Janulaitis, M. Victor. "Gaining Competitive Advantage," *Infosystems* (October 1984).

McFarlan, F. Warren. "Information Technology Changes the Way You Compete," *Harvard Business Review* (May–June 1984).

Millar, Victor E. "Decision-Oriented Information," *Datamation* (January 1984).

Porter, Michael. *Competitive Advantage*. New York: Free Press, 1985a.

Porter, Michael. *Competitive Strategy*. New York: Free Press, 1985b.

Porter, Michael. "How Information Can Help You Compete," *Harvard Business Review* (August–September 1985c).

The New York Times, December 7, 1984. "AT&T Is in Brain Power."

The New York Times, January 9, 1985. "GM Starts a New Card Subsidiary."

The New York Times, March 7, 1985. "Big New York Banks Link Teller Machines."

CHAPTER 4

Information Systems and Organizations

▬ OUTLINE

PRINTCO is a rapidly growing manufacturer of medium-speed dot matrix printers. The company uses a materials requirements planning (MRP) system to order parts for its products. Based on known order quantities and anticipated seasonal sales, the system automatically orders sufficient numbers of parts for all of its product runs on a routine basis. But information systems rarely fit the organization perfectly because of rapid changes in products, environments, and internal staff. PRINTCO's staff has had to revise their work procedures to make the system work effectively.

Buyers in Purchasing call Receiving every day to see if parts are sitting on the loading docks but have not yet been recorded in the system. If the parts are not on the docks, they call suppliers to complain. (The system had not been designed to start tracking parts as soon as they were unloaded, but rather when they arrived at the manufacturing facilities. The delay can be several days.)

In Customer Service, the staff keeps a manual warranty log for their customers because the MRP system puts out only a monthly report. The Data Processing Division has given the request for daily reports a low priority.

Commonly, workers walk from one side of the building to another—often taking 20-minute round trips—to verify data in the system. They must ensure that mistakes in ordering parts are not made. This avoids costly overstocking, something senior management watches very closely.

Adapted from Rob Kling and Suzanne Iacono, "Behind the Terminal: The Institutional Organization of Computing in Organizations," University of California at Irvine Public Policy Research Organization, 1984.

These are just some of the ways in which PRINTCO's employees work to support information systems. The effective operation of systems depends on both formal organizational structures and informal values, sentiments, and behaviors. Without close organizational and small-group support, PRINTCO's MRP systems would flounder. This chapter examines more closely the nature of organizations and their relationship to information systems.

In this chapter the student will learn:
■ The distinguishing characteristics of organizations.
■ The major types of organizations.
■ Theories about and concepts of organizations that help us understand their relationship with information systems.

- The role of the information system function within the organization.
- Models for describing the origins of systems in organizations.
- The impact of information systems on organizational structure, culture, political processes management, and work.
- Important organizational implications for the design and implementation of systems.

4.1 Introduction

As Chapters 1 and 2 have shown, there is a two-way relationship between organizations and information systems. On the one hand, information systems must be aligned with the organization in order to provide information needed by important groups. At the same time, the organization must be aware of and open itself to the influences of information systems in order to receive the strategic benefits of new technologies. Organizations must change their goals, operations, and relationships with outsiders in order to use advanced information technology. Information systems affect organizations, and organizations necessarily affect the design of systems.

What Is an Organization?

An organization can be simply defined as a *stable, formal social structure that takes resources from the environment and processes them to produce outputs*. This technical definition focuses on three elements of

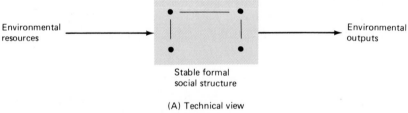

Environmental resources → Stable formal social structure → Environmental outputs

(A) Technical view

FIGURE 4.1
Two views of organizations. The technical view of organizations emphasizes their resource-transforming nature. A legal-rational view of organizations emphasizes group relationships, values, and structures.

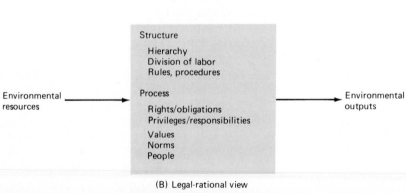

Environmental resources →

Structure
  Hierarchy
  Division of labor
  Rules, procedures

Process
  Rights/obligations
  Privileges/responsibilities

Values
Norms
People

→ Environmental outputs

(B) Legal-rational view

an organization (see Figure 4.1). An organization is *more stable* than an informal group in terms of longevity and routineness. Organizations are *formal* in a legal, rational sense because they are legal entities and must abide by laws. They have internal rules and procedures. Organizations are *social structures* because they are a collection of social elements, much as a machine has a structure—a particular arrangement of valves, cams, shafts, and other parts.

Organizations are, in part, information processing entities. However, it would be a mistake to view organizations or the human beings who work for them in this limited way.

Organizations process and use information *in order to produce outputs for an environment* (e.g., products and services). Most organizations are not designed primarily for processing information. A newspaper delivers news, not data or merely information. Even government agencies such as the Social Security Administration and the Internal Revenue Service, which are heavy users of information, have as their primary goal the delivery of pension and taxation services.

A more realistic definition of an organization is that it is a *collection of rights, privileges, obligations, and responsibilities that are delicately balanced over a period of time through conflict and conflict resolution.* The people who work in organizations develop customary ways of working, attachments to existing relationships, and arrangements with subordinates and superiors about how work will be done, how much work will be done, and under what conditions. Most of these arrangements and feelings are not found in any formal rule book.

Building new systems or rebuilding old ones involves much more than a technical rearrangement of machines or information flows. It involves changes in who owns and controls information, who has the right to access and update that information, and who makes what decisions about whom, when, and how.

Information systems can markedly alter life in the organization. Some information systems change the organizational balance of rights, privileges, obligations, responsibilities, and feelings that has been established over a long period of time.

What this means for the student is that one cannot design new systems or understand existing systems without a understanding of the nature of organizations.

4.2 Understanding Organizations

Understanding the nature of organizations has been a primary concern of the social sciences. This section will discuss the major findings and theories about organizations that are essential to understanding information systems.

TABLE 4.1
Characteristics of the Ideal Type of
Formal Organization

Clear division of labor

Hierarchy

Explicit rules and procedures

Impartial judgments

Technical qualifications for positions

Maximum organizational efficiency

Why Organizations Are So Much Alike: Characteristics

In some respects, all modern organizations are alike; they share certain characteristics. A German sociologist, Max Weber, was the first to describe these "ideal-typical" characteristics of organizations in 1911. He called them *bureaucracies* (see Table 4.1).

All modern organizations have a clear-cut *division of labor and specialization*. Experts are employed and trained for each position. These specialists are arranged in a *hierarchy* of authority in which everyone is accountable to someone and authority is limited to specific actions. Authority and action are further limited by a system of *abstract rules or procedures* that are interpreted and applied to specific cases. This creates a system of *impartial and universalistic decision making*; everyone is treated equally. Employees are hired and promoted on the basis of *technical qualifications and professionalism* (not personal connections). The organization itself is devoted to the *principle of efficiency*: maximizing output using limited inputs.

Formal organizations (bureaucracies) are so prevalent, according to Weber, because they are the most efficient form of organization. They are much more stable and powerful than mercurial charismatic groups or formal aristocracies held together by the right of birth.

Why Organizations Are So Different: Major Types

While all organizations have some of the characteristics of bureaucracy, they obviously have different levels of these characteristics and diverge in many other ways. Working in a circus is very different from working in a bank, a government agency, or a university. Organizational theorists have discovered a number of ways in which organizations differ from one another (see Table 4.2).

Organizations differ in terms of their ultimate goals and the types of power used to achieve them. Some organizations have coercive goals (e.g., prisons), others utilitarian goals (e.g., businesses). Still others have normative goals (universities, religious groups). The kinds of power and incentives differ accordingly. In a university with normative goals one can be persuaded to study in one's own interest,

TABLE 4.2
Types of Organizations

Author	Characteristic	Typology	Example
Etzioni (1975)	Types of power and goals	Coercive Utilitarian Normative	Military Business Church
Blau and Scott (1962)	Who benefits?	Members Clients Owners	Boy Scouts Welfare agency Business
Parsons (1960)	Social function	Economic Pattern Maintenance Integrative Political	Business Universities, schools Hospitals, courts Government
Gouldner (1954)	Leadership	Democratic Authoritarian Laissez-faire Technocratic Bureaucratic	Different types of leadership could occur in any organization
March and Simon (1958)	Task Technique Technology	Programmed Semi-programmed Unprogrammed Decisions	Inventory reorder Production scheduling Selecting strategy
Woodward (1965)	Environments		
Thompson (1967)	Uncertainty		

but one cannot be forced. Coercive power does not work well in normative organizations.

Organizations serve different groups. Some benefit primarily their members; others benefit clients, stockholders, or the public.

The social roles (or function) or organizations differ. Some organizations are primarily interested in politics (trying to change the distribution of benefits in society), while others play primarily economic roles (seeking to optimize the utilization of resources). Some organizations play integrative roles by trying to pull together diverse groups in a common enterprise—like hospitals devoted to the control of disease and courts devoted to the pursuit of justice. Still other organizations, such as universities, schools, and churches, work to preserve important social values (normative roles).

Clearly, the nature of leadership differs greatly from one organization to another, even in similar organizations devoted to the same goal. Some of the major leadership styles are democratic, authoritarian (even totalitarian), laissez-faire (leadership is absent), technocratic (according to technical criteria, formal models), or bureaucratic (strictly according to formal rules). These kinds of leadership can occur in any type of organization and seem to depend on chance and history.

Still another way organizations differ is in terms of the tasks performed, the technology, and the environment surrounding the organization. In some cases, organizations use routine tasks which could be programmed, that is, reduced to formal rules and requiring little judgement (e.g., inventory reordering). In other cases, organizations work with highly judgmental, nonroutine, tasks (e.g., a consulting company that creates strategic plans for other companies). Environments also differ. Some organizations find stable environments, comfortable niches, while others are constantly threatened by outside competitors, changing regulations, and lack of resources. In organizations where tasks are not programmable, where environments are changing, much more discretion must be given to lower-level employees. There must be much less bureaucratic red tape and fewer formal rules.

Theories About and Concepts of Organizations

Because of the diversity among organizations, there are many different theories about them. Each of these theories points to an aspect of organization that is important to take into account when building (or describing) information systems. While students do not need to know these theories in detail, they should be aware of them and of the facet of the organization on which they focus.

There are five major schools of thought about organizations. These schools are illustrated in Table 4.3.

The *classical or structural school* focuses on the relatively permanent characteristics of the organization in order to explain how organizations and people behave. Individuals generally do not count in this theory. This school focuses on structure (hierarchy, specialization, rules), goals, size, conflict, values, and standard operating procedures.

A directly opposite approach is taken by the *human relations school*. In this school, individual feelings, values, and attitudes are central in explaining why organizations behave the way they do. This school focuses on leadership, interpersonal relations, communication, cooperation, individual rewards, and job satisfaction. A major theme of this school is that good leadership leads to good morale among workers, and that the higher the morale, the higher the productivity.

The *managerial* or *scientific management school* focuses less on personal sentiments than on the correct, "scientific" organization of work and management. If the job is properly designed (after extensive analysis), if management provides the correct resources, the right strategic decisions, and the correct rewards, high levels of productivity result. This school seeks to explain organizational behavior in terms of management decision making and job design.

TABLE 4.3
Theories About Organizations

School	Authors	Concepts/Issues	Purpose
Classical/structural	Weber Perrow Parsons Allison	Structure-function Goals Authority Standard Procedures Size Specialization Conflict/politics Environment Values, norms, behavior Culture	To explain organizational and individual behavior using organizational level concepts. To explain societal behavior in terms of complex organizations.
Human relations	Roethlisberger and Dickson Homans Mayo Herzberg Argyris	Leadership Interpersonal relations Individual development Cooperation in groups Morale, job satisfaction Productivity Norms, sentiments, values	To explain organizational and individual behavior in terms of individual and interpersonal variables, concepts, and attributes.
Managerial	Fayol Taylor Barnard	Executive decision making Scientific management Persuasion Moral authority Organization of work Cooperation Rewards, contributions	To explain organizational behavior in terms the objective requirements of the organization, or the task. Individuals are driven by nonrational or irrational sentiments that are given direction by the organization.
Technology/environment	March and Simon Woodward Thompson Perrow	Decision making Uncertainty Bounded rationality Organizational goals History, sunk costs Satisficing behavior Communications Multiple goals Task and environment	To explain organizational structure and behavior in terms of the nature of decision making, the task at hand, or the environment. Existing technology and technique are important influences on organizational behavior and structure.
Institutional school	Selznick Perrow Messinger Skolnick Goffman	Structure and function Natural systems evolving Adaptation to environments History, past investments Culture, values, norms Organizational drift	To explain organizational and individual behavior in terms of organizational and institutional objectives of survival.

The *technology school* explains organizational behavior in terms of the nature of decision making, the task (or technology) at hand, and the environment. Organizational structure grows to cope with the uncertainty of decision making. (Formal rules reduce uncertainty. Hierarchy pushes nonroutine, important decisions up the organization to decision makers used to dealing with uncertainty.) Organizations and decision makers do not optimize because there are not enough resources to explore all alternatives. There are limits on rationality because human beings have limited information processing capacity. Organizations develop standard responses (standard operating procedures) as repertoires of proven and accepted solutions.

The *institutional school* explains organizational behavior largely in terms of the unique history of specific organizations. The Tennessee Valley Authority, the Federal Bureau of Investigation, General Motors, and DuPont are some of the organizations that have been studied in this manner. This school focuses on the unique mission and leaders of each organization and shows how they adapt over time to changes in the environment.

Levels of Analysis

Organizational theory applies to a wide range of behaviors that are lumped together in the word *organization*. In fact, however, there are different levels of organizational analysis and different theories that are appropriate to various levels of analysis of organizational behavior. This can be seen in Figure 4.2, which describes the levels of organizational analysis, and the principal concerns at each level, and gives an example of an information system designed to serve that level of organization.

At the individual and small-group levels of organization, information systems apply to a particular job, task, or project. The human relations and technology theories described in the previous section are especially appropriate at this level because they focus on personal and interpersonal factors. At the Department and Division levels, the structural and managerial theories identify relevant variables. At the organizational, interorganizational, and network levels, the institutional, technology, and structural theories are important.

Perhaps one of the most important—and least heralded—contributions of information systems is to support the large variety of work groups that spring up in organizations and are not even part of the formal organization chart. While the organization chart shows the formal relationships in an organization, much of the work of an organization, especially in the systems area, is done by informal task forces, interdepartmental committees, project teams, and committees. Table 4.4 presents the most important work groups and shows how systems can support them. These work groups generally have rapidly changing information needs, peak load work schedules associated with project deadlines, and high communication require-

Organizational level		Activity	Support systems
Individual	•	Job, task	Microcomputer application; personal client database; decision support systems
Group		Project	Project scheduling; access to mainframe data; access to external data sources; dynamic information requirements; group DSS
Department		Major function	Accounts payable; warehouse; payroll; human resources; marketing; stable information requirements; MIS; major transaction systems
Division		Major product or service	Systems to support production, marketing, administration, and personnel; access to organizational financial and planning data; MIS; major transaction systems; on-line interactive systems
Organization		Multiple products, services, and goals	Integrated financial and planning systems; MIS; on-line interactive systems; ESS
Interorganization		Alliance Competition Exchange Contact	Communication systems; intelligence, observation, and monitoring systems
Organizational network		Sector of economy: related products, services; interdependencies	Informal communication systems; industry and sector-level formal reporting systems

FIGURE 4.2
Organizational level and appropriate support systems. Systems are designed to support various levels of the organization.

ments. Office automation tools—the better ones having high-speed communication linkages—are one of the most recent system tools directed at work groups.

When designing an information system, it is important to have a keen sense of the scope or level of the organization that will primarily be affected by the system and an awareness of how far-reaching particular systems can be. For instance, systems designed to enhance division-level activities leading to the production of a particular service can affect an entire corporation, interorganizational relationships, and organizational sets. In other instances, such as microcomputer applications for individuals, the implications of systems may be limited to individuals or small groups.

TABLE 4.4
Work Groups, Problems, and Systems Support

Type of Work Group	Description	Problems	Systems Support
Hierarchical	Formal working relationship between Manager and staff	Frequent meetings; dispersed work environments	Video conferencing; electronic mail (one to many)
Interdepartmental	Sequential activities; "expediters," "fixers"	Need occasional direct communication	Electronic messaging (one to one)
Project teams	Formally defined groups; close day-to-day interaction	Meeting schedules	Scheduling and communication software; meeting support tools; document interchange
Committees	Formally defined groups; occasional interaction	High peak load communications, intermittent	Electronic bulletin boards; video conference; electronic mail; computer conferencing
Task force	Formally defined single-purpose group	Rapid communication; access to internal and external data	Graphics display; information utility; document interchange; meeting support tools
Peer groups/social networks	Informal groups of similar-status individuals	Intense personal communication	Telephone; electronic mail

	Problems of all work groups
	   Making arrangements
	   Attending meetings
	   Long agendas
	   Cost of meetings
	   Between-meeting activities		

Implications for the Design and Understanding of Systems

What is the importance of these theories of organizations for students of information systems? First of all, an awareness of these theories and the different variables that they describe and focus on should prevent the student from taking an excessively narrow view of the organization and its primary components. No one theory is adequate to describe all aspects of an organization, and no information system can be built without taking into account aspects of each of the theories presented in Table 4.3. For instance, information systems have to be built with an awareness of the following factors:

- The *level* of organization at which the system resides
- The *structure* of the organization: hierarchy, specialization, formal procedures

- The *sentiments and attitudes* of workers in the organization who will be using the information system
- The support and understanding of *top management*
- The *kinds of tasks and decisions* that the information system is designed to assist
- The *history of the organization*: past investments in information technology, important programs, and human resources
- The *environment* in which the organization must function

A second implication of this review is that each organization is a relatively unique combination of structure, leadership, people, goals, and environment. Therefore, systems built for one organization can rarely be transported directly to other organizations. Each organization's information requirements are largely unique.

4.3 How Organizations Affect Systems

Organizations design and use information systems. Each information system is fitted to a particular organization. There are four important questions to consider:

- How have organizations actually used information systems?
- How has the organizational role of information systems changed?
- Who is involved in the operation of information systems?
- Why do organizations adopt information systems in the first place?

In the following sections, we answer these questions.

How Organizations Have Actually Used Information Technology

Table 4.5 shows the changing applications of information systems over time.

The growing power of computer technology, both hardware and software, does not result simply in doing the old things faster or cheaper. New computing power is used to expand the kinds of work that computers can effectively do, releasing human potential for other tasks not suitable for machines.

There has been a clear progression from operations-level systems designed to make the elementary but vital transactions of an organization more efficient (like paying checks) in the 1950s, to management systems in the late 1960s (for monitoring and controlling), to planning and simulations in the 1970s. By the 1980s, information systems had expanded into areas more directly related to making specific decisions—custom-built decision support systems and early strategic planning systems. In the mid-1980s, organizations were beginning to take a strategic view of systems and beginning to plan and manage information as if it were like other resources—capital, physical resources, and labor.

TABLE 4.5
Changing Applications
of Systems

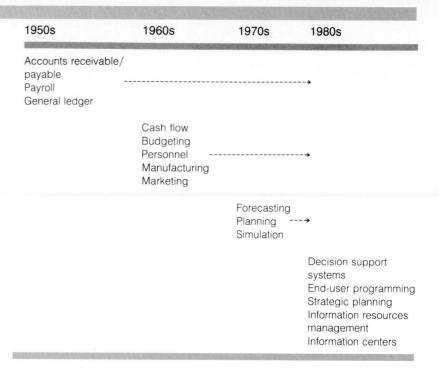

	1950s	1960s	1970s	1980s
	Accounts receivable/ payable Payroll General ledger	--→		
		Cash flow Budgeting Personnel Manufacturing Marketing	--------------------→	
			Forecasting Planning ---→ Simulation	
				Decision support systems End-user programming Strategic planning Information resources management Information centers

Information Centers

A brain child of IBM Canada in 1976, information centers have emerged as a major tool for delivering information services to users at higher management levels. Fortune 500 companies now have more than 3 centers on average. The information center gives access to corporate data and training to managers in non-data-processing areas. The centers train users in how to analyze corporate data themselves, without professional data processing intervention. The largest benefits to date are in the areas of routine report generation, which could not be done before, and in helping managers to make "what if" decisions.

Adapted from *Computerworld*, Oct. 28, 1985.

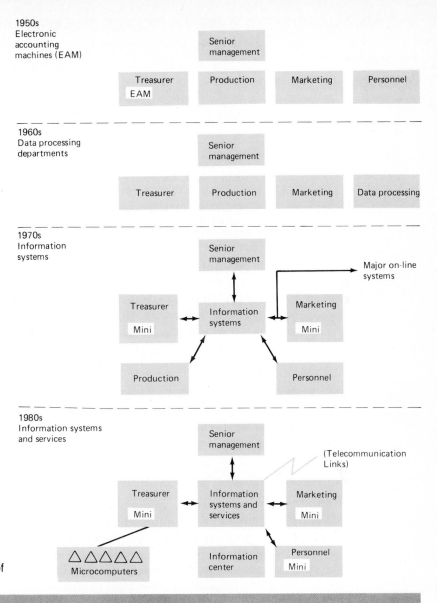

FIGURE 4.3
The organizational topology of systems.

How Has The Organizational Role of Information Systems Changed?

Figure 4.3 illustrates how the function of information systems has changed over time in the organization. Corresponding to the changes in applications previously described, there have been changes in the *technical and organizational configuration of systems*. In the 1950s, computers—then called *electronic accounting machines* (*EAM*)—were isolated machines performing limited functions and usually located in the office of the treasurer or the chief financial officer. The organization in this period was dependent on computers for a few critical functions, but could live on even if the machines broke down.

TABLE 4.6
Five Major Methods
of Delivering
Information Services

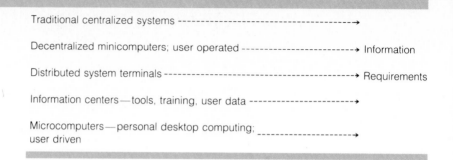

Traditional centralized systems ----------------------------------→

Decentralized minicomputers; user operated --------------------------→ Information

Distributed system terminals --------------------------------------→ Requirements

Information centers—tools, training, user data ----------------------→

Microcomputers—personal desktop computing; _____→
user driven

By the 1960s, as computers took on a broader array of applications, they tended to be large, centralized machines that served users at local and occasionally at remote sites, either with hard-copy printouts or sometimes with terminals. In this period, the function was referred to as *automatic data processing* or *electronic data processing*. Data processing was a major, centralized information factory in this period, producing major batch products for organizational users. By the end of the 1960s, most large organizations were dependent on information systems to maintain ongoing operations. They could not survive for more than a few days if these systems broke down.

By the 1970s and 1980s, technical configuration becomes more complex. Minicomputers and microcomputers at remote sites were employed directly by users for local needs. These smaller machines were tied into networks connected to large, centralized mainframes. Data were more distributed, and machine intelligence was much closer to the ultimate end users. Telecommunications links—the web holding these arrangements together—had become very important.

Instead of being an isolated factory making batches of information products, information systems are now integral, on-line, interactive tools deeply involved in the minute-to-minute operations and decision making of large organizations. Organizations are now critically dependent on systems. They cannot survive even occasional breakdowns. Therefore, system designers typically build in redundant capacity, additional machines, and disaster recovery plans.

Because of these changes in the technical and organizational configurations of systems, there are today many ways in which computer-based information systems can be used to meet an organization's information requirements. Table 4.6 lists the major alternatives.

Who Is Involved in the Operation of Information Systems?

Computer technology is similar to other kinds of technology, such as automobiles. In order to have and operate automobiles, a society needs highways, mechanics, gas stations, engine designers, police, and parts manufacturers. The "automobile" is a package of services, organizations, and people. Likewise with information systems: Com-

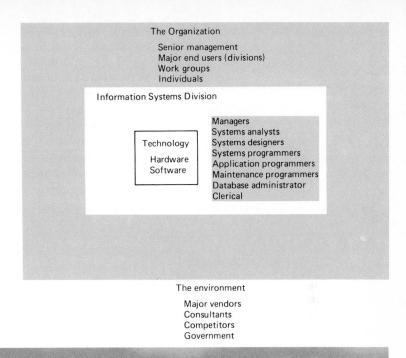

The Organization

Senior management
Major end users (divisions)
Work groups
Individuals

Information Systems Division

Technology

Hardware
Software

Managers
Systems analysts
Systems designers
Systems programmers
Application programmers
Maintenance programmers
Database administrator
Clerical

The environment

Major vendors
Consultants
Competitors
Government

FIGURE 4.4
The computer package. Many groups, individuals, and organizations are involved in the design and management of information systems. *Adapted from Kling and Dutton, 1982.*

puter technology requires specialized organizational subunits, information specialists, and a host of other supportive groups (Kling and Dutton, 1982).

The computer package is composed of three distinct entities (see Figure 4.4). An information system of any complexity requires a *formal organizational unit* or function—an information systems department, a management information systems department, or a management services group—the name varies from organization to organization. Further, having an information system in an organization implies a group of *information specialists*. Information specialists include both insiders and outsiders. Programmers, systems analysts, team leaders, project leaders, facilities managers, and data processing managers comprise the inside information specialists. In addition, external specialists such as hardware vendors and manufacturers, software firms, and consultants are frequently involved in the day-to-day operations and long-term planning of information systems.

A third element of the information systems package is *the technology* itself—both hardware and software.

Today the information systems group often acts as a powerful change agent in the organization. As noted in Chapter 1, the information system group is often the source of new business strategies and new information-based products. Increasingly, this group is taking on the role of information manager for the organization, coordinating both the development of technology and planned changes in the organization (to be discussed more fully).

The size of the information systems unit can vary greatly, depending on the role of information systems in the organization and on the organization's size. In most medium-sized firms, the information systems group is composed of 100 to 400 people and generally accounts for 1–20% of gross revenues, depending on the type of organization. Expenditures on computers and information systems are less in production-oriented organizations, somewhat more in mixed product and distribution organizations, and greatest in service organizations (especially those that sell information products like Dow Jones News), where information systems can consume considerably more than 40% of gross revenues.

With the changing role of the information systems group from the 1950s to 1980s came changes in its specialties and skills (see Table 4.7). In the early years, when the role of information systems was limited and the contacts between information systems and the rest of the organization were few, the information systems group was composed mostly of *programmers*. Today, in most information systems groups, programmers and systems analysts make up anywhere from 30% to 50% of the staff, but a growing proportion is allocated to the *systems analysis function*.

Systems analysts, as we discuss in later chapters, constitute the principal liaison between the information systems group and the rest of the organization. It is the systems analyst's job to translate business problems and requirements into information requirements and systems. Some organizations—principally banks—have created an entirely new job category called *business systems analysts* to emphasize that an understanding of both systems and business is required for successful systems.

In addition to programmers and analysts, the work of the information systems group is growing in size and complexity to the point where half of the staff is composed of *managers*. These managers are principally involved as leaders of teams of programmers and analysts, project managers, physical facility managers, telecommunications managers, heads of office automation groups, and finally, the data processing manager and related staff.

End users are not truly members of the information systems department, but they are certainly not outsiders. Users are representatives of departments outside of the information systems group for which applications are developed. These user groups are playing an increasingly large role in the design and development of information systems. Users are the clients of the information systems group, and they often pay for the projects out of their budgets. Sophisticated end users have grown increasingly important because they have taken over many of the design and programming tasks formerly

TABLE 4.7
Job Titles of
Information Specialists

Job Title	Description
Systems analyst	Works with users to define information requirements
Systems designer	Designs and chooses alternative systems to perform tasks specified by analysts
Applications programmer	Designs, codes, and tests computer programs based on the systems analyst's specifications
Maintenance programmer	Enhances and makes changes in existing programs based on the systems analyst's specifications
Systems programmer	Maintains operating system software that controls the schedule and flow of application programs
Program librarian	Maintains a library of programs
Database administrator	Defines and controls the organization's database
Office automation director	Develops policies and practices to further office automation
Microcomputer coordinator	Develops policies and practices to further the use of microcomputers
Telecommunications director	Develops and manages telecommunication links
Operator	Operates the mainframe computer
Data control clerk	Mounts tapes; handles card and other manual/clerical functions
Data entry clerk	Enters data through a keypunch machine or terminal
End users	Skilled users of information systems who help information systems specialists define the information requirements

monopolized by the information systems department. This phenomenon is discussed in Chapter 15.

The last element of the computer package is the technology itself, the hardware and software instructions. Separate chapters will be devoted to this issue, but three elements of the technology are important to mention. First, in the last 30 years, there has been a dramatic *enhancement in the price/performance ratio of computing hardware*. Second, there has been a commensurate radical reduction in the physical size of components and hence an exponential increase in the computing power available per cubic centimeter. The computing power available on some of the first third-generation IBM 360 general-purpose computers introduced in the early 1960s, which required several hundred square feet of office space, is now available on an IBM or Apple personal computer, which requires no more than 4 square feet of office space. Third, there have been vast improvements in the software or computer instructions that permit non-specialists to use the computer for a variety of applications.

Changes in the three elements of the computer package—the organizational unit, the people, and the technology—are closely interrelated. The changes in information systems experienced in the last 20 years occurred because of vast enhancements in the technology that made computers relevant and cost-effective for much broader groups within the organization. Today there are few functions or positions in the organization that do not utilize computers in some form.

Why Do Organizations Adopt Information Systems?

At first glance, the answer to the question "Why do organizations adopt information systems?" seems very simple. Obviously, organizations adopt information systems to become more efficient, save money, and reduce the work force. However, while this may have been generally true in the past, it is no longer the only or even the primary reason for adopting systems today.

Today systems are, of course, built with efficiency in mind, but they have become vitally important for simply staying in business. Information systems are like capital improvements such as buildings. Improvements in decision making (speed, accuracy, comprehensiveness), serving ever higher customer and client expectations, coordinating dispersed groups in an organization, and exercising tighter control over personnel and expenditures, become the principal rationales for systems.

More recently, the competitive aspects of systems, as described in Chapter 3, have become even more important. It may not be more efficient to gather funds using automatic teller machines (ATM) (compared to selling bonds in Europe), but to stay in the retail banking business, ATM systems are required today. It may not save money to build an integrated financial information system to serve senior managers at corporate headquarters, but such a system makes far better use of their time and permits much closer corporate control of remote divisions.

So, what seems like an easy question to answer—why do organizations adopt systems?—is quite complex. Some organizations are simply more innovative than others. They have values that are very supportive of any kind of innovation, regardless of its direct economic benefit to the company. In other cases, information systems are built because of the ambitions of various subgroups within an organization and the anticipated effect on existing organizational

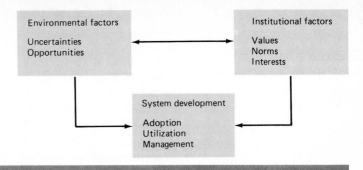

FIGURE 4.5
Factors in the organizational development of systems.

conflicts. And in some cases, changes in an organization's environment—government regulations, competitors' actions, changing costs—demand a computer system response.

A model of the systems development process that includes many factors other than economic considerations is given in Figure 4.5. This model divides the explanations for why organizations adopt systems into two groups: *external environmental factors* and *internal institutional factors* (Laudon, 1985).

Some external environmental factors are rising costs of labor or other important resources; important constraints such as the competitive actions of other organizations; changes in government regulations; and new sources of capital. In general, these can be thought of as *environmental constraints*. At the same time, the environment also provides organizations with *opportunities*: new technologies, the development of new production processes, the demise of a competitor, or a new government program that increases the demand for certain products.

Institutional factors are *internal* to the organization and include values, norms, and vital interests that govern matters of strategic importance to the organization. For instance, the top management of a corporation can decide that it needs to exercise much stronger control over the inventory process and therefore decides to develop an inventory information system. This kind of system is adopted, developed, and operated for purely internal, institutional reasons.

4.4 How Information Systems Affect Organizations

It is commonplace for newspapers and other popular media to portray the "impacts" of information systems and computers on organizations like a ship hitting an iceberg at sea. Instead, what is involved is an intricately choreographed relationship in which organizations and information technology mutually influence each other. Because information systems are used to promote organizational values and interests, they are deeply affected by the organization. What looks like an impact of technology is often a reflection of what the organization and the system designers consciously intended (or unconsciously created). While systems do not "impact" organizations in a simple sense, they do permit organizations to promote values and goals in a way that would be impossible without this technology. New information systems permit new organizational structures, goals, work designs, values and day-to-day behavior. These systems therefore do have an effect on *organizational actors* by widening their scope of action and enhancing their capabilities.

Systems and Organizational Structure

Organizational structure generally refers to the overall shape of the organization in terms of its hierarchy, centralization, and principal division of labor. Early research on information systems suggested that organizations would become more centralized and that middle management would tend to disappear over time because computers would give central, high-level managers all of the information they required to operate the organization without middle management intervention (see Figure 4.6).

Under the hypothesis of greater centralization, an organization chart would start to look like an inverted *T*. On the other hand, more contemporary research suggests that computerization gives more information to middle managers, permitting them to make more important decisions than in the past and reducing the need for large numbers of lower-level workers. Over time, this results in a diamond-like structure (Shore, 1983).

Contemporary research also recognizes that organizations have a great deal of control over the impacts of systems on structure. Important groups in the organization determine, either consciously

Normal shape

Expanding middle management
Decreasing unskilled jobs

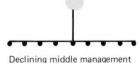

Declining middle management
Increasing unskilled jobs

FIGURE 4.6

Systems and organizational structures. There are many hypothesized impacts that systems may have on organizations. Systems may have no effect; they may expand the capabilities and numbers of middle managers; or they may reduce the number of middle managers. Each hypothesis is represented in the figure (reading from left to right). Most researchers have found, however, the organizational impacts reflect management choice as much as technological determinism.

A Financial Information System

Nothing sounds so apolitical as a modern financial information system (FIS) designed to speed the work of corporate accountants who have to report to federal agencies and stockholders. The Golden Triangle Corporation (GTC) began planning for FIS in 1972, and five years later there were still problems getting it to work properly. FIS was designed to centralize corporate financial reporting, to take over certain division accounting functions, and to serve both the divisions and the corporate headquarters. But the users—in this case, division accountants—were not consulted, the system was slow in recording new accounts, forced excessive time at data entry points, and removed some discretion from the divisions in reporting financial results. Often two sets of books were maintained: one automated (and incorrect) and one manual (correct but slow). Divisional accountants fought the corporate accountants to a standoff: FIS remained as a corporate consolidator of financial data, but it was denied the authority to become a more powerful, integrated financial control system.

Adapted from M.L. Markus, "Power, Politics, and MIS Implementation," *Communications of the ACM*, June 1983.

or unconsciously, what kinds of impacts on organizational structure will occur. Organizations can decide to centralize or decentralize power. In recent years, many organizations have shifted authority away from central headquarters, shrinking headquarters staff and placing more power in the hands of division managers and local factory managers. On the other hand, many organizations consciously seek to gather more information from operating units and to develop a large central corporate staff for both planning and operational control purposes.

Systems and Organizational Culture

Organizational culture refers to the central values, norms, and day-to-day activities of organizations. What are organizational values? *Values* are the announced and official goals and desirable conditions in the organization. *Organizational norms* refer to the actual day-to-day operational goals and behaviors in an organization.

In many instances, the values built into information systems do not adequately reflect organizational values. For instance, many cities have installed computer terminals in police patrol cars to check the license plates and registrations on motor vehicles. In order for these systems to achieve maximum benefit, it is assumed that police officers will spend a lot of time in their cars punching in license plate numbers. Supervisors in some cities have complained that young officers do just that. The result is fewer foot patrols, lower visibility of police on the streets, and a reduction in the flow of intelligence to local police precincts. Many jurisdictions are now limiting car terminals to traffic patrol units.

Systems and Politics

Because organizations are divided into specialized subgroups (e.g., marketing, accounting, production), different values represented by different groups arise in organizations. These groups compete for resources. These features of organizations create the group basis for politics in organizations. *Politics* means simply the competition between organizational subgroups for influence over the policies, procedures, and resources of the organization.

While anyone familiar with systems development projects is aware of the important role of politics in systems, most textbooks never mention the subject. But there is a growing research literature, and currently all information system students should be aware of the role of politics in systems (Laudon, 1974; Keen, 1981; Kling, 1980; Laudon 1986).

Information systems inevitably become bound up in the politics of organizations because they influence access to a key resource, namely, information. In powerful ways, information systems can affect who does what to whom, when, where, and how in an organization.

For instance, a major study of the efforts of the FBI to develop a national computerized criminal history system (a single national listing of the criminal histories—arrests and convictions—of over 36 million individuals in the United States) found that the state governments strongly resisted the FBI's efforts. The states felt that this information would give the federal government, and the FBI in particular, the ability to monitor how states use criminal histories and to control the interstate dissemination of criminal history information. This was a function that the states felt they could accomplish without federal interference. The states resisted the development of this national system quite successfully (Laudon, 1986).

Within organizations, even seemingly innocuous systems such as a new accounting system can have powerful political ramifications. If these new systems take functions and authority from one group and distribute it to others, they can inspire considerable resentment and counterimplementation resistance in an organization (Keen, 1981). For example, integrated human resources information systems typically attempt to include payroll, benefits, employment history, and medical information in a single, integrated database or data bank. However, many of these functions have traditionally been performed by separate subunits within the organization. Payroll functions are often performed in the financial officers' department (the Finance Department or the treasurer's office). These groups resist any effort to remove important functions from their jurisdiction.

Systems and Decision Making

The impact of information systems on decision making is described in greater detail in the following chapter. Information systems directly affect how decisions are made in an organization by altering the manner and frequency with which information is delivered to key decision makers.

Information systems speed up the decision-making process by making information more readily available to key decision makers at lower levels in the hierarchy and to a larger number of decision makers. This greater speed and scope of information dissemination is one of the most important effects of information systems to date.

Systems and Work

Information systems affect two aspects of work: the overall aggregate level of employment and the quality of work in specific organizations.

Early research suggested that information technology would significantly reduce the quality of work. It was feared that computers would bring about an inevitable decline in skills: Most of the intelligence involved in jobs would be absorbed by the machines. Career paths would shorten, and supervision would be closer and less humane. As jobs came to provide less and less autonomy, alienation from work would rise (Leavitt, 1958).

Early research also pointed to harmful changes in the social character of work. It was speculated that computers would increase the isolation and fragmentation of work by removing workers from group settings and placing them in small booths where they would work directly with video display terminals. The social network on the job would be destroyed. Informal communications would be replaced by formal communications. Briefly, there would be less face-to-face communication by workers. Workers would become closely tied to machines. Comradeship and high morale, which are typical of many office jobs, would be destroyed.

A related set of fears today about the impact of office systems on work concerns the redistribution of work both on and off the job. Office systems can be organized so that much work is done at home, especially by women with small children. This has the advantage of making work available to mothers who would like to stay at home, but at the same time it removes women from the office social network that is vital for promotion and advancement.

On the job, office systems can be organized so that all secretaries are placed in a central word processing pool, where they would serve all members of the organization. In this way, work would be relocated to specialized work centers. On paper, this centralization of clerical support has many advantages, including greater efficiency. It has the disadvantage, however, of reducing personal attachments

Designing It Right

If video display terminals are improperly designed, productivity can fall 20–30% from optimal levels, essentially wiping out the advances of technology. The National Institute of Occupational Safety and Health found that workers using properly designed work stations were 24% more productive than workers at poorly designed stations. Among the factors making for good design are furniture permitting the feet to rest flat on the floor, an angle between the upper and lower legs of 90 degrees, a back rest that supports the lower back, finger tips resting on the keyboard with the hands above the elbows, and the elimination of light glare from other sources. Regular rest breaks further enhance productivity. The cost of an ergonomically designed work station is $1361, as opposed to a poorly designed unit at $736. However, the gains in productivity from well-designed units pay for themselves through higher output in 4.78 months.

Adapted from *Computerworld*, October 28, 1985.

between managers and clerical workers, and it can reduce the effectiveness of clerical support.

Most of these negative implications and potentials for information technology have not been realized. Clearly, there are areas where particular jobs have lost skills. For instance, secretaries have been differentiated into word processing technicians and executive secretaries. Word processing technicians have a limited range of skills (mainly keyboard skills). In limited areas of certain industries, jobs have become isolated and more fragmented than in the past. In the insurance industry, the growth of very large keypunching sections, and in the airline reservation industry, the increasing number of reservation clerks working one-on-one before a video display terminal for up to eight hours a day with few or no breaks, are examples of jobs with a limited career path. Decision making is highly geared to the machine itself, and there are few, if any, social interactions.

On the other hand, many information technologies have enhanced the skills of jobs, extended career paths, created entirely new occupations (microcomputer coordinators, managers, etc.), and allowed more complex decision making and job enrichment.

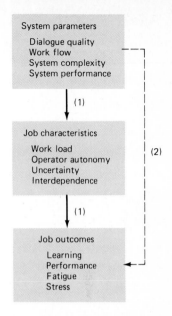

FIGURE 4.7
Computer systems and jobs. *From Turner and Karasek, 1984.*

Key: (1) Main powerful effects
(2) Weak, nonexistent effects

A detailed study of how computers affect jobs has found that the negative impacts of systems do not result directly from the computer, but instead, are filtered through the design of the job (Turner, 1984) (see Figure 4.7). The impact of systems on work depends, therefore, on how the systems are organized and how the work is designed.

4.5 Organizational Resistance to Change

Because information systems change important dimensions of the organization—its structure, culture, politics, and work—there is often considerable resistance to them.

Technology Is Only One Element

There are several ways to visualize organizational resistance. Leavitt (1965) used a diamond shape to illustrate the interrelated and mutually adjusting character of technology and organization (see Figure 4.8). Here changes in technology are absorbed, deflected, and defeated by organizational task arrangements, structures, and people. In this model, the only way to bring about change is to change the technology, tasks, structure, and people simultaneously. Other authors have spoken about the need to "unfreeze" organizations

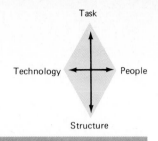

FIGURE 4.8
Technology and the organization. Implementing
information systems has consequences for job
tasks, people, and organizational structure.
From Leavitt, 1965.

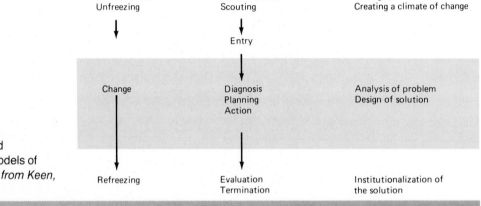

FIGURE 4.9
Lewin/Schein and
Kolb/Frohman models of
change. *Adapted from Keen,
1981.*

before introducing an innovation, quickly implementing it, and
"refreezing" or institutionalizing the change (Kolb, 1970; Alter and
Ginzberg, 1978) (see Figure 4.9).

Resistance Depends On Anticipated Effects

The model of systems development presented in Section 4.3 can be
extended to include questions of organizational change and resistance (see Figure 4.10). In this model, organizations adopt systems
because of environmental necessity and opportunities or because of
internal institutional factors. The impacts of these systems depend
heavily on organizational variables and on decisions made during the
adoption and implementation process. Impacts, in turn, feed back to
the environment and the organization itself (dotted lines) by creating
forces of change and resistance. In general, the larger the anticipated
impacts of systems, the greater the resistance. Massive systems
requiring a substantial amount of social change create a great deal
of resistance. Strong leadership and planning are required to overcome it.

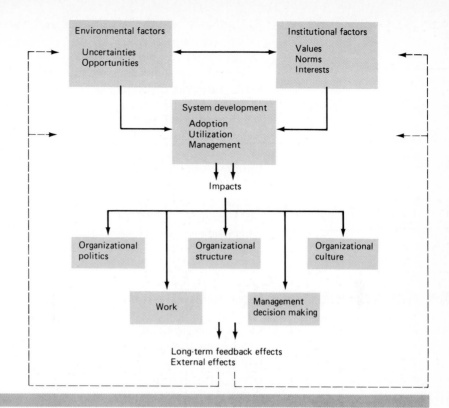

FIGURE 4.10
A model of the systems development/impacts process.

Implementation Is More Difficult Than Anticipated

A common experience of system designers and leaders is that the implementation of the system—getting the system to work as designed—is far more difficult than anticipated. Indeed, many systems failures are due to successful organizational resistance. Chapter 19 discusses system success and failure in greater detail.

Because of the difficulties of implementing systems, experienced systems observers like those previously cited have adopted very conservative models of social change through systems.

All of the models described in this section have one feature in common: They conclude that implementation of systems is difficult because of organizational change requirements. Briefly:

- Organizations do not innovate unless there is a substantial environmental change. Organizations adopt innovations only when they must do so.
- Substantial forces resisting change are rooted in the organization's structures, values, and interest groups.
- Organizational innovation is much more difficult and complex than simply purchasing technology. In order to reap the benefits of

technology, it must be utilized and managed properly. This, in turn, involves changes in the values, norms, and interest group alignments of the organization. Real change always involves a struggle over who does what, where, when and how.

- The function of leaders is to take advantage of external circumstances to solidify their power, and to use external opportunities to tilt the internal conflict in an organization in their favor and toward the successful development of their own agendas.

Bringing about change through the development of information technology and information systems is slowed considerably by the natural inertia of organizations. Of course, organizations do change, and powerful leaders are often required to bring about these changes. Nevertheless, the process, as leaders eventually discover, is more complicated and much slower than is typically anticipated.

4.6 Summary

One cannot understand or design an information system properly unless one understands the characteristics of the organization in which the system will reside. All modern organizations are hierarchical, specialized, and impartial, and use explicit rules and procedures with the objective of maximizing efficiency. Organizations differ in goals, groups served, social role, leadership style, incentives, and types of tasks performed.

Salient features of organizations that must be addressed by information systems include organizational level, organizational structure, types of tasks and decisions, the nature of management support, and the sentiments and attitudes of workers who will be using the system. The organization's history and external environment must be considered as well.

Theories highlighting facets of organizations that are critical to information systems can be broken down into five schools: (1) the classical or structural school, (2) the human relations school, (3) the managerial or scientific management school, (4) the technology school, and (5) the institutional school.

Computerized information systems are supported in organizations by a "computer package" consisting of a formal organizational unit or Information Systems Department, information specialists, and computer technology. The role of information systems and the computer package in the organization have become increasingly critical to both daily operations and strategic decision making.

Organizations adopt information systems for both external environmental and internal institutional reasons. The impact of information systems on organizations is not unidirectional. Information systems and the organizations where they are used interact with and influence each other. The introduction of a new information system will affect the organizational structure, goals, work design, values, competition between interest groups, decision making, and day-to-day behavior. At the same time, information systems must be designed to serve the needs of important groups.

Implementation of a new information system is often more difficult than anticipated because of organizational change requirements. Since information systems change important organizational dimensions, including the structure, culture, power relationships, and work activities, there is often considerable resistance to new systems.

Key Words

Organization
Social structure
Hierarchy
Division of labor
Structural school
Human relations school
Scientific management school
Technology school
Institutional school
Centralized systems
Decentralized systems

Programmer
Systems analyst
Business systems analyst
End user
Environmental factors
Institutional factors
Organizational structure
Organizational culture
Leavitt diamond
Implementation
Counterimplementation

Review Questions

1. What is an organization? How do organizations use information?
2. Compare the technical definition of organizations with the legal-rational definition.
3. What features do all organizations have in common?
4. In what ways can organizations diverge?
5. Name the five major schools of thought about organizations. What aspects of organizations does each try to explain?
6. Name the levels of analysis (work groups) for organizational behavior. What considerations about organizational levels must be addressed in information system design?
7. What aspects of organizations addressed by various theories of organizations must be considered when designing an information system?
8. Name the changing applications of organizational information systems from the 1950s to the 1980s. How has the role of information systems changed over this time period?
9. Name the three elements in the computer package. How has the role of each element in the organization changed over time?
10. Name some of the important information systems specialist jobs in the organization. What specialties and skills are characteristic of each? How have these specialties changed over time?

11. Describe the two models that explain why organizations adopt information systems.
12. What do we mean by the impact of information systems on the organization?
13. What is the relationship between information systems and organizational structure?
14. What is the relationship between information systems and organizational culture?
15. What is the relationship between information systems and organizational politics?
16. What aspects of work have been affected by information systems? How has each been affected?
17. Why is there considerable organizational resistance to the introduction of information systems? Describe two models that explain this phenomenon.

Discussion Questions

1. It has been said that when we design an information system, we are redesigning the organization. Discuss.
2. You are an information systems designer assigned to build a new accounts receivable system for one of your corporation's divisions. What organizational factors should you consider?
3. It has been said that implementation of a new information system is always more difficult than anticipated. Discuss.

Wallace International Makes Changes for Its New System

Wallace International, based in Wallingford, Connecticut, is a distinguished 150-year-old producer of silver flatware and holloware. Wallace sells both silverware sets and open stock; its sales are seasonal and are influenced by changing emphases in the retail market. Although it still draws on some traditional silversmith techniques, Wallace requires sophisticated computer systems to control its inventory, forecast marketing trends, and track costs.

Management decided to install a manufacturing resources planning (MRP) system in October 1982. The firm chose the MRP II software package from ASK Computer Systems, which included modules for general ledger, accounts payable, manufacturing management, order management/accounts receivable, fixed assets, and budgeting and analysis. A Hewlett-Packard HP3000 Model 68 was selected for the hardware.

Wallace made some changes in its operations to prepare for the new system. A successful MRP II system requires a high degree of inventory accuracy. To control access, Wallace had to secure its stockrooms by enclosing them in high metal fences. Pieces are counted when they are moved in and when they are shipped out. Wallace added cathode ray tubes to the stockrooms for on-line transactions.

Wallace also had to improve its housekeeping to make sure that supply materials and parts that moved from one operation to another remained orderly. Complete implementation of the MRP II software is now reducing the volume of sitting parts to a steady stream.

Wallace also took special steps to educate its personnel about the MRP II system. Wallace is unionized, and the Amalgamated Silversmiths recently joined with the International Service Workers' Union. Before making changes, the implementation team held orientation meetings with the shop union leaders. Enlisting their cooperation was a top priority, and they were among the first persons scheduled for training sessions. Wallace estimated that it took 4400 hours to educate all of its employees and felt that this extra time was well spent.

An ambitious endeavor from the start, the MRP II implementation was further complicated when Wallace was acquired by Katy Industries, Inc., of Elgin, Illinois, and when it purchased the International Silver Company in Meriden, Connecticut. Wallace was faced with two different billing procedures and invoices, a change in fiscal year, and the management of three different computers. It decided to implement the accounting functions of the ASK system before its production module. The installation of some of Wallace's MRP II functions was delayed because of this change in identity.

Wallace is pleased with MRP II's capabilities. It can review both in-house sales orders and market forecasts. The system can advise management when to purchase material and make deliveries, taking account of variables such as lead time, material on hand, ordered material, and work in process. The system also tracks work orders and canceled orders. The company attributes the success of this system not only to the software but also to the cooperation and hard work of its employees.

Adapted from "MRP II: A Manufacturer's Silver Lining," *Manufacturing Systems*, January 1985.

Case Study Questions

1. What organizational changes at Wallace were required to implement its MRP II system?
2. Why was it so important to enlist the union leaders' support for the MRP II system?
3. What organizational factors complicated the implementation of the MRP II system?
4. What levels of the Wallace organization were affected by the MRP II system?

References

Allison, Graham T. *Essence of Decision*. Boston: Little, Brown, 1971.

Alter, Steven, and Michael Ginzberg. "Managing Uncertainity in MIS Implementation," *Sloan Management Review*, Vol. 20, No. 1 (Fall 1978).

Anthony, R.N. *Planning and Control Systems: A Framework for Analysis*. Cambridge, Mass.: Harvard University Press, 1965.

Argyris, Chris. *Interpersonal Competence and Organizational Effectiveness*. Homewood, Ill.: Dorsey Press, 1962.

Barnard, Chester. *The Functions of the Executive*. Cambridge, Mass.: Harvard University Press, 1968.

Blau, Peter, and Scott, W. Richard. *Formal Organizations*. San Francisco: Chandler Press, 1962.

Etzioni, Amitai. *A Comparative Analysis of Complex Organizations*. New York: Free Press, 1975.

Fayol, Henri. *Administration industrielle et generale*. Paris: Dunods, 1950 (first published in 1916).

Gorry, G.A., and Morton, M.S. "Framework for Management Information Systems," *Sloan Management Review*, Vol. 13, No. 1 (Fall 1971).

Gouldner, Alvin. *Patterns of Industrial Bureaucracy*. New York: Free Press, 1954.

Herzberg, Frederick. *Work and the Nature of Man*. New York: Crowell, 1966.

Homans, George. *The Human Group*. New York: Harcourt Brace Jovanovich, 1950.

Keen, P.G.W. "Information Systems and Organizational Change," *Communications of the ACM*, Vol. 24, No. 1 (January 1981).

Keen, P.G.W., and Morton, M.S. *Decision Support Systems: An Organizational Perspective*. Reading Mass.: Addison-Wesley, 1978.

Kling, Rob. "Social Analyses of Computing: Theoretical Perspectives in Recent Empirical Research," *Computing Survey*, Vol. 12, No. 1 (March 1980).

Kling, Rob, and Dutton, William H. "The Computer Package: Dynamic Complexity," in *Computers and Politics* edited by James Danziger, William Dutton, Rob Kling and Kenneth Kraemer. New York: Columbia University Press, 1982.

Kolb, D.A., and Frohman, A.L. "An Organization Development Approach to Consulting," *Sloan Management Review*, Vol. 12, No. 1 (Fall 1970).

Laudon, Kenneth C. *Computers and Bureaucratic Reform*. New York: Wiley, 1974.

Laudon, Kenneth C. "Environmental and Institutional Models of Systems Development," *Communications of the ACM*, Vol. 28, No. 7 (July 1985).

Laudon, Kenneth C. *The Dossier Society: Value Choices in the Design of National Information Systems*. New York: Columbia University Press, 1986.

Lawrence, Paul, and Lorsch, Jay. *Organization and Environment*. Cambridge, Mass.: Harvard University Press, 1969.

Leavitt, Harold J., "Applying Organizational Change in Industry: Structural, Technological and Humanistic Approaches, in *Handbook of Organizations*, edited by James G. March. Chicago: Rand McNally, 1965.

Leavitt, Harold J., and Whisler, Thomas L. "Management in the 1980s" *Harvard Business Review*, (November–December 1958).

March, James G., and Simon, Herbert A. *Organizations*. New York: Wiley, 1958.

Mayo, Elton. *The Social Problems of an Industrial Civilization*. Cambridge, Mass.: Harvard University Press, 1945.

Mintzberg, Henry. *The Nature of Managerial Work*. New York: Harper & Row, 1973.

Parsons, Talcott. *Structure and Process in Modern Societies*. New York: Free Press, 1960.

Perrow, Charles. *Organizational Analysis*. Belmont, Calif.: Wadsworth, 1970.

Roethlisberger, F.J., and Dickson, W.J. *Management and the Worker*. Cambridge, Mass.: Harvard University Press, 1947.

Shore, Edwin B. "Reshaping the IS Organization," *MIS Quarterly*, (December 1983).

Thompson, James. *Organizations in Action*. New York: McGraw-Hill, 1967.

Turner, Jon A. "Computer Mediated Work: The Interplay Between Technology and Structured Jobs, *Communications of the ACM*, Vol. 27, No. 12 (December 1984).

Turner, Jon A. and Robert A. Karasek, Jr. "Software Ergonomics: Effects of Computer Application Design Parameters on Operator Task Performance and Health," *Ergonomics*, Vol. 27, No. 6, 1984.

Weber, Max. *The Theory of Social and Economic Organization*. Translated by Talcott Parsons. New York: Free Press, 1947.

Woodward, Joan. *Industrial Organization: Theory and Practice*. Oxford: Oxford University Press, 1965.

CHAPTER 5

Information, Management, and Decision Making

OUTLINE

(Continued on next page.)

In 1980 General Foods was a $7 billion sales food conglomerate in trouble: 39% of its revenues came from the no-growth coffee market, and the rest came from slow-growth products like cereals and powdered beverages. In 1981 the company's chairman and CEO, James Ferguson, started a wide-ranging restructuring program. Ferguson decided to add new high-growth products and to sell off ancillary fast food operations and concentrate on foods. The general objective was to make General Foods the market leader in all of its major product categories. To achieve this goal rapidly, Ferguson decided to buy other companies with well-established brand names rather than to invade markets. Thus, General Foods bought out Oscar Mayer & Company (the leading U.S. producer of branded meat products); two Northeast market leaders, Entenmann's, Inc. (baked goods), and the Ronzoni Corporation (pasta producer); and a West Coast baked goods leader, the Oroweat Foods Company.

Ferguson was motivated to restructure General Foods in part by changing market conditions in the food industry. Overall industry growth was down to 1% a year. The single mass food market dominated by mothers purchasing for their families (two children, mother, and father) had splintered into smaller, diverse segments such as working couples, working singles, teenagers (many cooking their own meals), and men cooking their own meals. And tastes had changed, with a new emphasis on convenient, low-calorie, healthy foods. This environmental change indicated that General Foods had to change its products, marketing, production, and distribution facilities.

Adapted from "General Foods' Strategy for Tomorrow," *Dun's Business Month*, May 1985.

The decisions facing James Ferguson of General Foods are typical of those facing many senior executives. What business should we be in? Where is our industry headed? Where are we strong and where are we weak? What should our strategy be? How can we design a strategy?

Many of these questions involve judgment; there are no easy, simple answers. Information systems and computers alone cannot provide solutions. In some cases, however, information systems can support the process of arriving at answers, sometimes in very powerful ways. In other cases, they may be of little or no use. To apply information systems effectively, one must first understand the nature of managerial activities and decision making.

In this chapter the student will learn:

- How information systems can support managers.
- Classical and contemporary descriptions of managerial activities and roles.
- How information systems should be designed to support managerial work.
- Levels, types, and stages of decision making.
- Models of individual and organizational decision making.
- How information systems can support decisions.

5.1 Introduction

In the previous chapter, we discussed how information systems must support organizations. We described the various aspects of organizations—hierarchy, specialization, and subgroups—that called for the development of different kinds of systems. Key figures in these organizations are managers, whose responsibilities range from making decisions, to arranging birthday parties, to writing reports, to attending meetings. Information systems must support managers in a number of ways if they are to help the organization at all.

To understand the proper role of information systems, we must examine what managers do and what information they need for decision making. We must also understand how decisions are made and what kinds of decision problems can be supported by formal information systems. We can then determine whether information systems will be valuable tools and how they should be designed.

5.2 What Managers Do

Obviously, information systems that claim to support managers cannot be built unless one clearly understands what managers do and how they do it. Management activities pervade the organization at all levels. Even lower-level clerks engage in some kinds of management activities by coordinating the flow of work, meeting deadlines, and maintaining quality.

Classical Descriptions of Management

For more than 50 years, since the 1920s, classical descriptions of what managers do were largely unquestioned. Henry Fayol and other early writers first described the five classical functions of managers: *planning, organizing, coordinating, deciding,* and *controlling* (see Table 5.1). This description of management activities has dominated the vocabulary of the management literature for a long time.

But as a description of what managers actually do, these five terms are unsatisfactory. For instance, what do managers do when

TABLE 5.1
The Classical Model of Management Activities

Planning

Organizing

Coordinating

Deciding

Controlling

they plan, and how do they plan? How do they actually decide things? How do managers control the work of others? What is needed is a more fine-grained understanding of how managers actually behave.

Behavioral Models: Mintzberg

Contemporary behavioral scientists have discovered from empirical observation that managers do not behave as the classical model of management led us to believe. Kotter (1982) has provided a description for the morning activities of the president of an investment management firm.

7:35 AM   Richardson arrives at work, unpacks his briefcase, gets some coffee, and begins making a list of activities for the day.

7:45 AM   Bradshaw (a subordinate) and Richardson converse about a number of topics and exchange pictures recently taken on summer vacations.

8:00 AM   They talk about a schedule of priorities for the day.

8:20 AM   Wilson (a subordinate) and Richardson talk about some personnel problems, cracking jokes in the process.

8:45 AM   Richardson's secretary arrives, and they discuss her new apartment and arrangements for a meeting later in the morning.

8:55 AM   Richardson goes to a morning meeting run by one of his subordinates. Thirty people are there, and Richardson reads during the meeting.

11:05 AM   Richardson and his subordinates return to the office and discuss a difficult problem. They try to define the problem and outline possible alternatives. He lets the discussion roam away from and back to the topic again and again. Finally, they agree on a next step.

TABLE 5.2 The Behavioral Model of Management Activities	High-volume, high-speed work
	Variety, fragmentation, brevity
	Issue preference current, ad hoc, specific
	Complex web of interactions, contacts
	Strong preference for *verbal media*
	Control of the agenda

The actual behavior of managers appears to be less systematic, more informal, less reflective, more reactive, less well-organized, and much more frivolous than students of information systems and decision making generally expect it to be. In the preceding example, it is difficult to determine which activities constitute planning, coordinating, and decision making.

A widely noted study of actual managerial behavior conducted by Mintzberg (1971) describes six characteristics of the modern manager (see Table 5.2). In general, these characteristics indicate a very different kind of managerial life from that portrayed by the classical model. First, modern researchers have found that the manager performs a great deal of work at an unrelenting pace and works at a high level of intensity. Some studies have found that managers engage in more than 600 different activities each day, with no break in the pace. Free time appears to be very rare. Even when they leave the office, general managers frequently take work home.

Second, the activity of managers is characterized by variety, fragmentation, and brevity. There simply is not enough time for managers to get deeply involved in a wide range of issues. Third, the attention of managers shifts rapidly from one issue to another, with very little pattern. A problem occurs, and all other matters must be dropped until it is solved. Mintzberg found that, in general, each activity of general managers lasted for less than 9 minutes, and only 10% of the activities exceeded 1 hour in duration.

Managers prefer speculation, hearsay, gossip—in brief, current, up-to-date, although uncertain, information. Historical, certain, routine information receives less attention. Managers want to work on issues that are current, specific, and ad hoc.

Fourth, as noted in the previous chapter, managers are involved in a diverse and *complex web of contacts* that together act as an informal information system. Managers converse with clients, associates, peers, secretaries, outside government officials, and so forth. In one

One might expect managers of information systems to be heavy users of formal information system reports and other products. As it turns out, however, these managers are like other managers. In a study of a small number of information system managers, Olson found that 76% of their time was spent in oral contacts: phone calls, office meetings, and casual conversations. Only 19% of their times was spent at their desk. They rarely looked at computer-based reports, and when they did, it was usually reports prepared for other organization units (e.g., marketing or personnel). There were few "decision support" aids. Olson found that, like the shoe-maker's children, information system managers seem to be the last to benefit from the technology they purvey.

Adapted from Margrethe H. Olson, "The IS Managers's Job," *MIS Quarterly*, December 1981.

sense, managers operate a network of contacts throughout the organization and the environment.

Fifth, several studies have found that *managers prefer verbal forms of communication* to written forms. In most studies, managers have been found to prefer verbal media, which provide greater flexibility, require less effort, and bring a faster response. Communication is the work of the manager, and he or she uses whatever tools are available to be an effective communicator (Olson, 1981).

Despite the flood of work, the press of deadlines, and the random order of crises, Mintzberg found that successful managers appear to be able to control their own affairs. To some extent, higher-level managers are at the mercy of their subordinates, who bring to their attention crises and activities that must be attended to immediately. Nevertheless, successful managers are those who can control the activities that they choose to get involved in on a day-to-day basis. By developing their own long-term commitments, their own information channels, and their own networks, senior managers can control their personal agendas. Less successful managers tend to be overwhelmed by problems brought to them by subordinates.

Managerial Roles

These studies of what managers actually do have led to a reconceptualization of managerial roles and the qualities of successful managers. Mintzberg conceives of managerial activities as falling into three categories: *interpersonal*, *information processing*, and *decision making*. Information systems, if built properly, can support these diverse roles in a number of ways (see Table 5.3).

An important interpersonal role is that of figurehead for the organization. Second, a manager acts as a leader, attempting to motivate subordinates and outsiders seeking their support. Lastly, managers act as a liaison between various levels of the organization and, within each level, among levels of the management team. Managers provide time, information, and favors, which they expect to be returned.

A second set of managerial roles Mintzberg called *informational roles*. Managers act as the nerve centers of their organization, receiving the latest, most concrete, most up-to-date information and redistributing it to those who need to know. Managers are therefore disseminators and spokesmen for their organization.

A more familiar set of managerial roles Mintzberg called *decisional roles*. Managers act as entrepreneurs by initiating new kinds of activities; they handle disturbances arising in the organization; they allocate resources to staff members who need them; and they negotiate conflicts and mediate between conflicting groups in the organization.

TABLE 5.3
Managerial Roles and
Support Systems

Role	Behavior	Support Systems
Interpersonal Roles		
Figurehead	---------------------→	None exist
Leader	-------Interpersonal------→	None exist
Liaison	---------------------→	Electronic Communication systems
Informational Roles		
Nerve center	---------------------→	Management information systems
Disseminator	-------Information-------→	Mail, office systems
Spokesman	-------processing-------→	Office and professional systems Work Stations
Decisional Roles		
Entrepreneur	---------------------→	None exist
Disturbance handler	------ Decision ------→	None exist
Resource allocator	------ making -------→	DSS systems
Negotiator	---------------------→	None exist

Source: Authors and Mintzberg (1971).

Table 5.3 notes that there are now many areas of management life where information systems do not make much of a contribution. These areas provide great opportunities for future systems and system designers.

In the area of interpersonal roles, information systems are extremely limited and make only indirect contributions, acting largely as a communications aid in some of the newer office automation and communication-oriented applications. These systems make a much larger contribution in the field of informational roles; large-scale MIS systems, office systems, and professional work stations that can enhance a manager's presentation of information are significant. In the area of decision making, only recently have DSS and micro-computer-based systems begun to make important contributions (see Chapters 10 and 16).

While information systems have made great contributions to organizations, until recently these contributions have been confined to narrow, transaction processing areas. Much work needs be done in broadening the impact of systems on professional and managerial life.

How Managers Get Things Done: Kotter

The classical school failed to describe *how* managers coordinate, control, and plan. Kotter (1982) has used the behavioral orientation to modern management to describe how managers work. Building on the work of Mintzberg, Kotter argues that effective managers are involved in three critical activities. First, general managers spend much time establishing *personal agendas and goals*, both short- and long-term. These personal agendas include both vague and specific topics and usually address a broad range of financial, product, and organizational issues. Second, and perhaps most important, effective managers spend a great deal of time *building an interpersonal network* composed of people at virtually all levels of the organization, from warehouse staff to clerical support personnel to other managers and senior management. These networks, like their personal agendas, are generally consistent with the formal plans and networks of an organization, but they are different and apart. General managers build these networks using a variety of face-to-face, interactive tools, both formal and informal. Managers carefully nurture professional reputations and relationships with peers.

A last function of the contemporary manager is *execution of personal agendas*. After they have developed networks and agendas, general managers use these networks for implementation. In Kotter's study, general managers called on peers, corporate staff, subordinates three or four levels below them, and even competitors in order to help them get things done. There was no category of people that was never used.

In the future, systems must be built that take into account the richness and diversity of managerial life. The following story sketches some possibilities.

A Day in the Life of the Future Manager

The mythical future manager works in the "smart" building wired with a local area network connecting all office equipment, a private branch exchange (PBX) handling voice and video traffic, and a fiberoptic cable connected to external telecommunications facilities sold by the phone company. It is a building like TRW Inc.'s new showcase "intelligent" building headquarters located on the outskirts of Cleveland, Ohio.

Our future manager, Mr. Taylor, dresses for work at 6:30 AM, when building computers start warming up the building and turning on lights and machinery. Mr. Taylor forgot to schedule a meeting with subordinates at 8:30 AM, so he goes to his living room and uses the phone to put a message on the company's mail system. The system recognizes his voice, has a business vocabulary of 10,000 words, and digitizes the message for storage and forwarding to his subordinates.

At 8:15 Mr. Taylor realizes that he needs some opinions from a co-worker 1500 miles away before he can conduct the meeting. He activates the teleconferencing equipment in a special room to call the executive through the PBX. At 9:30, after the meeting, Mr. Taylor checks the corporate databases to look at last week's performance, and checks the value of the peso, commodity prices, and real-time sales figures for his products.

At 10:30 a fire breaks out in the building. The building's management system detects the blaze, calls the fire department, pressurizes the floors above and below the fire, brings all elevators to the ground floor, starts the sprinkler system only in "hot" areas, and exhausts smoke at the fire origin. These decisions required 60 seconds (most of the time was used waiting for sensors to respond).

At 1 PM Mr. Taylor dictates some letters on the LAN system, which digitizes his voice, prints the copy on his desk top personal computer for review, and sends it at his command. By 4 PM Mr. Taylor is again talking with his colleague

What Managers Decide: Wrapp

Using the classical model of management, one might expect that managers make important decisions, and that the more senior the manager, the more important and profound the decisions will be. Yet in a frequently cited article written about general managers, H. Edward Wrapp (1984) found that good managers do not make policy decisions but instead give the organization a general sense of direction and become skilled in developing opportunities.

Wrapp found that good managers seldom make forthright statements of policy; often get personally involved in operating decisions; and rarely try to push through total solutions to or programs for particular problems. Wrapp described a number of myths about modern managers and compared them with the reality as he came to know it as a member of several corporate boards (see Table 5.4).

Contrary to these myths, Wrapp found that the successful manager spends much time and energy getting involved in operational decisions and problems in order to stay well informed; focuses time and energy on a small subset of organizational problems that he or she can directly affect successfully; is sensitive to the power structure of the organization because any major proposal requires the support of several organizational units and actors; and appears imprecise in setting overall organizational goals but nevertheless

TABLE 5.4
Some Myths About Top Managers

Life is less complicated at the top of the organization.

The top managers know everything, can command whatever resources are needed, and therefore can be decisive.

The top manager's job consists of making long-range plans.

The top manager's job is to meditate about the role of the company in society.

Source: Adapted from Wrapp (1984).

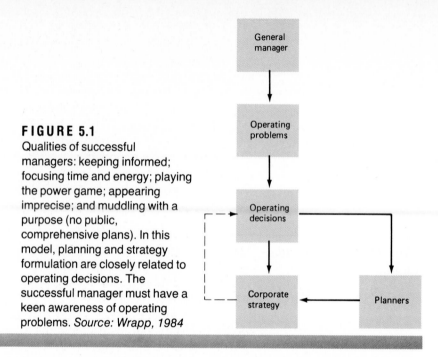

FIGURE 5.1
Qualities of successful managers: keeping informed; focusing time and energy; playing the power game; appearing imprecise; and muddling with a purpose (no public, comprehensive plans). In this model, planning and strategy formulation are closely related to operating decisions. The successful manager must have a keen awareness of operating problems. *Source: Wrapp, 1984*

provides a sense of direction. In this way, the manager maintains visability and avoids being placed in a policy straitjacket.

Contrary to the classical description, in which senior managers are thought of as making grand, sweeping decisions, Wrapp found that the contemporary manager muddles through organizational decisions with a purpose, as opposed to seeking to implement comprehensive, systematic, logical, well-programmed plans. Systematic, comprehensive plans are generally unable to exploit changes in the environment, and they are just as likely to create opposition in the organization as they are to gain support. For this reason, the manager seeks to implement plans one part at a time, without drawing attention to an explicit, comprehensive design.

Figure 5.1 illustrates Wrapp's conception of a good manager. Especially critical here is the notion of managers becoming involved in operating problems and decisions; second, corporate strategy derives from operating problems and decisions; and, third, the planning function is derived from a concise understanding of operating problems and decisions as opposed to a stand-alone entity.

Implications for Systems Design

The classical and contemporary views of what managers do are not contradictory. Managers do, in fact, plan, organize, coordinate, decide, and control. But the contemporary view of how they manage is much more complex, more behavioral, more situational—in a word, more human—than the classical view originally suggested.

This fact indicates that we need a more sophisticated view of formal information systems and information technology in the organization.

First, formal information systems are often used to plan, organize, and coordinate activities for managers. On the other hand, the experience of the Hewlett-Packard Corporation suggests that formal information systems are likely to be used by managers for a variety of other less obvious (but vital) tasks such as interpersonal communication, setting and carrying out personal agendas, and establishing a network throughout the organization. This should remind information system designers that there are multiple uses for their products and that the way systems are actually used may not, in fact, reflect the original intention of the designers.

Another implication of contemporary investigations of managers is that formal information systems may be more limited in their impact on managers than was heretofore believed. It may take several years for formal information systems to be designed, and by that time the situation of the firm and the managers themselves may have changed, so that the output of the system is no longer as relevant as it once was. Moreover, the output of formal information systems tends to be routine, and as we have seen, managers appreciate ad hoc, verbal, current, flexible sources of information. The formal output of systems may be briefly glanced at, but it is rarely studied in great detail by general managers.

Executives' Needs

A recent Hewlett-Packard Corporation study found that its top executives used their time in different ways from managers and professionals. Top executives spent 61% of their time in meetings; 25% on the telephone; 6.5% analyzing data prepared by subordinates; and even less time preparing documents or gathering information. Managers and professionals, on the other hand, spent more than 20% of their time creating documents and analyzing data. Like top managers, however, these groups spent considerable time on the telephone and most of their time in meetings. Hewlett Packard's executives most needed tools for communications.

Adapted from Robert Fuette, "Executive View of Microcomputers," *Infosystems*, August 1986.

Ad hoc (less formal) information systems that can be built quickly, use more current and up-to-date information, and can be adjusted to the unique situations of a specific group of managers are highly valued by the modern manager (see Chapter 16 for a description of DSS). Formal systems may have an important role to play at the operational level, but are less critical at the middle and senior management levels than was heretofore understood.

Last, systems designers and builders must appreciate the importance of building systems that can process information at the most general level; communicate with other sources of information, both inside and outside the organization; and provide an effective means of communication among managers and employees within the organization. The Hewlett-Packard Corporation, for example, found that its executives were most in need of tools for communication. These generalized computing systems, which are now technologically possible with the development of microcomputers, telecommunication networks, and related software, will have a powerful effect on the organization. These kinds of systems are discussed in later chapters.

5.3 Introduction to Decision Making

Perhaps no other management topic has received as much attention as management and organizational decision making. In classical theories of what managers do, decision making is often seen as the center of managerial activities, something that engages most of the time of managers. While we now know that this is not exactly the case, and that it can be easily overstated, decision making is nevertheless one of many management activities. It is one of the areas that information systems have sought most of all to affect (with mixed success).

In this section, we discuss the levels, types, and stages of decision making. In the following sections, we discuss the difference between individual and organizational levels of decision making.

Levels of Decision Making: Anthony

In Chapter 1 we described three organizational levels that correspond to the types of decisions made in organizations. Using Anthony's categories, decision-making activity in an organization can be divided into three types: strategic, management control, and operational control (Anthony, 1965).

Strategic decision making is concerned with deciding on the objectives, resources, and policies of the organization. A major problem at this level of decision making is predicting the future of the organization and its environment, and matching the characteristics of the organization to the environment. This process generally involves a small group of high-level managers who deal with very complex, nonroutine problems.

A second type of decision involves *management control*, which is principally concerned with how efficiently and effectively resources are utilized and how well operational units are performing. Management control involves close interaction with those who are carrying out the tasks of the organization; it takes place within the context of broad policies and objectives set out by strategic planners; and, as the behavioralists have described, it involves an intimate knowledge of operational decision making and task completion.

A third type of decision making is *operational control*, which involves making decisions about carrying out the specific tasks set forth by strategic planners and management. Determining which units in the organization will carry out the task, establishing criteria of completion and resource utilization, evaluating outputs—all of these tasks involve decisions about operational control.

Types of Decisions: Structured vs. Unstructured

Within each of these levels of decision making, Simon (1960) has developed a typology of human problem solving. He has classified decisions as being either *programmed* or *nonprogrammed*. Elsewhere in the literature, these decisions are referred to as *structured* and *unstructured*; we will use the latter forms here. Unstructured decisions are those in which the decision maker must provide judgment, evaluation, and insights into the problem definition. They are novel, important, and nonroutine, and there is no well-understood or agreed-upon procedure for making them (Gorry and Scott-Morton, 1971). Structured decisions, in contrast, are repetitive, routine, and involve a definite procedure for handling them so that they do not have to be treated each time as if they were new.

Types of Decision Support Systems

These two typologies of decision making—one based on levels in the organization and the other on the nature of human problem solving—have been combined to form a DSS typology, as illustrated in Figure 5.2 (Gorry and Scott-Morton, 1971). In general, operational control personnel deal with fairly well-structured problems. In contrast, strategic planners deal with highly unstructured problems. Nevertheless, each level of the organization contains both structured and unstructured problems.

In the past, most of the success in modern information systems came in dealing with structured, operational, and management control decisions. But now most of the exciting applications are occurring in the management and strategic planning areas, where problems are either semistructured or are totally unstructured. Examples include general DSS; microcomputer-based decision-making systems such as Lotus, dBase III, and other packages; and general planning and simulation systems (discussed in later chapters).

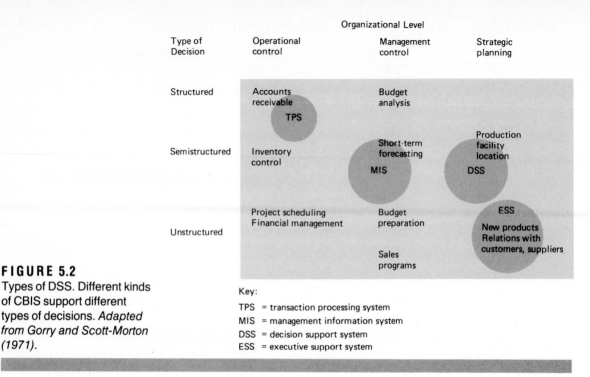

Organizational Level

Type of Decision	Operational control	Management control	Strategic planning
Structured	Accounts receivable **TPS**	Budget analysis	
Semistructured	Inventory control	Short-term forecasting **MIS**	Production facility location **DSS**
Unstructured	Project scheduling Financial management	Budget preparation	**ESS** New products Relations with customers, suppliers
		Sales programs	

Key:

TPS = transaction processing system
MIS = management information system
DSS = decision support system
ESS = executive support system

How Systems Support Decision Making: Simon

Making decisions is not a single activity that takes place all at once. It consists of several different activities that take place at different times.

Take any important decision that you as a student make—for example, whether or not to attend college—and ask yourself precisely when you decided to go to college. Chances are that the decision was made over a long period of time, had several influences, used many sources of information, and went through several stages. Next, ask yourself how information systems could help you make the decision. Let's try to breakdown decision making into its component stages.

Problems have to be perceived and understood; once perceived, solutions must be designed; once solutions are designed, choices have to be made about a particular solution; finally, the solution has to be carried out and implemented. Simon (1960) described four different stages in decision making (see Table 5.5): *intelligence, design, choice,* and *implementation.*

Intelligence involves identifying the problems occurring in the organization, why, where, and with what effects. This broad set of information-gathering activities is required to inform managers how well the organization is performing and where problems exist. Traditional MIS systems that deliver a wide variety of detailed information *can* be useful, especially if they are built to report excep-

TABLE 5.5

Stages in Decision Making, Information Requirement, and Examples

Stage of Decision Making	Information Requirement	Example System
Intelligence	Exception reporting	MIS
Design	Simulation prototype	DSS
Choice	'What-if' simulation	DSS; large models
Implementation	Graphics, charts	Microcomputer and mainframe decision aids, Gantt charts, etc.

Source: Author and adapted from Gorry and Scott-Morton (1971).

tions (with the added ability to call up text and additional detailed information).

The second phase of decision making involves *designing* many possible solutions to the problems. This activity may require more intelligence to decide if a particular solution is appropriate. Here more carefully specified and directed information activities and capabilities focused on specific designs are required. Smaller DSS systems are ideal because they operate on simple models, can be developed quickly, and can be operated with limited data.

The third stage involves *choosing* among alternatives. Here a manager can use information tools that can calculate and keep track of the consequences, costs, and opportunities provided by each alternative designed in stage 2. A larger DSS system is required because of the need to develop more extensive data on a variety of alternatives and the complexity of the analytic models needed to account for all of the consequences.

The last stage in decision making is *implementation*. Here managers can use a reporting system that delivers routine reports on the progress of a specific solution, some of the difficulties that arise, resource constraints, and possible ameliorative actions. Support systems can range from full-blown MIS systems to much smaller systems and project planning software operating on microcomputers.

Table 5.5 illustrates the stages in decision making, the general type of information required, and a specific example of an information system corresponding to each stage.

In general, the stages of decision making do not necessarily follow a linear path from intelligence, to design, choice, and implementation. Think again about your decision to attend a *specific* college. At any point in the decision-making process, it may be necessary to loop back to a previous stage (Figure 5.3). For instance, one can often come up with several designs but may not be certain whether a specific design meets the requirements for the particular problem. This requires additional intelligence work. Alternatively, one can be in the process of implementing a decision, only to discover that it is not working, forcing one to repeat the design or choice stage.

An important application of information systems directly tied to the intelligence-design-choice-implementation process is the use of systems in manufacturing to coordinate plans, actions, and day-to-day operations. MRP systems accomplish each of Simon's four stages of decision making.

Doing Simple Things Right

One reason for the decline of American manufacturing in the 1970s was the failure to do simple things right. Many manufacturers did not make the right things at the right time. One month they were saddled with tons of inventory. The next month they could not produce quickly enough. Once produced, products were often shipped with missing parts and had to be shipped back. Products were frequently shipped with the wrong parts, causing warranty problems and rework. The real problem was *control*—bridging top-level management plans, sales, middle-management activities, and day-to-day factory operations.

MRP systems are now designed to take into account senior management plans, sales, inventory of completed assemblies, parts, and shipping times in order to optimize factory utilization and other factors like quality.

One success story is that of the Megatest Corporation of San Jose, California, a maker of computer test equipment. Megatest grew rapidly from its beginnings in 1975 to the point where, in 1979, it had all of the traditional timing and supply problems: dated material plans, parts shortages, swelling inventories of not-yet-needed items, and half-finished assemblies. Employees were either idled due to parts shortages or asked to perform miracles in order to meet shipping dates when parts finally arrived.

After installing MRP, Megatest increased its shipments 47%, boosted labor productivity 100%, improved on-time delivery (from 54% to 95%), and attained a better quality of working life by reducing stress on managers and workers.

Adapted from "MRP II—A Strategic Tool for Survival," *Industry Week*, September 30, 1985.

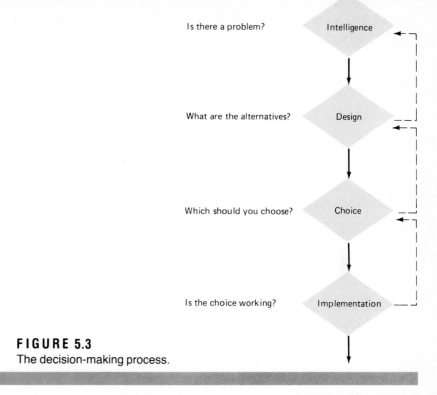

Is there a problem?   Intelligence

What are the alternatives?   Design

Which should you choose?   Choice

Is the choice working?   Implementation

FIGURE 5.3
The decision-making process.

From an information systems design perspective, the existence of various stages in decision making and the different requirements for each stage suggest that systems must have multiple general capabilities and must be flexible and easy to use.

Up to this point, we have assumed that decision making is accomplished by rational individuals. We have also assumed that an organization acts because individuals within it decide that it will act. We will now examine these two assumptions. First, what does *rational individual* mean? Second, how is individual decision making different from organizational decision making (and what difference does it make for systems design)?

5.4 Rational Individual Models of Decision Making

Because organizations are made up of individuals, it makes sense to build information systems that facilitate individual decision making. This activity requires a theory or model of decision making. There are a number of models that attempt to describe how individuals make

TABLE 5.6
Models of the
Rational Individual

Name	Basic Concept	Inference Patterns
Rational man	Comprehensive rationality	Establish goals, examine all alternatives, and choose the best alternative.
Satisficing model	Bounded rationality	Establish goals, examine a few alternatives, and choose the first alternative that promotes the goals.
Muddling	Successive comparison	Examine alternatives to establish a mix of goals and consequences; choose policies that are marginally different from those of the past.
Psychological	Cognitive types	All decision makers choose goals, but they differ in terms of gathering and evaluating information. Systematic thinkers impose order on perceptions and evaluation; intuitive thinkers are more open to unexpected information and use multiple models and perspectives when evaluating information. Neither is more rational than the other.

decisions (see Table 5.6). The basic assumption of all of these models is that human beings are rational.

The Rigorous Rational Model

Virtually all popular accounts of individuals (from leaders of industry to criminals), organizations, and nations utilize a *rational model* of human behavior. A cornerstone of all of these models is the idea that peoples, organizations, nations engage in basically consistent, value-maximizing calculations or adaptations within certain constraints. Since the time of Adam Smith, this assumption has been at the heart of consumer behavior and microeconomics, political philosophy (the individual as a free-willed value maximizer), and social theory (individual pursuit of prestige, money, and power).

The rational model is as follows: An individual has *goals or objectives* and has a payoff, utility, or preference function that permits him or her to rank all possible alternative actions in terms of their contribution to his or her goals. The actor is presented with and understands *alternative courses of action*. To each alternative is attached a *set of consequences*. The actor *chooses* the alternative (and consequences) that rank highest in terms of the payoff functions (i.e., contribute most to the ultimate goal).

In a rigorous model of rational action, the actor has comprehensive rationality (can accurately rank all alternatives and consequences) and can perceive all alternatives and consequences.

There are three criticisms of the rational model. First, in a human time frame, the model is computationally impossible. In a "simple" chess game there are 10^{120} moves, countermoves, and counter-countermoves from start to finish, and it would take a machine 10^{95} years operating at a rate of 1 million instructions per second (mips) to decide the first move! Second, the model lacks realism in the sense that most individuals do not have singular goals and a consciously used payoff function, and are not able to rank all alternatives and consequences. (To this it might be replied that realism is not required, only predictive accuracy.) Third, in real life the idea of a finite number of all alternatives and consequences makes no sense. In a maze constructed for a rat or in a game of tic-tac-toe, all alternatives and consequences can be meaningful and precise. In the real world of humans, specifying all of the alternatives and consequences is impossible.

Despite these criticisms, the rational model remains a powerful and attractive model of human decision making. It is rigorous, simple, and instructive.

Bounded Rationality and Satisficing: Simon

In answer to the critics, March and Simon (1958) and Simon (1960) proposed a number of adjustments to the rigorous rational model. Rather than optimize, which presumes comprehensive rationality, Simon argues that people *satisfice*—that is, choose the first available alternative that moves them toward their ultimate goal. Instead of searching for all of the alternatives and consequences, (unlimited rationality), Simon proposes that people limit the search process to sequentially ordered alternatives (alternatives not radically different from the current policy). Wherever possible, they avoid new, uncertain alternatives and rely instead on tried-and-true rules, standard operating procedures, and programs. Individuals have many goals—not a single consistent set—and therefore they try to divide their goals into separate programs, avoiding interdependencies wherever possible. In this way, rationality is *bounded*.

"Muddling Through": Lindblom

Lindblom (1959) proposed the most radical departure from the rational model in an article on the "science of muddling through." This method of decision making he described as one of "successive limited comparisons." First, individuals and organizations have conflicting goals—they want both freedom and security, rapid economic growth and minimal pollution, faster transportation and minimal disruption due to highway construction, and so forth. People have to choose among policies that contain various mixes of conflicting goals. The values themselves cannot be discussed in the abstract; they become clear only at the margin when specific policies are considered. Everyone is against crime; there is little need to discuss it. But many object to permitting the police to search homes without a court order (as called for in the Fourth Amendment). Hence, values are chosen at the same time as policies, and no easy means–end analysis is possible (if you believe in X, then choose policy X).

Because no easy means–end analysis is possible, and because people cannot agree on values, the only test of a "good" choice is whether people agree on it. Policies cannot be judged in terms of how much of X they provide, but rather in terms of whether or not the people involved in the choice agree on it. Labor and management can rarely agree on values, but they can agree on specific policies.

Because of the limits on human rationality, Lindblom proposes *incremental decision making*, or choosing policies most like the previous policy. Nonincremental policies are apolitical (not likely to bring agreement among important groups) and dangerous because nobody knows what they will lead to.

Last, choices are not "made." Instead, decision making involves a continuous process in which final decisions are always being modified to accommodate changing objectives, environments, value preferences, and policy alternatives provided by decision makers.

Psychological Types and Frames of Reference

Modern psychology has provided a number of challenges to the rational model. Psychologists have rarely challenged the basic premise that human beings are value maximizers and, in that sense, are rational. Instead they find that humans differ *in how they maximize their values* and in *the frames of reference they use to interpret information and make choices.*

Cognitive style refers to underlying personality dispositions toward the treatment of information, the selection of alternatives, and the evaluation of consequences. McKenney and Keen (1974) described two cognitive styles with direct relevance to information systems: systematic vs. intuitive types. *Systematic* decision makers approach a problem by structuring it in terms of some formal method. They evaluate and gather information in terms of their structured method. *Intuitive* decision makers approach a problem with multiple methods, using trial and error to find a solution, and tend not to structure information gathering or evaluation. Neither type is superior to the other, but some types of thinking are appropriate for certain tasks and roles in the organization.

The existence of different cognitive styles does not challenge the rational model of decision making. It simply says that there are different ways of being rational.

More recent psychological research, however, does pose strong challenges to the rational model by showing that humans have built-in universal biases that can distort decision making. Worse,

TABLE 5.7
Psychosocial Biases in
Decision Making

1. People are more sensitive to negative consequences than to positive ones; for example, students generally refuse to flip a coin for $10 unless they have a chance to win $30.

2. People have no sensible model for dealing with improbable events and either ignore them or overestimate their likelihood; for example, one-in-a-million lotteries are popular, and people have an exaggerated fear of shark attacks.

3. People are more willing to accept a negative outcome if it is presented as a cost rather than a loss; for example, a man will continue playing tennis at an expensive club, despite a painful tennis elbow, by accepting the pain as a cost of the game rather than quit and accept the loss of an annual membership fee.

4. People given the same information will prefer alternatives with certain gains rather alternatives with certain losses; people will gamble to avoid certain losses. For example, students and professional health workers were given the choice between alternative programs to fight a new disease that was expected to kill 600 people. When described in terms of lives saved, a large majority preferred a program that was certain to save 200 people over a program that had a possibility—but no certainty—of saving all 600. On the other hand, when presented in terms of lives lost, a large majority rejected a program that was guaranteed to lose 400 lives and preferred to gamble, against the odds, on a program that might save everyone but probably would lose everyone.

Source: Adapted from *The New York Times*, December 6, 1983, p. 6.

people can be manipulated into choosing alternatives that they might otherwise reject simply by changing *the frame of reference*.

Tversky and Kahneman (1981), summarizing a decade of work in the psychology of decision making, found that humans have a deep-seated tendency to avoid risks when seeking gains but to accept risks in order to avoid losses. In other words, people are more sensitive to negative outcomes than to positive ones. College students refuse to bet $10, for instance, on a coin flip unless they stand to win at least $30. Other biases are listed in Table 5.7.

Because losses loom larger than gains, the credit card industry lobbied retailers aggressively to ensure that any price break given cash customers would be presented publicly as a "cash discount" rather than a "credit card surcharge." Consumers would be less willing to accept a surcharge than to forego a discount.

Implications for System Design

The research on decision making has a number of implications for information systems design and understanding. First, decision making is not a simple process even in the rigorous rational model. There are limits to human computation, foresight, and analytical powers. These limits are conceptual, unrelated to considerations of computer size.

Second, decision situations differ from one another in terms of the clarity of goals, the types of decision makers present, the amount of agreement among them, and the frames of reference brought to a decision-making situation.

Third, an important role of information systems is not to make the decision for humans but rather to support the decision-making process. How this is done will depend on the types of decisions, decision makers, and frames of reference.

As a general rule, research on decision making indicates that information systems designers should design systems that have the following characteristics:

- They are flexible and provide many options for handling data and evaluating information.
- They are capable of supporting a variety of styles, skills, and knowledge.
- They are capable of changing as humans learn and clarify their values.
- They are powerful in the sense of having multiple analytical and intuitive models for the evaluation of data and the ability to keep track of many alternatives and consequences.

These elements of system design form the basis for DSS discussed in Chapter 16 and the rapid growth of end-user computing discussed in Chapters 10 and 15.

5.5 Organizational Models of Decision Making

For some purposes, it is useful to think of organizational decision making as similar to rational individual decision making. Organizations can be thought of as having singular goals, controlled by unitary rational decision makers who are completely informed, who chose among alternatives after weighing the consequences, and who act to maximize the goals of the organization. Thus, one can say, for instance, that General Motors "decided" to build a new type of automobile factory in order to make a profit on small cars.

But this simplified, shorthand way of talking about organizations should not conceal the fact that General Motors, and indeed any large organization, is composed of a number of specialized subgroups that are loosely coordinated, but each with a substantial life and capability of its own. What the organization ultimately does will be determined in large part by what the organizational subunits *can do*.

Organizations are also composed of a number of leaders who compete with each another for leadership. To a large extent, what the

TABLE 5.8 Models of Organizational Choice	Name	Basic Concept	Inference Pattern
	Rational actor	Comprehensive rationality	Organizations select goal(s), examine all alternatives and consequences and then choose a policy that maximizes the goal or preference function.
	Bureaucratic	Organizational output	Goals are determined by resource constraints and existing human and capital resources; SOPs are combined into programs, programs into repertoires; these determine what policies will be chosen. The primary purpose of the organization is to survive; uncertainty reduction is the principal goal. Policies are chosen that are incrementally different from the past.
	Political	Political outcome	Organizational decisions result from political competition; key players are involved in a game of influence, bargaining, and power. Organizational outcomes are determined by the beliefs and goals of players, their skills in playing the game, the resources they bring to bear, and the limits on their attention and power.
	Garbage can	Nonadaptive organizational programs	Most organizations are nonadaptive, temporary, and disappear over time. Organizational decisions result from interactions among streams of problems, potential actions, participants, and chance.

organization ultimately decides to do will be the result of political competition among its leaders and staff.

Each of these perspectives reflects a different organizational model of decision making that is very different from the individual models previously described (see Table 5.8). (See Allison, 1971; Laudon, 1974; and Laudon, 1986, on which our analysis draws.)

Bureaucratic Models

The dominant idea of bureaucratic models is that whatever organizations do is the result of standard operating procedures (SOPs) honed over years of active use. The particular actions chosen by an organization are an output of one or several organizational subunits (e.g., marketing, production, finance, personnel). The problems facing any organization are too massive and too complex to be attended to by the organization. Problems are instead divided into their components and parceled out to specialized groups. Competing with low-priced, high-quality Asian foreign cars, for instance, is a complex problem.

Blockade By the Book

In the evening of October 23, 1962, the Executive Committee of the President (EXCOM), a high-level working group of senior advisors to President John F. Kennedy, decided to impose a naval quarantine or blockade on Cuba in order to force the Soviet Union to remove its intermediate range ballistic missiles from the island, located 90 miles south of Miami.

The naval blockade was chosen only after the air force reported that it could not conduct what the politicians in EXCOM called a "surgical air strike" to remove the missiles. Instead the air force recommended a massive strategic air campaign against a number of ground, air, and naval Cuban targets. This was considered extreme by EXCOM, and the only other alternative seemed to be a blockade that would give Chairman Khrushchev plenty of time to think and several face-saving alternatives.

But EXCOM was worried that the navy might blunder when implementing the blockade and cause an incident, which in turn could lead to World War III. Secretary of Defense Robert McNamara visited the navy's Chief of Naval Operations to make the point that the blockade was not intended to shoot Russians but to send a political message.

McNamara wanted to know the following: Which ship would make the first interception? Were Russian-speaking officers on board? How would submarines be dealt with? Would Russian ships be given the opportunity to turn back? What would the navy do if Russian captains refused to answer questions about their cargo?

At that point, the Chief of Naval Operations picked up the Manual of Naval Regulations, waved it at McNamara, and said "It's all in there." McNamara responded, "I don't give a damn what John Paul Jones would have done. I want to know what you are going to do tomorrow!"

The visit ended with the navy officer inviting the Secretary of Defense to go back to his office and let the navy run the blockade.

Adapted from Graham T. Allison, *Essence of Decision*, 1971, pp. 130–132.

There are many aspects: production, labor relations, technology, marketing, finance, and even government regulation.

Each organizational subunit has a number of standard operating procedures, tried and proven techniques, which it invokes when dealing with a problem. Changing these standard operating procedures (SOPs) is rare, involves changes in personnel, and is risky (who knows if the new techniques work better than the old ones?)

SOPs are woven into the programs and repertoires of each subunit. Taken together, these repertoires constitute the range of effective actions that leaders of organizations can take. These are what the organization can do in the short term. As a recent U.S. president discovered in a moment of national crisis, his actions were largely constrained not by his imagination but by what his pawns, bishops, and knights were trained to do.

The organization generally perceives problems only through its specialized subunits. These specialized subunits, in turn, are concerned only with parts of the problem. They consciously ignore information not directly relevant to their part of the problem.

Although senior management and leaders are hired to coordinate and lead the organization, they are effectively trapped by parochial subunits that feed information upward and that provide standard solutions. Senior management cannot decide to act in ways that the major subunits cannot support.

Organizations do, of course, change; they do learn new ways of behaving; and they can be led. But all of these changes require a long time. Look around and you will find many organizations doing pretty much what they did 10, 20, or even 30 years ago. Consider the steel makers, car makers, post office, universities, hospitals—have they changed radically in the last 5 or 10 years? How about the last 30 years?

In general, organizations do not "choose" or "decide" in a rational sense; instead they choose from among a very limited set of repertoires. The goals of organizations are multiple, not singular, and the most important goal is the preservation of the organization itself (e.g., the maintenance of budget, manpower, and territory). The reduction of uncertainty is another major goal. Policy tends to be incremental, only marginally different from the past, because radical policy departures involve too much uncertainty.

Political Models of Organizational Choice

Power in organizations is shared; even the lowest-level workers have some power. At the top, power is concentrated in the hands of a few. For a variety of reasons, these leaders differ about what the organization should do. The differences matter, and competition for leadership ensues. Each individual in an organization, especially at the top, is a key player in the game of politics: bargaining through a number of channels among players.

In this view, what an organization does is a result of political bargains struck among key leaders. Its actions are not necessarily rational, except in a political sense, and the outcome is not what any individual necessarily wanted. Instead, policy—organizational action—is a compromise, a mixture of conflicting tendencies. Organizations do not come up with "solutions" "chosen" to solve some "problem." They come up with compromises that reflect the conflicts, the major stake holders, the diverse interests, unequal power, and confusion that constitute politics.

The top leaders of corporations are also subject to the influence of outside consultants, whose presentations may be flashy but faulty. The staff that surrounds senior managers also plays a role in the political conflict. The influence of the staff corresponds to the influence of their immediate boss and to the size of the deals they help to make. This competition for influence can sometimes lead large organizations astray, as the following example suggests.

Decision Making at the Top

In 1979 the Exxon Corporation, the world's largest private enterprise, bought out the Reliance Electric Company of Cleveland for $1.2 billion (twice its book value). Exxon had developed a technology to conserve energy in electric motors and hoped to gain a quick market entrance through Reliance.

The CEO at Reliance, B. Charles Ames, wondered if Exxon really knew what it was doing. The new technology did not look viable to Reliance engineers and production people. After 4 years following the merger, Reliance lost $85 million. The new technology had no viable market.

Ames, now CEO of a Cleveland machine tool builder, argues that top executives of acquiring companies do not have the expertise to make reasoned, intelligent judgments about the potential benefits of acquisitions. They are susceptible to fancy, polished presentations by consultants and their own staffs, who gain in power and influence if the deal goes through.

Merger experts estimate that one-third of corporate mergers are outright failures financially; three-fourths fail to achieve their objectives.

Adapted from "Why Mergers Fizzle," *Industry Week*, August 5, 1985.

Decision makers in this view are characterized by limited attention spans; participation in tens (sometimes hundreds) of games and issues; and susceptibility to misperception, extraneous influences, miscommunication, and pressures of impending deadlines. Players in the game focus almost entirely on the short-term problem: What decision must be made today? Long-term strategic thinking for the whole organization goes by the wayside as individual decision makers focus on their short-term interests and on the part of the problem they are interested in.

"Garbage Can" Models

All of the preceding models of organizational choice take as their starting point the basic notion that organizations try to adapt, and for the most part successfully, to changing environmental conditions. Presumably, over the long run, organizations develop new programs and actions in order to meet their goals of profit, survival, and so on.

Yet history indicates that many organizations do not survive. Between 1955 and 1975, only 53% of the Fortune 500 companies—the largest and most prosperous in the United States—survived. Fifty-year-old corporations represent only 2% of those that were initially created; 50-year-old federal agencies comprise only 4% of those ever created. In the future, 30% of today's corporations that are 50 years old or more can be expected to disappear (Starbuck, 1983).

These findings force us to recognize that organizations are not immortal and may even be temporary. When severely challenged by a changing environment, many organizations prove to be nonadaptive, incapable of learning, and unchanging.

A relatively new theory of decision making states that organizations are not rational. Decision making is largely accidental and is the product of a stream of solutions, problems, and situations that are randomly associated. That is, solutions become attached to problems for accidental reasons; organizations are filled with solutions looking for problems and decision makers looking for work.

If this model is true, it should not be surprising that the wrong solutions are applied to the wrong problems in an organization or that, over time, a large number of organizations make critical mistakes that lead to their demise.

Implications for System Design

While it is appropriate for students of information systems to consider themselves designers of systems to support management decision making, the research on organizational decision making should alert them to the fact that their sphere of action includes more than individual choice.

Systems must do more than merely promote decision making. They must also include the notion of making individual managers better managers of existing routines, better players in the bureaucratic struggle for control of an organization's agenda, and better political players. Last, for those who resist the "garbage can" tendencies in large organizations, systems should help bring a measure of power to those who can attach the right solution to the right problem.

Good information systems design must include the following:

- An awareness of the bureaucratic and political requirements of systems
- An understanding of how bureaucratic and political elements will use the information system for their own purposes
- Attention to the "symbolism" of systems, that is, how they will be perceived by important groups
- An understanding of compromises in system features to accommodate diverse interests
- An awareness and appreciation of the limits of organizational change in policy and in procedure
- Flexibility to permit changes in organizational repertoires and SOPs, that is, organizational learning and growth
- An honest and professional awareness of the limits of information systems

These implications form an important part of the system designer's tool kit.

5.6 Summary

Management and decision making are complex activities that involve many dimensions of human behavior. Early classical models of management stressed the functions of planning, organizing, coordinating, deciding, and controlling. Contemporary research has examined the actual behavior of managers to show how managers get things done.

Mintzberg (1971) found that managers' real activities were highly fragmented, variegated and brief in duration, with managers moving rapidly and intensely from one issue to another. Other behavioral research has found that managers spend considerable time pursuing personal agendas and goals and that contemporary managers shy away from making grand, sweeping policy decisions.

If information systems are built properly, they can support managerial roles—interpersonal, information processing, and decision making. Information systems that are less formal and highly flexible will be more useful than large, formal systems at higher levels of the organization.

An important contribution of modern systems is the support of individual and organizational decision making. Decisions can be either structured or unstructured, with structured decisions clustering at operational levels and unstructured decisions at strategic planning levels. The nature and level of decision making are important factors in building DSS.

Decision making itself is a complex activity at both the individual and the organizational level. Simon (1960) described four different stages in decision making: (1) intelligence, (2) design, (3) choice, and (4) implementation. Rational models of decision making assume that human beings can accurately choose alternatives and consequences based on the priority of their objectives and goals. But organizational models of decision making illustrate that the real decision making takes place in arenas where many psychological, political, and bureaucratic forces are at work. Thus, organizational decision making may not necessarily be rational.

The design of information systems must accommodate these realities, recognizing that decision making is never a simple process. Information systems can best support managers and decision making if they are flexible, with multiple analytical and intuitive models for evaluating data and the capability of supporting a variety of styles, skills, and knowledge. An honest and professional awareness of bureaucratic and political requirements and the limits of information systems is also essential.

Key Words

Behavioral models
Managerial roles
Interpersonal networks
Personal agendas
Structured decisions
Intelligence and design
Rational models
Bounded rationality

Muddling through
Frames of reference
Psychosocial bias
Organizational models
Bureaucratic models
Political models
Garbage can models

Review Questions

1. What are the five activities of managers described in the classical model?
2. Behavioral research has identified six characteristics of the modern manager. What are these characteristics and how do they relate to the classical model?
3. What specific managerial roles can information systems support? Where are information systems particularly strong in supporting managers, and where are they weak?
4. How do managers get things done and how can CBIS help?
5. What did Wrapp (1984) discover about the nature of managerial decisions? How do these findings compare with those of the classical model?
6. What are the implications of classical and contemporary views of managers for information systems design?

7. Define structured and unstructured decisions. Give three examples of each.
8. What are the four kinds of CBIS that support decisions? Which kind of system is most likely to support the decisions you described in problem 4?
9. What are the four stages of decision making described by Simon (1960)?
10. Describe each of the four rational individual models of decision making. What is the name, basic concept, and dominant inference pattern of each? How would the design of information systems be affected by the model of decision making employed?
11. Describe each of the four organizational choice models. How would the design of systems be affected by the choice of model employed?

Discussion Questions

1. With one other student, observe a manager for 1 hour. Classify the observed behavior in two ways, using the classical model first and then the behavioral model. Compare the results and discuss the difficulties of coding the behavior.
2. With two other students, identify and describe a decision that all of you have had to make (e.g., going to college, choosing a specific college, choosing a major). Use Simon's model of stages and show how an information system might have helped (or hindered) you in making the decision.
3. Take the same decision identified in problem 2 and apply each of the rational individual models to the decision process.
4. At your college or university, identify a major decision made recently by a department, an office, or bureau. Try to apply each of organizational models of decision making to the decision. How was information used by the various organizational participants? What are the implications for the design of information systems?

Executive Information Users

Floyd Kuehnis, managing partner of the San Jose, California, office of Peat, Marwick Mitchell, & Company, is one of the "new breed" of executive information users. He heads an office that uses a pilot system designed to boost upper management's productivity and to identify opportunities for office automation throughout the organization.

To expand its practice, Peat, Marwick must supply its managers with up-to-date information about its customer base. Effective personal contacts are essential. When managers make new contacts, they must be able to understand what these people do and respond with the right information. For example, if one manager wanted access to a venture capitalist who funds high-technology companies, it would be useful to get contact information from all 140 people in the branch office.

To meet this need, the San Jose branch office developed a pilot system that functions as a "giant Rolodex." The system supplies on-line information about every professional contact made by anyone within the Peat, Marwick San Jose office. Officially called the *Who and Referral System*, the pilot is known within Peat Marwick as the *War Machine*.

The War Machine maintains data on the type of contact (lunch, dinner, telephone call), the time and date of the contact, the individuals involved from each firm, and the resulting referrals. The War Machine is updated every time a Peat, Marwick representative meets with someone from another company, making the information available to anyone who uses the system. In effect, the War Machine serves as an automated "old boy" network.

The War Machine runs on six personal computers linked via a Wangnet local area network (LAN). One of the reasons Wang was selected for this application is that its software is menu driven. Peat, Marwick's staff at the manager and partner level is not heavily computer oriented. The Wang menus enable managers to nagivate easily through the system. Kuehnis and a senior manager designed the War Machine screens themselves in a single evening.

The project was approved by the chairman of the board because it was considered a good test for the entire organization. Eventually all 40 partners and managers in Peat, Marwick's San Jose office will be hooked into the War Machine network.

Adapted from Rita Shoor, "The New Breed of Executive Information Users," *Infosystems*, June 1986.

Case Study Questions

1. Why is this system especially appropriate for managers?
2. What kinds of managerial activities and roles are supported by this system?
3. What kinds of managerial decisions could this information system support?

4. Why was the choice of microcomputer-based, LAN technology appropriate for the managers using the War Machine? Could these functions be performed as well with a large, formal mainframe information system?

References

Allison, Graham T. *Essence of Decision—Explaining the Cuban Missile Crisis*. Boston: Little, Brown, 1971.

Anthony, R.N. "Planning and Control Systems: A Framework for Analysis," Harvard University Graduate School of Business Administration, 1965.

Cohen, Michael, March, James, and Olsen, Johan. "A Garbage Can Model of Organizational Choice," *Administrative Science Quarterly*, Vol. 17, (1972).

Gorry, G. Anthony, and Scott-Morton, Michael S. "A Framework for Management Information Systems," *Sloan Management Review*, Vol. 13 No. 1 (Fall 1971).

Huber, George P. "Cognitive Style as a Basis for MIS and DSS Designs: Much Ado About Nothing?" *Management Science*, Vol. 29 (May 1983).

Isenberg, Daniel J. "How Senior Managers Think," *Harvard Business Review* (November–December 1984).

Ives, Blake, and Olson, Margrethe H. "Manager or Technician? The Nature of the Information Systems Manager's Job," *MIS Quarterly* (December 1981).

Kotter, John T. "What Effective General Managers Really Do," *Harvard Business Review* (November-December 1982).

Laudon, Kenneth C. *Computers and Bureaucratic Reform*. New York: Wiley, 1974.

Laudon, Kenneth C. *Dossier Society: Value Choices in the Design of National Information Systems*. New York: Columbia University Press, 1986.

Lindbloom, C.E., "The Science of Muddling Through," *Public Administration* Review, Vol. 19, 1959, pp. 79-88.

March, James G., and Simon, Herbert A. *Organizations*. New York: Wiley, 1958.

Markus, M.L. "Power, Politics, and MIS Implementation," *Communications of the ACM*, Vol. 26, No. 6 (June 1983).

McKenney, James L., and Keen, G.W. "How Managers' Minds Work," *Harvard Business Review* (May–June 1974).

Mintzberg, Henry. "Managerial Work: Analysis from Observation," *Management Science*, Vol. 18 (October 1971).

Olson, Margrethe H. "The IS Manager's Job," *MIS Quarterly* (December 1981).

Simon, H.A. *The New Science of Management Decision*. New York: Harper & Row, 1960.

Starbuck, William H. "Organizations as Action Generators," *American Sociological Review*, Vol. 48 (1983).

Tversky, A., and Kahneman, D. "The Framing of Decisions and the Psychology of Choice," *Science*, Vol. 211 (January 1981).

Wrapp, H. Edward. "Good Managers Don't Make Policy Decisions," *Harvard Business Review* (July–August 1984).

Chrysler Corporation Systems Strategy: Technology Plus Management Theory Equals Formidable Automation Strategy

In 1980, the Chrysler Corporation lost a wopping $1.7 billion. It seemed headed down a one-way street toward bankruptcy. This was the worst of times for all American car makers (Ford lost $1.5 billion and GM lost $760 million). In 1980, Chrysler was $2.8 billion in debt, and the auto maker sought help from banks, a merger with Ford (which was rejected), and finally, government assistance.

The most ominous aspect of Chrysler's situation was its loss of customers. Chrysler's market share was dwindling as customers rejected Chrysler's poor-quality cars.

Today Chrysler is profitable once again. And it is gaining market share. According to Jean Claude Gruet, a Salomon Brothers automotive industry analyst, Chrysler is succeeding because of its product development, marketing, and manufacturing strategies. With the Caravan, it isolated and fulfilled a strong consumer need. Its decision to outsource the majority of its parts and materials (currently Chrysler buys 70% of its parts from outside suppliers, compared to GM's 40%) has enabled Chrysler to get lower-cost components.

Gruet also sees a connection between Chrysler's 6-year drive to implement tooling and computer equipment and the impressive gain in product quality and productivity that it has achieved. On the other hand, Gruet cautions, although automation leads to lower costs and higher quality, customers buy cars because they find them attractive. Ford is the leader of the Big Three when it comes to quality, but the Taurus and Sable are selling well because they appeal to a certain type of customer, not because they were produced in an automated factory.

Other security analysts are more bullish about Chrysler's role in factory automation. Even though price pressures from Asian producers will be increasing during the 1980s, Chrysler is expected by many analysts to remain profitable because of the new systems it has installed.

Baptism by Fire

Chrysler's financial crisis in the early 1980s galvanized its management to find ways to cut costs, increase inventory turnover, and improve quality. Chrysler responded nobly to these pressures.

Chrysler's new equipment and engineering expenditures went from $0.3 billion to $1.2 billion per year between 1981 and 1984. Capital spending swelled to $1.25–1.5 billion per year.

It is not the size of Chrysler's investment in high technology that is impressive (GM's investment is much larger) but the fact that Chrysler has received dramatic returns on its investment.

In 1980 Chrysler spent $100 million to modernize the plant that produced the K car in 1982. The K car is considered Chrysler's leading product of the 1980s. In 1983 the auto maker renovated its Windsor, Ontario, plant in a record 17 weeks (as opposed to the normal 12 to 18 months). This plant has the most advanced computer-based technology, including 123 robots, just-in-time scheduling, and in-line sequencing. Chrysler's product here, the Caravan, is its biggest hit of the decade.

Profit Motives

Unlike GM, Chrysler did not have the money to adopt a shotgun approach in which several high-technology paths are pursued simultaneously. According to Robert Brauburger, chief engineer of Chrysler's technical computer center, "Chrysler had to follow a single path and either guess right or be God awful wrong. Luckily, Chrysler guessed right."

Chrysler's director of information systems, G. Nichols Simonds, also points out that Chrysler was in a better position to concentrate on just those technologies that offered a high payoff. Chrysler is changing, according to Simonds, from being an auto manufacturer to being an assembler and distributor. The low degree of vertical integration at Chrysler lessens its need for leading-edge manufacturing technologies such as vision systems, programmable controllers, and robotics, all of which are far more important to GM and Ford.

Instead, Chrysler has been able to use the majority of its technical budget and innovations to set up a corporationwide communications system.

Telecommunications Infrastructure

Chrysler's telecommunications infrastructure is absolutely vital to the support of new production and scheduling disciplines such as just-in-time and in-line sequencing. The same network is used to support computer-integrated manufacturing (CIM), which includes computer-aided design (CAD), computer-aided manufacturing (CAM), and computer-aided engineering (CAE). All of the domestic manufacturers know that these techniques offer huge potential payoffs in the form of streamlined production, faster inventory turnover, lower labor costs, and higher quality.

In order to develop an integrated telecommunications structure, GM is struggling to achieve this capability; the costs are very high. A few years ago, it bought Electronic Data Systems for $2.5 billion to achieve this integration. Chrysler is managing to develop such a system far less expensively.

According to MIS Director Simonds, Chrysler has a history of centralized management, which resulted in a commonality and compatibility of computer systems. Integration was far easier here than at GM. At GM, whole divisions developed their own systems and networks.

Industry experts expect that GM will reap few immediate benefits from its high-cost, shotgun approach to factory automation. The trouble is that up to the past few years, GM's technology strategy reflected its highly fragmented internal organization. Each operating division had its own databases, its own office automation and robots, and other applications. To make matters worse, these systems were implemented on completely different types of equipment.

It was not until 1984 that GM instituted some degree of centralized control. In January of that year, GM announced a new regime in which product development for the five car divisions would be done by two centralized groups. One group would develop small cars and the other intermediate-sized and large cars. Engineering, product development, and manufacturing would become centralized instead of being parceled out.

GM hopes that this new organizational structure will bring about more effective cost control, scheduling, and quality control. On the other hand, before all of these good things can happen, the auto giant must set up a communications network among the computer systems that support the new groups; hence the purchase of Electronic Data Systems for $2.5 billion in 1984. As explained by Paine Webber's automobile industry analyst, Ann C. Knight: "Although General Motors is beginning to bring things together, they still will not be able to throw out all of the computers they've developed in the past. They never will be as homogeneous as Chrysler."

Managerial Insights

The new management team that took over at Chrysler in 1980, led by Lee Iacocca, instituted an aggressive policy to bring all computer-based systems (except CAD/CAM systems) under MIS control.

Even before the 1980s, Chrysler had decided that it needed a centralized, nonredundant database of CAD specifications that were accessible to all stages of production. In 1981, Chrysler installed a Cyber supercomputer mainframe built by the Control Data Corporation. Managers in all work areas and in all nine Chrysler plants had access to the same current design specifications. In addition, centralized business files for inventory, shipping, marketing, and a host of other related activities were put on the MIS mainframe.

All of this centralized management information makes scheduling and inventory control much easier to coordinate. Chrysler's cars and trucks share many of the same parts. Therefore, a centralized database, as opposed to a product database, makes sense.

The Cyber database also acts as the communications link between tooling and design managers, making it possible for tooling and design to go on concurrently. If there is a last-minute change in design because of advantages in shipping or manufacturing, it can be immediately taken into account by the tooling and manufacturing engineers.

Thirty-two mainframes and minicomputers from five different vendors communicate via a single corporationwide network. A mainframe-based gateway gives engineering work stations access to the MIS mainframe. This makes it easy to move data from one system, stage of production, or plant to another.

Lords of Discipline

Chrysler's advanced telecommunication system, coupled with its centralized MIS approach, has put it far ahead of GM and Ford in implementing the rigorous new techniques of manufacturing such as in-line sequencing and just-in-time inventory management.

In-line sequencing integrates the production cycles of various product lines into a seamless whole. The company knows exactly what it is making at any given moment, and the materials and parts flow into the factory in a continuous stream and appear exactly when they are needed. Chrysler has implemented in-line sequencing at its Sterling Heights, Michigan, and Windsor, Ontario, plants. It is moving to install it in all of its other seven major factories.

In-line sequencing offers many advantages in terms of cost and quality control. Knowing what must be produced at any given moment in advance, the company can arrange manpower and skills much more effectively to meet these demands. The result is higher-quality products and fewer delays on the assembly line.

Any delay on the assembly line can disturb the in-line sequence. For this reason, a new information system has been developed that allows workers on the line who spot a defect or other problem to feed the information into a computer. Then someone farther down the line can correct the problem without halting the sequence or the stream of goods. In the past, faulty products were simply pulled off the line and put into storage. The storage bin became huge.

Of course, in order to make in-line sequencing work, Chrysler had to arrange for its suppliers to deliver components and parts just in time to be assembled. This meant not just on the right day but also at the specified hour. In-line sequencing is a policy that was needed to implement just-in-time inventory scheduling. Suppliers could not be expected to meet a production schedule if the schedule kept changing.

Just-in-time management is obviously critical to a company that has 70% of its parts made by outside suppliers. By the end of 1985, 295 suppliers were delivering 541 truckloads ($15 million worth) of parts a day to Chrysler's plants on a just-in-time schedule.

Running on All Cylinders

In the last 2 years, Chrysler has been able to achieve an 8% reduction in inventory and an increase in average quarterly inventory turnover from 6.38 times in 1978 to 13.8 times in 1985.

Chrysler is not slowing down its factory automation efforts. Paine Weber predicts that Chrysler will spend between $1.25 billion and $1.5 billion per year for new engineering and equipment during the next decade. Part of that budget will go for CIM, and part will be used to bring other Chrysler facilities up to the desired level of technology. MIS Director Simonds foresees no end to the project of tying together various computer systems.

Supply-Side Economics: Integrating Chrysler's Suppliers

The Budd Company of Rochester, Michigan, is one of the major suppliers of parts to the automobile industry. Owned by the West German company Thyssen A.G., Budd supplies all four major American auto companies with sheet metal parts, wheel products, frames, and so forth. The company now supplies 85 to 90% of Chrysler parts on a just-in-time basis.

Richard Glazer, Budd's manager of sales administration, admits that Chrysler's procedures for just-in-time delivery and in-line sequencing impose strict delivery requirements. But there are many advantages for Budd.

On the requirement side, Glazer notes that in the past, Budd had the latitude to determine which parts to ship on a given day. Now Chrysler tells them to ship 50 parts at 2 PM, and it makes sure that it doesn't own those 50 pieces until that hour, when it actually needs them. Over time, these hours add up to important savings for Chrysler.

But there are savings in this method for Budd as well. Just-in-time inventory control and delivery eliminates the shop floor crises that can result from last-minute order changes or changes in the shipping/manufacturing release, which enumerates what Chrysler wants at what time during the week.

In the past, the worst panics occurred when a rush order for a single door or side panel came in that Budd was not even expecting to make on a given day. Those orders had to be filled and usually were very costly. Now, according to Glazer, if Chrysler says that it wants 100 pieces of a certain part by next Wednesday at 2 PM, the chances are very remote that the order will change.

Chrysler's production scheduling also benefits Budd's production cycle. Budd knows in advance exactly what Chrysler will need and at what time. This allows Budd to take the guess work out of manufacturing.

Vital Telecommunications Link

Chrysler has set up electronic links between its data center and those of its major suppliers like Budd. This linkage permits major suppliers such as Budd to extract manufacturing releases electronically through terminals installed in all of Budd's work areas. Even the shipping dock at Budd has a Chrysler terminal to verify current and future orders.

All of the major U.S. auto companies have set up such electronic supplier networks. Unfortunately, there are no standards for these networks, and each manufacturer has its own protocols. This imposes certain costs on the Budd Company and other suppliers. The Automotive Industry Action Group (AIAG) is working to develop a common industry standard.

Other Technologies

Bar coding is another technology that Chrysler will use in the future to make just-in-time inventory control more efficient. Each part's bar code will be entered directly into the supplier's computer, eliminating the need to write the part numbers manually on order slips. This should speed up inventory withdrawal and entry.

Adapted from Elisabeth Horwitt, "The Pride Is Back," *Business Computer Systems*, March 1986.

Part One Case Study Questions

1. In what ways have information systems at Chrysler played a strategic role? How has the structure of the industry itself changed with new systems?
2. Do you think that Chrysler has achieved a sustainable strategic advantage over other car manufacturers?
3. How was Chrysler's organizational structure important to the design of its information systems?
4. What is the relationship at Chrysler between the manufacturing process and the information systems?

PART TWO

Technical Foundations of Information Systems

Part Two lays out the technical foundation for understanding computers and information systems. The capabilities of information systems depend in part on the power of the underlying computer technology. Individual chapters explain how information is processed by computer software and hardware, and how information is stored in files and databases. Changes in telecommunications and microcomputers have introduced new opportunities and raised interesting issues.

Chapter 6 surveys the features of computer hardware which are very important for determining the usefulness of an information system. These include: the central processing unit and surrounding devices; contemporary input and output devices; distinctions between mainframes, mini-computers, and micro-computers; and future hardware technologies.

Chapter 7 defines the role of computer software in processing information, showing its relationship to computer hardware. It is through software that computer hardware becomes useful to human beings and organizations. There are three major types of software: systems software, application software, and dialogue/query software, each with unique functions. Selection of appropriate software requires an understanding of application requirements and knowledge of the capabilities of specific software products.

Chapter 8 describes the organization of information in files and databases. Without appropriate file organization and management techniques, organizations cannot properly access and utilize the information in their computer systems. Organizing information in databases is an antidote to traditional file management problems. Requirements for achieving a successful database environment include an organizational discipline, data modeling and planning methodology, and data base management technology. The chapter presents the components of a data base management system and the principal data base models.

Chapter 9 illustrates how deregulation and technical advances in telecommunications have created new opportunities and challenges for managers. Features of telecommunications technology of greatest interest to managers are: major types of telecommunications systems; measuring the capacity of telecommunications systems; how to plan for telecommunications systems; and costs and benefits of alternative telecommunications technologies.

Chapter 10 explores the impact of the microcomputer revolution. A mainframe computer of the 1960s can now be put on a desktop—your desk top. Microcomputers have put end users in direct control of some aspects of information processing. The soaring use of microcomputers has reduced application backlogs and met new information needs. But the growth of micros poses some unique challenges to management in order to obtain the promised benefits. Three visions of the role of microcomputers have emerged.

Part Two Case Study: "Capacity Planning at Ocean Spray". This case illustrates how one organization's deployment of computer hardware stood in the way of its changing business strategy. After moving to a decentralized, multi-system architecture in the 1970s, Ocean Spray had to recentralize with much higher-capacity mainframes. To ensure that computer hardware supports its business direction, Ocean Spray developed a capacity planning model.

CHAPTER 6

Computers and Information Processing

OUTLINE

(Continued on next page.)

159

Geosource, Inc., of Houston Texas, makes seismic equipment for the oil industry. The company needs customized computer chips for their sensing equipment, and they make their own on a desktop. They do not dress in white bunny suits, like most chip manufacturers' employees, and they need only a $2500 tool kit in a small box. David Sandifer, a Geosource engineer, writes a program for a sensing circuit on an IBM personal computer (PC) and connects the PC to an Altera Corporation complementary metal oxide semiconductor (CMOS) device the size of a shoe box that burns the program into a CMOS computer chip the size of a dime. This same chip can be erased with ultraviolet light and a new program burned in.

Before the development of these erasable, programmable, read-only memory (EPROM) chips, companies had to have chips custom made, which took months and cost hundreds of thousands of dollars. With custom-programmable chips, this process is reduced to minutes and the cost per chip to less than $50. User-programmable chips are expected to expand rapidly into new product areas by the 1990s.

Adapted from "Homemade Chips Advance," *The New York Times*, April 25, 1985.

User-programmable chips like those used by Geosource are just one of many advances in computer hardware that are changing products and information systems. A keen understanding of major trends in hardware is a crucial first step in finding competitive advantages in modern computer technology.

In this chapter the student will learn:
- How information is represented and processed in computer hardware.
- The major types of hardware used for information processing.
- The role of the central processing unit and surrounding hardware devices.

- The difference between digital and analog computers.
- How to distinguish generations of hardware and contemporary input and output devices.
- The most important future developments in hardware.

6.1 Introduction

At the heart of a contemporary information system is a collection of hardware devices that do the actual manipulation of numbers, symbols, and words. At the center of this computer system is the central processing unit (CPU). Strictly speaking, the CPU is the computer. The characteristics of the CPU, its speed, and its total capacity are very important in determining the usefulness of an information system in a modern organization. In this and the following two chapters, we will describe the hardware and software that permit a modern information system to function.

System Configuration

A contemporary computer system is composed of a CPU and four other hardware devices (see Figure 6.1). The CPU uses *secondary storage devices* (magnetic disks, tape) that feed information and programs into the CPU and store them for later use.

Information can be put into secondary storage and the CPU by several *input devices*. These include on-line terminals, card readers, and other devices that capture information from the environment, such as point-of-sale optical scanners (these will be described more fully at the end of the chapter).

A number of *output devices* receive information from the computer system and display it so that individuals can understand it. Such output devices include printers, terminals, cards, and other forms.

In contemporary systems, many *communication devices* act as an intermediary between end users and the CPU. These devices (described more fully in Chapter 9) are themselves computers that switch among users and control the telecommunications functions of the CPU. They also manage the input and output devices.

Time and Size in the Computer World

Before describing the CPU and other hardware, it is important to have a clear understanding of time and size in the computer world. Table 6.1 presents some key levels of time and size that are useful in describing the speed and capacity of modern computer systems.

Modern secondary storage devices generally operate at the level of *milliseconds* (thousandths of a second). This means that a modern disk drive can find your student record on a magnetic disk in 25 to 50 milliseconds. But it would take several seconds to find your name on a much slower tape system. (The reasons for this difference are

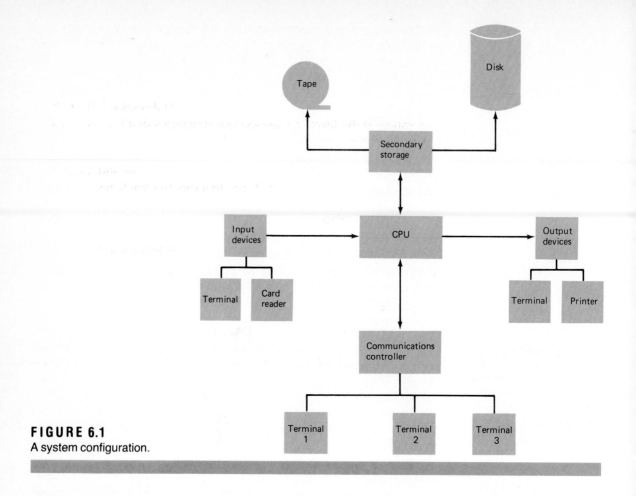

FIGURE 6.1
A system configuration.

TABLE 6.1
Size and Time in the Computer World

Time
Second	1	Time needed to find a single record on a tape
Millisecond	1/1000	Time needed to find a single name on a disk, 45 milliseconds
Microsecond	1/1,000,000	IBM PC Micro instruction speed, 2 microseconds for each instruction
Nanosecond	1/1,000,000,000	Mainframe instruction speed, one instruction each 30 nanoseconds
Picosecond	1/1,000,000,000,000	Switching speed of experimental devices, Josephson junctions

Size
Byte	A string of 8 bits	
Kilobyte	1000 Bytes.	PC Primary memory, 64 kilobytes
Megabyte	1,000,000 Bytes.	PC Hard disk storage; mainframe primary memory, 30 megabytes
Gigabyte	1,000,000,000 Bytes.	External storage disk and tape
Terrabyte	1,000,000,000,000 Bytes.	Social security programs and records

discussed in a later section.) Going somewhat faster in speed, an IBM PC can execute approximately 500,000 program instructions per second. This means that a PC can calculate $1 + 1 = 2$ about 500,000 times in 1 second, or 2 *microseconds* per instruction. In modern mainframes, the CPU can execute at a speed of approximately 30 million instructions per second (30 mips). At this speed, the CPU is operating at the level of nanoseconds (billionths of a second), or one instruction for every 30 nanoseconds.

Size, like speed, is an important consideration in a system. Information is stored in a computer in the form of 0s and 1s (binary digits, called *bits*), which are strung together to form bytes. One byte can be used to store one character, like the letter *A*. A thousand bytes are called a *kilobyte*. Small PCs have internal CPU primary memories on the order of kilobytes. A large PC CPU today can store anywhere from 640 kilobytes up to perhaps 16 megabytes (16 million bytes) of information. This means, theoretically, that the machine can store up to 16 million alphabetic letters or numbers. Modern storage devices, such as hard disk drives in a PC or disk packs in a large mainframe, store millions of bytes of information. A PC may have a 40-megabyte disk, whereas a large mainframe may have many disk drives, each capable of holding 1 gigabyte (16 billion bytes). Some large organizations, like the Social Security Administration or the Internal Revenue Service, have a total storage capacity—adding up all their disk drive capacities—measured in trillions of bytes. And if all of their records were added together, including those stored on punched cards, physical records, and tapes, the total would be at the terrabyte (thousands of billions of bytes) level of information storage.

Problems of Coordination

Size and speed are important issues in the development of information systems because of the vast differences in the size and speed of the major elements of computer systems. For instance, while CPUs operate at the level of microseconds, and in some cases nanoseconds, ordinary printers operate at the level of only a few hundred to a few thousand characters per second. This means that the CPU can process information far faster than a printer can print it out. For this reason, additional memory and storage devices must be placed between the CPU and the printer so that the CPU is not needlessly held back from processing more information as it waits for the printer to print it out.

One of the functions of communication devices and various kinds of memory buffers and storage areas in the system is to *stage* the flow of information into and out of the machine in such a way as to maximize the utilization of the CPU. A major development of the last 30 years in information systems has been the creation of operating systems software (see Chapter 7) and other buffering and storage devices, all of which combine to enhance the total utilization of the CPU.

Bits and Bytes: Digital and Analog Computers

Digital computers operate by reducing all symbols, pictures, and words to a string of binary digits called *bits*. Digital computers operate directly with binary digits, either singly or strung together to form bytes. A string of 8 bits is called a *byte*. Each byte can be used to represent a decimal number, a symbol, or part of a picture (see Figure 6.2).

Analog computers, on the other hand, do not operate on digits; instead, they represent digits and symbols through a continuous physical dimension such as voltage level, thickness of a material, or rotation of a shaft. Analog computers—one of which was the mechanical slide rule, which calculated mathematical results using the physical position of the slide rule—are used primarily in process control and in certain scientific applications such as controlling the density of materials being mixed together in a petroleum refinery.

Figure 6.3 shows how decimal numbers are represented using *true binary digits*. Each position in a decimal number has a certain value. At the bottom of the figure is a table that indicates the value of each place in the decimal number. Any number in the decimal system can be reduced to a binary number.

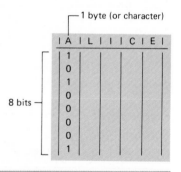

FIGURE 6.2
Bits and bytes. Every alphabetic character and decimal number, and other symbols ("$" , "%") can be represented by a binary code. In this example, the letter *A* is represented by an 8-bit binary code (ASCII).

10100, which is equal to:
$$0 \times 2^0 = 0$$
$$0 \times 2^1 = 0$$
$$1 \times 2^2 = 4$$
$$0 \times 2^3 = 0$$
$$1 \times 2^4 = \underline{16}$$
$$20$$

FIGURE 6.3
Representing decimal numbers in true binary.

Place	5	4	3	2	1
Power of 2	2^4	2^3	2^2	2^1	2^0
Decimal value	16	8	4	2	1

True binary cannot be used by a computer because, in addition to representing numbers, a computer must represent alphabetic characters and many other symbols used in natural language, like $ and &. This requirement led to the development of commonly agreed upon *binary codes* (like the Morse code in telegraphy).

There are two common codes: EBCDIC and ASCII. The first is the Extended Binary Coded Decimal Interchange Code (EBCDIC, pronounced ib-si-dick). This binary code, developed by IBM in the 1950s, represents every number, alphabetic character, or special character with 8 bits. For example, the decimal digit 9 is represented by the code 11111001. The following illustrates EBCDIC AND ASCII code.

Machine language is the underlying language of all electronic digital computers. There are a number of machine language codes.

Character	EBCDIC Binary	Character	ASCII-8 Binary
A	1100 0001	A	1010 0001
B	1100 0010	B	1010 0010
C	1100 0011	C	1010 0011
D	1100 0100	D	1010 0100
E	1100 0101	E	1010 0101
F	1100 0110	F	1010 0110
G	1100 0111	G	1010 0111
H	1100 1000	H	1010 1000
I	1100 1001	I	1010 1001
J	1101 0001	J	1010 1010
K	1101 0010	K	1010 1011
L	1101 0011	L	1010 1100
M	1101 0100	M	1010 1101
N	1101 0101	N	1010 1110
O	1101 0110	O	1010 1111
P	1101 0111	P	1011 0000
Q	1101 1000	Q	1011 0001
R	1101 1001	R	1011 0010
S	1110 0010	S	1011 0011
T	1110 0011	T	1011 0100
U	1110 0100	U	1011 0101
V	1110 0101	V	1011 0110
W	1110 0110	W	1011 0111
X	1110 0111	X	1011 1000
Y	1110 1000	Y	1011 1001
Z	1110 1001	Z	1011 1010
0	1111 0000	0	0101 0000
1	1111 0001	1	0101 0001
2	1111 0010	2	0101 0001
3	1111 0011	3	0101 0011
4	1111 0100	4	0101 0100
5	1111 0101	5	0101 0101
6	1111 0110	6	0101 0110
7	1111 0111	7	0101 0111
8	1111 1000	8	0101 1000
9	1111 1001	9	0101 1001

This code, can be used to code up to 256 different characters in one byte (2 to the eighth power equals 256).

Another commonly used code is the American Standard Code for Information Interchange (ASCII). This code was developed by the American National Standards Institute (ANSI) in the hope of providing a standard code that could be used by many different manufacturers in order to make their machinery compatible. Like EBCDIC, ASCII-8 is an 8-bit code. In general, EBCDIC is the primary mainframe IBM code that is used to coordinate both the CPU and peripheral devices. ASCII is used in data transmission and for microcomputers.

In actual use, EBCDIC and ASCII also contain an extra ninth parity or check bit, which is added for checking purposes. Machines are built as either *even parity* or *odd parity*. Assuming an even-parity machine, the computer expects the number of bits turned on in a byte always to be even (if the machine was designed as an odd-parity machine, the number of bits turned on would always be odd). When the number of bits in a byte is even, the parity bit is turned off. If the number of bits in a byte is odd, the parity bit is turned on to make the total number of on bits even. Because bits can be accidentally or mistakenly changed from on to off, when data are transferred from one device to another, or because of environmental disturbances, parity bits are used to assist in detecting these errors. All computer hardware contains automatic parity checking to ensure the stability of data over time.

Factories of the Future

The future of manufacturing is undergoing debugging at a General Motors truck assembly plant in Pontiac, Michigan. Engineers are installing a factory communication system that will allow computers, process controllers, robots, and other machines made by competing manufacturers to talk with one another.

The Pontiac system will connect 21 types of devices from 13 different suppliers in an effort to unite different "islands of automation." It is the first test of the manufacturing automation protocol, a growing body of standards and rules for electronic communication in the factory.

(Adapted from "Standardizing Automation," *The New York Times*, February 27, 1986).

The development of standard computing and telecommunication codes is especially important in factory automation. Until recently, robots, programmable machine tools, vision systems, conveyance devices, and CAD/CAM systems were speaking different languages because they were all made by separate manufacturers. The result was near chaos in General Motors assembly plants. One solution is the manufacturing automation protocol (MAP).

The Data Hierarchy: The Connection Between Bits and Systems

The only way a modern information system can store, process, and manipulate files and information is by breaking down all information (including pictures) into a series of bits. This process of reducing large information entities (e.g., a university database) into millions of bits stored in a computer is illustrated in Figure 6.4.

In Figure 6.4, a universitywide student *database* combines all of the information available in the university on students, including personal information, grades, and financial data. Within this student database, one can find a specific *file* on student grades. If we look at the student grade file, we see that it is composed of individual *records*. If we look at each of these records, we see that it consists of a number of *fields*: the name, the course taken, the date, and the grade. If we look at the fields, we see that they are represented by a series of *bytes*. That is, the name, for example, is broken down into its constituent letters, and each letter is represented by an 8-bit byte. And, of course, if we look at the byte itself, we see that it is composed of a string of *bits*—in this case, ASCII code.

	The Record Hierarchy	Example
A database containing information on all students in a university is composed of many files.	Database	Personal, financial, and course information on students
A file contains information on a specific topic, or group (e.g., a student grade file).	File	John Adamas A Mary Williams B Thomas Sloan B
A file is composed of many records that describe individuals or objects in the file. A student record contains information on the student name, address, course number, and grade.	Records	John Adamas A
Each record is composed of many fields that are items of information about the objects or persons in the file. A student grade file might have the following fields: name, ID, course, course date, final grade.	Fields	Name field: John Adamas
Each field is composed of a series of bytes.	Bytes	10100001 (Letter *A* in ASCII)
Each byte is composed of a string of bits.	Bits	+, − or 1, 0

FIGURE 6.4

From database to bytes and bits. All information in an information system is stored ultimately as bits on a storage device. These bits are aggregated into higher levels of information.

If the computer has to store a picture, it creates a grid overlay of the picture. In this grid or matrix, the computer measures the light or color in each box or cell, called a *pixel*. The computer then stores this information on each pixel. A standard high-resolution terminal has a 400×640 grid, creating 256,000 pixels. In a *bit map* terminal, each pixel can be addressed, requiring over 256,000 bytes of memory. Most terminals are lower-resolution *character mapped*, which permit 80 characters and 24 rows to appear on the screen, requiring only 80×24 bytes (1920 bytes). Obviously, the quality of the picture is higher in a bit-mapped terminal, but the memory requirements are larger.

Whether pictures or text are stored, it is through this process of reduction, which takes place almost at the speed of light, that a modern computer is able to operate in a complex environment. Now that we have seen how information is broken down into strings of bits and bytes, we can consider the physical devices that store and control this information.

6.2 The CPU

The CPU is the area of the computer system where the manipulation of symbols, numbers, and letters occurs. It is composed of three entities: *primary storage*, a *control unit*, and an *arithmetic-logic unit* (see Figure 6.5). Each of these parts operates on binary digits.

Primary Storage

Primary storage has three functions. It stores the complete program that is being executed (with the exception of virtual storage, discussed in Chapter 7). One of the major advances in computer systems in the 1940s was a stored computer program that could be executed very rapidly at electronic speeds.

Contrast a stored program to an unstored program. When you work with a hand calculator and calculate the percentage deduction for federal taxes for your paycheck, you are both the program and the programmer. You have to enter each step in the program separately. If you had to pay 1000 employees, you would have to "run" this

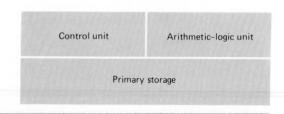

FIGURE 6.5
A CPU. All modern electronic digital computers consist of three functional units: the control unit, the arithmetic-logic unit, and primary storage.

FIGURE 6.6
Primary storage in a computer.
Primary storage can be thought of
as a matrix, each cell of which is a
mailbox. Each mailbox has a unique
address. In this example, we open
up mailbox (n, 1). It contains an
8-bit byte. In this example, the
8-bit byte represents the number 0
(in EBCDIC). Each mailbox
has room for one byte of data
or program.

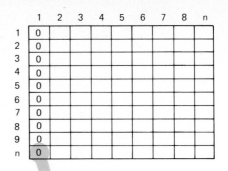

1 byte in each mailbox

Each mailbox contains
8 switches or transistors
that represent 8 bits

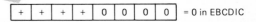

manual program all day long. A computer that can store such a program can pay the payroll in seconds.

Primary storage also stores the operating system programs that manage the operation of the computer. These programs are discussed in Chapter 7.

Finally, the primary storage area holds data that are being used by the program.

How is it possible for an electronic device like primary storage to actually store information? How is it possible to retrieve this information from a known location in memory? Figure 6.6 illustrates primary storage in an electronic digital computer. It makes no difference whether the storage devices themselves are made up of tubes, transistors, or magnetic core (to be described). Internal primary storage is often called *random access memory* (*RAM*). Unfortunately, this is somewhat of a misnomer; it should be called *direct access memory*. The advantage of electronic information storage is the ability to store information in a precise known location in memory and to retrieve it from that same location.

Figure 6.6 shows that primary memory is divided into memory cells. Each cell contains a set of eight binary switches or devices, each of which can store 1 bit of information. The set of 8 bits found in each memory cell is sufficient to store 1 byte, using either EBCDIC or ASCII. Therefore, in each memory cell, we could store one letter, one digit, or one special symbol (such as $).

Each memory cell has an individual address indicating where it is located in RAM. The computer can remember where all of the data bytes are stored simply by keeping track of their addresses.

The parallel with a mail delivery box, such as those found in apartment buildings, is entirely appropriate. Each memory location in primary storage has a specific address—a mailbox. Within this mailbox, 1 byte of information is stored.

Most of the information used by a computer application is stored on secondary storage devices such as disks and tapes, located outside of the primary storage area. In order for the computer to do work on information, information must be transferred into primary memory for processing. Therefore, data are continually being read into and written out of the primary storage area during the execution of a program. When a customer account has to be calculated, all of the data associated with that customer must be read into the primary storage area, where the CPU performs operations on it to calculate the account.

As we will see in the discussion of the various generations of computers, the nature of memory cells changes over time. The concept is the same, but the physical devices change. At the turn of the century, there were no electronic memory cells. Instead, each memory cell was represented on a physical card (the computer card), which had a column of bits. Depending upon which bits were punched out, an electromechanical card reader would know which alphabetic or numeric character was stored in that column. Computer punch cards still exist (the U.S. Treasury Department still issues checks on them).

In the 1940s, the first electronic computers relied on vacuum tubes. These tubes were replaced by transistors in the late 1950s. Integrated circuits took the place of transistors in the early 1960s.

Early computer systems had very modest amounts of primary storage. The first electronic computer had, at most, 1000 bytes of storage. The 1965 IBM 360s, which were the first third-generation computers, stored 64,000 bytes (64K) in primary storage. Today's microcomputers have up to 1 megabyte, and mainframes have 30 to several hundred megabytes in primary storage.

Magnetic core memory was a primary storage technology of the 1950s. It was composed of small magnetic donuts (much smaller than Cheerios), which could be polarized in one of two directions to represent a bit of data. Wires were strung along and through these cores to both write and read data. Of course, this system had to be assembled by hand and therefore was very expensive (see Figure 6.7). In addition, core memory was much slower than the semiconductor memory that replaced it in the form of transistors and integrated circuits.

Semiconductor memory first utilized transistors in the late 1950s, but these were rapidly replaced in the early 1960s by electronic circuits that could be reproduced photographically on miniaturized silicon chips. These were referred to as *integrated circuits*, which by the 1970s had become *very large integrated circuits* (*VLIC*). Using a variety of photographic reduction techniques, the development of semiconductors has revolutionized the computer industry. The cost of

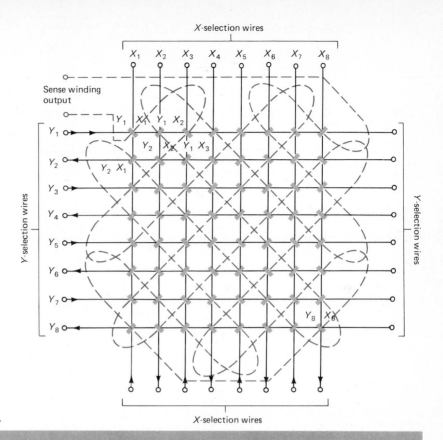

FIGURE 6.7
Magnetic core memory plane.

primary memory has fallen rapidly and its capacity has risen dramatically (see Figure 6.8). As a result, the cost of 100,000 calculations has fallen from several dollars in the 1950s to $0.0025 in the 1980s.

Today's semiconductor memory relies on small micro-sized transistors, which are placed on a silicon chip. Each of these transistors, or circuits, can store 1 bit of information. Photo 6.1 shows a modern RAM chip.

In these memory chips, a bit of data is represented by a circuit that either does or does not conduct electricity. One of the primary disadvantages of using semiconductors for primary storage is that when the supply of electricity is cut off, the CPU loses all of the data contained in primary memory, including the programs. Therefore, semiconductor RAM storage is volatile and is interrupted when power is disturbed.

Magnetic core technology does not lose data when power is interrupted. Moreover, it is impervious to radiation, which can destroy computer chips and alter their data content. For this reason, one of the remaining applications of the magnetic core is in operations where power may be interrupted and where programs

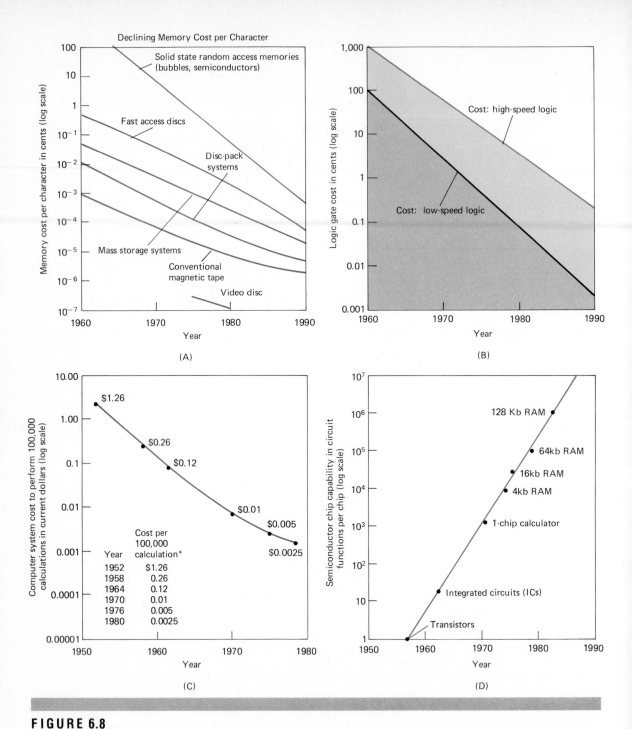

FIGURE 6.8

(A) Declining memory cost per character. (B) Declining logic cost per gate. (C) Drop in average computer system cost per 100,000 calculations from 1952 to 1980. (D) Increase in capability of semiconductor chips from 1956 to 1990. Adapted from Office of Technology Assessment, 1985.

PHOTO 6.1
IBM has developed a production memory chip that can store more than one million bits of information (1 megabit chip) on a chip about $\frac{1}{2}$ inch square. Photo supplied courtesy of the IBM corporation.

Obsolete Devices May Be Shuttle Key

IBM, the builder of the space shuttle's on-board computer systems, purposely avoided state-of-the-art technology when building the primary memories for the shuttle. Instead they used ferrite core memories developed in the late 1940s.

Ferrite core technology has two crucial advantages, even though it is more expensive than semiconductor memory. First, it retains data even if the power is cut off. Ferrite core stores data magnetically. Second, it protects data from radioactive belts around the earth that the shuttle flies through and that could change bits of data in a common semiconductor memory. Even in the event of a crash, the data in magnetic core are retained.

Adapted from the *New York Times*, March 16, 1986.

must be restored. The space program is one of the few remaining areas where magnetic core is still utilized.

Types of Semiconductor Memory

Several different kinds of semiconductor memory are available on chips today. RAM is used for volatile short-term memory in general-purpose computers. Read-only memory (ROM) can only be read from; it cannot be written to. ROM chips come from the manufacturer with programs already "burned in" or stored. ROM is used in general-purpose computers to store certain utility programs of the operating system and frequently used programs (such as BASIC A or computing routines such as calculating the square roots of numbers). Other uses for ROM chips are the storage of manufacturer-specific microcodes such as the Basic Input Output System (BIOS) chip used on an IBM PC, which controls the handling of data within the machine.

There are two other subclasses of ROM chips: programmable read-only memory (*PROM*) and erasable programmable read-only memory (*EPROM*). PROM chips are used by manufacturers as control devices in their products. They can be programmed once. In this way, manufacturers avoid the expense of having a specialized chip manufactured for the control of small motors, for instance; instead, they can program into a PROM chip the specific program for their product. PROM chips, therefore, can be made universally for many manufacturers in large production runs. EPROM chips are used for device control, such as in robots, where the program may have to be changed on a routine basis. With EPROM chips, the program can be erased and reprogrammed.

Arithmetic-Logic Unit

The arithmetic-logic unit (ALU) performs the principal logical and arithmetic operations of the computer. The ALU need only add and subtract numbers in order to do multiplication and division, as well as addition and subtraction. Multiplication is simply rapid addition, and division is rapid subtraction. In addition to performing these arithmetic functions, an ALU must be able to determine when one quantity is greater or less than another and when two quantities are equal.

Control Unit

The function of the control unit is to read the stored program, one instruction at a time, and to direct other components of the computer system to perform the tasks required by the program. The control unit first reads one line of the program (the instruction cycle). This is followed by an execution cycle in which the control unit retrieves information from memory and sends the information to the ALU, where an operation is performed on the information. The result is stored in primary memory. As the execution of each instruction is completed, the control unit advances to and reads the next line of the program.

6.3 Generations of Hardware

Table 6.2 indicates the major transitions in computer hardware from the mid-1940s to the present. Each of these transitions is referred to as a *generation*. There have been four major generations of computing equipment. In each of these generations, much more than computer hardware is involved. Computer hardware is directly related to the quality of telecommunications and the power of computer software.

First-Generation Vacuum Tube Technology: 1946–1956

The first generation of computers relied on vacuum tubes to store and process information. These tubes consumed a great deal of power, were short-lived, and generated a great deal of heat. Nevertheless, they were much faster than electromechanical devices like card sorters and relays.

Telecommunications was by teletype at a very slow rate—about 150 bits per second. The first-generation computer language was machine language. All machines used machine code, and programmers had to learn it in order to get the machines to work. In the early 1950s a second-generation language was developed that used many English language-like acronyms to speed programming; it was called *assembly language*. Words like *add, sub, num* could be used in programs, and a program called a *compiler* translated these words into machine language for programmers (see Chapter 7).

The maximum memory size was approximately 2000 bytes (2 kilobytes), with a speed of 10 kiloinstructions per second.

Second-Generation Transistors: 1957–1963

The second generation of computers relied on transistor technology and magnetic core memory. Each transistor had to be individually made and wired into a printed circuit board. While printed circuit boards were much more efficient than hard-wired vacuum tube machines, building computers remained a highly labor-intensive endeavor. Transistors were much more stable and reliable than vacuum tubes, generated less heat, and consumed less power. Still, they had to be assembled by hand and could not take shock loads or heat very well.

Digital telecommunications between computers was developed in this period. Communication speeds were now up to several hundred thousand bytes per second.

Perhaps the most profound breakthrough in this period was the development of higher-level languages, which permitted non-programming specialists to use computers. Languages such as FORTRAN (Formula Translation Program) and COBOL (Common Business Oriented Language), developed in this period, allowed specialists in mathematics and business to create custom-made programs and applications.

Memory size expanded to 32 kilobytes of RAM memory, and speeds reached 200,000 to 300,000 instructions per second.

TABLE 6.2
Five Generations of Computer and Communications Technologies

Generation	First	Second	Third	Fourth	Fifth
Years	1946–56	1957–63	1964–81	1982–89	1990–
Example computers	Eniac Edvac Univac IBM 650	NCR 501 IBM 7094 CDC-6600	IBM 360, 370 PDP-11 Spectra-70 Honeywell 200 Cray 1 Illac-IV Cyber 205	Crey XMP IBM 308 Amdahl 580	Extensive development of distributed computing Merging of telecommunications and computer technologies Extensive modularity
Telecommunications technology	Telephone Teletype	Digital transmission Pulse-code modulation	Satellite communications Microwaves Networking Optical fibers Packet switching	Integrated systems digital network (ISDN)	

Computer hardware	Vacuum tubes Magnetic drum Cathode ray tube	Transistors Magnetic core memories	ICs Semiconductor memories Magnetic disks Minicomputers Microprocessors	Distributed computing systems VLSI Bubble memories Optical disks Microcomputers	Advanced packaging and interconnection techniques Ultralarge-scale integration Parallel architectures Three-dimensional Integrated-circuit design Gallium arsenide technology Josephson junction technology Optical components Super conductive materials
Computer software	Stored programs Machine code Autocode	High-level languages Cobol Algol Fortran	Very high-level languages Pascal operating systems Structured programming Timesharing LISP Computer graphics	Ada Widespread packaged programs Expert systems Object-oriented languages	Concurrent languages Functional programming Symbolic processing (natural languages, vision, speech recognition, planning)
Computer performance (typical commercial machines)	2-kilobyte memory 10 kilo-instructions per second	32-kilobyte memory 200 KIPS	2-megabyte memory 5 mega-instructions per second	10–50-megabyte memory 30 mips	1 giga-instruction to 1 tetra-instruction per second

Third-Generation Integrated Circuits: 1964–1979

Third-generation computers relied on integrated circuits, which were made by printing transistors on silicon chips. These devices were called *semiconductors*. Magnetic disk technology was developed in this period. The first satellite telecommunications using microwave frequencies were created, and coaxial cable land telecommunications speeds advanced beyond the megabit per second range.

Very-high-level languages emerged in this period, allowing computer amateurs to do sophisticated statistical and word processing work on computers. Computer memories expanded to 2 megabytes of RAM memory, and speeds accelerated to 5 mips.

Fourth-Generation VLSIC: 1979–Present

The fourth generation, in which we are currently living, extends from 1980 to the present. Computers in this period use very-large-scale integrated circuits, which are packed with as many as 200,000 to 400,000 circuits per chip.

Costs have fallen to the point where desktop computers are inexpensive. Very-high-level languages have been further simplified by the use of menu-driven programs so that more and more nonspecialist end users can use machines. CPU memory sizes have expanded up to several hundred megabytes in commercial machines and speeds to 50 mips.

What Is a Microprocessor? What Is a Chip?

In the third generation, the early 1960s, integrated circuits were developed in which 3 to 15 transistors could be manufactured at once on a single chip of silicon. These circuits on a chip could be strung together to form the memory, logic, and control units of a computer. In the late 1970s, however, the Intel Corporation developed a method to put hundreds, and then thousands, of transistors on a single chip. These large-scale integrated (LSI) chips, and very-large-scale integrated (VLSI) chips, with hundreds of thousands of transistors per chip, integrated the computer's memory, logic, and control on a single chip; hence the name *microprocessor*, or computer on a chip. The most powerful microprocessor now used in personal computers is the 32 bit 16 megahertz chip such as the Intel 80386 (Photo 6.2).

Commonly available chips today are shown in Table 6.3. Chips are measured in several ways. You will often see chips labeled as 8-bit, 16-bit, or 32-bit devices. This refers to the *data word length*, or the number of bits that can be retrieved from memory in one cycle of the machine. An 8-bit chip can retrieve from memory 8 bits or 1 byte in a single machine cycle. A 32-bit chip can retrieve 32 bits or 4 bytes in a single cycle.

A second factor affecting chip speed is *cycle speed*. Every event in a computer must be sequenced so that one thing logically follows another. The control unit sets a beat to the chip. This beat is established by an internal clock and is measured in *megahertz* (millions of cycles per second). The Intel 8088 chip, for instance, has a clock speed of 4.4 megahertz, whereas the 80286 by Intel has a clock speed of 8 megahertz.

PHOTO 6.2
Intel's 80386 chip now used in
personal computers. Courtesy
of Intel Corporation.

TABLE 6.3
Computer Chips.
From *Introduction to Computers and Information Systems Without BASIC* by Thomas H. Athey and Robert W. Zmud. Copyright © 1986 by Scott, Foresman and Company. Reprinted by permission.

Microprocessor Chip	Manufacturer	Dataword Length	Microcomputers Using This Chip
6502	MOS Technology	8	Apple IIe Atari 800 Commodore 64
Z-80A	Zilog	8	Radio Shack Personal Desktop Sanyo Business Systems MBC/250 Epson QX-10
8088	Intel	16	IBM PC and XT COMPAQ Portable HP 150 (touch screen)
68000	Motorola	32	Radio Shack Model 16B Corvus Concept Apple Macintosh
80286	Intel	24	IBM-AT
80386	Intel	32	Compaq micro computers and advanced work stations IBM Personal System 2

Obviously, in order to get a computer to execute more instructions per second, and work through programs or handle users expeditiously, it is necessary to increase the word length of the processor and/or the clock speed.

While there has been enormous change in the technology, and in the associated costs and capacity of computers since the 1940s, the principal concept of a modern digital computer has remained basically the same. All symbols, numbers, and pictures are reduced to binary digits and strings of bits, or bytes. The computer operates on one instruction, and on individual bytes of data, one at a time. The technology of the hardware permits this processing of one instruction at a time, byte by byte, to proceed at an extremely fast rate. Nevertheless, digital computers can still do only one thing at a time. They are sequential processors. Modern digital computers are not parallel processors. The CPU cannot operate on multiple instructions and multiple elements of data at the same time. In the following chapter, we describe how software can be used to permit concurrent processing of multiple jobs by using several different processors that operate simultaneously.

Mainframes, Minis, and Micros

Computer systems are often categorized as mainframes, minis, or micros. As indicated in Table 6.2, however, the capacity of mainframes has expanded rapidly from a few thousand bytes to over several hundred million bytes within 40 years. The problem with the classification of machines into mainframes, minis, and micros is that the capacity of the machines changes so rapidly. Today, for instance, a microcomputer contains as much memory as a 1965 IBM System 360 mainframe computer (64K). Indeed, laptop computers in 1986 now exceed the 1970 mainframe in memory capacity.

In the 1986–1990 period, mainframe computers are generally those with 50 to several hundred megabytes of RAM. Minicomputers have 1 to 50 megabytes of RAM. And microcomputers range from 64 kilobytes to 4 megabytes of RAM. However, these distinctions can be expected to change fairly rapidly. Microcomputers are described more fully in Chapter 10. The most that can be said is that microcomputers are a class of machines that can be carried from room to room. Even some minicomputers fall into this category. But clearly, mainframe computers are too large to be carried by individuals or to be put on individual desks. So far, at least.

One way to quickly grasp the evolution of mainframe computers is to study the family tree of IBM computers in Figure 6.9. IBM makes up an estimated 70–90% of the U.S. mainframe market. The most famous IBM machines are the 360s and 370s. The 360 was the first powerful general-purpose commercial computer from IBM and was an enormous success. It was the first commercial mainframe to use integrated circuits.

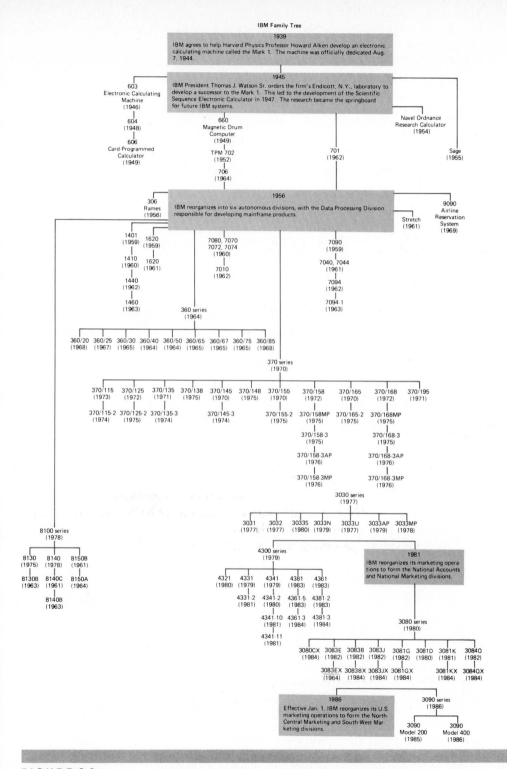

FIGURE 6.9

The IBM family tree. Copyright 1985 by CW Communications/Inc.,
Framingham, MA 01701—Reprinted from *Computerworld*.

TABLE 6.4
Five Generations of Mainframes at IBM

System Name	Year Introduced	Maximum Memory Size (in Megabytes)	Price per Megabyte* (in Thousands)	Cost per mip (in Thousands)
360	1964	1	$1600	$3500
370	1970	16	100	2000
3030	1977	32	25	400
308x	1981	126	16†	240
3090	1985	192	7	180

* Actual price at introduction.
† Before announcement of 3090.

Adapted from "Sierra Adds Power to IBM," The New York Times," Feb. 13, 1985.

TABLE 6.5
Currently Supported IBM Mainframe Products

System	3081 Model GX	3081 Model KX	3084 Model QX	3090 Model 200	3090 Model 400
Relative Performance	545	735	1,384	1,323	2,381
mips	12.5	16.3	29.1	29.3	52.7
Memory size in bytes (minimum-maximum)	16M–48M	16M–64M	32M–128M	64M	128M
Purchase price (memory size)	$2,550,000 (16M)	$2,995,000 (16M)	$5,610,000 (64M)	$5,000,000 (64M)	$9,300,000 (128M)
Machine cycle time (nsec)	24	24	24	18.5	18.5
Channels (minimum-maximum)	10–24	16–24	48	32–48	64–90
Cache (buffer) size	64K	64K	64K	128K	256K
Price (per 1M byte of main memory)	$12,500	$12,500	$12,500	$12,500	$12,500

Note: Mainframes can be distinguished from minicomputers and microcomputers by their faster execution speeds (mips) and maximum memory sizes. Note their price per megabyte of memory and compare this to minicomputer prices per megabyte in Table 6.6.

TABLE 6.6
Minicomputers by DEC

System Characteristic	VAX-11/780	VAX-11/782	VAX-11/785	VAX 8600	VAX 8650
mips	1.06	1.9	1.7	4.4	6.8
Memory size in bytes	1M–64M	4M–8M	2M–64M	4M–32M	4M–68M
Purchase price (memory size)	$145,000 (2M)	$320,000 (4M)	$195,000 (2M)	$350,000 (4M)	$475,000 (4M)
Machine cycle time (nsec)	290	290	166	80	55
Channels	1–8	1–8	1–8	1–12	1–12
Cache (buffer) size in bytes	8K	16K	32K	16K	16K
Price per extra megabyte of memory	$4500	$4500	$4500	$4000	$4000

Table 6.4 shows the power of the 360 and the follow-on models through 1986 to the 3090 or Sierra machines. Note the incredible drop in cost per million instructions per second. Table 6.5 shows IBM's currently supported (i.e., available from the manufacturer) machines.

Table 6.6 illustrates the power and speed of the minicomputers manufactured by the Digital Equipment Corporation (DEC). Minicomputers are considerably slower than mainframes, yet much faster and more powerful than microcomputers.

6.4 Secondary Storage

Modern computer systems use a number of different memory and storage devices in order to accomplish their tasks. We have already described the primary storage of the CPU, where information and programs are stored for immediate processing. However, there is also a need to store information outside of the computer in a nonvolatile state (not requiring electrical power) and to store volumes of data too large to fit into a computer of any size today (such as a large payroll or the U.S. census).

Large bodies of data must be stored on a medium that permits rapid transfer to the CPU. Table 6.7 indicates the range of storage devices found in a modern computing environment. Secondary storage refers to relatively long-term storage of data outside the CPU. The principal secondary storage devices used are disk technology and tape technology.

TABLE 6.7
Data Storage Devices in a Modern Computer

Type of Memory	Total Storage Capacity (Kbytes)	Access Time	Relative Rate (Operations per Second)	Storage Cost (Bytes per Dollar)
Register	0.1	0.01 microseconds	100,000,000	2
Cache	1	0.1 microseconds	10,000,000	20
RAM	1000	0.5 microseconds	2,000,000	200
RAM disk	1000	0.5 microseconds	2000	400
Hard disk	100,000	0.25 milliseconds	40	40,000
Floppy disk	2000	250 milliseconds	4	4,000
Optical disk	1,000,000	150 milliseconds	7	100,000
Magnetic tape	100,000	10 seconds	1/10	100,000

Source: *Introduction to Computers and Information Systems* by Thomas H. Athey and Robert W. Zmud. Copyright © 1986 Scott, Foresman and Company. Reprinted by permission.

Primary vs. Secondary Storage

Primary storage, such as found in the CPU, is where the fastest, most expensive technology is used. As shown in Table 6.7, there are actually three different kinds of primary memory: registers, cache, and RAM. Register is the fastest (and most expensive) memory, where small amounts of data and instructions reside for thousandths of a second just prior to use, followed by cache memory and RAM memory for large amounts of data. Access to information stored in primary memory is electronic and occurs almost at the speed of light.

Secondary storage is nonvolatile and retains data even when the power is turned off. There are many kinds of secondary storage; the most common are punched cards, magnetic tape, and magnetic disk. In general, secondary storage requires mechanical movement to gain access to the data; therefore, in contrast to primary memory, it is relatively slow.

Magnetic Tape

Magnetic tape is an older device that is still very important for the secondary storage of information. Generally, magnetic tape comes in 14-inch reels up to 2400 feet long and 0.5 inch wide. It is very similar to home cassette recording tape, but of higher quality. Figure 6.10 illustrates how information appears on magnetic tape using an EBCDIC coding scheme. Each byte of data utilizes one column on the tape. Each column is composed of 8 bits plus 1 check parity bit.

Information can be stored on magnetic tape at different densities. Low density is 1600 bytes per inch (bpi), and densities of up to 6250 bpi are common.

In addition to this commercial-quality tape, microcomputers and some minicomputers use small tape cassettes very similar to home recording cassettes to store information.

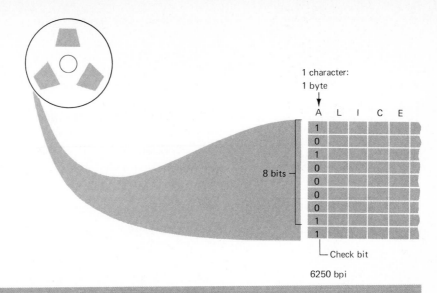

1 character:
1 byte

A L I C E

8 bits

1
0
1
0
0
0
0
1
1

Check bit

6250 bpi

FIGURE 6.10
Data are often stored on nine-track magnetic tape. Tape is a stable and inexpensive medium.

The principal advantages of magnetic tape are that it is very low in cost and that the data transfer rate, compared to that of computer cards, is very fast. A card reader can only read several hundred characters per second, whereas commercial tape devices transfer data at a rate of several megabytes per second. In addition, magnetic tape is a stable and compact way of storing very large volumes of information. It is a reliable technology because of several self-checking features (such as parity bits), and therefore it is an ideal form of backup storage for other more volatile forms of memory. Moreover, magnetic tape can be used over and over again, although it does age with time and care must be exercised in handling it.

The principal disadvantages of magnetic tape are that it is a sequential storage medium and is relatively slow. In order to find an individual record stored on magnetic tape, such as your professor's employment record, the tape must be read from the beginning up to the location of the desired record. This means that the CPU must read each name from "Abelson" all the way to your professor's name before it can locate your professor's record. Therefore, magnetic tape is not a good medium when it is necessary to find information rapidly (such as an airline reservation system). A second disadvantage of tape is, of course, that it is relatively slow compared to a CPU.

Other negative features of tape include the fact that it can be damaged, it is labor-intensive to mount and dismount, and the environment in which it is stored must be carefully controlled. Many have assumed that tape will soon go out of use, but it continues to exist in changing forms, as indicated in the following account.

Magnetic Disk

In the early 1970s, magnetic tape began to be replaced by a newer storage device called *magnetic disk* (see Figure 6.11). There are two kinds of disks: floppy disks (used in PCs) and hard disks (used on commercial disk drives and PCs).

As shown in Figure 6.11, a commercial disk pack has 11 disks, each with two surfaces—top and bottom. However, although there are 11 disks, no information is recorded on the top or bottom surfaces; thus, there are only 20 recording surfaces on the disk pack. On each surface, data are stored on tracks. The disk pack is generally sealed from the environment and rotates at a speed of about 3500 rpm, creating an air stream speed of about 50 mph at the disk surface.

Information is recorded on or read from the disk by read/write heads, which literally fly over the spinning disks. Unlike a home stereo, the heads never actually touch the disk (which would destroy the data and cause the system to "crash") but hover a few thousandths of an inch above it. A smoke particle or a human hair is sufficient to crash the head into the disk.

The read/write heads move horizontally (from left to right) to any of 200 positions called *cylinders*. At any one of these cylinders, the read/write heads can read or write information to any of 20 different platters (called *tracks*). There are 20 tracks at each cylinder.

When data are stored sequentially on a disk, they are stored by cylinder. When all of the tracks on a cylinder are filled up, the read/write heads move in one cylinder, fill up each of the tracks there, and move on.

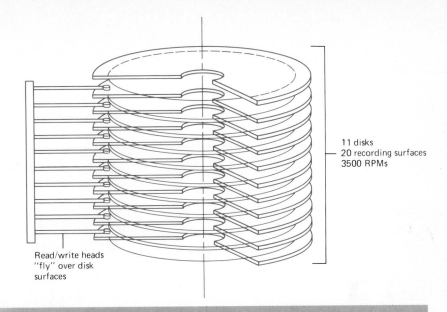

11 disks
20 recording surfaces
3500 RPMs

Read/write heads
"fly" over disk
surfaces

FIGURE 6.11
Illustration of a disk pack.

The speed of access to data on a disk is a function of the rotational speed of the disk and the speed of the access arms. In general, it takes about 38 milliseconds for the read/write heads to position themselves and 8 to 10 milliseconds for the disk pack to rotate until the proper information is located. More advanced and expensive disks have access speeds of 15–20 milliseconds and capacities of up to 1.5 gigabytes per unit.

Commercial hard disks have a *data transfer rate* of 10 megabytes per second compared to 3 megabytes, at most, for the new IBM drives previously described. Most traditional tape drives transfer at far slower speeds.

Figure 6.12 shows how records are stored on a single track of the disk. Each track, of course, contains several records. In general, 20,000 bytes of information can be stored on each track at densities of up to 12,000 bpi. Because there are 20 such tracks and 200 cylinders, the total capacity of the illustrated disk is 80 megabytes. As noted previously, advanced commercial disks have much higher storage capacities—over 1 billion bytes.

Microcomputers also use hard disks, which typically store up to 40 megabytes. These units now cost a few hundred dollars.

In addition to hard disks, PCs use floppy disks, which are flat, 5.25 inch disks of polyester film with a magnetic coating. These disks have a storage capacity ranging from 320K to approximately 1.2 megabytes. They were originally developed as secondary storage devices for minicomputers. They have a much slower access rate than

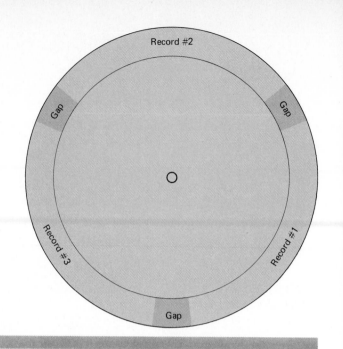

FIGURE 6.12
How records are stored on a single track of a disk.

Characteristic	IBM 3380	Tandon TM 705
Size (inches)	14	5.25
Capacity (megabytes)	1520	50.1
Access speed average (msec)	16	39
Number of surfaces	15	5
Price	$100,000	$1700

TABLE 6.8
Comparison of Mainframe (3380) and
Microdisk (Tandon 705)

hard disks, and therefore they are suitable only for microcomputers or PC use. Table 6.8 compares an advanced commercial hard disk to a PC hard disk.

Direct File Organization

On a magnetic tape there is only one way to store records: in sequential order. On a magnetic disk there are several different options, depending on the application.

Files can be organized sequentially, as on tape, although this misses the point of disk technology, which is the ability to access any record directly without reading all other records. How can you go to a record directly?

One common technique is to use an index. Just as in a card catalog at a library or a phone directory, an index can be created showing exactly where on the disk (what cylinder and track) each record is. This is called the *indexed sequential access* method.

Other methods of organizing the data on disk are simple direct, random direct, and virtual storage access method. In addition, files may be chained together on a disk, as will be discussed in Chapter 8.

Advantages of Disk Technology

Magnetic disks have several important advantages. First, they permit direct access to individual records. Each record can be given a precise physical address in terms of cylinders and tracks, and the read/write head can be directed to go to that address and access the information in about 20 to 60 milliseconds. This means that the entire file does not have to be searched, as in a tape file, in order to find one person's record. This creates the possibility for on-line information systems providing an immediate response, such as an airline reservation or customer information system. Disk technology is often referred to as *direct access storage devices* (*DASD*).

There are special devices that make disk technology even faster by reducing the movement of the read/write head. The disk can be coordinated with cache memory in the CPU to access many related records simultaneously, as in the story of Humana, Inc.

For on-line systems requiring direct access, disk technology is the only practical means of storage today. Records can be easily and rapidly retrieved. The cost of disks has steadily declined over the years. Moreover, as we will see in Chapter 8 in the discussion of file construction and databases, disk technology permits interrelationships among records to be built into the storage file itself. This system permits a single transaction to update or change data in a number of different files simultaneously and dramatically speeds the process of finding related records.

DASD is, however, relatively expensive compared to magnetic tape. Moreover, updating information stored on a disk destroys the old information. Unlike tape-based batch processing, which might include an old master file, a new master file, and a transaction file on three separate reels of tape, in disk technology there is only one copy of the information. Therefore, it becomes more difficult to back up and audit the transactions that take place on a disk. You can check this out by changing your seat selection on an airline reservation system and then asking the clerk to tell you where you wished to sit originally. You will find that the system has no memory for your previous selection because it has been wiped off the disk.

In addition, disk technology can crash. The disk drives themselves are susceptible to environmental disturbances; even smoke particles can disrupt the movement of read/write heads over the disk surface. Therefore, the environment must be relatively pure and stable. Disk technology cannot work in a space shuttle, for instance.

Unplugging a Bottleneck

Humana, Inc., is a large health care and hospital facility operator. Humana's 89 hospitals are on-line through a customer information and control system (CICS). This facility handles almost all business procedures and information for the on-line hospitals, including accounts receivable and payable, patient billing, ordering, and inventory. Several hundred terminals at headquarters use the same CPU, using the time-sharing option (TSO), a software product of IBM. The peak TSO load is 90 terminals, and response time had risen from 1.1 seconds to 3.3 seconds.

Analysis found that the bottleneck was the disk read/write time. Almost every job was calling for information from the disk one track and record at a time. What was needed was control over the disk drive itself so that entire blocks of data on one track, or related tracks, could be pulled off and stored in cache memory, where it was available for use at electronic speeds. Currently, it took the disk drive device 50 milliseconds to read a record. Humana wanted to cut this time to an average of 15 milliseconds by storing most of the needed information in cache memory.

Sybercache is a software product of StorageTek, Inc. It moves disk heads once and then takes entire tracks and stores them in cache memory if analysis shows that they are related.

Once installed, Sybercache brought access times down to 11 milliseconds, "device busy" went from 41% to 12%, and TSO response time dropped 31% to 2.29 seconds.

Adapted from *Infosystems*, October 1985.

Other Forms of Storage

Future storage technologies will involve optical storage and the use of lasers. Currently, compact disks (CDs) using laser storage are a popular medium for music. A number of optical data storage technologies are currently under development, and some will be on the market in a few years.

Unfortunately, optical storage on disks in which lasers burn in a pattern of bits and bytes is read-only storage. This is fine for prerecorded music. On the other hand, the disks can be inexpensive enough to allow one simply to buy a new disk rather than update the data on an old one.

A Computer That Does it All

Imagine a computer that can do it all: play a Mozart recording, record a baseball game for later playback, and handle your word processing and spread sheet needs.

Such a multipurpose machine is not far in the future because of magneto-optic technology. 3M, IBM, Control Data, and Eastman Kodak, along with several Japanese companies, have all begun huge research programs. The market is expected to be worth $11 billion by 1995.

Unlike today's compact disks, which permanently burn a pattern of music or data into an aluminum disk with a laser, a magneto-optic disk uses a laser to form patterns in a magnetic substrate on a compact disk. The advantage of magneto-optic over ordinary optic technology is that magneto-optic can be erased and rerecorded. The new technology permits very large data density and storage. It is expected that this new technology will provide powerful competition to traditional makers of disk drives, like IBM's 3380 drive.

Adapted from "Ever-Better Home Entertainment," *The New York Times*, March 30, 1986.

6.5 Input and Output Devices

Human beings interact with computer systems largely through input and output devices. Advances in information systems rely not only on the speed and capacity of the CPU but also on the speed, capacity, and usefulness of the input and output devices. These devices are often called *peripheral devices*.

Data Entry Devices

There are four major ways in which information can be put into a computer: punched cards, direct keying, interactive, and point of origin. Each of these methods has unique uses.

The 80-column punch card is still a familiar artifact of the computer age even though it was invented nearly 100 years ago by Herman Hollerith for use in the 1890 census. Punch cards were utilized through the 1970s as one of the principal methods of off-line storage of data and programs.

In punch cards, characters are coded on the card in columns by a combination of punches in different locations. The machine that reads them, the card reader, is an electromechanical device that senses the holes and solid parts of the cards.

Punch cards are a very stable, flexible storage medium. They can be used as original documents, signatures can be placed on them, they can be sent through the mail without being destroyed easily, and up to 80 bytes of information (80 columns) can be stored on a single card.

On the other hand, cards are very bulky and are sometimes difficult to work with (especially when they become stuck inside a card reading machine and are often destroyed). Card technology also requires a separate data entry or key punching staff to transform original source document information into punched card form. This creates the possibility of errors, lengthy verification procedures, and great expense. Punched cards are now a rarity in information processing, although in many corporations one can still find huge trays of cards storing data and programs being pushed around on heavy carts.

Direct Key Input Devices

Rather than punching information on cards and then entering it on the computer, in the 1970s technologists developed direct key-to-tape and key-to-disk data entry devices. In these systems, a small TV-like screen allows the operator to view data that have been keyed in for verification. Verification is usually accomplished by keying in the data twice and comparing the results. Once verified, the data are entered directly onto a magnetic tape or a magnetic disk for computer processing. These data entry systems can be stand-alone devices separated from the mainstream of data processing. Figure 6.13 shows an example of key-to-tape and key-to-disk data entry.

The advantages of direct key data entry are that much of the editing and verification of information can be performed at the time of data entry. Many keying errors can be detected before the data are loaded onto the mainframe system. Moreover, direct keying devices permit data entry to go on continuously without interfering with the operation of the main CPU. It is only when information processing begins that the keyed-in information is brought into the main CPU.

There are, however, several disadvantages of direct key systems. The keypunching stations themselves form a separate computer system and can be costly, especially for smaller firms. For larger firms, such as insurance companies and major financial institutions, separate data entry systems can be cost-justifiable. Nevertheless, a separate data keypunching staff is required. It would be much better if salespeople and other end users could key in data themselves. Moreover, in direct key systems, the information is entered in batches and the master files are updated on a nightly, weekly, or monthly basis. Hence the information in the master file is not current. An airline reservation system could not operate this way.

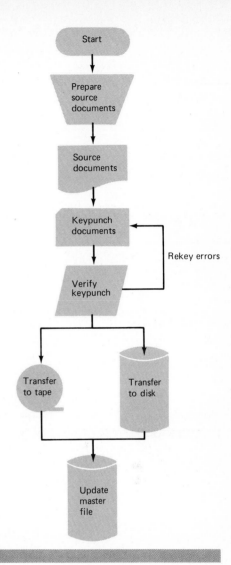

FIGURE 6.13
Key-to-tape and disk data entry.

Interactive Data Entry

Interactive data entry systems permit the data to be entered directly into the production master file through a data entry terminal or optical scanner, with either immediate processing against the master file or storage and batch updating for later processing (see Figure 6.14). The airline reservation system, for instance, uses interactive data entry, as do many customer information systems in financial institutions. In these systems, clerks or salespeople enter the transaction directly while dealing with the customer, and the main master files are updated immediately. In this manner, a separate data entry

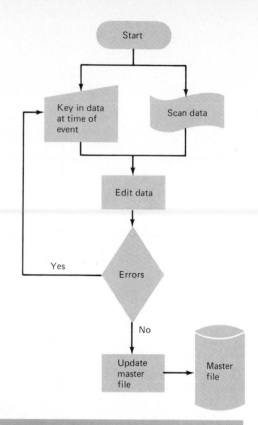

FIGURE 6.14
Interactive data entry.
Information about the
transaction is keyed in as the
transaction occurs. The master
file is usually updated at once,
although in some systems this
is done later.

staff and the cost associated with it are eliminated. Moreover, the cost of data entry is borne in part by the customer or client, as in automatic teller machines.

A number of advantages of interactive data entry are apparent. Aside from eliminating a separate data entry staff, many of the editing checks and verification of entries can be performed on-line and on an interactive basis with the use of templates or screens. If the wrong data are entered into a particular field, the machine will automatically inform the salesperson or clerk that an error has occurred.

There are also disadvantages. The data entry process can be slowed down when large number of users are entering data. The main CPU must have a very large capacity for on-line interactive data entry to take place, as the CPU is also dealing with other functions. On the other hand, the data in the master file are always up-to-date.

Point of Origin Automation

Point of origin automation is one kind of interactive data entry. It involves capturing information in computer-readable form at the time and location of the event. Point of sale systems, optical bar code scanners used in grocery stores, and other optical character recognition devices are examples of point of origin automation.

One of the advantages of point of origin automation is that the many errors that occur in keypunching are almost eliminated. Bar code scanners make fewer than 1 error in 10,000 transactions, whereas keypunchers make up to 1 error for every 1000 keystrokes. Moreover, source data automation permits information about events to be captured directly and immediately, with on-the-spot error correction. There is no separate keypunch staff. The computer-readable digits in the lower corner of personal checks are a computer-readable code that permits automation of data entry.

Other Input Devices

A number of devices are being developed to facilitate the interaction between computers and human beings. Voice recognition systems are currently being developed, which will have a vocabulary of 10,000 words and will be useful for office correspondence in a typical business. Other data entry devices include a portable lap top computer, illustrated in Photo 6.3. These computers can be carried by

PHOTO 6.3

The Portable Plus computer from Hewlett-Packard Company works with HP's battery-powered HP 9114 disk drive and battery-powered Thinkjet personal printer. It has a full 25-line LCD screen, weighs less than 10 pounds, and measures 13 × 10 × 3 inches. Photo courtesy of Hewlett-Packard Company.

salespeople and orders can be entered directly from the field via a customer telephone, permitting a direct and easy order entry capability.

Data Output Devices

The major data output devices are *cathode ray tube (CRT) terminals* (sometimes called *video display terminals* or *VDT*) and printers. The CRT is probably the most popular form of information output in modern computer systems. CRT text devices usually have the capability of displaying 80 columns and 24 lines of data. They can display both color and black-and-white characters.

Printers

Printers are used to produce a printed copy of information output. They include *impact printers* (a standard typewriter or a dot matrix) and *nonimpact printers* (laser and thermal transfer). Most printers print one character at a time, but some commercial printers print an entire line at a time.

Line printers capable of printing an entire line of output in a single step can print up to 2000 lines per minute (1600 characters per second). Printers working with microcomputers typically provide dot matrix print at a speed of 60–200 characters per second. Much slower letter-quality printers operate in the 10–50 character per second range.

In general, impact printers are slower than nonimpact printers. Laser printers for PCs can print eight pages per minute (130 characters per second). Dot matrix printer quality is generally much lower than letter quality and is used for less important documents and spread sheets.

Other Devices

There are some special-purpose devices in the systems environment that have unique capabilities. One is a computer output microfiche machine (COM) used by some insurance companies that need to store legal documents. A COM machine transfers information stored on a computer tape or disk to a piece of microfilm (called *microfiche*). These 4 × 6 inch microfiche cards can hold up to 270 pages of data with 99 lines per page. These machines are especially useful for producing parts lists for major assemblies such as automobiles and electrical components. The microfiche output can be duplicated and distributed to dealers. Retail supply depots for automobile parts or major appliance parts use microfiche to store information on parts in inventory.

Special-purpose graphics terminals used in CAD/CAM and commercial art have very high resolution capabilities (1000 × 1000 pixels). In addition, graphic documents can be created using plotters with multicolored pens to draw (rather than print) computer output. These

Sidney Writes Tickets

Sidney—a Citisource, Inc., device—is a limited-use personal computer that can be carried on a traffic cop's hip. It is designed to solve two problems: rejection of tickets by courts because of illegibility and quick identification of scofflaws and stolen vehicles.

Like other personal computers, Sidney has a processor, a screen, a keyboard, and a printer. These are squeezed into a package 9 inches long, 6 inches wide, and 6 inches deep weighing 5.5 pounds (not including batteries).

To write a ticket, Sidney prompts the officer through a series of decisions and beeps if a scofflaw or stolen vehicle is found. Special software allows the officer to enter as little information as possible: "P" for "Plymouth," "PO" for "Pontiac," and "POR" for Porsche.

The printer can produce a ticket in 25 seconds. At the end of the day, tickets and new information on stolen vehicles are transferred to a central computer when Sidney is recharged.

Adapted from "How Sidney of Citisource Produces Parking Tickets," *The New York Times*, January 22, 1986.

graphics devices are useful for illustrating major trends in data, such as profits and costs and sales.

As microelectronic components become smaller and more powerful, new jobs can be automated. One application currently being developed is, unfortunately, the automation of traffic ticket writing.

6.6 The Future

Advances in materials science, manufacturing, and concepts of computing promise to maintain the historic growth pattern in hardware power. Over the last 30 years, we have seen the cost drop by a factor of 10 each decade and the capability increase by a factor of at least 100 each decade (Office of Technology Assessment, 1985). There are four ways in which this momentum will most likely be maintained.

Increasing Switch Speed

A computer can work no faster than the speed required for each transistor, or switch, to turn on and off. In slow chips like the Intel 8088, used in many PCs, switches have a speed measured in nanoseconds (billionths of seconds). But some semiconductor experimental devices have been taken up to 20 picoseconds (trillionths of a second) before literally melting down (at these speeds, enormous heat is generated).

Some new experimental circuits are called *Josephson junctions*. While immersed in liquid helium at a temperature near absolute zero, these circuits have speeds of 4.2 picoseconds.

ATT's Bell Laboratories has recently tested a more ordinary semiconductor device immersed in liquid nitrogen that can operate at 5.8 picoseconds. Even more important, this same device can operate at room temperature at 10.2 picoseconds. This speed is thousands of times faster than that of commercial circuits (Datamation, 1986).

Shrinking Distances: Developing Superchips

A second way to speed up computation is to shrink the distance between components. Very fast switching devices or transistors are of little use if it takes a long time for information to flow among them.

The time it takes light (or electricity) to move 1/16th of an inch is 5.8 picoseconds. The Defense Department is sponsoring a $1 billion research program to develop a superchip by 1990. It is called a *very-high-speed integrated circuit*—(VHSIC, pronounced *vee-sic*). Using this chip, researchers have been able to shrink the distance between transistors on the chip from 3 microns (millionths of an inch) to 1.25 microns. The goal is 0.5 micron. A human hair is 100 microns thick. This size reduction will eventually permit clock speeds of up to 100 megahertz, 10 times faster than commercial chips today. (Office of Technology Assessment, 1985).

These faster chips may well provide better television pictures. Currently, chips are so slow that they can only modify and fine-tune television signals by rough aproximation. Superchips would permit nearly instantaneous picture processing and enhancement. (*New York Times*, 1985).

Limits to Hardware Solutions

Physical limits are being approached in the development of computer chips. Electrical signals can travel no faster than the speed of light, about 11.8 inches per nanosecond. Therefore, computers with a 1-nanosecond clock speed must be built within a cube approximately 12 inches per side so that an electrical signal can travel from one edge of the cube to another within 1 nanosecond. But this requires extremely tight packaging of circuits. In the largest supercomputer, the Cray-2, with a 4.1-nanosecond cycle time, there are more than 300 circuit modules, each 4 × 8 × 1 inch. Each of the modules generates 500 watts of heat and the whole machine generates 150 kilowatts—

the equivalent of 2000 75-watt light bulbs in a volume of 1 cubic foot! A super-supercomputer of the future operating at 1 nanosecond with current technology might generate well over 1000 kilowatts (National Bureau of Standards, 1986).

These physical limits to hardware stimulate interest in software solutions, which will be described here and in Chapter 7.

Parallel and Vector Processing

Superchips will do little good if they are put to work in the traditional sequential computer, which executes one instruction after another, as virtually all computers since 1940 have done. If problems could be broken down into common elements (vectors), and if these parts of programs could be processed in parallel (as opposed to sequentially), the overall computing speed could be radically increased even if there were no progress in materials.

What is parallel processing? Humans are frequently able to make amazingly correct judgments by considering a number of factors

Parallel Processing

Dr. Joseph F. Traub, chairman of Columbia University's computer science department, illustrates parallel processing with a 20-questions example. If I say I am thinking of a number between 1 and 16, let's suppose that the number is 11. You ask if the number is between 1 and 8 and I say no. You ask if it is between 9 and 12 and I say yes. You ask if it is between 9 and 10 and I say no. Finally, you ask if it is 11 and I say yes. You never need to ask more than four questions if you ask the right ones.

Computers work that way too—sequentially, one question at a time. But there are ways to ask all of the questions at once and get answers right away. Convert all of the numbers to binary so that 11 becomes 1011. Now you can ask, does the number have a 1 in the right-hand column? In the second column from the right? In the third colum? In the fourth column?

Here you also ask four questions, but the answers are independent of one another, meaning that they can be asked at once. A simple idea but profound in its consequences.

Adapted from "Hardest Questions Prove Alluring," *The New York Times*, April 23, 1985.

simultaneously. For instance, they can rapidly "size up" a highway situation in which an oncoming car has swerved into a driver's lane to pass another car. Most humans will almost instantly react with fear and drive over to the shoulder to avoid the oncoming car. A sequential computer would take a long time to conclude and act in a similar situation. An example of parallel processing has been described on the preceding page.

Getting a group of processors to attack the same problem all at once is easier said than done. It requires rethinking of the problems. Complex defense systems such as the Strategic Defense Initiative ("Star Wars"), which must track thousands of incoming supersonic projectiles, may require 10,000 processors working in parallel.

One way in which problems can be rethought is to break them down into vectors or similar operations. A supercomputer works in this fashion. A program can be broken down into groups of similar operations (e.g., additions, subtractions, square roots, and so forth). Each type of operation can be allocated to a specially designed processor that operates in parallel with others. In the end, the separate results must be brought together for a single solution.

So far, only parts of large programs can be split in this fashion. Nevertheless, processing can be speeded up to run 10 to 100 times faster than the fastest mainframe sequential processors.

Storage Technology

Magnetic storage media (tape and disk) will continue to be the main storage technologies and will be further enhanced in speed and capacity over the next decade. Industrywide user requirements for disk space are growing at a rate of 10% per year. Laboratory disk machines hold twice as much data per inch as existing models (densities of 25,000 bpi) and have a data transfer rate 50% higher than that of existing models (4.5 megabytes per second). Every 3 years, the data density capability doubles.

Optical disk storage is capable of much greater density than magnetic materials. Using a laser, binary patterns are burned into an aluminum disk similar to a home recording CD. One kind of data optical storage, *compact disk, read-only memory* (CD-ROM), is used to store large volumes of data such as those in dictionaries, encyclopedias, and other documents. Another type of storage called *write once, read many* (WORM), is used for backup storage of data that change over time, much like a tape backup. Erasable optical disks are also under development (National Bureau of Standards, 1986).

A single optical compact disk can store 550 megabytes, and much higher densities are possible. The disks do not need protection from the environment, can be stored like tapes, and never crash. On the other hand, the data transfer rate is slow (175,000 bytes per second), as is the access speed. Clearly, optical disks will play an important role in large-volume data storage.

6.7 Summary

The functionality of an information system, that is, how useful it is to the organization, depends in part on the power of the computer technology. The modern computer installation has five major components: a CPU, input and output devices, secondary storage, and a communications controller.

The CPU is the center of the computer, where the manipulation of symbols, numbers, and letters occurs. Its speed and capacity determine what kinds of information system functions the computer can handle. The CPU has three components: primary memory, an arithmetic-logic unit, and a control unit.

Digital computers store and process information in the form of binary digits called *bits*. A string of 8 bits is called a *byte*. There are several coding schemes for arranging binary digits into characters. The most common are EBCDIC and ASCII.

Computer technology has gone through four generations, from vaccum tubes to transistors, integrated circuits, and VLSIC. Each advance in technology has brought corresponding advances in telecommunications, input-output devices, and software. Depending on their size and processing power, computers are categorized as mainframes, minicomputers, or microcomputers.

Computerized data can reside in primary or secondary storage. Primary storage, the fastest and most expensive form of storage, is found in the CPU. Secondary storage is nonvolatile and is used for relatively long-term storage of data. The principal forms of secondary storage are tape and disk. Tape stores records in sequence, whereas disk permits direct access to specific records and is much faster than tape. Data entry has increasingly moved from a separate task accomplished by a data entry staff to on-line or point of origin data entry. Output devices, both printers and terminals, have increased in speed and density, permitting higher-quality graphics and letter-quality print.

The future will see steady and impressive progress toward faster chips at lower cost. The computing speed of chips is limited by the speed of light (the ultimate barrier) and by heat generation (a technical problem). Software innovations in parallel processing would permit must faster completion of certain tasks.

Key Words

CPU	Control unit
System configuration	Byte
Nanosecond	ASCII
Gigabyte	EBCDIC
Primary storage	RAM
Arithmetic-logic unit	ROM
	Magnetic core

Integrated circuits
PROM
EPROM
Computer generations
Microprocessor
Data word length

Cycle speed
Secondary storage
Direct access storage devices
Point of origin automation
Parallel processing
Optical storage

Review Questions

1. What are the major components of the CPU?
2. What major time and size distinctions are useful in the computer world?
3. Compare a microcomputer's primary memory size to that of a mainframe.
4. What problems of coordination exist in a computing environment and why?
5. Describe the relation between a bit and a student database.
6. What are ASCII and EBCDIC and why are they used? Why cannot true binary be used in a computer as a machine language?
7. What is the parity of a machine?
8. Describe how information is stored in primary memory.
9. Describe the major generations of computers.
10. What are the four different types of semiconductor memory and where are they used?
11. Describe the difference between a mainframe, a minicomputer, and a microcomputer.
12. What is the difference between tape and magnetic disk storage? Where is each useful?
13. Describe the major input and output devices.
14. What is interactive data entry?
15. What are the major limits to further advances in computer chips?

Discussion Questions

1. Assume that a recent technical breakthrough permits primary memory in computers to operate 10 times faster than before. Discuss some of the implications for an organization that utilizes this new technology.
2. A manufacturer of small motors would like to distinguish its products from those of others by introducing computerized controls over motor speed and power consumption. What kinds of hardware devices might be appropriate?
3. A small business is interested in computerizing some of its recordkeeping functions with a microcomputer. What considerations are important in deciding the size of primary and secondary storage? What special features for secondary storage should be considered?
4. A firm would like to introduce computers into its order entry

process but feels that it should wait for a new generation of machines to be developed. After all, any machine bought now will quickly be out of date and less expensive a few years from now. Discuss.

RISC at Hewlett-Packard

The Hewlett-Packard 3000 series of business computers is believed to be the second most widely used computer family in the world. When Hewlett-Packard introduced the Spectrum series 930 and 950 processors for the 3000 series, it claimed that their architecture would be the "data salvation" of information systems managers.

Both the 930 and 950 machines are based on reduced instruction set computing (RISC) architecture. Faster processing is possible because only the most commonly used instructions have been hard-wired into the system. They can be implemented directly by the CPU in tandem with new compilers. Instructions thus can be executed on virtually every machine cycle. Hewlett-Packard believes that this information architecture can meet all information system processing needs for at least the next decade.

The 930 and 950 processors are said to be fully compatible with existing Hewlett-Packard computer, software, and peripheral products. The company notes that application programs can be directly transferred to the new computers without compiling.

Information system managers often gauge a computer's performance by its mips (million instructions per second) rating. The series 930 machine executes 4.5 mips and the series 950 executes 6.7 mips. However, Hewlett-Packard believes that these new machines actually perform at much higher levels than their mips ratings. The company notes that mips ratings are inversely proportional to the average number of cycles required to execute each instruction. Computers based on RISC, unlike traditional mainframes, allow most instructions to be executed in a single cycle.

Hewlett-Packard claims that the RISC computers reduce cycle time by simplifying the data path. Traditional computers spend a considerable amount of cycle time performing routine tasks such as loading, storing, branching, and adding in response to the program code. The RISC processors store frequently used instructions and data in a large number of registers, which operate up to eight times faster than main memory. The RISC machines also feature a 128-byte cache memory, which matches the processor speed and acts as a buffer, thereby benefiting the main processor memory.

The series 930 supports up to 24 megabytes of main memory; the series 950, 64 megabytes. Hewlett-Packard says that its tests and evaluations demonstrate that the RISC processors have made substantial breakthroughs in increasing system performance while reducing computing costs. Both machines are smaller than their predecessors and consume less power. They support coprocessors and can function as multiprocessors; thus, they are suitable for more technical operations such as floating-point calculations.

Adapted from "HP Expects RISC Systems to Meet MIS Needs for Next Decade," *Infosystems*, May 1986.

Case Study Questions

1. Some analysts believe that Hewlett-Packard is staking its future on unproven mainframe technology. Discuss.
2. What kinds of systems are most likely to benefit from this type of computer hardware?
3. What criteria should an information system manager use in deciding whether to purchase a Hewlett-Packard RISC computer?

References

Athey, Thomas H., and Robert W. Zmud. *Introduction to Computers and Information Systems*. Glenview, IL: Scott, Foresman and Company, 1986.

Datamation. "Hardware Off-Line," April 1, 1986.

National Bureau of Standards. *Forecast of Technological Trends and Implications For Management*. Mimeo. Washington, D.C.: National Bureau of Standards, 1986.

New York Times. "Hardest Questions Prove Alluring," April 23, 1985.

Office of Technology Assessment. *Information Technology R&D*. Washington, D.C.: Office of Technology Assessment, U.S. Congress, 1985.

CHAPTER 7

Information System Software

▬ OUTLINE

205

In a recent survey of its work force, Corning Glass Works, Inc., in Corning, New York, found that 80% of its domestic workers were using personal computers (PCs) on the job. This high level of utilization reflected the Corning management's decision in recent years to move the entire company toward user-friendly computing environments where end users could directly control applications development. At the time, Corning knew that greater access to corporate data was needed. The number of mainframe accounts at Corning grew from 30 in 1980 to over 1600 in 1988. Now that Corning has raised its general level of computing, it is going back to specialized applications for specific jobs like sales, marketing, and manufacturing, according to the professional and office systems manager, Dennis Lockard. Two important constraints on further development of computing are its high cost and confusing software options. Lockard employs a staff of 12 to evaluate software for use at Corning. "100 copies of a $500 piece of software is $50,000. The hidden cost is having 400 to 500 users on different versions of the software, or in the worst case, on the wrong software altogether." Managing the software has become a full time job.

Adapted from "Looking at Corning Glass," *Business Computer Systems*, January 1985.

The usefulness of a computer depends on the software available and on the ability of management to evaluate, monitor, and control the utilization of software in the organization.

In this chapter the student will learn:
- The major types of software.
- How software has evolved and how it will develop in the future.
- The major types of information processing.
- The major computer software languages.
- How to select the proper software.

7.1 Introduction

In the last 20 years, a great deal of attention has been paid in the public media to advances in hardware. While these developments have been truly astounding, without systems and application software the computer revolution would have been stillborn. It is through software that computer hardware becomes useful to human beings and organizations. The functions of software are to (1) manage the computer resources of the organization, (2) develop tools that human beings can utilize to take advantage of these resources, and (3) act as an intermediary between stored information and organizations.

Major Types of Software

There are three major types of software: system software, application software, and dialogue/query software. Each of these kinds of software specializes in a unique set of capabilities.

The different kinds of software are illustrated in Figure 7.1. The software that operates on a computer can be thought of as a set of nested boxes, each of which must interact closely with the other boxes surrounding it. As shown in Figure 7.1, the system software surrounds and controls access to the hardware. Application software must work through the system software in order to operate. Last, dialogue and query languages frequently have to work through application software and translators, and finally through system software, in order to operate. Each of these kinds of software must be specially designed for a specific machine in order to ensure its compatibility.

System software includes the management software of computer resources, such as processing time, storage and memory, printers, terminals, communication links, and all of the peripheral equipment

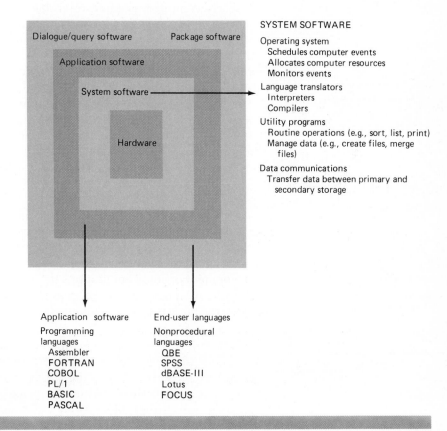

SYSTEM SOFTWARE

Operating system
  Schedules computer events
  Allocates computer resources
  Monitors events

Language translators
  Interpreters
  Compilers

Utility programs
  Routine operations (e.g., sort, list, print)
  Manage data (e.g., create files, merge files)

Data communications
  Transfer data between primary and secondary storage

Dialogue/query software   Package software
Application software
System software
Hardware

Application software

Programming languages
  Assembler
  FORTRAN
  COBOL
  PL/1
  BASIC
  PASCAL

End-user languages

Nonprocedural languages
  QBE
  SPSS
  dBASE-III
  Lotus
  FOCUS

FIGURE 7.1
Overview of software.

that surrounds a central processing unit (CPU). The special set of computer programs that manages and controls these aspects of the central processing organization and utility is called an *operating system*. Whenever users interact with a computer, even a PC or microcomputer, the interaction is controlled by and takes place through an operating system.

The first and second generations of computers in the 1940s and 1950s had no operating system. That is, human operators submitted each job, waited for the results, and, when there was time, loaded the next job. In other words, the operating system of the computer was the human user. In the early 1960s, and especially with the third generation of machines in the mid-1960s, operating systems appeared that took over the job of human computer operators.

These early operating systems automated job scheduling by storing programs that would be used as applications streamed into the computer. They also stored or *queued* jobs and applications that were waiting to be processed. In today's operating systems, a number of jobs are read onto disk and the operating system works its way through the queue.

Each computer manufacturer has its own unique operating software. Programmers who write system software are called *system programmers*. Occasionally, operating systems need modification; for this reason, every organization with a large computer installation employs several, sometimes a team of, system programmers to make changes in operating systems.

Application software refers to programs that are written for or by a user in order to accomplish a specific task. There are special software languages (to be described) that are used to develop applications. Programmers who write application systems are called *application programmers*.

A third kind of software, which appeared in the early 1980s, is a special kind of application software that has a variety of names: *end user, fourth generation, dialogue/query,* and *very-high-level* languages. Included are software tools that can be used directly by end users or by professional programmers. Chapter 15 provides an extended discussion of these software tools. In general, these tools permit the development of some applications by end users without professional intervention. They also make possible great productivity enhancements for professional programmers.

Generations of Software

Corresponding to the four generations of hardware evolution are the four generations of software development (see Figure 7.2). The first generation of software was the machine language used with the computers of the 1940s. Machine language—the 0s and 1s of binary languages—was the only way in which programmers could communicate with the computer. End users who wanted applications had to work with specialized programmers who could understand, think,

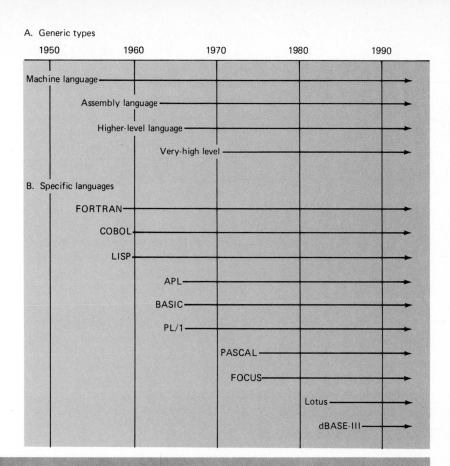

FIGURE 7.2
Generations of software.

and work directly in the machine language of a particular computer. Programming in 0s and 1s, reducing all statements such as *add*, *subtract*, and *divide* into a series of 0s and 1s, made early programming a slow, labor-intensive process.

The second generation of software occurred in the early 1950s with the development of assembly language, which permitted for the first time the use of language-like acronyms and words such as *add*, *sub* (subtract), and *load* in programming statements. Translation of assembly code into machine code was accomplished by a *compiler*— software that translates English language-like statements into a specific series of machine digits (0s and 1s).

The development of third-generation computer software extended from the mid-1950s to the 1970s. In this period, the first higher-level languages emerged. These were more sophisticated extensions of assembly language, permitting mathematicians for the first time to work with computers through the use of languages such as FORTRAN (FORmula TRANslation program). Mathematicians were now able to define variables with statements such as $Z = A + B$. The software translated these definitions and mathematical statements into a series of 0s and 1s. COBOL (COmmon Business Oriented Language) permitted the use of English statements such as *list employee number* and *sort employees* to be used by programmers, who did not have to think in terms of 0s and 1s.

These higher-level languages are so called because each statement in COBOL or FORTRAN generates multiple statements at the machine language level. The use of these complicated languages requires much faster, more efficient compilers to translate higher-level languages into machine codes.

A fourth generation of software development began in the late 1970s and is still in progress. In this period, packaged programs that perform limited functions first appeared. These programs do away, to some extent, with the need for application programmers. End users—noncomputer specialists—can interact with a computer directly, without the help of professionals. Using the software package LOTUS, for instance, users can create their own financial spread sheets and manipulate data without programmer intervention. Such sophistication by nonspecialists using FORTRAN would have been impossible in the 1960s and 1970s.

Relationship Between Hardware and Software

There is, of course, a clear relationship between the increasing capacity of hardware and software. Each new generation of software requires more and more primary storage area, faster compilers, and larger secondary storage. Higher-level language programs require a huge amount of memory. For instance, to load the Statistical Package for the Social Sciences (SPSS), the program alone may require over 200K (200,000 bytes of primary storage). If work space is included within primary memory, up to 512K may be required.

Four Major Trends in Software

There are four major trends in software that are likely to dominate throughout the 1990s: (1) the revolution in user interfaces, (2) the drive for data access, (3) the growing orientation toward personal use software, and (4) the development of huge, integrated programs operating on mainframes that support end users' needs for data and organizational needs for communication and control.

A long-term view of software shows that the major trend is to increase the ease with which users can interface with the hardware and software. In the next few years, this trend is expected to accelerate. Newer software is being designed that offers higher resolution for graphics and manuscript display to ease the interaction between humans and computers. There are also special monitors that allow high-resolution display. Software is becoming more interactive through the use of pointer devices such as the computer mouse, the touch screen, and the graphic pad. Compared to a keyboard, these

Voice Access to Computers

Kurzweil Applied Intelligence in Waltham, Massachusetts, is testing an automatic typewriter that will print any of 10,000 spoken words. Hundreds of office and factory workers, airline baggage handlers at Chicago's O'Hare airport, and F-16 pilots use voice recognition software to dial telephones, separate bags, and arm missiles. In older systems, the human voice was sampled and translated into zeros and ones. A special pattern for each phonetic sound by a given speaker was developed, and the computer would match up the speaker's digital voice pattern for the letter *s* with the stored digital template. New systems rely on a pattern recognition technology first advanced by Victor Zue, an MIT scientist. Zue found that no matter who speaks, every human generates a characteristic spectrogram or pattern when speaking the letter *s* in a word like *stop*. Zue taught himself how to recognize these patterns, and then he taught a computer how to recognize them. An important user of this breakthrough is the National Security Agency, whose supercomputers can pick out of millions of simultaneous conversations key words and suspicious calls.

Adapted from "His Master's (Digital) Voice," *Time* magazine, April 1, 1985.

permit much faster interaction between the computer and the user. Voice recognition software is another rapidly developing field.

A second major long-term trend that is expected to accelerate throughout the 1990s is data access for end users. When end-user computing and microcomputers first appeared in corporations, the central data processing groups often promised that their cherished data would never be made available to nonspecialists on a daily basis. This situation has changed dramatically to the point where the only question is how well users can be brought into direct contact with corporate data.

Virtually all major mainframe database management systems now have extraction programs that can send data to end-user networks, work stations, and PCs. There are more than 500,000 LOTUS 1,2,3 packages already in the marketplace, not to mention several hundred thousand other microcomputer word processor and number crunching software that uses corporate data. Almost all of the major PC software packages are now compatible with a wide variety of telecommunications networks linking them to mainframe files.

A third trend involves more marketing of software directly to individual end users. Up to the 1980s, software was marketed almost entirely by specialized software firms to specialist data processing personnel. Throughout the 1990s, we can expect to see software increasingly marketed to actual end users. This trend carries both risks and benefits. On the one hand, the marketplace will encourage the development of software that satisfies end users. On the other hand, end users are frequently incapable of making the best decisions about which software to buy. The risk of buying the wrong software will increase as individuals become bombarded with advertising claims that are difficult to evaluate.

A fourth major software trend derives from what we have already said. Significant advances in end-user computing, as well the

Can Software Control Star Wars?

A debate has split the academic and industrial software community concerning the feasibility of designing software which can operate an anti-ballistic missile defense of the United States. The programming tasks are enormous: the system would have to track about 30,000 warheads and 300,000 decoys, allocate weapons, keep track of warheads slipping through, and coordinate all defensive devices. From 10 million to 100 million lines of code would be required, according to experts at MIT. But as many large organizations from the IRS to NASA have found out, large programs brim over with errors and bugs, some of which are not revealed for years. Only through exhaustive testing and actual use do bugs appear. ATT found, for instance, that for every 1000 lines of code in its programs, there were 300 errors. Scientists do not know if the number of bugs grows exponentially or proportionally to the number lines of code. In any event, there would be no opportunity to test the space defense software. Modular approaches would be tried first, breaking complex programs into manageable modules. But the whole system would require effective communication between modules (more programs), and the whole system would be under enemy attack. It would have to work flawlessly the first time.

Adapted from "A Debate About Star Wars," *The New York Times*, September 15, 1986.

advent of sophisticated on-line customer account systems like bank teller machines and brokerage firm accounts, require the development of very large, sophisticated mainframe programs to manage data for the organization as a whole, prepare data for end users, integrate parts of the organization, and permit precise control and coordination of organizational decision making. These very large mainframe systems integrate what were once separate systems (e.g., accounts receivable and order processing) operated by separate departments (e.g., accounting and sales). Oddly enough, the growth and development of end-user computing with microcomputers will strengthen the coordinating and technical role of the central information systems group. In order to make a powerful contribution to the firm, microcomputers must be tied into corporate data and telecommunications networks.

Organizations are becoming increasingly dependent on these organizationwide systems. One example of the problems posed by very large systems is apparent in the proposed Strategic Defense Initiative.

7.2 Operating System Software

One way to look at a computer's operating system is as the system's chief manager. Operating system software decides which resources will be used, which programs will run, and how the programs will be translated into machine language.

Functions and Components of an Operating System

An operating system performs three functions. First, it *allocates resources* to the application jobs in the execution queue. It provides locations in primary memory for data and programs and controls the input and output devices such as printers, cathode ray tube (CRT) terminals, and telecommunication links.

Second, the operating system *schedules the jobs* that have been submitted. There are several ways in which jobs come to the attention of the CPU operating system. First, telecommunications links present many jobs to the CPU and handle the switch from one job to another. There is always at least one job waiting for the CPU from the telecommunications control devices. Second, a job can be submitted directly by a system operator. Third, batch jobs are executed, some of which may have a high priority, and the operating system must be aware of them. For instance, special priority classifications are given to payroll and administrative tasks of the organization. The operating system must schedule these jobs according to organizational priorities.

Third, the operating system *translates the higher-level language programs* and dialogue/query programs such as BASIC, COBOL, FORTRAN, and FOCUS, into machine language that the computer

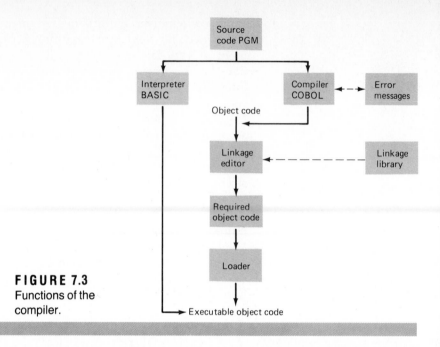

FIGURE 7.3
Functions of the
compiler.

can execute. This part of the operating system is called a *compiler* or *interpreter* and is described more fully in the section "Types of Programming Languages" (see Figure 7.3).

There are two major components of an operating system: *control* programs and *processing* programs. Control programs focus on the managerial aspects of executing a program. They load the program, supervise its execution, and read and respond to the job control statements in each program that tell the system what kinds of data and hardware are required for the job. Control programs also handle the input and output from the program. That is, they operate printers, CRT devices, and so forth.

In order to execute a program, however, a number of information processing tasks must be completed. The program must be compiled into object language. Certain routine tasks are referred to in all programs, and the operating system draws on these subprograms to accomplish them (such as taking a square root). These subprograms are called *processing programs*. They include utility programs (which can perform simple functions like copying, listing, and sorting) and statistical programs. Utility programs are normally supplied by computer manufacturers as one part of the operating system. They may be called by any application to be used by that program.

Obviously, the operating system of a major mainframe computer is itself a very large program. For this reason, only parts of the operating system are actually stored in the primary storage area. Most of the operating system is stored in a copy on a disk, to which the primary memory has very rapid access. Whenever parts of the operating system are required by a given application, they are transferred from the disk and loaded into the mainframe CPU. The device on which a complete operating system is stored is called *the system residence device*.

Multiprogramming

How is it possible for up to 1000 users sitting at remote terminals to use a computer information system simultaneously if, as we stated in the previous chapter, a computer can execute only one instruction from one program at a time? The answer is that the computer has a series of specialized operating system capabilities.

The most important of these capabilities is *multiprogramming*. Multiprogramming permits multiple programs to share a computer system's resources at any one time through concurrent use of a CPU. By *concurrent use* we mean that only one program is actually using the CPU at any given moment but that the input/output needs of other programs can be serviced at the same time. Small processors, termed *channels*, which are limited in their circuitry to input/output processing functions, actually provide all the input and output. Two or more programs are active at the same time, but they do not use the same computer resources simultaneously. With multiprogramming, a group of programs takes turns using the processor.

For instance, three programs in a multiprogram system can be stored in primary memory (see Figure 7.4). The first program executes until an input/output event is read in the program. At this point, the CPU directs a communication channel either to read the input and prepare it for entrance into the CPU or to take the output and print it on a printer. Meanwhile, the CPU begins to execute the second program until an input/output statement occurs. At this point, the operating system switches to the execution of the third program, and so forth, until eventually all three programs have been executed. Notice that the interruptions in processing are caused by events that take place in the programs themselves. In this manner, many different programs can be executing at the same time, although different resources within the CPU are actually being utilized.

The advantages of multiprogramming can be seen when one compares multiprogramming systems to the first computing systems, which executed only one program at a time. Before multiprogramming, whenever a program read data off a tape or disk or wrote data to a printer, the entire CPU came to a stop. Because the data transfer rate of input/output and secondary storage devices is extremely slow compared to that of mainframe computers, programs requiring extensive input and output—as most programs do, especially in business—run inefficiently. With multiprogramming, the CPU utilization rate is much higher.

	(A)		(B)		(C)
	Operating system		Operating system		Operating system
		16K	Program A	18K	Program A
	Single	16K	Program B	10K	Program B
	Program	16K	Program C	8 K	Program C
			Unused		Unused

FIGURE 7.4

Multiprogramming versus single-program execution.
Multiprogramming permits a number of programs to execute
concurrently. Several complete programs are loaded into memory.
Then, when individual programs reach an input or output event, the
operating system switches to a different program. This memory
management aspect of operating systems greatly increases
throughput by better management of high-speed memory and
slower input/output devices. (A) A traditional system with no
multiprogramming. (B) Memory divided into fixed partitions. This leads
to some waste, as no program is exactly the size of the partition.
(C) A variable-sized memory partition. From *Introduction to
Computers and Information Systems Without BASIC* by Thomas H.
Athey and Robert W. Zmud. Copyright © 1986 by Scott, Foresman
and Company. Reprinted by permission.

The result is much higher throughput—a measure of the total
amount of processing that a computer system can complete in a given
period of time.

Obviously, one constraint on multiprogramming is that the
number of lengthy programs that can be stored in main memory is
limited. However, virtual storage—to be described—reduces this
drawback.

Time Sharing

Time sharing is a second form of processor management. It is like
multiprogramming in that resources are shared but the basis for
sharing is *time driven* rather than *event driven*. In a time-sharing
environment, thousands of users are each allocated a tiny slice of
computer time (2 milliseconds). In this time slot, each user is free to
perform whatever operations are required; at the end of this period,
another user is given a 2-millisecond time slice of the CPU. This
arrangement permits many users to be connected to a CPU simultaneously, with each receiving only a tiny amount of CPU time.
However, it must be remembered that the CPU is operating at the

FIGURE 7.5

Time sharing in a multiprocessing system. A time-sharing system allocates a fixed amount of time to each user. This allows access to a CPU from many remote terminals. Often time-sharing systems are owned by vendors who sell computer time and charge a usage fee based on the time actually spent computing. The system shown here is also a multiprocessing system because it uses several different processors at once. A communications processor handles telecommunications and all remote terminals. Other processors are called *channels* and *secondary CPUs*. They handle input/output operations and can also act as a backup to the main CPU.

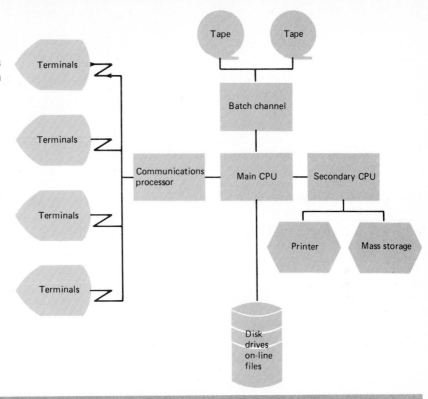

However, it must be remembered that the CPU is operating at the nanosecond level and in a brief 2 milliseconds, a CPU can accomplish a great deal of work (see Figure 7.5).

Virtual Storage

Virtual storage was developed after some of the problems of multiprogramming became apparent. First, in multiprogramming systems, two or three large programs can be read into memory, but unfortunately, a certain part of main memory generally remains underutilized because the programs add up to less than the total amount of CPU space available. Second, given the limited size of CPU memory, only a small number of programs can reside in primary storage at any given time. For example, many business programs may require up to 200K of storage, and the mainframe machine may have only 1 megabyte of storage. Therefore, only a few programs can reside in memory at any given time.

Virtual storage is based on the fact that in general, only a few statements in a program are actually being utilized at any given moment. In virtual storage, a program is broken into a number of separate segments called *pages* (see Figure 7.6). The actual breakpoint between pages can be determined either by the programmer or by the

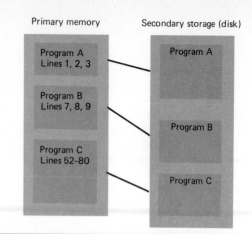

FIGURE 7.6

Virtual memory systems. In virtual memory operating systems, programs are broken down into pages or lines. Individual program pages are read into memory only when needed. The remainder of the program is stored on disk until it is required. In this way, very large programs can be executed by small machines. Alternatively, a large number of programs can be executed concurrently.

operating system. Generally, a single program module is considered to be a page of a program. In virtual storage and processing, every program is divided into pages, each of which is relatively small (about 2–4 kilobytes). This permits a very large number of programs to reside in primary memory, inasmuch as only one page of each program is actually located there.

All other program pages are stored on a peripheral disk unit until they are required for the program to execute.

This system provides a number of advantages. First, the CPU is utilized more fully. Many more programs can be in the CPU because only one page of each program actually resides there. Second, programmers no longer have to worry about the size of the primary storage area. Before virtual storage, programs could obviously be no larger than the CPU's main memory that stored them. With virtual storage, two things become possible: Programs can be of infinite length and small machines can execute a program of any size (admittedly, small machines will take longer than big machines to execute a large program). With virtual storage, there is no limit to a program's primary storage requirements.

Multiprocessing

Multiprocessing is the use of several independent computing units in the same system environment. This may involve the simultaneous use of two CPUs to accomplish the work in a given system, dividing the work between the CPUs. A more common form of multiprocessing involves the use of a single large main CPU that is connected to multiple channels. Each channel is a processing unit that handles input and output from the main CPU and coordinates the work of slower input/output devices (such as card readers and printers) (see Figure 7.5).

With a multiprocessing system, it is possible to service up to 1200 remote terminals through a communications processor while concurrently processing large batch jobs such as accounts receivable or payroll.

7.3 Types of Information Processing

There are two types of information processing that result from the hardware described in the previous chapter (data storage devices such as tape and direct access disk devices) and from the operating system software described in this chapter: batch processing and immediate processing.

Batch Processing

Batch processing occurs whenever changes or inquiries are sent to a file and stored for a while before processing. After this period, a processing run is made to update the file or to obtain the information requested. Batch runs can be made on any basis (daily, weekly, monthly, or as required). Figure 7.7 illustrates a typical batch sequential processing run utilizing sequentially organized data on magnetic tape. In this form of processing, the transactions are batched together and processed periodically on a sequential basis. Throughout the 1950s, 1960s, and 1970s, most data processing was done this way.

As long as tape was the predominant secondary storage medium, batch processing was the only method available. There was no direct access to data.

A second kind of batch processing that has become possible through the development of direct access storage devices (DASD) permits the updating of direct access files on a batch basis. Payroll or other benefit files can be stored on a DASD and updated once a week. This is becoming an increasingly common way of utilizing certain records, especially when the information does not have to be used on-line (that is, directly) for interactions with a client or customer.

Immediate Processing

In immediate processing, the transactions are processed to update a file or to make any changes in a file immediately or shortly after the transactions occur in the real world. This method is illustrated in Figure 7.8.

On-Line Direct Access

There are several variations on immediate processing. One variation is referred to as *on-line direct access systems*. This simply means that several terminals are in direct communication with the CPU (and therefore are on-line). These terminals are used to make changes in or retrieve data from files held on DASD.

Real-Time Systems

Another kind of immediate processing is called a *real-time system*. This includes any system that captures data about the environment

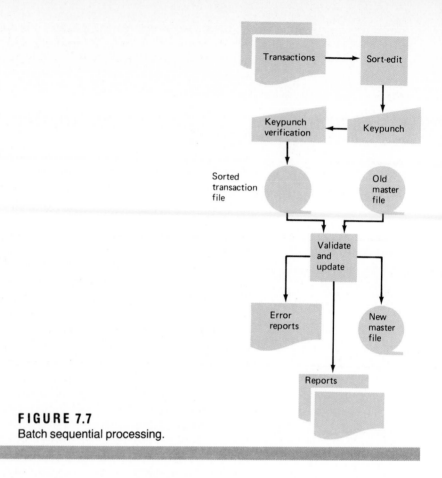

FIGURE 7.7
Batch sequential processing.

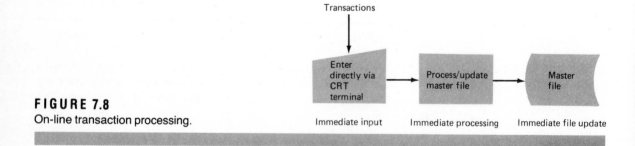

FIGURE 7.8
On-line transaction processing.

immediately or shortly after the event occurs. A point of sale system, which immediately records the sale of products in a grocery store, is a real-time system. An airline reservation system is another example. These real-time systems have the primary advantage of being able to provide timely information in a rapidly changing environment, such as in the reservation of airline seats. By contrast, there is little point in having a payroll or accounts payable processed by a real-time system.

Thus, in these terms, the airline reservation system is a real-time, on-line, direct access system. More simply stated, it is one kind of immediate, direct processing system.

7.4 Application Software

Up to this point, we have talked about operating system software that seeks to optimize the utilization of the hardware and to meet the demands of users. Application software, by contrast, is primarily concerned with accomplishing the tasks of end users. There are many different types of application programming languages.

Types of Programming Languages

The evolution of software was described in previous sections. At first, machine language was the only way to program a computer. In the early 1950s, machine language was replaced by the first language that used symbols rather than 0s and 1s. This first symbolic language was called *assembly language*. In the middle and late 1950s, there appeared the first *high-level languages* (FORTRAN and COBOL), which used no 0s and 1s but instead relied on English-like or mathematic-like phrases. In the late 1970s, very-high-level languages began to appear.

Assembly and high-level languages must be translated into machine code by a compiler, interpreter, or assembler. The high-level language is called *source code* and the machine language version is called *object code*.

Most high-level languages are translated into object code by a *compiler*—a piece of software that translates an entire program into machine code and lists all syntax errors in the source code. These *error messages* are then used to debug the program. The object code program is then stored and used in production, while the source code program is stored and used only for correcting the production program.

Some languages, like BASIC, do not use a compiler but an *interpreter*, which translates each source code statement one at a time into machine code and executes it. Interpreter languages like BASIC provide immediate feedback to the programmer if a mistake is made, but they are very slow to execute because they are translated one statement at a time.

An *assembler* is a software tool that translates assembly language into machine code.

Popular High-Level Languages

While managers should not be expected to have an intimate knowledge of programming, they should know the general nature and uses of the major programming languages. They should also have some experience in working with one program (e.g., BASIC) to understand the nature of programming and the difficulty of writing powerful software. We will now briefly describe the more popular high-level and very-high-level languages. Chapter 15 gives a comprehensive description of very-high-level languages.

Assembly Language

Many programmers still prefer to write programs in assembly language because it gives them close control over the hardware and very efficient execution. Like machine language, assembly language is designed for a specific machine and specific microprocessors. For instance, the Intel 8088 chip used in an IBM PC has its own assembly language. In general, there is a one-to-one correspondence between machine language and assembly language. Each operation in assembly corresponds to a machine operation. On the other hand, assembly language does make use of certain mnemonics (e.g., *load*, *sum*) and assigns addresses and storage locations automatically.

While assembly language gives programmers great control, it is costly in terms of programmer time, difficult to read and debug, and difficult to learn.

FORTRAN

FORTRAN (FORmula TRANslation) was developed in 1956 to provide an easier way of writing scientific and engineering applications. FORTRAN is especially useful in processing numeric data. Many kinds of business applications can be written in FORTRAN, it is relatively easy to learn, and contemporary versions (e.g., FORTRAN 77) provide sophisticated control structures. It is well supported by vendors.

FORTRAN is not very good at providing input/output efficiency or in printing and working with lists. The syntax is very strict and keying errors are common, making the programs difficult to debug.

COBOL

COBOL (COmmon Business Oriented Language) came into use in the early 1960s. It was originally developed because the Defense Department wished to create a common administrative language for internal and external software.

COBOL was designed with business administration in mind, for processing large data files with alphanumeric characters (mixed alphabetic and numeric data) and repetitive tasks like payroll. Its primary data structures are records, files, tables, and lists. COBOL is easily learned by business analysts. As the most widely used programming language, it is widely supported by external groups, and there is an abundance of productivity aids.

The weakness of COBOL is a result of its virtue. It is poor at complex mathematical calculations. There are many versions of COBOL, and not all are compatible with each other. Lengthy COBOL programs, some hundreds of thousands of lines long for major payroll programs, for example, can become so complex as to be virtually incomprehensible.

BASIC

BASIC (Beginners All-purpose Symbolic Instruction Code) was developed in 1964 by John Kemeny and Thomas Kurtz to teach students at Dartmouth College how to use computers. Today it is the most popular programming language on college campuses and for microcomputers. BASIC can do almost all computer processing tasks from inventory to mathematical calculations. It is easy to use, demonstrates computer capabilities well, and requires only a small interpreter.

The weakness of BASIC is that it does few tasks well even though it does them all. There are no sophisticated control or data structures, which makes it difficult to use in teaching good programming practices. While BASIC has only a few commands and is easily learned, subsequent versions of the language that have tried to add to the early syntax make the new versions of BASIC incompatible with the old ones. Therefore BASIC programs often cannot be moved from one machine to another. They are not "portable."

PL/1

PL/1 (Programming Language 1) was developed by IBM in 1964. It is the most powerful general-purpose programming language because it can handle mathematical and business applications with ease, is highly efficient in input/output activities, and can handle large volumes of data.

Unfortunately, the huge volume of COBOL and FORTRAN programs written in the private sector at great cost cannot simply be jettisoned when a newer, more powerful language comes along.

There are an estimated 12 billion lines of COBOL code in production in the United States. This represents an investment of over $2 trillion.

PL/1 has not succeeded largely because programmers trained in COBOL could not be convinced to learn an entirely new language and business organizations could not be convinced to spend millions of dollars rewriting their software. PL/1 is, moreover, somewhat difficult to learn in its entirety.

Other Languages

There are many other programming languages that do not have wide application in the business world. *PASCAL* was developed in the early 1970s as a tool for teaching programming by the Swiss computer science professor Niklaus Wirth. PASCAL has sophisticated control and data structures and a simple, powerful set of commands. PASCAL is weak at file handling and input/output, and is not easy for beginners to use.

Someday COBOL may be replaced by another language called *ADA*, which is being developed by the Defense Department. ADA is designed to standardize the development of military command/control operations. It is a sophisticated, efficient, and powerful language. As a result, it can be very complex and hard to understand. Nevertheless, for on-line applications like customer information systems, electronic funds transfer, and point of sale systems, it is a useful language.

In the mid-1970s, programmers at Bell Laboratories developed a language called C. This is a powerful language that, like assembly language, permits direct control over the hardware, but like high-level languages it also has powerful commands that permit the rapid development of programs. It is, unfortunately, not easily learned by the beginner.

How to Choose Programming Software

There are many programming languages to choose from. It is important for managers to know the differences between languages and very important to use clear criteria in deciding which language to use. The most important criteria will now be discussed.

Appropriateness

Some languages are general-purpose languages that can be used on a variety of problems, while others are special-purpose languages suitable for only limited tasks. Special-purpose graphics programs are excellent at creating tables but poor at routine processing of transactions. COBOL is excellent for business data processing but poor at mathematical calculations. Language selection involves identifying the use and the users.

Sophistication

High-level languages should have sophisticated control structures and data structures. *Control structures* shape the outcome of programs by providing clear, logical, structured programs that are easy to read and maintain. It may be impossible to create a table and then look up values in it unless the language has a table *data structure* capability. Languages should be selected that support many different data structures.

Organizational Considerations

In order to be effective, a language must be easily learned by the staff, easy to maintain and change, and flexible enough so that it can grow with the organization. These organizational considerations have direct long-term cost implications.

In general, sophisticated, well-structured languages are easier to learn and much easier to maintain over the long term than less sophisticated languages.

Support

It is important to purchase software that has widespread use in other organizations and is supported by many consulting firms and services. It is often less expensive to purchase software written elsewhere, or to have a service firm write it, than to develop the software internally. In these situations, it is crucial to have software that is widely used.

A different kind of support is the availability of software editing, debugging, and development aids. Because so many organizations use COBOL, there are hundreds of contemporary software devel-

Born-Again Systems

The Pacific Gas and Electric Company of San Francisco had a choice. It could totally rewrite its customer billing system or it could try to restructure the code into a manageable form. The customer billing system consisted of 900,000 lines of code written from 1969 to 1972. More than 4300 patches and changes had been made since then, only some of which were documented. Programs were taking too long to run and programmers could no longer understand their logic, let alone maintain and change them.

Rather than spend $13 million rewriting the applications, PG&E decided to hire a consulting firm to restructure the code, using one of the many new recoders on the market. IBM and several other vendors sell COBOL restructuring tools that can take tangled, complex COBOL programs and produce modularized modern programs.

Adapted from "Born Again Systems," *Computer Decisions*, April 8, 1986.

opment products available to assist the programming staff. The same cannot be said of ADA, a recently developed general-purpose language.

For instance, many organizations inherit poorly written, so-called spaghetti code programs that have been patched and repaired hundreds of times. After many years, perhaps decades, few people in the organization understand how such programs work. Maintenance is difficult and expensive. Now a number of new products can take poorly written COBOL programs and transform them into sophisticated, modular, documented COBOL, which is easier to maintain.

Efficiency   Although a less important feature than in the past, the efficiency with which a language compiles and executes remains a consideration when purchasing software. Languages with slow compilers, or interpreters like BASIC, can be expensive (in terms of programmer costs) to operate and maintain. In general, fourth-generation languages are very slow and expensive in terms of machine time. As discussed in later chapters, these languages are entirely inappropriate for high-speed transaction systems, which must handle thousands of transactions per second.

Some programming languages are more efficient in the use of machine time than others. PL/1, for instance, requires a large section in memory for its compiler, whereas PASCAL and BASIC have much

Software Selection Criteria at Fortune 1000 Companies

A recent survey of Fortune 1000 computer sites found that the most important software selection factor was documentation, cited by 72% of respondents. Documentation explains in plain English how a program works and is essential if on-site staff want to modify the software. Ease of use and production functionality were cited by 67% of respondents, and vendor support was cited by 53%. Less important criteria (fewer than 20% cited these factors) were price, vendor size, and vendor financial stability.

Adapted from "Third Annual Survey of Corporate Software Buyers," *Software News*, January 1985.

simpler interpreters that require little primary memory. In any event, efficiency should be judged in terms of both machines and personnel. As machine costs fall in price, personnel costs become very important in choosing a language. As machines become less expensive per unit of memory, languages that are inefficient in machine time but very efficient in programmer time will grow in importance.

7.5 Very-High-Level Languages

In the mid-1970s, a number of very-high-level computer languages appeared. With the development of microcomputers in the 1980s and the advent of database management systems, a flood of end-user and advanced languages appeared on the marketplace. Very-high-level languages are sometimes called *fourth-generation* languages, although the precise meaning of this term is not clear.

Very-high-level languages have become so important in the systems world that several chapters in this text focus on their specific use and role. Database management systems, described in the following chapter, usually contain an end-user, very-high-level language. The chapters dealing with microcomputers (Chapter 10) and end-user system development (Chapter 15) also contain examples of very-high-level languages.

There are two advantages of very-high-level languages. First, they allow nonprofessional end users to develop their own applications. Second, they offer order of magnitude increases in professional programmer productivity.

There are six types of very-high-level languages. *Query languages* (such as IBM's Query by Example) allow a user to query a file or database for an ad hoc (not predefined) inquiry. Such a query might be "List all employees in Department Y less than 50 years of age." *Report generators* are used to extract data from files and create customized reports. *Graphics languages* (such as SAS Graph) retrieve data from files and display it in user-defined graphic formats. *Application generators* contain preprogrammed modules that can generate applications based on the user's specification of what needs to be done. The decision on how to do it is left to the software, and the user simply specifies what needs to be done (an example for PCs is a relational database product like dBASE III Plus or Paradox).

Two kinds of very-high-level languages are used primarily by professional programmers to speed development. *Very-high-level programming languages* (like FOCUS or NOMAD 2) are general-purpose tools that can be used to develop applications with very few lines of code. Application development time can be compressed considerably for some simple applications. *Application packages* (like Management Science of America's MSA Payroll) are prewritten applications that can be modified for the user's organization and often have a special development language capability.

As we will discuss in Chapters 14 and 15, there are important limitations to these advanced tools. They are applicable only to certain limited areas of application development. Nevertheless, these new tools represent a major and growing trend toward end-user application development.

Software Solutions to Application Logjams

Fortune 1000 companies reported in a recent survey that application backlogs (applications waiting for development) were 15 months for mainframes, 9 months for minicomputers, and 6 months for microcomputers. Twenty-six percent of the respondents said that they would try to buy more ready-to-run packages in order to decrease the backlog. An equal percentage said that they would buy more program generators. Only 16% said that they would hire more software workers.

Adapted from "Third Annual Survey of Corporate Software Buyers," *Software News*, January 1985.

7.6 Summary

The usefulness of information systems depends to a great extent on the quality of software. The major types of software are system, application, and dialogue/query software. Each of these types serves a different purpose. Software has evolved along with hardware. The general trend is toward user-friendly high-level languages that both increase professional programmer productivity and make it possible for complete amateurs to use information systems.

Traditional programming languages, of course, are still important. Operating system software and large application development software like COBOL continue to play a predominant role in building large systems.

Operating system software acts as the chief manager of the information system, allocating system resources to many users. Many advances in computing like multiprogramming, time sharing, and virtual storage are dependent on operating system software.

Application software is used by application programmers and some end users to develop systems and specific applications for payroll and accounts receivable and for calculating projected sales.

Dialogue/query software usually cannot be used to develop an entire system. Instead it is used to permit untrained end users either to use a system or to build a simple application (e.g., to create a report).

Choosing the right software for a particular application requires some knowledge of the strengths and weaknesses of specific software products. Equally important is the support for software packages given by vendors, the ability of the organization to absorb new software, and the efficiency of the software in executing specific tasks.

Key Words

System software	Immediate processing
System programmers	On-line direct access
Application software	Real-time systems
Dialogue/query software	Assembly language
Generations of software	High-level language
User interface	Source code
Access to data	Object code
Multiprogramming	Compiler
Time sharing	Interpreter
Virtual storage	Assembler
Multiprocessing	Report generators
Batch processing	Application generators

1. What are the major types of software? How do they differ in terms of users and uses?
2. What are the major generations of software and approximately when were they developed? Give some examples of high-level application languages.
3. What is a high-level language?
4. What is the relationship between hardware storage capacity and speed, on the one hand, and the sophistication of software on the other hand?
5. What are the four major trends in software? Can you think of more than the four described in the text?
6. What is the operating system of a computer? What does it do?
7. What is the difference between an assembler, a compiler, and an interpreter?
8. Describe multiprogramming, time sharing, multiprocessing, and virtual storage. Why are they important to the operation of an information system?
9. Distinguish between batch processing and immediate processing. Describe different types of immediate processing.
10. Name three popular high-level programming (application) languages. Describe their strengths and weaknesses.
11. What are the major factors to consider when selecting application software?
12. What are very-high-level languages? Give some examples.

1. Explore with another student some useful applications in the college or university for voice recognition software.
2. Describe some of the new organizational and decision-making problems raised by software likely to be used in the Strategic Defense Initiative (described in the vignette entitled "Can Software Control Star Wars?")
3. Your firm wishes to develop a system that will process sales orders and update inventory. The programmers in your Information Systems department wish to use assembly language to write the programs for this system. Is this a good idea? Discuss.

The Software Interfacing Predicament

Data centers today are under pressure to do more for their organizations than ever before. With fewer technical resources, they must support increasingly sophisticated software for an expanding community of end users. End users complain because they spend too much time accessing layers of systems before they can get to the actual system that does their work. Many mistakes occur because screens and data are not presented to end users in a consistent way.

Data centers must also simplify software-to-software communication. Very few of their systems communicate with each other. Be-

cause software is not truly integrated, interfaces must be created between the software products that each data center uses for production control, tape management, or disk management. Two interfaces, one for each product, are required to connect two pieces of software. To connect three software products, six interfaces must be designed. Joining four products entails 12 interfaces, 3 per product. This interfacing predicament is illustrated in Figure 7.9. To interface 14 different products, a data center must support 182 different interfaces. To add just one new product, 28 new interfaces would be required to communicate with all of the others.

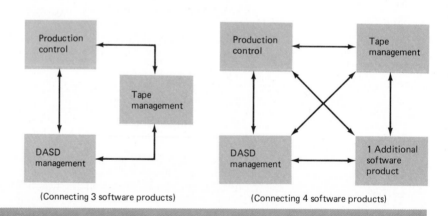

(Connecting 3 software products)   (Connecting 4 software products)

FIGURE 7.9

The interfacing predicament. This figure illustrates the increasing complexity of integrating different pieces of software within the same computing environment in the organization. To connect two different pieces of software, two interfaces are required (one per product). To connect three products, as illustrated above, requires six interfaces. It will take twelve different interfaces to connect four products (three per product), as illustrated above on the right. If a data center wishes to connect 14 different software products and interface to every one 182 different interfaces would be needed. Adapted from "A Software Architecture for the Future," *Infosystems,* June 1986.

UCCEL, a Dallas-based independent software supplier, is developing a solution called SYNOVA, which will enable software products to be fully integrated with each other and easily customized. Instead of interfacing products so that end users would have to navigate through various systems to access their data, UCCEL is trying to create a truly integrated software environment where users would only be concerned with accessing information. The current profusion of hard-coded interfaces between individual software products would be replaced by an integrating environment responsible for passing information to and from individual products, combining the information, and presenting it to the user as required.

SYNOVA session services are planned to allow easy access to concurrent sessions with different software products. These products include UCCEL products, products of other vendors such as the Customer Information Control System (CICS), one of IBM's on-line teleprocessing software systems; Information Management System (IMS), one of IBM's database management systems; IBM's Time-Sharing Option (TSO); Roscoe; and in-house developed software. Users can have access to more than one session at one time and can move freely among them from a single terminal.

In contrast, Virtual Telecommunications Access Method (VTAM), IBM's strategic access method, does not permit access to more than one application at a time. An end user working on one system who wants something from a different system must log off the first system and log on to the second. UCCEL estimates that in a typical data center it takes about 5 minutes to log off one system and log on to another. An end user who does this 12 times a day loses more than one-half of a working day per week.

SYNOVA dialogue services help data centers customize systems, consolidate screens, and make formats consistent between products. These capabilities can be of great value, for example, in tracking reports that are late or lost. Without integration of software products, one would have to check the report distribution system to see if the report was printed. If it was not, one would have to check the production system to see if the job to create the report had been run. If problems were detected, one would have to reference a problem management system to find out the status of the problem. Through SYNOVA's dialogue and communication services, on the other hand, all information concerning the report could be extracted automatically from various systems and presented to the user on a consolidated screen.

UCCEL expects SYNOVA to help data centers establish standards across products. Specialists who require months or years of training to learn the idiosyncracies of each software system will no longer be necessary.

Adapted from "A Software Architecture for the Future," *Infosystems*, June 1986.

Case Study Questions

1. UCCEL believes that the primary concern of data centers that adopt SYNOVA will shift to what kind of information is to be shared between products rather than how it is shared. Discuss.

2. Some authorities believe that it is not desirable for an organization to use too many different types of software. What problems discussed in this article support this point of view? What are some other reasons why an

organization might want to control the number of computer languages and types of software it supports?

3. Suppose you are a data center manager in charge of all of the operating system software for an organization. Under what circumstances might you consider adopting an approach such as SYNOVA? Under what circumstances would this approach not be desirable? Discuss.

CHAPTER 8

The Organization of Information: Files and Databases

OUTLINE

(*Continued on next page.*)

Robert Pennington, special agent for the Florida Department of Law Enforcement, uses a relational database called dBASE III PLUS on a personal computer (PC) to catch drug smugglers. In seconds the department gets information on criminals and suspects that once took days to gather.

Pennington notes that he has a file of associates of some criminals and a file of criminals, and in a few seconds he can create a new file of all criminals who have the same associates. With wiretap information, every call has data elements associated with it such as the number dialed, the time, and date. All of this information used to be put on 3 × 5 cards and filed in shoe boxes. When a supervisor wanted to know 'who called this number?', his department used to spend days sprawled on the floor sorting through the 3 × 5 cards.

Now the department has a file of target suspects and a file of all wiretap numbers. In seconds it can find out if suspects are calling its target numbers, or who is calling the target numbers, and then add their names to its associates file.

Adapted from "DBASE Tracks Crime On-Line," *Computerworld*, May 5, 1986.

Agent Pennington's system provides a good example of how hardware, software, and file organization techniques can contribute to flexible access to information. These techniques are referred to collectively as *database management systems*.

In the previous two chapters, we have described information system hardware and software. This background will prove useful in understanding database management systems and file organization. In this chapter the student will learn about:

■ File organization and management.
■ The traditional information processing environment.
■ A contemporary database environment.
■ Types of database structures.
■ The role of data dictionaries.
■ The organizational requirements for building databases.

The organizational themes introduced in this chapter are explored in greater depth in Chapter 20. The student should also review the case study "Social Security Administration: Systems Modernization Plan."

8.1 Introduction

While computer hardware and software are vital elements in information systems, they work efficiently only when information is properly organized. There are many elements to the proper organization of information. Hardware—in the form of high-speed computers, telecommunications, storage, and output devices—is important. Special software is required to organize properly an organization's files—database software. But more important is a rethinking of the role of information in the organization. Briefly, information must be seen as a resource that should be consciously managed. This is a new idea in the history of organizations, which have tended to think of information as a bureaucratic necessity, red tape, something of little value, and certainly not something to manage.

Related to this changing conception of information is a changing emphasis in information systems. In the past, great emphasis was placed on *efficient storage and processing* of large, predetermined reports and outputs (e.g., payroll checks). Once systems succeeded here, a new emphasis emerged in the late 1970s on *widely dispersed access* to corporate information by end users often untrained in the use of computers. This new emphasis required new techniques of file organization.

The Centrality of File Management to System Performance

One purpose of an information system is to provide users with timely, accurate, and relevant information stored in computer files. In many organizations these goals are not met because of poor file management despite the use of excellent hardware and software.

The importance of file management should be obvious to anyone who has ever written a term paper using a 3×5 card index (all of us?). No matter how efficient the storage device (a metal box, a rubber band), if the cards are organized in random order, the resulting term paper will have little or no organization. Of course, given enough time, the information could be put in order, but unless an organizational scheme is decided on early, it often cannot be imposed later. Moreover, if the scheme is flexible enough and well documented, it can be changed to take into account your change in viewpoint as you write the term paper.

So also with large organizations: When computer files are poorly managed, they lead to information processing chaos, high costs, poor performance, and little if any flexibility. This occurs despite the use of the most modern hardware and software. There must be a conscious effort to manage the organization's information.

Intersection of Users, Programmers, and Analysts

Because the organization of files is so important to system performance, determining the file structure in an organization requires the cooperation of three groups: users, programmers, and analysts. The users are required to inform systems analysts regarding their need for timely, accurate, and flexible information. Systems analysts are responsible for translating user requirements into an appropriate file structure. Working with programmers, analysts shape the file environment by choosing hardware and software to meet users' needs. Programmers ultimately work with the data management software to deliver the information.

We will first describe a traditional information system environment where files are not consciously managed. The student should review the case study "Social Security Administration: Systems Modernization Plan" as an example of what happens to large organizations that fail to manage files.

8.2 The Traditional Data Processing Environment

Gordius, King of Phrygia in Greek mythology, tied an intricate, complex knot in a rope, of which it was said that he who untied the knot would be master of Asia. As it turned out, Alexander the Great cut the knot and went on to become master of Asia. Many organizations in the 1970s found they had tied themselves into an information system Gordian knot of their own making. Here we describe the knot. In the following section, we show how to untie parts of the knot and cut through the rest.

The Gordian Knot: Divisions, Functions, Files, Documents, Data Elements, Users, and Programs

Most organizations began information processing on a small scale, automating one application at a time. Systems in any company tended to grow organically, opportunistically, and not according to some grand plan. Each division of a multidivision company developed its own applications. Within each division, each functional area tended to develop systems in isolation from other functional areas. Accounting, finance, manufacturing, and marketing all developed applications suitable to their purpose.

Within each division, each functional area, and each "system," several, perhaps hundreds, of applications were developed. Figure 8.1 illustrates the traditional approach to information processing.

Each application, of course, required its own file and its own computer program in order to operate. In general, the files in an application area were some version of the functional area master file. For instance, there was one very large master personnel file containing most of the basic information on all employees in the company, including current position and salary. However, over time, a number

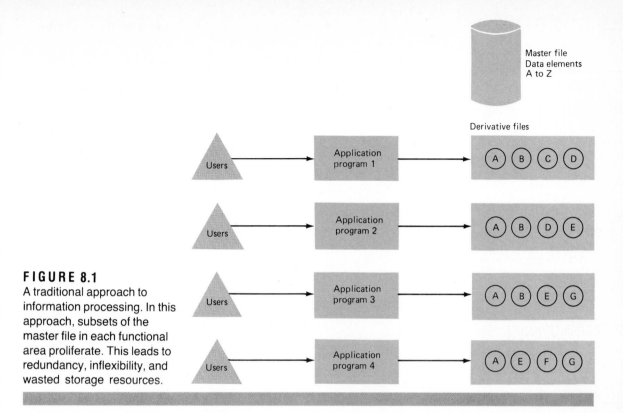

of smaller files extracted from the larger master file were spun off for processing efficiency as well as specialized applications. So, a payroll file was developed, followed by a medical insurance file, a pension file, a mailing list file, a list of employees who joined the company via prior acquisitions (who were paid using a different payroll program), and so forth until tens, perhaps hundreds, of files and programs existed.

In the company as a whole, there were several master files created, maintained, and operated by separate divisions or departments. Figure 8.2 shows three separate master files: customer, personnel, and sales. In order to create a simple report on, for instance, a list of sales personnel by annual sales and by principal customers, a complex "matching" program had to be undertaken in which each of the three files was read and pertinent records were copied and then recombined into an intermediate file. This file then had to be sorted in the desired sequence (sales personnel ranked by highest sales). Then a final report was issued. When data were stored on cards or tape, considerable labor costs were involved.

Of course, every data element in the various files, required a set of documents to support the file and help collect information. Often

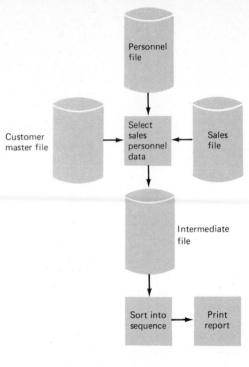

FIGURE 8.2
The pre-database environment. In a traditional file environment, a simple report consisting of a list of sales personnel by annual sales and principal customers required reading three separate files and creating an intermediate file and several programs. The lower panel shows the information selected from each file.

	Customer master file	Personnel file	Sales file
Salesperson data			
Number		X	
Name		X	
Sales data			
Amount of sales			X
Customer data			
Name	X		
Address	X		

the same data element was collected on multiple documents by different divisions and departments.

In time, the file structure of the organization became so complex that programmers developed specialties by focusing on subsets of files and programs. Eventually, the programs became totally dependent on a few programmers who understood the programs and files. If these programmers became ill or left the company, important applications failed.

There are several terms to describe this situation: the *traditional environment*; the *flat file organization* (because most of the data are organized in flat files); and the *data file* approach (because the data and business logic are tied to specific files and related programs). By any name, the situation results in growing inefficiency and complexity.

Some Problems

It should be apparent that after this process of automation goes on for several years (5–10), the organization becomes quickly tied up in knots of its own creation.

Some of the obvious problems will now be discussed.

Complexity

There now are hundreds of programs and applications, with no one in the organization who knows what they do, what data they use, what documents are needed, and who is using the data. There is no central listing of data files, data elements, or definitions of data. The organization is collecting the same information on far too many documents.

Data Redundancy

There are three kinds of data redundancy. First, divisions will collect the same information repeatedly from the client. Second, within the same division, many functional areas will collect the same information. For instance, within the commercial loans division, marketing and credit information functions need much of the same customer information. Third, the same information will be collected on multiple documents. (How many times, on how many documents, has the university asked you to fill in your name and address?)

Data Confusion

The same data element will have different meanings and definitions in different parts of the organization. Simple data elements like the fiscal year, employee identification, and product code can take on different meanings as programmers and analysts work in isolation on different applications.

Program–Data Dependence

Every computer program has to describe the location and nature of the data with which it works. These data declarations can be longer than the substantive part of the program. In a traditional environment, any change in data requires a change in all of the programs that access the data. Changes, for instance, in tax rates or zip code length require changes in programs—which may cost, in some cases, millions of dollars.

Costly Program Development

The development of new applications takes more time and money than it would otherwise. Programmers have to write complicated programs, stripping data elements from a variety of files to create new files. New programs require new arrangements of data. Users are dissatisfied with lengthy development periods.

Costly Maintenance

A large part of the programming effort involves updating data elements that are scattered throughout hundreds of files. In many instances, applications work with outdated data simply because of the difficulty of making updates.

Lack of Flexibility

A traditional system can deliver routine scheduled reports after extensive programming efforts, but it cannot deliver ad hoc reports or respond to unanticipated information requirements in a timely fashion. The information required by ad hoc request is "somewhere in the system" but is too expensive to retrieve. Several programmers would have to work for weeks to put together the required data elements in a new file. Users—in particular, senior management—begin to wonder at this point why they have computers at all.

Poor Security and Lack of Privacy

Because there is little control or management of data, access to and dissemination of information are virtually out of control. What limits on access exist tend to be the result of habit and tradition, as well as of the sheer difficulty of finding information.

Lack of Data Sharing and Availability

Because pieces of information in different files and different parts of the organization cannot be related to one another, it is virtually impossible for information to be shared or accessed in a timely manner.

Origins and Evolution of Database Software

When records were stored sequentially on cards and tape, the first efforts to deal with the record storage problem focused on efficient sorting and "stripping" *utility programs* that could remove the required data from multiple files. *Report generator programs* were developed to reduce the complexity of the programming needed to produce a report.

By the late 1960s and early 1970s, *file management systems* like Informatics, Inc.'s, Mark IV had been developed. These software packages permitted programmers and trained end users to access traditional COBOL files and to retrieve, manipulate, and print data. File management systems are an advance over traditional utility programs because they are easier and faster to use and can combine data from separate files rapidly and efficiently.

As disk technology became more common in the early 1970s, new ways of storing and manipulating data emerged. One technique was to chain records together on a disk by using embedded pointers. Pointers are actually new data elements that are added to each record and link records together.

Figure 8.3 shows a traditional flat file in the top panel. In the next panel, the records have been linked together using the attribute "sex." With these pointers embedded in the records, a list of all female employees can be easily produced without reading all of the records. The difficulty with this system is that the complexity of the file increases rapidly with the addition of more and more pointers.

Attribute name

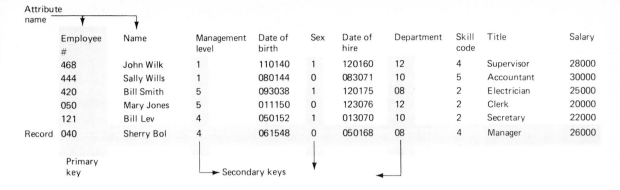

Employee #	Name	Management level	Date of birth	Sex	Date of hire	Department	Skill code	Title	Salary
468	John Wilk	1	110140	1	120160	12	4	Supervisor	28000
444	Sally Wills	1	080144	0	083071	10	5	Accountant	30000
420	Bill Smith	5	093038	1	120175	08	2	Electrician	25000
050	Mary Jones	5	011150	0	123076	12	2	Clerk	20000
121	Bill Lev	4	050152	1	013070	10	2	Secretary	22000
Record 040	Sherry Bol	4	061548	0	050168	08	4	Manager	26000

Primary key → Secondary keys

The use of embedded pointers to link records

Employee #	Name	Management level	Date of birth	Sex	Date of hire	Department	Skill code	Title	Salary	Embedded pointer
468	John Wilk	1	110140	1	120160	12	4	Supervisor	28000	420
444	Sally Wills	1	080144	0	083071	10	5	Accountant	30000	050
420	Bill Smith	5	093038	1	120175	08	2	Electrician	25000	121
050	Mary Jones	5	011150	0	123076	12	2	Clerk	20000	040
121	Bill Lev	4	050152	1	013070	10	2	Secretary	22000	468
040	Sherry Bol	4	061548	0	050168	08	4	Manager	26000	444

The use of an inverted file derived from the preceding file

Sex	Employee #
1	468
	420
	121
0	444
	050
	040

This inverted file is stored like any other file on tape or disk. For each special report, an inverted file must be created and stored.

FIGURE 8.3

Pre-database techniques for storing records. In a traditional two-dimensional flat file, information on entities is stored as individual records, each record containing the attribute values of the entity. This is a useful storage technique for answering the question "What are the properties of a given entity?" Different storage techniques are needed to answer the question "What entities have a given attribute value?" For instance, which employees are male (or female), or what are the skills of employees? To answer these questions in a tape or sequential file environment, the only alternative was to sort the file repeatedly until the records were arranged in the desired order. With the development of disks, more sophisticated techniques emerged. In one technique, pointers and chains were created by adding data elements to each record, linking records together. In a second technique, inverted files were created in which records were arranged by attribute, not by primary key. This system required knowing in advance precisely what attributes would be used to sort the records.

A second alternative is to invert the file. Like a subject catalog in a library, an inverted file lists entities by some attribute. In the bottom panel of Figure 8.3 an inverted file has been created, listing employees by sex. This file is stored on disk as a new file. The problem with inverted files is that for each special report a new file has to be created, and eventually disk storage space is depleted.

With these new techniques for storing and arranging data, generalized *database management systems* began to appear. Among the first was IBM's Information Management System (IMS), followed quickly in the mid-1970s by a number of others. After spread sheets and word processing software, database software is the most popular use of microcomputers. Over 500,000 copies of dBASE III—one of the most popular microcomputer products—are now being used.

8.3 A Modern Database Environment

Database technology and organization can find the common thread in the information processing Gordian knot and cut through many of the remaining problems.

Definition of a Database Management System (DBMS)

A *database* is a set of data organized to serve many applications efficiently by centralizing the data and minimizing redundant data. A *database management system* (*DBMS*) is simply the software that permits an organization to centralize data, manage them efficiently, and provide access to the stored data by application programs (see Figure 8.4).

There are four elements in the definition of a database that should be emphasized. First, there is the physical reality of data that reside on some physical device (usually a disk pack). This is called the *database*. Within this database are all of the *data elements* used by a functional area in the organization such as personnel. In contrast to the traditional systems, here the data are stored in one location, defined once and consistently, and used for all applications in that area.

The second element of the DBMS is a software package. This acts as an interface between application programs and the physical data files. When the application program calls for a data element like annual earnings, the DBMS finds this element in the database and presents it to the application program; the programmer does not have to define the data and then tell the computer where they are. Most of the data definition statements found in traditional programs are not needed. A DBMS package includes a special *data definition language* used by database programmers that provides this link between application programs and data files.

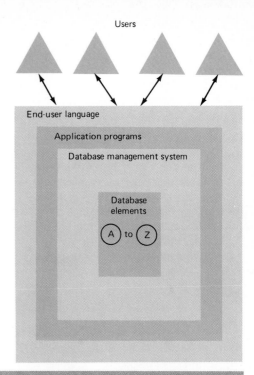

FIGURE 8.4

In a modern database environment, data are centralized in a single database. This database is created and maintained by a comprehensive software package, the database management system (DBMS). Within the DBMS, application programs are written to serve user needs. A key part of contemporary DBMS is a user-friendly language that even novice programmers can use.

The third element of the DBMS is a set of application programs that request data elements from the database. Application programs can be written in traditional languages like COBOL. Data elements called for by the COBOL programs are found and delivered by the DBMS. The programmer does not have to specify in detail how or where the data are to be found.

A DBMS comes with a package of software (see Figure 8.5). It generally includes a data definition language, a data manipulation language, and a query language. The data definition language is the formal language used by programmers to develop the database. Generally, the use of this language is reserved for systems developers.

Most DBMSs come with their own application development language called a *data manipulation language*. This is a user-friendly fourth-generation language containing a number of commands that permit end users and programmers to manipulate data in the database. Some commands from the most popular personal computer DBMS (dBASE III) are shown in Table 8.1. Examples of the use of database commands are given later in the chapter.

Complex programming tasks cannot be performed efficiently with typical DBMS languages. However, most mainframe DBMSs are

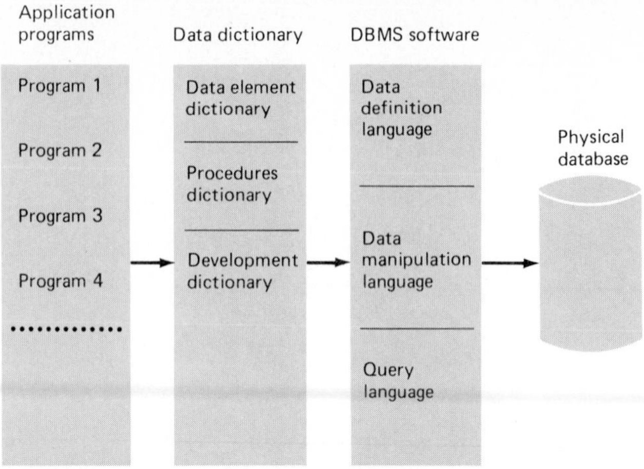

FIGURE 8.5

Elements of a DBMS. In an ideal database environment, application programs work through an active data dictionary that catalogs data elements and procedures (e.g., accepted means of calculating the return on investment for a specific firm). Application programs are written in a data manipulation language that is an integral part of the DBMS.

TABLE 8.1
dBASE III User-Friendly Database Language

Creation of Files	
Create	Creates a new database file
Join	Combines specified records and fields from two files
Sort	Creates a sorted version of a file
Copy	Copies a file in use to another file
Data Display	
Average	Displays the average for records specified
Count	Counts number of records specified
Report	Displays a report of the data
Text	Displays a block of text
Manipulating Data Bases	
Append From	Adds records from other files to dBASE III files
Erase	Deletes files from the directory
Use	Specifies the file to be used

Source: Adapted from *dBASE III User Manual*, Ashton-Tate Corporation, Torrance, California, 1985.

compatible with COBOL and FORTRAN, permitting greater processing efficiency and complexity.

Using the data manipulation language, programs can be written for a DBMS that permit ultimate end users (clerks, managers, and complete novices) to enter a few simple queries to produce reports. Most DBMSs have a query language capability.

The fourth element of a DBMS is a *data dictionary*. This is simply an automated file that stores definitions of data elements and data characteristics such as usage, physical representation, ownership (who in the organization is responsible for maintaining the data), authorization, and security. Many data dictionary products can produce lists and reports of data utilization, groupings, program locations, and so on.

Most data dictionaries are entirely passive; they simply report. More advanced types are active; changes in the dictionary automatically update all related programs. For instance, to change zip codes from five to nine digits, one could simply enter the change in the dictionary without having to modify and recompile all user programs using zip codes. Data dictionaries are discussed more fully in Chapter 20.

Logical and Physical Views of Data

Perhaps the most important feature of a DBMS is that it separates the logical and physical views of the data, relieving the programmer or end user from the task of understanding where and how the data are actually stored. Suppose, for example, that a professor of information systems wanted to know at the beginning of the semester how each of his current students in Information Systems 201 performed in the prerequisite computer literacy course (Computer Literacy 101) and what their current majors are. Using a DBMS supported by the registrar, the professor would like something like the report shown in Table 8.2:

TABLE 8.2
The Report Required by the Professor

Student Name	ID No.	Major	Grade in Computer Literacy 101
Lind	468	Finance	A−
Pinckus	332	Marketing	B+
Williams	097	Economics	C+
Laughlin	765	Finance	A
Orlikowsky	324	Statistics	B

Ideally, for such a simple report, the professor could sit at an office terminal connected to the registrar's database and write a small application program in the DBMS language to create this report.

The professor creates the desired logical view of the data (Table 8.2) and uses it to shape the application program. The DBMS then translates it into a physical view of the data. Finally, the DBMS assembles the requested data elements, which may reside in several different files and disk locations. For instance, the student major information may be located in a file called "Student Majors," whereas the grade data may be located in a file called "Transcripts". Wherever they are located, the DBMS pulls these pieces of information together and presents them to the professor according to the logical view requested.

The actual application program used by the professor might look something like Table 8.3:

TABLE 8.3
Application Program Used by the Professor

Use	'student majors'
Select	student name from 'student majors' where comp lit 101 not equal 0 and where Info Sys 201 = Current
Use	'transcript'
Join	'student majors' with 'transcript'
Project	student name, student ID, major, grade comp lit 101
Print	

Here two files (the student major file and the student transcript file) are joined and certain selected information is abstracted from the combined file. This abstracted information is then printed as the report.

Several DBMSs working on both mainframes and microcomputers permit this kind of interactive report creation.

In the real world, there are few registration systems that permit this kind of inquiry; most university registration systems were created in the 1960s and are of the traditional, flat file variety. In order to produce the report shown in Table 8.2, a COBOL programmer would have to be hired and about 200 lines of code written (at a rate of 20 lines per day), requiring 10 days of work, several test runs, debugging, and so forth. The labor costs alone would be around

$3000. Several files would have to be accessed, stripped of the relevant information, and a third file created. Hopefully, no data inconsistencies would be found.

Imagine the cost to the university if all professors requested this or similar reports. If the university tried to meet the demand, its information processing costs would balloon rapidly. Instead, most universities simply say that the information is "in the system somewhere but is too expensive to retrieve." Only an information systems professor could understand this reply.

Purposes of a DBMS

The preceding example illustrates several purposes of the DBMS. The advantages of this system are as follows:

- *Complexity* of the organization's information system environment can be reduced by central management of data, access, utilization, and security.
- *Data redundancy* can be reduced by eliminating all of the isolated files in which the same data elements are repeated.
- *Data confusion* can be eliminated by providing central control of data creation and definitions.
- *Program–data dependence* can be reduced by separating the logical and physical aspects of data.
- *Program development and maintenance costs* can be radically reduced.
- *Flexibility* of information systems can be greatly enhanced by permitting rapid and inexpensive ad hoc queries of very large pools of information.
- *Access and availability* of information can be increased.
- *Security and privacy* can be controlled.

Given all of these benefits of DBMS, one might expect all organizations to change immediately to a database form of information management. But it is not that easy, as we will see later.

Types of Database Structures

There are three logical database structures: hierarchical, network (or plex), and relational. In their evolution, early DBMSs were entirely hierarchical, with network and relational structures coming later. Each logical structure has certain *processing advantages* (and disadvantages) and certain *business advantages* in the sense of supporting particular business needs.

All database designs are concerned with the proper organization of information. Every information system—including a 3 × 5 card box of research notes—must keep track of certain *entities* (people, places, things) that have certain *attributes* (color, size, address, type) and certain *relations* among them [e.g., King Henry (1491–1547) (entity—a person) murdered (attribute—he was a murderer) his wife (Anne Boleyn—another entity), and King Henry was English (a relation)]. Hence a 3 × 5 card index might have an entry for King Henry describing his many attributes, one of which is murderer, and pointing to other entities or relations such as Anne Boleyn, England, and perhaps even "famous murderers."

A DBMS must be able to organize information as well as a card index file. There are three different ways in which the DBMS keep track of entities, attributes, and relations.

Hierarchical DBMS

Hierarchical DBMSs present data to users in a tree-like structure. The most common hierarchical DBMS is IBM's IMS. Within each record, data elements are organized into pieces of records called *segments*. To the user, each record looks like an organization chart with one top-level segment called the *root*. An upper segment is connected logically to a lower segment in a parent–child relationship. A parent segment can have more than one child but a child can only have one parent.

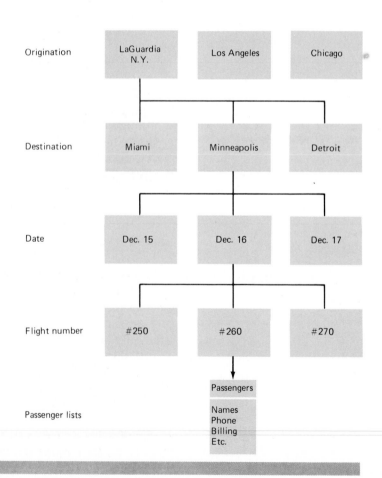

FIGURE 8.6
A hierarchical database structure for airlines reservations.

Figure 8.6 shows a hierarchical structure similar to the one used by airline reservation systems. The root segment is "Origination," which contains information about airports where flights originate. The first child is "Destinations" and contains information on where flights go. The second child is "Date" (airlines generally accept reservations one year in advance). The third child is "Flight Number" because on any given day there may be multiple flights to a single destination. The fourth child is "Passenger Lists," which contains information on the passengers (e.g., name, local phone number, when the reservation was made, billing address, form of payment, and, in some cases, seat location).

Behind the logical view of data are a number of *physical links* and *devices* to tie the information together into a logical whole. In a hierarchical DBMS the data are physically linked to one another by a series of pointers that form chains of related data segments.

Other means are also used to structure the data physically on the disk. The data can be broken down into directories and subdirectories. For instance, the information on international flights can be stored in a separate area from that on domestic flights and can be further stored in subdirectories on the basis of continents.

Figure 8.7 illustrates the use of pointers. Pointers are data elements attached to the ends of record segments on the disk directing the system to related children. In our example, if the root was LGE (New York's La Guardia Airport), the end of the Origination segment would contain a series of pointers to all of the destinations. In turn, at the end of the Destinations segment, there are pointers to the dates when the airline flies to that destination.

Because there are so many airports where flights originate, it would be convenient if the system could rapidly find the appropriate root segment, the origination airport. Rather than read each data segment (of which there are millions) one at a time until the right one (the root originating airport) is found, all originating airports can be stored in an *index* that lists the originating airports and their precise location on disk (see Figure 8.8). Once this root segment is identified, pointers take over to guide the search of the database.

Network DBMS

*Network DBMS*s are a variation of hierarchical DBMS. Indeed, databases can be translated from hierarchical to network and vice versa in order to optimize processing speed and convenience. Whereas hierarchical structures depict one-to-many relationships, network structures depict data logically as many-to-many relationships. The most common network DBMS for mainframe computers is IDMS from Cullinet Software.

A classic many-to-many relationship in which network DBMSs excel in performance is the student–course relationship. There are many courses in a university and many students, and students are usually enrolled in many courses. Another classic example of a

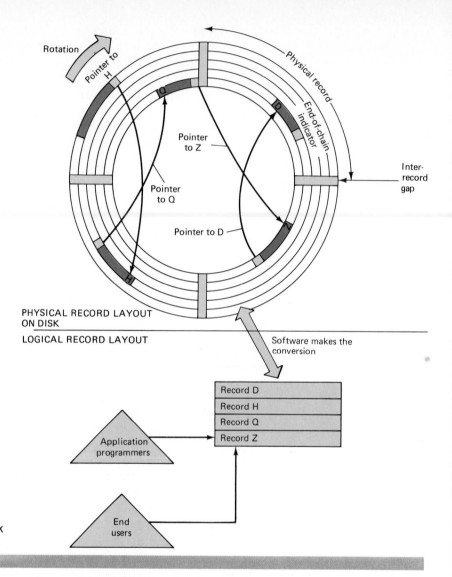

FIGURE 8.7
Pointers used on a disk to link records in a database.

FIGURE 8.8
Use of an index to speed access to a root data element in a hierarchical database.

Index of originating airports		Data elements
Airports	Disk location (track and cylinder)	
Chicago	01,001	
Los Angeles	01,005	
New York	01,006	
....		

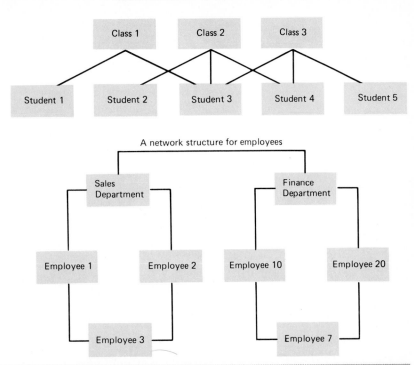

A network structure for students in a university

A network structure for employees

FIGURE 8.9
A network structure for
students in a university.

many-to-many relationship is the employee–department relationship (see Figure 8.9). During the course of their career, employees may work in many departments. A typical need of personnel managers is to know quickly where in the corporation an employee has worked and where he or she should be rotated for further training.

The data in Figure 8.9 could be structured hierarchically. But this could result in considerable redundancy; the same student would be listed on the disk for each class he or she was taking instead of just once. Network structures reduce redundancy and, in certain situations (where many-to-many relationships are involved), respond more quickly. However, a price is paid for this reduction in redundancy and speed: The number of pointers in network structures rapidly increases, making maintenance and operation more expensive.

The physical storage of data in network structures is similar to that of hierarchical structures. Pointers, indices, and directories are used to navigate through the database. All application programs must use these pointers and devices.

**Advantages and
Disadvantages**

There are several advantages to hierarchical and network databases. The principal ones are organization and access to data, efficient processing of transactions, and the ability to attach a large number of variable-length records to a given root. In our case, an airline could triple or quadruple the number of its flights from La Guardia to Denver's Stapleton Airport by simply adding record segments with no changes in file structure. This feature fits in very well with airline industry business practices, which call for rapid expansion of service to meet new demands. In network systems, employees can work in many different locations, with the information system adding additional record segments to department roots.

Also, because of its processing efficiency, a hierarchical structure is ideal for reservation transaction processing systems, which must handle millions of *structured routine requests* each day for reservation information. Here, once again, the logical structure of the business and of related business practices fit nicely with the structure and capability of the database technology.

Unfortunately hierarchical and network structures also have many disadvantages. All of the access paths, directories, and indices must be specified in advance. Once specified, they are not easily changed without a major programming effort. Therefore, these designs have *low flexibility*.

For instance, if you called an airline and said, "My parents gave me a ticket for a flight to an exciting resort, leaving from New York's La Guardia Airport, but did not tell me exactly where or when; where am I going?", you would discover that there is no way that the system can find the answer in a reasonable amount of time. This path through the data was not specified in advance. Or if the FBI called a major airline and asked about the movements in the last six months of a suspected terrorist traveling under a known assumed name, the airline could respond only after several months of programming effort (the records are kept for a period of 5 years on backup tapes).

Both hierarchical and network systems are programming intensive, time-consuming, difficult to install, and difficult to remedy if design errors occur. Ad hoc, English language-like inquiries to hierarchical designs are not well supported.

Relational DBMS

Relational DBMSs are the most recent and exciting database development. The most common mainframe relational database products are DB2 from IBM, Oracle from the Oracle Corporation, and INGRES from Relational Technology. For PCs, the leading products are Ashton Tate's dBASE III and Ansa Software Corporation's Paradox.

Relational DBMSs present data to users in the form of simple two-dimensional tables called *relations*. Most business information has always been organized in tables (see Figure 8.10). The relational model's tables are remarkably similar to ordinary flat files; therefore, we will refer to these tables as *files.*

Figure 8.10, for instance, shows a supplier file, a parts file, an

Supplier file

| Supplier name | Address | Credit | Part numbers | Supplier ID no. |

FIGURE 8.10
A relational database structure. Terminology in relational systems can be confusing. Records appear to be stored in flat files. These files are referred to in manuals and other literature as *relations* or *tables*.

Part file

| Part no. | Supplier ID no. | Name | Description |

Order file

| Order no. | Supplier ID no. | Delivery date | Order date | Totals |

Quotation file

| Supplier ID no. | Part no. | Quote price | Delivery time |

order file, and a quotation file. In each file, the rows are unique records and the columns are fields.

Most of the time, these files are used separately to produce reports such as a list of suppliers. Often, however, information from a number of files is needed. Here is the strength of the relational model: It can relate any piece of information stored in one file to any piece stored in another file *as long as the two tables share a common data element.*

For instance, in Figure 8.10 suppose we wanted to find the names and addresses of suppliers who could provide us with part 152 in less than 4 weeks. We would need information from two files: the supplier file and the quotation file (a file showing the most recent quotation and delivery time of specific parts by supplier ID). Note that these two files have a shared key (data element): supplier ID.

In a relational database three basic operations are used to develop useful sets of data: *select*, *project*, and *join*.

The select operation creates a *subset of all records in the file* that meet stated criteria. "Select" creates, in other words, a subset of rows that meet certain criteria. In our example, we want to select records (rows) from the quotation file where delivery time is less than 4 weeks and where the part number equals 152.

The join operation combines relational files to provide the user with more information than is available in individual files. In our example, we want to join the now shortened quotation file (only quotes involving part 152 and a delivery time of less than 4 weeks will be presented) and the supplier file into a single new result file.

The *project operation creates a subset of columns in a file*, permitting the user to create new tables that contain only the information required. In our example, we want to extract from the new result file only the following columns: supplier ID, name, address, part number, quote price, and delivery time.

Data are stored on the disk in many different ways. In certain instances, records are stored in flat files as users create them in some sequential order. In others, the tables are *virtual tables* put together by the system when called up by the user, and the actual records are stored using any of several different addressing techniques. Users can also create indices and inverted indices for frequently used relations.

Advantages and Disadvantages

The strengths of relational DBMSs are great flexibility in regard to ad hoc inquiries, power to combine information from different sources, simplicity of design and maintenance, and the ability to add new data and records without disturbing existing programs and applications. Unlike hierarchical DBMSs, the access paths are not prespecified. No great programming talent is needed to develop reports or make ad hoc queries to the relational DBMS.

The weakness of the relational DBMS is poor processing efficiency. These systems are painfully slow because they typically require many accesses to the data stored on disk in order to carry out the select, join, and project commands. Selecting one part number from among millions, one record at a time, can take a long time. Of course, the database can be indexed and "tuned" to speed up selecting. Relational systems do not have the large overhead of pointers carried by hierarchical systems.

Nevertheless, as indicated in the following story, hierarchical systems contain many desirable features that are not found in relational systems today. In the opinion of many, relational systems are not yet ready for high-volume production environments.

Even when tuned, relational systems are too slow for large-volume transaction processing systems (e.g., airline reservation systems or common on-line motor vehicle registration operations). Moreover, large relational databases can have a considerable amount of redundancy—the same data element stored in other, perhaps several, tables. This can present storage problems in some installations and may require a considerable investment in new hardware.

Also, updating of these data elements is not automatic in many relational DBMSs. For example, changing the employee status in one table will not necessarily change it in all tables. This means that more time will be spent in updating.

Despite these very real drawbacks, the major hardware and software vendors are rapidly improving relational database performance and functionality.

In the future, relational systems are expected to increase in speed, and special-purpose computers devoted to high-speed relational data processing will further add to this increase. Some relational systems now promise dynamic updating.

Relational Products Fail to Meet Some DBMS Criteria

Most relational products do not have *referential integrity*. For instance, in business logic, a purchase order cannot be written for a nonexistent vendor. In a hierarchical system, you can enforce this relationship through pointers from one data element to another.

Referential integrity ensures that changes made in one part of the database are automatically made in related parts. For instance, if you record the sale of an item in the sales file, you want the inventory file reduced by one. You want automatic updating. Most relational products—like IBM's Release 2 DB2—do not have this. Updates of tables and views have to be done one at a time.

Most relational products, lacking inter-item data pointers, cannot work efficiently in production environments. For instance, a purchase order is logically associated with a single vendor. Having accessed an order record, the DBMS should be able to access the associated vendor record with no more than one additional I/O action. In hierarchical systems, this is accomplished through pointers which point to the vendor information. In relational systems without pointers, an index of vendors indicating the precise disk address of the vendor must be searched first, and then the information is accessed (resulting in two I/O actions). If an index is missing because it was not anticipated, a full data file search is needed, reading one record at a time, resulting in perhaps hundreds of I/O actions.

Adapted from "Relational Products Failing to Meet Basic DBMS Criteria," *Computerworld*, April 15, 1985.

Table 8.4 summarizes some of the important characteristics of the three different approaches to databases.

Distributed Processing and Distributed Databases

Beginning in the early 1970s, the processing of information became more distributed with the growth of powerful telecommunications networks and the decline in computer system costs. Instead of relying on a single centralized mainframe computer to provide service to remote terminals, organizations began to install minicomputers and

DB2 Pushing IMS into the Grave

IBM's Release 2 of its relational database product for mini and mainframe computers, DB2, is about 30% faster than Release 1 and in some operations approaches the 18-year-old hierarchical Information Management System (IMS) in speed.

DB2 Release 2 can perform as many as 47.2 transactions per second (twice as fast as Release 1), which is just as fast as the standard IMS (although a special version of IMS called Fast Path can achieve speeds of 100 transactions per second). On the other hand, to achieve these speeds, DB2 may require up to twice as much processing power. That translates into much larger machines—which IBM also sells.

IBM is apparently abandoning its dual-product database strategy and focusing on increasing the speed and functionality of its relational product, DB2. The transition to DB2 will be painfully slow, however, because of the enormous number of applications written in the older IMS language.

To ease the transition, and to compete with third-party relational systems costing hundreds of thousands of dollars, IBM has aggressively priced DB2 at $16,000 for the initial license and a $2675 per month fee. While the fees add up, third-party systems have recently announced large price reductions.

Adapted from "New DB2 Pushing IMS into Grave," *Computer Decisions*, January 1986.

TABLE 8.4

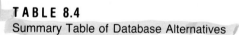

Summary Table of Database Alternatives

Type of Database	Processing Efficiency	Flexibility	End-User Friendliness	Organizational Change	Programming Complexity
Hierarchical	Very good; up to 100 transactions per second	Low	Low	High	High
Network	Very good; up to 75 transactions per second	Low	Low, moderate	High	High
Relational	Poor but improving; 20–50 transactions per second	High	High	Medium to high	Low

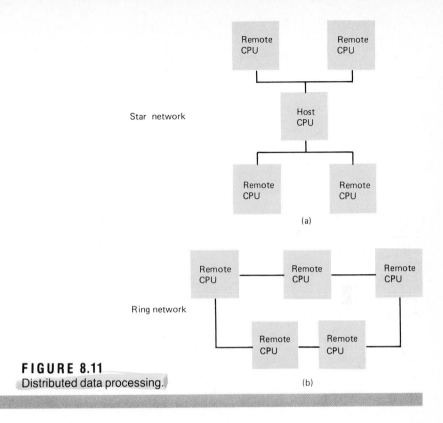

Star network

(a)

Ring network

(b)

FIGURE 8.11
Distributed data processing.

small mainframes at remote sites. These distributed processors directly serve local and regional branches, offices, and factories. Figure 8.11(A) illustrates a distributed processing system arranged in a star network, and Figure 8.11(B) illustrates a ring network. A fully connected network in which every distributed processor is connected to every other processor is also possible; however, this is not a common configuration.

It is only a short logical step from distributed processing to distributed databases. While early distributed systems worked with a single centralized database, over time the smaller local systems began to store local databases as well. It soon became obvious that the central database could be entirely distributed to local processors as long as some mechanism existed to provide proper updating, integrity of data, sharing of data, and central administrative controls (Martin, 1976).

There are several ways of distributing a database. The central database can be *partitioned* so that each remote processor has the necessary data on customers to serve its local area (see Figure 8.12). Changes in local files can be justified with the central database on a batch basis—often at night. Another strategy is to *duplicate* the central

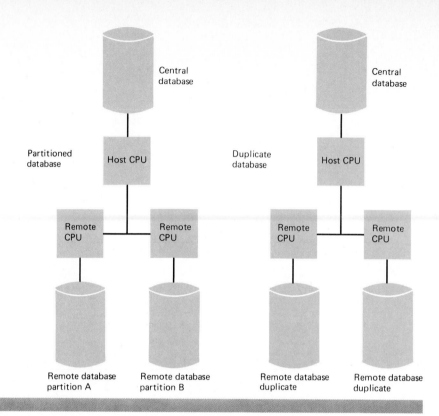

FIGURE 8.12
Distributed databases.

database at all remote locations. This also requires updating of the central database on off hours. Still another possibility—one used by very large databases like the FBI's National Crime Information Center—is to maintain only a central name *index* and to store complete records at local levels. A query to the central name index identifies a location where the full record can be found. Here there is no central database and no updating costs. Another variation is an *ask-the-network* schema. There is not even a central index of names. Instead, all remote processors are polled to find a complete record. The complete record is then transferred to whatever processor requests it (Laudon, 1986).

Both distributed processing and distributed databases raise interesting issues and problems. Distributed systems reduce the vulnerability of a single, massive central site. They permit increases in systems power by purchasing smaller, less expensive minicomputers. Finally, they increase service and responsiveness to local users.

Distributed systems, however, are dependent on high-quality telecommunications lines, which themselves are vulnerable. Moreover, local databases can sometimes depart from central data standards and definitions, and pose security problems by widely distributing

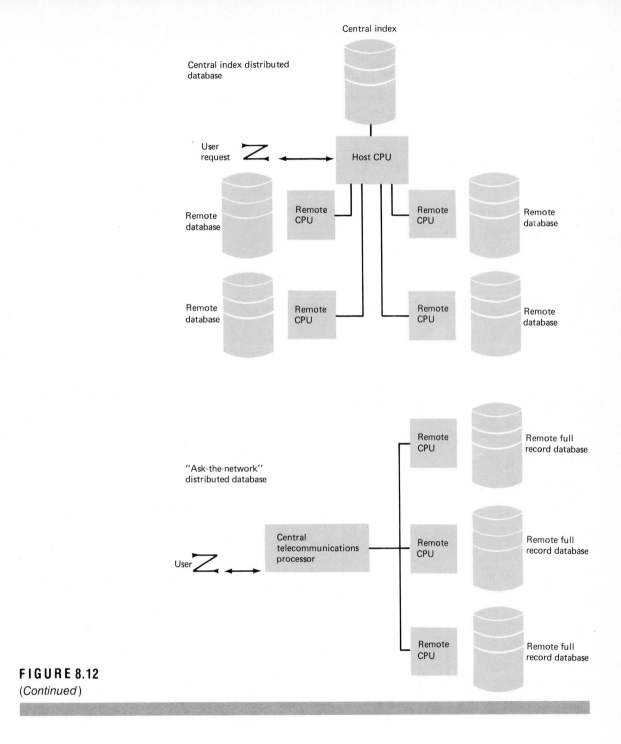

FIGURE 8.12
(*Continued*)

access to sensitive data. The economies of distribution can be lost when remote sites buy more computing power than is needed. Sometimes, increasing the size of the central system is more economical. DBMS vendors have only recently begun to offer distributed DBMS (DDBMS).

Despite these drawbacks, distributed processing is growing rapidly. With the advent of microcomputers (see Chapter 10) and powerful telecommunications systems (see Chapter 9), more and more information services will be distributed. For large national organizations working in several regions, the question is no longer whether to distribute but how to distribute in such a way as to gain economies and responsiveness without sacrificing data and system integrity. Newly available distributed DBMS are providing one answer (Martin, 1983).

8.4 Management Requirements for Database Systems

Much more is involved in the development of database systems than simply selecting a logical data structure. Indeed, this may be among the last decisions. The database is an *organizational discipline, a method*, rather than a tool or technology. It requires *organizational* and *conceptual change.*

Without management support and understanding, database efforts fail. The critical elements in a database environment are (1) data administration, (2) data modeling and planning methodology, (3) database technology and management, and (4) users. This environment is depicted in Figure 8.13 and will now be described.

Data Administration

Database systems require that the organization recognize the strategic role of information and begin actively to manage and plan for information as a corporate resource. This means that the organization must develop a *data administration function* with the power to define corporatewide information requirements and with direct access to senior management. The chief information officer or vice president of information becomes the primary advocate in the organization for database systems.

In a traditional environment, files and programs were constructed by each department to fulfill specific needs. Now, with DBMS, files and programs must be built that take into account the full organization's interest in data. For instance, whereas in the past the treasurer could insulate his data and applications from others in the organization, now some information that once "belonged" to the treasurer will be shared through the DBMS with other users in other departments. Quite naturally, the treasurer may worry that other

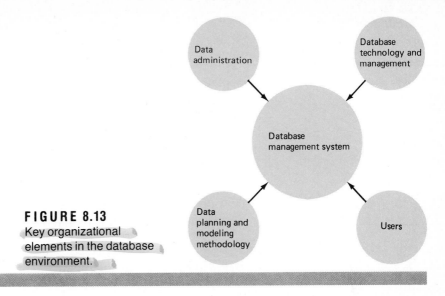

FIGURE 8.13
Key organizational elements in the database environment.

users will not treat financial data with the same care and concern as the treasurer's personnel.

Data Modeling and Planning Methodology

Because the organizational interests served by the DBMS are much broader than those in the traditional environment, new methods of planning for data and modeling relationships are required.

Data base design involves three steps:

- Gathering data requirements for the organization as a whole.
- Developing logical data relationships for the organization.
- Implementing the physical representation of data in a DBMS.

Enterprisewide (as opposed to application-specific) information requirements analysis is needed to develop DBMS systems. The purpose of enterprise analysis is to identify the key entities, attributes, and relationships that constitute the organization's data. These techniques are described in greater detail in Chapters 13 and 20.

Once the organization's key data are identified, the analyst must define the logical relationships between the data, a step known as *data modeling*. Can a client own more than one automobile? Can a customer have more than one reservation on the same flight? These relationships must be represented in any database.

Last, the designer must organize the database in such a way as to optimize access, flexibility, and efficiency. Here is where the choice of a hierarchical versus a relational system is made.

Database Technology and Management

DBMS requires new technology (both hardware and software) and new management structures. An intensively used DBMS can literally bring down a corporation's main time-shared computer system. Large corporate DBMSs generally run on their own hardware, isolated from other corporate systems yet compatible with them. As previously described, the DBMS requires new software and a new staff specially trained in DBMS techniques. Most corporations develop a *database design and management group* within the corporate information system division. This group:

- defines and organizes database hardware and software.
- develops security procedures to safeguard the database.
- develops database documentation.

In close cooperation with users, the design group establishes the physical database, the logical relations among elements, and the access rules and procedures.

Users

The DBMS involves a wider community of users than traditional systems. Relational systems with fourth-generation query languages permit unsophisticated, untrained employees to access large databases. In addition, users include sophisticated professionals. In order to optimize access for nonprofessionals, more resources must be devoted to training end users. Professional systems workers must be retrained in the DBMS language, DBMS application development procedures, and new software practices.

8.5 Organizational Obstacles to Database

Hierarchical database technology first became commercially available in the early 1970s. Since then, more sophisticated and efficient database designs have appeared. Nevertheless, progress in installing database technology in organizations has been much slower than anticipated. Why? Three reasons stand out. (See Chapter 20 for an extended discussion of these issues.)

Organizational Politics

The database approach requires widespread organizational change in the role of information (and information managers), the allocation of power at senior levels, the ownership and sharing of information, and patterns of organizational agreement.

For instance, a database approach to personnel requires that virtually all information about employees be centralized in the personnel department. This includes all employees regardless of division, includes payroll data formerly controlled by the treasurer, and may lead to the sharing of confidential personnel information formerly held at local plants.

As discussed in Chapter 4, politics in organizations is inevitable because real interests—pay, confidentiality, promotion, and the nature of work—are involved. DBMS challenges the existing arrangements in an organization, and for that reason often generates political resistance. At times this resistance can be strong enough to discourage the idea of using databases; at other times, it simply slows down implementation.

Cost/Benefit Considerations

The costs of moving to a database environment are palpable, up front, and large in the short term (3 years). Most firms buy a commercial DBMS package and related hardware. The software alone can cost $1 million for a full-function package with all options. New hardware may cost an additional $1–2 million. A new telecommunications system may be required, adding additional millions. What good is a DBMS if end users cannot obtain easy access at remote locations? Perhaps an entire fleet of PCs is required to obtain the most benefits.

It soon becomes apparent to senior management that a database system is a huge investment.

Unfortunately, the benefits of the DBMS are often intangible, back-loaded, and long term (5 years). The systems that the DBMS seeks to replace generally work, although they are inefficient. Moreover, several million dollars have been spent over the years designing and maintaining existing systems. People in the organization understand the existing system after long periods of training and socialization.

For all of these reasons, and despite the clear advantages of the DBMS, the short-term costs of developing a DBMS often appear to be nearly as great as the benefits. When the short-term political costs are added to the equation, it is convenient for senior management to defer the database investment.

As Lord Keynes noted, in the longer term "We are all dead." Therefore, the obvious long-term benefits of the DBMS tend to be severely discounted by managers, especially those unfamiliar with (and perhaps unfriendly to) systems.

Wrong Approach

Many organizations, seeking to avoid large commitments and organizational change, begin (and end) by buying a DBMS package and placing it in the hands of a low-level database group in the Information Systems Department. DBMS applications are encouraged by this group whenever opportunities arise. Generally, this leads to a

Choosing A DBMS

Without careful preparation, the benefits of a DBMS will not be realized. Some of the important factors are:

1. *software/hardware environment:* DBMS should be compatible with your existing software programs; hardware limitations should be considered.
2. *human resource environment:* the sophistication and types of users, as well as the organizational structure (centralized versus decentralized), affect how well a DBMS will work.
3. *application system environment:* the types of applications which require DBMS support should be carefully examined.
4. *security and integrity:* DBMS can create security problems by making data easily and widely available.
5. *long-range planning:* a specific DBMS should be compatible with the long-range information processing strategy.

Adapted from "Choosing Your First (Or Second or Third) DBMS,"*Computerworld*, February 18, 1985.

piecemeal approach to database use; that is, small database systems will be developed for various divisions, functional areas, departments, and offices.

This common, low-visibility approach has many advantages, among which are the slow development of expertise with DBMS and the lower short-term cost. Unfortunately, this approach is very slow, results in the building of incompatible databases throughout the company, and fails to address the key organizational issue: What is the role of information and who will manage it for the organization as a whole?

The key to successful long-term development of database systems is the triad approach outlined in the previous section. Along with DBMS technology (and a small systems group that understands it), the organization must develop a data administration function at the highest corporate level. A third key element is the adoption of a data planning methodology. These activities are described in later chapters.

Some of the more important factors to consider in selecting a DBMS are described in the story above.

8.6 Summary

Along with hardware and software, the proper organization of information is vital to successful information processing. It may also be vital to organizational effectiveness and survival. There is a growing recognition that information is a strategic resource and that widely dispersed end users must have rapid and flexible access to corporate information. The database approach is an organizational philosophy and technology that makes these new approaches possible.

In a traditional data processing environment, applications—and related data files and programs—were developed in an uncoordinated fashion. This resulted in hundreds of files and programs, great complexity, data redundancy, data inconsistency, and high costs. Most important, in this environment there was little ability to respond quickly and flexibly to ad hoc requests.

Database management systems (DBMS) are the software that permits centralization of data and data management. Database software includes a data definition language, data manipulation language, and a data dictionary capability.

The most important feature of the DBMS is its ability to separate the logical and physical views of data. The user works with a logical view of data, which is translated automatically by DBMS software into a physical view. The DBMS retrieves information so that the user does not have to be concerned with its physical location. This feature separates programs from data and perhaps from the separate management of data.

There are three kinds of logical database structures: hierarchical, network, and relational. Each has unique advantages and disadvantages. Hierarchical systems are low in flexibility but high in processing speed and efficiency. Relational systems are slow but very flexible. The choice depends on the business requirements.

It is no longer necessary for data to be centralized in a single, massive database. Data can be distributed to remote processors and databases in order to increase responsiveness and reduce vulnerability and costs. New software is available to ensure data integrity and compatibility.

Development of a database environment involves much more than selection of technology. It involves a change in the corporation's attitude toward information. The organization must develop a data administration function and a data planning methodology.

The DBMS has developed more slowly than was originally anticipated. There is political resistance in organizations to many key database concepts, especially sharing of information that has been controlled exclusively by one organizational group. There are difficult cost/benefit questions in database management. Often, to avoid raising difficult questions, database use begins—and ends—as a small effort isolated in the Information Systems Department. Remedies to this approach are discussed in Chapters 13 and 20.

Key Words

File management	Logical and physical views of data
Traditional data processing environment	Hierarchical DBMS
Flat file organization	Network DBMS
Data redundancy	Relational DBMS
Data confusion	Pointers
Program–data dependence	Inverted lists
Flexibility	Distributed databases
Database	Distributed data processing
Database management system (DBMS)	Data administration
Data definition language	Data modeling
Data manipulation language	Data planning methodology
Data dictionary	Cost/benefit considerations

Review Questions

1. Why is file management important for overall system performance?
2. What are the roles of users, analysts, and programmers in file design and management?
3. Describe the traditional data processing environment in terms of divisions, functions, files, documents, data elements, users, and programs.
4. Why do files proliferate in a traditional environment?
5. In what sense are programs and data linked together in the traditional environment?
6. List and describe some of the problems of the traditional data processing environment.
7. How would you define a database and a database management system?
8. Name and briefly describe the four elements of a DBMS.
9. What is the difference between a logical and a physical view of data?
10. List some of the purposes of a DBMS.
11. What three aspects of information are all database designs concerned with? (Hint: think of King Henry.)
12. Describe the three different database structures and the advantages and disadvantages of each.
13. What is a distributed database and how does it differ from distributed data processing?
14. What are the three key elements of a database environment? Describe each briefly.
15. Describe and briefly comment on the major organizational obstacles to building a database environment.

1. The registrar at your university is interested in developing a student registration database. List four of the most important information requirements of a registration system and recommend a database structure (e.g., relational, hierarchical).
2. Compare the manual database system used by libraries to a contemporary PC database package like dBASE III, Paradox, or Microrim's Rbase 4000. How does the library organize information on books?
3. As an information system manager, you are concerned that the percentage of your staff working on maintenance of existing programs is growing and the percentage working on new applications is declining. How could a database environment change this trend?
4. Consider two strategies for building a database environment. One strategy recommends that a small group be created in the Information Systems Department to begin exploring database applications throughout the firm. The other strategy recommends the creation of a vice president of information and subsequent development of important database applications. Explore and describe the costs and benefits of each strategy.

CASE STUDY

Customer Information Files in the Insurance Industry

In insurance companies (and banks as well), information technology followed product lines. The corporation's file systems were set up to support specific products. Automobile systems followed auto policies, life insurance had its own system, and health coverage had a third system.

The insurance industry is being forced to change this pattern as banks and brokerage firms have begun to offer insurance products. Insurance companies would like to develop a total "customer approach" and begin offering bank-like and brokerage-like services.

These are the findings of a major new study by the Life Office Management Association (LOMA), a trade association in Atlanta.

The study found that insurance companies will need to develop giant new databases called *customer information files (CIFs)*. CIFs have been used by banks for several years. Instead of organizing around product lines, CIFs collect information about customers who buy any of the company's products. They track current and prospective customers according to name and address, demographic data, relationship with other customers, preferences in billing, and other information.

The benefits of these CIFs are several. All employees throughout the insurance company can access customer information; salesmen can use the information to pitch particular products, cutting sales costs; customer financial statements can be consolidated; and customers can review their status more easily. Finally, CIFs support cross-selling, target marketing, customer profitability analysis, and customer monitoring—capabilities that banks have enjoyed for years.

Developing CIFs is not easy. Most insurance companies have not even begun; most companies still struggle with the old product-based systems.

CIFs require relational systems because the older hierarchical systems are too structured and inflexible. Nonprogrammers must be able to access the data quickly; therefore, user friendliness and query-like languages are most important. Only relational systems offer these advantages.

The Travelers Corporation, a major insurance company located in Hartford, Connecticut, is developing a CIF using IBM's DB2 relational DBMS.

CIFs are difficult to justify in terms of cost. They cost millions of dollars in the short term but probably do not produce quantifiable benefits for several years. On the other hand, they are increasingly needed simply to stay in business. Companies will have to increase their data processing (DP) budgets by 10–15% to build these systems, the study found, despite the falling costs of hardware. In order for these huge database systems to work, new hardware, new office telecommunications, and more investments in personal computers (PCs) are required. The big expenses in these systems are for software, expertise, and training. Average DP expenditures simply will not be enough.

CIFs also place demands for change on the systems professionals in a company. They must now interact more closely with users, acting both as professional systems people and as guides for end-user managers. Last, the professionals must live in a world where more computer processing power will be used by end users at PC terminals than by major production systems.

Adapted from "Insurers' Next Move: Customer Info Files," *Information Week*, July 7, 1986.

Case Study Questions

1. How does the dilemma of the insurance industry illustrate the need for appropriate file management techniques?

2. Developing a CIF is not easy. Why?
3. Why is a relational model appropriate for this application?

References

Buday, Robert. "Insurers' Next Move: Customer Information Files," *Information Week* (July 7, 1986).

Computer Decisions, "New DB2 Pushing IMS Into Grave," January 1986.

Computerworld, "Choosing Your First (Or Second or Third) DBMS," February 18, 1985.

Computerworld, "Relational Products Failing to Meet Basic DBMS Criteria," April 15, 1985.

Computerworld, "Dbase Tracks Crime On-Line," May 5, 1986.

Curtice, Robert M., and Jones, Paul E., Jr. "Database: The Bedrock of Business," *Datanation*, June 15, 1984.

Date, C.J. *An Introduction to Data Base Systems*, 3rd ed. Reading, Mass: Addison-Wesley, 1981.

IBM Corporation, "IBM Data Base 2 General Information," San Jose Corporation, 1983.

Laudon, Kenneth C. *Dossier Society. Value Choices in the Design of National Information Systems.* New York: Columbia University Press, 1986.

Martin, James. *Principles of Data Base Management.* Englewood Cliffs, N.J.: Prentice-Hall, 1976.

Martin, James. *Managing the Data Base Environment,* Englewood Cliffs, N.J.: Prentice-Hall, 1983.

CHAPTER 9

The Telecommunications Revolution

OUTLINE

Prudential-Bache Securities, Inc., spends more than $100 million a year for communications. Since it is one of the largest global investment firms, its telecommunications group must support trading and operations, 300 branch offices, and internal corporate communications as well. Recently, its corporate headquarters moved a few blocks from its former headquarters in New York City to a new building, leaving data processing and other operational groups behind. This created a massive communications problem: how to connect the company's headquarters and traders economically with its computers a few blocks away.

Now that the telecommunications industry has been deregulated, the Corporate Communications Department knew that it would be less expensive to bypass the local telephone company and set up their own communications highway between the two buildings. Cost analysts found that a Prudential network would cost 80% less than the use of the local phone company's circuits. But how could it be built? Microwave and infrared systems were out of the question; they relied on a clear line of sight, and other tall buildings were in the way. Fiber optics was a new and powerful but untested technology. Prudential had little experience here. Any system would have large front-end capital costs.

Prudential approached the local phone company with its problems and desire to bypass expensive local telephone cables. The phone company, recognizing that it could lose Prudential as a customer if it was unable to come up with an alternative, offered to build and lease to Prudential a state-of-the-art fiber optic system connecting Prudential's buildings. The cost would be 60% less than commercial rates charged for coaxial cable circuits, and the phone company would be responsible for the technically complex job of building and maintaining the network. Today Prudential leases 9 primary fiber optic cables, 9 backup cables, and 3 coaxial copper wire cables from a local cable television company just in case the state-of-the-art fiber optic system does not work out as planned.

Adapted from "Broker Picks Fiber Optics for Bypass," Computerworld, April 29, 1985.

In a world of growing distribution of data and machine intelligence, telecommunications will play the vital role of connecting the hardware and, just as important, the people behind the terminals. Many of the technological advances in computing and information systems would be impossible without similar strides in telecommunications. Table 9.1 shows some of the common tasks performed by computer systems that would be impossible without advanced telecommunications. The

TABLE 9.1
Common Tasks Performed by Computer Systems
Requiring Telecommunications

Application	Example	Requirements
Business		
On-line data entry	Inventory control	Transactions occurring several times/second; direct response required
On-line text retrieval	Hospital information systems; library systems	Response required in real time; high character volumes
Inquiry/response	Point of sale system; airline reservation system; credit checking	Transactions several times/second; instant response within seconds
Remote job entry	Calculating payroll	Transactions weekly or monthly; batch processing; no immediate response
Administrative message switching	Electronic mail	Short response and delivery times (minutes to hours)
Process control	CAM; numeric control of machine tools	Continuous input transactions and on-line responses required
Intercomputer data exchange	International transfer of bank funds	Infrequent but high-volume bursts of information; transfer of large data blocks; on-line immediate response
Home		
Inquiry response	Home banking; shopping; ordering	On-line transactions collected with high frequency
Text retrieval	Home education	High-volume, rapid transmission
Special entertainment	Sports; polling and political participation	High-capacity video and data capabilities

building of modern telecommunications networks has been likened to the building of canals and railways in the 19th century and the building of highways and air routes in the 20th century. Some states have begun building "digital thruways" to entice business investment.

Chances are that most managers will be participating in or making important telecommunications decisions throughout their career. Organizations now have more options in telecommunications. They face new unregulated markets in systems and are now forced to develop their own expertise in telecommunications.

This chapter will prepare you to make the right telecommunications decisions. In this chapter the student will learn:

- How the changing telecommunications environment affects modern managers.
- What managers should know about telecommunications technology.
- The definition and function of telecommunications systems.
- The major types of telecommunications systems.
- How to measure the capacity of telecommunications systems.
- How to plan for telecommunications systems.
- How telecommunications are used for strategic advantage.

9.1 Introduction

We are currently in the middle of a telecommunications revolution in the United States that has two components: rapid changes in the technology of communications and equally important changes in the ownership, control, and marketing of telecommunications services. These developments are inseparable. The overall corporate and information system plans of large organizations require for their success a keen awareness of these new developments in telecommunications.

Telecommunications Technology and Institutional Change

For most of the last 100 years since Alexander Bell invented the first "singing telegraph" in 1876, telecommunications was a monopoly either of the state or of a regulated private firm. In the United States, American Telephone and Telegraph (AT&T) was the largest regulated monopoly, providing virtually all telecommunications services. In Europe and the rest of the world there is a state post, telephone and telegraph authority (PTT). These monopolies had the advantage of developing nationwide, compatible, stable, and unitary systems of interconnected parts, all of which share the same standards. The disadvantage, as with any monopoly, is a lack of innovation and active efforts to prevent technical change because of the cost of the monopoly's huge, installed base of copper wires, standards, machines, and equipment. In the United States, this situation changed in 1984 when the Department of Justice forced AT&T to give up its monopoly and allow competing firms to sell telecommunications services and equipment.

The end to AT&T's monopoly created a huge market for new telecommunications technologies and devices, from cheaper long-distance service from new companies like SPRINT and MCI, to telephone answering equipment, to cellular car telephones, to private satellite communications systems like those owned by Boeing Aircraft, Tymnet, and other companies.

What Managers Should Know and Why

These rapid changes in technology and environment are placing a strain on many corporations and providing new strategic opportunities for others. In the 1960s, few companies had a separate telecommunications function. By the 1970s the advent of time-sharing computing had made telecommunications essential to information processing systems. Telecommunications management emerged as a specialist occupation. Then the alternatives were relatively simple: All local and long-distance communications were handled by the reliable phone company. Communications within the firm's building were handled either by the local phone company or by the firm itself. The telecommunications managers simply had to track the cost of local calls, direct distance dialing, WATS lines, and private leased lines.

In the 1980s the alternatives are much more numerous and confusing. Entire new classes of communications equipment have emerged. Today managers must know the alternative technologies and systems available to their organization, the costs and benefits of each, the capabilities of various devices, and a method for determining telecommunications requirements.

9.2 Overview of Telecommunications

Defining Telecommunications Systems

One *definition of telecommunications* is simply the electronic linking of geographically separated devices. A *telecommunications system* is defined as a set of *compatible* telecommunications devices that link geographically separated devices. The purpose of a telecommunications system is to develop a *network of interconnected components*. The system employs a language to achieve compatibility among the components. This language is called a *protocol* and is similar to a code such as Morse code. Telecommunications devices talk with one another through this protocol or code.

Functions of Telecommunications Systems

In order to achieve a network of interconnected components, telecommunications systems perform a number of separate functions. As outlined in Table 9.2, a telecommunications system *transmits* information, establishes the *interface* between the sender and the receiver, *routes* messages along the most efficient paths, performs elementary *processing* of the information to ensure that the right message gets to the right receiver, performs *editorial* tasks on the data (such as checking for errors and rearranging the format), and *converts* messages from one speed (say, the speed of a computer) into the speed of a communications line or from one protocol to another. Lastly, the telecommunication system *controls* the flow of information. Many of these tasks are accomplished by computer. Modern telecommunica-

TABLE 9.2
Functions of Telecommunications

Function	Definition
Transmission	Media, networks and path
Interface	Path—Sender—Receiver
Routing	Choosing the most efficient path
Processing	Getting the right message to the right receiver
Editorial	Checking for errors, formats, and editing
Conversion	Changing speeds and codes from one device to another
Control	Routing messages, polling receivers, providing network structure maintenance

tions systems are virtually indistinguishable from computer systems. Both technologies work together.

Major Types of Telecommunications Systems

There are several different types of telecommunications systems in the United States, some of which are quite recent. One way to think of these systems is to classify them by geographical scope.

Computer Telecommunications

Computer telecommunications systems tie together the components of modern, time-shared, distributed computer systems. Generally, these systems range from a few meters to large, multibuilding systems covering several hundred meters.

Local Networks

Local networks tie together computers and other equipment over areas ranging from a few meters up to several square city blocks. Two kinds of systems we will discuss later are private branch exchanges and local area networks.

Wide Area Networks (WANs):

WANs tie together components over areas ranging from several city blocks to entire cities. A college campus system is typically a WAN. For instance, MIT is installing a WAN to tie together the various voice and digital components on its campus (see the following account).

Long-Haul Networks

Long-haul networks connect cities and countries, handling voice, digital, and video images. Two kinds of systems will be described: public switched telephone systems and value-added networks.

MIT's Wide Area Net Connects Many Local Networks

MIT is building a fiber optic wide area network to connect together more than 3,000 micro computers spread out across MIT's campus. The wide area net is a backbone fiber optic cable which itself is controlled by several computers. This backbone system will be able to translate different communications protocols from the micro computers made by different manufacturers. Thus Apples will be able to talk with IBM PCs in the same network. The micro computers are organized into 8 different local area networks located in dormitories and faculty offices.

From "Wiring MIT for Computers," *The New York Times*, February 17, 1984.

9.3 Basics of Telecommunications

This section introduces the necessary vocabulary for discussing telecommunications. At the most basic level, it is important to see how signals are represented.

Types of Signals: Analog and Digital

Signals are represented in two ways: analog and digital. An analog signal is represented by a continous waveform that passes through a communications medium (see Figure 9.1). In this signal, a positive voltage represents a +1 and a negative charge represents a 0. This voltage switch is used to represent one binary event. A binary event is called a *baud*. In one baud, we can send one bit (either a 0 or a 1).

In general, in the telecommunications field, *bits per second* is the standard measure used to express the speed of a medium (rather than bytes per second).

A digital signal is a discrete rather than a continuous waveform. If a telecommunications system, like a telephone, is set up to process analog signals—the receivers, transmitters, amplifiers, and so forth—a digital signal cannot be processed without some alterations.

All digital signals must be translated into analog signals before they can be transmitted in an analog system. The device that performs this translation is called a *modem*. A modem translates the digital signals of a computer (basically on and off charges) into a continuous, audible signal.

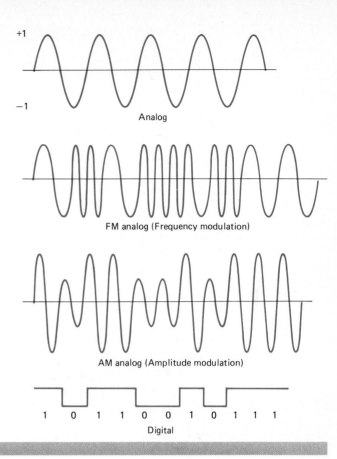

+1

−1

Analog

FM analog (Frequency modulation)

AM analog (Amplitude modulation)

1 0 1 1 0 0 1 0 1 1 1

Digital

FIGURE 9.1
Analog and digital signals.

Measuring the Capacity of Telecommunications: Bandwidth

It should be obvious that if one cycle or one binary event change is required to send one bit per second, then *the capacity of the medium is a function of the frequency of that medium.* That is, the more cycles per second that can be squeezed into a telecommunications medium, potentially the more bits per second can be sent down the line.

For instance, a long jump rope can oscillate at a rate of about 1 cycle per second. If you shake at a much faster rate, the rope cannot follow. A jump rope can therefore send about 1 bit per second. On the other hand, light waves oscillate (have a frequency) at a rate of up to several trillons of cycles per second and can be used to carry a correspondingly large amounts of information (billions of bits per second).

Frequency refers to how often the continuous analog wave repeats itself per unit of time, generally 1 second. This is expressed as cycles per second, which has been renamed *hertz*. The frequency spectrum goes from zero to trillions of hertz. The frequency spectrum is divided into bands, which are allocated by the government to selected uses.

TABLE 9.3
Telecommunications
Speed and Cost

Type	Speed	Cost
Teletype	150–300 BPS	Low
Voice wire	300–9600	
"Conditioned" wire	56–150K	
Microwave	56–256K	
Coaxial cable	56K–400 MEG	
Fiber optic cable	500K–500 MEG	High

BPS = bits per second; K = kilobits per second;
MEG = megabits per second.

For instance, the AM radio band that operates from 560 to 1560 kilohertz is allocated solely for AM commercial radio transmissions.

All telecommunications media can be described in terms of their *bandwith*, which is the difference between the highest and lowest frequencies that can be transmitted down a single line. The greater the range of frequencies that a transmission medium can accommodate, the greater the telecommunications capacity of the medium expressed in bits per second (Table 9.3).

There are several ways in which the efficiency of an existing medium can be expanded. One of these ways is through *multiplexing*. A multiplexer divides the bandwidth of a given transmission medium into several discrete channels on the basis of either frequency (e.g., commercial radio bands are divided into stations) or time. The same frequency division can be used in a cable, in twisted wire, or in a fiber optic device to increase the number of independent channels along which a signal can be sent.

Obviously, the greater the bandwidth, the more distinct channels that can be placed in a transmission medium. Signals can also be *time multiplexed*. Here all of the medium's capacity is given over to a particular group of signals for a short period of time, then to another group of signals, and so on. One kind of time multiplexing is called *packet switching*.

Types, Speed, and Cost of Telecommunications Media

There are five different kinds of telecommunications media: twisted wire, coaxial cable, microwave and other radio transmission, fiber optics, and satellite (see Table 9.3). The cost of these media can be given only in the most general terms because it depends entirely on how intensely each medium is used. A satellite link, for instance, can be purchased for several thousand dollars per month (which is expensive indeed). However, if a company uses the link 100% of the time, the cost per bit of data is much lower than that of leasing a telephone line from AT&T. The object here is to utilize the link as much as possible.

Two new technologies may be less familiar to some readers. *Fiber optics* is a small but growing part of the telecommunications business. It employs a glass cable that is a little thicker than a small plastic fishing line. Because of the high frequency of light, the transmission capability of fiber optics is enormous—on the order of 100 megabits to several gigabits per second. It is possible to splice and connect fiber optic cable almost as easily as copper cable.

Satellite technology, a few years older than fiber optics, utilizes microwave radio to communicate from local earth stations to satellites. It operates channels in the range of 250 kilobits per second. The cost of satellite, like fiber optic technology, is high compared to that of in-place telephone wire. On the other hand, the amount of data that can be transmitted is very large.

9.4 Types of Telecommunications Systems

There are four different telecommunications systems with which the student should be familiar: computer telecommunications, local networks, long haul networks, and wide area networks.

Computer Telecommunications

Figure 9.2 illustrates the typical telecommunications arrangements in a large, contemporary mainframe computer environment. The central feature of this environment is a large centralized main computer that is time shared by several remote installations.

All of the telecommunications workload has been shifted from the main computer to a second computer called a *front-end processor*. The front-end processor is a general-purpose communications processor attached to a mainframe. In addition to acting as the communications conduit to the mainframe, it performs error control, formating, editing, controlling, and routing, as well as speed and signal conversion. Analog signals from remote sites are translated into digital signals by a modem.

In order to increase the efficiency of transmission speeds, several devices are employed to enhance the speed of telecommunications over ordinary voice phones. One of these devices is a *remote concentrator*, a programmable telecommunications computer that concentrates messages from terminals until enough messages are ready to be sent economically. The concentrator then "bursts" signals to the mainframe. Another device to enhance the speed of telecommunications is

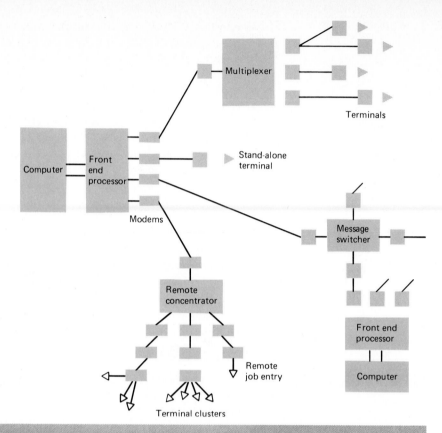

FIGURE 9.2
Computer network typology.
(Adapted from Loomis, 1983.)

a *multiplexer*, which operates at a remote site. It can take several high-volume applications, divide up the communications bandwidth, and send the messages simultaneously to the host computer.

Still another device that enhances the flexibility and versatility of the host computer is a *message switcher*. This is a programmable telecommunications computer that allocates computer host time to remote terminals seeking access to the host computer. The message switcher acts like a traffic cop, determining which messages will come through to the mainframe.

PBXs and Computerization of the Telephone

A PBX is an electronic switch that transfers telephone calls—hence a private branch *exchange*. It is simply a branch exchange owned by a private company as opposed to a regulated monopoly or utility.

While the first PBXs performed limited switching functions, in the last few years models have appeared that store, forward, transfer, hold, and redial telephone calls. PBXs can also be used for call accounting (tracing the origin of all calls made from a company's telephone). In this manner, the overall telecommunications pattern of an organization can be routinely examined.

In addition to performing these voice functions, PBXs are increasingly playing a central role in the new office. Their purpose here is to switch digital information among computers and office devices. For instance, you can write a letter on a microcomputer in your office, dial up the local copying machine, and have the hard copy of your letter printed. You can also send a copy to your secretary's file and distribute copies to other people in the office through the electronic mail system. All of this activity is possible with a digital PBX connecting "smart" machines in the advanced office.

The great advantage of digital PBXs over other alternatives to be discussed is that a phone jack can be found almost anywhere in the office building. Equipment can therefore be moved when necessary with little worry about rewiring the building. A hard-wired computer terminal or PC connected to the mainframe with a coaxial cable must be rewired at considerable cost and delay every time it is moved. A PC connected to a network or mainframe by telephone can simply be plugged and unplugged anywhere in the building utilizing the existing telephone lines.

Some of the new PBX systems sold by Intecom and American Telecom are illustrated in Figures 9.3 and 9.4. One notable aspect of these systems is the mixture of media in the same network. Slower communication lines connect remote devices to concentrators, which in turn communicate with mini- and mainframe computers in bursts

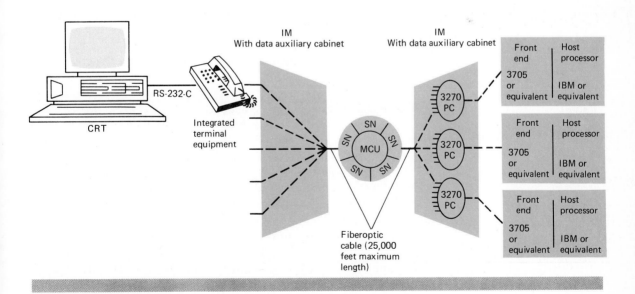

FIGURE 9.3

A PBX integrates several different devices. In this example, an Intecom IBX S/80 made by Intecom uses different cables operating at different speeds to integrate terminals, telephones, and computers.

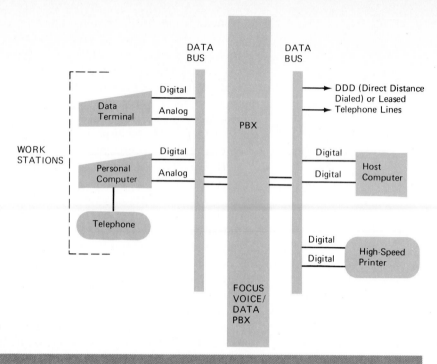

FIGURE 9.4
American Telecom's FOCUS
PBX architecture.

over media with much higher capacity—in the case of Intecom, a 40-megabit fiber optic cable. These systems have a considerable data and voice capability. The question is: Do you need all this capability? We will show how to answer this question in a later section.

Local Area Networks (LANs)

A LAN is a system that allows several different people to use computers, disk drives, files, and/or printers at the same time. In this sense, a LAN is like a PBX. The difference is that a LAN is totally user installed, is not part of the telephone system, requires new wiring, and often uses a *technology with much higher capacity*.

Most LANs allow users to share hardware that is located within about a 2000-foot radius. A cable connects all of the elements of the system at each site. Most users never need to know anything about how the LAN works because powerful computers built into the network itself control the movement of data. LANs differ from mainframe computer networks [like IBM's System Network Architecture (SNA)], in which only the central main computer has the power to do data processing. In a LAN, computing power is widely distributed among a number of intelligent devices.

LANs differ from PBXs in several ways. First, LANs are designed to work in a restricted area, generally on the order of thousands of feet. PBXs using the existing telephone system have no such limits.

Second LANs operate at much higher speeds than a modem or a PBX, on the order of 6–50 megabits per second. In contrast, a fast PBX operates at 56 kbps (56 kilobits or 56,000 bits per second). Thus, LANs are recommended for applications requiring high volumes and high transmission speeds. For instance, because a picture consumes so many bits of information, a LAN is necessary for video transmissions and graphics.

LANs are totally controlled, maintained, and operated by end users. This has the advantage of allowing user control, but it also means that the user must know a great deal about telecommunications equipment. With PBXs, there is much more support by the vendor. Often this is the local telephone company, which will exist 5 years from now and has an excellent service record.

There are a number of reasons why organizations are now purchasing LANs. First, expensive hardware and software can be shared by various computer systems. Expensive letter-quality printers can be shared by several PCs. Second, LANs can lead to greater productivity because users are no longer dependent upon a centralized computer system (which can fail) or upon the availability of any single peripheral device such as a printer. Finally, there are many new applications that require high-density LANs for implementation. Electronic mail, video, teleconferencing, on-line data acquisition and distribution, and so forth, require multichannel, high-capacity lines.

The typical hardware in a LAN is a collection of PCs, peripheral devices (printers, copying machines), and perhaps a gateway to a time-sharing or central computer, depending on how the network is arranged.

There are four important criteria that are used to judge LANs: How *flexible* is the system (can new users be added, and how many)? What is the *actual performance* (as opposed to the advertising claims)? How *reliable* will the system be in the face of various sorts of disturbances? What is the *true cost* of the system, including software, implementation, rewiring, training, and the opportunity cost of use?

Long-Haul Networks and Value-Added Networks (VANs)

Once an organization decides to transmit information beyond its local buildings and neighborhood, it becomes dependent upon public utilities and private providers of long-distance communications. Here the user has five choices.

One of the options is to rely on direct distance dialing (DDD) provided by the local phone company and AT&T's Long Lines Division. DDD over voice lines is relatively slow (1200 bits per second), is the most expensive form of telecommunications (about $25–35 per hour), and in many respects is not very reliable given the noise of voice switching circuits, which introduce errors into digital transmissions of data. (On my PC at home, I cannot communicate reliably with my university mainframe computer 30 miles away in New York City between 12 noon and 5 P.M. because the demand on

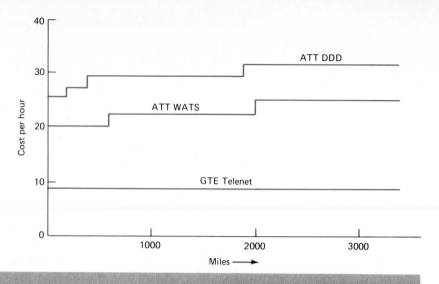

FIGURE 9.5
Cost of telephone circuits compared to that of packet switched VANs.

the voice-switched networks increases dramatically at these hours, as does the attendant noise in the circuitry.)

A second alternative is to use the wide area telephone service (WATS) lines offered by local telephone companies and AT&T. WATS lines are semidedicated telephone lines utilizing normal voice circuits that cost less than DDD lines because the user pays a monthly fee for access. The fees are lower because AT&T is wholesaling its service, providing the user with a somewhat lower-priced line and guaranteeing a stream of income from that line. WATS lines operate at 1200 bits per second, are subject to the same noise and error problems of regular telephone lines, and are expensive (on the order of $20–25 per hour) (see Figure 9.5). Moreover, the user must pay for a WATS line whether or not it is being used. Ordinary DDD lines are paid for only when they are utilized. Therefore, WATS lines are advisable only when there is a large, continuous stream of communications to be transmitted at relatively slow speeds.

A third alternative, also provided by local telephone companies at AT&T, is to lease a private, dedicated communications channel or line. These leased lines are generally coaxial cable lines of very high capacity (1.544 megabits per second is an AT&T standard), and they are much less noisy and less prone to error than voice-grade lines. However, they are expensive, ranging in price from $400 per month for a 10-mile leased line up to several thousand dollars per month for longer-distance lines. The user pays for these lines whether or not they are used. Therefore, leased lines are attractive to very large corporations or government agencies with huge masses of data to move on a routine, daily basis. Moreover, like DDD and WATS lines, leased lines are distance sensitive; the greater the distance, the greater the cost.

A fourth alternative is virtually insensitive to distance: satellite transmission. A number of companies now offer voice and digital long-distance communications via satellite: Satellite Business Systems (a corporation two-thirds owned by IBM and one-third by Aetna Life Insurance), Vitalink, ITT, AT&T, and Western Union.

There are several ways in which a company can use satellite telecommunications. One way is to dial up the satellite company via an ordinary telephone modem, operating at 1200 bits per second, and transmit a message to the satellite station, which in turn transmits it to a distant satellite station via a transponder on the satellite.

A fifth alternative is to bypass the telephone companies altogether. One can purchase an earth station and transmit directly to satellites owned and operated by the providing companies. The Vitalink Corporation, for instance, sells small earth stations carrying two 56-kilobit-per-second channels for about $130,000. This is just the right amount of data capability for intensive networking applications such as video conferencing or connecting 50 or 60 remote terminals to a mainframe located far away.

In the above five alternatives, the user is totally responsible for the telecommunications contents and management. This means that the user has to establish the most efficient routing of messages, accomplish error checking and editing, take care of any required changes in speed or communications protocol, and assume full responsibility for the management of the telecommunications function. But there is another option: value-added networks (VANs).

A VAN is a computer-controlled, multimedia/multipath, private (nonregulated), packet-switched, data-only telecommunications system. An example of a national packet-switched VAN is shown in Figure 9.6—the Arpanet, which is operated by the Advanced Research Projects Agency of the Department of Defense and connects the computer science departments in the United States to a single network, along with other government installations.

Figure 9.6 (lower panel) shows the major components of a packet-switched network—in this instance, the network provided by Tymnet, Inc. A network supervisor, which is a computer, controls the network and communications among the nodes of the system, which may be located in different cities or different countries. The user's computers are connected to the VAN nodes either by ordinary telephone lines or by dedicated communications lines leased perhaps from a local telephone company or installed directly by the VAN network. The long-distance connections between the network computers, and between the network computers and the network supervisor, are composed either of satellite linkages, leased lines from other companies, leased private lines, or simply private lines installed by the VAN or some combination of these systems.

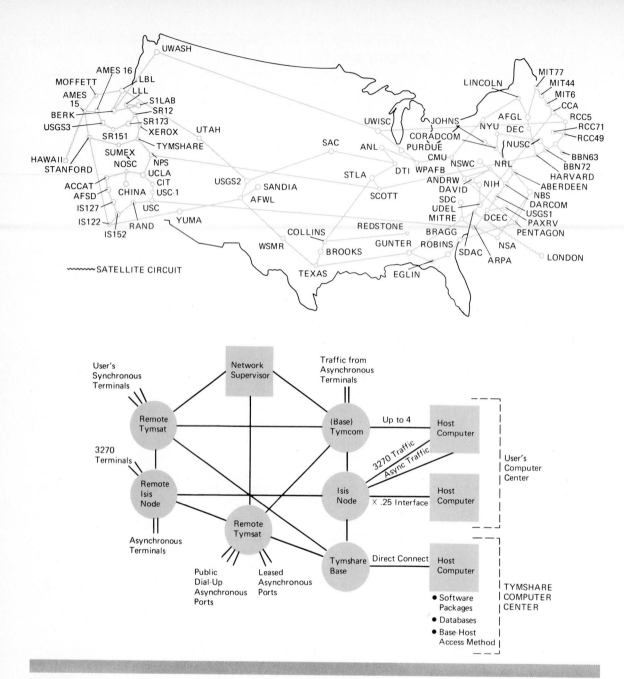

FIGURE 9.6

Top panel: Arpanet VAN. Lower panel: Tymenet VAN. (Adapted from Loomis, 1983.)

VANs achieve economies compared to traditional long-distance telecommunications by utilizing a new technology of telecommunications called *packet switching.* In this system, a lengthy block of text or a stream of data is broken up into *packets*, small bundles of data approximately 300 bits long. Control information is attached to the front and back of this packet. The entire packet is then sent down a communications line in a single bundle (see Figure 9.7). This is much faster than a traditional communications protocol, which requires a series of check, control, and acknowledge bits for each byte sent.

But packet switching also achieves economies by utilizing existing telecommunication facilities more efficiently than a traditional communications network can. Compared to leased lines, for instance, which a user may use intensively for 1 hour and then not use for 3 or 4 hours, a VAN gathers information from many users, divides this information into small packets, and continuously uses a long-distance communications line to send the packets to the recipients. In this way, existing communications facilities are utilized more fully, spreading the fixed costs of communications lines over a larger user base.

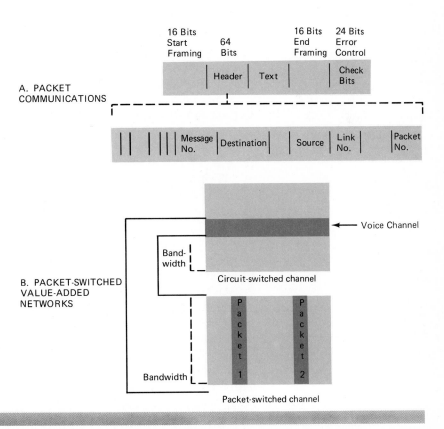

FIGURE 9.7

With these high volumes, VANs can utilize the full bandwidth available on any given communications line and utilize it more intensively (see Figure 9.7, lower panel).

This new technology leads to long-distance communication costs that are roughly one-third those of DDD ($6–8 per hour; see Figure 9.5 which shows the cost for GTE's Telenet VAN). This can save large corporations hundreds of thousands of dollars a year in communications costs.

In addition to their low costs, VAN networks provide total end-to-end management of the telecommunications function. The ability of VANs to assume full responsibility for managing a customer's network, from point of entry to point of departure, has led many customers to choose these systems. The VAN assumes responsibility for routing, error checking and editing, protocol conversion from one kind of computer to another, any changes in required speeds, faster setup time (leased lines from AT&T now require over 100 days to install), and, finally, end-to-end service by one company. The ability to communicate among different brands of computers is especially attractive to very large companies like General Motors, which have different brands of computer hardware in different parts of the company. VANs also permit smaller companies, which have little or no expertise and limited budgets, to utilize some of the most advanced telecommunications technology available.

The meaning of *value added* should now be clear: VANs provide a number of telecommunications/computing services for the fees they charge and hence "add value" to communications.

There are a growing number of competitors in the VAN market. In the late 1970s, IBM, Aetna Life Insurance, and Comsat (a domestic satellite communications corporation) jointly invested $1 billion to found Satellite Business Systems, which was intended to be a vendor of teleconferencing and sophisticated long-range networking.

Fortune 500 companies, such as Boeing, Chemical Bank, and General Motors, are now developing their own VANs and selling spare data services as well. Computer companies such as General Electric, IBM, and AT&T offer VANs, as well as the Bell operating companies and other communications companies such as MCI and Western Union. Table 9.4 provides a list of some of the largest providers of VAN service.

General Electric's Mark Net is one of the most extensive packet-switched VAN services, with connections to up to 600 U.S. cities and 150 countries. It supports protocols for communication between most major mainframe computers.

The VAN's typical transmission speed is about 2.4–9.6 kilobits per second. This is much slower than the 1.5 megabits of a dedicated leased line or a satellite link. On the other hand, it is much faster than AT&T voice communication lines, which operate at 1200 bits per second and are noisy. If more speed is needed, the user can purchase

TABLE 9.4
VAN Services

Company/Network	Number of Cities	Electronic Mail	Time Sharing	Major Customers and Allies
ATT Information Services NET	200	No	Yes	Ford Motor Co., Northwest Industries
GEISCO Mark Net	600	Yes	Yes	Kodak, Wang
Tymnet, Inc. Tymnet	500	Yes	Yes	Pacific Telecom, Chase Manhattan
GTE Telenet	350	Yes	No	Citibank, Medical Data
IBM Corp. Information Network	256	Yes	Yes	Insurance agents
Compuserve	250	Yes	Yes	VISA
RCA Cyclix	100	No	No	Republic Airlines, Burroughs

Source: Adapted from Elisabeth Horwitt, "Long Distance Networks," *Business Computer Systems*, December 1984.

a Vitalink satellite earth station and transmit directly to VAN satellites at 56 kilobits per second.

9.5 How Organizations Use Telecommunications for Competitive Advantage

The American Hospital Supply Corporation, described in Chapter 2, was one of the first companies to realize the strategic significance of telecommunications. The company placed its own computer terminals in hospital supply rooms and provided a direct telecommunications link with its central headquarters via a VAN. Customers could dial up a local VAN node and send their orders directly to the company. Since then, several other corporations have realized the strategic potential of telecommunication/computer systems.

General Mills: Changing Relations with Customers

The Super Value Supermarket chain urged General Mills to set up a network service incorporating the electronic data interchange/uniform customer standard (EDI/UCS), which is the grocery industry's standard for electronic invoicing and order entry. Super Value wanted General Mills to create a network that would permit supermarkets to transmit their orders directly to General Mills instead of going through local salespeople and the postal service. This is very similar to American Hospital Supply's strategy of placing terminals and communication links in its customers' order network.

General Mills could have set up 40,000 miles of leased lines between its customers and central headquarters just to carry thousands of 20- to 30-second transactions. Obviously, this would have entailed a huge expense. An alternative way had to be found to create a single network that would accommodate customers using different and incompatible hardware and software systems.

Tymnet solved both of General Mills's problems by acting as an intermediary between General Mills and supermarket chains. Supermarkets today that want to order foods from General Mills simply contact the nearest Tymnet user access node, usually via a dial-up telephone. The order travels from this access node through Tymnet's high-speed network, where General Mills maintains a mailbox. The order is automatically converted from the customer's format to the EDI/UCS format. Twice a day the General Mills mainframe computer reads its mailbox at Tymnet and downloads its mail, and twice a day

Ryder's Fleet Control Service

Ryder Truck Rental, the nation's largest truck rental firm, offered its customers a Fuel Credit Service, allowing renters to stop at Ryder stations for fuel and supplies on credit. When Ryder bought out Truck Stops of America, it offered the service to all fleet owners in a much larger number of stations. A driver wanting credit stops at a station and gives his card to an attendant, who enters the number electronically into the Fleet Control Service. The driver's purchase and location is sent over General Electric Information Services Company's VAN called "Mark Net." The information is stored there and sent later to the fleet owners so they can keep track of expenses. The system can also be used in reverse: messages can be left for drivers.

From Elisabeth Horwitt, "Long Distance Networks," *Business Computer Systems*, Decenber 1984.

General Mills sends invoices back to the supermarket via the same link. General Mills does not have to pay for unused line time, which would be necessary with a leased line.

Ryder Truck Rental: Fleet Control

A different example of the use of a VAN is that of the Ryder Truck Rental Corporation's Fleet Control Service.

Obviously, VANs are not for all situations. They are best at moderate-speed, high-volume, frequent long-distance communications. They do raise security problems because company data can be mixed in with data from other companies—although very few problems have been reported. In addition, the customers lose control of their own telecommunications by participating in a VAN. In some instances, this may create the perception of a potential security problem.

9.6 Management Issues and Decisions

The starting point for rational planning of telecommunications is to forget about the "features" of systems and instead try to understand the requirements of your organization. A telecommunications plan is more likely to succeed if it advances the key business goals of the company. Cutting costs and installing advanced systems for their own sake is rarely sufficient to justify large telecommunications projects today.

The Telecommunications Plan

There are four elements that should be a part of any strategic telecommunications plan. First, start with an audit of the communications functions in your firm. What are your voice, data, video, equipment, staffing, and management capabilities? For each of these areas, identify and evaluate your strengths, weaknesses, exposures, and opportunities. Then identify priorities for improvement.

Second, you must know the long-range business plans of your firm. These plans can come from planning documents, interviews with senior management, and annual reports. Your plan should include an analysis of precisely how telecommunications will contribute to the specific 5-year goals of the firm and to its longer-range strategies (e.g., cost reduction, distribution enhancement).

Third, identify how telecommunications support the day-to-day operations of the firm. What are the needs of the operating units and their managers? Telecommunications managers must spend a good deal of time with operational personnel to understand user needs. Try to identify critical areas where telecommunications does or can make a large difference in performance. In insurance, these may be systems that give field representatives quick access to policy and rate information; in retailing, inventory control and market penetration; and in industrial products, rapid, efficient distribution and transportation.

Fourth, develop indicators of how well you are fulfilling your plan for enhancing telecommunications. Try to avoid technical measures (e.g., transmission rates enhanced from 300 to 1200 baud) and focus on business measures (e.g., sales force utilization of high-speed data lines increased from 10 to 40%).

Implementing the Plan

Once a business telecommunications plan is developed, the initial scope of the telecommunications project must be determined. Deciding on which telecommunications technology to adopt, and under what circumstances, can prove difficult, given the rapid rate of change in the technology and in the related costs of telecommunications. Currently, for instance, with the divestiture of AT&T, long-distance communication rates are falling rapidly and local communication rates are rising. As a result, telecommunications in general are becoming less and less sensitive to distance as a criterion.

There are six factors that managers should take into account when deciding what kind of telecommunications network to participate in or to install.

The first, and most important, factor is *distance*. If communication will be largely local and entirely internal to the organization's buildings and social networks, there is little or no need for VANs, leased lines, or long-distance communications. Another factor to consider is *security*. The most secure means of long-distance communications is through lines that are owned by the organization. The next most secure form of telecommunications is through dedicated leased lines. VANs that slice up corporate information into small packets are among the least secure modes. Finally, ordinary telephone lines, which can be tapped at several locations, are even less secure than VANs.

A second factor to consider is whether *multiple access* is required throughout the organization or whether it can be limited to one or two nodes within the organization. A multiple access system requirement suggests that there will be perhaps several thousand users throughout the corporation; therefore, a commonly available technology such as installed telephone wire and the related technology of a PBX is recommended. If, on the other hand, access is restricted to fewer than 100 high-intensity users, a more advanced, higher-speed, more exotic technology like a fiber optic or broad band LAN system may be recommended.

A third and most difficult factor to judge is *utilization*. There are two aspects of utilization that must be considered when developing a telecommunications network: the frequency and the volume of communications. Together, these two factors determine the total load on the telecommunications system. High-frequency, high-volume com-

TABLE 9.5
Installation Factors in Telecommunications Systems

- Distance
- Security
- Multiple access
- Utilization
- Thruway effect
- Installation

munications suggest the need for high-speed LANs for local communication and leased lines for long-distance communication. On the other hand, low-frequency, low-volume communications suggest dial-up, voice-grade telephone circuits operating through a traditional modem.

Fourth, it is important to avoid overkill by buying a state-of-the-art, high-capacity, but expensive and unreliable system. A 10-megabit-per-second data exchange rate sounds wonderful, but for many applications it simply isn't necessary. In a local office where CRT displays, communicating word processors, and microcomputers are being connected, a broadband LAN with megabit data rates is probably excessive. A PBX working in the kilobit range (up to 56 kilobits) is totally adequate for this kind of digital communication. Telephone manufacturers have demonstrated that users can build their own inexpensive LANs using existing telephone wires and plugging their machines into the local telephone network.

Fifth, it is wise to recall the *thruway effect*: The easier it is to use a communications path, the more people will want to use it. Therefore, most telecommunications planners estimate future needs on the high side. And they still often underestimate the need.

Sixth and finally, one must consider the difficulties of *installing* the telecommunications system. Are the organization's buildings properly structured to install fiber optics? In some instances, the buildings have inadequate wiring channels underneath the floors, which makes installation of fiber optic cable extremely difficult. These difficulties can be exaggerated by uncertain technologies. In the case of fiber optics, the ability of field workers to weld, splice, and install fiber optics properly has been a problem. There is much more experience with traditional coaxial cables, which are somewhat easier to snake around poorly wired buildings. Table 9.5 summarizes these implementation factors.

A Decision Support Table

Figure 9.8 presents a decision support table that can be useful in weighing the factors previously discussed and deciding what kind of telecommunications capability is required.

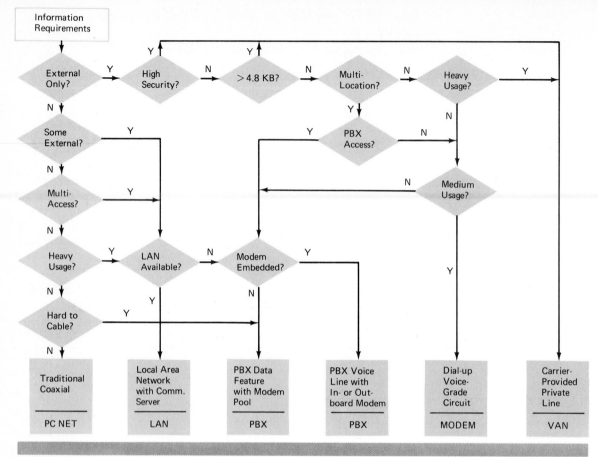

FIGURE 9.8
Data communications decision-support table.

9.7 Summary

Information processing today is vitally dependent on telecommunications links, both local and long distance. Changing technology, economics, and public policy have increased the number of alternative communication systems and placed greater responsibility on the organization for making communications decisions.

A telecommunications system is a set of compatible telecommunication devices used to develop a network of components. These systems involve the interface between devices, the actual transmission facility, routing of messages along the most efficient lines, processing of information in the system, editing of information, and often converting information from one format to another.

There are four major types of systems distinguished by geographic or distance criteria: short-range computer telecommunications, local area networks, wide area networks, and long-haul networks.

Telecommunications signals and related equipment are based on either analog or digital signals. A modem is a device that translates from analog to digital and vice versa. The capacity of a telecommunications medium is determined by the frequency at which it can operate; the higher the frequency, the higher the capacity (measured in bits per second). The principal media are twisted copper telephone wire, coaxial copper cable, microwave radio, and fiber optic cable.

A telecommunications system generally uses many different media and machines to accomplish its purpose.

A computer short-range telecommunications network uses modems, multiplexers, concentrators, and message switchers to optimize the flow of messages from remote terminals to central mainframes.

Short-range office and building systems (local networks) are of two types: PBXs and LANs.

There are two types of long-haul networks: the public switched telephone system and newer, private operated VANs.

The choice among systems requires a strategic telecommunications plan to ensure that the telecommunications system serves the organization's objectives and operations. The important factors to consider are distance, security, access, utilization, and installation. Making the right choice of systems can be of critical importance for the long-run performance of the company.

Key Words

Telecommunication functions	Message switcher
Analog	Remote concentrator
Digital	Coaxial cable
Bypassing	Fiber optics
Baud	Microwave
Bits per second	PBX
Hertz	LAN
Frequency	VAN
Bandwidth	WAN
Multiplexing	Packet switching
Modem	Long-haul network
Duplex	Protocol
Front-end processor	

Review Questions

1. What is the significance of telecommunications deregulation for managers and organizations?
2. What are the principal functions of all telecommunications systems?
3. Distinguish between an analog and a digital signal.

4. What is the relationship between bandwidth and the capacity of a line?
5. Name 5 different types of telecommunications media and compare them in terms of speed and cost.
6. If a line has capacity of 1200 bits per second, approximately how long would it take to transmit this book? (Assume that there are 200 words per page and spaces do not count as characters. Do not include graphics).
7. Name and describe the functions of the typical components of a computer telecommunications system.
8. What are the major communication systems in a large country like the United States?
9. Distinguish between a PBX and a LAN.
10. Name and describe 5 long-distance telecommunication options.
11. Define the following:
    - Modem
    - Multiplexing
    - BAUD
    - Value-Added Network
    - Packet switching
12. What are the major components of a telecommunications plan?
13. What are the principal factors to consider when making a telecommunications decision?

Discussion Questions

1. Your firm has just decided to build a new headquarters building in a suburban setting. You have been assigned to work with the architect on plans for making the new building intelligent, that is, capable of supporting the computing and telecommunications needs of the business. What factors should you consider?
2. Your boss has just read in a leading business magazine that fiber optic networks are the wave of the future. You are directed to explore how the firm can use these LANs. What words of caution and what factors should the boss consider?
3. You are an electronic parts distributor to television repair shops throughout the country. You would like to edge out regional competitors and improve service. How could you use computers and telecommunications systems to achieve these goals?

Telecommunications Makes USA Today *a World-Wide Newspaper*

When readers of *USA Today* sit down with the morning paper and a cup of coffee in Singapore, London, New York, Chicago, and Minneapolis, they can thank William O. Hider for the fact that they are all looking at precisely the same paper in terms of content, color, and format. This uniformity is made possible by a telecommunications system built by Hider for the Gannett Company, owners of *USA Today*. *USA Today* is a world-wide newspaper—the first of its kind—and its competitive position depends on a strategic satellite based telecommunications network.

The heart of the *USA Today* system is an American Satellite Company 7-meter dish antenna system that sits atop Gannett's Washington, D.C., headquarters. The system has a 300-kilobit per second bandwidth, divided into two 150-kilobit-per-second channels sending data to a Western Union's WESTAR III satellite. The satellite relays data to 31 print locations across the world, each equipped with a 5-meter satellite dish.

The system transmits black-and-white pages in 3 minutes and color pages in 6 minutes. The receivers translate the signals to printing plates, using a variety of internal communication systems. A total of 1.2 million copies of the paper are distributed worldwide each day—a feat impossible before satellite telecommunications.

The system is not foolproof, but because its function is so critical, Gannett has developed several backup systems. A private line leased from AT&T provides each site with backup in case of network failure. A backup satellite broadcasting facility 10 miles away from Gannett's headquarter system, connected with a 1.54-megabit T1 line from AT&T, stands ready to come on-line in case the network system is hit by lightning or worse.

Transmission of the daily newspaper is a round-the-clock affair, requiring precision and considerable testing. From 6 A.M. Eastern Standard Time to 2 P.M., technicians at the 31 sites and headquarters send test pages to calibrate equipment. Tints are established, for instance, to accuracies within 4%. Each of the paper's four sections is then sent and completed by midnight. Second and third editions are sent through 4 A.M.

Hider maintains that the satellite system, costing $300,000 per month to maintain and operate, costs half what a terrestial system would cost and has far fewer errors inherent in noisy land circuits. Fiber optics may change this situation, Hider admits, and then Gannett will take another look at land communications.

Adapted from "*USA Today*: Satellite Network Delivers Daily," *Computerworld*, October 14, 1985.

Case Study Questions

1. How is *USA Today's* business strategy linked to its telecommunications system?
2. Can other competitors develop a similar system?
3. What technological changes must *USA Today* track very carefully?
4. What special problems does this system have to prepare for?

References

Glatzer, Hal. "The Promise of LANs: MIS Back in Control," *Software News* (March 1985).

Glatzer, Hal. "Before Hooking Up, It Helps to Understand LAN Concepts," *Software News* (March 1985).

Harvard Business School. "Local Area Networks. Technical Note." Cambridge, Mass.: President and Fellows of Harvard College, 1984.

Horwitt, Elisabeth. "Long Distance Networks," *Business Computer Systems* (December 1984).

Housely, Tervor. *Data Communications and Teleprocessing Systems.* Englewood Cliffs, N.J.: Prentice-Hall, 1979.

Kass, Elliot M. "Value Added Networks," *Information Week* (January 14, 1985).

Loomis, Mary E.S. *Data Communications.* Englewood Cliffs, N.J.: Prentice-Hall, 1983.

McKean, Kevin. "The Computerization of the Telephone," *Personal Computing* (July 1984).

Seaman, John. "Local Networks: Making the Right Connection," *Computer Decisions* (June 1982).

CHAPTER 10

The Microcomputer Revolution

▬ OUTLINE

(Continued on next page.)

299

Nick Tarlson, vice president of finance for Brae Electric in San Francisco, recently received a call from the president of a large energy company who proposed a merger. The president asked for a quick response. After the call, Nick turned to his microcomputer and loaded up an integrated communications/spread sheet package. Nick dialed up Disclosure II, an on-line data base filled with financial information on most large corporations. In a few minutes Nick had the data on the screen, downloaded it into his spread sheet and began the analysis. Was the proposed merger feasible? What are the risks? Is the price right? After a few hours of analysis, Nick concluded that the other company had several financial weaknesses and therefore that the price was too low to cover the inherent risks. He told the president that afternoon. Both parties knew that Nick was right and that he had the negotiating advantage.

Adapted from "Tapping Into On-Line Data Bases," *PC World*, May 1985.

Brae Electric is one of many companies in which end users are using information systems based on microcomputers. There are many ways in which organizations can use microcomputers to reduce application backlogs and meet new information needs. To utilize micros effectively, however, their capabilities and challenges to traditional information processing management must be clearly understood.

In this chapter the student will learn:
■ How to define a microcomputer.
■ How organizations are using microcomputers.
■ Capabilities and limitations of microcomputers.
■ Different models for integrating microcomputers into the organization.
■ Management problems created by microcomputers.
■ Strategies for managing microcomputers effectively.

10.1 Introduction

One of the most exciting trends in information systems is the explosive development of microcomputers. It began in 1975 with machines like the Altair, which had a tiny memory of 256 bytes, no operating system, and no disk or tape storage. Today microcomputers can be purchased with up to 16 megabytes of internal memory, up to 230 megabytes of disk storage, and a sophisticated operating system that permits multiple, simultaneous uses. These machines are as powerful as mainframe computers of the mid-1960s. See Table 10.1 for characteristics of the IBM Personal System 2.

The sales of microcomputers have soared beyond the expectations of virtually all manufacturers and organizations. Currently, over 4 million microcomputers are sold each year (about 3 million to the business market), and approximately 15 million microcomputers

TABLE 10.1

The latest microcomputers from IBM, the Personal System/2, utilize faster chips (the 80286 and 80386), which in turn permit much larger RAM memories. The Model 80, for instance, is $3\frac{1}{2}$ times as fast as IBM's earlier fast machine (the AT) and can have a RAM memory of up to 16 megabytes.

	Model 30	Model 50	Model 60	Model 80
Potential system speed	Up to $2\frac{1}{2}$ times PC XT	Up to 2 times PC AT	Up to 2 times PC AT	Up to $3\frac{1}{2}$ times PC AT
Microprocessor	8086	80286	80286	80386
Standard memory Expandable to	640KB[a]	1MB[a] 7MB	1MB 15MB	Up to 2MB 16MB
Diskettes used	$3\frac{1}{2}$-inch, 720KB	$3\frac{1}{2}$-inch, 1.44MB	$3\frac{1}{2}$-inch, 1.44MB	$3\frac{1}{2}$-inch, 1.44MB
Fixed disk[b]	20MB	20MB	44,70MB	44,70 115MB
Maximum configuration[c]	20MB	20MB	185MB	230MB
Expansion slots	3	3	7	7
Operating system(s)	PC DOS 3.3	PC DOS 3.3 & Operating System/2	PC DOS 3.3 and Operating System/2	PC DOS 3.3 and Operating System/2
Price	$1,695–$2,295	$3,595	$5,295–$6,295	$6,995–$10,995

[a] KB = kilobyte; MB = megabyte.
[b] Model 30 also comes in a diskette-based configuration.
[c] Models with 44MB fixed disk are expandable to 88MB

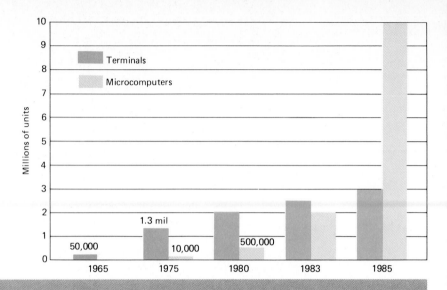

FIGURE 10.1
Growth of terminals and microcomputers.

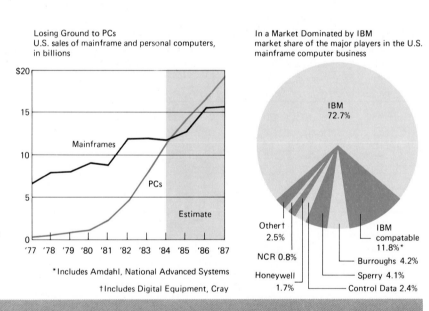

FIGURE 10.2
Plight of the mainframe makers. From: David E. Sanger, "Bailing Out of the Mainframe Industry," *The New York Times*, February 5, 1984. Copyright © 1984 by The New York Times Company. Reprinted by permission.

are currently installed in large organizations. Already more microcomputers than terminals have been installed. By 1990 it is expected that there will be well over 50 million microcomputers installed in all locations (see Figure 10.1).

Microcomputers have extended the end-user computing phenomenon that began with time-shared mainframes and continued with time-shared minicomputers. As micros have grown in power, they have seriously eroded the minicomputer market and have rapidly extended computing to users who had never before had contact with computers.

The year 1984 was a watershed for microcomputers because, for the first time, the value of microcomputers sold in the United States exceeded that of mainframes (see Figure 10.2).

What Is a Microcomputer?

There is no one definition of a microcomputer. Mainframe computers in the 1960s were considered to be those that had internal memories of at least 64K; in the 1970s mainframes were considered to be those with a minimal memory of 1 megabyte. Minicomputers in the 1970s had a main memory ranging from approximately 256K to 1 megabyte.

Obviously, these definitions are no longer valid. Microcomputers today contain up to 16 megabytes of memory. Minicomputers (e.g., an IBM System 36) start with RAM memories of 1 megabyte, and go up to 70 megabytes. They are more sophisticated than micros because of their operating systems (the ability to do multiprocessing and multiprogramming), but even here micros are catching up. Large commercial mainframes today begin with memories in the 20-megabyte range.

A microcomputer can no longer be defined as having a particular memory size. The best that can be said is that microcomputers have a smaller memory than mainframes and generally a less sophisticated operating system than minis and mainframes. Even these limitations may disappear, as indicated by the experimental machines now being tested on college campuses.

A Scholarly IBM Machine

At Stanford, Berkeley, Carnegie-Mellon, and Brown it is known as the "3-M" machine. It soon will be a new addition to IBM's expanding line of "desk top" computers. The machine will have one million bytes of internal memory, the central processor will execute one million instructions per second, and the graphic display screen will have a resolution of one million pixels (a 1,000 by 1,000 square matrix). Berkeley would like to connect 30,000 of these machines into a campus network. The difficult part will not be the hardware capacity, but the cost: university officials want to sell the machine for about $3,000 to students.

From "A Scholarly' IBM Machine," *The New York Times*, October 18, 1984.

Microcomputers can also be defined as computers that sit on a desk, can be carried from room to room, and *can be operated by end users*. Mainframe computers do not sit on desks, are much larger physically, and require separate rooms, air conditioning equipment, and so forth. Moreover, their operating system software is so sophisticated that years of training are required to use it successfully.

Another criterion for defining a microcomputer is cost. A microcomputer can be thought of as a computer owned by an individual. However, even this definition will probably be unsatisfactory by 1990. With some assurance, we can say that what we call a mainframe today (a machine with 20 megabytes) will be called a microcomputer by 1990.

Of all of the criteria just cited to distinguish micros from mainframes, the most important is the notion that microcomputers originated and are now intended for end users—non-data-processing employees ranging from clerical workers to professional money managers and senior executives who must process documents rapidly and access information in order to do their jobs better.

10.2 Why Microcomputers?

There are several explanations for the explosive growth of microcomputers.

Price–Power Relationships

Enhanced computing power coupled with falling prices is an important part of the explanation for the microcomputer revolution. Figure 10.3 shows the dramatic price power–relationships and their change from 1970, projected to 1995. The falling cost combined with the rapidly increasing capability of the hardware means that the supply of computing power has been rapidly expanding while the cost of the machinery has been falling. This unusual economic situation, which is contrary to the experience of other goods (when prices fall, the supply usually dwindles), is part of the explanation. The year 1980, when sales for microcomputers began to grow rapidly, was a watershed because the computers then available (the early Apples and the Radio Shack TRS-80) were expandable to 64K of internal memory, which was the power of the IBM third-generation mainframe machines (IBM 360) of 1964 and 1965. In September 1981 IBM released its first PC with 64K of memory.

End-User Software

The growth of internal memory alone is worth little unless there is software available to do useful things with the hardware. The sales of microcomputers began to expand rapidly in the early 1980s because internal memory was becoming large enough to operate useful software programs that were very easy to use (i.e., no prior computer experience was required). Easy-to-use programs require a large

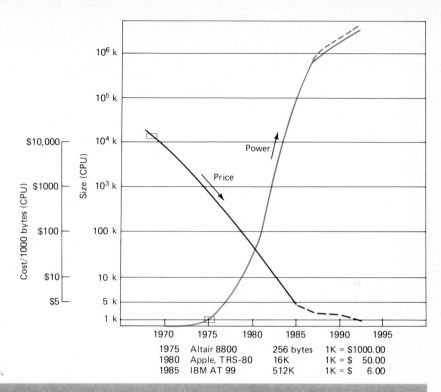

FIGURE 10.3
Price-power relationships of
microcomputers 1970–1995.

1975	Altair 8800	256 bytes	1K = $1000.00
1980	Apple, TRS-80	16K	1K = $ 50.00
1985	IBM AT 99	512K	1K = $ 6.00

amount of memory to operate due to the overhead of menus, screens, and help files.

In 1980 the first financial spread sheet package, VisiCalc, was introduced. This software permitted accountants and other financial analysts with no mainframe or computer programming experience to manipulate large, sophisticated financial spread sheets and tables. While it took a year or two for electronic spread sheet software to take off in the marketplace, by 1983 financial spread sheets were the most common use for microcomputers. The successor to Visicalc, Lotus 1-2-3, is the largest-selling software in history (see Table 10.2 for a list of popular microcomputer software packages and capabilities). Word processing software also appeared in the early 1980s and, together with spread sheet software, made it possible to use microcomputers in many areas of the organization.

Electronic Services

A third reason for the rapid growth of microcomputers is that more and more services were being made available to owners of microcomputers. The supply of information services and utilities began to grow rapidly after 1980. In the early 1980s, The Source and other companies grew up to act as information utilities for owners of microcomputers. Many more home uses were being found for

TABLE 10.2
Some Microcomputer
Software Packages

Name	Description
Graphwriter	Fully capable graphics package; produces professional transparencies, slides, and charts
Lotus 1-2-3	The most popular electronic spread sheet
dBASE III	A powerful relational database
LANLink	A software-based system to connect PCs into a LAN
SideKick	A desktop manager that permits multiple jobs to be run on the PC in separate windows.
PC/FOCUS	A fourth-generation language database and information manager compatible with a mainframe fourth-generation language
Microsoft Word	One of hundreds of word processing programs available for the PC.

microcomputers in addition to hobbyist uses. Homeowners could tie into utilities containing information on airline reservations, ticket availability for popular shows in certain towns, long-range weather forecasts, retrieval of stock information through the Dow Jones News Service, retrieval of archival data (such as the archives of *The New York Times* through a service called NEXIS), and legal research through a service called LEXIS (see the vignette "On-line Databases" for a description of some powerful public databases open to microcomputer users).

Telecommunications Networks

A related development in the 1980s is the rapidly expanding telecommunications sophistication of homes in the United States. Two developments account for this trend: the growth of cable television systems and the advent of inexpensive modems (which translate digital signals to analog signals that can be carried over ordinary telephone systems).

The advent of microprocessors—which themselves made microcomputers possible—also made possible a much more rapid, dense telecommunications network in the United States. Consider, for instance, the growth of cable television and communications systems. By 1985 there were 4500 local cable stations serving 30% of U.S. households with approximately 40 million viewers. Purchasers of cable television services receive not only entertainment but can also access digital services. About 10% of cable television users have two-way cable systems, providing a natural market for providers of

TABLE 10.3	Service	Description
Home Digital Services for Microcomputers	CompuServe, Inc.	Mail, consumer shopping, business
	Dialog Information Services, Inc.	Business, technical information
	Dow Jones News/Retrieval	Business, financial information
	Mead Data Central	Full text news, business, law
	The Source	Consumer information

digital services. Some of the current services available on cable are home banking, home shopping, access to information services, home security, polling, and home study and education. At times these services involve the use of a cable as well as telephones. For instance, a home shopping service can show video pictures of sale items to homeowners utilizing the greater bandwidth of cable television, who can then use the telephone to place an order.

While cable television is a new telecommunications system, opening up new digital opportunities to both businesses and homes, the most extensive telecommunications network is the telephone system. Fifty million U.S. households have a telephone. This represents as enormous market for digital microcomputer services (see Table 10.3 for a list of some home services available through the telephone system).

Indeed, there are so many on-line databases available to managers that choosing among them is difficult. The following vignette provides some criteria to use when choosing a database.

Needs of Large Organizations

While the sales of microcomputers to homeowners were disappointing, the sales to large organizations exceeded expectations. Several large firms are installing 1000 to 10,000 microcomputers at a time and are planning to put them on the desks of all clerical and managerial workers by the 1990s. Many managers will have more than one microcomputer: one on their desk, one in their car, and one at home.

Large organizations hope that microcomputers can be attached to mainframe computers to permit *desk-top processing* of large information files. Large organizations also hope that microcomputers can *reduce the backlog* that exists at most data processing installations for applications requested by users. Microcomputers, in other words, are one *alternative to expanding mainframes*.

One dramatic consequence of microcomputers is that for the first time everyone in a large organization can use a computer at the same

On-Line Databases

There are more than 300 on-line digital services providing more than 3000 databases to microcomputer users. In order to choose what is right for you, you must first *determine your needs*. What do you need quickly, and regularly? What expense will you incur? What are your current expenses for journals, research assistants, and staff? Second, *shop for the right database*. Many services give you more than you want (stocks, airline reservations, and mail). Some offer nighttime service at much lower cost. Third, *choose the right software*. You may want to postpone selecting communications software until you find the right service. Some services require that you use their software; others permit a variety of communications software packages. Last, *look for services that provide training*. Some services provide free training time or even classes. These are worth the savings in communications costs.

Based on Tapping into On-line Databases," *PC World*, May, 1985, pp. 120–125.

time. Assuming, ceterus paribus, that a worker with a computer is more productive than one without a computer, the gains in overall productivity can be enormous (see Figure 10.4.)

For instance, with the largest mainframe computers, sophisticated operating systems permit up to 2000 users to share the computing facilities simultaneously. With the addition of more users, the mainframe operating system slows down considerably, the delay and response time increases from seconds to minutes, and major production jobs have to be canceled because of insufficient computing power. Of course, the corporation can purchase a new mainframe computer for $5 to $6 million and double the size of computing available from 2000 to 4,000 users. And, of course, it must markedly expand its telecommunications capabilities as well. This is a very large expense and may not be necessary. With microcomputers, everyone, regardless of the number of people at the installation, can use a computer and have computing resources available. Microcomputers can be purchased in much smaller bundles of computing power; there is no limit on the number of such machines; and extensive use of microcomputers by large groups of people does not prevent other people from having access to computers.

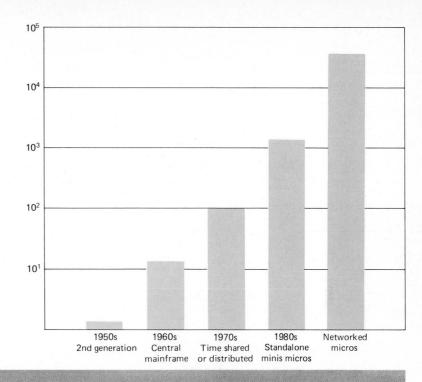

FIGURE 10.4
Number of people who can be computing simultaneously at any site.

But managers consider much more than simply avoiding expensive mainframe expenditures when they purchase 20,000 microcomputers. They are hoping to achieve *gains in productivity, innovation, better decision making*, the ability to offer *new services and products* to customers, and *improvement in the quality of work life* by relieving frustrations and adding new dimensions to work. It is these visions of the future—rather than cost avoidance—that are the most powerful driving forces behind the explosive growth of the microcomputer market.

10.3 Three Visions of Microcomputers in the Organization

Microcomputers had a controversial beginning, and there are still strong differences of opinion concerning where they fit in the overall corporate information systems processing operation. In the early 1980s, microcomputers were a maverick invention of small entrepreneurs and marketers. They were bootlegged into organizations by interested hobbyists and non-data-processing personnel looking for

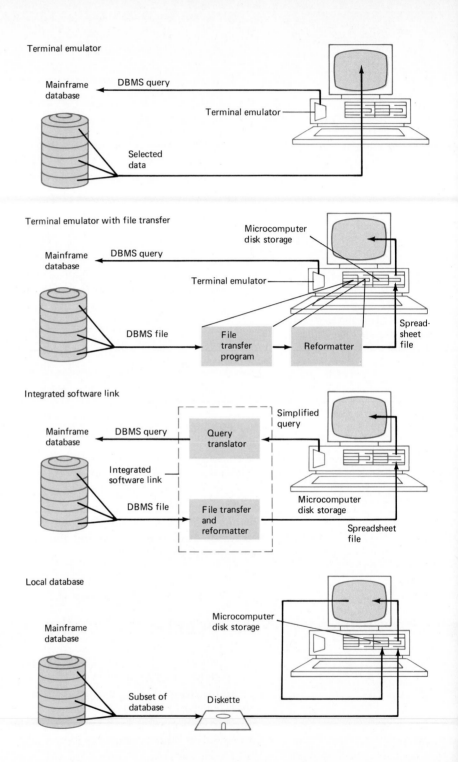

Terminal emulator

Mainframe
database

DBMS query

Terminal emulator

Selected
data

Terminal emulator with file transfer

Microcomputer
disk storage

Mainframe
database

DBMS query

Terminal emulator

Spread-
sheet
file

DBMS file

File
transfer
program

Reformatter

Integrated software link

Simplified
query

Mainframe
database

DBMS query

Query
translator

Integrated
software link

Microcomputer
disk storage

DBMS file

File transfer
and
reformatter

Spreadsheet
file

Local database

Microcomputer
disk storage

Mainframe
database

Subset of
database

Diskette

local PCs that could handle some office jobs. Microcomputers were not fostered, developed, innovated, or invented by large mainframe manufacturers. They originated in the backyards and garages of inventors such as Steven Jobs (the founder of the Apple Computer Corporation) and other entrepreneurs. The world of large mainframe computers largely ignored microcomputers or thought of them as mere toys.

There are three major views of how micros should fit into the firm. There is, of course, some overlap among these views, and organizations can adopt all of them at the same time. Nevertheless, these views reflect distinct models of how to incorporate micro-systems into the organization. They also represent marketing strategies of the major micro and mainframe vendors.

The Data Processing Vision

In the data processing vision, microcomputers are seen as subservient to and closely integrated into the mainframe corporate environment. There are several ways in which this is seen as taking place, but in the final analysis, microcomputers are conceived as appendages of the mainframe data processing environment.

Microcomputers can be integrated into the mainframe data processing environment in several ways (see Figure 10.5). Software can be developed so that microcomputers can emulate ordinary terminals. This is the most primitive use of a microcomputer because no use can be made of its local intelligence. Data cannot be downloaded from the mainframe into a micro program like Lotus. Moreover, the user must be familiar with mainframe applications software, which is generally not user friendly.

FIGURE 10.5
Microcomputers can access data from a mainframe in a number of ways. (1) Through a *terminal emulator*, the microcomputer can act like a computer terminal. Data are not downloaded into the microcomputer. However, the user can select data from a mainframe database and display it on the microcomputer terminal. (2) Using a *terminal emulator with file transfer*, plus reformatting programs, data can be downloaded, manipulated, and stored in the microcomputer. (3) *Integrated software links* provide an interface that simplifies the interaction between the microcomputer and data on a mainframe database. The link translates an end-user query selected from a menu into a database management system (DBMS) query language. (4) A fourth method is to utilize a local database version of a mainframe DBMS. The microcomputer version is loaded via diskette with a subset of the mainframe database. An example would be an application using PC FOCUS. Adapted from David H. Freedman, "Tapping the Corporate Database," *High Technology*, April, 1984.

A second way of integrating micros into the mainframe environment is to add file transfer capability to emulation. This requires mainframe software to produce micro-compatible files and the purchase of special micro software to accept these files (see "Fidelity's Micro–Mainframe Links"). In this manner, information can be transferred and reformated through a transfer program and placed in the microcomputer. This is called *downloading* of information files. For instance, corporate financial data for the year can be downloaded into a microcomputer, where a program such as Lotus can be used to manipulate them.

Another and more sophisticated way of integrating the microcomputer into the firm is the use of integrated software links combining emulation, file transfer, and user-friendly applications

Fidelity's Micro–Mainframe Links

Micro users at Fidelity Investment Co. in Boston wanted some way to use mainframe data on their micros with software packages like Lotus 1-2-3. The firm had 350 IBM micro computers and stored its corporate data on IBM mainframes. There was no connection between mainframes and micros; users typically had to re-key data from mainframe reports to micros. They needed a software that would provide the mainframe–micro connection, could work with a variety of micro software, would be compatible with different kinds of machines, and would provide data security. The firm chose Linkware Corporation's Linkware: Information Server. The product is a file server which is installed on the mainframe computer and prepares mainframe data for transfer to a number of micro computers. About 25 users have been given copies of the micro software needed to download mainframe data. The user types in the Linkware command on his micro and is presented with a list of the mainframe libraries he is permitted to search. The data can then be converted to micro compatible form and downloaded to the micro which is connected to mainframe via coaxial cable. The process is completely reversible for uploading data and files to the mainframe. Secretaries, financial analysts, and managers are the current users.

Adapted from "File Server, Micro Software Merge to Give Investment Firm Universal Access," *Computerworld*, April 29, 1985; p. 53.

software that can run on the micro. In this manner, data are not transferred to Lotus or dBASE III but instead to an integrated spread sheet or DBMS produced by the same manufacturer as the mainframe hardware or software. This user-friendly interface permits unsophisticated end users to query the corporate database and request downloading of information into a microcomputer-usable format. After the data are downloaded and formated, they can be used directly with integral microcomputer software.

This is the most sophisticated linkage between microcomputers and the corporate mainframe. It is sometimes called a *tight link*. Several major corporations are involved in testing and developing such mainframe–micro software (IBM, Cullinet, and Lotus). Some fourth-generation mainframe packages currently have PC versions that can accept mainframe data. A language called FOCUS has some of these abilities.

Still another way that the microcomputer can be integrated into the corporate mainframe environment is to produce subsets of corporate databases on diskettes (or in some electronic form such as a file in a minicomputer) in a format readable by micro software. The idea of the information center originates with this kind of downloading. In an information center, corporate data relevant to end users are downloaded on a routine basis, such as once a week. End users work on these data using microcomputers.

The data processing vision of microcomputers is primarily emphasized by large mainframe manufacturers.

The Logical Office

A radically different vision of the role of microcomputers in the organization focuses on the new relationship between individuals and the work that micros makes possible. This new relationship has been dubbed the *logical office*. As one wag put it, "a logical office is wherever your head is at when you think about business. A physical office is wherever your body is at when it acts as if it is doing business" (see Figure 10.6).

With microcomputers, people can do work in many locations—in the car, on the train, at home, in different parts of the organization, on airplanes when traveling, and so forth. Work no longer has to be associated with a single physical location. Proponents of this view argue that the only reason work is associated so strongly with a physical location is that the traditional information processing and communications technologies require central offices. People go to offices because that is where the telephones, the secretaries, and the filing cabinets are located. Microcomputers and high-speed telecommunications change this picture: Work can now be distributed more evenly in space and time. There is no need for a central office or a 9 to 5 job.

A logical office requires a logical desk, which can be provided by a highly capable and truly portable microcomputer—one that could

FIGURE 10.6
The logical office. A logical desk requires very portable and capable PCs.

be carried from place to place, weighs approximately 8 pounds, and has approximately 1 megabyte of internal memory and 1 megabyte of disk storage. This machine could handle correspondence, place orders, stay in touch with the stock market, and contact fellow employees via electronic mail. The Data General/One is a step toward such a machine (see "Hardware for the Logical Office"). Many other corporations have developed similar machines (Radio Shack, Hewlett-Packard, and Compaq).

Hardware for the Logical Office

Truly portable lap top computing began with the Radio Shack Model 100. But with only 24K of memory it could not do much except write a few letters. But the new Data General/One packs more punch: 128K (upgradable to 512K) memory, 720K disk built in, and a full 80 column, 25 line screen. A modem and extra disk drives can be added for communications and additional storage. A miniature printer is even available. Unfortunately, the price is high (about $4,500), the screen is difficult to read, and the options [are] expensive. Still, mobile professionals from writers to salespeople and engineers would argue that this is an acceptable price to pay for having vital data and texts at their finger tips.

Adapted from "DG/One For the Road," *PC World*, May, 1985, pp. 158–162.

The Automated Office

In a third vision, the microcomputer is the centerpiece of the office of the future (see Figure 10.7). Here the microcomputer plays a central role in integrating the diverse machines found in the office. Increasingly, this machinery is being developed with partial and local intelligence. Copying machines are being built that have small memories and can be linked to other communication networks. Inexpensive electronic typewriters can also be used as computer printers. Color graphics plotters and slide producers accept digital input. Telephones are increasingly relying on digital communications. Printing machines are now being built that can operate in a totally digital environment; typesetting can be accomplished with a microcomputer.

In this view, the PC can be used to control and coordinate the flow of documents and work in an office, largely independently of the mainframe computer. Powerful PCs can control telecommunications networks that link other PCs, copying machines, printing machines, and secretarial and management work stations. Microcomputers can also be used as large file servers—communicating with the mainframe on a routine basis, downloading important files to be used in an office, and then distributing this information to other office

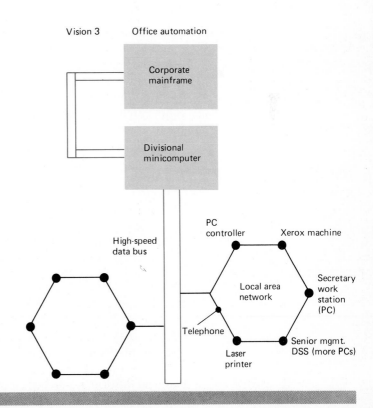

FIGURE 10.7
Vision 3: Office automation.

microcomputers. In this vision, highly capable microcomputers—with an internal memory of 1 to 2 megabytes and a storage capacity of up to 60 megabytes—can be used as the overall coordinator of the office of the future and of the telecommunications links that make it work. Although they are connected to the mainframe and minicomputers of the corporation by high-speed data links, micros in this view operate on an independent, highly autarchic basis. Under the control of users, they operate user-friendly software, and they do not require the intervention of mainframe information systems personnel.

This vision is strongly supported by the Apple Computer Corporation. Currently, Apple sells the only 16-bit microcomputer with a built-in LAN capability and an optional laser printer at very reasonable prices. The Apple "Lisa," a still larger machine, is more than capable of acting as an overall automated office coordinator. The Xerox Corporation is also a leading proponent of the automated office using smart machines connected to its Ethernet LAN. (Local Area Networks are discussed in the preceding chapter.)

10.4 The Reality: Some Problems

Bits and pieces of each of these grand visions of microcomputers are clearly visible in large and small corporations throughout the country. Many large organizations have chosen a single path, while others—unsure of what model is correct—are experimenting with all three.

It is clear that we are only in the very early stage of microcomputer and end-user computing. Most knowledgeable observers now believe that it will take at least a decade to fully utilize the potential of existing microcomputer equipment, let alone that of equipment yet to be developed.

The Micro–Mainframe Connection

The vision of microcomputers as fully integrated, end-user, desktop computers used as professional and managerial work stations cannot be implemented easily at the present time. Mainframe software cannot operate on microcomputers and was not designed to output data in a format suitable for use with micro software. Mainframe files are too large either to communicate rapidly with a micro or to store in a micro. The telecommunications infrastructure of most corporations would quickly be overwhelmed if large numbers of micro users started transferring large files. It is very expensive to convert large corporate files to micro-compatible form. Establishing information centers that store downloaded mainframe data compatible with micros and keep this information updated and current is also an expensive undertaking. The cost to a large corporation of installing financial information centers permitting widespread access to its financial data by financial professionals is about $10 to $30 million. At this stage, no one knows precisely what dollar benefits are produced by such investments or how much of what kinds of data to put on an end user's desk.

Moreover, using micros as terminal emulators is not a satisfactory solution because it misses the whole point of microcomputers as user-friendly, end-user–controlled, intelligent devices. Most end users have unfriendly attitudes toward data processing and do not know or understand mainframe software. Therefore, terminal emulator micros are useful only in professional data processing shops—hardly an end-user revolution.

Independence of End Users

Many worry that the data processing vision, with its emphasis on mainframe compatibility and required telecommunications links, will stifle the independence and creativity of end users and reduce their ability to define their own information needs. Large mainframe manufacturers are urging their users to develop integrated systems that make a microcomputer simply an intelligent terminal. This seems sensible: Documents can be transferred over a whole range of machines, from mainframe, to minicomputer to microcomputer, using a single communication standard. But such a strategy also has a number of negative consequences: Users become totally dependent on the mainframe and its vendor; as a result, prices for key elements may rise; the ability to use certain software provided by other vendors may decline; and micro users may lose influence on central data processing requirements. The original appeal of microcomputers was that they permitted stand-alone applications and promoted independence from centralized data processing departments.

Organizational Resistance

Equally important is organizational resistance. It takes many hours for employees to learn how to use microcomputer software (it took the author about 8 hours to learn how to use the graphics portion of a popular spread sheet program proficiently). Training is often incomplete or lacking altogether in many firms. Senior management is often skeptical of the benefits of establishing integrated managerial work stations. A safer approach is to simply purchase stand-alone micros and see how they are used. Later, as the demand for access to corporate databases increases, it is hoped that the machines can be integrated. Hence the development of integrated work stations will take many years.

Similar problems plague the realization of the logical office and the automated office. Existing machines are simply too small for serious, remote work except in certain situations—like writing short letters on an airplane or entering small customer orders. As the centerpiece of the automated office, micros simply are poorly designed. They cannot handle multiple jobs at one time (they have no multitasking operating system), they are poor at handling communications, and they are insufficient to act as file servers for a large

TABLE 10.4
What Micros Can and Cannot Do Well

Micros *can*:
Provide superior software applictions: word processing, spread sheets
Support small, department-based, stand-alone applications
Provide controlled, consistent response time
By pass data processing for *certain* applications
Reduce some of the hidden backlog

Micros *cannot*:
Process large amounts of data
Communicate very large files rapidly
Support large transaction-driven systems (major applications)
Automatically back up files
Print large amounts of data rapidly
Rapidly upload/download from the mainframe
Develop large programs for the mainframe
Support complex boolean logic
Create applications generalizable to other business areas
Reduce the maintenance backlog of mainframe systems

office. At the moment, these operations require minicomputers and mainframe software.

Micros are no panacea for the backlog of applications faced by most information systems groups. They are too small for most applications and are poor at handling transaction processing tasks. Micros may actually increase the backlog of applications due to the "freeway effect." Once end users realize the value of information held in large corporate files, and once the skills to analyze data on micros become more widespread, they may request more information from the information system group.

On balance, there are some things microcomputers can now do well and others that are best left to other machines (see Table 10.4). Yet software, telecommunications, and hardware limitations are all changing rapidly. It is less a question of which microcomputer vision will succeed than of which one is best for a specific organization and how can it be implemented.

10.5 How Micros Are Used Today and Will Be Used in the Future

Surveys and interviews with a wide variety of corporate microcomputer users have found that firms are at different stages in the use of micros. While almost no firms have yet developed integrated microcomputer "systems" in the sense of very-large-scale integration

TABLE 10.5
Stages of Microcomputer
Development

Stage 1: Stand-alone microcomputers (50% of firms)

Stage 2: Some terminal emulation (40% of firms)

Stage 3: Integrated networks (10% of firms)

of micros into corporate information systems, many have begun building telecommunications networks that will act as the integrative links for microsystems envisaged by proponents of managerial work stations, logical offices, and automated offices. In this section, we will review the results of a recent survey completed by one of the authors of some of the largest and most sophisticated microcomputer users in the nation (Laudon, 1985). The survey and supporting interviews involved 25 financial service firms in the New York metropolitan area. While not representative of all firms using micros, these leading-edge firms provide a number of insights into how very large organizations are using micros and what kinds of problems have been encountered.

The large corporations in our survey fall into one of three stages in the use of micros. Table 10.5 uses the degree of networking and network integration as a measure of sophistication in the uses of microcomputers. In the largest category (50%), the firms' micros are used as stand-alone devices totally unconnected to corporate data processing. A second group of firms (40%) is using micros as terminal emulators connected to the existing time-shared mainframes. A small number of leading-edge firms (10%) have developed high-speed, integrated telecommunications networks that make micros a part of the overall information network. Here managerial and professional work stations are the predominant goal of micro use. The telecommunications systems also permit micros to play a useful field role as a logical office (users can dial into a corporate mainframe and read their correspondence or send correspondence to a letter-quality printer) and a larger role in office integration.

Current and Future Uses

When companies are asked how micros are currently used and will be used in the near future, it becomes clear that spread sheets (and related modeling/analysis of data) and word processing are still the predominant uses (see Figure 10.8). However, in the near future (3 years), these firms expect to use the micros in more interesting ways: Searching corporate databases, processing mainframe records, and remote work are the most important anticipated applications. Other high-growth applications are internal/external communications (electronic mail), graphics, planning, and learning.

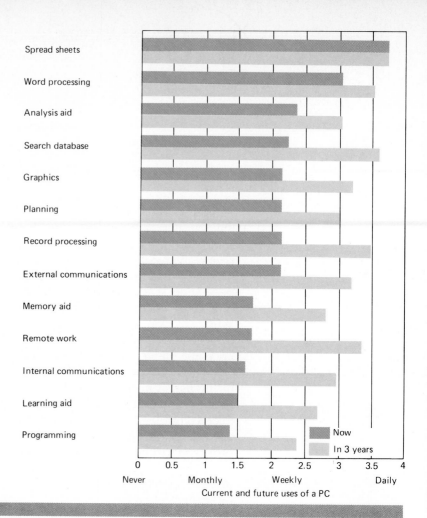

Spread sheets

Word processing

Analysis aid

Search database

Graphics

Planning

Record processing

External communications

Memory aid

Remote work

Internal communications

Learning aid

Programming

Now
In 3 years

| 0 | 0.5 | 1 | 1.5 | 2 | 2.5 | 3 | 3.5 | 4 |

Never   Monthly   Weekly   Daily

Current and future uses of a PC

FIGURE 10.8
Uses of microcomputers.

Users of Micros

The largest groups of users of micros today are professional and middle management employees (about 35% of these workers use micros), followed closely by clerical workers (see Figure 10.9). Senior managers are far less likely to use micros. The most intense users of micros in terms of hours per week are clerical and middle management groups, who average about 12 hours.

It is clear that micros have made a large impact on work life. On the other hand, the microcomputer revolution has a long way to go: 65% of middle management does not use micros at all. In smaller or less advanced firms, the number of managers who have no contact with micros is probably much larger.

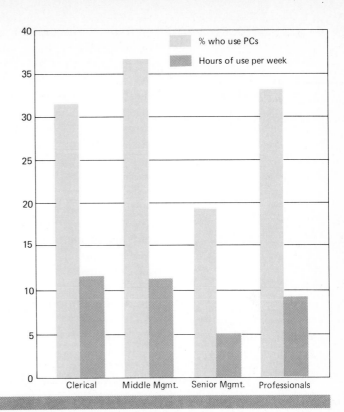

FIGURE 10.9
Extent and intensity of PC use.

10.6 Management Problems and Issues

More than any other recent information technology, end-user computing and the microcomputers that support it pose challenges to the way organizations think about and use information. Having barely adjusted to the first wave of stand-alone micros, managers are now learning that in order to be really useful, the micros must be connected to other corporate information systems and databases.

Micros Empower People   Micros represent a loss of control by traditional management techniques and specific managerial groups over the computing resource. Micros are, after all, a little like mass literacy. They are a form of magic insofar as they empower a large number of people to do and to understand things that heretofore were restricted to a small group of professionals located in the Data Processing Department. Its as if people have suddenly learned how to read, gaining access to secret texts and data. Personal computing represents a loss of control by the priests of information. The sanctity, accuracy, integrity, and uses of heretofore protected information are challenged by PCs. Insofar as microcomputers allow ordinary untrained employees access to important data, they threaten the traditional control over information.

Security Problems

It is important to realize why corporate data have traditionally been tightly controlled. Limitations on access to these data were in part technological; it was impossible to disseminate information widely in a timely fashion. But many of these limitations also have to do with the desire to protect confidential information. If certain information becomes public, it could harm the corporation by exposing its decision making to public criticism, to competitors, and to government agencies. Data are also restricted so that employees do not take advantage of corporations, either through direct embezzlement of funds or through the sale of information to outsiders.

These are all important reasons for restricting access to information. End-user computing—with micros in particular—threatens data protection by permitting large numbers of employees to access confidential information.

Changes in the Distribution of Power

Microcomputers also pose a challenge by permitting people throughout the organization to form independent judgments rather than receiving interpretations from on high. These employees can therefore learn to act on the basis of information that they themselves possess and create, rather than being told how to act. The ability to make informed decisions and judgments, and the ability to act in a rational manner without the intervention of personal authority, are pushed down in the organization with PCs.

With micros, for instance, junior loan officers can track loan portfolios and make independent judgments about new loan agreements in the coming days and weeks rather than waiting for a monthly MIS report to be read by their boss, who will instruct them monthly regarding the nature of the portfolio for the following month.

Micros change the distribution of power, perquisites, advantage, and resources in organizations. Insofar as information confers power, independence, and advantage, then, PCs are very interesting.

Loss of Management Control

But there is a third, more concrete reason why micros pose a unique challenge to management. In the 1950s and 1960s, information systems were confined to one to three data processing centers in the organization. By the 1970s, large organizations had anywhere from 5 to 15 data centers involving networks of minicomputers and mainframes. Nevertheless, the information processing function, that is, the information resources of the company, were confined to relatively small cells where key decisions were slowly made, thoroughly analyzed, and the data processing and human and technological resources carefully balanced, weighed, and measured. With microcomputers, however, the organization is composed not of 1, 2, 10, or

Decentralization Dilemma at SSA

In March of 1981 the Social Security Administration (SSA), which each month sends checks to more than 40 million Americans participating in SSA programs, contracted with the Paradyne Corporation to install 1800 new terminals in 1350 field offices located around the nation. These terminals would initially have a limited local intelligence (memory and storage) to replace existing dumb terminals installed in 1975. SSA hoped by 1985 to enhance the terminals by adding more memory (about 1 megabyte) and a large local storage capacity (60 megabytes). These terminals would then become microcomputers. This additional intelligence would be used to develop local applications, perform communications systems functions locally, and to permit the storage of some data locally which heretofore was stored exclusively at the massive SSA Computer Center in Baltimore, Maryland. SSA hoped this would also reduce telecommunications costs and reduce the load on the existing system. With more work done locally, there would be less need to communicate with the central system.

But the central system in the early 1980s was itself in a state of crisis. The central computers were operating at capacity, data were stored on 500,000 outmoded tapes, the telecommunications systems were subject to frequent overload and breakdown, and the existing software was a maintenance nightmare because it lacked documentation and was not developed according to modern standards.

SSA ultimately pulled back from developing a highly decentralized system based on the Paradyne microcomputers. One important consideration was that the local computers would in effect create 1350 data centers (each local office becomes a data processing center). It was not clear that all these centers could be coordinated. Who would control data definitions, uses of machines, compatibility of application systems? As one SSA staffer put it, "If we couldn't run a central data center well, the idea of 1350 data centers was ludicrous."

From "Social Security Administrations Data Communications Contracts with Paradyne Corporation Demonstrate the Need for Improved Management Controls," General Accounting Office, Comptroller General of the United States, July 1984, and interviews with SSA personnel conducted by the author.

20 data centers but of a 1000, 5000, 20,000 data centers; conceivably, every employee in the future will become a data center by virtue of having access to a very powerful microcomputer. Each employee will become a player in the definition of data and information, in its collection, storage, and dissemination. This was one of the factors in the decision of the Social Security Administration in the 1980s to pull back from its early plan to radically decentralize computing power.

In this milieu, a number of simple management questions that could be answered in the traditional computing environment of the 1970s become problematic:

- What is a good, cost-effective use of a computer?
- How are computers currently being used?
- Who is using them? Where did they get them?
- Who is responsible for the data in micros?
- How many machines do we have? What software is being used?
- Who's in charge of the uses, the software, the hardware purchase and maintenance?
- How much are we spending on micros?
- What is the total cost of hardware and software purchases, annual maintenance, training costs, communications, and opportunity costs?

Managers who have had no exposure to data processing or information systems, who hardly know a mainframe from a disk drive, are being forced to think about these questions with very few intellectual tools, very few guidelines, very little prior research, and very little understanding of what other organizations are doing.

Survey Results

Our survey of leading firms provides several insights into the problems encountered with microcomputers (see Figure 10.10). Four issues stand out. In descending order of importance, they are security, utility, quality, and support. Some specific problems encountered are the following.

Security

Key financial information on operating units in major corporations can be stored on high-density floppy disks (720-kilobyte disks). Hard *bernoulli* disks, which can store up to 60 megabytes and are easily removed and concealed, are sufficient to capture very large data files, such as executive compensation, personnel, product testing, and marketing information files. Most firms generally prevent uploading from micros to mainframe operating applications, but significant downloading is occurring, which results in wide distribution within the firm of sensitive data. By and large, no special security precautions are being taken. In one instance, a disgruntled broker at a major stock brokerage house copied the names of all of the firm's large

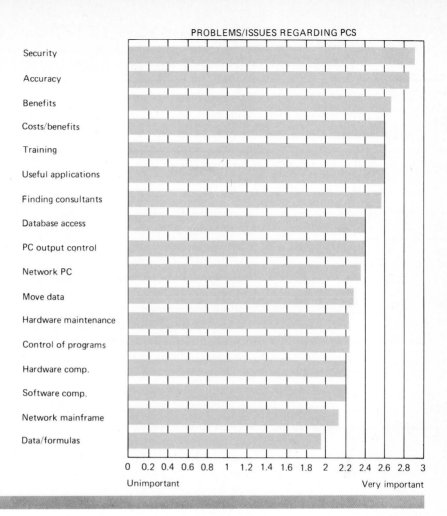

PROBLEMS/ISSUES REGARDING PCS

Security
Accuracy
Benefits
Costs/benefits
Training
Useful applications
Finding consultants
Database access
PC output control
Network PC
Move data
Hardware maintenance
Control of programs
Hardware comp.
Software comp.
Network mainframe
Data/formulas

0   0.2 0.4 0.6 0.8   1   1.2 1.4 1.6 1.8   2   2.2 2.4 2.6 2.8   3
Unimportant   Very important

FIGURE 10.10
Problems and issues in
PC use.

clients and their recent transactions on several floppy disks before erasing the brokerage firm's copy and then quitting.

Utility

Measuring the benefits of micros and understanding their cost/benefit applications is the second most important category of problems after security. Micros rarely result in real cost avoidance (e.g., fewer managers and/or clerical workers or lower administrative costs). In fact, these costs may rise. One firm reports, for instance, that it now prints over 300 pages of computer output per employee per day from all sources and states that micros have added significantly to this burden. Instead of reducing costs, micros can temporarily increase them. However, they have intangible benefits: more information distributed to more people, more informed decisions, better modeling of data, better correspondence, and more of it. In the long run, more business can be done with the same workforce. Nevertheless, in the short term, interesting questions are raised. Does it make sense for a $70,000-a-year executive to spend 50% of his or her time in programming? A well-trained programmer might cost less and be more effective.

Quality

Several items in our survey reflect a growing concern about the quality of data, formulas, and models in microcomputer programs. End-user computing rests fundamentally on amateur keypunching, programming, and modeling. Unlike mainframe systems, there is no quality control, no keypunch error checking, and no formal training in systems design, programming, and documentation of programs. Large Lotus 1-2-3 spread sheets can have thousands of cells and 100 formulas, some of them interrelated, and employ several canned and custom-built formulas. Generally, no one except the originator of these spread sheets checks the cell entries, formulas, or algorithms. Nevertheless, important decisions are made on the basis of these models and spread sheets.

Recognizing this problem, several large banks have placed a prominent seal on reports emanating from the Data Processing Division (indicating authenticated reliable information) and prohibit the dissemination of information produced on a micro outside of the originating department.

Support

Several issues presented in Figure 10.10 focus on the quality of support that end users receive in the organization. Many organizations have purchased large numbers of micros with inadequate attention to training users and no provision for internal consulting to handle exceptions and special applications. In the rush to bring micros into the organization, incompatible hardware and software has been purchased and little provision has been made for its maintenance. Unlike mainframes, no maintenance is provided as part of the purchase price.

10.7 Some Solutions

From the beginning, there has been controversy about how micros should be managed. In the early years, micros had to be bootlegged into corporations over the objections of data processing professionals, who saw them at best as toys and at worst as a threat to the integrity of corporate information management. In many organizations, individuals were permitted to purchase any equipment they desired so long as a rationale existed. Other organizations sought to control micros rigidly from the beginning and only slowly to introduce them into selected areas. What is the correct management approach?

Management Stages

Much seems to depend on how advanced and sophisticated the applications are. As organizations move through the three stages of microcomputing suggested in the previous section, from stand-alone device to increasingly integrated machines, they increase the intensity of management and create new management positions.

When micros are used solely as stand-alone devices serving individual needs (stage 1), an overly restrictive management policy makes little sense; innovations could be crushed before they have a chance to develop. As micros enter stage 2 and become networked as terminal emulators, and in other ways become integrated with the mainframe, more stringent management policies controlling hardware and software purchases are advised, if only to ensure the compatibility and portability of results from micro to mainframe. In stage 3, as micros become a full-fledged, integral part of the corporate information processing network, decision making about micros must become more centralized and more corporatewide. The reason for this is clear: Micros in this environment must be compatible with expensive telecommunications networks and new mainframe software. Typically, a new entity is established independently of data processing to impose corporate controls. This new management entity is often called the *PC coordinator, end-user computing center,* or *information center.* As suggested by the experience of *The New York Times,* to be described, new management skills and people are also required.

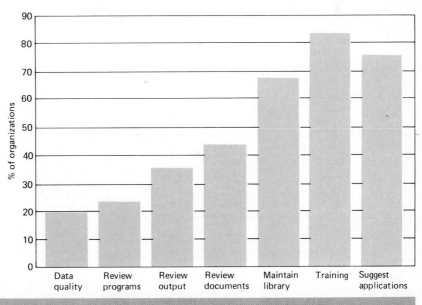

FIGURE 10.11
Specific management controls in organizations.

Management Controls

What specific practices should be used to control micros? Figure 10.11 illustrates some of the practices followed by leading corporate users. Few organizations control or review data quality, programs, or output. More than 50% of the organizations surveyed do maintain libraries of software and applications (if only to prevent reinventing

Issue	Individual users (1)	PC user groups (2)	Division manager (3)	PC coordinator (4)	Data processing (5)	Other (6)	No one (7)
Hardware purchase	XXXXXXXX	XXXX	XXXXXXXXXX XX	XXXXXXXXXX X	X	XX	
Software purchase	XXXXXXXXXX XXXXXX	XXXX	XXXXXXXX	XXXXXX		XX	
Version control	XXXXXXXXXX		XX	XXXXXXXX	X	X	XXX
Data definitions	XXXXXXXXXX XXXXX	XX	X	XX	XXXX		XXX
Hardware maintenance	XXXXXX		XX	XXXXXXXXXX XXXXX	XXXX	X	X
Access to central data	XXXXX	X	XXX	XXXXXXXXXX XXX	XXXXXXXXXX XX	XX	XXXX
Network to other PCs	XXXX	XX	XXXX	XXXXXXXXXX XX	XXXXXXX	XX	XXXX
Network to firm telecommunications	XXX	XX	XXX	XXXXXXXXXX XX	XXXXXXXXXX X	X	XX
Training/consulting	XXXXX		XX	XXXXXXXXXX XXXXXX	XXX	XXX	
New applications	XXXXXXXXXX XXXXXXXXX	XX	X	XXXXX	XXXX	XX	X
Accuracy of PC data	XXXXXXXXXX XXXXXXXXXX	X	XXX	XXXX		X	XXX
Security of PC data	XXXXXXXXXX XXXXXX	XX	XX	XXXXX	XX		XX
Controlling dissemination of PC reports, data	XXXXXXXXXX XXXXX	XXX	XXXXX	XXXX			XXX
Specific day-to-day uses and applications	XXXXXXXXXX XXXXXXXXXX	XXX	XXXX	XXX	XX	X	XX
Maintaining a library of PC applications	XXXXXXXXXX	XX	XXX	XXXXXXXX	XX	X	XXXXX X

FIGURE 10.12

Who is most important in making the following kinds of decisions?

the wheel every time an individual needs a particular program), conduct training seminars, and have an employee (usually a micro-computer "buff") who suggests and advertises new applications.

The more sophisticated organizations become in their use of micros, however, the more attention they pay to data and program quality. A full-time microcomputer specialist is often hired to closely review and edit micro programs.

Another question is, who should make decisions about micros? Figure 10.12 is a matrix of decision makers and decision issues and shows the pattern of decision making found in leading microcomputer user organizations. Figure 10.13 shows the average scores for the various decision makers found in Figure 10.12. In general, data processing and PC coordinators are powerful in the areas of mainte-nance, access to central databases, telecommunications, and training. Individual users are powerful in making decisions about hardware and software purchases, applications, accuracy, and security.

As the overall scores of decision making show, individuals still play the most powerful role in managing micros, followed by the corporate PC coordinator.

Increasingly, large organizations are creating a new title and career, *microcomputer manager*.

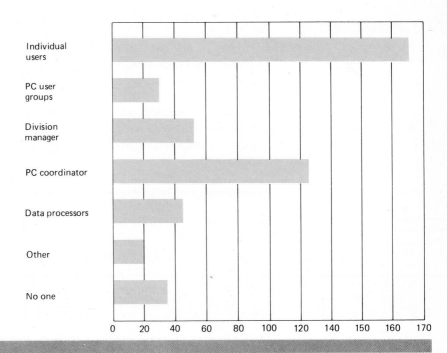

FIGURE 10.13
Overall scores for decision groups in Figure 10.12.

Birth of the Micro Manager

In the late 1970's the *New York Times* budget department purchased an IBM 5110 to expedite the budgeting cycle. The entire system was written in APL—a professional programming language. That machine was replaced in 1984 with an IBM personal computer using Lotus 1-2-3. The micro system permitted multiple passes during the budget development cycle which was not possible with old system. Other applications followed by the thousands.

As the money spent on these machines and software grew, the micro revolution could not be controlled by data processing management. A micro manager was needed.

Adapted from "Increased Personal Computer Use Demands New Breed of Manager," *Computerworld*, July 15, 1985.

10.8 Summary

The most rapidly changing area in information systems is end-user computing, made possible by the advent of microcomputers. Microcomputers can best be distinguished by their use and intended function, not their size. They have less memory and operating system capability than minicomputers and mainframes but can be used by individuals on their own. Microcomputers are designed to help non-data-processing personnel access and model data and prepare documents. Micros have become popular because they combine enhanced computing power, low cost, and software oriented toward end users.

There are three major views of how micros should be used: (1) as appendages of large mainframes, (2) as logical desks, and (3) as the centerpiece of automated offices. Software has been developed to make micros emulate mainframe terminals or receive data downloaded from mainframe databases. As logical offices micros enable work to be performed at multiple locations. PCs can also be used to control and coordinate the flow of documents and work in an office environment independently of the mainframe computer.

Microcomputers are best suited for small, department-based, stand-alone applications and have superior capability for word processing and spread sheets. They are inappropriate, however, for applications that require processing large amounts of data and large files, and they cannot develop large programs for mainframes.

In the future, micros will be more closely integrated with corporate data processing. This will require strengthening the management of microcomputers and imposing controls and quality assurance procedures (since micros have enpowered end users to create their own applications and data outside of the traditional managerial framework for information systems.) However, in order to serve end-user requirements, individuals will continue to play a powerful role in decision making about microcomputers.

Key Words

End-user computing	Automated office
Microcomputer	Security
Spread sheet packages	Quality control
Downloading	Microcomputer manager
Uploading	Micro–mainframe connection
Logical office	

Review Questions

1. How would you define a microcomputer? How does it differ from a minicomputer or a mainframe?
2. Why have micros proliferated in organizations?
3. What needs of large organizations can microcomputers meet?
4. Describe the three visions of how microcomputers should fit into the firm. Which individuals and groups support which vision?
5. Define the logical office. How is it enhanced by microcomputers?
6. What problems have arisen from the introduction of microcomputers into large organizations?
7. What data processing functions can microcomputers perform well? What functions can't they perform?
8. Name the three stages of microcomputer development in large organizations. How are micros used in each stage?
9. What are the predominant uses for microcomputers at the present time? What will be the predominant uses in the future?
10. What management problems and issues are raised by the widespread use of microcomputers in the firm? Suggest some solutions.

Discussion Questions

1. Some managers have said, "Now that we have microcomputers, we can do our computer work ourselves. We don't need the Data Processing Department any longer." Discuss.
2. Many organizations have a 2- to 3-year backlog of computer applications because the demand for new applications cannot be met by their Data Processing Departments. How can microcomputers be used to reduce this backlog?

Insurance Agents Buy Their Own Micros

New York Life Insurance Company has embarked on a drive to put an IBM PC on each of its agents' desks. The company recommended that agents with a minimum of 4 years' experience purchase a microcomputer system. The agents had to purchase the desktop computer with their own funds. Approximately 3500 of New York Life's 10,000 agents were initially eligible, and 3000 chose to make the investment.

The agents are self-employed but closely tied to the home office. Without micros they would have to maintain their client files manually or write letters to the homes office whenever they needed sales illustrations. With PCs, agents can do their own sales illustrations, maintain electronic client files, and access New York Life's mainframes directly for information.

New York Life helped its agents purchase their PCs at a discount and provided them with three software packages that they could use with minimum training. Independent software firms created programs for sales illustrations and client and prospect files. The agents also use word processing software from the Multimate International Corporation and a communications program.

New York Life's vice-president in charge of the PC campaign has observed that life insurance has undergone dramatic changes. Financial packages such as the industrywide universal life insurance introduce annual variables into a policy. (New York Life uses a version of the package called Target Life.) The product has become difficult to sell without an automated illustration package.

New York Life is trying to further enhance its agents' desktop computing by linking their tools more closely to its five IBM 3080 series mainframes in the home office. The company is upgrading its Facts network, which links its Clinton, New Jersey, data center to its 220 general offices around the country to accomodate individual agents. A terminal emulation package can link agents' PCs to an IBM Series/1 minicomputer in the general offices. Agents can thereby access a host computer by dialing into the Series/1. New York Life built its network around IBM's Series/1 minicomputer and PCs to ensure they can communicate with its mainframes.

New York Life has formed its own microcomputer user group. To troubleshoot problems, it publishes a newsletter and provides a home office hot line.

Adapted from "Insurance Firm Sells Its Agents on Buying Their Own Micros," *Computerworld*, April 15, 1985.

Case Study Questions

1. What model of the microcomputer in the organization has New York Life adopted?
2. Why have microcomputers become essential tools for the insurance industry?
3. What measures did New York Life take to make sure that microcomputers were successfully integrated into its organization?

References

Bender, Eric. "Firms Warned on Intuitive Micro Purchase Decisions," *Computerworld* (December 1984).

Benson, David H. "A Field Study of End-User Computing: Findings and Issues," *MIS Quarterly* (December 1983).

Canning, Richard G. "Coping with End-User Computing," *EDP Analyzer* (February 1984).

Coon, Jennifer L. "Documentaing Micro-Computer Systems," *EDPACS*, the EDP Audit, Control and Security Newsletter (October 1983).

Data Decisions. "Micros at Big Firms: A Survey," *Datamation* (November 1983).

Datamation. "Adventures in Micro Land," *Datamation* (November 1983).

Ferris, David. "The Micro–Mainframe Connection," *Datamation* (November 1983).

Johnson, Jan. "In Search of Missing Links," *Datamation* (November 1983).

Keen, Peter G.W., and Woodman, Linda A. "What to Do with All Those Micros," *Harvard Business Review* (September–October 1984).

Laudon, Kenneth C. "From PC's to Managerial Workstations," New York University Symposium on Micros, Managers and Mainframes, New York City, May 22, 1985.

"Micros at Big Firms: A Survey," November 1983. (A report prepared by Data Decisions, 20 Brace Road, Cherry Hill, New Jersey 08540.)

Murphy, John A. "Tighter Links Open PC–Mainframe Gate," *Software News* (December 1984).

Parker, Wayne. "From Altair to AT," *PC World* (March 1985).

Rockart, John F., and Flannery, Lauren S. "The Management of End-User Computing," *Communications of the ACM* (October 1983).

Capacity Planning at Ocean Spray

Ocean Spray Cranberry, Inc., is a cooperative owned by 800 cranberry and other fruit growers. Once a tiny regional operation located in Plymouth, Massachusetts, Ocean Spray became a Fortune 500 company in 1985. Revenue in 1986 was $630 million and has been growing at the rate of 15% per year.

Ocean Spray's growth has resulted from a reformulation of its original cranberry juice drink to make it taste better and from expansion of its product line to include other juices like grapefruit and guava juice. Ocean Spray has benefited as well from changing public tastes toward natural fruit products, a concern with diets in general, and the image of Ocean Spray products as unaltered, healthy, and natural.

Decentralization

Rapid growth, the development of national markets, and branching into new products have proved a challenge for the company MIS department. The company had gone from a centralized minicomputer to a decentralized multisystem MIS in the 1970s. It is now recentralizing with much higher-capacity hardware.

In the mid-1970s, MIS installed a Burroughs B1800 minicomputer to handle all computing at a central facility. This was adequate when the company was a small regional producer with only a few processing plants. As the number of processing plants expanded, however, the local plants began begging for more processing power and faster service from the central MIS. The old Burroughs was "bending at the knees," according to Thomas Modestino, MIS director. A second Burroughs mini was added, but even this was inadequate. The business had changed. There were now six processing plants that received orders from the sales staff. It was taking 24 hours just to post orders to plants on a batch basis from the central MIS.

In 1982 Ocean Spray converted to a host IBM 4331 Model Group 2 at headquarters and installed a number of Wang VS 80 minicomputers at the processing plants.

The shift to IBM host equipment was a difficult transition. All of the software had to be converted or rewritten because of incompatibilities between Burroughs and IBM. It was a traumatic shift for employees who were used to the friendly operating systems of Burroughs. Systems workers lost productivity as they were forced to learn IBM's more complex and difficult systems languages.

The shift to IBM was made because Ocean Spray wanted the flexibility to take advantage of the much larger amount of third-party software written for IBM operating systems. Also, IBM had a large range of machines so that Ocean Spray could upgrade within the IBM line as MIS demands increased.

Ocean Spray shifted to decentralized minicomputers to ensure better service to local processing plants. Indeed, as Modestino notes, the systems world was moving toward decentralization in the early 1980s, and the new minicomputers were cheap, powerful, supportive of this move.

The Wang VS 80 minis were used to process orders during the day and to batch-upload those orders to the host 4331 at night. Also, the remote minis were used for local purposes such as office automation and local regulatory compliance in diverse regions in Florida, Massachusetts, and Washington. Wang VS 90s and VS 100's were added at central headquarters to support the uploads and headquarters office automation.

Getting the Wang VS minis to talk with the host IBM consumed enormous resources. As many as 10 consultants at a time were needed, producing a consulting bill that Modestino called "startling."

Recentralization

The minicomputer, decentralized solution worked for a time. But in a few years, Ocean Spray outgrew the system. Serious problems arose in coordinating the minis with the host, in controlling application development at so many sites, and simply in finding information.

For instance, it became difficult to track an order that might be on any one of three systems (the remote VS, the headquarters VS, or the headquarters host). The order processing system was slowed as orders moved through three systems. It often took 24 hours from receipt of an order at a remote site to the return of the shipment order to that location from headquarters. Maintenance was a problem as well because many of the remote sites were far from cities where maintenance staffs of manufacturers were located.

In 1984 Ocean Spray began recentralizing its MIS. It purchased an IBM 3083 to centralize order processing once again. Now an order can be processed at headquarters and printed out within minutes at a remote plant that fills the order and ships it.

The VS 80 minis are being removed from the remote sites. In their place are powerful new PCs that pick up many of the local applications. IBM System 36s (an IBM mini) are used at remote sites for office automation of entities like electronic mail and as telecommunications controllers for dumb 3270 terminals connected to the host mainframe.

Asked if it was not unusual to recentralize, Modestino noted that the trend may be toward centralization in the industry. "As you get into minicomputers, you have to ask what you are doing with a mini that a PC can't do as well. Also, you won't hear many people disagree that it is better to have all of your data stored in one place. What we said was 'Let's store it once, accurately, and in one place.'"

Related Software and Hardware

The move toward centralization and growth of PCs has caused MIS to become much more involved in key aspects of the company and training. Ocean Spray did not want to restrict access to data; just the opposite—they hoped to make corporate information more available even as they centralized in some areas.

Ocean Spray now has about 110 PCs at headquarters and remote locations. A total of 150 people use IBM 3270 terminals. To train users, MIS opened up an information center in 1985 to provide mainframe-based decision support tools to sales and marketing personnel.

The firm has installed and is modifying a manufacturing software system that emphasizes electronic ordering, invoicing, and bill payment. Within 5 years, electronic orders are expected to jump from 5% of all orders to 70–80%.

Forty salesmen in offices across the U.S. use PCs to access the mainframe. They use Applied Data Research, Inc.'s, Datacom/DB database system to pull down reports on their specific product lines. These daily reports—which used to be sent by express mail—show actual sales levels, planned sales levels, and how sales relate to costs.

Ocean Spray's principal decision support tool is Integrated Planning, Inc.'s Strategem, which is used by sales and logistics analysts. A common application is to compare the cost of shipping from alternative sites in filling a specific order.

Ocean Spray is also developing uses for Comserve Corporation's AMAPS manufacturing software. This package should help Ocean Spray optimize its production processes and reduce costs.

Capacity Planning

One of the more difficult tasks for MIS directors is estimating future computing needs. Next year

[1987] Ocean Spray is moving up to an IBM 3090 Model 150. Modestino uses a home-grown planning model to help determine the system's capacity.

The planning model is located in a looseleaf notebook filled with color charts and graphics that Modestino can show to senior management to justify requests for equipment. He developed the model by taking a cross-sectional survey of typical job mixes on the 3083. He then interviewed the managers responsible for these applications in the user departments to determine the likely growth of these applications in the next 5 years.

Modestino then projected CPU demands for each major application on a 6-month basis for the next 5 years. It is difficult to factor in new product introductions, unanticipated changes in market conditions, potential shifts in organizational structure, and changes in computer software that can greatly increase the demand. These factors are unknown, and they can be anticipated only by providing a certain amount of excess capacity. Another factor that is difficult to estimate is the total communications load. Like highways, as remote microcomputers become more powerful, as telecommunications becomes easier and cheaper, more and more demand is stimulated. Peak hour congestion becomes a problem, and demand quickly grows to capacity. In some organizations, telecommunications demand grows 100% each year.

With his model in hand, Modestino traveled to an IBM facility in Raleigh, North Carolina, to test his sample job mix on various IBM processors. The tests, using 14 hours of CPU time, showed which processor could handle his processing load and at what point each system would be overloaded. The tests indicated that the 3083 now installed is operating at 85% of capacity. This does not leave sufficient CPU power for growth and unanticipated demands. Therefore, a 3090 Model 150 will be installed next year. The model shows that this will be sufficient up to late 1988.

Adapted from James Connolly, "Capacity Plan: Ocean Spray MIS Prepares to Meet 1990," *Computerworld*, September 22, 1986.

Part Two Case Study Questions

1. Why did Ocean Spray develop a decentralized strategy in the 1970s?
2. What went wrong with the decentralized system?
3. Describe the hardware elements involved in recentralization. Did Ocean Spray really recentralize? What computing power is left in remote sites?
4. What are the problems involved in moving from one manufacturer like Burroughs to another like IBM?
5. How does the new centralized system differ from the original centralized system?
6. Make a list of factors to take into account when planning for the future capacity of a system.
7. How will the addition of 150 microcomputers potentially complicate MIS control over data and programs?

PART THREE

Building Information Systems: Contemporary Tools, Techniques, and Approaches

Building an effective information system is both a skill and an art, requiring sensitivity to both technical and organizational concerns. The proliferation of microcomputers, fourth-generation languages, and decision-support systems coupled with rising demand for artificial intelligence applications, has spawned many different methodologies and tools for building systems. This section presents the principal tools, techniques, and approaches that are used today to analyze, design, and build information systems. For information systems to perform successfully, an understanding of implementation and information systems controls is also crucial.

Chapter 11 presents the principal tools and techniques used today to analyze and design information systems. They are: flowcharts, decision tables, decision trees, pseudocode, structured analysis, structured design, and HIPOs (Hierarchical Input-Process-Output). A separate section on systems analysis and design exercises provides an opportunity for students to apply these techniques.

Chapter 12 is an overview of systems analysis and design. It describes the basic stages and activities that must be completed to develop an information system. Systems analysis and design combine technical responsibilities with the process of planned organizational change. End users and technical specialists have specific responsibilities throughout the entire system-building process. This chapter focuses primarily on the traditional "systems life cycle" approach to building information systems.

Chapter 13 describes several alternative approaches to constructing information systems. The process of creating a new information system is replete with risks and uncertainties, necessitating more flexible alternatives to traditional "life cycle" methodology. One of the most problematic aspects of systems development is requirements analysis. Careful selection of alternative strategies for systems development and requirements analysis can help reduce risks. The chapter presents a decision tree for choosing appropriate strategies for requirements analysis and systems development.

Chapter 14 introduces the practice of prototyping and the use of software packages as important, nontraditional, systems-building alternatives. For certain types of applications these approaches can fashion systems more rapidly and effectively than traditional "life cycle" methodology. However, system builders must clearly understand their strengths and limitations. An entire section is devoted to guidelines for evaluating software packages.

Chapter 15 examines end-user computing, the development of information systems by end users with little or no formal data processing assistance. "Fourth-generation" languages and other sophisticated software tools enable end users to access data directly, create entire systems on their own or minimize the role of professional programmers in the development process. Capabilities of "end-user" software, the role of information centers, and management issues posed by end-user computing are carefully analyzed.

Chapter 16 focuses on decision-support systems, which are more user oriented, interactive, and helpful to managers faced with unstructured problems than traditional information systems. Examples of successful decision-support systems illuminate the distinctive features of DSS. Building DSS is a departure from the traditional "life cycle" approach because of different requirements, tools, and organizational arrangements.

Chapter 17 traces developments in artificial intelligence and their impact on business applications. Applications of direct relevance to general business are primarily "expert systems" that automate selected aspects of the decision-making process. This chapter provides numerous examples of major types of expert systems; illustrates their capabilities and limitations; and describes many successful applications. Building expert systems entails "knowledge engineering," which must painstakingly capture the decision rules and knowledge of experts.

Chapter 18 demonstrates why and how special measures must be taken during design and operation of information systems to ensure they are effectively controlled. Without proper safeguards information systems are highly vulnerable to destruction, abuse, error, and loss. Both general and application-specific controls can be applied to ensure that information is accurate, reliable, and secure. An appropriate control structure for an information system will consider costs and benefits. This chapter highlights the importance of information system security and auditing.

Chapter 19 looks at the factors responsible for the success and failure of information systems. A high percentage of information system failures can be attributed to organizational factors. To better understand these factors the entire process of implementation must be examined with special attention to the role of end users; the level of management support; dimensions of project risk; and the role of the systems builder as a change agent. While not all aspects of implementation can be controlled, a contingency approach to project management, and efforts to secure management and end-user support, can help minimize risks and problems.

Part Three Case Study: "Using Critical Success Factors". This case illustrates the benefits of using a requirements analysis strategy that can identify organization-wide needs. An insurance corporation used Critical Success Factor methodology to assess organizational rather than project-specific information requirements. The process led to a fundamental reconceptualization of the nature of the company and a long-term information systems plan. This case study also points out that the CSF method proved most valuable for defining senior managers' information needs.

CHAPTER 11

Tools and Techniques for Systems Building

▬ OUTLINE

(*Continued on next page.*)

Arthur Young & Company, a leading accounting and consulting firm, has produced an automated tool called Information Engineering Workbench (IEW) to help with systems analysis and design. IEW automates many of the labor-intensive definition, analysis, and planning activities that must be accomplished before programming can begin. IEW components include a data flow diagrammer to define basic processing steps; an entity diagrammer to identify entities such as processes or departments and their relationships; a decomposition diagrammer to furnish detailed information; and an action diagrammer to provide high-level information about a system. Although this tool is based on artificial intelligence rules, it cannot be employed effectively unless its users have a command of systems analysis and design techniques. According to James P. Horan, Arthur Young's southwest regional director of information technology practice, IEW is like a power drill. Anyone can buy one, but sophistication and expertise are required to use it with maximum benefit.

Adapted from "AI Tool Helps Systems Analysts with Applications Development," *Information Week*, February 17, 1986.

Automated tools can expedite systems analysis and design, but system builders must first understand basic system-building tools and methodologies. In this chapter the student will learn:

- The major tools and techniques for systems analysis and design.
- How to use each tool for documentation and analysis.
- The kinds of problems each technique can help solve.
- The strengths and weaknesses of each technique.
- How to choose appropriate analysis and design tools.

11.1 Introduction

Many techniques have been developed to document and describe the way systems work. The tools and methodologies discussed here are among the most widely used for systems analysis and design. They include flowcharts, decision tables, decision trees, pseudocode, structured analysis, structured design, and hierarchical input-process-output (HIPO). Each of these approaches can help system builders structure, clarify, and communicate system problems and solutions.

Requirements of Design Tools

System builders' choice of tools and approaches will depend largely on the nature of the system problem to be addressed. It may be necessary to use a combination of these aids or to create new graphic or analytical tools appropriate to the problem. Whatever design or analysis aid or combination of aids is selected, it should:

- Be easy for analysts and users to understand.
- Be relatively easy to modify if requirements or design decisions change.
- Use graphic representations to convey information.
- Eliminate unnecessary or excessive detail.
- Visualize a system in levels of abstraction, breaking design down into successive levels of detail that can be handled by system builders one at a time.
- Support analysis of both data and activities.
- Integrate analysis with design activities so that the documentation and findings of the analysis stage can be translated more easily into design.
- Promote clarity, simplicity, and reliability of software (*EDP* Analyzer, 1979).

11.2 Flowcharts

Flowcharting is the most popular and the oldest design tool. *System flowcharts* detail the flow of data throughout an entire information system. *Program flowcharts* describe the processes taking place within an individual program in the system and the sequence in which they must be executed. Flowcharting is no longer recommended for program design because it does not provide top-down modular structure as effectively as other techniques. However, flowcharting remains a popular tool for systems analysis and design.

System Flowcharts

The *system flowchart* is a graphic way of depicting all of the procedures that take input data and convert them to their final output form. Using specialized symbols and flow lines, the system flowchart shows all of the processes taking place; the data acted on in each step; and the relationships between the processes. It is superior to narrative descriptions of the system because, in easily understood graphic form, it:

- Shows the overall structure of the system.
- Traces the flow of information and work.
- Shows the physical media on which data are input, output and stored.
- Highlights key processing and decision points.

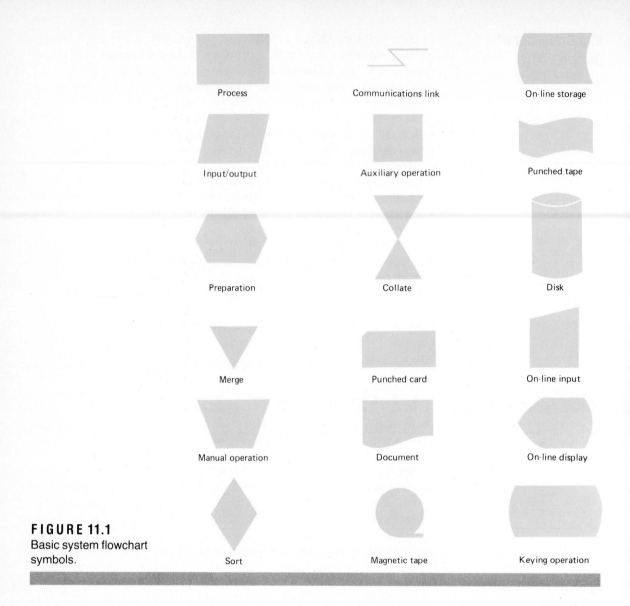

FIGURE 11.1
Basic system flowchart symbols.

Process

Communications link

On-line storage

Input/output

Auxiliary operation

Punched tape

Preparation

Collate

Disk

Merge

Punched card

On-line input

Manual operation

Document

On-line display

Sort

Magnetic tape

Keying operation

System Flowchart Symbols

Figure 11.1 contains the basic symbols for system flowcharting. The plain rectangle is a general symbol for a major computer processing function. Flow lines show the sequence of steps and the direction of information flow. Arrows are employed to show direction if it is not apparent in the diagram.

System flowcharts can encompass different levels of detail. Figure 11.2 illustrates a high-level overview flowchart of a payroll system. Figure 11.3 is a detailed flowchart for one portion of the payroll system, transaction editing and validation.

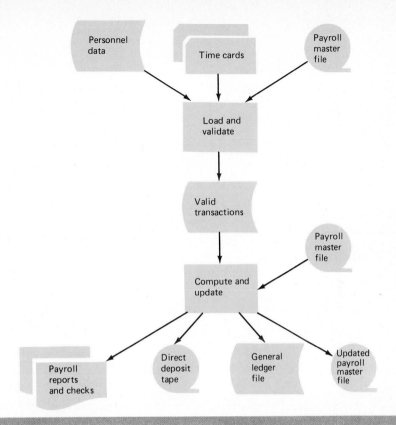

FIGURE 11.2

System flowchart for a payroll system. This is a high-level system flowchart for a batch payroll system. Only the most important processes and files are illustrated. Data are input from two sources: timecards and payroll-related data (such as salary increases) passed from the personnel system. The data are first edited and validated against the existing payroll master file before updating the payroll master. The update process produces an updated payroll master file, various payroll reports (such as the payroll register and hours register), checks, a direct deposit tape, and a file of payment data that must be passed to the organization's general ledger system. The direct deposit tape is sent to the automated clearing house that serves the banks offering direct deposit services to employees.

Advantages and Disadvantages of Flowcharts

The system flowhcart provides little detail on how processes are actually accomplished. It does not furnish details of programs within a system; instead it reduces an entire program or set of programs to a single box. (Detail on the way the programs work will be provided by the program flowchart, program structure chart, or another program design tool.) The system flowchart provides a concise, powerful

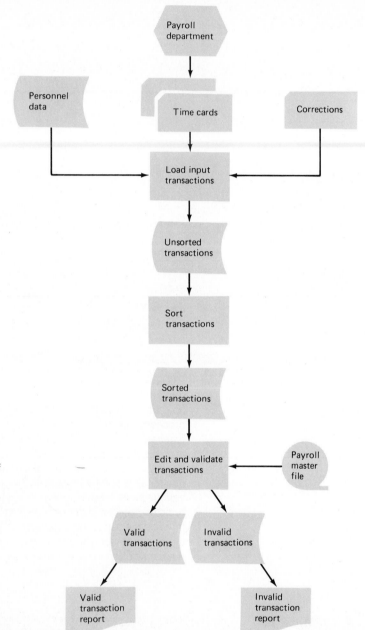

FIGURE 11.3

Detail payroll system flowchart. This flowchart is a detailed view of the portion of the payroll system in Figure 11.2 that is concerned with transaction editing and validation. Transactions are loaded from input, sorted, edited, and validated against the payroll master file. Separate files are created to separate invalid from valid transactions. Valid transactions are passed on for further processing. Invalid transactions are corrected and resubmitted. Reports listing both valid and invalid transactions are produced.

overview of the system. Its strength lies in the way it highlights the physical media used in the system, the various work stations through which data pass, and the sequence of activities.

System flowcharts are used extensively in two major areas:

1. To show all inputs, major files, processing, and outputs for a system.
2. To document manual procedures. In systems where the information flow entails a large number of documents, flowcharts can show the origination, processing, and destinations of each document and the procedures employed by users.

11.3 Documenting Decision Rules

Several sets of tools are used for documenting decisions rules and for structuring processing logic for computer programs. These tools are decision tables, decision trees and pseudocode.

Decision Tables

Decision tables are considered very useful for documenting situations in which the decision process is highly structured and clearly understood. Decisions are portrayed graphically in a table expressing a series of conditions. When certain conditions are met (Yes, No), decisions are made according to specified rules. The table must specify all possible conditions that affect the decision.

Figure 11.4 illustrates the most widely used decision table format. It consists of:

1. A header identifying the table.
2. Condition stubs with entries for each possible condition.
3. Action stubs with entries for each possible action that could be taken. Such actions will be determined by the conditions present and the decision rules governing the decision process. The figure illustrates the following logic for sending money market account statements:

> The money market fund will send monthly statements of account balances to all investors, whether those accounts have had activity or not. However, investors with account balances less than $500 will be sent warning notices of low balances along with their monthly statements unless their accounts have had activity during the past month.

Decision tables have been hailed for facilitating communication between users and analysts and for expressing logic in more compact form than flowcharts or other forms of documentation. By breaking down decision logic, they also help to translate human rules into a

Send monthly statement	1	2	3
Condition stub			
1. Balance >= $500	Y	N	N
2. Account activity during past month	-	Y	N
Action statements			
3. Send monthly statement only	X	X	
4. Send monthly statement with warning			X

(Condition entries / Action entries)

FIGURE 11.4

Decision table for logic for sending monthly money market account statements. The money market fund will send monthly statements of account balances to all investors. However, investors with less than $500 in their accounts will be sent warning notices with their monthly statements if their accounts have not had any activity during the past month.

form that can be captured by computer programs. Programs known as *decision table processors* can even translate decision table specifications into programming languages such as COBOL or FORTRAN.

Decision Trees

Decision trees are another graphic method of documenting decision rules. They look somewhat like flowcharts without symbols or processing boxes. They present conditions and actions sequentially, showing decision paths that may be taken. The diagram resembles the branches of a tree. Different alternatives branch out from an initial decision point.

The initial decision is the root of the tree. Branches proceed from left to right. The nodes of the tree show conditions. The next path to follow depends on the outcome of a determination about which condition exists. On the right side of the tree are the actions that can be taken, depending on the sequence of conditions and alternatives that are followed. How the branches develop depends on the nature of the decision being made—the conditions and alternatives. Figure 11.5 illustrates a decision tree for the same decision rules for money market statements documented as a decision table in Figure 11.4.

Some authorities consider decision trees easier to understand than decision tables. They are especially useful for highlighting decision paths and the sequence of decisions rather than the criteria for selecting a given path. However, if a system is highly complex, with many sequences of steps and combinations of conditions, decision trees may cloud the analysis. Documentation of too many

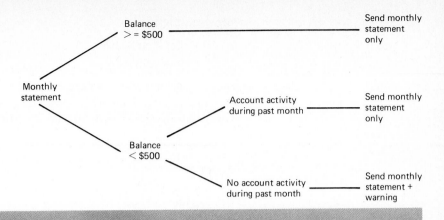

FIGURE 11.5
Decision tree for logic for sending monthly money market account statements. This figure shows how a decision tree would illustrate the same monthly money market account statement logic shown in decision table format in Figure 11.4.

In the figure:
- Monthly statement
  - Balance >= $500 → Send monthly statement only
  - Balance < $500
    - Account activity during past month → Send monthly statement only
    - No account activity during past month → Send monthly statement + warning

branches and paths becomes unwieldy. In such instances, decision tables are preferred.

Pseudocode

Pseudocode, sometimes called *structured English,* is a method of expressing program logic using plain English statements rather than a programming language. It uses narrative statements rather than graphic symbols such as trees or tables to describe a procedure. An advantage of pseudocode is that system builders can concentrate on developing processing logic independent of the syntax guidelines (rules for formulating instructions) of any programming language. If the logic is sound, pseudocode can be easily translated into a programming language.

Pseudocode is used for communicating processing specifications that shape program design. It is also a helpful method for documenting decision rules during analysis and requirements definition. It can be understood by analysts, programmers, and often users. We have worked on projects where pseudocode has been used both to structure program logic and to provide user documentation for the decision rules governing programmed calculations and input data validation routines.

Pseudocode uses the same logic patterns as the basic control structures of structured programming (described in further detail in Section 11.5). These are:

1. *The sequence structure,* single steps or actions that follow one another without interruption. The series of actions does not depend on the existence of any condition.
   The pseudocode for the sequence structure is:

   > Do Action 1
   > Do Action 2.

For example:

> Read customer bill
> Print customer bill.

2. *The decision structure*, where two or more actions can be taken depending on which satisfies a stated condition.
The pseudocode format for the decision structure is:

> IF (condition 1 is true)
>   Do X
> ELSE
>   Do Y
> ENDIF.

For example:

> IF (transaction key = master file key)
>   Update Master File
> ELSE
>   Reject Transaction
> ENDIF.

3. *The iteration structure*, where certain actions are repeated over and over while a specified condition occurs or until a condition occurs.
The pseudocode format for the iteration structure is:

> DO WHILE (condition 2 is true)
>   Action Z
> DOWEND.

For example:

> DO WHILE (End of file switch is off)
>   Read each student record
>   Add 1 to student record counter
> DOWEND.

TABLE 11.1
Pseudocode for Money Market Fund
Monthly Statement

> Money Market Fund Monthly Statement:
> IF investor's balance is greater than or equal to $500
>   Send monthly balance statement only
>   ELSE
>   IF account fund has had activity
>   Send monthly balance statement only
>   ELSE
>   Send monthly balance statement + warning notice
> ENDIF.

Table 11.1 shows how the same decision rules for money market fund monthly statements illustrated in the Figure 11.4 decision table and the Figure 11.5 decision tree would be expressed in pseudocode.

11.4 Structured Analysis

Structured analysis is a widely used method for defining system inputs, processes, and outputs and for breaking systems down into subsystems. It offers a logical graphic model of information flow, partitioning a system into modules that show manageable levels of detail. The structured approach

- Views a system from the top down, progressing from the highest, most abstract level to the lowest level of detail.
- Specifies the interfaces that exist between modules.
- Rigorously specifies the processes or transformations that occur within each module.

Structured analysis can be applied to systems analysis, requirements specification, and design and serves as the starting point for structured software design described in Section 11.5.

Data Flow Diagrams

Structured analysis is highly graphic, relying mainly on diagrams rather than narrative text. Its primary tool is the *data flow diagram*, a graphic representation of a system's component processes and the interfaces between them. Data flow diagrams show how data flow to, from, and within an information system and the processes that transform the data. Data flow diagrams also show where the data are stored.

Data flow diagrams are constructed using four basic symbols, which are illustrated in Figure 11.6. These symbols consist of:

1. The *data flow* symbol, an arrow showing the flow of data.
2. The *process* symbol, rounded boxes or bubbles depicting processes that transform the data.
3. The *data store* symbol, an open rectangle indicating where data are stored.
4. The *external entity* symbol, either a rectangle or a square indicating the sources or destinations of data.

Data flows show the movement of data between processes, external entities, and data stores. They always contain packets of data, with the name or content of each data flow listed beside the arrow. The flows are of known composition and represent data that are manual or automated. Data flows consist of documents, reports, data

Data flow

Process

FIGURE 11.6

Data flow diagram symbols. Data flow diagrams can be constructed by using these four symbols. Arrows represent the flow of data. Processes transform input data flows into output data flows. Data stores are collections of data used or maintained by the system. External entities are sources or destinations of data and help to define the boundary of a system.

Data store

External entity

from a computer file, or data from a telecommunications transmission. These can be either inputs or outputs.

Processes portray the transformation of input data flows to output data flows. An example is a process that transforms a sales order into an invoice or calculates an employee's gross pay from his or her time card. The convention for naming a process consists of combining a strong verb with an object. For example, we could call the process that calculates gross pay CALCULATE GROSS PAY. Each process has a unique reference number (such as 1.0, 2.0, etc.) so that it can be easily distinguished from other processes in the data flow diagram.

Data stores are either manual or automated inventories of data. They consist of computer files or databases, file cabinets, card files, microfiche, or a binder of paper reports. The name of the data store is written inside the data store symbol.

External entities are originators or receivers of information. They consist of customers, suppliers, or government agencies, which are external to the organization, or employees or departments within the organization. External entities are sometimes called *outside interfaces* because they are outside the boundary or scope of the system treated by the data flow diagram.

Figure 11.7 shows a simple data flow diagram for a mail-in university course registration system. Students submit registration

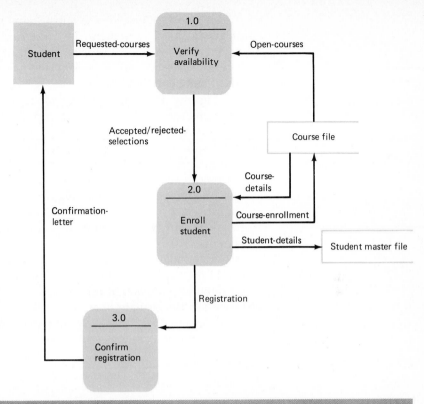

FIGURE 11.7
Data flow diagram for a mail-in university registration system. Process 1.0 determines whether courses selected by students are still open by referencing the university's course file. If the course is still open, Process 2.0 enrolls the student and updates the course file with the student's name and identification number and recalculates the class size. It flags courses with maximum enrollment as closed. This process also updates the university's student file with information about new students or student address changes. Process 3.0 then sends each student a confirmation of registration letter.

forms with their name, identification number, and the numbers of the courses they wish to take. In process 1.0 the system verifies that each course selected is still open by referencing the university's course file. The file distinguishes courses that are still open from those that have been canceled or filled. Process 1.0 then determines which of the student's selections can be accepted or rejected. Process 2.0 enrolls the student in the courses for which he or she has been accepted. It updates the university's course file with the student's name and identification number and recalculates the class size. If maximum enrollment has been reached, the course number is flagged as closed. Process 2.0 also updates the university's student master file with information about new students or changes in address. Process 3.0 then sends each student applicant a confirmation of registration letter listing the courses for which he or she is registered and noting the course selections that could not be fulfilled.

The diagrams can be used to depict higher-level processes as well as lower-level details. Through *leveled* data flow diagrams, a complex process can be broken down into successive levels of detail. An entire system can be divided into subsystems with a high-level data flow diagram. Each subsystem, in turn, can be divided into additional subsystems with second-level data flow diagrams, and the lower-level subsystems can be broken down again until the lowest level of detail has been reached.

Figures 11.8(A), 11.8(B) and 11.8(C) show leveled data flow diagrams for a pension recordkeeping and accounting system. Figure 11.8(A) is the most general picture of the system. It is called a *context diagram*. The context diagram always depicts an entire system as a single process with its major inputs and outputs. Subsequent diagrams can then break the system down into greater levels of detail.

The next level of detail, Figure 11.8(B), shows that the system is comprised of five major processes: tracking participation in the pension plan (1.0); tracking service that can be credited to pension benefits (2.0); capturing employee earnings data (3.0); maintaining actuarial tables (4.0); and calculating pension benefits (5.0). Figure 11.8(C) explodes process 5.0, CALCULATE BENEFIT, into greater detail. It shows that this process can be further decomposed into processes to calculate final average earnings (5.1); the normal retirement benefit (5.2); the early retirement benefit (5.3); the survivor's benefit (5.4) and to generate benefits statements (5.5).

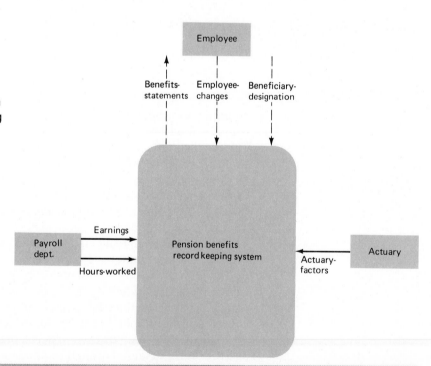

FIGURE 11.8A
Context diagram for a pension recordkeeping and accounting system. This diagram provides an overview of the entire pension recordkeeping and accounting system, showing its major inputs and outputs. The context diagram depicts the entire system as a single process that can be exploded into more detailed data flow diagrams at lower levels. Data flow to and from this pension recordkeeping and accounting system, with the employee, payroll department, and actuary as external entities.

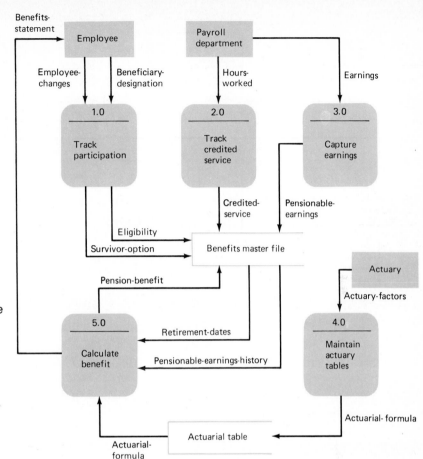

FIGURE 11.8B
First-level data flow diagram for a pension recordkeeping and accounting system. The data flow diagram explodes the context diagram into a more detailed picture of the pension recordkeeping and accounting system. It shows that the system consists of five major processes: tracking participation (1.0), tracking credited service (2.0), capturing earnings (3.0), maintaining actuary tables (4.0), and calculating the benefit (5.0). These processes, in turn, can be broken down into more detailed data flow diagrams.

Other Structured Analysis Tools

Other tools for structured analysis include a *data dictionary*, which contains information about individual pieces of data and data groupings within a system. The data dictionary defines the contents of data flows and data stores so that system builders understand exactly what pieces of data they contain. For example, a data dictionary entry for the data flow "Retirement-Benefits" in Figure 11.8(C) might look like this:

Retirement-Benefits = Normal-Retirement-Benefit-
Amount + Normal-
Retirement-Date + Early-
Retirement-Benefit +
Early-Retirement-Date + Survivor-Option

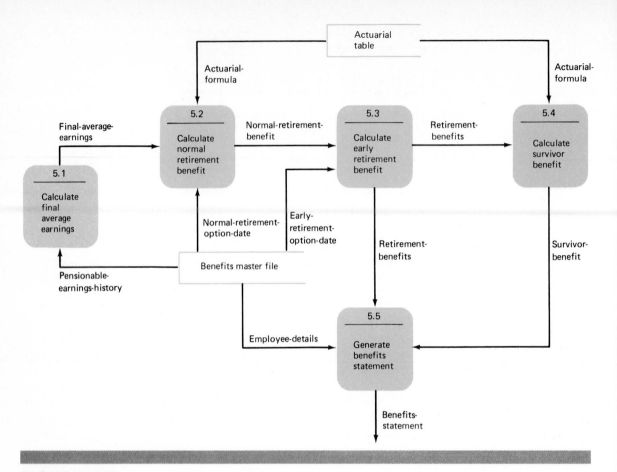

FIGURE 11.8C
Second-level data flow diagram for a pension recordkeeping and accounting system. The diagram breaks down process 5.0 (calculate benefit) into further detail. It shows that calculating pension benefits entails processes to calculate final average earnings (5.1), normal retirement benefit (5.2), early retirement benefit (5.3), and survivor benefit (5.4), and a process to generate benefits statements (5.5).

This means that the data flow called "Retirement-Benefits" consists of the data items Normal-Retirement-Benefit-Amount, Normal-Retirement-Date, Early-Retirement-Benefit, Early-Retirement-Date, and Survivor-Option. The dictionary also provides information on the meaning and format of each data item and the data flows and data stores where it is used. Sometimes the dictionary also includes information about frequency, volume, values, users, security, and processes.

The data dictionary used in structured analysis can be expanded and used throughout the system development cycle to help system builders keep track of all of the details about data, functions, and processes that accumulate for every system. The role of data dictionaries in system building and information management is discussed further in Chapter 20.

Process specifications describe the transformations occurring within the lowest-level bubbles of the data flow diagrams. They express the logic for each process using one of three methods:

- *Structured English*, or pseudocode
- *Decision tables*
- *Decision trees*

These methods are described in Section 11.3. Process descriptions are often written with pseudocode rather than decision tables or decision trees because they are easier to translate into program code.

Steps in Structured Analysis

The process of structured analysis consists of these procedures:

- Study and *model the current system*, using data flow diagrams.
- Derive a *logical equivalent* of the current environment that is divorced from the physical aspects of the physical model. The logical model emphasizes *what* is done (what data flows and transformations occur) rather than *how* it is done or who or what does it, which are treated in the physical model.
- Derive a *logical model for the new system*, using data flow diagrams, the data dictionary, and process specifications.
- *Establish a human–machine boundary* to constrain the model. This shows which parts of the system will be manual and which will be automated. Several *alternative physical system models* will be produced, using data flow digrams.
- Measure *cost and benefits* by performing a cost/benefit analysis of each physical alternative. (Cost/benefit analysis is discussed in Chapter 21.)
- *Select the best option*, passing hardware, budget, and time requirements back to management.
- *Package the specifications* into a structured specification document. This document is an integrated set of data flow diagrams for system functions, data dictionary descriptions of data flows and data stores, process specifications, and input and output documents, plus security, control, conversion, and performance requirements.

Advantages and Disadvantages of Structured Analysis

Structured analysis has been praised for organizing the data about a proposed system in a manner that can help both the analyst and the user cope with complexity. The structured model portrays the components of a system and the parts of those components from the highest level down to the lowest level of detail. Compared to earlier approaches, which dwelled on the physical aspects of system hardware and operating procedures, structured analysis focuses more on data flows and transformations. Analysts and users alike can more readily grasp the essential processes and flows required in the new system.

Structured analysis alone cannot bridge the classic user–analyst communication gap that has troubled so many development efforts. However, structured specifications are highly graphic. Users may find them easier to digest than the "Victorian novel" narrative traditionally used for functional specifications. Structured documentation may also be more easily modifiable than unstructured narrative, so that there is less pressure to "freeze" specifications.

On the other hand, structured analysis does not deal with important design concerns such as hardware, timing, procedures, and controls. These aspects of system building are better treated by other methodologies. System builders have also pointed out that the methodology loses its usefulness if too many levels of detail are introduced.

11.5 Structured Design

Structured design is primarily a software design discipline, but it is often associated with structured analysis and other structured approaches. Structured design encompasses a set of design rules and techniques that promote program clarity and simplicity, thereby reducing the time and effort required for coding, debugging and maintenance (Stevens, 1974). Sometimes structured design is also referred to as *top-down design* or *composite design*. The main principle of structured design is that a system should be designed from the top down in hierarchical fashion and refined to greater levels of detail. The design should first consider the main function of a program or system, then break this function into subfunctions and decompose each subfunction until the lowest level of detail had been reached. In this manner, all high-level logic and the design model are developed before detailed program code is written. If structured analysis has been performed, the structured specification document can serve as input to the design process.

As the design is formulated, it is documented in a *structure chart*. The structure chart shows each level of design, its relationship to other levels, and its place in the overall design structure. The highest levels are the most abstract, with lower levels containing increasingly greater detail. Figure 11.9 shows a structure chart that can be used for the payroll system in Figure 11.2. If a design has too many levels to fit onto one structure chart, it can be broken down further on more detailed structure charts. For example, details for processing gross pay on the structure chart of Figure 11.9 are treated in the detailed

FIGURE 11.9
High-level structure chart
showing the highest or most
abstract level of design for a
payroll system. Such a chart
provides an overview of the
entire system.

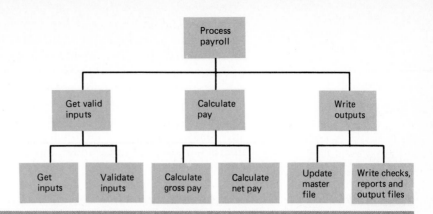

FIGURE 11.10
Detailed structure chart
showing further information on
the calculation of gross pay for
the payroll system illustrated
in Figure 11.9. This structure
chart shows an intermediate
level of design. A more
detailed structure chart would
still be required to show the
lowest levels of design for
gross pay calculations.

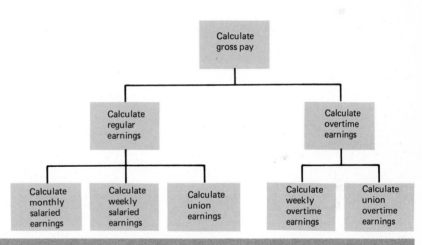

structure chart in Figure 11.10. A structure chart may document one program, one system (set of programs), or part of one program.

Modularization

Modularization follows from top-down development. Each of the boxes in the structure chart represents a component *module*. Programs can be partitioned into modules, each of which constitutes a logical unit that performs one or a small number of functions. Ideally, modules should be independent of each other. They should be interconnected so that they have only one entry to and exit from their parent modules. They should share data with as few other modules as possible.

There should be no obscure connections with other modules that would create a "ripple effect," whereby a change to module A creates unanticipated changes in modules B, D, and F. Minimizing connections among modules, or *coupling*, minimizes paths by which errors can be spread to other parts of the system.

Each module should also be kept to a manageable size. An individual should be able to read the program code for the module and easily keep track of its functions. Within each module, program instructions should not wander and should be executed in top-down fashion.

Structured Programming

Structured programming extends the principles governing top-down design and modularity to the writing of program code. It is a method of organizing and coding programs that simplifies control paths so that the programs can be easily understood and modified. Structured

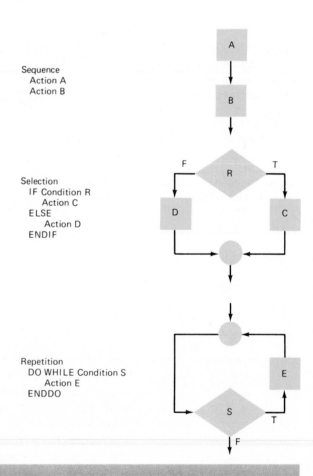

Sequence
    Action A
    Action B

Selection
    IF Condition R
        Action C
    ELSE
        Action D
    ENDIF

Repetition
    DO WHILE Condition S
        Action E
    ENDDO

FIGURE 11.11
Basic control constructs. This figure illustrates the three basic control constructs used in structured programming.

programming reduces the complexity created when program instructions jump forward and backward to other parts of the program, obscuring the logic and flow of the program.

Proponents of structured programming have shown that any program can be written using the three basic control constructs, or instruction patterns, introduced in the discussion of pseudocode in Section 11.3: (1) simple sequence, (2) selection, and (3) repetition. These control constructs are illustrated in Figure 11.11.

The *sequence* construct executes statements in the order in which they appear, with control passing unconditionally from one statement to the next. The program will execute statement A and then statement B.

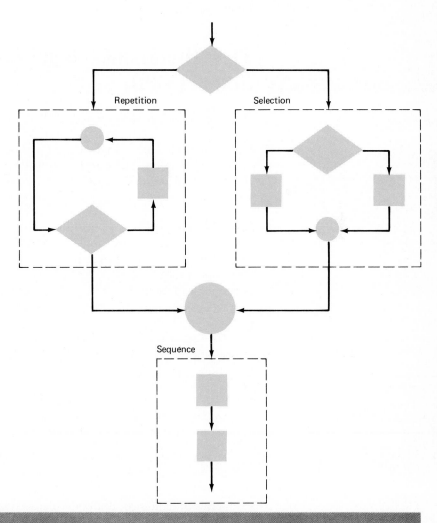

FIGURE 11.12
Nested control constructs. The control structures can be nested, but they will still have only one point of entry and only one point of exit.

The *selection* (decision) construct tests a condition and executes one of the two alternative instructions based on the results of the test. Condition R is tested. If R is true, statement C is executed. If R is false, statement D is executed. Control then passes to the next statement.

The *repetition* (iteration) construct repeats a segment of code as long as a conditional test remains true. Condition S is tested. If S is true, statement E is executed and control returns to the test of S. If S is false, E is skipped and control passes to the next statement.

Any one or any combination of these control structures can accommodate any kind of processing logic required by a program. There is a single entry and exit point for each structure. The control structures can be strung one after the other or nested, as shown in Figure 11.12. Structured programming control structures can be used in any programming language.

11.6 Hierarchical Input-Process-Output (HIPO)

HIPO is a methodology used to display a program or procedure graphically in a system in terms of the functions to be performed. The HIPO method was originally developed by IBM for its large, complex operating systems but has become a widely used tool for documenting application designs. It can be used to communicate system specifications throughout the design process.

Purpose of HIPO

In a complex system, it is easy to lose track of its intended functions (what the system does). Single functions may be fragmented among several modules, or a single function may be implemented in more than one module. HIPO enables system builders to understand, describe, and document the system's component modules in a way that keeps track of the details without losing sight of the larger picture.

HIPOs are primarily graphic. Through a structured set of method-of-operation diagrams, they help system designers and users answer these key questions:

- What does the system or module do?
- How does it do it?
- What are the inputs and outputs?

  HIPOs consist of:

- A visual table of contents (VTOC).
- A series of diagrams, each of which is related to one function of the system.

Documenting the Hierarchy of Functions

The *visual table of contents* (*VTOC*) is a hierarchy chart showing the relationships among each of the diagrams/functions in the HIPO package and the contents of each diagram. The VTOC provides a brief description of each module and identifies it by number. Each box in the VTOC represents only one diagram. The lower the level in the hierarchy, the greater the level of detail. Boxes at the lowest level of the VTOC hierarchy represent detail diagrams, while those at the upper and intermediate levels represent overview diagrams.

The number of levels of boxes in the VTOC depends on the complexity of the system. While there are no rules limiting the number of levels, HIPOs appear cumbersome when there are more than four or five.

Each diagram, corresponding to a VTOC box, shows:

- The *process*, or series of steps that supports the described function.
- The requirements of, or *inputs* to that process.
- The results, or *outputs*, of that process.

Upper-level or *overview diagrams* are abstractions of the major functions of the system and serve as pointers to more detailed diagrams at lower levels. Low-level *detail diagrams* show actual inputs, outputs, and processes, with detailed layouts of data and processing logic. Boxes are used to isolate special processing, and arrows show both flow of data and flow of control. A detail diagram may also contain an *extended description* or narrative explanation of the process depicted.

Figures 11.13 and 11.14 are part of a HIPO for an accounts receivable system. Figure 11.13 illustrates the VTOC, which is always the first diagram in a HIPO package. It shows the main modules of the accounts receivable system. Since this is a very complex system, this VTOC can only show functions at a very high level. Each of the modules in the hierarchy is described briefly. The numbers reference the numbers of other documents where more detail can be found. For example, to find out more about the process CALCULATE CURRENT BALANCES one must look at document 3.1.

Figure 11.14 is an intermediate overview diagram corresponding to VTOC Box 2.2. It can be considered a *process overview diagram*, and shows that the customer changes function can be subdivided into functions for reading, validating, and building customer change transactions, with customer standing data changes and the customer master file as input and transaction files and a transaction audit trail as output. Flowchart symbols are used to show storage media for the inputs and outputs. The arrows show data flow. This function can be broken down into even greater detail. The numbers at the bottom reference other documents where still more detail can be found.

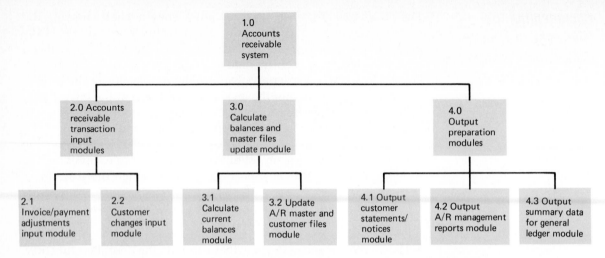

1.0 Accounts Receivable System

Controls all processing for data input, updating of files, and creation of reports

2.0 A/R Transaction Input

Controls all entry and editing of data from invoices and customer payments, adjustments from the Accounting Department, and customer standing data changes

2.1 Invoice/Payment Adjustments Input

Entry and validation of input data from invoices, customer payments, and adjustments

2.2 Customer Changes

Entry and validation of input data from changes in customer standing data

3.0 Calculate and A/R Master Update

Controls calculation of current account balances and updating of A/R and customer master files

3.1 Calculate Current Balances

Calculation of customer account balances using payment and adjustment input data

3.2 Update A/R Master and Customer Files

Updating of accounts receivable and customer master files with new customer balances and changes in customer standing data

4.0 Output Preparation

Controls output of reports to customers and management and of data for general ledger system

4.1 Output Customer Statements/Notices

Formatting and printing of monthly statements to each customer with recent charges, credits, and outstanding balance

4.2 Output A/R Management Reports

Formatting and printing of essential management reports such as aged trial balance, accounts receivable register, and customer status reports.

4.3 Output Summary for General Ledger

Summarization, formatting, and output of data required by the general ledger system

FIGURE 11.13

HIPO VTOC for an accounts receivable system. The three highest levels of function for the system are illustrated here.

Advantages and Disadvantages of HIPO

HIPOs have been praised for facilitating top-down modular design. They focus on organizing a system in terms of its functions, partitioning it into modular components that can be related to each other. HIPOs also help system builders visualize design at different levels of detail. The HIPO approach can be used to develop the preliminary conceptual design and the final design at detailed levels. Another

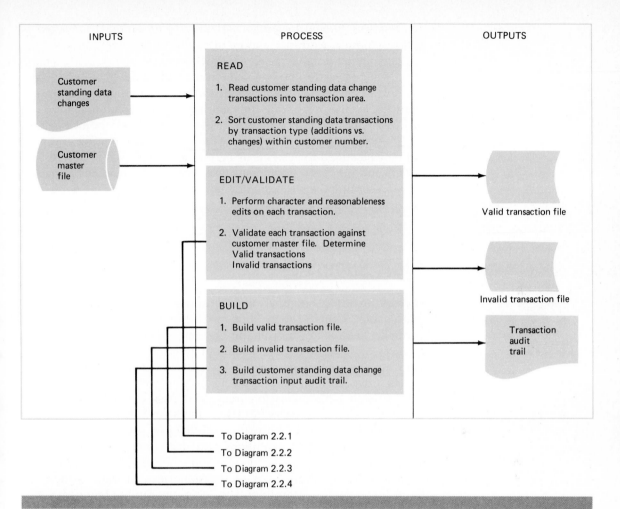

INPUTS	PROCESS	OUTPUTS

READ

1. Read customer standing data change transactions into transaction area.

2. Sort customer standing data transactions by transaction type (additions vs. changes) within customer number.

Customer standing data changes

Customer master file

EDIT/VALIDATE

1. Perform character and reasonableness edits on each transaction.

2. Validate each transaction against customer master file. Determine
   Valid transactions
   Invalid transactions

Valid transaction file

BUILD

1. Build valid transaction file.

2. Build invalid transaction file.

3. Build customer standing data change transaction input audit trail.

Invalid transaction file

Transaction audit trail

To Diagram 2.2.1
To Diagram 2.2.2
To Diagram 2.2.3
To Diagram 2.2.4

FIGURE 11.14

Intermediate overview HIPO diagram. The diagram corresponds to Box 2.2 of the HIPO for the accounts receivable system in Figure 11.13. It provides more detail about the Customer Changes Input Model and is an intermediate diagram. The numbers at the bottom of this diagram reference other documents where more detail can be found about the processes to use in validating transactions and building valid and invalid transaction files and an input transaction audit trail.

advantage of HIPOs is that they facilitate documentation. Documentation that explains the system is a by-product of design.

On the other hand, HIPOs have been criticized for being very time-consuming to produce. They are often left incomplete because so much extensive documentation is required. Their explanatory value is also limited beyond a certain level of detail. If a system is highly complex, warranting more than four or five levels on a VTOC, the documentation may be too overwhelming to digest. HIPOs have not always proved to be good communication aids.

Critics of HIPOs also note that the methodology encourages analysts to focus on one process at a time, slighting multiple processes and the interactions between them. Others point out that HIPOs were originally developed as tools for programming and may not be well suited to systems design. Finally, it should be noted that HIPOs and other methodologies with modular approaches are good for representing the structure of a system but cannot easily depict the timing and sequence of processes and flows.

11.7 Summary

Each of the design and analysis tools and methodologies discussed in this chapter helps system builders to visualize and understand a particular feature of information systems. System flowcharts detail the flow of data and work throughout an entire information system. They are useful for portraying the physical aspects of a system: inputs, outputs, major files, and the sequence of procedures.

Decision tables, decision trees, and pseudocode are primarily used to describe processing logic. Decision tables portray decisions graphically in table form, expressing a series of conditions. Decision trees present conditions and decision paths sequentially, using a diagram that resembles the branches of a tree. Pseudocode expresses the program logic of decision rules in plain structured English statements rather than specific programming languages.

HIPOs organize inputs, outputs, and processing procedures in terms of the hierarchy of a system's component functions. Component functions are broken down into successive levels of detail, using graphic symbols and narrative.

Structured analysis highlights the flow of data and the processes through which it is transformed. Its primary tool is the data flow diagram, a network representation of a system's component processes and the interfaces between them.

Structured design and structured programming are software design disciplines that produce reliable, well-documented software with a simple, clear structure that is easy for others to understand and maintain. Structured design is based on the principles of modularization and top-down development. Structured programming is a method of organizing and coding programs that simplifies control paths. Any program can be written using three basic control constructs: sequence, selection and repetition.

Key Words

System flowchart
Program flowchart
Decision table
Pseudocode
Structured English
Sequence structure
Iteration structure
Decision structure
Structured analysis
Data flow diagram
Process
Data store

External entity
Context diagram
Process specification
Human–machine boundary
Data dictionary
Structured design
Structure chart
Modularization
Structured programming
Hierarchical input-process-output (HIPO)
Visual table of contents (VTOC)

Review Questions

1. Why do system builders need special tools or methodologies for analysis and design? What are the features of a good design tool?
2. Describe the use of system flowcharts.
3. Name three techniques for documenting decision rules. Compare the features of each.
4. Name the three basic control structures used in structured programming and pseudocode. Describe how each works.
5. What is structured analysis? What is the role of the following in structured analysis: data flow diagrams, data dictionary, process specifications?
6. Compare data flow diagrams with flowcharts. What features of systems does each highlight?
7. What are the principles of structured design? What is the role of structure charts in structured design?
8. Define modularization and structured programming. What is their relationship to structured design?
9. What is a HIPO? What is the role of the following in a HIPO: VTOC, the overview diagram, detail diagram?
10. Which of the techniques and tools discussed in this chapter would be most easily understood by users?

Discussion Questions

1. Compare the strengths and weaknesses of flowcharts, structured analysis, and HIPOs. How would you decide which of these tools to use?
2. Which of the design and analysis tools described in this chapter would be most important in describing TPS, MIS, DSS, ESS, and OAS?

Coopers & Lybrand's Project Tool Kit

Coopers & Lybrand is a leading accounting and consulting firm with numerous offices. Its systems development projects range from customized systems built from scratch to implementing packages developed by Coopers & Lybrand and other vendors. The firm also provides consulting on strategic planning, systems migrations, and conversions. To establish companywide standards for its profusion of assignments, the firm adopted a standardized "tool kit."

Michael W. Bealmear, the company's national director of system development, notes that since the firm maintains many offices, the tool kit provides a uniform approach. Coopers & Lybrand can pull people from any of its offices to work on projects elsewhere, confident that they will apply the company's methods and standards.

Coopers & Lybrand acquired exclusive rights to adopt SDM/Structured, a graphic and database-oriented methodology, from AGS Management Systems, Inc., and the AGS Structured Analysis/Design package. For automated design and analysis tools, the company chose Nastec's DesignAid.

DesignAid is one of a series of CASE 2000 systems development tools offered by the Nastec Corporation. (CASE stands for Computer-Aided Software Engineering.) The tool integrates text processing with over 50 predefined graphics symbols and facility for free-hand drawing to support various design techniques. All design and documentation tasks are performed on-line and catalogued in a design dictionary. The tool can create nested data flow diagrams and scan them for accuracy and completeness.

All of the packages in the tool kit are portable and personal computer based. However, their results can be implemented on IBM, Burroughs, Univac, and Honeywell mainframes or on Digital Equipment VAX, Hewlett Packard HP 3000, or Wang VS minicomputers.

Business functionality is not a determining factor for using automated design tools. Development techniques vary by type of application. Commerical applications may have different requirements than real-time tasks or process control operations. Good design tools have sufficient flexibility to help develop any of these applications.

The tools are especially useful in relatively large, complex projects. Automated design work stations then provide a flexible, standardized way to describe and share the components of each project without generating volumes of paperwork. Diagrams and documents can be easily revised or corrected as with word processing. Good automated design tools are one way to promote design experimentation and overcome the rigidity of traditional "life cycle" methods.

Adapted from Don Leavitt, "Design Tools: The Real Starting Point," *Software News*, February 1986.

Case Study Questions

1. Discuss the advantages and disadvantages of adopting a standard automated analysis and design tool kit.
2. In what kinds of projects might the costs of standard methodologies outweigh the benefits?
3. If you were building a standard tool kit for your organization, how would you decide what analysis and design tools to include?

Exercises

1. Illustrate the decision rules for the following in a decision tree, decision table, and pseudocode:

   The university provides scholarships to students under the following conditions: Freshmen must have a grade point average of at least 3.3. Upperclassmen must have a grade point average of at least 3.5.

2. Illustrate the decision rules for the following in a decision tree, decision table, and pseudocode:

   Customers may purchase heating oil from the Warm and Toasty Heating Oil Company under different arrangements. Customers who pay cash immediately upon delivery or send in checks for payment within 10 days of delivery will pay five cents less per gallon than customers who pay after 10 days. Customers will be charged an 18% annual interest rate for bills that have not been paid within 30 days of the billing date.

3. Illustrate the decision rules for the following in a decision tree, decision table, and pseudocode:

   Authors' royalties are computed on the basis of sales volume. Royalties are 7.5% of a book's retail price for sales of up to 10,000 books; 10% for sales of 10,000–15,000; and 12% of all sales above 15,000. No royalty can be paid to the author until royalty earnings have paid back the author's prepublication advance.

4. Use data flow diagrams to describe the processes and flows for some part of a business or other kind of organization with which you are familiar. How well does this tool help you understand its operations? Can you identify any areas for improvement based on your analysis?

5. Develop a data flow diagram for the following:

   Realty Rentals maintains a rental roll for the residential apartment complexes it owns. Whenever the rent is changed, the rental control clerk completes a rental change form showing the apartment number and the new rent. The clerk enters this information into the company's microcomputer, which maintains files on all of Realty Rental's units. The microcomputer updates the files with the new rental changes and prints out a report showing the apartments, their rental change, total number of units with rental changes, and total amount of rentals.

6. Develop a data flow diagram for the following:

   Sales orders are received by the sales order clerk and batched. The total value of the orders and the total number of orders are written on a batch header slip. The orders and header figures are keyed into CRT terminals to produce a transaction file. The sales orders and header slip are returned to the sales department and filed by date. Computer programs edit and validate the transaction file, producing a report showing the total value of orders and total number of orders. The Sales Department reviews this report and rejects the batch if the totals do not agree with the manual totals on the batch header.

7. Develop a context diagram and first-level data flow diagram for the following:

The accounts payable system is responsible for tracking and paying the money that a business owes its suppliers. The system maintains a master file for all suppliers with whom the company deals. It contains data about suppliers (name, address, payment terms) and details about outstanding transactions, invoice history, payment history, and account balances. After reviewing and approving suppliers' invoices and credit memos, the Accounts Payable Department inputs data from these documents to update the accounts payable master file. It produces checks to pay authorized invoices, a cash disbursement report of all checks written, and an accounts payable transaction register. The system summarizes the total value of the transactions for posting to the general ledger system. The accounts payable system also summarizes items or balances, producing lists of balances and exception reports (such as debit balances) for management review. The system accommodates adjustments to correct erroneous postings or invoice amounts. It also summarizes data and reports on adjustments.

8. Use a system flowchart to describe a computer-based system with which you are familiar. On the basis of your flowchart, point out the advantages and disadvantages of the system.

9. Many supermarket chains today use point of sale terminals. The containers of nonperishable items such as laundry detergent or breakfast cereal are marked with universal product code bars. When customers check out their groceries, the cashier passes each coded item through an optical character recognition scanner, which reads the bar code. The scanner is connected to the supermarket chain's mainframe, which contains prices and inventory levels for each code. The computer calculates the item's price and updates its inventory master file. The computer then transmits price information back to the checkout register. Prices for perishable items such as meat and produce are entered into the register manually. In this manner, the supermarket can restock and track sales trends automatically. Draw a system flowchart for this system.

10. Draw a system flowchart to document the following system:

Order processing is an accounting application that records and screens customer orders and assists with inventory control. Purchase orders from customers are input on-line through point of sale terminals at various locations throughout the company's sales territory. Computer processing references a customer master file with data on each customer such as name, address, discounts, and credit standing. The computer also references an inventory master file to determine if particular goods are on hand prior to producing shipping orders. Items not on hand are placed on back order and the inventory master file is updated to reflect goods that are shipped. Back orders must be maintained on the current order file to initiate a shipping order when goods become available. The system outputs shipping orders and management reports such as "Orders Processed" and "Back Orders."

11. The fixed assets system maintains computerized information about a company's fixed assets. A fixed assets master file contains information such as the cost of fixed assets, depreciation rates, and accumulated depreciation to date. Input transactions for purchases, capitalized wages and materials, disposals, and adjustments are first prepared on hard copy and then entered via CRT terminals.

Changes to standing data, such as depreciation rates, are prepared and entered the same way. The system calculates and summarizes depreciation and profits and losses on disposals. It supplies data to the general ledger system and various management reports. Routine reports are produced on the following: summary and analysis of additions, disposals, depreciation, and adjustments; listings of depreciation rate changes, profit or loss on disposals; and lists of balances. The system also produces exception reports such as those on fully depreciated assets and assets not inspected. Use this information to develop part of the HIPO for this system. Your description should include the HIPO VTOC and an intermediate process overview diagram for one of the system's functions.

References

DeMarco, Tom. *Structured Analysis and System Specification*. New York: Yourdon Press, 1978.

Dijkstra, E. "Structured Programming," in *Classics in Software Engineering*, ed. Edward Nash Yourdon. New York: Yourdon Press, 1979.

Donaldson, J.R. "Structured Programming," *Datamation*, Vol. 19 (December 1973), pp. 52–54.

Gane, Chris, and Sarson, Trish. *Structured Systems Analysis: Tools and Techniques*. Englewood Cliffs, N.J.: Prentice-Hall, 1979.

Katzan, H. *Systems Design and Documentation: An Introduction to the HIPO Method*. New York: Van Nostrand Reinhold, 1976.

Ross, D.T., and Schoman, K.E., Jr. "Structured Analysis for Requirements Definition," *IEEE Transactions on Software Engineering*, Vol. SE-3 (January 1977).

Stay, J. "HIPO and Integrated Program Design," *IBM Systems Journal*, Vol. 15, 1976.

Stevens, W., Myers, G. and Constantine, L.L. "Structured Design," *IBM Systems Journal*, Vol. 13, (May 1974), pp. 115–139.

"The Analysis of User Needs," *EDP Analyzer*, Vol. 17 (January 1979).

Yourdon, Edward, and Constantine, L.L. *Structured Design*. New York: Yourdon Press, 1978.

CHAPTER

12

Systems Analysis and Design: I

OUTLINE

(Continued on next page.)

The Antitrust Division of the Department of Justice was routinely losing track of the cases it was prosecuting because an existing batch system was out-of-date, inaccurate, and slow. Division management had to wait months for reports, 330 lawyers with no computer expertise could not track current or related cases, and 70 managers could not obtain up-to-date caseload reports. A parallel manual system of index cards had grown up among the lawyers in order to track current cases. Management statistics were nonexistent.

A new Antitrust Management Information System was part of the answer, along with a new philosophy of user–system interaction. The new system would have to be user driven and controlled because programmers were in short supply and the variety of requests was too great. Users would have direct access to the database with no programmer intervention.

The systems staff, after months of study, developed easy-to-use data screens driven by function keys and menus. After studying information flows and needs, the systems staff developed on-line screens for a prototype version of the system. Once users had critiqued the screens, they were redone and tested again. Only then did the systems staff proceed to detailed design and programming. The users now enter data directly, and the data tend to be more accurate and up-to-date.

Rather than purchase their own hardware, the system designers chose to run the system on a time-shared computer (IBM 3033) operated by Computer Network. The software used is Cullinet's IDMS/R database management system. Users access the database via Wang Laboratories' VS 100 work stations (with IBM 3270 emulation capabilities) connected by dedicated lines through an on-site communications controller with a 4.8-kilobit per second capacity.

Adapted from "Anti-trust Agency Develops Litigation Tracking System," *Computerworld*, January 13, 1986.

The Antitrust Division's tracking system is a powerful example of the many factors at work in the analysis and design of an information system. Among these factors are organizational goals, philosophy of information processing, user needs, technological capabilities, job design, and organizational change.

In this chapter we discuss systems analysis and design. The student will learn:

- What and who is involved in building systems.

- The role of systems analysis and design.
- The life cycle methodology.
- How resources are allocated in the life cycle.

12.1 Introduction

Building systems involves many people and can take a long time—several years in the case of large systems. This chapter presents an overview of the process of building systems. We identify who does what to whom, where, when, and how. Later chapters will cover special subjects in greater detail.

Different Kinds of Systems, Organizations, and Techniques

There are many different kinds of systems and many different situations in which each is conceived and built. There is no one right way to build a system. Systems differ in terms of their size, technology, and complexity. Organizations differ in terms of the skills of their data processing staff, experience, and past investments in equipment.

The size of the system effort—expressed in dollars for the whole project—is one way to understand the diversity of systems. *Typical medium-sized* systems in Fortune 500 corporations are budgeted at $500,000 to $1 million. Projects costing over $1 million are considered *large*. Projects costing less than $500,000 are considered *small*.

At the upper end of large systems are superprojects like the Social Security Administration's Systems Modernization Plan, which was originally budgeted at $500 million but is currently budgeted at around $1 billion and will be completed in 1992. This is the largest civilian systems development project in history. At the lower end of small systems is an executive support application developed for one senior executive using a microcomputer and budgeted at $10,000.

In most organizations, more than 75% of the systems development projects are small, but they consume less than one-third of the development resources. In other words, most of these resources are consumed by a small number of medium-sized to large projects.

Another way to think about the diversity of systems is to consider the amount of full-time staff involved. Small projects generally require fewer than 5 professionals; medium-sized projects may demand up to 10 to 15; and large systems may involve 100.

Because of the diversity of systems and situations, a number of methods have been developed to build systems (see Table 12.1).

In this chapter we focus on the traditional systems life cycle—the first method mentioned in Table 12.1. We will consider a large project—say, the development of a human resources database, budgeted at around $4 million, involving about 25 full-time systems

TABLE 12.1
Major System Development
Methods and a
Brief Description

Method	Description
Traditional systems life cycle	A formal series of stages through which a system progresses
Phased commitment	A long-term method whereby the system is developed in a series of phases
Evolutionary	A less formal method whereby the ultimate goal is not known in advance
Packages	Purchase of software from outside vendors
Prototyping	Development of system models to clarify final objectives
End-user development	Informal method without intervention of data processing specialists
Service bureau	Purchase of systems or services from outside vendors

personnel for 2 years. In later chapters we will describe the alternative methods and the conditions under which they can be used.

Planned Organizational Change in a Sociotechnical System

Any technology involves much more than hardware. It also includes jobs, skilled people, management, and organization. This has led to the notion of *sociotechnical systems*; that is, to the idea that technologies have to be understood in terms of their total relationship to people and organizations (Blauner, 1964). New information systems are sociotechnical systems; they involve an arrangement of both technical and social elements to form a single entity (Bostrom and Heinen, 1977).

This view involves important practical considerations. In the sociotechnical philosophy, one cannot install new technology without considering the people who must work with it (Bostrom and Heinen, 1977). Building new information systems includes much more than installing a new computer. Frequently, new systems mean new ways of doing business and working together.

One of the most important things to know about systems analysis and design is that it is one kind of planned organizational change. The building of systems involves changes in work, management, and social organization. The nature of tasks, the speed with which they must be completed, the nature of supervision (its frequency and intensity), and who has what information about whom will all be decided in the process of building an information system. This is especially true in contemporary systems, which deeply affect many parts of the organization as the following example illustrates.

The sociotechnical perspective means that system builders have general organizational as well as technical responsibilities. There are four organizational areas where systems analysts and designers are held accountable by senior management. First, they are responsible for the technical quality of the information system. Analysis and design involves a close examination of organizational decision making and the related information flow. Builders of information systems are responsible for ensuring that the processes that are automated are timely, efficient, and highly accurate. The computerized system must

Where Is Your Boss?

It's 7 A.M.—do you know where your boss is? Employees at Thermo Electron Corp., Banco Internacional de Columbia, Northwest Industries, and over 50 other corporations believe they know. These organizations have recently installed management systems that allow senior executives to bypass their staffs, division chiefs, and other layers of bureaucracy for up-to-the-minute information on business activities. Depending on the system, some CEOs can get information as detailed as the name of the bank officer who signed off on a bad loan, to the factory floor manager in charge of production for a given week, to the phone number of any person in the company.

Put bluntly, these systems scare the daylights out of subordinates. Staff groups and data processing managers fear that their influence will wane, and operating managers fear a loss of autonomy and microscopic scrutiny from above. Many senior executives are aware of these problems and rarely call lower managers directly. And they try to make sure that their subordinates see the same information they do so that lower-level managers have a chance to prepare for questions. Thermo Electron's chairman, rather than calling subordinates with his computer analysis, will convey the results in the course of a scheduled meeting to try to convince the manager to see the problem his way. Ultimately, the local manager makes the decision.

Adapted from "Direct Data: Some Computer-Savvy Officials Bypass, and Irk, Their Corporate Aides in Getting Information," *The Wall Street Journal*, Wednesday, January 12, 1983.

provide for the proper filtering of data to avoid overloading workers and managers with too much information.

Second, builders of systems are responsible for the *user interface*. The user interface is a set of software tools that permit often untrained clerical, managerial, and supervisory workers to interact directly with an information system. These tools must be designed in a flexible manner to permit change over time. The interface must encompass considerable education and retraining of the work force, take into account the human factors involved in working with the system, and include the development of understandable software and error codes.

A third area of responsibility for systems builders is the overall *impact on the organization*. Builders must take into account how the system will affect the organization as a whole, focusing particularly on organizational conflict and changes in the locus of decision making. Builders must also consider how the nature of work groups will change under the impact of the new system and how much change is needed.

Finally, builders of information systems have overall managerial responsibility for *the process of design and implementation*. Systems can be technical successes but organizational failures because of a failure in the social and political process of building the system. Analysts and designers are responsible for ensuring that key members of the organization participate in the design process and are permitted to influence the ultimate shape of the system. This activity must be carefully orchestrated by information system builders.

Where Do Ideas for Systems Come From?

Systems originate at different points in the organization. Generally, there are three sources: end users, data processing, and senior management.

End-user demands are the source of most system projects. One of the most common situations occurs when operations personnel sense that something is wrong with an existing transaction system. The system may break down frequently, fail to record new transactions properly, or fail to meet new expectations. Alternatively, middle management in an end-user area, such as personnel, may find an existing MIS inadequate to meet new demands for pensions and benefits.

A second source of systems is data processing. New technologies may present the organization with new opportunities to reduce costs or pursue new lines of business. One responsibility of the Information Systems Division is to track information technology and introduce appropriate technologies into the firm. This might be thought of as *technological push*.

A third source of new systems is senior management. In developing strategic plans for the organization, senior management may conclude that new kinds of information systems will be required to support new business activities. Or it may be apparent that competitors have taken strategic advantage of new information technology, threatening the organization. A technological response of similar dimensions is often required. These kinds of systems can be thought of as the result of *strategic pull*.

Who Is Involved in Building Systems?

Because of the organizationwide impact of contemporary systems, a number of groups, both inside and outside data processing, are involved in building systems.

Some of the major groups involved are shown in Table 12.2. In the development of large systems, senior management is an important actor, providing overall strategic direction (making sure that systems are coordinated with strategic plans) and, equally important, providing funding and strong support. The lack of senior management involvement is probably the single most common cause of long-range strategic systems failure in organizations.

A number of professional groups are also involved in developing systems. Systems require contracts with outside vendors and sometimes involve copyright permissions; therefore, legal professionals are involved. Contracts call into play procurement specialists within the organization, and both of these groups are key players in the systems building process. They lend their organizational and legal expertise to the systems effort.

Two intermediate management groups are important to systems building: middle management and supervisory management. Typi-

TABLE 12.2	Groups	Role
Groups Involved in Building Systems	**Organizational groups**	
	Senior management	Provides funding and support
	Professional experts	Provides legal, procurement, and organizational expertise
	Middle management	Provides entry and support
	Supervisory management	Provides entry and critical insights
	Factory and/or clerical workers	Provides information, job, and task details
	Data processing groups	
	Senior data processing management	Coordinates system development and planning
	Project management	Manages a specific project
	Senior analysts	Coordinates systems analysts, designers, and procurement personnel
	Systems analysts	Determines new system requirements, concepts, and procedures
	Programmers	Responsible for technical realization of the new system.

cally, systems are built at the office or division level. This necessarily involves middle managers, who are crucial in providing analysts and designers with access and support during the design effort. Middle managers who are responsible for specific organizational divisions must be willing to reveal their decision-making process to outside systems analysts. They must be frank and forthcoming with data and insights into the nature of their business before effective systems can be built.

Just below the supervisory level, on the factory floor or in the local office, supervisory management plays a critically important role in providing insights as to how the business works now and how it might be enhanced. This group also provides entry and information to the builders.

Last, if information systems are to be used by factory and clerical workers, they too must be interviewed and interacted with during the building of a system. This ensures that the system will help them to do their jobs better and will provide them with information.

In the data processing area, five major groups are involved in the building of systems (see Table 12.2). Senior data processing management coordinates the overall organizational system development and planning effort. It is their responsibility to establish system priorities in cooperation with the organization's non-data processing senior

Shortages, Backlogs, Costs, and Development Methods

Several studies indicate that the application backlog in major data processing centers is growing from 25 to 40% per year. The majority of organizations have a backlog of 1 to 4 years. Computing expenditures as a percentage of corporate budgets grew from 1% in 1965 to 2% in 1978 and are expected to rise to 13% in 1990, according to the U.S. Department of Labor.

The Pentagon recently estimated that to fulfill its mission critical programs by 1995, it will need an additional 1 million systems experts. If no productivity increases occur in system development methodologies, by 1998 industry will require more than 30 million system workers of all kinds. There are only 4 million system workers now.

Adapted from Kosynski 1984–1985.

management and to ensure adequate budgeting and management in order to deliver projects on time.

Project managers have the most direct responsibility for any given systems effort because it is they who manage projects. They must ensure that adequate resources are available to build the system, that personnel are hired and retained to fulfill the promises of the system, and that the target dates are properly met and within budget.

Three technical groups are involved in building systems: senior analysts, systems analysts, and programmers. Senior analysts are systems analysts with many years of experience who coordinate the efforts of a team of systems analysts in building large systems. Beneath them, and working under their direct supervision, are systems analysts, who are primarily responsible for the development of new system requirements and for the actual design or technical realization of the system. Programmers, in turn, are technical personnel who are ultimately responsible for writing the code and connecting the elements of the system to render it fully operational.

How Is Systems Development Managed?

There are many more ideas for system improvement and development than there are resources. The organization must develop a technique for ensuring that the most important systems are attended to first, that unnecessary systems are not built, and that end users have a full and meaningful role in determining which new systems will be built and how.

Figure 12.1 shows the elements of a management structure for developing new systems. (A detailed discussion of issues in the management of systems is presented in Chapter 21.) At the apex of

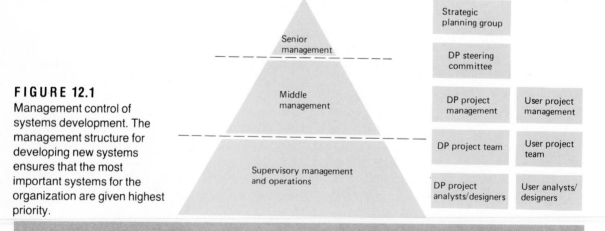

FIGURE 12.1
Management control of systems development. The management structure for developing new systems ensures that the most important systems for the organization are given highest priority.

this structure is the corporate strategic planning group and the data processing steering committee.

The *corporate strategic planning group* is responsible for developing the strategic organization plan. This plan may require the development of new systems. An important function of this committee, then, is to give overall strategic direction to the data processing area. A second less obvious function is to educate senior management about the systems area so that they understand how dependent the organization is on systems.

The *data processing steering committee* is the senior management group with direct responsibility for systems development and operation (Nolan, 1974). It is composed of division directors from the end-user and data processing areas. The steering committee reviews and approves plans for data processing in all divisions; seeks to develop common systems that can be shared; seeks to coordinate and integrate systems; sometimes becomes involved in selecting specific project alternatives; and approves training for new systems. Increasingly, the data processing steering committee is becoming a powerful gatekeeper of systems development.

The next level of management, the *project management team*, is concerned with the management of specific projects. Generally, this is a small group of senior data processing managers and end-user managers with responsibility for a single project.

The *project team* is composed of the systems professionals (analysts and programmers) who are directly responsible for building the system. As previously indicated, ultimate end users (e.g., the Personnel Department) frequently have their own systems professionals who participate directly in the project. Indeed, many large organizations have created a new job title, "business systems analyst," to identify, recruit, and reward systems personnel who work directly for user departments. This is quite a departure from the past, where the Data Processing Department was the sole source of systems professionals.

A typical project team consists of systems analysts, functional analysts (specialists from relevant business areas), application programmers, and perhaps database specialists. This team is responsible for most of the development activities. For certain applications, legal staff representatives and behavioral specialists may be consulted. Discussions with managers from both user areas and information systems will take place at key decision points.

The mix of skills and the size of the project team vary from one application to another. Obviously, complex, far-reaching applications, such as a general ledger system or an accounts receivable system integrating corporate headquarters with a number of semi-autonomous operating units will require a much larger project team than a small system to computerize automobile insurance records for one operating unit's cars. Sometimes, two or three teams operating simultaneously will be needed for large projects.

However, there is a limit to the number of people who can work effectively on a project at any one time. A project that would take 50 man-years cannot be completed by 50 people working for 1 year. There are too many task dependencies (tasks that cannot be started until others are completed) and inefficiencies caused by coordinating the work of so many people. For each application, there is a project team of optimal size. Up to a certain point, people can be added to a project team to raise its overall productivity, but beyond that point, every additional member successively *decreases* productivity. (This is discussed in later chapters on the management of systems.)

Clearly, not all systems must be approved by all levels of project development management. In our assumed large human resource database project, this effort would probably be initiated by the Human Resources Department and proposed first by the data processing committee. Managers from other departments would have to approve the project (recognizing that their own projects might have to wait until this one is completed). Next, the corporate planning group would be informed of the desire to build a new system: given the size of the project, its approval would also be required. A project management team composed of human resources and data processing management would be formed. This group would pick a project team composed of project managers, systems analysts, and programmers.

With this organizational background, we can now take a closer look at the systems development life cycle and consider what systems analysts actually do.

12.2 Overview of the Systems Development Life Cycle

All projects in organizations have a life cycle—a beginning, a middle, and an end. In the information systems world, all projects go through a systems development life cycle. With some projects, especially small ones, this is largely an informal series of stages. With very large projects, however, the development life cycle involves a much more formal approach.

When a formal systems development life cycle is used to manage large projects, it is called the traditional systems life cycle. This method of developing systems was first used with large transaction processing systems in the 1950s. For most medium-sized and large projects, it is still the principal method of development.

In the systems life cycle, the development process is partitioned into distinct stages. Each stage consists of basic activities that must be

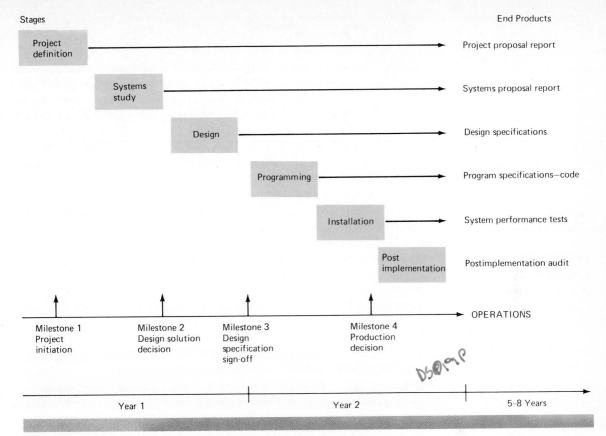

FIGURE 12.2
Model of the system development life cycle, showing each stage with
its end products and key decision milestones. A typical medium-sized
development project requires 2 years to deliver and has an expected
life span of 5–8 years.

performed for successful completion of the development effort. In
each of these stages, users, managers, and data processing staff have
specific responsibilities. The stages are usually handled sequentially,
with a formal *sign-off* or agreement between data processing personnel and end users as each stage is passed.

The various stages of the systems development life cycle are
illustrated in Figure 12.2. In Sections 12.3 and 12.4, these stages are
described in greater detail.

The terminology and activities assigned to each stage differ from
one organization to another (and from one textbook to another).
Some life cycle methodologies group programming and design
together in a single phase. Others define project definition and
system study as the prefeasibility and feasibility stages. Nevertheless,

the basic sequence of system development activities and control procedures are the same.

As shown in Figure 12.2, each of the major stages in the life cycle has a product or output that is required before the next stage can proceed. The project definition stage results in a proposal for the development of a new system. The system study stage provides a detailed systems proposal report outlining alternatives and establishing the feasibility of the general objective. The design stage results in a report on the design specifications for the system. The programming stage results in actual computer code. The installation stage involves using the new system to ensure that it passes certain benchmark tests and performs properly. Last, the postimplementation stage involves continual maintenance, updating, auditing, and management of the system.

What Is Systems Analysis?

Systems analysis and design involves the building of systems. Systems analysts are the architects of systems, whereas programmers are the carpenters. Systems analysis and design are two different activities performed by systems analysts. They are described in this chapter.

There are four major objectives of systems analysis (see Table 12.3). First, the systems analyst *defines the overall objective* of the systems project, establishing its approximate overall costs and estimated benefits; deciding who will use the system; determining its scope; and working out a time frame and budget for its development.

The key to building any large information system is a thorough understanding of the existing organization and system. Thus, the second objective of the analyst is to create a road map of the *existing organization/system*, identifying the *creators of data* and the primary users of data. A primary purpose of this study is to identify the primary *stakeholders* within the organization. These people are the primary owners and users of data; they have a direct interest in the information affected by the new system. In addition to these organizational aspects, the analyst also briefly describes the existing hardware and software that serve the organization. A related area is a

TABLE 12.3
Objectives of the
Systems Analyst

Define the overall objectives of the system

Identify the operation and problems of existing systems

Identify the requirements and objectives of the new system

Identify areas of required organizational change

gross estimate of the benefits and costs of the existing system. More detailed cost/benefit analyses will be done later.

Perhaps the most difficult task of the systems analyst is to *define the specific information requirements* of the new system. This is the area where many large system efforts go wrong and the one that poses the greatest difficulty for the analyst. Here the analyst must establish the specific objectives and requirements of the new system, and describe the data flows and the processing of information. The information requirements must be based upon a keen analysis of decisions in the organization. The result is a statement of the detailed requirements of the system: who gets what information, when, where, how often, and in what form.

What Is Systems Design?

The three objectives of systems design are shown in Table 12.4. In comparison to systems analysis, systems design is more technical. However, it is not as technical as programming.

There are three major system designer activities. First, the designer is responsible for considering *alternative hardware and software configurations* for carrying out and developing the system as described by the analyst. This may involve analysis of the performance of different pieces of hardware and software, security capabilities of systems and their auditability, and the portability or changeability of systems hardware.

Second, the designer is involved in the detailed *construction of the physical database*, changes in clerical and managerial procedures required to support the system, new telecommunications facilities, and physical facility changes.

Third, designers are responsible for the *management and control of programming*. The detailed programming specifications, coding of data, documentation standards, and software tools are all the responsibility of the design staff. In addition, designers are responsible for the procurement of hardware, consultants, and software needed by the system.

With this understanding of systems analysis and design, we can take a closer look at the systems development life cycle.

TABLE 12.4
Objectives of Systems Design

Devise detailed system solutions

Deliver the functions required by the analyst and, ultimately, by the user

Manage the technical realization of systems

12.3 Systems Analysis Stages of the Life Cycle: Project Definition and Systems Study

Project definition and systems study involve the systems analyst. Here the overall rationale for the new system is developed (project definition) and the existing system—if there is one—is given a rigorous critique. Gross alternative systems are also considered, and the costs and benefits of change are roughly estimated.

Project Definition Stage

In the project definition stage, a preliminary survey is made to answer the questions "Why do we need a new system project?" and "What do we want to accomplish?".

Some reasons for initiating a systems project are as follows:

1. *To solve a problem* in an area where the current system is not functioning as required.
2. *To incorporate new requirements*, which may necessitate additions, modifications, or replacements of existing systems.
3. *To improve existing systems*, for example, by reducing operating costs or response time.

Systems analysts identify the general objectives of a new system and develop a project plan. They define the project scope: its duration, complexity, and expense. Unless system planners set boundaries on a system, the project will bog down by intruding in nonessential areas and undertaking too much.

System Rationale Statement

Using our example of a large human resources system, the project scope statement might say:

> The project will encompass all human resource functions (equal employment opportunity, compensation, employment, personnel development, benefits) except relocation, health, and safety. The new system will require an interface with the payroll department but will not include the payroll system or payroll processing.

The customers or people expected to use the new system will be identified:

> This system will be used by the entire human resources network in Corporate and the operating units. It will not be used by the Trust Unit, which funds and administers employee before- and after-tax savings plans and the pension trust.

Project Feasibility

In addition to establishing the overall rationale for the new system, in this stage the analysts must attempt to determine the feasibility of the project. Three major areas of feasibility must be addressed:

1. *Technical feasibility*: whether the proposed solution can be implemented with the available hardware, software, and technical expertise.
2. *Economic feasibility*: whether the benefits of the proposed solution outweigh the costs. (Chapter 21 treats cost/benefit analysis in detail.)
3. *Operational feasibility*: whether the proposed solution is desirable within the existing managerial and organizational framework.

Formal feasibility reports are generally prepared at two points during systems analysis. In the project definition stage, when a new system is initially proposed, preliminary analysis will assess *project feasibility*. The project feasibility study will roughly determine the economic and technical feasibility of developing the system. Later, as the systems analysis is completed in the systems study stage, the feasibility of alternative solutions will be carefully evaluated in great detail.

The end product of the project definition stage is a project plan that can be shown to management. The plan describes in detail the remaining life cycle activities (design, programming, testing, etc.) and the tasks (documentation, flow charts, coding, debugging, etc.) for each phase. It spells out the individuals and skills required for each task and the number of man-days and dollars that will have to be allocated. The plan also pinpoints milestone tasks with dates to compare the project performance to the project plan.

The project plan is the essential proposal document utilized by the data processing steering committee to decide among alternative investments of systems development funds. It is therefore crucial.

Systems Study Stage

This phase answers the following questions:

- What does the existing system do?
- What inputs, outputs, and processing are involved?
- What are the strengths, weaknesses, trouble spots, and problems?
- What should the new or modified system do to meet user requirements?

To answer these questions, the project team embarks on an extensive information-gathering effort. Existing systems, both automated and manual, are meticulously documented and analyzed.

Essential sources of information include the following:

1. *Existing documents and work papers.* These include manuals or written outlines of procedures for existing manual or computer-based systems; appropriate technical documentation; operating statistics and cost data; organization charts; job descriptions; letters; memos; and all forms, files, and reports associated with the function under investigation.

   Collecting and shifting through such documents can be very tedious and time-consuming. Sometimes there is no way to ensure that all critical documents have been gathered. Wihout considerable discussion with users, it is hard to determine which pieces of information on the documents must be captured in the new system and which ones are extraneous. Key pieces of information may reside in the user's heads rather than in the documents themselves. Therefore, documentary information is usually supplemented with personal interviews.

2. *Observation.* This gives the analyst a firsthand look at the practices and procedures of a given system. From such observations volumes and layouts of transactions may be noted and bottlenecks or procedural problems discovered. Suppose, for example, that a large number of transactions from an accounts payable edit program are rejected because the amount fields have blanks in the second decimal place. This may indicate a poorly designed input transaction form or a lack of strict data entry procedures.

3. *Questionnaires.* These are useful when many people must be polled to gather the requisite information. Questionnaires are an efficient and relatively effective technique if the questions are clear and well written and if the analysts know exactly what kind of information to elicit. Information derived from questionnaires can be used to supplement other sources or to gain insights that would not be possible through the examination of existing documents and papers.

4. *Interviews.* This is a valuable but costly technique. Large amounts of time must be allocated to preparing questions, researching the background and activities of interviewees, and analyzing the results. Depending on the nature of the information sought, the interview sessions themselves may last for half an hour or several days. Therefore, this technique is not cost effective for polling large numbers of people. It is most efficiently used when in-depth information is required from a few key individuals. These may include the most experienced order entry clerk, who knows the most about transactions that must be input into the system, or high-level executives with decision support requirements to be incorporated.

Information Requirements Determination

All of the facts gathered during the systems study phase will be used to determine information system requirements.

At the most basic level, *the information requirements of a new system involve identifying who needs what information, where, when, and how.*

Requirements analysis carefully defines the objectives of the new or modified system and develops a detailed statement of the functions that the new system must perform. Requirements must consider economic, technical, and time constraints, as well as the goals, procedures, and behavior of the organization.

Faulty requirements analysis is a leading cause of systems failure and high systems development costs (see Chapter 19). A system designed around the wrong set of requirements will either have to be

The System Understands

A customer walks into a Motor Vehicle Bureau office to renew registration for the family car. After some pertinent data—plate number, and so on—is keyed in, the system takes over, analyzes the input entry, decides which entities need updating, and that the registration and plates need replacing.

A new registration document is printed and the customer is surprised to learn that the new registration shows a different owner ID number, the address is specified in a different way, and new plate numbers have been issued.

This new information was not solicited from the customer but decided on by the system. The information in the system is now more accurate. The system is designed to understand the principles of vehicle registration and data cleanup policies in effect and to act on them when appropriate. The system acts in much the same way clerks would act at the counter—correcting information as they went along in the course of a transaction. Only now the corrections are made by the system.

The Vehicle Registration System was implemented by the Ontario Ministry of Transportation and Communications. It is an on-line distributed IMS system handling 72 million transactions per year. The application logic supporting the over-the-counter registration business occupies 1.8 megabytes of executable code.

Adapted from Philip Edwards, "The System Understands," *Datamation Magazine*, August 15, 1985.

discarded because of poor performance or heavily revised. Therefore, the importance of requirements analysis cannot be underestimated.

Developing requirements specifications may involve considerable research and revision. A business function may be very complex or poorly defined. There may be no existing manual system or routine set of inputs and outputs. Procedures may vary from individual to individual. Such a situation will be more difficult to analyze, especially if the users are unsure of what they want or need—which is extremely common. To derive information systems requirements, analysts may be forced to work and rework requirements statements in cooperation with users. Although this is laborious, it is far superior to and less costly than redoing and undoing an entire system.

In many instances, business procedures are unclear or users disagree about how things are done and should be done. Systems analysis often makes an unintended contribution to the organization by clarifying procedures and building organizational consensus about how things should be done.

In many instances, building a new system creates an opportunity to redefine how the organization conducts its daily business. In the preceding vignette, the analysts made a marked improvement (from the consumer's point of view) in existing procedures.

Requirements Determination Techniques

Because of the importance of information requirements analysis, much has been written about how it should be done (Davis, 1977, 1981, 1982). In the following chapter, we describe the major strategies for determining information requirements. All of them rely to varying degrees on four underlying techniques of data collection:

1. *Polling*: contacting users, either through questionnaires or interviews and asking them to state their requirements.
2. *Data analysis*: deriving requirements from existing information systems.
3. *Prototyping*: experimenting with an evolving information system.
4. *Object system analysis*: building requirements from an "ideal" or conceptual system model.

Polling is the most obvious way to find out what kinds of information managers need, as well as when, how, and where. Questionnaires can be a highly cost-effective way to gather this information, but they are appropriate only when a limited number of responses is sufficient. In new systems, those with no mechanical or manual predecessor, a clearer understanding of information requirements often necessitates the use of personal interviews. Both techniques assume that managers know what kinds of information they need and want. Often this assumption is incorrect.

Data analysis is a bottom-up approach that focuses on data needs at the operational level of the organization. Requirements are derived primarily from files, documents, or reports (time cards, paychecks, sales slips, sales summaries, invoices, etc.) that currently support operational activities or management decisions. This material may be supplemented by interviews with management. Data analysis is most useful in defining operational requirements, especially for operational systems such as payroll or order processing.

Prototyping involves constructing a model system with which users can experiment. By working with an actual system, users will have a clearer idea of what the system can do for them and what they want. Created with special application tools that facilitate modifications, the prototyped system can be revised to incorporate requirements that emerge from experience and actual use. (Prototyping is discussed in detail in Chapter 14.)

Object system analysis derives requirements from ideal or conceptual models of systems rather than from actual systems or data flows. It is used primarily for building systems to support key management decisions and strategic organizational objectives. One form of requirements modeling is called *decision analysis*. This analysis derives requirements from decisions at the managerial level. From fine-tuned interviews and work sessions with key managers, analysts define the decisions essential to support strategic organizational objectives. The decision process is documented and analyzed with decision tables, decision flowcharts, or decision trees. Requirements can then be derived from the information needed for each decision.

Cost/Benefit Analysis

A major consideration in assessing the feasibility of a proposed system or design alternatives is cost/benefit analysis (Emery, 1971; Nolan, 1974; Parker, 1982). It would be foolish to develop a new system without knowing what it will cost to implement and operate and whether it will generate savings to offset these expenses. Cost/benefit analysis is a decisive step in the systems development effort:

- It accounts for all costs and benefits associated with the proposed system that will affect the organization.
- It lists clearly defined assumptions about the analysis—how costs and benefits will be measured for the system—and sets forth a common monetary base.
- A favorable outcome of the cost/benefit analysis provides one rationale for the project.

Cost/benefit analysis for systems is discussed in some detail in Chapter 21.

12.4 Systems Design Stages of the Life Cycle: Design to Postimplementation

Design

The design of an information system is the overall plan or model for that system. Like the blueprint of a building or house, it consists of all of the specifications that give the system its form and structure. Whereas the requirements developed during systems analysis show *what* a system should do, the design shows *how* the system will operate. Information systems design is an exacting and creative task demanding imagination, sensitivity to detail, and expert skills.

Conceptual and Physical Design

The design of an information system can be broken down into stages. *Conceptual design* (sometimes called *logical design*) lays out the components of the system and their relationship to each other as they would appear to users. It describes inputs and outputs, functions to be performed, and the flow of processing. It may also outline operating and user procedures, audits, and controls.

Physical design is the process of translating the abstract conceptual model into the specific technical design for the new system. It produces the actual specifications for programs, hardware, telecommunications, security, and backup. Some life cycle methodologies include *physical database design* (the actual layout of data as they would be organized for physical storage) within physical design. Others treat it as a separate phase.

Design Alternatives

Before the design of an information system is finalized, analysts will evaluate various *design alternatives*. Based on the requirements definition and systems analysis, analysts construct high-level conceptual design models. They then examine the costs, benefits, strengths, and weaknesses of each alternative based on the design factors to be described. Examples of design alternatives for a corporate cost system are illustrated in Figures 12.3(A) and 12.3(B). The first alternative maximizes the efficiency and economy of processing. The second features more timely information and reduced manual effort, but at greater processing cost.

There are three basic design solutions for every systems problem:

1. To do nothing, leaving the existing situation unchanged.
2. To modify or enhance existing systems.
3. To develop a new system.

There may be several design options within solutions 2 or 3. A written systems proposal report will describe the costs and benefits, advantages and disadvantages of each alternative. It is then up to

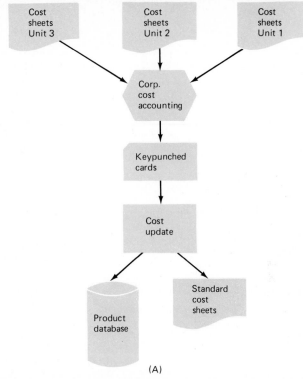

(A)

FIGURE 12.3A
Conceptual design alternative 1. This design entails relatively inexpensive and efficient computer processing but extensive manual preparation of data. There is also a time lag between the preparation of operating unit cost sheets and the point when this information is reflected on the product database.

1. Operating units prepare cost sheets with product cost data by plant. Sheets are mailed to Corporate Cost Accounting at corporate headquarters.

2. Corporate Cost Accounting reviews cost sheets and prepares transaction forms, which are keypunched.

3. The corporate product database is updated twice weekly via batch processing. The database maintains standard product cost data by plant and links local product numbers to corporate product numbers. The update also produces standard cost sheets.

4. Copies of the standard cost sheets are mailed back to the operating units.

management to determine which mix of costs, benefits, technical features, and organizational impacts represents the most desirable alternative.

Design Components

The *design process* describes all of the components of an information system and the way they fit together to form a unified whole. Basic design components consist of the following:

- *Outputs*: what the information system produces. Outputs can consist of reports, hard copy, files, or any medium on which information is stored.
- *Inputs*: the data fed into the information system for processing to output.

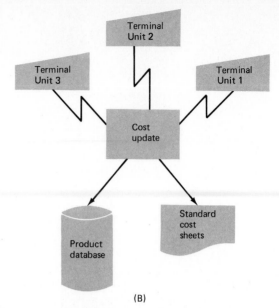

(B)

FIGURE 12.3B
Conceptual design
alternative 2. This design
is relatively expensive in
terms of hardware, software,
and security and recovery
procedures required to
maintain the integrity of the
database. On-line processing
is also more expensive than
batch processing. However,
the design considerably
streamlines manual activities
and provides up-to-the-minute
information to both corporate
cost accounting and the
operating units.

1. Operating units enter their own product cost data on-line via local CRT terminals with tele-communications links to the central corporate mainframe.

2. Through extensive on-line editing, the operating unit product data are edited. Errors are corrected and the data immediately update the corporate product database.

3. Up-to-date product cost information is available immediately after update. The system produces hard-copy standard cost sheets or allows the operating units to perform on-line inquiries about product cost information.

- *Processing*: all of the automated or manual procedures or activities through which data are transformed from input to output.
- *Database*: the medium and format for storing either manual or automated information in the system. A database may consist of paper files in a cabinet or computerized data on magnetic tape or disk.
- *Procedures*: all of the activities performed in the operation and use of an information system.
- *Controls:* both manual and automated processes and procedures that ensure that information systems are performing as required. Controls specify standards for acceptable performance and methods for measuring actual performance in relation to these standards.

Like houses or buildings, information systems may have many possible designs. They may be centralized or distributed; on-line or batch; fully manual, partially manual, or fully automated. Each design represents a unique blend of all of the factors—technical and organizational—that shape an information system.

Factors Shaping Design

What makes one design superior to others is the ease and efficiency with which it fulfills user requirements within a specific set of technical, organizational, financial, and time constraints.

Each design reflects a balance between five major factors:

- *User information requirements*: what information in what form and time frame the system must produce.
- *System requirements*: demands on the system other than information. These demands include performance level, reliability, maintainability, flexibility, implementation time, and anticipated life expectancy.
- *Information processing technology*: available manual and automated tools for processing data. These include manual processing, mainframes, minicomputers, microcomputers, telecommunications networks, programming languages, database management systems, and data storage devices.
- *Systems development methodologies*: the various approaches and methodologies for building information systems, such as top-down or bottom-up development; prototyping; structured analysis and design; or information engineering (These methodologies are discussed in subsequent chapters.)
- *Organizational characteristics*: the tasks, technology, people, structure, and culture of the organization. A proper system is one that optimizes the fit among these elements. System design is also shaped by the availability of financial and material resources.

The Role of Users

Design cannot be directed by technical specialists alone. It demands a very high level of participation and control by users. User information requirements drive the entire system-building effort. Users must have sufficient control over the design process to ensure that the system reflects their business priorities and information needs, not the biases of the technical staff.

Working on design increases users' understanding and acceptance of the system, reducing problems caused by power transfers, intergroup conflict, and unfamiliarity with new system functions and procedures. As Chapter 19 points out, insufficient user involvement in the design effort is a major cause of system failure.

Some MIS researchers have suggested that design should be "user-led" (Lucas, 1974). However, other researchers point out that systems development is not an entirely rational process. Users leading design activities have used their position to further private interests and gain power rather than to enhance organizational objectives. Users controlling design can sabotage or seriously impede the implementation effort (Franz and Robey, 1984).

The nature and level of user participation in design vary from system to system. There is less need for user involvement in systems with simple or straightforward requirements than in those with requirements that are elaborate, complex, or vaguely defined. Transaction processing or operational control systems have traditionally required less user involvement than strategic planning, information reporting, and decision support systems. Less structured systems need more user participation to define requirements and may necessitate many versions of design before specifications can be finalized.

Different levels of user involvement in design are reflected in different systems development methodologies. Chapter 13 describes how user involvement varies with each development approach.

TABLE 12.5
Detail Design Considerations

Ouput
  Medium
  Content
  Timing

Input
  Origins
  Flow
  Data entry

Use interface
  Simplicity
  Efficiency
  Logic
  Feedback
  Errors

Database design
  Logical data relations
  Volume and speed
  requirements
  File organization and design
  Record specifications

Processing
  Computations
  Program modules
  Required reports
  Timing of outputs

Manual procedures
  What activities
  Who performs them
  When
  How
  Where

Controls
  Input controls (characters, limit,
  reasonableness)
  Processing controls (consistency, record
  counts)
  Outputs controls (totals, samples of output)
  Procedural controls (passwords, special forms)

Security
  Access controls
  Catastrophe plans
  Audit trails

Documentation
  Operations documentation
  Systems documents
  User documentation

Conversion
  Transfer files
  Initiate new procedures
  Select testing method
  Cut over to new system

Training
  Select training techniques
  Develop training modules
  Identify training facilities

Organizational changes
  Task redesign
  Job design
  Office and organization structure design
  Reporting relationships

Detail Design ▬▬▬▬▬ *Detail design* provides the remaining specifications that transform the high-level, abstract design plan into a functioning system of people and machines. The level of detail design extends down to the last byte in the system and must be complete before programming begins. Detail design specifications address a number of areas (see Table 12.5).

Programming ▬▬▬▬▬ The process of translating design specifications into software for the computer constitutes a smaller portion of the systems development cycle than design and perhaps testing activities. But it is here, in providing the actual instructions for the machine, that the heart of the system takes shape.

During the programming stage, system specifications prepared during the design stage are translated into program code. On the basis of detailed design documents for files, transaction and report layouts, and other design details, specifications for each program in the system are prepared. Program specifications include the following:

- A brief narrative description of what the program will do.
- Type of programming language.
- Input and output descriptions.
- Processing schedule.
- Processing detail specifications such as use of tables, types of computations, logic, editing, sorting, etc.
- Limitations and restrictions, such as sequence of input data, control statements, etc.

Some development projects assign programming tasks to programmer specialists whose work consists exclusively of coding programs. Other projects prefer programmer/analysts who both design and program functions. Since large systems entail many programs with thousands, even hundreds of thousands, of lines of code, programming teams are frequently used. Moreover, even if an entire system can be programmed by a single individual, the quality of the software will be higher if it is subject to group review. Structured *walk throughs*, where programs are subject to peer review under formal rules, have been institutionalized in many information systems departments to ensure high-quality software (Weinberg, 1972).

Installation ▬▬▬▬▬ As a stage in the systems life cycle, *installation* consists of the final steps that put the new system into operation: testing and conversion.

Testing ▬▬▬▬▬ Exhaustive and thorough testing must be conducted to ascertain whether the system produces the right results. Testing answers the question "Will the system produce the desired results under known conditions?".

The amount of time needed to answer this question has been traditionally underrated in systems project planning. As much as 50% of the entire software development budget can be expended in testing. Testing is also time-consuming: Test data must be carefully prepared; results reviewed; and corrections made in the system. In many instances, parts of the system have to be redesigned. Yet, the risks of glossing over this step are enormous.

Testing a system involves three activities:

- *Unit testing*, or program testing, consists of testing separately each program in the system. While it is widely believed that the purpose of such testing is to guarantee that programs are error free, this is realistically impossible. Testing should be viewed instead as a means of locating errors in programs, focusing on finding all the ways to make a program fail. Once pinpointed, problems can be corrected.
- *System testing* tests the functioning of the system as a whole. It tries to determine if discrete modules will function together as planned and whether discrepancies exist between the way the system actually works and the way it was conceived. Among the areas examined are performance time; capacity for file storage and handling peak loads; recovery and restart capabilities; and manual procedures.
- *Acceptance testing* provides the final certification that the system is ready for conversion. Systems tests are evaluated by users and reviewed by management. When all parties are satisfied that the new system meets their standards, the system is formally accepted for installation.

Test Plans

It is essential that all aspects of testing be carefully thought out and as comprehensive as possible. To ensure this, the development team works with users to devise a systematic test plan. The test plan includes all of the preparations for the series of tests previously described.

Figure 12.4 shows an example of a test plan. The general test condition being tested here is a record change. The documentation consists of a series of test plan screens maintained on a database— perhaps a micro database, which is ideally suited to this kind of application.

Users play a critical role in the testing process. They are the only ones who understand the full range of data and conditions that might occur within their system. Moreover, programmers tend to be aware only of the conditions treated in their programs; the test data they devise are usually too limited. Therefore, input from other team members and users will help ensure that the range of conditions included in the test data is complete. Users can identify frequent and less common transactions, unusual conditions to anticipate, and most

FIGURE 12.4

A sample test plan to test a record change. Various conditions to be tested, requirements for each condition tested, and expected results must be included. Test plans require input from both end users and information system specialists.

Procedure	Address and Maintenance "Record Change Series"		Test: Series 2		
Prepared By:		Date:	Version:		
Test Ref.	Condition Tested	Special Requirements	Expected Results	Output On	Next Screen
2	Change records				
2.1	Change existing record	Key field Other fields	Not allowed		
2.2	Change nonexistent record		"Invalid key" message		
2.3	Change deleted record	Deleted record must be available	"Deleted" message		
2.4	Make second change	Change 2.1 above	OK if valid	Transaction file	V45
2.5	Insert record		OK if valid	Transaction file	V45
2.6	Abort during change	Abort 2.5	No change	Transaction file	V45

of the common types of errors that might occur when the system is in use. User input is also decisive in verifying the manual procedures for the system.

Conversion

Conversion is the process of changing from the old system to the new. It answers the question "Will the new system work under real conditions?". Four main conversion strategies have been developed:

- *Parallel strategy.* Both the old system and its potential replacement are run together for a time until everyone is assured that the new one functions correctly. This is the safest conversion approach because, in the event of errors or processing disruptions, the old system can still be used as a backup. However, this approach is very expensive, and additional staff or resources may be required to run the extra system.
- *Direct cutover.* At first glance, this strategy seems less costly than parallel conversion. The old system is discarded on an appointed day and replaced completely with the new system. There are no parallel activities. However, this is a very risky approach and potentially more costly than parallel activities if serious problems with the new system are found. There is no other system to fall back on. Dislocations, disruptions, and the cost of corrections may be enormous.

- *Pilot study.* The new system is introduced only to a limited area of the organization, such as a single department or operating unit. When this pilot version is complete and working smoothly, it is installed in the rest of the organization, either simultaneously or in stages.
- *Phased approach.* The new system is introduced in stages, either by functions (e.g., hourly employees paid weekly first, salaried monthly employees 6 months later for a new comprehensive payroll system) or by organizational unit (e.g., corporate headquarters first, outlying operating units 4 months later).

Conversion Plan

A schedule of all of the activities required to install the new system is detailed in a formal *conversion plan*. The most time-consuming activity is usually the conversion of data. Master files and any requisite table files for the new system must be loaded and verified. If the data were previously maintained manually, all of them must be entered into the new system manually. Conversion programs can be written to transfer data that have already been automated from the old set of files to the new.

Postimplementation

After the system is installed and conversion is complete, the system is said to be in *production*. During this stage, it will be reviewed by users and technical specialists to determine how well it has met its original objectives and whether any revisions or modifications are in order. The formal review process after installation is called the *postimplementation audit*. Changes in hardware, software, documentation, or procedures to correct errors, meet new requirements, or improve processing efficiency are termed *maintenance*.

Postimplementation Audit

The *postimplementation audit* is a formal review that compares the actual performance and costs of the system to the objectives and cost/benefit estimates formulated during the systems analysis phase. The audit does the following:

- It compares the actual implementation time and cost to the schedules and budgets originally proposed for the development project.
- It compares the actual operating costs to the preimplementation estimates.
- It reviews operational activities, documentation, security provisions, and controls.

In addition to examining system usage logs and statistics for operating costs, frequency of errors, and incidence of production problems, the evaluation includes some measurement of user satisfaction. Users are asked through questionnaires or interviews to rate the system's accuracy, response time, reliability, and ability to satisfy their information requirements. The audit should also review organizational impacts: changes in job functions, work groups, and behavior.

The postimplementation audit should be (and most often is) conducted by the corporate auditing department using trained dating processing auditors.

Maintenance

The average life span of an information system is 4 to 6 years. (An occasional long-lived application will remain in production for 10 years or more.) During this time, the system must be *maintained*. It may sound odd that an information system must be maintained like a car. The reasons are as follows:

- Hardware and software must be periodically tuned to function effectively or modified to meet new technical or user requirements.
- The organization changes and new information requirements emerge.
- The environment changes (e.g., new government regulations or industry practice) and creates new information requirements.

Studies of maintenance have examined the amount of time required for various maintenance tasks (Lientz and Swanson, 1980). Approximately 20% is devoted to debugging or correcting emergency production problems; another 20% is concerned with changes in data, files, reports, hardware, or system software. But 60% of all maintenance work consists of making user enhancements, improving documentation, and recoding system components for greater processing efficiency. The amount of work in the third category of maintenance problems could be reduced significantly through better system analysis and design practices. Some tools—in the form of systems engineer work stations—are now available to improve the process of designing systems.

Because of the soaring costs of data processing personnel and limited flexibility of most information systems, maintenance has become a very expensive, inefficient process. One study showed that maintenance was 50 times more costly per instruction than the original cost of development. Today maintenance consumes over 50% of software budgets. Typically, more than one-half of the Data Processing Department's professional staff is involved in maintenance. This problem is discussed in Chapter 21.

As an information system ages, maintenance costs tend to escalate. The system becomes increasingly less efficient to maintain. Finally, a point is reached where maintenance costs surpass the cost of replacing the entire system. In purely economic terms, a case can be made for creating a new system.

Automated System Development Tools

A study by TRW, Inc., found that as many as 64% of system errors can be traced to the analysis and design phase. As errors move through the development cycle, the cost of correcting them increases 100 times or more.

Systems analysts complain that they do not have enough time to get applications developed, completed applications often do not meet users' needs, and costs are soaring beyond budget limits. They say they lack tools. But some recent products on the market may help.

Manual techniques for developing software have improved greatly over the years. Computer Sciences Corporation (CSC) estimates that there has been a 10% compound growth in productivity since 1980. But manual tools—graphics templates, project controllers, handwritten documentation, and manual error checking—are still awkward, error-prone, and slow.

A number of integrated software development tools are now on the market that can run on mainframes, minicomputer work stations, or even microcomputers. They offer high-speed graphics capabilities for drawing systems, data dictionaries to integrate parts of large projects, documentation support incorporating text with graphics, automatic error checking for consistency between graphics and the data dictionary, and project management functions.

Adapted from "Structured Analysis Can Streamline Software Design," *Computerworld*, December 9, 1985.

12.5 Resource Allocation in the Life Cycle

Ideally, a considerable amount of resources should be devoted to the project definition and systems study stages. The literature suggests that about one-quarter of a project's time and cost should be ex-

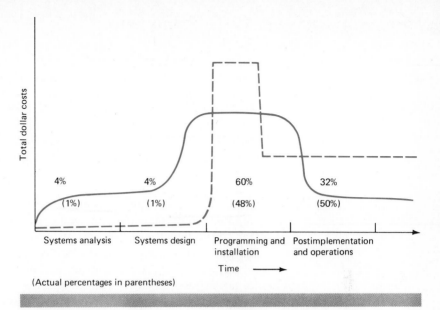

FIGURE 12.5
Ideal and actual software life cycle costs. Ideally, relatively balanced amounts of time are allowed for analysis, design, programming, and installation. About 8% of costs are allocated ideally to analysis and design, 60% to programming and installation, and 32% to long-term maintenance. Actually, however, the early stages of analysis and design receive far less resources than is desirable. Programming and installation (including all important testing) also receive less time and fewer resources than is desirable, reflecting pressure to deliver a workable system as soon as possible. As a result, systems maintenance is far more expensive than is desirable—about 50% of total software costs over the expected life span of the system. (Adapted from Alberts, 1976.)

pended here. About 50% of project resources should be allocated to the design and programming stages. Installation and postimplementation ideally should require one-quarter of the project's resources (Alberts, 1976).

Figure 12.5 compares the ideal software systems life cycle costs over time (solid line) with the actual experience with several large system efforts (dotted line). Clearly, the early stages of a study often receive far less resources than is desirable. Moreover, maintenance costs (postimplementation) are enormous, far larger than anticipated.

In the next chapter, we will consider some of the causes and consequences of poor resource allocation in systems development.

12.6 Summary

There are many different ways to build systems because there are different kinds of systems and different organizational situations. Information systems are one kind of sociotechnical system. Systems building is a form of planned organizational change that involves many different people in the organization. A change in systems involves changes in work, management, and the organization.

Ideas for systems can originate from operations personnel, data processing personnel and senior management. We have characterized these sources of system initiation as end-user demand, technology push, and strategic pull. In contrast to the past, most organizations today have a well-established management structure for controlling the development of systems. All medium-sized and large systems involve senior management and division managers, along with data processing professionals. Large and medium-sized organizations usually have a corporate information system steering committee to allocate resources to system projects.

All systems building projects, regardless of the method used to build them, go through a life cycle. One of the most common methods of.system development is the systems development life cycle. This approach partitions the development process into a distinct sequence of tasks, showing the flow of work, user/technical responsibilities, and resulting end products.

Traditional life cycle methodology remains a popular systems development approach. It provides a framework in which the development process can be structured and managed. This methodology works best when requirements can be specified in detail before design and programming commence. It will continue to remain appropriate for large-scale operational applications where requirements are highly structured and easily defined and for complex technical systems.

Systems analysts and designers act as the architects of systems. They work closely with users to ensure that systems fulfill user requirements and can be easily controlled by users.

Ideally, about one-quarter of a project's resources should be devoted to the definition and systems study stages. Usually much less is spent here. Last-minute programming corrections and long-term maintenance consume more resources than is desirable. Better design options and techniques are required. These are discussed in the next chapter.

Key Words

Systems development life cycle	Technological push
Project definition	Strategic pull
Data processing steering committee	Systems study

Systems analysis
Feasibility
Requirements determination
Data analysis
Object system analysis
Decision analysis
Cost/benefit analysis
Programming
Conceptual design
Physical design
Installation
Testing

Unit testing
Systems testing
Acceptance testing
Test plan
Conversion
Parallel strategy
Direct cutover
Pilot study
Phased approach
Postimplementation audit
Maintenance

Review Questions

1. What is a sociotechnical system? Why are information systems considered sociotechnical systems?
2. What are the four organizational areas of responsibility for systems analysts and designers?
3. List the three sources of ideas for new systems.
4. Name the major organizational groups involved in building information systems. What is the role of each?
5. Name the groups responsible for the management of systems development. What are the responsibilities of each?
6. What is the traditional systems life cycle? Name the various stages in the life cycle and the activities that occur in each stage.
7. What is the difference between systems analysis and systems design?
8. What is feasibility? Name and describe each of the three major areas of feasibility for information systems.
9. What are information requirements? Why have they proved so difficult to determine correctly?
10. Name and describe four requirements determination techniques.
11. What is the difference between conceptual design of an information system and physical design?
12. What are the basic components of information system design?
13. What is detail design? What aspects of design does it encompass?
14. What is the difference between information system design and programming?
15. Why is the testing stage of systems development so important? Name and describe the three stages of testing for an information system.
16. What is conversion? Why is it important to have a detailed conversion plan?
17. What is the postimplementation audit?
18. Why has maintenance proved to be such a problem in information systems?

Discussion Questions

1. It has been said that the design of an information system is an iterative process. Discuss.
2. It has been said that design cannot be directed by technical specialists alone. Discuss.
3. Information systems often have to be redesigned after testing. Discuss.
4. Evaluate the strengths and weaknesses of the four main strategies for information systems conversion. Which conversion strategy would you use for the following?
   - A transaction tracking system for the purchase and sale of stocks on the New York Stock Exchange
   - A process control system at a chemical plant
   - A monthly batch system to record student attendance at a 2000-student high school
   - A corporate accounting system that will tie together local general ledger systems from 10 operating units
5. The history of many systems development projects has shown that it is extremely difficult to estimate the total cost of a proposed information system. Discuss.
6. Discuss the roles of users and information processing specialists in the following systems development activities:
   - Study of existing systems
   - Requirements determination
   - Assessment of feasibility
   - Design
   - Testing
   - Conversion
   - Postimplementation audit

Tools for Helping Users, Analysts, and Programmers to Understand Each Other

A systems development methodology is a set of procedures used to develop a project. A methodology helps to answer the question "What should we do and in what order?". Methodologies are created and sold by software and accounting firms to other organizations, who buy them in the hope of building higher-quality systems at a lower cost. Methodologies also help in auditing development projects by keeping track of project milestones and costs.

A difficult problem in system development projects is often a lack of understanding and communication between users, analysts, and programmers. Lack of agreement on simple things like what to call a file, what to call a data element, and how to draw or sketch out systems can produce major errors in analysis and design. Historically, systems analysts evaluated applications and turned over their findings to programmers, who then wrote the code. Often this set off a cycle of reviews, corrections, rewriting, and respecification of the system. Users, in desperation, would often say, "Give us what you have now."

In medium-sized to large projects, thousands of documents are generated, ranging from sketches of subsystems to data definitions to program documentation. Just keeping track of these documents and making sure that everyone has the needed materials can be a nightmare. Lack of automated tools is a major source of failure in systems projects.

Only about 10% of MIS shops have done anything to reduce the confusion. By using an agreed-on systems methodology, however, a great deal of time can be saved.

A major originator of systems methodology tools is Milton Bryce, president of M. Bryce and Associates. This company has introduced three tools: structured systems analysis, chronological decompositions, and layered documentation.

A systems methodology is simply an administrative framework like Bryce's 5-stage systems life cycle (feasibility, general design, detailed design, programming, and implementation) plus some obvious techniques.

At the heart of Bryce's method (the software is called Pride) is the information resource manager (IRM). In addition to being a data dictionary of all data elements in a system and a listing of where they appear in programs and other documents of the project, the IRM tracks files, records, programs, jobs, and manual procedures.

More recent additions to the systems developer tool kit are products that not only implement a methodology (such as the systems life cycle) but also include an integrated graphics tool to draw system documents. One such tool is Nastec Corporation's DesignAid. DesignAid operates on an expanded PC and is easy enough for users and professional designers to share. Project documents can be shared if the PCs are connected to a local area network or to a mainframe. DesignAid uses a data dictionary to keep track of data definitions. If data elements are used inappropriately in the system diagrams, the data dictionary automatically informs the user.

Adapted from "Putting the Horse Before the Cart," Infosystems, September 1986.

Case Study Questions

1. Why should an organization invest in a design methodology? List some of the benefits.
2. What might be some of the pitfalls of a design methodology?
3. Who should participate in methodology selection? What criteria should be used?

Bond Portfolio Management System

System Design Exercise

Background

The Golden State Casualty Insurance Company is considering placing certain portfolio management operations on the computer. Golden State currently manages a bond portfolio in excess of $1 billion. This portfolio consists of more than 3000 separate bond issues. For tax reasons, a large number of these are tax-exempt municipal bonds. All other issues are corporate bonds.

Golden State has just signed an agreement to manage the bond portfolio of another insurance company, Lone Star Casualty Insurance, a company in which Golden holds a minority interest. Lone Star currently has a bond portfolio whose par value is in excess of $400 million, with more than 1000 separate issues.

A plan adopted at the recent board meeting of Golden State is to spin off the investment operations of Golden State to a separate corporation, Bond Investment Advisors (BIA). This corporation would be completely owned by Golden State, and its principal responsibility would be to manage bond portfolios. Initially, BIA's clients would be Golden State and Lone Star. If BIA proves successful in its operation, it will expand this service to other organizations.

Economic Justification

You are a principal in a well-known consulting firm and have just examined the records of Golden State. In your letter to the president of Golden State, you note that a staff of 3 full-time accountants and 20 clerks is required to maintain the bond accounting records. Furthermore, and much more seriously, the vice president of finance of Golden State, who will be the new president of BIA, is currently devoting more than two-thirds of his time to clerical and record-keeping activities. His three accountants are also devoting equivalent efforts to essentially clerical tasks.

As a result of your management review, you have been asked by Golden State to design an overall bond accounting and portfolio management system for BIA.

Objectives and Goals of the System

The principal goals of the system are to produce the following:

1. Monthly and annual accounting reports. One set of reports should show, by type of bond (municipal or corporate), the par value, market value, book value, cost, purchase date, coupon rate, and maturity dates of the bonds owned as of a certain date. The other set of reports should show the purchase, sale, interest received, and amortization of bonds during the specified accounting period.
2. Portfolio management reports that give information beyond the accounting reports. This includes changes in market values, ratings, after-tax yields to maturity, and sensitivity of market value to interest rates. A list of bonds maturing in the next month is also required for the next month.

On your first visit with the client, you obtained a copy of the current bond card used by the Accounting Department. Some of the items on the card are described in Exhibit 1.

You are to design a computerized system to produce appropriate accounting and portfolio management reports. Elements that you should consider in the design are:

- A system to maintain and produce on a regular basis both the accounting and portfolio reports.
- Conversion procedures to convert from a manual system to a computer-oriented system.

A systems design report should contain, at a minimum, details on the following:

1. Management summary
    1.1 Benefits
    1.2 Implementation schedule
2. Overall systems flow
3. Forms/screen design
4. Report specification
5. File design
6. Conversion procedure

Problems in the world of business usually are not precisely defined. This exercise is deliberately vague. If you need to make assumptions in order to complete this assignment, state what those assumptions are and why you believe they are justified.

Specifically, you should be concerned with the number of transactions, the use of reports, on-line or batch system, type of computer, and so on.

In designing the system, you should assume the following:

- All bonds pay interest semiannually. Interest is due January 1 and July 1.
- No bonds are in default.
- Bonds are amortized on a straight-line basis.
- For this problem, accrued interest and commissions may be disregarded.
- The settlement date and purchase date are the same day.
- Given White's rating for bonds and the maturity and coupon rate, a computer program has been developed that calculates the market yield to maturity.
- The calendar year consists of 360 days per year, with 12 months of 30 days each.

Exhibit 1
Bond Card

Bond #1234
Date purchased: 01/01/70
Description: Minneapolis Water Works
Cost: 900,000.00
Par: 1,000,000.00
Coupon: 6%
Yield to Maturity: To be calculated
Maturity date: 01/01/90

Book	Value	Interest	Received
01/01/70	900,000	7/2/71	30,000
01/01/71	905,000	1/1/72	30,000
01/01/72	910,000	7/5/72	30,000
01/01/73	915,000	1/3/73	30,000
01/01/74	920,000	7/4/73	30,000
01/01/75	925,000	1/2/74	30,000
01/01/76	930,000	7/3/74	30,000
01/01/77	940,000	1/4/75	30,000
01/01/78	945,000	7/6/75	30,000
01/01/79	950,000	1/3/76	30,000
01/01/80	955,000	7/1/76	30,000
		1/5/77	30,000
		7/3/77	30,000
		1/3/78	30,000
		7/6/78	30,000
		1/3/79	30,000
		7/2/79	30,000
		1/4/80	30,000

References

Ahituv, Niv, and Neunann, Seev. "A Flexible Approach to Information System Development," *MIS Quarterly* (June 1984).

Alberts, David S. "The Economics of Software Quality Assurance." Washington, D.C.: *National Computer Conference, 1976 Annual Proceedings*.

Blauner, R. *Alienation and Freedom: The Factory Worker and His Industry.* Chicago: University of Chicago Press, 1964.

Bostrom, R.P., and Heinen, J.S. "MIS Problems and Failures: A Socio-Technical Perspective; Part I: The Causes," *MIS Quarterly*, Vol. 1 (September, 1977), pp. 17–32; "Part II: The Application of Socio-Technical Theory," *MIS Quarterly*, Vol. 1 (December 1977), pp. 11–28.

Brooks, Frederick P. "The Mythical Man Month," *Datamation* (December 1974).

Davis, Gordon B. "Determining Management Information Needs: A Comparison of Methods," *MIS Quarterly*, Vol. 1 (June 1977), pp. 55-67.

Davis, Gordon B. "Information Analysis for Information System Development," in *Systems Analysis and Design: A Foundation for the 1980's*, ed. W.W. Cotterman, J.D. Cougar, N.L. Enger, and F. Harold. New York: Wiley, 1981.

Davis, Gordon B. "Strategies for Information Requirements Determination," *IBM Systems Journal*, Vol. 1 (1982), pp. 4–30.

Emery, James C. "Cost/Benefit Analysis of Information Systems." Chicago: *Society for Management Information Systems Workshop Report No. 1*, 1971.

Franz, Charles, and Robey, Daniel. "An Investigation of User-Led System Design: Rational and Political Perspectives," *Communications of the ACM*, Vol. 27 (December 1984).

Ginzberg, Michael J. "The Impact of Organizational Characteristics on MIS Design and Implementation." Working Paper CRIS 10, GBA 80-110. New York University Center for Research on Information Systems, Computer Applications and Information Systems Area, 1980.

Gould, John D., and Lewis, Clayton. "Designing for Usability: Key Principles and What Designers Think," *Communications of the ACM*, Vol. 28 (March 1985).

Grudnitski, Gary. "Eliciting Decision Makers' Information Requirements," *Journal of Management Information Systems* (Summer 1984).

King, William R. "Alternative Designs in Information System Development," *MIS Quarterly* (December 1982).

Kosynski, Benn R. "Advances in Information System Design," *Journal of Management Information Systems*, Vol. 1 (Winter 1984–1985).

Lientz, Bennett P., and Swanson, E. Burton. *Software Maintenance Management.* Reading, Mass.: Addison-Wesley, 1980.

Lucas, Henry C., Jr. *Toward Creative Systems Design*. New York: Columbia University Press, 1974.

Nolan, Richard L. *Managing the Data Resource Function*. St. Paul, Minn.: West Publishing, 1974.

Parker, M.M. "Enterprise Information Analysis: Cost-Benefit Analysis and the Data-Managed System," *IBM Systems Journal*, Vol. 21 (1982), pp. 108–123.

Rockart, John F. "Chief Executives Define Their Own Data Needs," *Harvard Business Review*, Vol. 57 (March–April 1979).

Vitalari, Nicholas P. "Knowledge as a Basis for Expertise in Systems Analysis: Empirical Study." *MIS Quarterly* (September 1985).

Weinberg, Gerald M. *The Psychology of Computer Programming*. New York: Van Nostrand Reinhold Company, 1972.

Zmud, Robert W. "Design Alternatives for Organizing Information Systems Activities," *MIS Quarterly* (June 1984).

CHAPTER 13

Systems Analysis and Design: II

■ OUTLINE

The Carter Automotive Company of St. Louis is one of the country's largest automotive parts manufacturers, a supplier of components for cooling, fuel, and electrical systems. When Ron Perez joined Carter's data processing operation a few years ago, there was a tremendous backlog of requests for applications development stored in two huge looseleaf file folders. No one had even estimated how many years of work were represented by these outstanding requests for service.

The existing systems were out of date, some running partially on punched cards, and the staff had little experience with large system development.

When a request came in for an integrated order entry system to incorporate billing, inventory control, and systems analysis, Perez felt that some way had to be found to leverage the limited staff and hardware resources. He considered buying an off-the-shelf package (which would have to be customized for the firm and maintained) or purchasing of a fourth-generation language (which would permit much faster development of many systems, not just the current order entry system). Carter decided to purchase the fourth-generation language Gener/OL from Pansophic Systems, Inc.

Perez reported that "Gener/OL has permitted us to program five times faster than before. We can develop systems in weeks instead of months and years." Programmers learned the new language in a few days.

An unanticipated benefit of this fourth-generation language was its ability to involve users more closely in the analysis and design of systems. Analysts, after interviewing users, develop initial screen designs and then invite the users to comment at the terminal. The systems that are developed this way are much more reflective of users' real needs.

Adapted from "Language Tool Drives Auto Parts Maker's Progress," *Computerworld*, September 16, 1985.

The Carter Automotive story dramatizes both the pressures on data processing staffs to develop better systems more quickly and the new opportunities for developing systems in different ways. This chapter is concerned with alternative development strategies and techniques for developing information requirements.

In this chapter the student will learn:
- The strengths and weakness of systems life cycle methods.
- The risks and uncertainties of system development.
- Major alternatives to the systems life cycle.
- Alternative information requirements analysis techniques.
- How tools can improve analysis and design.

13.1 Introduction

Traditional life cycle methodology remains a dominant systems development approach. It will continue to remain appropriate for large TPS and MIS systems where requirements are highly structured and well defined (Ahituv and Neunann, 1984). It will also remain appropriate for highly complex technical systems such as satellite image processing, air traffic control, space launches, and refinery operations. In these kinds of applications, there is a need for complete, formal requirements analysis, predefined specifications, and tight controls.

However, the systems development life cycle methodology has several limitations:

- *The conventional development cycle is very costly.* A tremendous amount of time must be spent gathering information, preparing systems analysis documents, and writing specifications.
- *The time needed to develop a system through the life cycle is often lengthy and prolonged.* It may take years before a system is finally installed. If development time is prolonged, requirements may have changed before the system is operational. The system that took so many years and dollars to construct may be obsolete while it is still on the drawing board (Brooks, 1974).
- *Life cycle methodology is relatively inflexible.* It is possible to revise requirements as new needs arise, but the process is very expensive. The life cycle approach does allow for some iteration to ensure that requirements can be met. Whenever requirements are incorrect or deficient, the sequence of life cycle activities can be repeated. A project can go back to the requirements determination stage to obtain correct specifications. The sequence of life cycle activities can be repeated as often as necessary until requirements have been correctly finalized. Some writers have called for a more dynamic systems life cycle approach (Snyder and Cox, 1985). However, the addition of any iteration to the life cycle process dramatically raises development costs and delays completion time.
- *Life cycle methodology discourages change.* Because of the time and cost of repeating the sequence of activities, the methodology freezes specifications early in the development process. Users are asked to sign off on written specifications documents. Once user approval is secured, the specifications are frozen. Often users approve specifications documents without fully comprehending their contents. Only during programming and testing is it discovered that the specifications are incomplete or not what the users had in mind. It has traditionally been difficult for users to visualize a final system from specification documents. They typically are not sure of exactly what they want until they see or use it. Proper specifications cannot always be captured the first time around, early in the life cycle when they are easy to change.
- *Life cycle methodology is ill suited to decision-oriented applications.* The decision-making environment is relatively unstructured and fluid. Requirements constantly change or have no grounding in well-defined models or procedures. Often it may not be possible for

decision makers to specify their information needs in advance. They may have to experiment with concrete systems to clarify the kinds of decisions they wish to make. This high level of uncertainty calls for an iterative approach to requirements specification that cannot be easily accommodated by the life cycle approach.

In many respects, the strengths of the systems development life cycle—formal stages, planned end products, rigorously defined requirements and specifications—are also its principal weakness. There are many situations where these virtues are vices.

Major Risks and Uncertainties of Systems Development

Every project carries with it certain risks and uncertainties. *Risks* are negative outcomes that have a known or estimated probability of occurence based on experience or some theory. *Uncertainties* are negative outcomes that have unknown probabilities because of lack of experience or lack of theory (Alter and Ginzberg, 1978).

Risks and uncertainties can be handled in various ways. Risks are known and calculable negative outcomes, and these can be leveraged or ensured against in a number of ways. For instance, they can be balanced in a portfolio (McFarlan, 1981). Development costs are more of a risk than an uncertainty, and a number of management actions can be taken to ensure that these costs are kept within bounds; the same is true of development time. Additional staff can be hired, packages can be used to help in certain areas, and parts of a project can be cut off or developed later if the costs and delivery dates are exceeding the schedule.

An uncertainty is more difficult to manage. For instance, understanding user requirements is a major uncertainty; no one can attach

TABLE 13.1
Major Risks and Uncertainties of System Development

Development costs

Development time

Understanding user requirements

Long-term maintenance

Implementation

Establishing system benefits

Impact on the organization

Skills of personnel

Technology

a probability to a project team's failure to understand user requirements. However, uncertainties can studied and, hopefully, reduced over time by careful methods.

Table 13.1 lists the major risks and uncertainties associated with information system development. Based on our experience in the field, we have ranked these risks in order, with the most important and common ones first.

Cost Overruns Plague Project

In 1978 California's Department of Motor Vehicles (DMV) initiated a 5 year project to automate the registration of licensing of 17 million drivers and collect $2 billion in DMV-related fees each year. In 1986 the project was 3 years behind schedule and up to $58 million over budget.

The project was divided into four phases. Phase I involved installing distributed minicomputers to 157 field offices in a distributed network from 1979 to 1984. This phase was about a year behind schedule. Phase II involved linking the field offices to state central computers, installing terminals for field office clerks to work with, and redesigning work in the field office. This is where the real trouble started.

Delays in obtaining telecommunications lines delayed the project for 6 months. Without equipment, the DMV trained employees before the technology was installed. Most had to be retrained when the equipment arrived. Project managers thought that with the new equipment employees could do several tasks at once, completing typical transactions in 5 minutes. This was not true. Workers had to be retrained in aspects of office work where they had no experience. Then DMV management complicated matters by laying off keypunch operators in anticipation of productivity savings from the new system. These productivity gains did not occur, and temporary keypunch clerks had to be hired at a cost of $5 million.

Phase III of the project has been delayed from 1984 to 1987. As one manager noted, "We made a decision that it's not wise to do too many things at once. We've lowered our expectation levels on the learning curve, and our planning parameters are better."

Adapted from "Cost Overruns Plague California DMV Automation Project," *Computerworld*, January 20, 1986.

At the top of the list are development costs and time. In our experience, large systems development projects are often 30% over budget and require 50% more time than the early estimates developed in the project plan of a traditional systems life cycle. Unfortunately, large-scale projects have developed a reputation for being *much more costly, and much later, than expected.*

The preceding example describes a cost overrun in a large public sector system. While systems in the private sector tend to be much smaller, the costs overruns are nevertheless substantial and common.

A second major problem in system development has been the difficulty in understanding user requirements. Data processing professionals often have a poor understanding of what users truly desire. Often the result is systems that are underutilized or simply fail. (These are described in Chapter 19.)

As experience with large systems grows, it is also becoming apparent that long-term maintenance costs are far higher than was originally anticipated. To make matters worse, cost estimates developed in cost/benefit studies of systems rarely include maintenance costs, and when they do, they are woefully underestimated, as indicated by the following recent survey.

Why are maintenance costs so high? A changing environment is clearly one major reason. The firm may experience large internal changes in structure and leadership, or change may come from the environment. These organizational changes affect information requirements.

But an equally common cause of long-term maintenance problems is faulty systems analysis and design, especially information

Maintenance Problem Escalating

A survey of 37 Fortune 500 companies by the Quality Assurance Institute found that on average 51% of data processing budgets went for maintenance of old programs. Nearly 80% of the companies said that they had major systems maintained by specific individuals because no one else understood the program logic. Less than 15% of the respondents used a formal method for determining when programs should be rewritten, and only 16% of respondents said that they required older systems to conform to current programming standards.

Adapted from "Survey Finds Maintenance Problem Still Escalating," *Computerworld*, January 27, 1986.

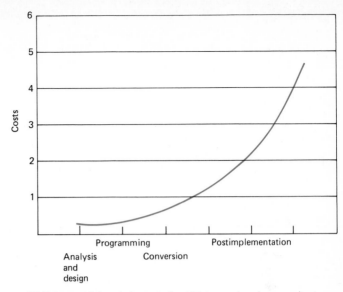

(A) Estimates of the relative cost of repairing errors based on consultant reports and the popular trade literature

FIGURE 13.1
The cost of errors over the life cycle. The most common, most severe, and most expensive system errors develop in the early design stages. They involve faulty requirements analysis. Errors in program logic or syntax are much less common, less severe, and less costly to repair than design errors. (Adapted from Alberts, 1976.)

Error Type	% of Total Errors	Relative Severity	% of Total Cost of Errors
Design	66%	2.5	83+%
Logic	17%	1.0	8+%
Syntax	17%	1.0	8+%

(B) Origin, frequency, and severity of errors in large national defense and space programs

requirements analysis. Some studies of large TPS systems by TRW, Inc., have found that a majority of system errors—64%—result from early analysis errors (Mazzucchelli, 1985). Figure 13.1 illustrates the cost of correcting errors. Part (A) is based on the experience of consultants such as ourselves and others reported in the literature. Part (B) shows the results of a quality assurance study of large national defense software projects.

If errors are detected early, the cost to the development effort is small. But if they are not discovered until after programming, testing, or installation has been completed, the costs can soar astronomically. A minor logic error, for example, that could take 1 hour to correct during the analysis and design stage would take 10, 40, and 90 times as long to correct during coding, conversion, and operation, respectively.

TABLE 13.2
The Maintenance Problem

Annual personnel hours	
Maintain and enhance current systems	48.0%
Develop new systems	46.1%
Other	5.9%
20% of the survey allocated 85% of its efforts to maintenance and enhancements	
Frequency of activity	
Errors—emergency	17.4%
Change—data, inputs, files, hardware	18.2%
Improve—user enhancements, efficiency, documentation, etc.	60.3%
Other	4.1%

Source: Adapted from Bennett P. Lientz and E. Burton Swanson, *Software Maintenance Management.* Reading, Mass.: Addison-Wesley, 1980 and L. H. Putnam and A. Fitzsimmons, "Estimating Software Costs," *Datamation* (Sept. 1979, Oct. 1979 and November 1979.)

Table 13.2 indicates the size of the maintenance problem. In one-fifth of data processing shops, 85% of personnel hours are allocated to maintenance, leaving little time for new systems development. In most shops, nearly one-half of professional personnel time is spent in the maintenance of existing systems.

A number of other problems listed in Table 13.1 are also important in large-scale projects. It is often difficult to establish the precise benefits of the system to the organization, and this problem becomes more difficult as the nature of systems changes from clerical and paper processing systems, where benefits are easy to measure, to decision support systems, where benefits are less easy to quantify. Other problems, such as the skills of the data processing staff, the nature of the technology, and the size of the system, which can overwhelm inexperienced data processing staffs, are also important.

Some Solutions

There are three solutions to the risks and uncertainties previously described. First, we can create new strategies, other than the systems development life cycle, for the development of systems that solve some of the these problems. These strategies will be described in section 13.2.

Second, we can look for better techniques to establish information requirements of end users. These are described in section 13.3.

A last area to consider is the use of automated tools to speed up and make more precise the analysis and design process. These topics are explored briefly here and discussed in greater detail in the following chapter.

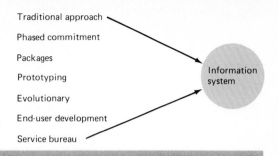

FIGURE 13.2
Alternative strategies for developing systems. There are seven alternative strategies for building information systems. Choosing an appropriate strategy depends on a project's risk and uncertainty for a particular organization.

13.2 Alternative Strategies for Developing Systems

Figure 13.2 shows seven alternative strategies for developing sytems. Each of these strategies has specific strengths and weaknesses, and must be selected carefully in accordance with the risks and uncertainties of the specific project.

Phased Commitment

We have already described the traditional systems development life cycle. One major alternative is *phased commitment*, a strategy in which projects are developed using a traditional life cycle approach but the project itself is broken down into several phases. This is especially useful when the technology is uncertain or when the ultimate configuration of the system will be decided later. In some instances, systems require either a new technology or a new set of organizational arrangements, which themselves will require 4 to 5 years to develop. In this situation, a large project can be broken down into phases, with the easy tasks accomplished first and the more difficult ones put off until later.

For instance, the Social Security Administration is developing its Systems Modernization Plan over a 10-year period, with the early phases focusing on hardware acquisition and telecommunications networks. Later phases will focus more on difficult software and database design issues.

Packages

A second alternative strategy is to *buy a package*, as opposed to developing a system in house. Even when packages are purchased, however, the organization must do a thorough analysis of its needs, define the project, and go through a series of stages similar to those of a systems development life cycle. Nevertheless, packages are appropriate where the information requirements of the organization are well known, where the system is large and would be difficult to develop internally, where the technology is certain, and where the underlying system is complex (such as a payroll system). Packages are described in greater detail in Chapter 14.

Prototyping

Prototyping is another alternative technique for developing a system. Generally, it is useful in situations where the system and the number of users are relatively small. In this instance, prototypes—literally, simulations or mockups of systems—can be developed on a desktop computer for a user; in this way, the user's requirements can be quickly determined. The prototype that is agreed upon with the user can then be used as a template to create the actual system. This alternative is also described in detail in Chapter 14.

Evolutionary Strategy

An *evolutionary* strategy is appropriate in a situation that is not envisioned at all in a systems development life cycle. In some instances, users do not know what they want; their needs become apparent to them only when a general capability is delivered and they find out how the system may be used. This is typically the case, for instance, with microcomputers. Few people know in advance precisely how they will use it until it is installed on their desk with a generalized set of computing, communications, and data storage capabilities. Then specific needs can be explored.

Evolutionary design usually begins with a broad discussion of user information needs (rather than a project plan). One or two specific target capabilities are selected, and a system that can accomplish these tasks is delivered. This initial system is designed to have adequate expansion capability so that additional applications can be developed. As users become accustomed to the system, they develop new applications and needs. Hopefully, the early applications are compatible with these new needs and applications. In the end, evolutionary designs lead to a series of related applications that could not have been envisioned when the project started. The emphasis in this alternative is on close interaction between users and the development staff. This technique is especially valuable for DSS systems, described in detail in Chapter 16.

End-User Development

A further alternative to consider is *end-user development*. We devote Chapter 15 to this subject because it is an exciting new form of systems development. End-user development is useful when users know what their needs are and the system is not particularly large, sophisticated, or complex. For instance, desktop database, DSS, and ESS, can all be partly designed by end users. Because the end user totally controls the design effort, there is little need to go through a traditional systems design life cycle. Moreover, today, end users are much more sophisticated about information systems than they were in the 1960s. Therefore, they can play a larger role in systems design.

End-user development does not necessarily mean total end-user control of projects. There are many ways in which end-user development can be assisted by professional systems personnel, such as when prototyping tools are appropriate or access to specialized telecommunications and database facilities is required (Kraushaar and Shirland, 1985).

Service Bureau

A last alternative for developing systems is to have a *service bureau* do the required information processing or design a system for the organization (so-called turnkey systems). This approach is useful when the organization has a clear knowledge of its needs, the system involved is quite large, the technology is certain, and the skills required to develop the system are beyond the grasp of the internal staff. Service bureaus develop packages as well as expertise in specific kinds of systems, (e.g., accounts receivable, payroll, personnel). They can either provide a customized turnkey system or design a system specifically for the organization. Service bureaus are often less expensive than internal development because of their expertise and experience with other organizations.

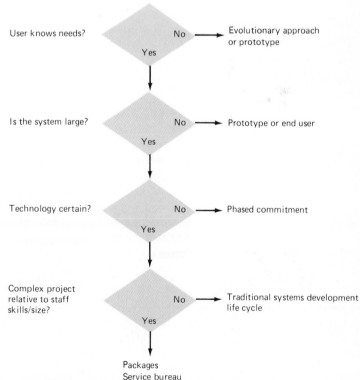

FIGURE 13.3

Fitting the technique to the system. The technique of system development should be chosen on the basis of the system being developed, its inherent and relative risks, the nature of the technology, and the extent of user understanding.

Figure 13.3 shows a decision tree for choosing the appropriate strategy for systems development. The factors to take into account are user needs, the size of the system, the certainty of the technology, and the complexity of the system relative to the organization's data processing skills and staff.

13.3 Alternative Requirements Analysis Techniques

One of the major causes of information systems failure, aside from poor project management and the choice of wrong strategies, is the difficulty of understanding the information requirements of an organization. This is probably one of the more complex and least well examined aspects of building systems. For that reason, we will spend some time reviewing the variety of techniques for establishing information requirements and discussing the situations in which they are appropriate.

**Why Requirements
Analysis Is Difficult**

While it may seem easy to establish the information requirements for a system by simply asking, interviewing, or using some other data collection instrument, this task is far from simple (Munro and Davis, 1977; Davis, 1982).

The first problem is that the organizational environment may change between the time when the system is initially conceived and the time of its implementation several years later. Managers and personnel can change rapidly, so that the people for whom the system was originally designed are no longer making the actual decisions. The persons originally involved may have moved on, and the new incumbents may not even understand the need for the system.

A second class of problems involves the difference between *real organizational needs* and *management perceived needs.* Managers have their own agendas, as described in previous chapters, and they may believe that in order to achieve them, an information system is required. For instance, managers may desire a certain system because it will help them in other jobs or because it will give them experience in an area of the systems world that will enhance their career or mobility. However, these kinds of systems are not necessarily needed by the organization.

Another difficulty is the possibility that systems analysts may be talking to the wrong people when designing a system. For instance, a system to be used primarily by clerical workers should be constructed on the basis of extensive interviews and discussions with these workers. However, middle managers who manage clerical workers may have their own ideas about how the system should be developed. In this instance, a system may be developed that supports the manager's beliefs about how the work should be done rather than one that actually reflects the needs of the workers.

In the area of managerial support systems—reporting, DSS, and ESS—managers may not always know what they require. For instance, if you ask managers what information they require in the area of product quality, they may not know precisely how they use information or where it comes from; in some cases, the information may change from product to product. Therefore, it is not always easy for managers to state explicitly how they use information and what information is required (Grudnitski, 1984).

An even more common difficulty with requirements analysis is that the systems analyst may not understand what the managers are saying. Analysts frequently come from a programming or other technical background and are themselves not the best communicators. They may have their own notions of what an information system should do, and they may bias the information system toward their own conceptions as opposed to those of management (Vitalari, 1985).

The last difficulty involves the fact that many business functions are not easily defined, are complex, or are poorly documented. This is especially true of totally new systems. Some information systems are relatively easy to build because they are based upon existing manual systems. Long before computers came along, there were payroll, accounts receivable, accounts payable, and many other manual transaction processing systems.

When a manual system already exists, the development of a computerized system is made easier by prior organizational decisions about where information is created, who uses it, and the basic information requirements of the system. But with an entirely new system, this is not true. Here one must develop new creators of information and users, new kinds of decisions have to be envisioned, and the process is much more creative but nevertheless much more likely to produce systems that are not really used.

For all of these reasons, it is not uncommon for systems to be developed that do not fully meet the information requirements of management or the organization. However, there are a number of approaches that can be used to ensure that, as far as possible, the systems meet existing information requirements and that systems that anticipate future requirements can be built. We will discuss these alternative techniques.

Major Approaches to Defining Information Requirements

There are six major approaches to defining information requirements (see Table 13.3). We will now describe the premise, the methods, and the strengths and weaknesses of each of them.

TABLE 13.3
Requirements Analysis Techniques

Null approach

By-product approach

Key indicator approach

Bottom-up project approach

Enterprise analysis

Critical success factors

Null Approach

The premise of the null approach is that the higher you go in an organization, the more difficult it is to specify information requirements systematically. In this view, MIS reports to managers are simply not used and are irrelevant. Managers rely on informal, oral, subjective communications. Moreover, the business environment changes so rapidly that any formal statement, any effort to freeze information requirements, is fruitless (Rockart, 1979). What is needed, in this view, is ad hoc, situational data suitable for specific, ever-changing problems—in particular, a generalized computing-telecommunications capacity that can provide a wide variety of specific information and information sources, rather than highly defined, "canned" reports.

The methods used in the null approach are case studies and close observation of executives to discover real information needs. In general, analysts following this approach seek to supply executives with desktop computing and telecommunications capabilities.

The strength of the null approach is that it has a strong behavioral foundation (see Chapters 4 and 5). Much of what executives actually do cannot be expressed in formal information systems. This approach also has the advantage of not imposing a rational or normative model of decision making on managers. It is a highly flexible approach to the information requirements of senior managers (Rockart and Treacy, 1982).

The principal weakness of this method is that it fails to account for the use of systematic information at middle and lower levels in the organization. Much of the information that managers do look at is systematic and can be specified in advance. This method fails to account for the fact that senior management often is *required* to look at certain systematic data (e.g., financial, employment, production data).

Overall, the null approach appears to be most fruitful at the senior executive level, where information requirements are always changing and largely situational.

By-Product Approach

The premise of the by-product approach is that the most important contribution of information systems to the organization is the automation of basic clerical and transaction processing activities such as payroll, accounts receivable, accounts payable, billing, inventory, and the like. Summary and exception information *by-products* from these operational systems will tell managers what they need to know about how the firm is operating on a regular and routine basis.

Rather than developing extensive MIS or ESS, the by-product approach encourages the mining of existing information captured by the firm's transaction systems.

The principal method for the by-product approach is first to establish what information is available in existing operational systems. Then an effort is made to match these data to management requests for information. One result is that data processing ends up "selling" to management, much as the librarian informs potential clients of new book acquisitions.

The strength of the by-product approach is that it focuses on the automation of operational systems, providing a strong foundation for information processing. It is based on well-defined, elementary measures of firm performance that are required for planning daily operations. Moreover, because it forces daily processing to "sell its wares" to user groups, it educates users about the available information and maximizes the use of an available resource (information). It is also a low-cost approach that does not require the development of major new management systems.

Last and perhaps most important, the by-product approach is a common MIS approach. Indeed, historically, MIS often result from the efforts of the data processing group to make its information more available to management.

One weakness of the by-product approach is that it implies the paper processing tail wagging the information dog. That is, the information delivered to management is almost totally dependent on what data are available in existing transaction systems. This would seem to put the cart before the horse. Second, this method results in the useless reports and information that clog the information channels of many organizations. The poor reputation of the data processing division is based largely on the fact that so many useless reports are generated. These result largely from a by-product approach to the information function.

A key weakness of the by-product (and other approaches to be discussed) is that it does not have an organizational or environmental orientation. It does not ask managers to look at the environment and to shape their information requests in terms of what is happening outside or within the firm. This method does not call for any analysis of decision making to determine if the right information is being used to make critical decisions.

Key Indicator Approach

The premise of the key indicator approach is that most organizations operate in environments where the marks of success are well known. It is also assumed that the specific measures of firm performance that managers should pay attention to are well understood and agreed upon throughout the industry. These are called the *key indicators*, and it is argued that they can easily be provided by systems. Key indicators include market share, unit cost, return on investment, stock market price, and labor unit costs.

The principal method of the key indicator approach is to identify (1) appropriate industry indicators and (2) key management indicators of successful organizational performance. Information on these key indicators is then gathered, and simple exception reports are developed to report when the organization departs from expectations. Graphic displays are frequently used to focus on the key indicators. End users typically call up information in the form of prespecified graphics or tables.

The strength of this method is that it has a broader vision of the environment and the firm than any of the methods previously discussed. It identifies factors that management should observe, and it focuses attention on demonstrably proven indicators.

The weaknesses of this method are also obvious. It can be biased toward quantifiable and financial data. Moreover, it assumes that the key indicators are already well established, whereas in many industries or organizations this may not be the case. In a mature industry, the key indicators are well understood. In younger industries, this is less true.

Moreover, information requirements may change faster than the key indicators. There can be structural changes in the industry or tactical decisions that the firm itself must make in order to preserve its situation within the industry. Systems based upon key indicators cannot focus rapidly on new key indicators.

Last, the key indicator approach imposes a closed normative model of what managers should consider. This may bias performance toward short-term goals and toward what was important in the past. A key indicator of success in World War II, for instance, may be a poor indicator of success in subsequent wars. In other words, what is known to have been a key indicator of success in the past may not be so in the future.

Bottom-Up Project Approach

The premise of the bottom-up approach to systems is that data processing should respond to problems perceived by current managers. That is, it should analyze existing decision and data needs as they are perceived by specific subunits of the organization. Normative models of what management should be looking at, grand visions of data processing in the firm, as well as key indicators imposed from outside, are not particularly useful. In the bottom-up approach, the role of data processing is simply to respond to users' requests on a project-by-project basis.

The principal method in this approach is to interview users and try to identify their information requirements. Wherever possible, existing systems are used. There are no grand redesigns of systems in this view. Responsiveness to user requests is a key measure of the success of the data processing division.

The project model and the by-product method are two of the main modes of system development in both the public and private sectors. Responding to user requests is a very safe position; few, if any, organizational changes or challenges are anticipated. This approach is highly responsive to managers and divisions that control central budgeting and are politically influential. The bottom-up approach is a politically wise strategy that results in custom-fit applications for each division and each major user group.

The weaknesses of this approach should also be clear. There is no organizationwide perspective. Managers and environments change, but there is no provision for ending applications. This method tends to overwhelm the data processing capacity because data processing resources are allocated wherever users want them. This method often results in many large-scale system projects an organization with little or no coordination between them.

Enterprise Analysis (Business Systems Planning)

Enterprise analysis argues that the information requirements of a firm can only be understood by looking at the entire organization in terms of *organizational units, functions, processes,* and *data elements.* This method starts with the notion that the information requirements of a firm or a division can be specified only with a thorough understanding of the entire organization. This method was developed by IBM in the 1960s explicitly for establishing the relationship among large system development projects (Zachman, 1982).

The central method used in the enterprise analysis approach is to take a large sample of managers and ask them how they use information, where they get the information, what their environment is like, what their objectives are, how they make decisions, and what their data needs are.

The results of this large survey of managers are aggregated into subunits, functions, processes, and data matrices (see Figure 13.4). Figure 13.4 shows parts of two matrices developed at the Social Security Administration as part of a very-large-scale systems redevelopment effort called the *Systems Modernization Plan,* which began in 1982 and will run through 1992.

PROCESS/ORGANIZATION MATRIX

ORGANIZATIONS (columns):

1. Commissioner
2. DC programs and policy
3. AC disability insurance
4. AC retirement and survivors ins.
5. AC supp. security income
6. AC government affairs
7. O policy
8. O actuary
9. O hearings and appeals
10. DC management and assessment
11. AC assessment
12. O field assessment
13. O human resources
14. O material resources
15. O financial resources
16. O training
17. DC systems
18. AC system integration
19. AC system requirements
20. AC system operations
21. DC operations
22. AC field operations
23. Region
24. District/branch
25. Teleservice center
26. AC Central operations
27. O Program service center
28. Process center
29. Module
30. D International opers.
31. Module
32. O Disability opers.
33. Module
34. Central records
35. Module (cert. and coverage)
36. Data operations centers
37. Disability determination service

PROCESSES (rows):

PLANNING
- Develop agency plans
- Administer agency budget
- Formulate program policies
- Formulate admin. policies
- Design work processes

GENERAL MANAGEMENT
- Manage public affairs
- Manage intergovernmental affairs
- Exchange data
- Maintain administrative accounts
- Maintain programmatic accounts
- Conduct audits
- Establish organizations
- Manage human resources
- Provide security
- Manage equipment
- Manage facilities
- Manage supplies
- Manage data
- Manage workloads

PROGRAM ADMIN.
- Issue social security numbers
- Maintain earnings
- Collect claims information
- Determine eligibility/entitlement
- Compute payments
- Administer debt management
- Generate notices
- Respond to programmatic inquiries

SUPPORT
- Provide quality assessment

KEY

M = major involvement
S = some involvement

DC = deputy commissioner
AC = associate commissioner
O = office

FIGURE 13.4A

Process/organization matrix. This figure indicates who in the organization participates in specific processes and the nature of their involvement.

The matrix below reproduces Figure 13.4B. Rows are organizational **PROCESSES** (grouped into PLANNING, GENERAL MANAGEMENT, PROGRAM ADMIN., and SUPPORT); columns are **DATA CLASSES** (LOGICAL APPLICATION GROUPS). **C** designates creators of data; **U** designates users of data.

PROCESSES \ DATA CLASSES	Actuarial estimates	Agency plans	Budget	Program regs./policy	Admin. regs./policy	Labor agreements	Data standards	Procedures	Automated systems documentation	Educational media	Public agreements	Intergovernmental agreements	Grants	External	Exchange control	Administrative accounts	Program expenditures	Audit reports	Organization/position	Employee identification	Recruitment/placement	Complaints/grievances	Training resources	Security	Equipment utilization	Space utilization	Supplies utilization	Workload schedules	Work measurement	Enumeration I.D.	Enumeration control	Earnings	Employer I.D.	Earnings control	Claims characteristics	Claims control	Decisions	Payment	Collection/waiver	Notice	Inquiries control	Quality appraisal
PLANNING																																										
Develop agency plans	C	C	C	U	U			U			U	U	U	U	U	U	U		U	U				U	U	U	U		U	U	C			C		C			C		U	U
Administer agency budget	C	U	C	U	U			U			U	U				U	U	U				U			U	U	U		U		C						C				U	U
Formulate program policies	U	U	U	C	C			U				U	U	U								U					U		U		C			U		U						
Formulate admin. policies	U	U	U	U	C	C		U						U				U	U						U	U	U		U		C						U					U
Formulate data policies	U	U	U	U	U		C	U	U		U	U		U				U																								
Design work processes	U	U	U	U	U		U	U	U	C	U	U		U	U	U	U											U	U			U			U		U					U
GENERAL MANAGEMENT																																										
Manage public affairs				U	U			U	U	C	C	C	C	C																												
Manage intrgovt. affairs	U	U	U	U	U			U		C	C	C	C	U																												
Exchange data				U	U			U			U	U	U	U	U	U				U									U	U	U	U	U	U	U		U		U			
Maintain admin. accounts			U	U	U			U						U	C	C	U		C						C	C	U															
Maintain prog. accounts			U	U	U			U						U	U	C	C								C	U	U		C									U	U			
Conduct audits				U	U			U				U	U	U	U	U	U	C		U					C	U	C	U													U	
Establish organizations			U	U	U	U		U											C	C	C	C	C			U																U
Manage human resources			U	U	U	U		U											C	C	C	C	C	C																		
Provide security	U	U	U	U	U		U	U	U					U						U				C	C	C	C	C	U													U
Manage equipment	U	U	U	U	U		U	U	U					U										C	C	U	C	U	U													
Manage facilities	U	U	U	U	U		U	U	U					U										C	U	U	U	U														
Manage supplies	U	U	U	U	U		U	U	U															C	U	U	U															
Manage workloads	U	U	U	U	U		U	U	U						U										U	U	U	U	U	C	U			U	U	U					U	U
PROGRAM ADMIN.																																										
Issue social security numbers				U	U			U						U																C	C											
Maintain earnings				U	U			U						U																C	C	U	U	U								
Collect claims information				U	U			U																						C	C	U	C	U	C	C	U	U	U			
Determine elig/entlmt.			U	U	U			U																						C	U	U	C	U	U	C	U	C			U	
Compute payments		U	U	U	U			U		U				U																U	U	U	U	U	U	U	U	C	C		U	
Administer debt management				U	U			U						U			U	U												U	U	U	U	U	U	U	U	U	C	U	U	
SUPPORT																																										
Generate notices				U	U			U																						U	U	U		U	U	U	U	U	U	C		
Respond to prog. inquiries	U	U	U	U	U			U																						U	U	U		U	U	U	U	U	U	C	U	U
Provide quality assessment					U			U																						U	U	U		U	U	U	U	U	U	U	U	C

FIGURE 13.4B

Process/data class matrix. This figure depicts what data classes are required to support particular organizational processes and which processes are the creators and users of data. *C* designates creators of data; *U* designates users of data.

Figure 13.4(A) shows a process/organization matrix identifying those persons in the organization who participate in specific processes, such as planning. Figure 13.4(B) shows a process/data class matrix depicting what information is required to support a particular process, which process creates the data, and which uses it. (C in an intersection stands for "creators of data"; u stands for "users of data").

The dark crosshatching in Figure 13.4(B) indicates a *logical application group*—a group of data elements that support a related set of organizational processes. In this case, actuarial estimates, agency plans, and budget data are created in the planning process. The planning process, in turn, is performed by the Commissioner's office, along with Deputy Commissioners and Assistant Commissioners.

This suggests, then, that an *information system* focused on actuarial, agency plan, and budget *data elements* should be built for the *Commissioners* in order to support *planning*.

In this manner, the creators and users of data within an organization are identified. Together they form a *logical application group*—a unit in the organization where users, creators, and functions intersect. This information on data creators and users can be employed to identify where information systems should be improved or developed. Gaps are also identified and new systems are proposed where necessary.

One strength of enterprise analysis is that it gives a comprehensive view of the organization and of systems/data uses and gaps. It is an important antidote to excessive use of the by-product and bottom-up perspectives.

Enterprise analysis is especially suitable for start-up or massive change situations. For instance, it is one of the methods being used by the Social Security Administration to bring about a long-term strategic change in its information processing activities. This organization had never before performed a comprehensive analysis of its information requirements. Instead, it had relied on a bottom-up method of responding to whatever users requested, as well as on by-product approaches where most emphasis was placed on simply performing elementary transaction processing. Enterprise analysis is now used to develop a comprehensive view of how the Social Security Administration currently uses information.

Enterprise analysis has recently been semiautomated to speed up and make more accurate the requirements definition phase, as described in the following account.

Another strength of enterprise analysis is that it helps to produce an organizational consensus by involving a large number of managers and users of data. It helps the organization find out what it should be doing in terms of information processing simply by requiring many managers to think about information (Doll, 1985).

The weakness of enterprise analysis is that it produces an enormous amount of data that is expensive to collect and difficult to

Information Quality Analysis—
Automating Enterprise Analysis

In the past 5 years, more than 400 European and U.S. firms have used IBM's Information Quality Analysis (IQA), which is an automated, less time-consuming version of its Business Systems Planning (BSP) technique. The flow of data and information used to make decisions in an organization is examined, and data that are missing, inaccurate, late, incomplete, underautomated, or improperly distributed are identified.

As in BSP, data are provided by joint participation of users, managers, and information system professionals. With IQA, however, the analysis is assisted by ISMOD, an integrated set of simulation programs that allows participants to rapidly diagnose problem areas and formulate information system plans. ISMOD automates data entry, database creation, data manipulation, and data analysis functions.

When corporations like Bethlehem Steel used the technique, a number of unanticipated benefits emerged. Participants were stimulated to reexamine their own roles and objectives; new energy and job interest resulted. A sense of participative management was also encouraged.

Adapted from "Information Quality Analysis," *Infosystems*, December 1985.

analyze. It is a very expensive technique with a bias toward top management and data processing. Most of the interviews are conducted with senior or middle managers, with little effort to collect information from clerical workers and supervisory managers. Moreover, the questions frequently focus not on the critical objectives of management and where information is needed, but rather on what *existing* information is used. There is little or no normative perspective in enterprise analysis. The result is a tendency to automate whatever exists. In this manner, manual systems are automated. But in many instances, entirely new approaches to how business is conducted are needed, and these needs are not addressed.

Strategic Analysis: Critical Success Factors

The strategic analysis or critical success factor approach argues that the information requirements of an organization are determined by a small number of *critical success factors* (*CSFs*) of managers. CSFs are

TABLE 13.4	Example	Goals	CSF

Critical Success Factors and Organizational Goals	Profit concern	Earnings/share
		Return on investment
		Market share
		New product
			Automotive industry
			  Styling
			  Quality dealer system
			  Cost control
			  Energy standards

	Nonprofit	Excellent health care Meeting government regulations Future health needs	Regional integration with other hospitals Efficient use of resources Improved monitoring of regulations

Source: Adapted from Rockart (1979).

operational goals. If these goals can be attained, the success of the firm or organization is assured (Rockart, 1979; Rockart and Treacy, 1982).

The case study at the end of this chapter describes how the CSF method is used (Shank et al., 1985).

CSFs are shaped by the industry, the firm, the manager, and the broader environment. This broader focus, in comparison to that of previous methods, accounts for the description of this technique as "strategic." An important premise of the strategic analysis approach is that there is a small number of objectives that managers can easily identify and information systems can focus on.

The principal method used in CSF analysis is personal interviews—three or four—with a number of top managers to identify their goals and the resulting CSFs. These personal CSFs are aggregated to develop a picture of the firm's CSFs. Then systems are built to deliver information on these CSFs. (See Table 13.4 for an example of CSFs. For the method of developing CSFs in an organization, see Figure 13.5.)

The strength of the CSF method is that it produces a smaller data set to analyze than enterprise analysis. Only top managers are interviewed, and the questions focus on a small number of CSFs rather than a broad inquiry into what information is used or needed. This method can be tailored to the structure of each industry, with different competitive strategies producing different information systems. The CSF method also depends on the industry position and even the geographical location. Therefore, this method produces systems that are more custom-tailored to an organization.

A unique strength of the CSF method is that it takes into account the changing environment with which organizations and managers must deal. This method explicitly asks managers to look at the

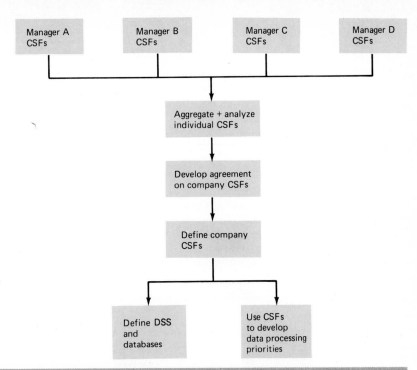

FIGURE 13.5
Using CSFs to develop systems. The CSF approach relies on interviews with key managers to identify their CSFs. Individual CSFs are aggregated to develop CSFs for the entire firm. Systems can then be built to deliver information on these CSFs. (Adapted from Bullen and Rockart, 1981.)

environment and consider how their analysis of it shapes their information needs. It is especially suitable for top management and for the development of DSS and ESS. Last, the method produces a consensus among top managers about what is important to measure in order to gauge the organization's success. Like enterprise analysis, the CSF method focuses organizational attention on how information should be handled.

The weakness of this method is that the aggregation process and the analysis of the data is an art form. There is no particularly rigorous way in which individual CSFs can be aggregated into a clear company pattern. Second, there is often confusion among interviewees (and interviewers) betwen *individual* and *organizational* CSFs. They are not necessarily the same. What can be critical to a manager may not be important for the organization. Moreover, this method is clearly biased toward top managers because they are the ones (generally the only ones) interviewed. Indeed, the method seems to apply only to management reporting systems, DSS, and ESS. It assumes that successful TPSs already exist. Last, it should be noted that this method does not necessarily overcome the impact of a changing environment or changes in managers. Environments and managers change rapidly, and information systems must adjust

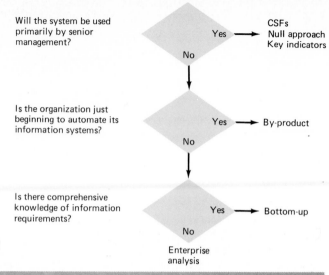

Will the system be used primarily by senior management? → Yes → CSFs / Null approach / Key indicators

No ↓

Is the organization just beginning to automate its information systems? → Yes → By-product

No ↓

Is there comprehensive knowledge of information requirements? → Yes → Bottom-up

No ↓

Enterprise analysis

FIGURE 13.6

Deciding on a requirements analysis technique. This decision tree helps system builders to choose the appropriate technique. Factors to be considered include: (1) the client, (2) the organization's experience with information systems, and (3) the organization's knowledge of information requirements.

accordingly. The use of CSFs to develop a system does not mitigate these factors.

Choosing an Approach to Information Requirements

Each of the methods just described has advantages and disadvantages. Much depends on the circumstances. Three factors are important to consider when choosing a technique. First, *who is the client*? Is the system designed primarily for senior management, middle management, or transaction processing? Second, *what is the organization's experience* with information systems? Is it just beginning to automate its manual systems, or does it have a long history of successful TPS? Third, *how much does the organization know* about its information requirements? Does it have a firm understanding of its broad needs, or has it never conducted such a study?

These three factors are used in a decision tree in Figure 13.6 to help choose a requirements analysis technique.

13.4 Better Analysis and Design Tools

In the 1950s, information systems were single-purpose, limited in scope, well-defined, and relatively isolated from the rest of the business. Programmers built systems using machine language finely adjusted to the specific characteristics of the machine they were working on. Given the kinds of systems to be built and the primitive nature of the tools, there was little need for development strategy, requirements definition techniques, or specialized tools.

In the 1980s, the information systems that must be built are complex, integrated, multipurpose, highly visible, and closely tied to day-to-day business operations. Information system departments are under growing pressure to produce more complex, user-friendly, integrated systems more rapidly. They are expected to do this in the face of a rapidly growing demand for systems (with application backlogs of 2 to 4 years), a shortage of skilled analysts and programmers, high turnover (see Chapter 21), and relatively tight budgets (Konsynski, 1984–1985).

The strategies outlined in this chapter for developing systems and techniques for requirements analysis are one part of the tool kit now available to help speed up systems development and to produce higher-quality systems. In general, there are three kinds of tools available to expedite the systems development process:

- *Definition techniques:* concerned with defining the requirements of the new system. These techniques shape both the initial view of the system and all aspects of design. Examples of such techniques previously described are enterprise analysis and CSF. Also included are data administration tools such as data dictionaries, which codify, centralize, and standardize the access and use of data elements in an organization.
- *Software engineering:* generally, computer-aided procedures and techniques to facilitate the development of systems. Included here are advances in programming practice, automated code generators, and programmer tool environments (Alavi, 1985).
- *End-user and package approach:* all efforts that seek to change the relationship between end users and systems personnel. This may include giving all responsibility for the system to users (as in microcomputer applications) or including end users more systematically in the design process. Other end-user approaches include the development of fourth-generation languages permitting users to define their own reports, and information centers where user data are kept in a readily accessible format.

Each of these tools is discussed in greater detail in other chapters. One tool—data administration—cuts across all three areas. Proper administration of data elements in an organization can be useful for system definition, software engineering, and end-user development. Chapter 20 focuses on this subject. Software engineering techniques are described in Chapter 11, which focuses on tools and techniques. Package acquisition, prototyping, and end-user systems development opportunities are discussed in Chapters 14 and 15.

13.5 Summary

The traditional systems development life cycle is appropriate for certain kinds of systems under some conditions. However, this methodology has several drawbacks. Moreover, the costs of making errors in analysis and design are significant. It is therefore important to consider different development strategies for different situations. The major development strategies outlined in this chapter are phased commitment, packages, prototyping, evolutionary, end-user development, and service bureaus. None of them are foolproof, but each has advantages over the life cycle approach under certain circumstances.

One of the most likely areas where systems go wrong is in the early definition stage, when the information requirements of the system must be specified. Six techniques were described for eliciting information requirements: null, by-product, key indicators, bottom-up, enterprise analysis, and CSF.

The alternatives described in this chapter are some of the many advances in systems analysis and design that have occurred in the last decade. Additional advances have taken place in software engineering and end-user involvement. Software engineering tools seek to ensure that systems are properly analyzed and designed by professionals. End-user involvement seeks to put more responsibility on end users to participate in the design process or to actually design the system. These new development techniques are described more fully in the following chapters.

Key Words

Project risk
Project uncertainty
Maintenance
Phased commitment
Packages
Prototyping
Evolutionary approach
End-user development

Service bureau
Requirements analysis
Null approach
By-product approach
Key indicators
Bottom-up approach
Enterprise analysis
Critical success factors

Review Questions

1. Describe the five major limitations of the systems development life cycle methodology.
2. Define the difference between a risk and an uncertainty. What can be done about either?
3. Describe the major risks and uncertainties in systems development.
4. Why are the maintenance costs of systems high?
5. List and briefly describe the seven strategies for developing systems.

6. One of the examples in this chapter involved the California Department of Motor Vehicles system. What approach or strategy would be appropriate for this system? What kinds of failures did this system experience, and what improvements would you make?
7. What are the major factors to consider when choosing a development strategy? Try to draw a decision diagram.
8. Why is it so difficult to understand information requirements? Can't analysts just ask people what they want?
9. Describe the six major approaches used to define information requirements.
10. What are the major factors to consider when choosing a requirements gathering approach?

Discussion Questions

1. You have just been hired as a vice president of data processing by a large manufacturer. Your mandate is to reduce the 3-year backlog of applications to less than 6 months. What system development approach(es) do you recommend? (You can make any assumptions you wish as long as you are explicit.)
2. One of the strengths of the evolutionary approach is that information requirements will emerge over time as users become familiar with the technical capabilities of information systems. What are some of the drawbacks?
3. Using service bureaus wherever possible, and buying packages, means that less time and money are spent on internal training and expertise. Discuss this statement and describe some of the drawbacks of this approach.
4. The basic function of data processing is to serve other parts of the organization that need information. Discuss.
5. The only way to understand what information is needed is to do a comprehensive study of how various groups in the organization actually use information. Discuss.

Flexible Systems at Kinney Shoe

Executives at the Kinney Shoe Corporation in New York are finding a new report on their desk every Monday morning. It lists the previous week's sales and compares them with sales figures from the same week a year ago and with budget projections.

Philip W. Richards, senior vice-president for finance at Kinney Shoe, calls it the "report card for the business."

The old system reported the same information but took two more days to do it. The format was confusing: Eight divisions used a ponderous store-by-store reporting procedure. Each division reported sales in a different way. If a managers needed inventory data, it was necessary to subtract sales from inventory and enter this information in the system.

Kinney wanted to reverse its priorities. Instead of having management reports defined in terms of what data were available, Kinney wanted top managers to specify what the reports should contain. Moreover, managers change their minds. Sometimes they want more, sometimes less information. Sometimes they want to know sales just in Los Angeles; at other times, they may be traveling to Florida and want to see what impact a sales campaign has had there. Kinney executives knew that a system must be flexible, not just a routine MIS reporting system set in stone.

Kinney has decided to use of point of sale terminals to capture and transmit data from 3111 stores to its data processing center. It then extracts the information it needs for top-down reports, as well as for its regular batch process reports. Kinney has set up a two-tier system: a quick-turnaround batch system based on changing manager needs and a longer-term batch system for more stable and predictable management reports.

In this manner, Kinney's MIS department can respond to executive requests for special information with 1 week's advance notice. Each week's results are reported by 11 A.M. on Sunday over portable teletype units to district managers.

All of this was made possible by reorganizing Kinney's reporting system. From 1980 to 1983, Kinney replaced a mixture of manual receipts and scanning cash registers with IBM 3680 point of sale terminals. The terminals send results to an IBM 3083 mainframe computer. The data collected include the store/department number, stock number, gender and size code, retail price, and discounts. The 3680 terminals can be programmed to collect additional information when Kinney requires it.

The information on sales, which average $2.5 million per day for eight divisions, drives Kinney's basic accounting and merchandising systems including order picking, inventory control, cash management, and warehouse control.

Adapted from "Kinney Revamps Data Collection to Fit Managers' Needs," *Computerworld*, June 10, 1985.

Case Study Questions

1. How would you characterize Kinney's original system in terms of the alternative requirements analysis techniques?
2. You are a consultant called in to rebuild Kinney's original system. What kind of strategy would you choose and what requirements analysis technique would you use?
3. What kinds of improvements in Kinney's new system would you recommend?

References

Ahituv, Niv, and Neunann, Seev. "A Flexible Approach to Information System Development," *MIS Quarterly* (June 1984).

Alavi, Maryam. "High Productivity Alternatives for Applications Software Development," *Journal of Information Systems Management* (Fall 1985).

Alter, Steven, and Ginzberg, Michael. "Managing Uncertainity in MIS Implementation," *Sloan Management Review* Vol. 20 (Fall 1978).

Brooks, Frederick P., Jr. "The Mythical Man Month," *Datamation* (December 1974).

Bullen Christine V. and Rockart, John F. "A Primer on Critical Success Factors," Center for Information Systems Research, Sloan School of Management, 1981.

Davis, G.B. "Strategies for Information Requirements Determination," *IBM Systems Journal*, Vol. 21 (1982).

Doll, William J. "Avenues for Top Management Involvement in Successful MIS Development," *MIS Quarterly* (March 1985).

Grudnitski, Gary. "Eliciting Decision Makers' Information Requirements," *Journal of Management Information Systems* (Summer 1984).

Konsynski, Benn R. "Advances in Information System Design," *Journal of Management Information Systems* (Winter 1984–1985).

Kraushaar, James K., and Shirland, Larry E. "A Prototyping Method for Applications Development by End Users and Information Systems Specialists," *MIS Quarterly* (September 1985).

Mazzucchelli, Louis. "Structured Analysis Can Streamline Software Design," *Computerworld* (December 9, 1985).

McFarlan, F. Warren. "Portfolio Approach to Information Systems," *Harvard Business Review* (September–October 1981).

Munro, Malcolm C., and Davis, Gordon B. "Determining Management Information Needs: A Comparison of Methods," *MIS Quarterly* (June 1977).

Rockart, John F. "Chief Executives Define Their Own Data Needs," *Harvard Business Review* (March–April 1979).

Rockart, John F., and Treacy, Michael E. "The CEO Goes On Line," *Harvard Business Review* (January–February, 1982).

Shank, Michael E., Boynton, Andrew C., and Zmud, Robert W. "Critical Success Factor Analysis as a Methodology for MIS Planning," *MIS Quarterly* (June 1985).

Snyder, Charles A., and Cox, James F. "A Dynamic Systems Development Life Cycle Approach: A Project Management Information System," *Journal of Management Information Systems* (Summer 1985).

Vitalari, Nicholas P. "Knowledge as a Basis for Expertise in Systems Analysis: Empirical Study," *MIS Quarterly* (September 1985).

Zachman, J.A. "Business Systems Planning and Business Information Control Study: A Comparison," *IBM Systems Journal*, Vol. 21 (1982).

Zmud, Robert W. "Design Alternatives for Organizing Information Systems Activities," *MIS Quarterly* (June 1984).

CHAPTER 14

Alternative System-Building Methodologies: Prototyping and Packages

OUTLINE

Capital Bankers Life Insurance Company had been growing 225% annually for 3 years. Because its programmers could not keep pace, there was a 6- to 8-month backlog of projects. Thanks to new productivity-promoting programming software installed in June 1983 and changes in system development methodology, this backlog has been cut in half. Much of the remaining backlog can be attributed to increased demand rather than to data processing development bottlenecks.

Capital's data processing staff works with users to design prototypes of their information systems with Rexcom, a fourth-generation language and relational database management system. Basic functional requirements are defined at the start of each project, and programmers then build experimental screens and databases with Rexcom. The prototype systems include simple edits and data manipulation. Users then work with the prototypes to enter test data and generate reports. The prototypes are refined and transformed into production systems. The entire process of planning and implementing typical applications (which support new types of insurance policies) takes 2 weeks.

According to Capital's data processing manager, prototyping gives his company an edge over organizations that use traditional techniques because it creates new policy applications and strategic systems more rapidly. One prototyped application that allows insurance agents in the field to enter policy data on-line into the company's host computer and print out policies in their offices has made Capital an industry leader because it can offer its independent agents instant policy turnaround.

From "Prototyping System Halves Insurance Firm's Backlog," *Computerworld*, August 26, 1985.

Capital's experience shows that there are alternative approaches to systems building that can fashion systems more rapidly and effectively than the traditional life cycle methodology. For some organizations, such as Capital, alternative systems-building approaches may be of strategic importance.

In this chapter the student will learn:
- How prototyping and the use of application software packages provide alternative approaches to system building.
- How prototyping and the use of application software packages differ from traditional life cycle methodology.
- The advantages and disadvantages of using software packages.
- The strengths and limitations of prototyping.
- How to evaluate software packages.
- Which kinds of systems and projects are most conducive to the use of prototyping or software packages.

14.1 Introduction

As information systems have grown progressively more complex, the development cycle has lengthened. The conventional life cycle approach to systems building is time-consuming, costly, and ill-suited to sophisticated decision-level applications. The limitations of this approach and the shortage of data processing specialists have created a 3- to 4-year applications backlog in many organizations.

Systems builders have started to explore alternative approaches to systems development that can solve these problems. They are looking for tools and methods that can reduce the time, cost, and inefficiency in specifying requirements and in translating them accurately into information system design. They are also searching for methodologies that make more use of the skills and talents of end users and lessen the need for professional data processing specialists. This chapter examines the use of prototyping and application software packages as major nontraditional systems-building alternatives. Chapter 15 explores end-user development as a third important alternative.

14.2 What Is Prototyping?

For increasing numbers of applications, it may be useful to build a preliminary model of the system, or *prototype*, before finalizing the system's design. The prototype is a working version of a system or part of the system, but it is meant to be only a preliminary design. Once operational, the prototype will be further refined until it conforms precisely to users' requirements. For many applications, a prototype will be extended and enhanced over and over again before a final design is accepted. Once the design has been finalized, the prototype can be converted to a polished production system.

The process of building a preliminary design, trying it out, refining it, and trying again has been called an iterative process of systems development. Of course, as noted in earlier chapters, traditional systems development approaches have involved some measure of reworking and refinement. However, prototyping is more explicitly iterative than the conventional life cycle approach and actively encourages and facilitates system design changes. It has been said that prototyping replaces unplanned rework with planned iteration, with each version more accurately reflecting users' requirements.

Information systems prototyping differs in some ways from the concept of prototyping in manufacturing. These differences are summarized in Table 14.1.

With declining costs for computer processing time and with the advent of application development aids and fourth-generation languages, prototyping has become a viable and increasingly attractive

TABLE 14.1
A Comparison of Manufacturing with Information Systems Prototyping

Manufactured Product Prototype	Information System Prototype
Prototype is developed over a long period of time	Initial prototype developed over a short period of time
Prototype costs more than the final production version	Prototype costs less to develop than production versions developed with traditional methodologies
Multiple production versions are manufactured	A single production version is produced (except in a commercial environment)

Adapted from Jenkins, 1985.

systems development methodology. For certain functions it is possible to rapidly create files, transactions, reports, and programs. An entire system or parts of a system such as reports or screens can be up and running in several weeks or months. For example, the Hughes Aircraft Company redeveloped an old batch financial system into a much more sophisticated on-line, menu-driven system in 4 months for a total cost of $50,000 ("Attacking the Backlog Problem," 1984).

The prototype version will not have all the final touches of the complete system—reports, sections of files, and input transactions may not be complete; processing may not be very efficient—but a working version of the system or part of the system will be available for users to evaluate. They can start interacting with the system, deciding what they like or dislike, what they want and don't want. Since most users cannot describe their requirements fully on paper (McCracken, 1980), prototyping allows them to work with a system in order to determine exactly what they need. The methodology anticipates that they will change their minds; these changes can be incorporated easily and inexpensively during an earlier stage of development.

When Prototyping Is Desirable

Prototyping is most useful when there is some uncertainty about requirements or design solutions. We can expect to see prototyping applied under the following circumstances.

User Requirements Are Not Clear

Inherent in certain types of applications is a high level of uncertainty about requirements. Requirements may be difficult to specify in advance or they may change substantially as implementation progresses. This is particularly true of decision-oriented applications, where requirements tend to be very vague. Management realizes that better information is needed but is unsure of what this entails.

For example, a major securities firm requests consolidated information to analyze the performance of its account executives. But what should the measures of performance be? Can the information be extracted from the personnel system alone, or must data from client billings be incorporated as well? What items should be compared on reports? Will intermediate processing based on some form of statistical analysis be involved?

For many decision-support applications such as this one, it is unlikely that requirements can be fully captured on the initial written specifications. The final system cannot be clearly visualized because managers cannot foresee how they will use it. By working with an experimental model, users can immediately start to interact with a live system. They can evaluate it by the way it actually works and in so doing clarify their requirements. Through trial and error, they can use and revise the prototype repeatedly until it precisely fits their needs. Requirements will be specified dynamically and will be much more complete than traditional methodologies would permit.

Prototyping is especially valuable for the design of user interface areas. User needs and reactions are strongly dependent on the context. For example, until users are confronted with a concrete data entry screen, it may not be possible to know whether they will prefer key-driven or typed commands. User needs and behavior are not entirely predictable (Gould, 1985).

Design Solutions Require Further Evaluation

In other instances, end-user requirments may be clear enough, but the systems development team may be unsure of certain technical aspects of the design solution. For example, a company may want to link three different commercial software packages together into one system. But the design team is unsure of exactly how to link them and which modules should perform which functions. Which functions should be handled by the package and which ones by in-house code? By experimenting with different prototypes linking the packages, the systems team and the users will be able to determine which combination optimizes processing efficiency and ease of use.

In another example, a major supermarket chain contemplates revamping its inventory control system. It wants easy on-line access to its master files from multiple locations. The application will entail extensive use of screens for on-line data entry and for retrieval of key pieces of information. But the systems project team is unsure of how the screens should flow on-line and needs to fine-tune screen formats as well. So the team decides to prototype many of the screens, using IBM's Development Management System, a tool for generating interactive applications. The screens are quickly developed, showing users how they will flow and allowing them to interact.

How Prototyping Differs from Traditional Development Methodology

Prototyping is different from traditional systems life cycle methodology in many ways. These differences will now be discussed.

Different Application Development Tools

Prototyped systems must be created very quickly, within days or weeks rather than months or years. Prototyping therefore requires software development aids that will create files, screens, reports, and program code much more quickly than conventional programming languages. Such software tools include the following:

- *Fourth-generation languages*, ultra-high-level languages that are largely nonprocedural and use English language-like syntax. Such languages are considered more user-friendly and easy to learn than conventional programming languages. They are generally associated with file management and database features that facilitate updating, ad hoc information retrieval, report generation, and screen generation.
- *Application generators*, tools that produce procedural source code for screens, reports, and basic processing. For example, the benefits system package marketed by Genesys Software Systems, Inc., includes standard processing logic for basic calculations such as social security. Through processing tables for user-defined calculations and special areas to add custom source code, unique forms of processing, such as accrued benefits for a company's pension plan, can be added. The applications development package also includes an on-line retrieval language, custom report generators, and screen generators. With these tools the package can create code for calculations, updating, and reporting for almost any benefits plan in much less time than is needed for coding in conventional languages.
- *Libraries of reusable code*, where parts of programs such as input/output routines, files definitions, on-line input, and editing routines are stored as separate and independent modules in on-line libraries. The appropriate modules can then be accessed and reused for other applications.

These tools are discussed in more detail in Chapter 15.

There is More Interaction With Users

Users interact with a working system much earlier in the design process. Rather than being presented with a final production version at the end of the development cycle, they can experiment with a series of trial systems throughout the design process. As they react to and refine each version of the prototype, users become more intimately involved in the design effort (Cerveny et al., 1986).

A Different Mix of Programming and Systems Analysis Skills Exists

Somewhat less attention is paid to interviewing and information gathering for initial requirements specification. Instead, more time is spent capturing requirements by working directly with users as they interact with the prototype. If new application development aids are employed, less time is devoted to writing code. There is a reduced need for conventional programming skills. Systems professionals are expected to spend even more time with users and to work well with them.

Requirements Are Determined Dynamically

The development process still necessitates a preliminary definition of requirements, but this occurs at a much more general level than with conventional methodologies. After a few basic requirements have been determined, a prototype is constructed. Detailed requirements are developed by users as they interact with the prototype.

The Systems Development Process Is Explicitly Iterative

A prototyped system is designed, evaluated, and revised over and over again. With each successive version, new requirements and refinements are incorporated. With conventional development methodologies, the design must capture the correct version of the system the first time around. If prototypes can be created quickly and inexpensively, this is no longer necessary. The development team has the luxury of refining the design over time. If the prototype is not exactly what users want, it can be discarded and rebuilt or extended to incorporate requirements that cannot be anticipated before the system is actually used.

Figure 14.1 shows a four-step model of the prototyping process. It consists of the following:

1. *Identify the user's basic requirements.* The system builder works with the user only long enough to capture his or her basic needs.
2. *Develop a working prototype.* The system builder creates a working prototype quickly, most likely using one of the tools previously described to speed application development. The emphasis is on speed rather than efficiency. The prototype may only perform the most important functions with a small file of data.
3. *Use the prototype.* The user is encouraged to work with the system in order to determine how well the prototype meets his or her needs. Revisions of this version of the system are expected.
4. *Revise and enhance the prototype.* The system builder notes all changes requested by the user and refines the prototype accordingly. After the changes have been made, the cycle returns to step 3. Steps 3 and 4 are repeated until the user is satisfied.

The approved version of the prototype then becomes an *operational prototype* that furnishes the final specifications for the application. Sometimes the prototype itself is adopted as the production version of the system.

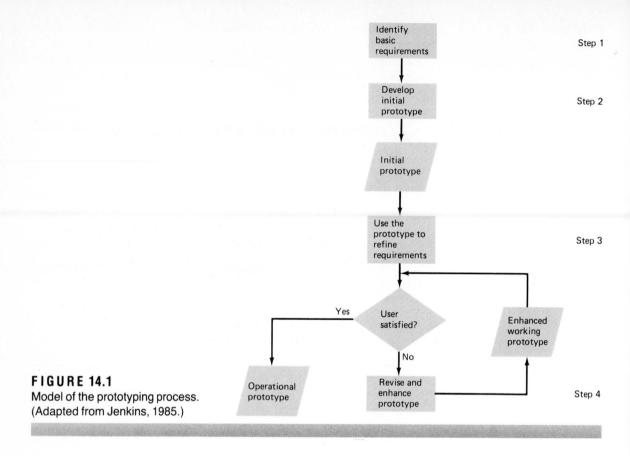

FIGURE 14.1
Model of the prototyping process.
(Adapted from Jenkins, 1985.)

TABLE 14.2

Comparison of Prototyping and Conventional Systems Development
Methodology

	Conventional Systems Development	Prototyping
Requirements analysis	Time-consuming, lengthy, formal operation.	Rapid determination of basic requirements.
System specifications	Lengthy specification document. User is unsure of what he or she is approving.	Produced by the prototype. User sees the results and may make repeated modifications.
Coding and testing	Slow and expensive.	Rapid and relatively inexpensive. Conversion to more efficient code is simplified.
Documentation	Time-consuming and requires additional effort.	May be partly automated.

The differences between prototyping and conventional systems development methodology are summarized in Table 14.2. With prototyping the entire systems development process is more rapid, iterative, and informal than it is with conventional development methodology.

Problems with Prototyping

Prototyping has been widely hailed as a panacea for the problems attending the traditional systems development process. It encourages intense end-user involvement throughout the systems development life cycle. It is more likely to produce systems that fulfill user requirements. It promises to eliminate excess development costs and design flaws occurring when requirements are not fully captured the first time around. User satisfaction and morale are usually heightened because users can be presented with an actual working system, preliminary though it may be, in a very short period of time. Several estimates have shown that prototypes that fully capture user requirements can be created in 10–20% of the total estimated development time ("Developing Systems by Prototyping," 1981). Prototyping is especially useful for the sophisticated decision support applications that are becoming increasingly popular.

However, prototyping may not be appropriate for all applications. It should not substitute for careful requirements analysis, structured design methodology, or thorough documentation. Nor can it totally replace conventional development methodologies and tools. Both the methodology and the development tools currently used for prototyping introduce several problems, which will now be discussed.

Prototyping May Not Be Appropriate for All Applications

Applications that are oriented to simple data manipulation and records management are considered good candidates for prototyping, as illustrated by the prototyping plans of the Union Mutual Life Insurance Company. However, systems based on batch processing or relying on heavy calculations, complex algorithms, and extensive procedural logic are generally unsuitable for the prototyping process.

Prototyping is also meant for smaller applications. Large systems must be subdivided so that prototypes can be built one part at a time (Alavi, 1984). This may not be possible without a thorough requirements analysis using the conventional approach, since it may be hard to see at the outset how different parts will affect each other.

Essential Steps in Systems Analysis May Be Glossed Over

Basic systems analysis and requirements gathering cannot be short-circuited. The appeal of an easily and rapidly developed prototype may encourage the development team to move too quickly toward a working model without capturing even a basic set of requirements. This may be especially problematic when a large, complex system is involved. It may not be clear how prototypes can be created for a big

Union Mutual's Prototyping Plans

> Union Mutual Life Insurance Company of Portland, Maine, is launching prototyping projects in each of its seven strategic business units, ranging from employee benefits to investments. It expects the most likely candidates to be on-line, transaction-oriented applications that emphasize record maintenance and manipulation with many data elements, such as a distributed claims management database. "Number-crunching" batch systems are not considered suitable for prototyping because they lack interactive screens for transactions that users can visualize and modify.
>
> From Amy Bernstein, "Shortcut to System Design," *Business Computer Systems*, June 1985.

system or its parts unless prototyping is preceded by a comprehensive and thorough requirements analysis.

Once finalized, the prototype often becomes part of the final production system. If the prototype works reasonably well, management may not see the need for reprogramming and redesign. Such hastily constructed systems may be difficult to maintain and support in a regular production environment. Since prototypes are not carefully constructed, their technical performance may be very inefficient. They may not easily accommodate large quantities of data or a large number of users.

Documentation and Testing May Be Insufficient

The ease with which a prototyped system is built may prove deceptive; it will still need thorough documentation and testing. Testing may be treated casually because it is assumed that it can be handled by users; it is further assumed that any oversights in testing can be easily corrected later. Because the system is so easily changed, documentation may not be kept up-to-date.

Prototyping Tools Have Certain Limitations

The short-cut development tools used for prototyping may not be appropriate for building complex, sophisticated systems. Fourth-generation languages have proved most valuable for simple, ad hoc reporting but often they are not technically feasible for developing large, complex systems.

These tools were conceived for building very simple systems with small files. They cannot easily accommodate processing that involves complex calculations or logic. Any attempt to do so requires so much manipulation that coding becomes much more time-consuming and error-prone than it would be with conventional programming languages. Current prototyping technology does not allow for much experimentation with different response times. Facilities for fine tuning of measurement are limited as well.

Despite these limitations, we feel that prototyping is still under-utilized as a development methodology. It may not be suitable for all applications, but there are clearly systems or parts of systems that would benefit from its use. On-line screens, for example, are one area where users typically request changes in the initial design. This area is very conducive to prototyping. Prototyping can also flourish for decision support applications, where requirements are nebulous and the system cannot be clearly visualized. As such applications proliferate, prototyping will become a popular development strategy.

14.3 Software Packages

A *package* is one or a series of related software programs commercially available for sale or lease. Software packages may range from a simple task (e.g., printing address labels on a microcomputer) to over 400 program modules with 250,000 lines of code for a complex mainframe system such as the one for the general ledger. Table 14.3 provides examples of applications for which packages are commercially available.

Packages have flourished because there are many applications that are common to all business organizations—for example, payroll, accounts receivable, general ledger, or inventory control. For such universal functions with standard accounting practices, a generalized system will fulfill most organizations' requirements. Therefore, it is not necessary for a company to write its own programs. The prewritten, predesigned, pretested software package can be substituted instead. Since the package vendor has already done most of the design, programming, and testing, the time frame and costs for developing a new system should be considerably reduced.

Packages are likely to be chosen as a development solution under the following circumstances:

1. *Where functions are common to many companies.* For example, every company has a payroll system. And payroll systems typically do the same things: They calculate gross pay, net pay, deductions, and taxes. They print paychecks and registers. Payroll has always been a popular candidate for packages.
2. *Where data processing resources for in-house development are in short supply.* The limited supply of trained and experienced systems

TABLE 14.3
Examples of Application Packages

Accounting	Letter writing/mailing
Accounts payable	Library systems
Accounts receivable	Life insurance
Architecture	
	Management decision making
Banking systems	Mathematical/statistical
Bond and stock management	modeling
Check processing	Order entry
Computer-aided design	
Construction costing	Payroll
	Performance
Data management systems	measurement
Document processing	Process control
Electrical engineering	Query languages
Education	
	Real estate management
Financial control	Remote job entry
Forecasting and modeling	Report generators
	Route scheduling
General ledger	
Graphics	Sales and distribution
Government purchasing	Savings systems
	Stock management
Health care	
Health insurance	Tax accounting
Hotel management	Telecommunications
Installment loans	Utilities control
Insurance	Work scheduling
Inventory control	
Job accounting	
Job costing	

professionals means that many companies do not have staff that is either available or qualified to undertake extensive in-house development projects. (The following example of service stations typifies the plight of many small businesses, which cannot afford any custom programming at all.) Under such circumstances, packages may be the only way that a new system can be developed. Unless data processing services and activities are a major source of revenue (as is the case with banks or insurance companies), most companies do not have the budget to develop all of their systems in-house. Consequently, the most cost-effective development strategy is likely to involve a software package.

Software for Service Stations

Service stations are an industry in transition. Major franchisers are closing out unprofitable stations, forcing small stations out of business. Profit margins on gasoline sales are shrinking. Small independent stations are doing more repair work than ever to stay in business and increasingly require assistance with billing, bookkeeping and inventory management. Because most can't afford custom systems, Computer Possibilities Unlimited of Hartsdale, New York, designed Servistat, a personal computer package for service stations and repair shops. The package enables service station owners to track inventory and to print out repair estimates, job tickets and invoices. It automatically updates inventory house charges and customer files. It also measures mechanics' productivity and the profit margin on all jobs.

From "Computer Consultant Keeps User in Mind," *The New York Times Westchester Weekly*, Feb. 2, 1986.

Advantages

It is tempting to view packages as the long-awaited antidote to escalating software and development costs. Applications software packages can shorten the development process in the following areas:

Design

Design activities may easily consume up to 50% or more of the development effort. Since the specifications, file structure, processing relationships, transactions, and reports have already been worked out by the package vendor, most of the design work has been accomplished in advance.

Testing

Programs are extensively pretested before they are marketed so that major technical problems have been eliminated. Testing can be accomplished in a shorter period. The remaining problems will lie primarily in data and operations. Many vendors supply sample test data and assist with the testing effort.

Installation

Vendors supply tools and assistance for major mainframe systems such as payroll or accounts receivable.

Maintenance and Support

Much of the ongoing maintenance and support for the system is provided by the vendor. For large systems such as benefits or payroll, the vendor is responsible for making changes to keep the system

Tax Calculation Package Speeds Invoice Computations

When Prime Computer, Inc., a computer systems vendor, bills its customers, its invoices must include any state, county or local taxes for the areas where the customers are located. To eliminate the need to research and compute each local tax manually, the company automated its tax calculations with the Sales/Use Tax package from AVP Systems. This package computes the tax for different localities and integrates the information into Prime's billing and accounting system. In addition to reducing invoice preparation time and calculation errors, the package helps Prime keep its tax information up-to-date. AVP sends Prime monthly updates of changes in tax rates. The updates eliminate problems keeping up to date with tax changes that Prime experienced prior to package installation. Once, Prime did not learn about a New York City tax change until it had processed 40 invoices. Prime's tax department spent a full day correcting the erroneous invoices.

Adapted from "Calculation Aid Speeds Company's Tax Computations," *Computerworld*, April 8, 1985.

up-to-date and in compliance with changing government regulations. The vendor supplies periodic enhancements or updates, which are relatively easy for the client's staff to apply. This strength of packages is illustrated by the Prime Computer Company's experience with its automated tax computation system.

Fewer internal data processing resources are necessary to support a package-based system. Since 50–80% of data processing budgets are consumed by maintenance costs, the package solution is one way to cut these costs and free the time of the internal staff for other applications. Packages help to minimize dislocations created by rapid data processing staff turnover. The package vendor maintains a permanent support staff with expert knowledge of the package. If a company's data processing personnel supporting the system terminate or change jobs, the vendor remains a permanent source of expertise and help.

Documentation — System and user documentation is prewritten and kept up-to-date by the vendor.

Organizational Advantages

An attractive feature of packages for management is the way they can reduce some of the organizational bottlenecks in the development process. Much of the wrangling with users in the design stage to work and rework specifications has been eliminated. Users can be more easily convinced to accept the system as is, because specifications have been fixed. Even though they must bend their procedures to conform to the package, they will lean toward a package because external design work is perceived as superior to an in-house effort. The package vendor offers a fresh start by a third party who is in a stronger position to take advantage of other companies' experiences and state-of-the-art technology.

Packages have strong 'political' appeal to management because major software costs are fixed. Implementation can be accomplished more rapidly and with less cost. Problems with the system can be attributed to the limitations of the package rather than to internal sources. Thus, the major contribution of packages may be their capacity to end major sources of organizational resistance to the development effort.

Disadvantages

Rarely noted are the disadvantage of packages, which can be considerable, even overwhelming, for a complex system. It is much easier to design and code software that performs one process or activity very well than it is to create a system with numerous complex processing functions. Commercial software has not yet achieved the level of sophistication and technical quality needed to produce multi-purpose packages that can do everything well that users want. The following vignette shows the need for a specialized package for processing employee retirement benefits because this function was not handled well by the more comprehensive, all-purpose personnel packages.

In some circumstances, packages may actually hamper the development effort, as indicated by the following discussion.

Conversion

Although vendors often provide conversion software and consulting help, a package may actually prolong the conversion process, especially if conversion to the package is from a sophisticated automated system. In such cases, conversion costs have been known to be so astronomical as to render the entire development effort unfeasible. Conversion to a package is easiest from simple manual applications or from automated applications that are not very sophisticated.

Design and Customization

To maximize market appeal, packages are geared to the most common requirements of all organizations. But what happens if an organization has unique requirements that the package doesn't address? To varying degrees, packages anticipate this problem by providing features for customization that do not alter the basic software. Package design can incorporate parameters supplied by

Specialized Products for Human Resources Management

National FSI, Inc., in Dallas offers a highly specialized software package for processing employee retirement benefits. It can perform both recordkeeping and analyses for pension and profit-sharing plans. According to W.D. McFarlin, the firm's president and CEO, vendors tend to handle certain requirements very well and their adjuncts less well. The larger, more comprehensive Human Resources Management Systems tend to treat retirement in a secondary manner compared to their offerings for payroll/personnel. Retirement is a complicated application area that requires a high degree of specialization.

Adapted from Michael J. Major, "HRMS: Last of the 'General' Computing Frontiers," *Software News*, January 1986.

clients for data elements and processing unique to their company. Customization facilities include the following:

- Use of tables for processing or adding data elements that can be specified by users.
- Modular design that allows clients to select the modules with the kind of processing they need.
- User exits—places in program code where clients can exit from package processing to call modules they write themselves.
- Flexible file structure—the ability to accommodate data elements other than those provided with the package by setting aside portions of records or segments for in-house fields.

It is standard policy among vendors to refuse to support their products if changes have been made by altering the package source code. Some packages have been so heavily modified with user source code changes that they are virtually unmaintainable. In addition to making maximum use of the package's customization tools, one way to prevent this situation is to add *front* or *back ends*—programs that run before or after the package and do not interfere with the package software. These front or back ends may be much more extensive than the package software itself. One payroll system we worked on used the best payroll package software on the market. Yet so many

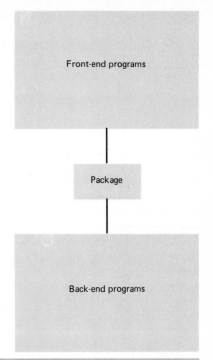

FIGURE 14.2
A heavily customized package. To customize some packages may require so much modification that large front-end and back-end programs must be written to handle processing requirements that can not be met by the package. If extensive customization is required, these extra programs may be more elaborate than the package itself.

important requirements remained unmet that huge front and back end programs were added. The final structure of the system looked like Figure 14.2.

What this illustrates is that so much modification and additional programming may be required to customize a package that implementation is seriously prolonged. Customization that is allowed within the package framework may be so expensive and time-consuming that it eliminates many advantages of the package. Figure 14.3 shows how package costs in relation to total implementation costs rise with the degree of customization.

Even when a package is cost-effective, implementation costs in addition to the initial purchase price of the package must be anticipated. An internal study by one company of the cost and time required to install six major application packages (for manufacturing resources planning, the general ledger, accounts receivable, and fixed assets) showed that total implementation costs ranged from 1.5 to 11 times the purchase price of the package. The ratio was highest for packages with many interfaces to other systems. The same study showed that mangement and support costs for the first year following installation averaged twice the original package purchase price. (Source: authors)

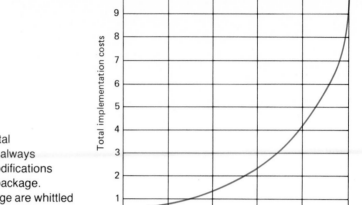

FIGURE 14.3
The effects of customizing a package on total implementation costs. Installing a package always requires some modifications. But as the modifications rise, so does the cost of implementing the package. Sometimes savings promised by the package are whittled away by excessive changes. As the number of lines of code changed approaches 5% of the total lines in the package, the costs of implementation rise fivefold.

Package Evaluation Criteria

These are some of the basic criteria for evaluating an application package (Timmreck, 1975):

Functions Included

The functions included vary by application. But for the specific application, the following considerations are important:

- How many of the functional requirements will the package meet?
- How many of these functions are standard?
- Which functions can be supported only by modifying the package code?
- How extensive are the modifications required?
- Which functions can't be supported at all by the package?
- How well will the package support future as well as current needs?

Flexibility

- How easy is the package to modify?
- What customization features are included (user exits, user data areas, table processing)?
- Is the vendor willing to modify the software for the client?

Maintenance

- Does the vendor supply updates or enhancements to the system?
- How easy are these changes to apply?

- What is the minimum internal staff necessary for ongoing maintenance and support (applications programmers, analysts, database specialists)?
- Is the source code clear, structured, and easy to maintain?

User Friendliness
- How easy is the package to use from a nontechnical standpoint?
- How much training is required to understand the package system?
- How much user control does the package allow?
- Can users make table changes or take charge of security functions? Or must everything be handled by data processing specialists?

Computer Resources
- What model computer can the package run on?
- What operating system is required?
- Is the package release dependent?
- How much input/output and core resources does the software take up?
- What are the package's disk storage and tape drive requirements?
- How much computer time is needed to run the package?
- Can the package run in the client's current operating environment (computer model, operating system, database management system, etc.)?

Installation Effort
- How much change in procedures would the package necessitate?
- How difficult would it be to convert from the current system to the package system?

Documentation
- What kind of documentation (system and user) is provided with the package?
- Is it easy to understand and use?
- Is the documentation complete, or must the client write additional instructions in order to use the package?

Vendor Quality
- Is the vendor experienced in this application area?
- Does the vendor have a strong sales and financial record?
- Will the vendor continue to remain in business and support the package?
- What kinds of support facilities does the vendor provide for installation and maintenance (support staff, hotlines, training facilities, research and development staff)?
- Is the vendor responsive to clients' suggestions for improvements?
- Does the vendor have an active user group that meets regularly to exchange information on and experiences with the package?

Cost
- What is the purchase or lease price of the basic software?
- What does the purchase price include (add-on modules, on-line, retrieval, or screen generator facilities, consulting time, installation support)?

- Is there a yearly maintenance fee and contract?
- What are the annual operating costs for the estimated volume of processing expected from the package?
- How much would it cost to tailor the package to the user's requirements and install it?

Database Characteristics

- What kind of database/file structure does the package use?
- Do the standard fields in the file correspond to the data elements specified by the application requirements?
- Does the information architecture support processing and retrieval requirements?
- Are there provisions to add customized user fields for data elements that are not standard with the package?
- Do the size and format of package data elements meet application requirements?

These criteria should be ranked in importance. A common practice is to assign weights with the most critical criteria ranked highest. Vendor scores for each point are multiplied by their relative weight and totaled. One can then select the vendor with the highest weighted total. Sometimes, however, this approach does not work well because vendor scores are often too close to allow the client to select a winner. Alternatively, the vendor with the highest weighted total may be deficient in some of the most critical areas. Therefore, some analysis of the trade-offs between high overall rating and superior scores in critical areas may be in order.

Impact of Packages on the Systems Development Process

The choice of packaged software will have a decided effect on systems development activities. Table 14.4 illustrates an application package life cycle, noting the specific activities, such as package selection and demonstration, required by a package development strategy.

Conversion will consume significantly more time and resources if a package is replacing a sophisticated automated system. Considerable effort must be applied to translate previously existing files and processing procedures in order to conform to those prescribed by the package design.

The *system study* stage of the systems life cycle will include a package evaluation effort. This is usually accomplished by sending various package vendors a written "Request for Proposal" (RFP). The RFP contains a structured set of questions to which vendors prepare written responses. Depending on the requirements and time frame, the RFP can be employed to single out the strongest packages for further evaluation or to make a final selection. To evaluate a package successfully, the RFP and the package evaluation criteria must be based on a complete set of user requirements.

TABLE 14.4
Application Package Life Cycle. This chart summarizes how system "life cycle" development activities would be altered when a software package solution is chosen.

Project definition
  Establish the need for the system
  Estimate costs and benefits
  Select the project team

Systems study
  Identify user needs
  Prepare requirements statement
  Initial vendor/package screening
  Evaluate package vs. in-house development
  Prepare the conceptual design

Package selection
  In-depth package evaluation
  Vendor negotiations
  Database options
  Recommend the optimal package

Package installation
  Load programs on the computer
  Demonstrate package for users
  Conduct pilot of package
  Begin the training on the package

System design
  Detailed design interface
  Screens, reports, files
  Design processing flows
  Design conversion

System development
  Program interfaces
  Data and file conversions
  Produce documentation
  Run system parallel: optimize
  Run system conversion: turnover
  Terminate old system

Maintenance and support
  Correct problems
  Enhancements to system
  Install new software releases

Additional information can be obtained from the following sources:

- Question-and-answer sessions with vendors.
- Live demonstrations of the package software system.
- Questionnaires, interviews, and on-site visits to the vendor's clients who are using the package.

Sometimes vendor evaluations will focus on these sources and dispense altogether with the RFP. Experts disagree on how much weight to place on the RFP for package evaluation. One group believes that a voluminous RFP can accurately measure a package's functional and technical strengths; the quality of the response is commensurate with the quality of the product. Another group believes that RFPs elicit little new information; vendors receive so many each year that they cannot afford to lavish much time on each response. This group recommends sending abbreviated RFPs covering only critical requirements or dispensing with them altogether. Many organizations base package selection on subjective feelings about a vendor or "gut" impressions. Even if an RFP is not employed, the project team should work out a formal set of evaluation criteria.

Design activities will have a different focus. Requirements and specifications will still have to be developed, but they will be matched with package features rather than being translated directly into design. Instead of tailoring the design directly to the requirements and specifications, the design effort will consist of trying to mold user requirements to the package. One of the principal themes of this book has been the need to design systems that fit well with the organizations they serve. But when a package solution is selected, this fit may be much harder to attain. The organization no longer has total control over the design process.

Even with the most flexible and easily customized package, there are limits to the amount of tailoring allowed. Prevailing wisdom suggests that even the best packages cannot be expected to meet more than 70% of the organization's requirements. The remaining requirements will be unfulfilled or must be met in other ways.

With all of the customization possible, a package may not process as efficiently as an in-house custom-designed system. Major requirements may remain unmet. In data processing, a package is considered good if it can satisfy 70% of an organization's requirements. But what about the remaining 30%? They will have to go unmet by the package or be satisfied by other means. If the package cannot adapt to the organization, the organization must adapt to the package. One of the most far-reaching impacts of packages, therefore, is the effect they have on organizational practices and procedures. The kind of information a company can store for an application such as accounts receivable, for example; the kind of processing it can perform with this information; and the way in which it organizes, classifies, inputs, and retrieves this information from the system will be increasingly determined by the packages it is using.

14.4 Summary

Prototyping and application software packages represent two important alternative approaches to the costly and time-consuming life cycle methodology for systems development. They enable certain kinds of information systems to be built more rapidly and cost-effectively than with conventional methodology.

Prototyping is an iterative design process. A system is designed rapidly for users to experiment with and is refined repeatedly until it meets all of the users' requirements. Once the design is finalized, the prototype is converted to a finished production version. Prototyping often makes use of software tools that can rapidly create an entire system or parts of a system for users to evaluate.

Prototyping is especially useful for decision support applications, clarification of design solutions, and design of user interfaces. However, it may not be suitable for all applications and should not substitute for careful requirements analysis and thorough documentation and testing. Some prototype systems put directly into production may be too inefficient technically or operationally to accommodate many users or large, complex files.

Application packages are commercially marketed, predesigned, precoded, pretested software that can help reduce development time and cost. Packages are best suited for applications with generic requirements and simple functions.

To meet an organization's unique requirements, packages may require extensive modifications that can substantially raise development costs. When evaluating an application software package as a design alternative, the most important criteria to consider are (1) the functions included, (2) flexibility, (3) ease of maintenance, (4) user friendliness, (5) required computer resources, (6) the installation effort, (7) the quality of documentation, (8) the purchase cost, (9) database characteristics, and (10) the reputation and support services of the vendor. A package may not be a feasible solution if implementation necessitates extensive customization and changes in the organization's procedures.

Key Words

Prototyping
Fourth-generation languages
Application generators
Software packages

Customization
Vendor
Request for Proposal (RFP)

Review Questions

1. What do we mean by information system prototyping?
2. Under what conditions is prototyping a useful application development approach? What kinds of problems can it help to solve?
3. What kinds of software tools are most conducive to prototyping?
4. Describe five ways in which prototyping differs from traditional system development methodology.
5. List and describe the steps of the prototyping process.
6. List and describe four limitations of prototyping.
7. What is an application software package? Under what circumstances are such packages most often chosen?
8. What are the principal advantages of packages in the areas of design, testing, installation, maintenance and support, and documentation? Why do packages have a strong appeal to management?
9. List and describe several disadvantages of packages.
10. What is package customization? Under what circumstances can this become a problem when implementing a software package?

11. List the main criteria for evaluating an application software package.
12. How is the system development process altered when an application package is being considered and selected?
13. What is the potential organizational impact of selecting an application software package?

Discussion Questions

1. A widely cited research report found that prototyping facilitated communication between users and information system designers but that designers who used prototyping had difficulty controlling and managing the design process. Discuss.
2. It has been observed that successful prototyping depends less on the selection of software tools than on the corporate culture. Discuss.
3. Some have said that the best way to avoid using professional programmers is to install an application software package. Discuss.
4. One data processing industry publication stated that, at best, in-house development of a system that is already available in package form is apt to cost 15 times as much and take three to four times as long to recover the out-of-pocket investment. Discuss.
5. Experienced information system builders have noted that a strong project team is even more essential for successful implementation of a package than for in-house development. Discuss.

CASE STUDY

Software Packages at the Crane Carrier Company

The Crane Carrier Company of Tulsa, Oklahoma, builds garbage trucks, cattle cars, cement mixers, and other vehicles. It also owns and operates a nationwide network of 23 parts depots that sell engines, transmissions, and other truck parts to other companies. Diversification and successful expansion led to the need by 1982 to upgrade its basic business systems.

The company installed an IBM 4341 (small mainframe) to supplement and eventually replace its Sperry Corporation 9080 computer. It also purchased software packages to run on the IBM machine from Management Sciences of America (MSA) for the following applications:

accounts payable, general ledger, and payroll. These packages were installed one at a time, with payroll going on-line in November 1983. The MSA payroll package replaced Crane's home-grown payroll system, which had run on the Sperry computer.

Crane runs five separate payrolls for employees in its manufacturing plant in Tulsa and its depots throughout the country. An executive payroll and a payroll for other salaried employees are run once a month. Payrolls for office workers and workers in the plant, who are paid hourly, are run once a week. A payroll for drivers who deliver parts and equipment is run twice a week.

With the MSA payroll, Crane has cut the

time it spends preparing its payroll in half. It can complete its payroll cycle, which includes entering time card data and cutting and distributing checks, in 2.5 days. The payroll cycle under the old home-grown system took 4 working days.

Workers' time card data and other information is keyed into the system using an IBM 3278 terminal. Programs edit and validate this input, flagging unusual entries and errors and showing whether the payroll information is in balance. Crane's payroll supervisor makes corrections and checks the validation audit trail reports before processing paychecks.

The vendor provides Crane with tax bulletins to keep abreast of tax changes. The old in-house system was occasionally lax in keeping up with such changes because it depended on the local parts depots to report state tax changes to the company's central office. Tax updates that involve fewer than 50 lines of program code change are sent on hard copy and keyed into Crane's system. Larger changes are supplied on tape.

The package can generate reports of federal, state, and local unemployment tax deductions and required payroll registers. It will also produce monthly or quarterly reports for state and federal tax authorities. The payroll supervisor can select the reports to print by keying in a code on a control card. More customized reports required by the firm's managers, such as a list of all employees in order of date of hire, can be produced through the package's special report generator.

Crane's future plans include installation of the IBM PC to supplement the 3278 terminal using MSA's Peachlink software to access the mainframe. Crane is also installing an interface to tie in the payroll package with its general ledger package.

Adapted from "Applications Package Halves Processing Time for Truck Firm's Five-part Payroll System," *Computerworld*, January 28, 1985.

Case Study Questions

1. What steps do you think the Crane Carrier Company took to assess the feasibility of installing its payroll package? What kinds of questions might it have asked?
2. What would be the role of end users in evaluating and adopting this package?
3. What factors might explain why Crane was so successful in adopting this package?
4. What problems might this company have experienced in implementing its payroll package?
5. If software packages are recommended for more than one information system in an organization, is it advantageous to install packages from the same vendor, as Crane did for the general ledger, accounts payable, and payroll? Are there any disadvantages?

References

Alavi, Maryam. "An Assessment of the Prototyping Approach to Information System Development," *Communications of the ACM*, Vol. 27 (June 1984).

"Attacking the Backlog Problem," *EDP Analyzer*, Vol. 22 (December 1984).

Cerveny, Robert P., Garrity, Edward J., and Sanders, G. Lawrence. "The Application of Prototyping to Systems Development: A Rationale and Model," *Journal of Management Information Systems*, Vol. 3 (Fall 1986).

"Developing Systems by Prototyping," *EDP Analyzer*, Vol. 19 (September 1981).

Gould, John D., and Lewis, Clayton. "Designing for Usability: Key Principles and What Designers Think," *Communications of the ACM*, Vol. 28 (March 1985).

Janson, Marius, and Smith, L. Douglas. "Prototyping for Systems Development: A Critical Appraisal," *MIS Quarterly*, Vol. 9 (December 1985).

Jenkins, A. Milton. "Prototyping: A Methodology for the Design and Development of Application Systems," Working Paper, School of Business, Indiana University, 1983.

Jenkins, A. Milton. "Prototyping: A Methodology for the Design and Development of Application Systems," *Spectrum*, Vol. 2 (April 1985).

Martin, J., and McClure, C. "Buying Software Off the Rack," *Harvard Business Review* (November–December 1983).

Mason, R.E.A., and Carey, T.T. "Prototyping Interactive Information Systems," *Communications of the ACM*, Vol. 26 (May 1983).

McCracken, D.D. "Software in the 80's: Perils and Promises," *Computerworld Extra!*, September 17, 1980.

Timmreck, Eric M. "Performance Measurement: Vendor Specifications and Benchmarks," in *The Information Systems Handbook*, ed. F. Warren McFarlan and Richard C. Nolan. Homewood, IL: Dow-Jones-Richard D. Irwin, 1975.

CHAPTER 15

End-User Systems Development

OUTLINE

(Continued on next page.)

469

In the late 1970s, the Santa Fe Railroad realized that its shipments could no longer be tracked manually. It was being fined by the Interstate Commerce Department for not maintaining accurate records. Although the Santa Fe desperately needed an automated shipment tracking system, its backlogged data processing department could not begin work on a new system for 3 years.

Instead, non-data processing staff in the railroad's operations department developed their own system using MAPPER, a Sperry Univac software system running on Series 1100 computers. MAPPER, which stands for "Maintaining, Preparing and Processing Executive Reports," is an on-line system which enables users to create files, reports and processing procedures at display terminals. It can print reports or transmit them from terminal to terminal. A team of four got the system running at its first freight yard location within 18 months. Santa Fe's system has grown into a comprehensive facility that can pinpoint the location of any Santa Fe shipment in the country.

To coordinate the system, the railroad established a central information systems staff composed of 14 former station masters and clerks. This group uses MAPPER to create local applications. The system is credited with reducing the Santa Fe workforce from 34,000 to 28,000.

Adapted from "Nonprocedural Languages Bringing Up the Fourth Generation," *Computer Decisions*, December 1983.

The Santa Fe Railroad's shipment tracking system is a prime example of an information system developed entirely by end users. End-user development has emerged as another important alternative approach to systems building.

In this chapter the student will learn:
- What kinds of information systems can be developed by end users.
- How end-user development differs from conventional life cycle methodology.
- The strengths and limitations of the special software tools for creating end-user applications.
- The advantages and disadvantages of end-user development.
- The impact of end-user development on the organization.
- Why special policies and procedures are required to manage this powerful trend.

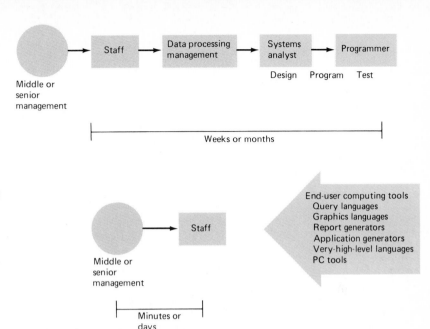

15.1 Introduction

In many organizations, a growing percentage of information systems are developed by end users with little or no formal data processing assistance. This phenomenon is called *end-user development*.

What Is End-User Development?

The increasing sophistication and power of computer hardware and software has created special tools with which end users can develop their own information systems. Through such user-friendly tools, end users can access data, create reports, and perform their own information processing. Entire systems can be developed by end users alone, without professional systems analysts or programmers. Alternatively, end users may still rely on information systems specialists for technical support but perform many development activities themselves that were previously undertaken by data processing personnel. The idea of end users having direct control over their own computing has been termed *end-user computing*. This concept is illustrated graphically in Figure 15.1.

Why End-User Development Is Growing

The trend toward end-user development is expected to continue for the following reasons:

1. Conventional approaches to applications development are very time-consuming and labor intensive. The data processing staff

cannot keep up with the rising demand for new systems. An applications backlog of 3 to 4 years has been documented for many organizations (Martin, 1982). The only way this backlog can be reduced is by finding ways of developing applications outside of the traditional data processing domain.

2. Technical advances have produced a new generation of software that is considerably more user-friendly than earlier programming tools. This end-user software is not always superior to traditional programming software. However, it has supplied tools for reporting, ad hoc queries, graphics, modeling, and some kinds of file creation and updating that can be employed directly by users without formal data processing training. Decreasing hardware costs have made it economically and technically feasible for such tools to be used even it they are less computer-efficient than traditional development methods.

3. The widespread use of computers in business has made more and more organizations dependent on information from automated systems for analysis, planning, and control. Both staff and line managers require immediate access to decision-level information, which often cannot be supplied by existing information systems. New applications must be rapidly created to make this information available.

TABLE 15.1 Categories of End Users	Type of User	Description
	Nonprogramming user	Accesses the system through highly structured, predefined menus or screens
	Command-level user	Uses high-level command or simple query languages
	End-user programmer	More sophisticated user of query languages and user-friendly programming tools to solve own business problems
	Functional support specialist	Writes programs and uses other end-user development tools to support other end users in the same functional area
	End-user support specialist	An information systems professional dedicated to facilities that support end-user computing activities
	Data processing professional	Develops applications with end-user facilities rather than with conventional data processing tools

Adapted from Rockart and Flannery (1983).

End-user development encompasses both end users and information system professionals. Researchers have identified several classes of end users, each of which approaches information systems with varying degrees of sophistication. There are also several categories of information system professionals who work closely with end users and their special computing tools. Table 15.1 depicts the spectrum of end-user computing.

15.2 End-User Computing Tools

End-user applications have been developed for both mainframes and microcomputers. There are seven major categories of software for end-user applications:

1. Query languages
2. Report generators
3. Graphics languages
4. Application generators
5. Very-high-level programming languages
6. Application packages
7. Personal computer tools

Query Languages

Query languages are high-level languages for retrieving data stored in databases or files. They are usually interactive, on-line, and capable of supporting requests for information that are not predefined. They are often tied to database management systems. Query languages can search a database or file, using simple or complex selection criteria to display information relating to multiple records. Available query language tools have different kinds of syntax and structure, some being closer to natural language than others (Vassiliou, 1984–1985). Some support updating of data as well as retrieval. An example of a typical ad hoc query is "List all employees in the Payroll department." Figure 15.2 illustrates how two different query languages express this request.

Query: "List all employees in the Payroll department."

Using Query-By-Example

EMPLOYEE	EMPLOYEE #	NAME	DEPARTMENT
		P.	PAYROLL

Using FOCUS

```
>> TABLE FILE EMPDEPT
> PRINT EMP_NAME IF DEPT EQ 'PAYROLL'
> END
```

FIGURE 15.2
A simple query using two different query languages.

Report Generators

Report generators are facilities for creating customized reports. They extract data from files or databases and create reports in many formats. The more powerful report generators can manipulate data with complex calculations and logic before they are output. Some report generators are extensions of database or query languages. The more complex and powerful report generators may not be suitable for end users without some assistance from professional data processing specialists.

Graphics Languages

Graphics languages retrieve data from files or databases and display them in graphic format. Users can ask for data and specify how they are to be charted. Some graphics software can perform arithmetic or logical operations on data as well.

Application Generators

Application generators contain preprogrammed modules that can generate entire applications, greatly speeding development. A user can specify what needs to be done and the application generator will create the appropriate code for input, validation, update, processing, and reporting. The most full-function application generators consist of a comprehensive, integrated set of development tools: a database management system, data dictionary, query language, screen painter, graphics generator, report generator, decision support/modeling tools, security facilities, and a high-level programming language. For unique requirements that cannot be met with generalized modules, most application generators contain *user exits* where custom-programmed routines can be inserted. Some application generators are interactive, enabling users sitting at a terminal to define inputs, files, processing, and reports by responding to questions on-line.

Very-High-Level Programming Languages

Very-high-level programming languages are designed to perform coding with far fewer instructions than conventional languages such as COBOL or FORTRAN. Programs and entire applications based on these languages can thus be written in a much shorter period of time. Simple features of these languages can be employed by end users. However, these languages are designed primarily for data processing professionals as alternatives to conventional programming tools.

Application Packages

Application packages consist of prewritten application software that is marketed commercially. They are available for major business applications on mainframes, minicomputers, and microcomputers. Through input of parameters, they may be tailored to an organization's unique requirements. Although application packages for large complex systems require installation by data processing professionals, some packages have been marketed directly to end users. Turnkey systems can be installed without the help of the data processing department. Application development based on packages is discussed in detail in Chapter 14.

Mobil Oil Programmers and Managers Work Together

Professional programmers in the information systems group of Mobil Oil Corporation's marketing division develop, update and maintain databases that are used by managers for reports and ad-hoc queries. Both programmers and managers use the same fourth-generation computing tools. These consist of SAS, a financial analysis package, IFPS, a modeling package, and FOCUS, a database management and reporting system. Marketing managers also use microcomputer versions of FOCUS and IFPS. In addition to developing databases for managers, the information systems group uses fourth-generation tools to create applications too sophisticated for nonprogrammers.

Adapted from Horwitt, (1985).

PC Tools

PC tools consist of microcomputer products with capabilities similar to those of the mainframe tools previously described. They include word processing software, graphics software, electronic spreadsheet software, application generators/database management systems, and programming languages such as BASIC and PASCAL. PC tools and end-user personal computing are discussed in detail in Chapter 10.

Figure 15.3 shows examples of available products for each of these categories of end-user development tools.

15.3 Fourth-Generation Languages

A common term for the languages described in Section 15.2 is *fourth-generation languages*. This term has been widely misused, and there is much confusion about what it actually means. We feel that it is an appropriate term for classifying languages that are designed to improve the efficiency of the development process.

In general, fourth-generation languages:

Features

- Can provide order-of-magnitude productivity gains that obtain at least a 10-to-1 increase in productivity over traditional methods.

Oriented toward end users				Oriented toward IS professionals	

PC tools	Query languages/ report generators	Graphics generators	Application generators	Application packages	Very-high-level programming languages
Lotus 1-2-3	Easytrieve	Tell-a-Graf	FOCUS	MSA Payroll	APL
dBASE III Plus	Intellect	SAS Graph	DMS	Maxicalc	Nomad
Wordstar	Query-By-Example		SAS	AVP Sales/Use Tax	
Javelin	SQL		Mapper	AMAPS	
Flow	RPG–III		ADS/Online		
Charting II+	Inquire		Ideal		
	Mark IV		Natural		
			CSP		

FIGURE 15.3

The spectrum of end-user computing tools. The major categories of end-user computing tools and commercially available products in each category are illustrated. Tools range from those that are simple and designed primarily for end users to complex tools designed primarily for information system professionals. (Adapted from Mimno, 1985.)

- Are less procedurally oriented than conventional languages, emphasizing *what* needs to be accomplished rather than *how*. Instructions can be written with much less detail than with lower-level programming languages.
- Can be used by less skilled programmers.
- Often have features suitable for direct use by end users so that some capabilities can be mastered with 2 days or less of training.

Classification

Fourth-generation languages can be classified in the following ways (Synders, 1984):

Degree of Integration with Database Management Systems

Some fourth-generation languages are based on their own database management system. For example ADS/O (ADS/Online) is closely integrated with IDMS, Cullinet's database management system. Natural is based on ADABAS, Software A.G.'s database management system. Other languages such as FOCUS from Information Builders, Inc., Ramis II from the Mathematica Products Group and PACBASE from CGI support different database management systems such as IBM's IMS and other database management software.

Procedural versus Nonprocedural

A procedural language specifies *how* something is accomplished and the sequence of computer processing steps. A nonprocedural language specifies *what* is to be accomplished, with little detail as to the method. A common fallacy has been to define fourth-generation languages as being nonprocedural. While many of these languages (especially the more user-friendly query languages, report generators, graphics packages, and application generators) are primarily nonprocedural, some have procedural facilities. Very-high-level programming languages such as NOMAD and APL are also considered heavily procedural but have nonprocedural facilities suitable for end users. With highly concise code and order-of-magnitude productivity advantages, such languages fall within the domain of fourth-generation tools.

Batch versus On-Line

Some fourth-generation languages are designed to be used off-line. An individual requesting information will fill out forms, and submit them to the computer center, receiving a report in a few hours or the next day. Mark IV by Answer Systems Inc. is a noteworthy example of this type, with forms for defining reports, transactions to update files, logical and arithmetic manipulations on data, and tables. Figure 15.4 illustrates a Mark IV request form and the resulting report. Many fourth-generation tools, however, are designed for on-line use. An individual can specify a query at a terminal and receive a response in seconds or minutes. Languages that support update processing include on-line screens for transactions and processing logic. Figure 15.5 shows a sample report and instructions for FOCUS, a primarily on-line tool.

Suitable for Users or Data Processing Professionals

Some of these tools are designed to improve the productivity of programming professionals; others are primarily for direct use by end users. Examples in the former category include ADS/Online by Cullinet and Natural by Software A.G., which are sophisticated, high-level application generators. Query languages such as Query-by-Example by IBM or Cullinet's On-line English are oriented toward end users. Some application generators, such as Sperry's MAPPER or FOCUS from Information Builders, Inc., have many features that are easily learned by end users. However, their more complex applications require professional data processing assistance. Many of these fourth-generation tools have one set of functions for end users and another set primarily for data processing professionals.

Advantages

A principal strength of fourth-generation languages is the speed and ease with which they can create certain kinds of applications. Application design knowledge is built into many of these fourth-generation tools. When products are linked to a database, the data are already organized and defined. Specific functions are precoded, requiring only customization via input parameters. With most of the leading fourth-generation languages, it is relatively easy to access data, produce reports or graphs, or generate simple data entry and editing transactions. The principal strengths of these tools will now be discussed.

INFORMATION REQUEST

Informatics Inc

PAGE ____ OF ____

REQUEST NAME	FORM CODE	REPORT DATE	REQUESTOR NAME	TELEPHONE/EXTENSION	DIVISION/DEPARTMENT	MAXIMUM ITEMS SELECTED
EXAM 2	IR	JULIAN				

REPORT FORMAT

SELECTION CONTROL — SUMMARY REPORT ONLY — VERTICAL SPACING — FORMS CONTROL — WIDTH OF PAGE — HEIGHT OF PAGE — LINE NUMBERS

DECK

RECORD SELECTION

FORM CODE	SEQUENCE NUMBER	LOGIC LEVEL	CONNECTOR	FIELD NAME A	OPERATION	BLANK	C (B)	FIELD NAME B OR CONSTANT
P R								
P R								
P R								
P R								
P R								
P R								
P R								
P R								
P R								
P R								
P R								
P R								
P R								
P R								
P R								
P R								

REPORT SPECIFICATION

FORM CODE	SEQUENCE NUMBER	NUMBER SPACES BEFORE COLUMN	FIELD NAME	SORT/BREAK SEQUENCE	DESCENDING?	CONTROL SUBTITLE	TOTAL	CUMULATIVE	COUNT	MINIMUM	MAXIMUM	AVERAGE
R 1			SUPLR-NO	1	1P							
R 1			PART-NO	2								
R 1			CITY			G						
R 1			UNITCOST								G	
R 1			QANONHND				1					
R 1												
R 1												
R 1												
R 1												
R 1												
R 1												
R 1												
R 1												
R 1												
R 1												
R 1												

TITLE

T 1 0 0 1 PARTS LISTING BY SUPPLIER NUMBER #

MK IV IR03 COPYRIGHT © 1969 INFORMATICS INC.

*KEYPUNCHING NOTE THIS NAME MUST APPEAR IN COLS 1 8 OF ALL CARDS PUNCHED FROM THIS FORM.

LITHO IN U.S.A.

FIGURE 15.4A

Sample request form for a report in Mark IV, a batch-capability fourth-generation tool. The "Information Request" contains the logic and report specifications that will produce the report "Parts Listing by Supplier Number." Proprietary and confidential information of Answer Systems Inc. Reproduced by permission of Answer Systems Inc.

Productivity

Many organizations such as John Deere and Heatilator have reported appreciable gains in application development productivity achieved with fourth-generation tools.

Analysis of productivity-building techniques based on conventional languages, such as structured programming, has shown that the maximum gain that can be expected is an improvement of 25% (Jones, 1979). In comparison, studies of fourth-generation productivity have found gains of 300–500% in organizations that have de-

33333

PART NO	CITY	UNIT COST	QUANTITY ON HAND
10030	03	$15.043	15
10060	03	14.141	25
10090	01	4.404	
10120	01	5.050	
10150	03	.082	
10180	01	21.762	

SUPLR-NO GRAND	TOTAL COUNT AVG.			
	COUNT	20		40
	AVG.		$14.262	

FIGURE 15.4B
Mark IV Report, "Parts Listing by Supplier Number." This report was generated by the Mark IV request. Proprietary and confidential information of Answer Systems. Reproduced by permission of Answer Systems Inc.

Example:

```
Recap line
TABLE  FILE  PROD
SUM  AMOUNT  AND  UNITS  AND  COUNT
BY  AREA  BY  MONTH  FROM  1  TO  3
ON  AREA  COMPUTE
UNITPRICE = AMOUNT/UNITS ;
AVE SHIPMENT = UNITS/COUNT ;
END
```

The report appears as:

AREA	MONTH	AMOUNT	UNITS	COUNT
EAST	1	4528.00	200	8
	2	1200.00	100	3
	3	6240.00	460	14
**EAST		UNITPRICE 15.55		
		AVE SHIPMENT 30.80		
NORTH	1	1400.00	200	7

.
.
etc.

FIGURE 15.5
Sample report and instructions for FOCUS, a primarily on-line, fourth-generation tool. (Reprinted by permission of Information Builders, Inc., New York.)

veloped applications with fourth-generation tools (Green, 1984–1985; Harel, 1985). While these gains are not yet on the order of magnitude (10 times) originally claimed for fourth-generation methods, they are still very impressive. Fourth-generation languages have recharted the direction of information system development.

Fourth-Generation Productivity Gains

A new employee inexperienced in programming rewrote three COBOL applications at John Deere, Inc., using ADF (IBM's Application Development Facility). His productivity was twice that of the COBOL effort on the first application; 32 times on the second application; and 46 times on the third. Heatilator, Inc., a firm specializing in manufacturing office furniture, reduced MIS staff by 80% while increasing user satisfaction by developing applications via software packages, a relational database, end-user programming, and query languages, all running off a Prime superminicomputer. MIS expenses have been reduced by 50%.

Adapted from Green (1984–1985).

User Involvement and Satisfaction

Fourth-generation tools enable end users to take a more active role in the systems development process. Users can create entire applications themselves or with much less assistance from data processing professionals. The tools often support prototyping, creating experimental systems that can be revised quickly and inexpensively to meet changing requirements. (Chapter 14 discusses prototyping in detail.) With end users playing a much larger role in application creation, fourth-generation tools have helped break down the barrier between users and programmers that has hampered conventional systems development.

New Functions

Finally, fourth-generation tools have new capabilities, such as graphics, spread sheets and modeling, and ad hoc information retrieval, that meet important business needs.

Limitations

Although many fourth-generation languages are rich enough in functions to replace conventional tools for many business applications, their capabilities are still limited. Most of these tools were designed for simple systems manipulating small files. At this point, fourth-generation languages are not suitable for certain kinds of applications.

Processing Efficiency

Fourth-generation languages are not suitable for all applications. Processing is relatively inefficient, and the languages consume large amounts of computer resources. At this stage, most fourth-genera-

Jersey Vehicle Registration Backlog Linked to Computer

New Jersey has had to spend $160,000 a month in overtime to clean up a backlog of 1.4 million vehicle registration and ownership records that resulted largely from the improper choice of programming language for its new computer system. H. Arthur Smith, a spokesman for the Motor Vehicles Division, noted that something that should take 2 hours a day to run into the system was taking 10–20 hours. Division employees were spending up to 5 minutes to get the computer to accept a single transaction, compared to the response time of 3 to 5 seconds planned in the original design. The fourth-generation language Ideal was used for the entire project, against the advice of its manufacturer. Ideal's manufacturer, Applied Data Research, stated that Ideal was not designed for the 15% of the system dedicated to high-volume transaction processing of all registration and title work originating in New Jersey's regional agencies. Price-Waterhouse, the accounting firm that designed the system, has agreed to pay for reprogramming in COBOL, a task that could require 30,000 man-hours and a cost of $2 million.

Adapted from "Jersey Struggling to Cut Vehicle Registration Backlog Linked to Computer," *The New York Times*, October 3, 1985.

tion languages process each transaction too slowly and at too high a cost to make these systems suitable for applications with large volumes of transactions. Slow response time and computer performance degradation often result when large files are used. The predicament of the New Jersey State Division of Motor Vehicles shows the problems that can ensue when a system requiring massive transaction processing is developed with an inappropriate fourth-generation tool.

Complex Logic Requirements

At this point, most fourth-generation tools will not replace conventional languages for applications with complex updating requirements. For example, applications such as those for the design of nuclear reactors, optimal production scheduling, or tracking daily trades of stocks, bonds, and other securities involve complex processing and often the matching of multiple files. Procedural logic must be used to specify processing functions, utility functions, error-handling conditions, specialized interfaces, and highly customized reporting. The logic for such applications is more easily expressed and controlled by conventional procedural code. The specification of procedural logic with fourth-generation languages is slow compared to the specification of nonprocedural functions, such as the generation of screens, reports, or graphics. For applications based on a large amount of specialized procedural logic, the overall productivity advantage of fourth-generation tools may be lost (Martin, 1982; Morison, 1985).

Security and Integrity Controls

Some fourth-generation on-line tools still lack the security and integrity features that are built into Customer Information Control System (CICS) and other teleprocessing monitors based on conventional languages. The teleprocessing monitor controls the scheduling and movement of communications messages or records within a host computer for on-line systems.

Limited Role in the Development Process

The contribution of fourth-generation tools lies mainly in the programming and detail design areas of the system development process. But these tools in themselves have little impact on other aspects of implementation. Productivity in analysis, procedural changes, conversion, and other design areas is largely independent of the choice of programming tool. Nor can fourth-generation languages overcome traditional organizational and infrastructural problems—such as the lack of well-defined, and well-integrated databases, standardized data management techniques, and integrated communications networks—that typically hamper information system implementations (Grant, 1985).

15.4 Information Centers

The *information center*, a relatively new concept, is a special facility that provides users with direct access to information processing resources. Information centers feature hardware, software, and technical specialists that support end-user applications development. With information center tools, users can create their own computer reports, spread sheets, or graphics or extract data for decision making and analysis with minimal technical assistance. Information center consultants are available to instruct users and to assist in the development of more complex applications.

Functions

Information center staff combine expert knowledge of the hardware, software, and databases for end-user applications with strong communications skills. They function primarily as teachers and consultants to users, but they may also take part in the analysis, design, and programming of more complex applications. Typical support activities include the following:

- Education in high-level languages and development tools
- Assistance in accessing data
- Assistance in debugging
- Assistance with applications, queries, and reports employing high-level languages
- Consultation on appropriate tools and methodologies for developing applications
- Generation and modification of prototypes
- Providing reference materials on information center resources
- Liaison with other information processing groups (such as database specialists) that support information center resources
- Maintaining a catalogue of available applications and databases

Tools

Information center hardware may consist of mainframes, minicomputers, PCs, or a combination of these machines. Typical software tools include the following:

- Graphics software
- Word processing software
- Modeling or planning software, including spread sheets
- Report generators
- User-friendly fourth-generation languages (s) for queries or simple applications
- High-level programming languages for end-user–based applications development

Example of an Information Center

The Exxon Corporate Headquarters Client Support Center is one of 16 information centers established by the Exxon Corporation. It provides consulting, training, and technical assistance in end-user computing to 1200 professionals, managers, and support personnel in Exxon's New York corporate headquarters. The Client Support Center is part of Exxon's Communications and Computer Sciences Department, which is responsible for many information resource functions. A separate data resource management function ties end-user computing to traditional computing applications through extract databases.

The Client Support Center staff consists of one secretary and four information system professionals. They furnish management overviews; consulting to determine if an application is suitable for end-user computing; tool selection, security, and control; equipment installation; and training, technical assistance, and limited troubleshooting. The center does not write applications, and limits consultation and technical assistance to 4 hours per application.

Training courses maximize hands-on exercises. The Client Support Center supports a mixture of mainframe and microcomputer tools. It suggests the use of microcomputers to solve small problems and terminals connected to the mainframe to solve large problems. Software on both mainframes and micros provides similar functions: analysis and modeling, database query and report writing, graphics, and communications. The center plans to add executive tools, networking, professional office automation, and improved query facilities to its services (Johnson, 1984).

FIGURE 15.6
The information center is in the information systems area but is separated functionally from conventional applications development.

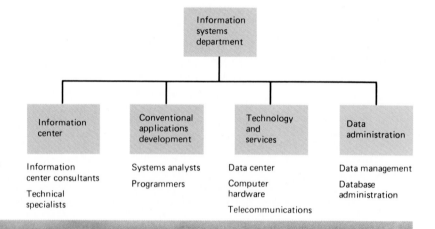

FIGURE 15.7
Each functional area in the organization has its own information center. The information center function is based entirely in the end-user business area.

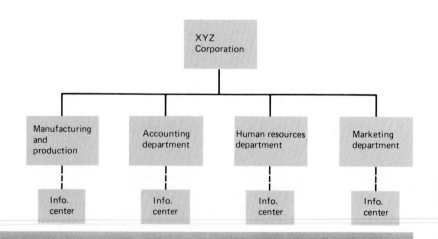

The Role of Information Centers

Exxon's Client Support Center is one of many different kinds of information centers. Some are part of the organization's Data Processing Department. Some are fully based in the end-user business areas. Some information centers, such as Exxon's Client Support Center, support only applications that can be developed by end users themselves. Others furnish data processing specialists to work closely with users. Figure 15.6 illustrates a common arrangement whereby the information center is part of the traditional Information Services Department but is separate from conventional application development. Figure 15.7 illustrates the concept of information centers based in end-user business departments.

Information centers also differ in the amount of data they make available to users. Some, such as the Exxon center, extract data from production systems and make them available for user manipulation and analysis. Others support data from the user's own applications. Still others operate major information retrieval systems to which new data can be added. The information center concept is illustrated in Figure 15.8.

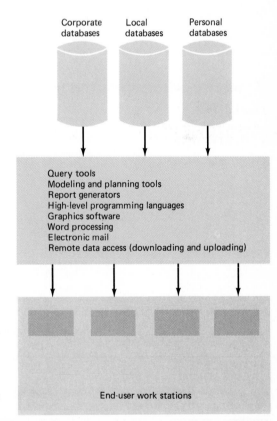

FIGURE 15.8
This information center makes software tools for graphics, reporting, retrieval, modeling, and electronic mail available to end users at special work stations. End users can use these tools to access data that is companywide or limited to their specific department or work unit.

Information centers facilitate application development by users and provide a framework in which it can be managed.

- They prevent the creation of redundant applications.
- They promote data sharing and minimize integrity problems (see Chapter 20).
- They ensure that the applications developed meet audit, data quality, and security standards.
- They promote efficiency in the development of end-user applications.

15.5 Management of End-User Development

The surge of end-user computing is creating both benefits for and challenges to the organization. It is now possible for users to develop many applications entirely on their own. More complex applications based on end-user computing tools may still require technical assistance from the data processing staff, but they can be created much

TABLE 15.2
Conventional Versus
End-User Development

	End-User Development	Conventional Development
Development tools	Fourth-generation languages.	Conventional programming languages (COBOL, PL/1, etc.).
Specifications	Requirements/specifications developed rapidly and often dynamically through prototyping. Specifications often revised.	Lengthy formal requirements analysis and specifications. Specifications hard to revise.
Staffing	Primarily users with minimal data processing assistance; less use of coding specialists.	Primarily professional programmers and analysts.
Development time	Significantly reduced. Often days or several months.	Often many months or years.
Controls/standards	Often informal and undocumented, based in end-user departments.	Usually formal, documented and administered by a central information system department.

more rapidly and informally than traditional systems outside the constraints of the formal data processing environment. The development of information systems outside the conventional framework poses new challenges for the organization.

Comparison of Conventional and End-User Development

To appreciate the management issues posed by end-user development, one must clearly understand the differences between end-user development and the conventional pattern. Table 15.2 summarizes these differences.

Benefits of End-User Development

The primary benefits of end-user computing are as follows:

- *Improved requirements determination.* With users developing their own systems, there is less need to rely on data processing outsiders for requirements analysis and less chance that requirements will be distorted by the user–technical communications gap.
- *Control of the implementation process by users.* Users are more likely to use the systems they design and develop themselves.
- *Reduced application backlog.* User-developed systems can help relieve the application backlog by transferring the responsibility for development from data processing staff to end users. The productivity of professional data processing specialists can also be boosted by the use of fourth-generation languages.

Problems with End-User Development

There are organizational risks to end-user computing because it is occurring in a new environment outside of traditional organizational mechanisms for information system management and control. Most organizations have not yet developed strategies to ensure that end-user–developed applications meet organizational objectives or meet quality assurance standards appropriate to their function. The most critical challenges posed by end-user computing are the following:

- *Insufficient review and analysis when user and analyst functions are no longer separate.* Without formal data processing analysts, user-developed applications have no independent outside review. There is no independent source of analysis or alternative solutions. It may also be difficult for users to specify complete and comprehensive requirements.
- *Lack of proper quality assurance standards and controls.* User-developed systems are often created rapidly, without a formal development methodology. While there are productivity and design advantages to be gained by avoiding conventional development methodologies (see Chapter 14), user-developed systems often lack appropriate standards, controls, and quality assurance procedures. (Information system controls are treated in detail in Chapter 18.) There may

not be adequate disciplines for testing; documentation; controls for the completeness and validity of input and updating; audit trails; operating controls; project controls; and standards for stable interfaces among subsystems.

- *Uncontrolled data.* With end-user computing tools, non–data processing groups can easily create their own applications and files. Private files will proliferate, many with the same pieces of information. Each user application may update and define these data in a different way. Without formal data administration disciplines, it will become increasingly difficult to determine where data are located and to ensure that the same piece of information such as product number or earnings is used consistently throughout the organization. Data administration issues are discussed in detail in Chapter 20.

- *Proliferation of private information systems.* Users can create their own private systems that are hidden from the rest of the organization. Such systems can be used to conceal information from other groups. Undocumented private systems cannot be easily turned over to other individuals who take over a position (Davis and Olson, 1985).

Policies and Procedures to Manage End-User Computing

If end-user computing is to serve larger organizational goals, organizations must develop appropriate strategies for quality assurance, management, and control (Rockart and Flannery, 1983). These may include the following:

Support Facilities

In addition to central information centers, it may be necessary to establish distributed centers that can provide training and computing tools tailored to the needs of different operating units and business areas.

Education

Multiple levels of education will be required by end-user areas. It will be necessary to provide training in end-user tools that is appropriate for each of the types of end users described in Section 15.1.

Application Development Priorities

End-user applications should not continue to be developed randomly. The organization should incorporate end-user systems into its strategic systems plans. Methodologies such as business systems planning and critical success factors (discussed in Chapter 13) can help identify end-user applications with the greatest payoff or determine the most effective use of end-user information resources.

Data Administration Disciplines

Policies and procedures should be developed to control the creation and use of data. Special attention should be paid to safeguarding the integrity and security of multiuser databases that are shared by many different business areas. Data administration strategies are discussed in Chapter 20.

Well-Defined Controls

End-user–developed applications require well-defined control processes. Standards and procedures appropriate for the end-user computing environment should be developed for the following situations:

- Cost-justification of end-user system projects.
- Hardware and software for user-developed applications, with companywide standards for PCs, word processing software, database management systems, graphics, and retrieval tools.
- Quality assurance reviews, specifying whether only individual end users or analysts from outside functional areas such as data processing or internal audit should review end-user systems projects.
- Application controls, such as testing, documentation, accuracy and completeness of input and update, backup, recovery, and supervision. Chapter 18 treats these issues in detail. The control process should flag critical applications that feed other important systems. Such systems warrant more rigorous standards for documentation, editing, and other controls.

15.6 Summary

The development of information systems by end users, either alone or with minimal technical assistance, is called *end-user development*. End-user–developed applications can be produced more rapidly and inexpensively than conventional systems because they are easier to build and because more of the work can be done by the end users themselves.

End-user development has been facilitated by software tools such as query languages, report generators, graphics languages, application generators, very-high-level programming languages, application packages, and PC software. These software tools require less professional programming assistance than conventional tools.

A number of these tools are considered fourth-generation languages because they have features that can be used by end users or less skilled programmers and because they can substantially increase productivity in the development of certain types of applications. Fourth-generation languages are best suited for applications with relatively simple processing logic and small files.

Information centers help promote and control end-user development. They provide end users with appropriate hardware, software, and technical expertise to create their own applications and encourage adherence to application development standards.

The primary benefits of end-user development are improved requirements determination, reduced application backlog, and increased end-user participation in and control of the systems development process. However, end-user development has introduced new organizational risks by propagating information systems and data resources that are not easily controlled by traditional means. Organizations must develop new policies and procedures concerning system development standards, training, data administration, and controls to manage end-user computing effectively.

Key Words

End-user development   Application package
Query language   Fourth-generation language
Report generator   Procedural language
Graphics language   Nonprocedural language
Application generator   Information center
Very-high-level programming language

Review Questions

1. What do we mean by end-user development?
2. Identify and describe the categories of end-users that can exist in an organization.
3. Name and define each of the major end-user computing tools.
4. What is the difference between an application generator and an application package? Between high-level and very-high-level programming languages?
5. Define fourth-generation languages. What are the major differences between these languages and conventional programming languages?
6. What are the strengths and limitations of fourth-generation languages?
7. What is an information center? How can information centers support end-user computing?
8. What are the principal benefits of end-user development?
9. What problems for the organization are created by end-user development?
10. Name some policies and procedures for managing end-user development.

Discussion Questions

1. Several authorities have claimed that fourth-generation languages will soon replace conventional programming languages such as COBOL for implementing the vast majority of information system applications. Discuss.
2. You are the director of data processing for a medium-sized firm. Several end-user departments have asked you to help them locate and evaluate various end-user computing tools. What criteria would you use?
3. Your company has asked you to develop an information center. What would be your strategy regarding: software selection, hardware, staffing, and rules and guidelines?

COBOL Dumped at Morgan Stanley

Morgan Stanley, a leading U.S. investment bank, decided to tackle its application backlog problem with a strategy that maximizes the use of fourth-generation languages. During the late 1960s and early 1970s, the bank began a 10-year period of high growth. It moved into new business areas such as real estate development and management; asset management; stock trading; and stock borrow and loan. In 1983 the firm had approximately 2300 employees and revenues in excess of $300 million. Morgan Stanley plays a prominent role in the underwriting field and in numerous mergers and acquisitions. It accounts for a significant percentage of the dollar volume traded on the New York Stock Exchange (but only a small portion of total Exchange transactions.)

In the late 1970s, Morgan Stanley began a major productivity drive. Key steps included the following:

- Stabilizing existing processing systems to survive for several more years.
- Implementing an on-line processing system to replace old bookkeeping systems and provide appropriate management information.
- Using very-high-level languages for all systems development.
- Significantly upgrading its computer hardware to accommodate new applications and development tools.
- Implementing a management training program that could supply all MIS management from internal sources.

The firm started experimenting with very-high-level languages in the late 1970s. It used APL for a number of analytic applications and used APL-D1 (IBM's APL data interface product) and in-house tools to make data available to end users. In 1980 it developed pilot applications with Natural, a very-high-level programming language integrated with the ADABAS database management system. Due to the success of the pilots and other applications developed in Natural, Morgan Stanley's MIS management decided to use Natural for all on-line and batch database and transaction processing systems.

The firm still uses APL for applications requiring sophisticated financial and analytic models. Morgan Stanley has used packages and outside services when appropriate for applications such as the general ledger and payroll. It claims that it no longer does any COBOL, assembly, or PL/1 development. All internally developed applications are based on either Natural or APL.

Initially, there was some programmer resistance to these changes. The technical staff claimed that traditional languages were more efficient and flexible. Morgan Stanley countered by securing agreement among high-level management that productivity gains were mandatory in systems development and by making managers at all levels responsible for the productivity of their staff. Hiring practices were altered to recruit liberal arts graduates with no systems experience who could be taught Natural from the ground up. An "up or out" policy for all systems development staff combined with strong management directives forced obstructionists to either conform to the new policy or leave.

Morgan Stanley claims that management trainees with 2 years' experience have proved to be three or four times as productive with Natural as senior programmers were with COBOL. To further enhance productivity, the firm is enhancing the capabilities of its data dictionary for systems documentation and management; developing tools to generate programs for end users and systems development staff; and revising traditional systems development methodology. Instead of producing detailed specification documents for application systems, the firm is encouraging a more informal approach to documentation. End users and systems development staff work closely together and develop programs based on verbal agreements. Programs written in Natural or APL can be easily revised.

Morgan Stanley envisions MIS becoming primarily a data administration and operations organization. By using the highest-level languages available, it anticipates that end users will develop 90% of their applications, at a lower cost to the firm than if they were developed by MIS. The firm sees the information center not as a small component of MIS but as its essence in the future.

Adapted from Abbey (1984).

Case Study Questions

1. Morgan Stanley is considered a leader and innovator in the use of fourth-generation tools for application development. Would you recommend this firm's strategy to another company? Discuss.

2. What factors explain Morgan Stanley's success in adopting fourth-generation languages and promoting end-user development?

References

Abbey, Scott G. "COBOL Dumped," *Datamation* (January 1984).

Atre, Shaku. "The Information Center and Productivity Tools: Working in Harmony," *Computerworld Focus* (1985).

Christoff, Kurt A. "Building a Fourth Generation Environment," *Datamation* (September 1985).

Cobb, Richard H. "In Praise of 4GLs," *Datamation*, (July 1985).

Davis, Gordon B., and Olson, Margrethe H. "Support Systems for Knowledge Work," in *Management Information Systems*, 2nd ed. New York: McGraw-Hill, 1985.

Grant, F.J. "The Downside of 4GLs," *Datamation* (July 1985).

Green, Jesse. "Productivity in the Fourth Generation," *Journal of Management Information Systems*, Vol. 1 (Winter 1984–1985).

Harel, Elie C., and McLean, Ephraim R. "The Effects of Using a Nonprocedural Computer Language on Programmer Productivity," *MIS Quarterly* (June 1985).

Horwitt, Elisabeth. "A New Language for Managers," *Business Computer Systems* (January 1985).

Johnson, Richard T. "The Infocenter Experience," *Datamation* (January 1984).

Jones, T.C. "The Limits of Programming Productivity," Guide and Share Application Development Symposium, Proceedings, New York: Share, 1979.

Kull, David. "Nonprocedural Languages Bringing Up the Fourth Generation," *Computer Decisions* (December 1983).

Martin, James. *Application Development without Programmers*. Englewood Cliffs, N.J.: Prentice-Hall, 1982.

Mimno, Pieter. "Power to the Users," *Computerworld* (April 1985).

Morison, Robert, "4GL's vs. COBOL," *Computerworld* (August 1985).

Rockart, John F., and Flannery, Lauren S. "The Management of End-User Computing," *Communications of the ACM*, Vol. 26 No. 10 (October 1983).

Rowe, Lawrence A. "Tools for Developing OLTP Applications," *Datamation* (August 1985).

Synders, Jan. "In Search of a 4th Generation Language," *Infosystems* (October 1984).

Vassiliou, Yannis. "On the Interactive Use of Databases: Query Languages," *Journal of Management Information Systems*, Vol. 1 (Winter 1984–1985).

CHAPTER 16

Building Decision Support Systems

OUTLINE

494

In a crisis, decisive action is required, and there may be myriad factors to consider and goals to pursue. Such a crisis occurred at the Pfizer Pharmaceutical Company, and a computer-based decision support system (DSS) helped Pfizer make the right decisions in a timely fashion.

In the mid-1970s, Rachelle Laboratories had begun selling an antibiotic that was identical to the one patented and sold by Pfizer. Pfizer contended that its patent had been violated and sued.

To support its legal staff during the 6-week trial in 1984, Pfizer put together a team of lawyers and systems staff professionals and built a model of the market for its antibiotic. The DSS was placed in a "war room" three blocks away from the court house, complete with terminals connected to Pfizer's mainframe in Connecticut, printers, and microcomputers.

With the trial underway, Pfizer measured the impact of claims made by witnesses, estimated how much revenue had been lost to Rachelle by the competing drug's sales, and estimated how Pfizer might have charged more for its product in the absence of Rachelle infringement. Using this information, Pfizer forced Rachelle's lawyers to yield on important points and convinced the jury that important losses to Pfizer were involved.

Pfizer won the largest judgment on patent infringement in U.S. history—$55.8 million.

Adapted from "Enriching the Decision Making Process." *Computer Decisions*, March, 1984.

The Pfizer system provides an interesting example of a new kind of information system called a *decision support system (DSS)*.

In this chapter the student will learn:
- The difference between DSS, MIS, and the use of microcomputers.
- The origins and philosophy of DSS.
- New technology, roles, and organizational arrangements for DSS.
- How to analyze and design a DSS.
- How to control DSS development through a systems life cycle.

16.1 Introduction

In the early 1970s, a number of companies began developing information systems that were quite different from traditional MIS systems. These new systems were *smaller* (in terms of labor and cost). They were also *interactive*, designed to help end users utilize *data* and *models* in order to discuss and decide (not solve) *semistructured and unstructured problems* (Keen, 1976; Henderson and Schilling, 1985).

Defining DSS

These characteristics can serve as a definition of *decision support systems (DSS)*: interactive systems under user control, providing data and models as a basis for discussing and deciding semistructured and unstructured problems.

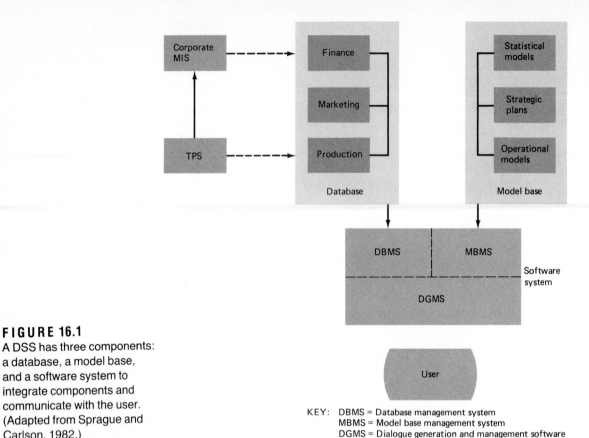

FIGURE 16.1
A DSS has three components: a database, a model base, and a software system to integrate components and communicate with the user. (Adapted from Sprague and Carlson, 1982.)

KEY: DBMS = Database management system
MBMS = Model base management system
DGMS = Dialogue generation and management software

Early examples of DSS are Getty Oil's Plan Analysis and Modeling Systems (PAMS) and American Airlines' An Analytical Information Management System (AAIMS), built in the late 1970s. Both of these systems allowed managers to interrogate corporate and industry databases directly and permitted analysis of the data with financial, statistical, and other analytic models.

Figure 16.1 is a schematic diagram of a DSS. The important point here is that a DSS is an *integrated* system that combines data, models, and interactive, user-friendly software into a single powerful system under user control from early inception to final implementation and daily use (Sprague and Carlson 1982).

The relationship between DSS and the organization's existing TPS and MIS are left deliberately vague in Figure 16.1 (dotted lines). In some cases, DSS are linked closely to existing corporate information flows. More commonly, however, DSS are isolated from major organizational information systems. DSS tend to be stand-alone systems, although it is obviously better if they are integrated into

FIGURE 16.2
DSS database. (Adapted from Sprague and Carlson, 1982.)

External
data

Finance

Marketing

Personnel

Manufacturing

FIGURE 16.3
DSS model base. (Adapted from Sprague and Carlson, 1982.)

Strategic models

Tactical models

Operational models

Analytic routines

organizational systems when this is a functional requirement. Figures 16.2 and 16.3 expand the database elements and the model base elements of a DSS, indicating in greater detail the components of a DSS.

DSS is a Philosophy

Schematic diagrams of DSS fail to convey their purpose. Stated simply, the philosophy of DSS is to give users the tools necessary to analyze important blocks of data, using sophisticated models in a flexible manner that users can easily control. DSS are intended to *do things*, not simply to supply information. They are designed to *deliver capabilities*, not simply respond to information needs (Keen, 1976; Keen and Morton, 1982; Sprague and Carlson, 1982).

The best way to understand the difference between DSS and a more traditional approach to systems support of decision making is to consider the analysis of a stock investment decision in Figure 16.4. As good analysts developing an MIS, we use a flowchart to document and mimic the decision-making process of the investment advisor. We have arrived at a version of investment advisor after studying several textbooks, interviewing actual advisors, and spending some time in the field looking at several investment offices.

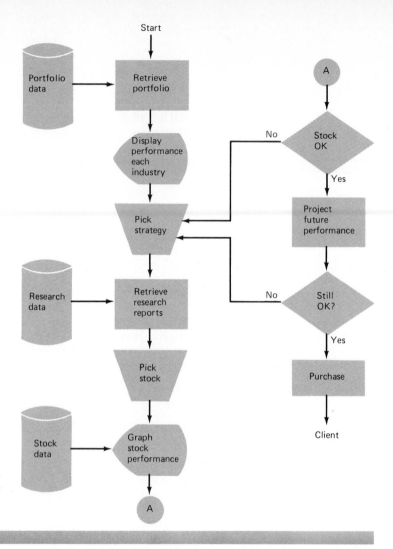

FIGURE 16.4

Flowchart analysis of an investment decision. In a traditional approach and system, the analyst seeks to obtain a consensus view of how decisions are reached. This consensus view is frozen as the system is developed. It is difficult to change. (Adapted from Sprague and Carlson, 1982.)

After doing this work, we have decided that the investment advisor reviews portfolios, individual company research data, and stock data (the databases). In general, the advisor reviews individual portfolios by comparing each stock to its industry performance. If the stock is performing well for its industry, it is kept; if it is performing poorly, it is sold. If it is sold, a new stock is purchased to replace it. This calls for an examination of institutional analyses of companies and stock performance. On the basis of a promising report and good price performance, the stock is added to the portfolio.

Figure 16.4 mimics this decision process. If the DSS or MIS is built along these lines, the decision-making pattern is frozen and

Representations

| Portfolio lists | Graphs | Research reports | Simulation outputs | Interface language |

Operations

| List operations | Graph operations | Report operations | Simulation operations | Procedure operations |

Memory aids

| Work space representations operations | Storage | Databases |

Control aids

| Menus | Training documents |

FIGURE 16.5
DSS approach to investment decisions. In a DSS approach to systems, the emphasis is on providing capabilities to answer questions and reach decisions in a variety of ways. (Adapted from Sprague and Carlson, 1982.)

built into the system. Indeed, the analyst might very well draw Figure 16.4, submit it to investment advisors, and have them review and sign off as a good representation of what the system should do. At this point, the system is frozen. If new advisors come along with different decision processes, the whole system will have to be changed or the new advisors will have to change their decision making process.

Figure 16.5 shows a different way of building a system to support the same—and many other—decision processes. In this figure, a DSS is portrayed as a *set of capabilities* that would be useful in a number of decision processes used in making investment decisions.

Four capabilities are portrayed in Figure 16.5, and all DSS can be characterized in this manner (Sprague and Carlson, 1982).

- *Representations*: conceptualizations of information used in making decisions such as graphs, charts, lists, reports, and symbols to control operations (a procedure construction language syntax).
- *Operations*: logical and mathematical manipulations of data such as gathering information, generating lists, preparing reports, assigning risks and values, generating statistics, and simulating alternatives.
- *Memory aids*: databases, views of data, work spaces, libraries, links among work spaces and libraries, and other capabilities to refresh and update memory.
- *Control aids*: a language (software) permitting user control of representations, operations, and memory. Included here are menus, function keys, conventions, training, "help" commands, and tutorials. Also important is the ability to develop new analysis procedures from standard arithmetic operations.

In essence, a DSS is a *decision-making scratch pad*, backed up by databases, that decision makers can use to support many decision-making processes.

This approach to DSS as *a set of capabilities* goes to the heart of the DSS philosophy and provides a benchmark against which we can compare and critique any DSS in the market.

Characteristics of DSS: What It Means to Support Decisions

With this understanding of the components and philosophy of DSS, it is possible to discuss more precisely what is meant by *decision support*. (Here it may be helpful to review Chapter 5, where management decision making was discussed from several perspectives.) Because DSS promise to support decision making, it is important to understand the unique characteristics of DSS that support this claim.

Designed for Semi Structured and Unstructured Problems

DSS are designed to support semistructured and unstructured problem analysis. In Chapter 5 we introduced the distinction between structured, semistructured, and unstructured problems. Structured problems are repetitive, routine, and for which known algorithms provide solutions. Unstructured problems are novel, nonroutine, and for which there is no algorithm for solution. One can discuss, decide, and ruminate about unstructured problems, but they are not solved in the sense of finding an answer to an equation (Henderson and Schilling, 1985). Semistructured problems fall between structured and unstructured problems.

Along with other characteristics to be discussed, DSS are designed to support important decisions often made by senior executives. (Keen, 1976; Keen and Morton, 1982).

Support for All Stages of Decision Making

In Chapter 5 we introduced Simon's description of decision making, which consists of four stages: intelligence, design, choice, and implementation. Traditionally, electronic data processing (EDP) and MIS have provided managers with intelligence (information) on day-to-day operations, and management science and operations research (MS/OR) have provided management with models for making choices. DSS is designed to incorporate the data of MIS/EDP and the models of MS/OR. DSS is intended to help design alternatives and monitor the adoption or implementation process.

Figure 16.6 shows the elements of a DSS that was used to allocate police resources over a geographic area. Here it can be seen that a DSS is an integrated tool involving data (including maps of the patrol region), models, and user-friendly software to support many stages in decision making. This example is described in greater detail in Section 16.4.

Support for Decision Making at Different Levels

While many early DSS were aimed at senior management, most users of DSS are found at middle management levels. There are many reasons for this, but experience indicates that a well-designed DSS can be used at many levels of the organization. Senior management

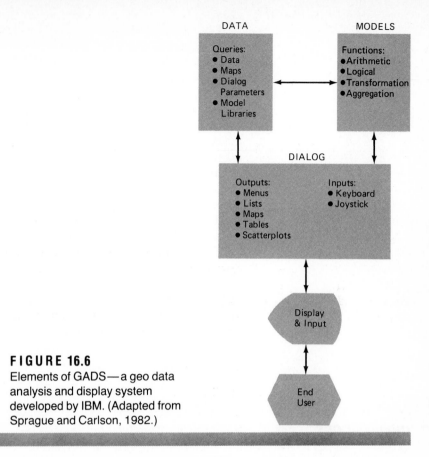

DATA

Queries:
● Data
● Maps
● Dialog Parameters
● Model Libraries

MODELS

Functions:
● Arithmetic
● Logical
● Transformation
● Aggregation

DIALOG

Outputs:
● Menus
● Lists
● Maps
● Tables
● Scatterplots

Inputs:
● Keyboard
● Joystick

Display & Input

End User

FIGURE 16.6
Elements of GADS—a geo data analysis and display system developed by IBM. (Adapted from Sprague and Carlson, 1982.)

can use a financial DSS to forecast the availability of corporate funds for investment by division. Middle managers within divisions can use these estimates and the same system to make decisions about allocating division funds to projects. Capital project managers within divisions, in turn, can use this system to begin their projects, reporting to the system (and ultimately to senior managers) on a regular basis how much money has been spent.

Support for Organizational (Group) Decision Making

As noted in Chapter 5, it is a mistake to think that decisions are made by individuals in large organizations. In fact, most decisions are made collectively. Rational, bureaucratic, political, and "garbage can" models of organizational choice were described in Chapter 5. Frequently, decisions must be coordinated with several groups before being finalized. In large organizations, decision making is inherently a group process.

DSS are uniquely suited to support a number of organizational processes such as decision making and political competition. As previously noted, DSS are highly flexible and can support a number of different assumptions and decision processes. An organization-wide DSS should permit different groups, using different assumptions, to analyze the same problem and come up with interesting, unique answers (Henderson and Schilling, 1985).

In a vignette described later concerned with allocating police patrol beat resources, a community group may wish to maximize the police presence, in contrast to the police department's objective of maximizing arrests. These different assumptions *may* lead to a different allocation of police to beats. There may be a compromise solution that affords good police visibility and a good chance of making arrests (Keen and Morton, 1982). A DSS that can help to design different solutions and describe their consequences is useful in making explicit the real policy choices and consequences facing an organization. Such a DSS *can* clarify the political debate and make explicit the bureaucratic resource constraints in any problem.

Ease of Use

DSS should provide session control for end users. That is, end users should be able to find relevant data, choose and operate relevant models, and control operations without professional intervention. Professionals are, of course, needed to build the databases, model bases, and control language. Experts should be available for consultation, training, advice, and support, but sessions should be end user driven.

Origins of DSS

It is difficult to understand the significance of DSS without considering where it fits into the evolution of information technology in organizations. In some respects, DSS is a natural evolution that began with EDP and the first transaction processing system and culminated in the late 1960s with MIS and the first management reporting systems.

Yet, by the 1970s, dissatisfaction with MIS was emerging in the end user community. The ability of MIS to support decision making directly was limited. MIS systems were not interactive, required intervention by analysts and designers just to get information, and project development took too long to permit the use of relevant information in day-to-day decision making. Rather than supporting management decision making directly, MIS systems were often nothing more than report generators (Keen, 1976; Keen and Morton, 1982).

Moreover, advances in technology by the mid-1970s had made different kinds of systems possible. With minicomputers, processing power could be distributed to users (as opposed to being centralized in the data processing department). Operating systems permitted interactive, time-shared sessions. More user-friendly software was being developed, especially report generators and statistical packages. The first databases and fourth-generation languages were created in this period. Equally important was the development of powerful graphics software and hardware that could display choices and alternatives to a large number of users.

These technical advances revolutionized end-user expectations. Batch reports put out by MIS departments simply could not match the appeal of interactive terminals under user control analyzing corporate data with the aid of powerful statistical models.

In this period, there was an active reconsideration of decision making. There was a growing awareness that many decisions faced by ordinary managers would never be amenable to operations research techniques. Yet there was also the belief that systematic use of information technology could make an important contribution to decisions under conditions of uncertainty.

DSS often has a different organizational position than MIS. In the 1970s, many large MIS groups were unable or unwilling to respond to the growing interest in and demand for DSS by end users. (A similar situation has occurred with office automation and microcomputing.) DSS groups often spring up as separate entities in end-user divisions or as a central corporate DSS group operating under central head-quarters staff control. As Keen (one of the earliest writers on DSS) has noted, DSS started as a fringe group opposed by data processing departments (Keen and Morton, 1982).

Today many of the ideas of DSS are common and are integrated into existing MIS. Indeed, one result of the DSS movement was the development of better MIS. The MIS described in Chapter 2 is an interactive, user-friendly, database MIS accessing corporate data. If external data and more modeling capability were added, this MIS would qualify as a DSS. In fact, because many DSS concepts have been added to MIS, the distinction between the two kinds of systems is becoming increasingly difficult to make.

A large part of DSS must be understood in terms of the growing belief in end-user computing, the technical possibilities of distributed processing and data, and the growing sophistication of support for organizational decision making.

Different Types of DSS

In the last 10 years since the development of DSS, many different types of DSS have emerged. Table 16.1 describes the principal dimensions of different kinds of DSS found by various researchers. Two of these distinctions bear further description.

Clearly, some DSS systems are more data oriented than others. This is particularly true of DSS that migrate out of MIS areas. Other DSS are more model oriented, often forgetting completely about how the data enter the system. At the extreme, DSS consisting of only data or only models are not true DSS at all. The concept of DSS requires that data and models be integral parts of the system.

A second important distinction, to be described more fully, can be made between *DSS generators* and *specific DSS*. DSS generators are

TABLE 16.1
Different Types of DSS

Alter (1977)	Data oriented versus model oriented
Canning (1982)	Reporting versus decision analysis
Donovan and Madnick (1977)	Ad hoc versus institutional One-time versus recurring problems
Sprague and Carlson (1982)	Specific DSS versus DSS generators
Bonczek et al. (1982)	Procedural versus nonprocedural
King (1983)	Very large versus small
Henderson and Schilling (1985)	Public versus private

Source: Adapted from Ginzberg and Stohr (1982) and Keen and Morton (1982).

collections of tools that permit the development of many specific DSS. Specific DSS are systems devoted to the analysis of a particular set of problems (e.g., marketing, production, inventory).

The Difference Between DSS, MIS, and Microcomputing

The development of inexpensive, powerful microcomputers, spurred by equally powerful advances in software design, has furthered the principal goal of DSS: to give tools to end users. Simultaneously, MIS systems have added many DSS features and have attempted, with limited success, to adopt more user-friendly software, giving end users direct control over sessions.

While all of these advances have been positive for end users and managers, they have made the job of textbook writers and researchers more difficult because the distinctions between DSS, MIS, and microcomputer use are more and more difficult to make.

Table 16.2 summarizes the differences between MIS, DSS, and microcomputing as of this writing. DSS has been placed between MIS and microcomputing to suggest that DSS is a bridge between them. In philosophy, DSS and microcomputing are identical; both promise end-user control of data, tools, and sessions. MIS remains largely devoted to the professional mode; users receive information from a professional staff of analysts, designers, and programmers.

In terms of their objectives, MIS focuses on structured information flows to middle managers. DSS is aimed at top managers, with emphasis on change, flexibility, and a quick response. With DSS there is less of an effort to link users to structured information flows and a correspondingly greater emphasis on models, assumptions,

TABLE 16.2
Difference between DSS,
MIS, and microcomputing

Dimension	DSS	Microcomputing	MIS
Philosophy	Provide integrated tools, data, models, and language to users	Provide computing power to end users and simple models	Provide information to end users
Objectives	Directly impact key decisions and enhance effectiveness of decision making	Increase productivity of knowledge and office workers	Enhance control and monitoring power of managers
Systems Analysis	Establish what tools are used in the decision process	Identify what software packages suitable for task at hand	Identify information requirements
Design	Iterative process	Customize package to task	Deliver system based on frozen requirements

and display graphics. Microcomputing focuses on automating well-defined, specific tasks (e.g., document preparation, spread sheet analysis.) Until recently, there was little concern with systematically tying microcomputers into corporate or external data flows (this situation is now changing).

Perhaps the greatest differences can be found in systems analysis and design. Microcomputing is almost entirely dominated by packages. Users establish their needs and buy a package, but then are limited to changing the capabilities of the package. If information requirements expand, they must buy a new package. Analysis and design are done by end users.

Both DSS and MIS rely on professional analysis and design. However, whereas MIS follows a traditional systems development life cycle, freezing information requirements before design and throughout the life cycle, DSS systems are consciously iterative, are never frozen, and in a sense are never finished. This topic will now be discussed more fully.

16.2 Framework for Developing DSS

Developing a DSS requires new kinds of tools, a different concept of who is involved in building systems, and new organizational arrangements.

DSS Technology

DSS technology can be divided into three levels. The application system level technology is called *specific DSS*. This includes the hardware and software that decision makers use to guide their decision making. The Pfizer system described at the beginning of this chapter and Getty Oil's PAMS and American Airlines AAIMS, mentioned subsequently, are additional examples. The case study at the end of this chapter describes a specific DSS used by Hertz to allocate its fleet of rental cars. Voyage Estimator, described in Chapter 2, is a specific DSS used to make decisions about ship scheduling. Each of these examples points to a *specific* problem that a system helps to solve. A Lotus spread sheet used to make financial projections and test assumptions is a specific DSS. Table 16.3 describes some recent commercial specific DSS.

A second level of technology is called *DSS generators*. Generators are a package of related technologies, both hardware and software, that provide the tools for building specific DSS. Mainframe systems such as Boeing's Executive Information System (EIS), the Execucom Systems Corporation's Interactive Financial Planning System (IFPS), and EXPRESS, marketed by Tymshare, are all examples of mainframe software DSS generators. These packages contain data management, graphic display, financial and statistical modeling, and query language capabilities.

More recent additions to this market are decision analysis systems that employ selective artificial intelligence qualities to help decision makers arrive at decisions and summarize the results. Some examples of recent DSS generators are presented in Table 16.3.

TABLE 16.3 Recent DSS Generators	Name	Description
	Reflex (PC) Analytica Corp.	Data base product providing different views of financial data, as well as flexible graphics and report facilities
	Lightyear (PC) Lightyear, Inc.	Decision modeling package
	Decision-Analyst (PC) Executive Software, Inc.	Decision modeling package
	EIS Executive Information System Boeing Computer Services	Financial modeling system

IBM's Geodata Analysis and Display System

In the early 1970s, IBM developed an interactive system to enable noncomputer people to access, display, and analyze data that have geographic content and meaning. Geographic data problems were chosen because this area of decision making is underdeveloped.

The first application of GADS was to analyze calls for police service by type, geographic zone, time of day, and so on. The rapid feedback and display potential allowed police officers to design more efficient allocations of police personnel on beats.

Over a 6-year period, GADS was used to develop 17 specific DSS involving over 200 users. These included police applications, school district boundary decisions, urban planning, fire service, human service delivery, commuter bus route planning, shopping center location, and customer engineer territory planning.

Adapted from Sprague and Carlson (1982).

DSS generators have experienced tremendous market growth since the arrival of microcomputers. Integrated spread sheet packages, database packages with graphics, and related graphic support tools are examples of DSS generators that can be used to develop a large number of specific applications.

An early DSS generator, still used, is IBM's Geodata Analysis and Display System (GADS) system. This is a powerful DSS generator useful in solving problems with geographic components, as described in the preceding account. GADS is introduced here and described in greater detail in Section 16.4.

While each of these capabilities had been available in the past as separate packages, they had never been combined into easy-to-use, integrated tools.

A major area of growth again is in microcomputer generators. While the early spread sheet packages such as Visicalc had limited analytic, data handling, and graphics abilities, more recent packages could certainly qualify as DSS generators. At the same time, microcomputer-based database management packages have come to include data analysis and graphics.

A more fundamental level of DSS technology is *DSS tools*. These are the building blocks of generators. Included are special-purpose languages, such as APL, that permit the rapid development of applications, screens, menus, and interactive dialogue. Also included are graphics subroutines of languages, special-purpose graphics hardware, and supportive telecommunications hardware.

Each of these levels of technology involves a different set of roles.

Roles: Users, Builders, and Toolsmiths

Along with the development of end-user computing and the growth of more user-friendly mainframe software, a number of new roles have emerged in the organization that link technical specialists with ultimate end users. Unlike a more traditional arrangement, with a professional systems staff, on the one hand, and a user group, on the other, DSS entails a more elaborate division of labor and more specialized roles.

Five roles are involved in DSS, each related in a unique way to the technologies previously described (Sprague and Carlson, 1982) (see Figure 16.7).

1. *The manager or end user* is the person or group who is ultimately responsible for making key organizational decisions, operates in an environment of uncertainty, and faces bureaucratic constraints

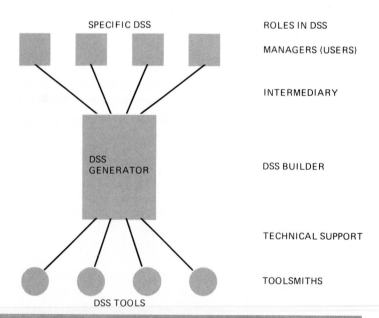

FIGURE 16.7
Roles and tools in DSS. (Adapted from Sprague and Carlson, 1982.)

and political competition in the effort to reach an organizational decision. A DSS must provide information on how things are going, help to design alternatives, aid the user in arriving at a decision that others will support, and finally, facilitate the implementation.

2. *The intermediary* is a skilled staffer who helps to schedule the manager's or task force's work load. This person plays an important gatekeeper role by determining what problems come to the attention of the manager, what information is presented, and how it is presented, and is influential in scoping the solution.

3. *The DSS builder* is generally a member of a special DSS group (to be described) who uses a DSS generator to build the capabilities desired by end users. This person must be familiar with the business problem but must also have a keen understanding of how to make the technology work (although not necessarily to understand how it works). This occupational role has seen the largest growth (and has experienced the greatest shortages) of any role described here.

4. *The technical supporter* is a member of the data processing group or department who develops or installs DSS generators and tools. DSS require links to corporate databases, graphics software, display hardware, and a host of highly technical facilities.

5. *The toolsmith* is a member of the data processing staff who develops new technology, new graphics, and new software to serve DSS applications. Toolsmiths often work for private vendors that develop DSS packages or for service bureaus that deliver DSS services, rather than for end-user organizations. This person is most often a computer scientist or systems engineer.

Organizational Arrangements

A number of organizational issues must be decided before the development of DSS begins. Who will take responsibility for the development and guidance of DSS? Should DSS be developed piecemeal, in one department after another, or for the organization as a whole? What is the justification for an organizational approach? Each organization will resolve these issues differently.

There are three different kinds of organizational arrangements for DSS.

The initiative for most DSS development has come from the user area. This method may be called an *ad hoc approach*. Traditional MIS departments have usually responded to end-user requests for development by offering technical assistance. But the development effort is typically controlled by users.

Unfortunately, with this pattern of development, DSS is not adopted throughout the organization; some departments, typically finance, are far more advanced than others; and significant resources are wasted as each department reinvents the systems of others. There is little or no sharing of experiences across departments. Moreover, the MIS department plays only a reactive role and is often hostile to DSS. Senior management is not involved. Resources are scarce.

A more practical but uncommon strategy is to develop a *DSS group within the organization that reports directly to senior management*. Sometimes this group is labeled the *advanced systems group* and is composed of representatives from the corporate data processing steering committee (mostly end-user managers), data processing management, and senior staffers. This group is given the mandate to develop a corporatewide DSS, establish priorities for applications, and ensure cooperation among users and with the MIS group. When a decision is made to support a particular DSS effort, a task force composed of DSS, MIS, and management specialists is created to design and implement the system.

This corporate approach requires senior management involvement and resources in the form of visibility, legitimacy, and funding (Sanders and Courtney, 1985; Meador and Keen, 1984; King, 1983).

A third arrangement is a *DSS group within the information system or data processing department*. This approach has the advantage of creating a skilled core group capable of understanding the technology and data resources of the organization. It can coordinate organizational efforts, save resources, and permit the orderly development of DSS tools and generators. But the drawback of this approach is that DSS may never escape the information system department. It may be perceived as a data processing group and may not be able to encourage DSS development in user areas.

The location of the DSS must be adapted to the characteristics of the organization. If the end users are hostile to the MIS group, ad hoc development appears best. If the MIS group has a history of close, cooperative and successful relations with end users, then DSS should be located here for a more systematic program of DSS development. Clearly, the most powerful location for DSS is attachment to senior management as a staff function. Here the DSS group can command widespread visibility and significant organizational resources.

16.3 The Process of Developing a DSS

Building a DSS is different from building a TPS or MIS system. DSS generally use smaller amounts of data, do not need on-line transaction data, involve a smaller number of important users, and tend to employ more sophisticated analytic models than other systems. Because DSS are customized to specific users and specific classes of decisions, they require much closer participation of users. In addition, they must be flexible and must evolve as the sophistication of users grows. In this section, we describe how to build such systems.

In order to build effective DSS, a new strategy and design process is needed.

Strategy

There are many different ways of developing DSS, each suited to different conditions. These options include quick-hit development of a few specific DSS, phased development of a related series of specific DSS, and development of a full-service DSS generator (Sprague and Carlson, 1982).

The *quick-hit approach* essentially involves scanning the organization to find easy, rapid development opportunities characterized by willing users, a well-understood problem, and readily apparent, fruitful approaches using information technology—in short, low-risk, high-payoff development. Hopefully, the required tools and techniques can be purchased from a vendor and applied directly.

The problem with this approach is that development tends to be unplanned and ad hoc (a virtue becomes a vice). Different DSS are developed, with no sharing of capabilities or experience. The specific DSS constructed have no general capabilities and may not be adaptable to future problems, forcing total redesign in the near term.

The quick-hit method is the most conservative and most popular approach to DSS development. It does not require a central DSS group; users can develop systems as needed; and the short-term investment is minimal (although the long-term one may be more expensive).

The *staged development approach* attempts to build a string of specific DSS, one at a time, but in a coordinated fashion that involves, the sharing of software, hardware, and, most important, expertise among projects. Generally, this approach requires a central corporate DSS group. The DSS group has the opportunity to engage in a systematic program of development, while appearing to work on only one project at a time. Therefore, this strategy seems conservative but is in fact more ambitious. The disadvantages of this approach are a delay in developing the first system and the risk that later systems cannot use the technology of earlier ones. There may not be a synergistic effect in which later systems build on earlier capabilities. Nevertheless, this is the second most common approach to DSS development and the most common one wherever the organization has a DSS group.

The most ambitious strategy requires senior management support for the development of a DSS generator or general DSS capability prior to developing specific DSS. This is essentially a multiyear effort, perhaps requiring up to 3 years with current technology. The effort focuses on developing a powerful set of tools, an integrated DSS generator, and supportive hardware and physical facilities. A few large companies have taken this approach. IBM's GADS (see Section 16.4) is one example of a powerful DSS generator. The case study at the end of the chapter describes Hertz's DSS, which is an application of a DSS generator. While this approach has the advantage of taking a long-term, coherent view of DSS, it runs the risk of encountering technological and market obsolescence (e.g., the fall in the price of terminals and microcomputers in the last few years).

There is no one best strategy. The strategy chosen should be linked to the organization, the users, the tasks, and the builders. If we divide strategies into two groups, the less ambitious and the more ambitious, it is clear that a more ambitious strategy is possible for a firm that has had considerable experience with information technology, has identified tasks susceptible to this apprach, and has supportive users and willing builders. Any organization where one or more of these conditions does not exist should opt for a less ambitious strategy.

Analysis

In the traditional systems life cycle, analysis is concerned with two stages: project definition and systems study (in which the old system is critiqued and a new system proposed). The end result is a list of information requirements and the broad outlines of a future system.

But the purpose of DSS is not to deliver a system in response to a specific set of information needs. Its purpose is to deliver *a set of process-independent capabilities.* We alluded to these capabilities earlier in this chapter as representations, operations, memory aids, and control mechanisms (the ROMC approach).

The purpose of systems analysis in DSS construction is to identify a problem and a set of capabilities that users consider helpful in arriving at decisions about that problem.

How can one identify a problem susceptible to DSS techniques? First, problems should be identified by users. Hence, users must have some knowledge of DSS techniques. Second, there must be a body of data to work with and analyze. Third, the problem must one for which no simple formula provides a solution. Fourth, there must be some systematic way of thinking about the problem (graphs, lists, charts, operations, etc.) that a DSS can automate or assist. Fifth, the problem must be important enough to engage the time and energy of management groups ranging from first-line supervisors to senior management. Hopefully, the amount of time spent deciding on the problem using traditional methods can be estimated. The analyst should try to show how a DSS can reduce management costs.

What kinds of capabilities should be considered? The ROMC method directs the analyst to specific capabilities. For example, representations may include a list, a graph, a cross-tabulation, or virtually any symbolic conceptualization of a problem that can be represented in two or three dimensions. Representations should be kept simple. Maps, pie charts, PERT charts, and tabular data entry forms are examples. Representations should not confuse the viewer; they are intended, after all, to clarify. A seven-dimension regression equation is probably not simple enough.

Typical operations are the ability to plot, scale, draw, forecast, print, and display any data in the system. Other implicit statistical functions include the basic arithmetic operations, means, standard deviations, correlation, and regression.

Memory aids distinguish DSS from simple microcomputing. DSS have databases both internal and external to the organization; they have work spaces and the ability to profile data, to trigger alarms when critical values in streams of data are exceeded, and to manipulate data files (merge, join, sort, etc.).

Exemplary control aids are user-friendly front-end languages, ample use of function keys at terminals, and a menu-driven capability, as well as the ability to run commands for experienced users (turning off the menu). A DSS generator has all of these capabilities. A systems analyst then need only select those that are specifically needed for a given system.

Design

In the traditional systems life cycle, design involves the development of detailed logical and physical design specifications of the system, programming, and installation. The major product of the design is a system that meets a specific list of requirements.

But in DSS there is no list of information requirements, and initially the user does not know what the final system will look like. All of the vital features of the system that are decided up front in the traditional life cycle methodology are decided at the end in DSS design.

DSS must therefore use a dynamic (changing, evolving) method that is iterative (repetitive). The reasons for this are several. The users do not know and cannot specify in advance the functional requirements of the system. They need an initial system to react to. Their perception of the problem or the task will change as experience with the system grows. The users themselves change as they learn. They themselves cannot agree on how to handle a task or problem. Hence different users want different systems.

With DSS, the trick is to know how to design a system under these conditions of uncertainty, disagreement, and differences in style. What is needed is a system that can be customized for a large number of users.

Iterative design utilizing prototyping is the solution (see Chapter 14). It has three stages.

- *Stage 1.* Develop a small, stable, simple system that will fit on the user's desk, if possible. No complex analysis is involved. The user and the designer simply spend an afternoon together, with the user describing the problem and the designer creating screens (representations) of it on the spot until the user has selected a number of representations that appear to be useful. Here early analysis and early design occur all at once.

- *Stage 2*. Refine, expand, and modify the system in a series of cycles. In each cycle the analyst/designer reanalyzes the problem, designs new elaborations of the system, implements them for the user, and evaluates their use. The user participates directly in establishing the technical capabilities of the system.
- *Stage 3*. Evaluate the system after each cycle. The use for a DSS can disappear as a problem disappears. (Remember the oil shortage crisis?) Continual evaluation is a key virtue of DSS. Users must ask: Does the system help me? Does it save time? Are my decisions more effective, and if so, how? Is the DSS better than nothing at all? The DSS staff must ask: Is this DSS a worthwhile use of our time? Is the company receiving value for the effort? How can we quantify the value of making more effective decisions?

Implementation

In the traditional systems life cycle, the information system staff, after gathering information requirements, essentially disappears from the user area for several months. A system is then designed to meet the information requirements and is delivered on a certain date to the user area. Then a period of implementation begins. This can be a wrenching experience for users and systems personnel alike. The users may discover that the system is not what they wanted and are shocked at certain of its aspects. The designers, who may not have interacted with the users for a long time, may become defensive and insist that the system works exactly according to specifications. The entire situation is often characterized by enormous communication and language gaps.

In DSS there is no separate implementation stage. The system is always being implemented and, therefore, in a sense, is never implemented. It continues to grow. As a DSS goes through iterative cycles, users and systems personnel are in daily contact. The users see the system develop before their eyes. There is generally little opportunity for communication gaps to develop and no opportunity for any party to be shocked by the other's work.

Nevertheless, there are certain elements of implementation that tend to stabilize a DSS. Implementation involves *developing documentation* on the system. An important problem with DSS is that they develop in a totally ad hoc manner. There must be documentation on applications to ensure transportability and user-independent existence.

Implementation also involves developing a *training program*. Most end users will be keyboard literate, but most will need training in the specific DSS syntax, operations, controls, and representations. This is also an ideal opportunity to educate users about the role of DSS and to search for new DSS applications.

Finally, implementation involves an ongoing process of system *evaluation and tracking*. User surveys, observation, testimonials, and usage patterns are all important ways in which a DSS can be evaluated. These data can be especially useful to the DSS group, clarifying its contribution to the firm, helping it to understand what users like (and dislike), and allowing it to identify problems in its internal operations and personnel.

A Dynamic Systems Development Life Cycle for DSS

The different purposes and requirements of DSS that distinguish them from TPS and MIS systems lead to the differences in analysis and design methods previously described. There are also large differences among DSS. Some are very large efforts, involving important organizational actors; others are small, involving only a few managers in a single division. Therefore, the life cycles for different kinds of systems will vary accordingly. Figure 16.8 presents an overview of the iterative DSS systems life cycle, which provides for several different variations.

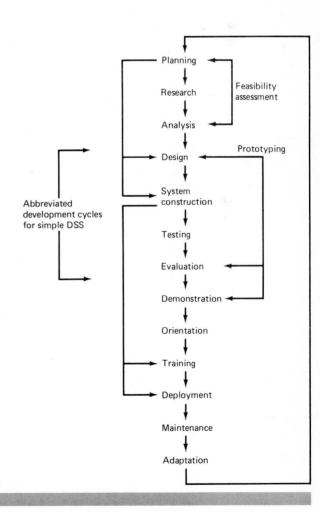

FIGURE 16.8
The DSS systems life cycle. This life cycle can follow many different paths, depending on the complexity of the system. The emphasis is on iteration and flexibility of design to meet changing conditions and new perceptions of requirements. (Adapted from Meador and Keen, 1984.)

Full-scale, organizationwide DSS may continually cycle through the 13 stages of the DSS life cycle shown in Figure 16.8. However, this situation is rare. The vast majority of DSS are smaller, ad hoc, and specific. These systems will go through truncated cycles. Prototyping and exploration of management decision making is perhaps the most powerful DSS technique and is a great advantage over traditional development methods.

Factors in DSS Success and Failure

As experience with DSS has grown, a number of factors have been identified as important to their success and failure. The success factors are not very different from those of MIS and other systems. These factors are described in detail in Chapter 19.

A study of 124 organizations with DSS applications discovered that user training, top management support, length of use, and novelty of the application were the most important factors in DSS success. Success is defined as perceived improvements in decision making and overall satisfaction with the DSS (Sanders and Courtney, 1985).

A smaller study of 34 DSS found that a top management orientation of the DSS (helping to make important decisions) and return on investment are the most important factors in the approval process for DSS (Meador and Keen, 1984; King, 1983). This is an important finding because it highlights what organizations are looking for when they develop DSS. Organizations need support for senior management decision making, which requires custom-built, flexible, and easy to use systems that address important organizational problems.

16.4 Example of a DSS: GADS

One of the earliest large DSS was the Geodata Analysis and Display System (GADS), begun in the 1970s by the IBM Research Laboratory at San Jose, California. The goal was to develop a system that could aid in making decisions involving geographic content and location, because the researchers felt that this was an underdeveloped area of business and government application. Researchers had in mind problems such as allocation of police resources, assignment of salespersons to areas, human service delivery to neighborhoods, development of human service geographic indicators, and urban development.

GADS is an interactive system with user-friendly characteristics, enabling users to manipulate maps (representations) and data and to present graphic displays of solutions. Users can load different maps, data, and analysis routines to solve many different problems. In a

6-year period, 17 specific DSS were developed:

- Police
  Personnel allocation
  Burglary analysis
  Calls for service analysis (two separate applications)
- School
  Attendance boundary formation (four applications)
  School closing
- Urban planning
  Urban growth policy evaluation
  Urban growth modeling
- Fire
  Inspection planning
  Fire equipment planning
- Human service delivery evaluation
- Commuter bus route planning
- Shopping center location
- Customer engineer territory planning

An example of how GADS is used is provided by a police allocation application. GADS helped a city to allocate its police to beat patrols. The cost was several hundred thousand dollars less than that proposed by solutions developed by manual methods and provided a solution that was acceptable to the police officers.

The city first attempted to use a data-oriented DSS. Reports were developed on calls for service, workload, response times, and so forth. The data were plotted manually on maps, and management used these maps to develop alternative decisions. The objectives were a balanced workload and cost reduction.

This semiautomated method failed. It produced costly, unbalanced plans. A consultant was called in to devise a solution. Based on his interviews and on an effort to develop an even distribution of police over time, the consultant built a model to allocate police automatically. The resulting model was rejected by police officers on several qualitative grounds. In particular, it was felt that the central business district was underpoliced, and police officers rejected the proposed schedule changes.

Last, GADS was employed to develop an allocation plan. Using graphics display panels, a large group of police officers and city personnel worked out several alternative patrol beat plans, criticizing each as the results (in terms of workloads, personnel, and budgets) were observed. Finally, a plan was adopted and approved by police officers and city budget officials. This plan was less expensive and was closer to users' objectives than either the data-oriented or the model-oriented plan.

16.5 Summary

DSS are interactive systems under user control that provide data and models to support unstructured decisions. DSS are designed for senior management decision making, although they are equally useful for middle managers with semistructured problems.

The emphasis in DSS is on the delivery of capabilities rather than information. The four central capabilities of a DSS are representations, operations, memory aids, and control aids. In this sense, the DSS is a decision-making scratch pad.

DSS play a different role than either MIS or microcomputing. DSS are designed for semistructured decisions. They attempt to support all stages and multiple levels of problem solving, and they can be very useful for group decision making.

DSS technology is divided into three categories. Specific DSS focus on the solution of specific problems identified in advance. DSS generators are a package of related capabilities that can be used to generate many specific DSS. At a more basic level are DSS tools—the building blocks of DSS generators. Special-purpose computer languages, graphics hardware and software, and supportive communications hardware are potential DSS tools.

The strategy used to develop DSS depends on the organization. In most instances, an ad hoc approach is followed. This method requires no permanent commitment. A DSS group attached to senior management provides a more powerful and systematic approach, but this arrangement is not common. An intermediate strategy calls for a DSS group within a larger, more powerful MIS department.

Users must play an active role in the analysis and design of DSS. For this reason, a different systems development life cycle is used. The DSS life cycle is iterative and dynamic. DSS are never finally designed, but rather are continually being altered and redesigned. Successful implementation of DSS requires top management support, training, and continuous user involvement.

Key Words

Decision support system (DSS)
Specific DSS
DSS generators
DSS tools
Representations
Operations

Memory aids
Control aids
Unstructured decisions
Group decision making
DSS strategy
DSS life cycle

Review Questions

1. Describe important elements of the DSS philosophy. What is a DSS supposed to do?
2. What are the four capabilities of all DSS?
3. How can DSS support unstructured decisions?

4. What stages of decision making can DSS support? Give examples.
5. What is group decision making, and how can DSS support it?
6. Describe five characteristics that distinguish DSS from each other.
7. What are some of the differences between DSS, microcomputing, and MIS?
8. What is the difference between specific DSS, DSS generators, and DSS tools?
9. Describe the five roles that are important in the development of DSS. What difficulties might emerge in coordinating these roles?

[handwritten margin note: manager, intermediary, builder, tech support, toolsmith]

10. Describe three different organizational arrangements for the support of DSS.
11. Describe three different strategies for developing DSS within an organization.
12. How does analysis differ for DSS and MIS systems?
13. How does design differ for DSS and MIS systems?
14. Describe the DSS systems development life cycle.

Discussion Questions

1. Some have argued that all information systems support decision making. Conceptually, a DSS is just a good MIS. Discuss.
2. What kinds of skills must you, as an end user of systems, have in order to participate in the design and use of a DSS?
3. Identify an organization with which you are familiar. Describe and justify an organizational location for the DSS group and a strategy for development, and identify specific areas where DSS could help decision making.

CASE STUDY

Fleet Planning at Hertz

In the last decade, the car rental business has changed dramatically. A growing demand for rental vehicles, more car rental companies, and intense competition for new customers have changed the industry. Car rentals used to be a convenience; now they are an integral part of the transportation system. Many airports around the country would not be able to handle the volume of arriving and departing passengers were it not for the rental car fleets. Throughout this period, Hertz has enhanced its position in the marketplace.

One the reasons for Hertz's success is the ability of its management to plan for and re-spond to changing market conditions. Hertz is able to continuously assess and evaluate fleet requirements versus anticipated demand because of an interesting decision support system.

Demand for automobiles depends on overall industry growth, prices, promotional policies and advertising, and competitive conditions. In determining how many cars will be demanded for a given day and hour, Hertz relies on local assessments of the marketplace. Once their demand assessment has been made, supply is treated as a variable that can be controlled. Relative to a given demand level, an appropriate number of cars is needed to satisfy the customer and to ensure a high level of service.

Because of the long lead time required to establish the overall supply of vehicles, the process of guaranteeing that supply has to begin months in advance. Once a correct fleet level is achieved among a group of cities, the next step is to determine the appropriate distribution strategies on a day-to-day and hourly basis.

The decision support system (fleet planning model) was developed by the Hertz Operations Research Group. This group developed an interactive, computer-based model that is used jointly with management to address each of the three parts of the fleet planning process; long-term, short-term, and immediate or hourly.

The system described here deals directly with the heart of the car rental business. Vehicles are added to and deleted from the fleet, inventory is distributed from city to city, and business levels are monitored and controlled hour by hour, all with the assistance of this decision support tool. The decision support tool is used interactively with managers; the computer model does not actually make the decision, but it helps managers to do so. Field managers who are responsible for the overall level of profit in their area are not willing to surrender the responsibility of decision making to a computer model they do not understand. They are more than willing, however, to take advice from a decision support system, especially if, over the long term, this advice actually works and makes sense.

Design

From the beginning, input from the field was critical to the design effort. The important elements of fleet planning and management decision making were extracted from local officials and employees, and were put together into a comprehensive decision support system that serves as a powerful computational aid. The tools developed were intended to assist the manager's judgment, experience, and insight, not to replace them.

In this manner, the model is part of the decision-making process and the manager relates to it as his tool for better, more timely, and more rational decision making.

The Long-Term Problem of Fleet Planning

Planning for an adequate fleet is a complex process. The proper level depends on local demand, which fluctuates from month to month. The strategy is to develop a fleet in an area that closely coincides with the forecasted peaks and valleys of demand resulting from special events, seasons of the year, and underlying business growth. Too many cars in a city mean an unnecessary expense, and too few cars means lost opportunities and profits. The problem is to achieve an optimal fit between demand and supply.

Hertz has several ways of increasing its fleet. Hertz can purchase, lease, purchase with a buy-back arrangement, or transfer from another location. When disposal is necessary, Hertz sells its cars retail or wholesale, transfers them to another city where demand exists, or turns them back to the leasee or the dealer. Each of these methods has benefits and drawbacks. The typical fleet supply strategy uses several of them each month to adjust the overall level of the fleet in each city. These overall fleet considerations are also adjusted and related to specific models of cars.

The Process

The fleet planning model (FPM) is an analytical tool that helps management to develop an appropriate level of supply and to evaluate the adequacy of the resulting fleet given local demand. This model is illustrated in Figure 16.9. A set of equations establishes the relationship between the fleet and rental-related variables for each month in the planning horizon. The model then generates the financial and operational statistics that measure the viability of a proposed plan.

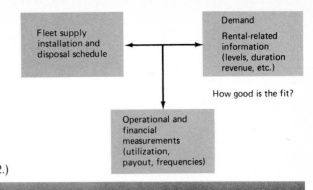

FIGURE 16.9
The FPM. (Adapted from Edelstein and Melnyk, 1982.)

For example, let us assume that there is an increase in demand, which will result in more revenue and a greater use of a given fleet. This may or may not be feasible. Increasing the fleet in a given month may eliminate a current shortage but create a surplus fleet in later months.

Hertz may or may not offset this surplus by selling or otherwise disposing of cars. The model evaluates several of these strategies and trade-offs. A whole series of alternatives can be developed quickly and easily.

The Database

The data used and generated by the models are stored in a database. Managers at all levels of the organization can retrieve this information and design reports to meet their needs. Senior management generally focuses on the overall direction of the business by running a division-level report over a specific time period such as weekly, monthly, or quarterly. Zone managers commonly rank their cities by specific criteria to judge relative performance and to identify problem cities. Reports can be generated based on actual performance.

In addition to these specific reports, a complete description of the current fleet is available to assist in the planning process. For instance, fleet age information can be generated to forecast profit and loss for planned car sales. Inventory reports for specific model

cars can be produced to identify imbalances in model and size mixes. This instantaneous accessibility to critical current and past information provides a strong foundation for the development of new strategies.

The Short-Term Problem: Daily Fleet Planning

Once the overall fleet level is determined and fixed in a given time period, the operational problem of managing the fleet on a day-to-day basis must be considered.

The Problem

Operations are set up either as "independent cities" or as "pools." An independent city owns its fleet of vehicles, and all fleet-related decisions are made by the local city management. In a pool, the fleet is shared by a group of cities. Each city is run by its own management, but fleet administration is centralized. Distribution and control of the fleet rest with the distribution manager. This manager works closely with each of the cities and the zone manager, who has overall responsibility for the pool. Most of Hertz's major field operations are organized in pools consisting of 2 to 15 cities, with fleets ranging from 2000 to 15,000 cars.

The distribution process consists of three steps, as shown in Figure 16.10. The first step is

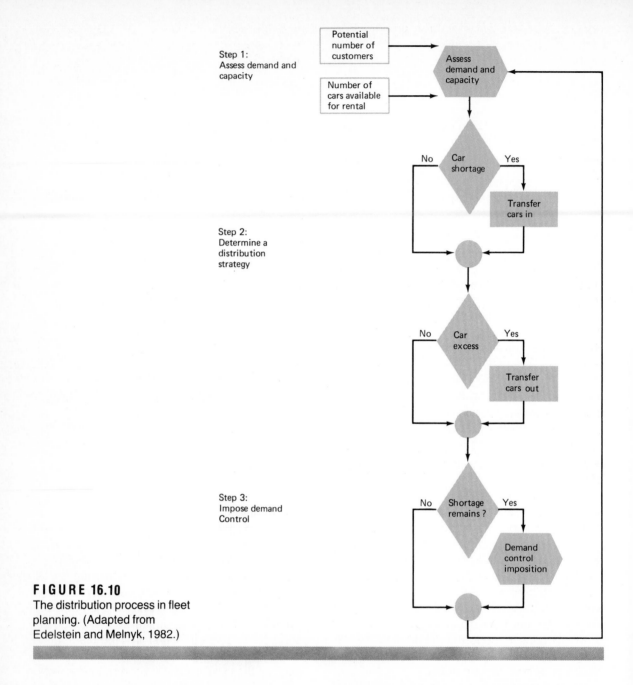

FIGURE 16.10
The distribution process in fleet
planning. (Adapted from
Edelstein and Melnyk, 1982.)

a demand potential and capacity assessment.
Before any distribution decision can be made,
two critical numbers for each city, for each day
in the planning horizon, have to be determined:
the number of customers (the demand poten-

tial) and the number of cars available for rental
(the rental capacity).

The second step is to determine a *distribution strategy*. The rental capacity estimate is
compared to the demand potential in each city

to determine which cities have shortages and which have excesses. The appropriate vehicle transfers are then proposed.

An additional management tool is control over *demand*. If it is concluded that shortages will remain in some cities even after transfers have been made, management can control demand. Demand can be restricted by the zone manager by limiting reservations and renting only to customers with reservations.

However, the most critical determination of all, available capacity, is highly complex and uncertain. New cars are always being installed and others are always being retired. Cars are going into and out of the repair shops or being moved from city to city. New cars are being returned from previous rentals, and some cars disappear from cities because of Hertz's policy of "rent it here, leave it there."

The overall problem is to forecast future demand and fleet availability accurately for each city during each day in the planning horizon. Based on this determination, various transfers and demand control policies have to be assessed.

The Process

Daily, each city manager completes a form that includes actual data from the prior day and projections for future days for his city. These data are telecopied to the distribution manager. He, in turn, inputs these data and some of his own into the daily planning and distribution aid (DPDA) via a time-shared terminal. These data are fed to the model, which is a set of recursive, sequential equations describing the timing of arrivals, check-ins, and flows between cities.

The model produces a report forecasting the situation in each city for the coming week. A sample report is shown in Table 16.4. In this illustration, city 1 has anticipated shortages during the middle of the week and on the weekend. City 2 has shortages predicted for the end of the week.

Based on these projections, some transfer of cars from 2 to 1 seems logical. The question is: how many and when? Given the counts for

the timing of rentals, check-ins, and customer flow between city locations, the model can quickly simulate the impact of any transfer and/or demand control policy and help to establish the most balanced solution.

Table 16.5 shows a final strategy to use the fleet effectively while guaranteeing a high level of service. Many cars are moved to city 1 from city 2. In spite of this, demand control is still needed to keep fleet supply and rental demand in balance. For this reason, demand in city 1 for Tuesday is reduced by 100.

The Database

A database develops as a by-product of runs using this model. This database allows managers to study in detail the car rental business patterns in any city over any period of time. For example, suppose a proposal to charge the customer for not returning the car to the renting city (a dropoff charge) is being considered. What impact will this have on car rentals? The system provides a detailed check-in analysis indicating the degree of current customer movement between pools of cities. This information is useful in determining when and where the charge should apply. After such a policy is invoked, the report is used to monitor its impact.

Another example of secondary uses of the database is in estimating the average revenue per rental. In some instances, this can decrease or increase simply because of changes in the rental length. A rental length analysis report displays length-of-rental statistics for each of the pool cities for all periods and shows how changes in average revenue can be related to length-of-rental statistics.

The Immediate Problem: Hourly Availability of the Fleet

Once a transfer or control policy has been determined that establishes the overall supply in a given city, the focus is on getting through the current day and guaranteeing immediate vehicle availability for arriving Hertz customers.

TABLE 16.4
Anticipated Fleet Distribution

	City # 1						
	Monday	Tuesday	Wednesday	Thursday	Friday	Saturday	Sunday
Idle	443	73	0	0	12	137	0
Check-ins	194	311	411	462	633	176	329
Intercity transfers	0	0	0	0	0	0	0
Available fleet	631	383	411	462	645	313	329
Demand projection	570	600	501	447	500	380	500
Cars left over	61	−217	−90	15	145	−67	−171

	City # 2						
	Monday	Tuesday	Wednesday	Thursday	Friday	Saturday	Sunday
Idle	70	112	119	92	76	46	0
Check-ins	94	71	80	116	95	87	85
Intercity transfers	0	0	0	0	0	0	0
Available fleet	163	182	198	206	169	133	84
Demand projection	99	95	86	107	139	141	79
Cars left over	64	97	112	99	30	−8	5

Source: Adapted from Edelstein and Melnyk, 1982.

The Problem

The DPDA provides a picture of total fleet availability versus demand for a given day. Demand and availability may have to be adjusted to guarantee a car for each customer. This overall adjustment needs to be refined. It may be necessary to develop a demand control measure at a major airport by limiting reservations.

The amount of such demand control depends on the specific hourly rental patterns.

The number and distribution of check-ins for that day must also be considered. Other factors affecting fleet availability, such as the number of cars returning from maintenance, new arrivals, or cars leaving the fleet, must also be evaluated.

The Process

Several times a day, the manager enters data on the current status of his business—the number of cars available and a forecast of

TABLE 16.5

Corrected Fleet Distribution

	City # 1						
	Monday	Tuesday	Wednesday	Thursday	Friday	Saturday	Sunday
Idle	443	163	44	42	110	247	81
Check-ins	195	321	441	492	653	186	339
Intercity transfers	80	40	0	0	0	0	0
Available fleet	621	524	484	533	763	431	412
Demand projection	570	500	481	447	500	380	400
Cars left over	51	24	3	86	263	151	12

	City # 2						
	Monday	Tuesday	Wednesday	Thursday	Friday	Saturday	Sunday
Idle	70	82	49	12	26	16	10
Check-ins	94	72	79	106	65	75	65
Intercity transfers	−44	−40	0	0	0	0	0
Available fleet	120	112	127	116	90	92	74
Demand projection	99	95	76	76	79	88	69
Cars left over	21	17	51	40	11	4	5

Source: Adapted from Edelstein and Melnyk, 1982.

rentals and check-ins for the rest of the day. The model uses this input, as well as the relative pattern based on rental and check-in flow histories, to determine fleet availability hour by hour. A sample report is shown in Table 16.6. The report predicts no cars available for the midday hours. This advance notice of an expected shortage allows local management to augment the fleet with transfers, accelerated repair work, and other supply tactics.

Perspective

All fleet-related decisions throughout the country are made with these systems. Fleet plans generated by the FPM are the basis for generating orders for new cars and for disposing of vehicles. These plans are reviewed several times a month, with a planning horizon of 1 year in each city in the country. Plans are revised and results are continuously evaluated. The system has great flexibility to focus on specific

TABLE 16.6 Anticipated Hourly Fleet Distribution	Hours	Start	Check-ins	Adjust	Avail. fleet	Rentals	Cars Left
	AM 7–8	180	20	0	200	43	156
	8–9	156	17	0	173	53	120
	9–10	120	17	26	163	63	101
	10–11	191	15	0	116	64	−51
	11–12	51	17	−5	63	84	−20
	PM12–1	0	20	0	20	82	−62
	1–2	0	27	−20	7	19	−12
	2–3	0	37	0	37	5	−32
	3–4	32	54	30	116	8	108
	4–5	108	61	0	169	50	119
	5–6	119	42	0	161	21	140
	6–7	140	32	0	174	13	161
	7–8	161	15	0	176	40	136
	8–9	136	10	0	146	18	128
	9–10	128	10	0	138	18	120
	10–11	120	2	0	123	5	118
	11–12	118	2	0	120	6	114

Source: Adapted from Edelstein and Melnyk (1982).

regions and diversified markets. Emerging trends can be analyzed, identified, and adjusted to. Senior management can "pull up" the latest fleet plan for any city in the country at any time. This flexibility stimulates analysis and leads to better fleet planning.

The DPDA has been used successfully to manage special events such as the Olympics, the Superbowl, the Florida Christmas season, and business conventions in a number of cities.

If a competitor runs out of cars or stops taking reservations, the impact on Hertz's business can be quite significant. The model allows the company to adapt to these circumstances.

The success of these models demonstrates how system technology can be applied creatively to a complex business environment. The keys to success are field involvement from the outset, user-oriented design, and strong senior management support.

Adapted from "Decision Support Models for Fleet Planning" by M. Edelstein and M. Melnyk, The Hertz Corporation. In *Decision Support Systems*, ed. M.J. Ginzberg, W. Reitman, and E.A. Stohr. New York: North Holland, 1982.

Case Study Questions

1. How does Hertz's DSS fit into the decision-making process? How does this system differ from an MIS system?
2. What are the strategic implications and uses of the Hertz system? How might such a system be used to gain strategic advantage?
3. How does senior management use the data created by the DSS?
4. What are the major risks and weaknesses of this model when it is used for tactical (short-term) decision-making? What other sources of data would you want to consider in planning weekly and daily demand and fleet supply?

References

Alter, Steven. "A Taxonomy of Decision Support Systems," _Sloan Management Review_, Vol. 19 (Fall 1977).

Bonzcek, R.H., Holsapple, C.W., and Whinston, A.B. "Representing Modeling Knowledge with First Order Predicate Calculus," _Operations Research_ (1982).

Canning, Richard. "Interesting Decision Support Systems," _EDP Analyzer_, (March 1982).

Donovan, J.J., and Madnick, S.E. "Institutional and Ad Hoc Decision Support Systems," _Data Base_, Vol. 8 (Winter 1977).

Ginzberg, M.J., Reitman, W.R., Stohr, E.A. (editors) _Decision Support Systems_. New York: North Holland Publishing Co., 1982.

Ginzberg, Michael J., and Stohr, Edward A. "Decision Support Systems: Issues and Perspectives," in _Decision Support Systems_, ed. M.J. Ginzberg, W.R. Reitman, and E.A. Stohr. New York: North Holland, 1982.

Henderson, John C., and Schilling, David A. "Design and Implementation of Decision Support Systems in the Public Sector," _MIS Quarterly_ (June 1985).

Keen, Peter G.W. "Interactive Computer Systems for Managers: A Modest Proposal," _Sloan Management Review_, Vol. 18 (Fall 1976).

Keen, Peter G.W., and Scott Morton, M.S. _Decision Support Systems: An Organizational Perspective_. Reading, Mass.: Addison-Wesley, 1982.

King, John. "Successful Implementation of Large Scale Decision Support Systems: Computerized Models in U.S. Economic Policy Making," _Systems Objectives Solutions_ (November 1983).

Meador, Charles L., and Keen, Peter G.W. "Setting Priorities for DSS Development," _MIS Quarterly_ (June 1984).

Meador, Charles L., and Ness, David N. "Decision Support Systems: An Application to Corporate Planning." _Sloan Management Review_, Vol. 15 (Winter 1974).

Sanders, G. Lawrence, and Courtney, James F. "A Field Study of Organizational Factors Influencing DSS Success," _MIS Quarterly_ (March 1985).

Sprague, R.H., and Carlson, E.D. _Building Effective Decision Support Systems_. Englewood Cliffs, N.J.: Prentice-Hall, 1982.

C H A P T E R 17

Artificial Intelligence: Business Applications

OUTLINE

(Continued on next page.)

Aldo Cimino is nearing retirement, and the Campbell Soup Company is worried. Mr Cimino, who has worked for Campbell for 44 years, is the only employee who knows everything there is to know about the 72-foot-high cookers that fill up to 800 soup cans a minute at Campbell factories.

Late last year, a number of software engineers began interviewing Mr. Cimino, trying to organize and codify a lifetime's worth of experience and knowledge about how to can soup. The idea was to capture his expertise in an inexpensive computer system so that problems of production could be diagnosed instantly simply by asking maintenance workers a few questions.

As Mr. Cimino noted, "You have only a short period of time to correct problems with the cookers. Otherwise, you lose the soup." Mr. Cimino appeared on a televised symposium produced by the Texas Instruments Corporation, which is designing an expert system for the Campbell Soup Company. More than 34,000 people, including production experts from General Motors, tuned in all day to the Texas Instruments seminar, trying to learn how to build expert systems for their companies.

Adapted from "Computers Are Getting Smarter," *The New York Times*, December 15, 1985.

The Boeing Company faced a similar problem. The typical design of a large aircraft has a life span of 10 years. In the late 1970s, Boeing's management realized that two of its key aircraft designs—models 57 and 67—were reaching the end of their life at the very time when several senior tool design engineers were due to retire. This raised the prospect of having to rely on a young, untried generation of designers to design the next cycle of aircraft.

Boeing first tried to create design teams that paired junior and senior engineers, with each team using its own CAD work station. This proved to be a good short-term solution, but Boeing still wanted more effective and dependable ways to disseminate expertise among its workers. The company wanted to prevent valuable knowledge from being lost when individual workers retired. As a result, Boeing developed a dozen expert systems: computer programs that mimic the problem-solving and goal-oriented thought processes of human experts.

In 1983, Boeing was one of the first large American corporations to open its own artificial intelligence center at its information systems education facility in Belleview, Washington. The center conducts research for Boeing in robotics, expert systems, natural languages, and voice simulation.

Twelve large expert systems are currently under development at Boeing, including a helicopter repair advisor, a deep-space station designer, a system to diagnose airplane engine troubles, and a program that advises division managers on data-based management system purchases.

Adapted from Elisabeth Horwitt, "Exploring Expert Systems," *Business Computer Systems*, March 1985.

Boeing and Campbell Soup illustrate the kinds of projects that Fortune 500 companies are pursuing in the area of artificial intelligence. The student should be aware of developments in this field and their potential impact on organizations.

In this chapter the student will learn:
- What artificial intelligence is and is not.
- The various types of artificial intelligence efforts.
- Why businesses are interested in artificial intelligence.
- What expert systems are.
- How to build expert systems.

17.1 Introduction

The effort to use computers to understand or imitate aspects of human intelligence began in the 1950s. In 1956 Marvin Minsky (now at MIT), Claude Shannon of Bell Laboratories, and other innovators in the early study of computers and intelligence met at a conference at Dartmouth College. John McCarthy, then an assistant professor of mathematics at Dartmouth, coined the term *artificial intelligence* for the theme of the conference. The conference's high point was the unveiling of what some people thought was the first expert system, Logic Theorist. It processed nonnumerical symbols instead of crunching numbers, and it proved several theorems in the *Principia Mathematica* of Alfred North Whitehead and Bertrand Russell. No magazine would publish the proof of the theorems because it had been produced by a machine. This was the first software that claimed to have properties of artificial intelligence.

Ever since that time, skeptics, pundits, journalists, and serious scholars have argued over what artificial intelligence means.

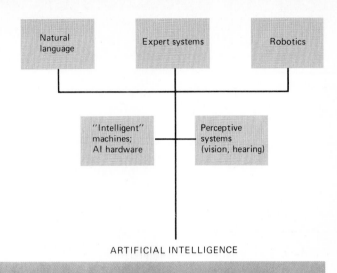

Natural language

Expert systems

Robotics

"Intelligent" machines; AI hardware

Perceptive systems (vision, hearing)

ARTIFICIAL INTELLIGENCE

FIGURE 17.1
Artificial intelligence family tree.

What Artificial Intelligence Is and Is Not

Artificial intelligence is commonly defined as the effort to develop computer-based systems (both hardware and software) that behave as humans. Such systems would be able to learn natural languages; accomplish coordinated physical tasks (robotics); develop and utilize a perceptual apparatus that informs their physical behavior and language (visual and oral perception systems); and, finally, exhibit logic, reasoning, and intuition, qualities that we associate with human beings. Figure 17.1 illustrates the elements of the artificial intelligence family tree. A fifth important element here is the physical hardware that performs these tasks.

The student can rest assured that no system yet developed comes close to possessing any of these human qualities. What has been developed is nevertheless of profound interest.

Artificial intelligence is without doubt the most controversial subject in computer science and information systems circles, as well as in the broader community of scholars and decision makers.

Since the Renaissance, men and women, in their physical form and mental accomplishments, have been at the center of the cultural universe, the measure of all things. Now to be joined by a lowly machine, an artificial, inanimate object, represents a challenging cultural revolution that most persons resist.

Critics of the study of artificial intelligence argue that it is a waste of time and resources, a study dotted with significant failures and few accomplishments, that succeeds only insofar as it denigrates the power and elegance of human thought processes. At worst, critics

The Artificial Intelligence Scam

Artificial intelligence is the snake oil of the information age. This is not the first time a tribe of wild-eyed academics has stormed down from the hills to take over the real world. Many will remember the early claims of total management information systems in which managers would sit a la NORAD (North American Air Defense Command) and direct their corporations. This kind of MIS was simply out of sync with the reality of decision making in corporations.

Expert systems can be helpful. We need packages with the experience and expertise of nuclear physicists and airline tariff wizards. What we don't need is the snake oil hype—the notion that in some mysterious way a logic processor and an-as-yet-unwritten expert system generator will magically extract the expertise of humans by watching them.

AI is a bust. The Tokyo bureaucracy is cutting fifth generation funding. People have discovered that computer chess involves no AI whatsoever. Real success will not happen. There is little in the bag for real problems in real organizations out in the real world. What is good—expert systems—is not new and requires the same grinding effort and understanding of the computer that all the earlier advances in the field demanded.

Adapted from Herb Grosch, "The Artificial Intelligence Scam," *Management Technology*, March 1984. Grosch is a Swiss-based consultant who has been prominent in the development of systems since 1935.

argue, artificial intelligence insults the very nature and role of human beings.

Moreover, critics point out, the current media fascination with machines that think obscures the fact that leading artificial intelligence thinkers have been wrong in the past. More than a quarter of a century ago, Herbert Simon and Alan Newell (1958) claimed: "There are now in the world machines that think, that learn, and that create. Moreover, their ability to do these things is going to increase rapidly until—in the visible future—the range of problems they can handle will be coextensive with the range to which the human mind has been applied." Not even the most ardent supporters of artificial intelligence today believe that such machines are now available or likely to be in the foreseeable future.

A New Knowledge Transfer Technology

For nearly 500 years, books have been the primary means of retaining and transmitting knowledge. But passive books cannot explain their knowledge. AI systems can. Knowledge transfer in the past has been a major human bottleneck. The computer has created both the need and the opportunity to enhance knowledge distribution through knowledge-based expert systems.

There are three major trends. First, AI will spawn many new products. Second, knowledge engineering will rapidly penetrate industrial and commercial organizations. Third, knowledge systems will be more closely integrated with data processing.

AI will create widespread home banking and financial planning; a centralized electronic university; the replacement of the library-as-archive by the library as information-network-access-node; electronic accountants and consultants; expert-to-expert and company-to-company knowledge transfers.

In the long run, knowledge systems will increase individual and social potential by preserving know-how, distributing knowledge more effectively, and improving the performance of tasks that require expertise.

Adapted from Frederick Hayes-Roth, "Knowledge Based Expert Systems," in *Spectrum of the IEEE*, October 1984. Hayes is the cofounder and chief scientist of Teknowledge, Inc., a major artificial intelligence firm.

Supporters of the study of artificial intelligence point to the noble goal of using it as a way of understanding human intelligence and as a vehicle for distributing expertise. Artificial intelligence systems, if they could be developed, might lead to a quantum leap in social wealth and well-being. It has been claimed that several successful artificial intelligence systems have been developed that work in the real world. These successes support the further commitment of resources.

The new technology, supporters argue, will increase individual and social potential by distributing knowledge more widely.

Supporters dismiss the critics as Luddites standing in the way of science and technology, which they see as supporting the rapid

"No plausible claim to intellectuality can possibly be made in the near future without an intimate dependence on this new instrument [artificial intelligence]. Those intellectuals who persist in their indifference, not to say snobbery, will find themselves stranded in a quaint museum of the intellect, forced to live petulantly, and rather irrelevantly, on the charity of those who understand the real dimensions of the revolution and can deal with the new world it will bring about."

Adapted from Edward A. Feigenbaum and Pamela McCorduck, *The Fifth Generation: Artificial Intelligence and Japan's Computer Challenge to the World*. Reading, Mass: Addison-Wesley, 1985.

exploitation of artificial intelligence. History, they argue, is propelling artificial intelligence forward.

Manufacturers of artificial intelligence software and hardware have established impressive growth patterns; the sales of some companies are growing at a rate of 50–70% per year. Extrapolating from their initial success, they have issued provocative predictions about the future in which artificial intelligence is seen as an ineluctable juggernaut sweeping the field. The head of IBM's artificial intelligence group recently claimed that IBM surveys of market potential indicate that "The MIPS [million instructions per second] spent on knowledge processing will surpass MIPS spent on data processing" sometime in the 1990s (*Government Computer News*, September 12, 1986).

The largest manufacturer of dedicated artificial intelligence machines, Symbolics, Inc., has sold 2000 of its Symbolics 3600 machines—about 60% of all such AI machines. This machine uses a special language, LISP, and enormous power (a 36-bit processor that can address up to 30 megabytes of RAM memory and up to 1 gigabyte of virtual memory) to create expert artificial intelligence systems. The president of Symbolics, Inc., Russell Noftsker, sees a bright future for his firm and for the artificial intelligence industry.

In this chapter, we will try to avoid making judgments about whether artificial intelligence is a worthwhile pursuit. Instead, we will give the views of both critics and supporters, as well as some real-world examples. The student can decide whether artificial intelligence is a worthwhile pursuit with potential real-world benefits.

AI Moves Into the Mainstream

By 1990 knowledge-based advisory systems built and delivered on symbolic processing machines will be the ground floor, even in general-purpose computing. This is an unstoppable trend.

Commercial uses of the computer right now are primarily for managing and digesting records—processing those records to enhance management understanding. In the near future, more intelligence will reside in the system.

The system should draw conclusions and tell you what's going on in your business, as opposed to just running out reams of paper that you have to dig through and understand. DP shops are looking for these kinds of capabilities now.

Adapted from "Pushing AI Into the Mainstream," *Computerworld*, February 24, 1986.

Human and Artificial Intelligence

Before describing artificial intelligence, it is worthwhile to distinguish more fully between *artificial* and *human* intelligence.

Much of the controversy that surrounds artificial intelligence results from the poor choice of words used to describe the activity. The term *artificial intelligence* is flamboyant and provocative. If the term *advanced programming* had been used in 1956 by John McCarthy to describe the Logic Theorist, much of the controversy might never have occurred. However, most of the public interest and funding might also have disappeared.

Successful artificial intelligence systems are neither artificial nor intelligent. This raises the question, "what would a truly *artificial* intelligent system look like?" A thermostat or an autopilot are the best examples of systems that solve problems in a goal-oriented, machine-like, artificial way. Yet no one calls thermostats or autopilots intelligent.

All successful artificial intelligence systems are based on human expertise, knowledge, and selected reasoning patterns (syllogisms, rules of thumb, etc.). Successful artificial intelligence systems are, if anything, "naturally" intelligent. They act like textbooks. Indeed, it will be shown that artificial intelligence systems can be developed only when human knowledge can be effectively expressed in simple textbook form (e.g., "if x, then do y"). Successful artificial intelligence systems—like textbooks—cannot learn without being rewritten. Existing artificial intelligence systems do not come up with new and novel solutions to problems.

Now let us examine *human* intelligence. As it turns out, human intelligence is vastly complex and much broader than computer or information systems. Philosophers, psychologists, and other students of human cognition have all recognized that key aspects of human intelligence are beyond description and therefore are not easily imitated by a consciously designed machine. If a problem cannot be described, it cannot be programmed. At least four important capabilities are involved in human intelligence: reasoning, behavior, the use of metaphor and analogy, and the creation and use of concepts.

- *Human intelligence is a way of reasoning.* One part of human intelligence can be described as the application of rules based on human experience and genetics. (Whether this rule-governed behavior takes the form "if *x*, then *y*" is not known.) These rules, although not always consciously invoked, are an important part of the knowledge carried by all human beings as an inheritance from the broader culture and the human gene pool.
- *Human intelligence is a way of behaving.* Even if humans do not actually invoke rules, they are obligated to act as if they did by a culture and a society that values reasonable, intelligent behavior. Human intelligence, at the very least, consists of acting in a way that can be described as intelligent.
- *Human intelligence is the development and use of metaphors and analogies.* What distinguishes human beings from other animals is their ability to develop associations and to use metaphors and analogies such as "like" and "as". Using metaphor and analogy, humans create new rules, apply old rules to new situations, and at times act intuitively and/or instinctively without rules.
- *Human intelligence involves the creation and use of concepts.* It has long been recognized that humans have a unique ability to impose a conceptual apparatus on the world around them. Meta-concepts such as cause and effect and time, and concepts of a lower order such as breakfast, dinner, and lunch, are all imposed by human beings on the world around them. Thinking in terms of these concepts, or "frames," and acting on them are central characteristics of intelligent human behavior.

Artificial intelligence, then, refers to an effort to develop machines that can reason, behave, compare, and conceptualize, as just described. While this may be a noble effort, clearly none of the successful systems described in this chapter come close to achieving this form of human intelligence. What has been developed is, however, of interest. Moreover, no theoretical proof or empirical evidence prevents the development of systems capable of exhibiting some kinds of intelligent behavior.

FIGURE 17.2
Evolution of artificial intelligence. Artificial intelligence has evolved toward more limited and specific goals.

General Problem Solvers "Logic theorist"	Power Approach Chess players Decision tree analysis		Applied AI Expert systems Robotics Perception systems Natural language Parallel processors, neural net machines	
1950	1960	1970	1980	1990

The Development of Artificial Intelligence

Artificial intelligence has gone through three stages (see Figure 17.2). Much of the early work was characterized by the development of weak methods and general problem solvers. The Logic Theorist previously described was an example of efforts in the 1950s to develop machines that would exhibit some general characteristics of human problem solving. Researchers recognized that problem solving involved moving toward a goal or solution. Programming a machine to try out various solution paths, or means to a goal, was one of the early conceptual methods used to build intelligent systems.

Systems in this period faced two problems. Problem-solving skills could not be described well or transferred from one field to another, and the machines were not big enough to try enough alternatives rapidly.

In the 1960s, third-generation hardware provided what seemed to be a solution in the form of greater storage capacity and much higher speeds. These more powerful machines were applied to the old paradigm of evaluating all alternative paths to a goal until the right one was found.

At the same time, what was thought to be an interesting problem changed. Instead of evaluating a few hundred alternatives, researchers became interested in truly mammoth problems, like chess where there may be 10^{120} possible moves at various points in the game. An extremely large, fast machine is needed to evaluate all of these alternatives. Indeed, the problem is beyond the capability of the largest supercomputer today.

A key innovation of the 1960s was the search for heuristics, or rules for pruning the number of alternatives to be evaluated in chess programs. Successful chess programs of the 1960s were the first to embody expert knowledge in the form of rules that limited and guided the evaluation of alternative moves. Another advance in this period was the development of languages such as LISP that provided a more efficient programming environment to describe and work with rules. Chess programs today operate on large mainframes and can play at the master's level.

Despite these advances, researchers recognized that systems that could play chess were not useful for anything else. They did not exhibit any general form of intelligence. Moreover, the chess systems were not particularly intelligent. They still mechanically searched huge decision trees that required enormous computing power.

In the 1970s artificial intelligence entered its third and present stage: the expert systems or knowledge-based approach to artificial intelligence. Artificial intelligence researchers have given up the pursuit of a generalized problem-solving capability and are trying to develop more elegant approaches to the problem of intelligent behavior. Expert systems focus on systematically representing the knowledge and rules of highly limited and specific domains of human experience. Expert systems use these rules to arrive at known solutions to well-understood problems. Considerable computing power is required, but it is used to evaluate which rules apply to a given situation.

In the other areas of artificial intelligence, such as natural language, robotics, and visual systems, there has been a similar retreat from the early unattainable goals to more domain-specific areas. In the 1980s, natural language systems are being developed that are appropriate for limited areas such as office use; visual systems are being developed with highly limited applications, such as pattern recognition of maps and factory visual systems; and robots are being developed that look nothing like the androids of the 1950s but instead consist of a series of appendages that can assemble specific products in a specific setting.

Nevertheless, as the following story indicates, researchers have not given up the quest for a machine that can think and behave in a general sense like a human being. Unfortunately, the researchers cannot explain why the machine acts like human.

Computers That Come Close to Thinking

Scientists have now developed a radically new type of computer that can learn how to read—called a *neural net computer*. What distinguishes the neural net computer from regular computers is a radical departure in architecture. The design for all current computers was laid down by the mathematician John von Neuman in the 1940s. In this design there is a physical separation of the computer's memory and processor with a communications link in between. This provides for tight control but also slows the machine down because the processor spends most of its time waiting for data to be taken out of storage or sent back. The von Neuman computer could never attain the hyperfast speed required to attack some of the thorniest problems confronting science and engineering—such as how to recognize a face in a crowd.

The neural net computer avoids this bottleneck by mimicking the brain's fast web of interconnected neurons. When a neuron fires in the brain, it broadcasts a signal to thousands of other neurons, which in turn alert millions of others. In a second, entire regions of the brain are involved and processing happens everywhere at once.

Neural net computers do something similar, but on a smaller scale. The brain has an estimated 10 billion neurons and 1000 times that many interconnections, or synapses. The largest neural net machines have 250,000 processors and 5.5 million connections.

Some of these neural net machines are uncanny in their ability to act like humans. One small machine can teach itself how to read and speak. Starting out with babble, it can acquire overnight the language skills of a 6-year-old child. No one programs the machine except to tell it when it makes a mistake. After that, it is trial and error. The machine can process so many alternatives and possibilities of speech and words that eventually it will find the correct pattern of pronunciation, assuming that it has a human teacher.

A different neural computer designed by the California Institute of Technology and AT&T's Bell Laboratories can solve the very complicated traveling salesperson problem in a fraction of the time required by ordinary supercomputers. A computer called Wisard can learn to recognize images in much the same way people do.

Unfortunately, no one can fully explain how a neural network computer creates organized behavior on its own. "It's something that emerges from the local interactions in this incredible ensemble of interconnected components," says John Seely Brown, director of the Intelligence Systems Lab at Xerox Corporation. Somehow, "Important computational properties arise spontaneously," says John Hopfield, professor of biology and chemistry at CalTec.

Adapted from "Computers That Come Awfully Close to Thinking," *Business Week*, June 2, 1986.

Super Structure: IBM's New AI-Based Tool

IBM has developed a new AI tool that attempts to transform an unstructured mass (some would say mess) of COBOL code into elegantly structured, modern, standard COBOL. IBM claims that the new product can extend the life of programs by putting them into structured form, salvage large parts of old programs for reuse in modular form, and enforce software standards. IBM hopes that this will reduce the enormous resources devoted to maintaining old programs, freeing resources for new hardware and software development, and indirectly help the sales of IBM hardware. Especially critical is new hardware based on new architectures that will require rewriting of old programs. This product will ease the transition.

Adapted from "IBM's COBOL AI Tool May End Code Mess," *Computerworld*, September 12, 1985.

Why Business Should Be Interested In Artificial Intelligence—Why Worry?

Given the experimental nature, high costs (to be described more fully), and limited accomplishments of artificial intelligence systems, why should business be interested in them at this point? The most important reasons are the following:

- To preserve knowledge that might be lost through the retirement, resignation, or death of an acknowledged expert.
- To clone experts mechanically, so that their knowledge can be used to train and instruct others.
- To store information in an active form—to create a knowledge base—that many employees can examine, much like an electronic textbook or manual.
- To create a mechanism that is not subject to human feelings like fatigue and worry. This may be especially useful when jobs may be environmentally, physically, or mentally dangerous to humans. These systems may also be useful advisors in times of crisis (see the case study at end of this chapter).
- To eliminate routine and unsatisfying jobs that are currently held by human beings.

- To maintain the strategic position of a company in an industry. Expert systems, like other systems, can be used as a marketing device, to reduce the cost of production, or to improve existing product lines.

All of these contributions of artificial intelligence have potential strategic importance.

Clearly, most progress in artificial intelligence of direct relevance to general business has been made in expert systems. We will now describe these systems in greater detail.

17.2 Knowledge-Based Expert Systems

While manufacturing companies have traditionally focused on artificial intelligence for robots and vision systems to assist assembly, management and service industries in particular are more interested in expert systems.

Expert systems automate parts, and in some cases all, of the decision-making process. They are thus more like automated DSS and may be considered a special kind of DSS.

What Is an Expert System?

An *expert system* is a knowledge-intensive program (software) that solves a problem that normally requires human expertise. An expert system can merely assist decision making by asking relevant questions and explaining the reasons for adopting certain actions. Some of the common characteristics of expert systems are the following:

- They solve problems as well as or better than human experts.
- They use knowledge in the form of rules or frames.
- They interact with humans.
- They can consider multiple hypotheses simultaneously.

Expert systems are therefore different from thermostats and auto-pilots insofar as they attempt to base their actions on human knowledge.

It should also be clear what expert systems are not. Today expert systems are quite narrow, shallow, and brittle. They lack the breadth of knowledge and the understanding of fundamental principles of a human expert. Expert systems today do not "think" as a human being does. A human being perceives significance, works with abstract models of causality, and can jump to conclusions. Expert systems do not resort to reasoning from first principles, do not draw analogies, and lack common sense.

Paradox

Paradox is a relational database system for PCs that uses artificial intelligence techniques to guide the user through stages in the development of a database. The system, using menus, interacts with the user to create data files and data elements and to manipulate data files. Instead of the user having to specify all of the procedures for combining files, for instance, in Paradox the user specifies what information is wanted. The system then finds the information and writes a program to combine the files and display the results.

Above all, expert systems are not a generalized expert or problem solver. They typically perform very limited tasks, such as interpreting, diagnosing, planning, and scheduling, that can be performed by professionals in a few minutes or hours. Problems that cannot be solved by human experts in the same short period of time are far too difficult for an expert system.

Major Types of Expert Systems

The least expert or lowest-level expert systems are those that can be viewed as an *assistant*. This system helps a decision maker by doing the routine analysis and pointing out those portions of the work where human expertise is required. The assistant expert system, like a robot, does the tedious work while the human thinks. This kind of expertise is being built into some software, such as the Ansa Corporations' Paradox database management system for PCs.

A far more powerful assistant system is the Dipmeter Advisor System developed by Schlumberger Limited, a major oil industry service corporation that provides geological advice to drilling companies. Dipmeter reads charts produced by instruments lowered into new wells. After reading the charts, the system decides whether the well is likely to contain oil.

A second-level system is that of a *colleague*. With an expert system of this type, the user discusses the problem until a joint decision is reached. When the system is going wrong, the user adds more information to get it back on track. Financial Advisor, a system that falls into this category, will be described.

A third-level system is a *true expert system* that advises the user without question. Despite many popular discussions, there are no practical areas today in which decision making has been given over to an expert system.

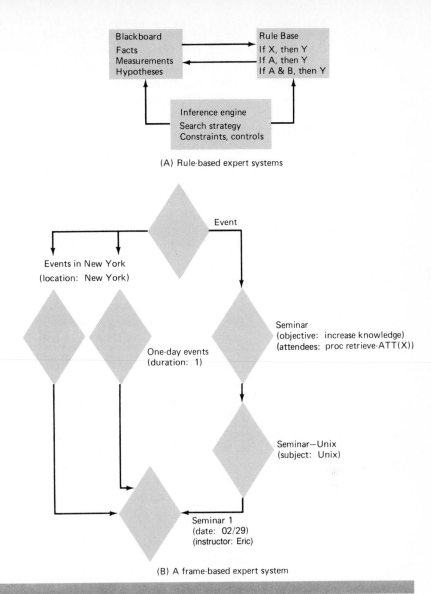

Blackboard
Facts
Measurements
Hypotheses

Rule Base
If X, then Y
If A, then Y
If A & B, then Y

Inference engine
Search strategy
Constraints, controls

(A) Rule-based expert systems

Event

Events in New York
(location: New York)

Seminar
(objective: increase knowledge)
(attendees: proc retrieve-ATT(X))

One-day events
(duration: 1)

Seminar—Unix
(subject: Unix)

Seminar 1
(date: 02/29)
(instructor: Eric)

(B) A frame-based expert system

FIGURE 17.3
Rule- and frame-based expert systems. The most common kinds of expert systems are rule-based and frame-based systems. (Adapted from Firdman, 1986.)

How Expert Systems Work

All expert systems use one of two techniques developed in the 1970s: rule-based systems and frame-based systems.

The basic structure of *rule-based systems* is depicted in Figure 17.3. The underlying assumptions of these systems are that an expert exists, that his or her skills can be extracted *effectively* as rules of thumb, and that these rules can be incorporated in an expert system through knowledge engineering. There are three components of rule-based systems: the rule base (also called the *knowledge base*), a blackboard (a listing of facts), and an inference engine (a program to search the rules and facts and come up with a solution).

The *rule base* is a collection of statements in the form "If *x* then *y*," where *x* represents a condition and *y* an action. In a business application, the rule base is a collection of business rules—the underlying decision criteria that are actually used to operate a business.

For instance, a business may decide to send employees to seminars only if the seminar is held within 250 miles of the company's location and if the employee shows an interest in attending. The two business rules related to seminars are as follows:

- *R1*. Send employees to seminars only if the seminar is held within 250 miles of the company's location.
- *R2*. Send employees to seminars only if they are interested in attending.

The *blackboard* in a rule-based system is a collection of facts about the real world. These facts are supplied by the user. In the preceding example, blackboard items would be "John Doe is an employee. John Doe works in New York. New York is 70 miles from a seminar on expert systems. John Doe is interested in attending the seminar on expert systems."

The *inference engine*, the only procedural part of the rule-based system, is the set of procedures that actually solves a given problem. The inference engine follows a predetermined strategy to search the rule base and the blackboard.

Two kinds of strategies guide the inference engine: forward chaining and backward chaining.

A forward-chaining strategy begins with a premise and looks through the rule base and the blackboard to find possible solutions. The machine tries to answer the question "What can be inferred from all of the elements on the blackboard by using all of the rules of the rule base?" To answer this question, a forward-chaining control mechanism matches the conditional part (*x*) of every rule with all of the elements on the blackboard. The action part (*y*) of any rule that matches the elements is added to the blackboard as a newly inferred fact. The process continues until the control mechanism can make no further inferences.

For instance, using our example, suppose we load the blackboard with the names of all of the employees in the company, the names of all seminars, the names of all seminars in which specific employees have indicated an interest, and a distance between all of these employees and all of the seminars. We can then construct a forward-chaining control mechanism to search the rule base. There it will find the two established business rules (if an employee lives within 250 miles of the seminar, and if the employee shows an interest in the seminar, the employee should be sent to the seminar). We can then instruct the computer, once it understands these two rules, to go back to the blackboard and create the set of employees who (1) live within 250 miles of a seminar and (2) have shown an interest in attending.

In contrast to a forward-chaining expert system, which begins with the question "What can be inferred from all of the elements in the data base and the rule base?", a backward-chaining control mechanism starts with a tentative solution (a hypothesis or goal) and then looks through the rule base and the blackboard to find justifications for that hypothesis. The question asked of a backward-chaining control mechanism is "Can the given hypothesis be justified by the elements on the blackboard and by applying the rules from the rule base?".

A backward-chaining control mechanism matches the hypothesis with the action part (y) of every rule. The conditional part (x) of any rule that matches the hypothesis is tested against the blackboard. Any match of a rule condition with a blackboard element justifies the hypothesis. All mismatches point out other possible hypotheses that the control mechanism can test in turn.

To continue our simple example, the hypothesis the system must test is: John Doe should attend the seminar on expert systems in Chicago. A backward-chaining expert system would then ask: "What are the rules in the rule base pertaining to attendance at seminars?". Once the system identifies the rules (the x conditions permitting attendance (y)), the system inquires: "Does John Doe work within 250 miles of Chicago and is he interested in the seminar?". Having searched the blackboard and found that the answer to both questions is yes, the expert system would then affirm the hypothesis.

Frame-based systems are different from rule-based systems and are a more recent innovation. Whereas rule-based systems stay within predefined boundaries, frame-based systems are dynamic entities that continually grow as the system attempts to model related knowledge entities. Figure 17.3 shows the elements of a frame-based system.

Frames are collections of knowledge that describe related concepts by listing each concept's features and showing the relationships to other concepts. *Slots* are specific pieces of information (typically, values and procedures) attached to frames. In Figure 17.3 the systems knowledge base consists of events and their characteristics (subject matter, objectives, duration, location, instructor, date, attendees). Each diamond on the diagram represents a frame and each set of brackets represents a slot. A frame-based system, then, is a collection of frames, each of which defines a concept from a different point of view or at a different level of abstraction.

An important control mechanism in frame-based systems is known as *inheritance* (the lines in the diagram that connect the frames). These inheritance mechanisms ensure that subclasses inherit the features and relationships of their superclasses. The expert system illustrated in Figure 17.3 understands that Seminar 1 takes place on April 29 and is taught by Paul, and also that it increases knowledge, lasts for 1 day, covers the topic of UNIX, and is held in New York.

Until recently, frame-based systems operated exclusively in research laboratories. However, these systems promise flexibility and the ability to relate a vast amount of information with only a few concepts.

Examples of Successful Expert Systems

There are many successful expert systems. However, there is no accepted definition of *successful*. What is successful to an academic ("It works!") may not be successful to a corporation ("It cost a million dollars!"). While some of the better-known expert systems are quite large and cost millions of dollars (Schlumberger's Dipmeter Advisor System is alleged to have cost $21 million over 10 years), others are less expensive and tackle interesting but smaller problems. Many of the most celebrated systems are not used to facilitate routine decision making. Finding out which successful systems are used on a daily basis is difficult because corporations treat this information as proprietary. Nevertheless, we can briefly describe some of the better-known commercial products.

- *Planned Design Management System* (*PDMS*) is a British engineering modeling software system that helps to design oil and gas production facilities. PDMS prompts the user for inputs and checks them for validity, commenting in a conversational manner when inputs are outside the expected limits. It submits a resulting file to a drafting program, which analyzes input data to select the drawing scale that will best display the design details.
- The Securities and Exchange Commission (SEC) requires that all publicly held companies submit detailed financial statements to the SEC on a monthly and a quarterly basis. These statements are used to investigate possible violations of security laws, but the financial information is of enormous utility to competitors and other persons interested in the financial health of firms. The Arthur Andersen Company developed an expert system to read corporate proxy statements with a sophistication unmatched by the average human investigator. When the system is asked to identify, for instance, companies that have taken actions in the past year to dodge a leveraged buy-out attempt, it searches for concepts rather than specific words, just as a knowledgeable investor would.
- *Weld Scheduler* is a system built by the Babcock & Wilcox Company of Lynchburg, Virginia. It specifies welding procedures and inspection requirements for the on-site construction of coal and oil-fired boilers. This system combines the expertise of design and welding

engineers. Its output is a set of instructions to welding technicians at the construction site. The system runs on an IBM PC.

- *Expert Publishing System* is an expert system built by Composition Systems, Inc., of Elmsford, New York. It is designed to eliminate the crisis atmosphere of daily newspaper operations. The system ties together advertising, page design, and production. It manages newspaper space allocation for ads and news, coordinates order processing from the sales and advertising offices, and gives advice on real-time, continuous page layout. This system also helps to configure the presses and mediates between the conflicting demands of the editorial, advertising, and production departments.

- *Credit Advisor* is a system built by Bruce Olson, vice president of Sea First Bank, Seattle, Washington. The system is designed to be used as a bank credit examiner. Three separate knowledge bases incorporate bank rules and policies for auto leasing installment loans, new car loans, and the bank's personal revolving line of credit system. Most consumer credit is granted according to a technique called *credit scoring*. Olson incorporated into his system 10 pages of scoring rules taken from a manual that accompanied the bank's computer software system. This expert system, taking information from the client, is used to coordinate the granting of credit to the client in all three areas in which the bank is involved. (*Computerworld*, July 14, 1986).

- *MYCIN* diagnoses and prescribes treatment for meningitis and bacteremia infections. It was developed by the Stanford University Medical Experimental Computer Facility in the mid-1970s.

- *Steamer* teaches naval officers, through simulation, the techniques needed to run a steam propulsion plant similar to those used in many ships. The U.S. Navy Personal Research and Development Center developed it in cooperation with Bolt, Beranek, and Newman in the 1980s.

- *R1* (also known as *XCON*) configures VAX-11/780 and other computers on a daily basis for the Digital Equipment Corporation (DEC). DEC and Carnegie-Mellon University first developed this system in the early 1970s.

- *Dendral* estimates the molecular structures of unknown compounds by analyzing mass spectrographic, nuclear magnetic resonance, and other data. Stanford University developed this system in the late 1970s.

- *Delta* uses diagnostic strategies to identify and help maintenance workers correct malfunctions in diesel locomotives. It was developed by General Electric in the early 1980s.

Table 17.1 describes other well-known expert systems in terms of their size and programming languages. As can be seen, these systems generally have at least several hundred rules. R1/XCON, for

TABLE 17.1

Well-Known Expert Systems

Name of System or Project	Brief System Description	Method of Verification	No. of Rules	Programming Language
Auditer	Selects procedures to be used by independent author	Scientific (blind verification by panel of experts) (BV)	Fewer than 50 (experimental)	AL/X
Crib	Diagnosis of faults in computer hardware and software	Field use	1500	Coral and Plan
Heuristic Dendral	Identification of organic compounds by analysis of mass spectrograms	Field use	400	Interlisp
MYCIN	Diagnoses certain infectious diseases and recommends appropriate drugs	Scientific (BV)	400	Interlisp
Prospector	Aids geologists in evaluating mineral sites for potential deposits	Field use	Largest Knowledge base; 212 assertions and 133 inference rules	DEC 10
Puff	Analyzes results of pulmonary function tests for evidence of disorder	Field use	250	Emycin
R1	Configures the VAX-11/780 computer system	Field use	772	OPS4 (implemented in MACLISP)
Raffies	Diagnoses faults in computer hardware and software	Field use	Precompiles the data base for CRIB	Coral and LISP
Sacon	Advises structural engineers in using the structural analysis program MARC	Field use	170	Emycin (implemented in Interlisp)
Taxadvisor	Provides estate planning recommendations for clients	Scientific (BV)	275	Emycin (implemented in Interlisp)
VM	Provides care suggestions for patients needing breathing assistance	Field use	120	Interlisp

Adapted from Robert Michaelson and Donald Michie, "Expert Systems in Business," *Datamation*, November 1983.

example, started out with 772 rules but has expanded to about 3500. Many expert systems not listed here did not succeed.

Approaches and Tools for Expert Systems

There are three general approaches to expert systems: purchase of fully developed systems, purchase of artificial intelligence shells, and custom-built systems.

One approach to expert systems is to buy a system that has been fully developed for a specific application. One well-known system is the *Financial Advisor System* produced by Palladian Software, Inc., of Cambridge, Massachusetts. Financial Advisor helps executives analyze a proposed investment in a new plant, warehouse, or product, or even the acquisition of another company. The system has gathered the expertise of financial analysts in many corporations and made this knowledge base (set of rules) available to other corporations. The system runs on a Texas Instruments Explorer or Symbolics 3600 and uses data from an IBM or DEC mainframe.

Here is how the system works. Assume that a company is thinking about marketing a new product. When it is first released, the product will have no direct competition. If it is successful, however, competitors can be expected to bring out similar products in a short time.

To analyze this situation, the first step is to build a business case for the product. The system helps managers and staff to create this business case by asking for data to be entered: the equipment that will be used to produce the product, the capital cost, the plants that will be used, how many people will be needed, the useful life of the equipment, the discount rate, and so forth.

Compare this approach to that of an ordinary spread sheet. With a spread sheet the user has to know all of the factors to be included in the business plan. With an expert system such as Financial Advisor, the many factors that should be considered in any investment are included by the system. Some of the intelligence thus lies in the system, not in the user. On the other hand, if the user does not want to consider a factor or wants to enter new, nonstandard factors, the system can be adjusted.

When the business case is built, the analysis starts. The year-by-year net cash flow is computed and displayed graphically. The discounted cash flow is also computed. At this point, the user begins to interact with the system by changing some of the variables. If a discounted cash flow tends toward zero or even goes negative, the human analyst can make some changes. Perhaps less expensive equipment can be used. The cheaper equipment will have a shorter useful life, and the system will ask for the new useful life. The cheaper equipment will require earlier replacement, and the system will automatically factor this information into its calculation of cash flow. The system will also ask about various competitive responses

TABLE 17.2
Expert System Tools

Area	Name	Vendor	Applications
End-user applications	Questware	Dynaquest	PC hardware and software selection
	Logician	Daisy	Electronic design
	TKI Solver	Software Arts	Equation solving
	SMP/Macsyma	Inference Symbolics	Mathematical simplification and problem solving
Commercial Applications tools	S.1	Teknowledge	Industrial diagnostic and structured selection problems
	M.1	Teknowledge	Microcomputer tool for small expert system applications
Research and experimentation	KEE	Intellicorp	Extended programming environment; frames
	Art	Inference	Varied representations and inference techniques
	Rosie	Rand Corp.	Legible, intelligible symbolic programming language
	KL-Two	BBN, ISI	Knowledge representation schemes
Support systems	Commonlisp	DEC, LMI, Symbolics	New attempt to standardize LISP
	Interlisp	Xerox, ISI	Mature programming environments
	Franzlisp	Berkeley	Unix-based LISP
	Machines	LMI, Xerox, Symbolics	Integrated graphics, personal work station
	Prolog	Expert Systems, LMI	Formal semantics, logic-based programming language

Source: Adapted from Frederick Hayes-Roth, "Knowledge Based Expert Systems," *Spectrum IEEE*, October 1984.

and then compute the critical values. This process can be repeated at higher levels of management and by different managers individually as they probe the effects of changes in the assumptions on the final outcome.

Financial Advisor provides an excellent example of an intelligent DSS. It can also be seen how close DSS as a concept is to expert systems. Unlike the interaction with a DSS, users of an expert system are systematically led through a set of assumptions and exposed to a body of knowledge that is much broader than their own. Nevertheless, the difference between a DSS and an expert system is one of degree, not concept.

A second approach to expert systems is to build a new one using an *artificial intelligence shell*. (Table 17.2 describes expert system tools at various levels, ranging from shells to programming languages.) A *shell* is a piece of software that uses a predetermined strategy (backward chaining or forward chaining) and a limited, reasonably user-friendly language to develop small expert systems. With artificial intelligence shells the user has to supply the knowledge to the system. This is very different from buying a packaged expert system, as previously described.

A good example of an expert system shell is M.1, manufactured by Teknowledge, Inc., of Palo Alto, California. This system sells for $10,000 and operates on large PCs. While the price may seem high, it is considerably less than the $100,000 to multi-million-dollar systems that operate on mainframes.

M.1, according to the manufacturer, is best suited to structured selection applications. Teknowledge defines such problems as those that a human expert can solve in less than 30 minutes, do not involve extensive calculations, can be solved through a telephone discussion with an expert, and have only a few dozen conclusions to choose from.

In general, M.1 can be used to create "intelligent manuals" that clients can consult in a question-and-answer fashion. The demonstration disk of M.1's capabilities includes a wine advisor (which recommends what type of wine to serve with meals), a bank services advisor (which matches banking requirements with bank services), and a photography advisor (which uses information about environmental conditions to recommend which shutter speed and film type to use).

Artificial shells come in all shapes and sizes. Lightyear (from Lightyear, Inc.) is not a true expert system but rather helps the decision maker to define and weight criteria. Lightyear is a more common decision analysis tool. Figure 17.4 illustrates how a decision maker faced with a coup d'etat in Oceania might use Lightyear to analyze alternatives and constraints. A much more tightly rule-governed decision tree is illustrated by the use of M.1 to diagnose a problem with a PC monitor (Figure 17.5). M.1 comes much closer to

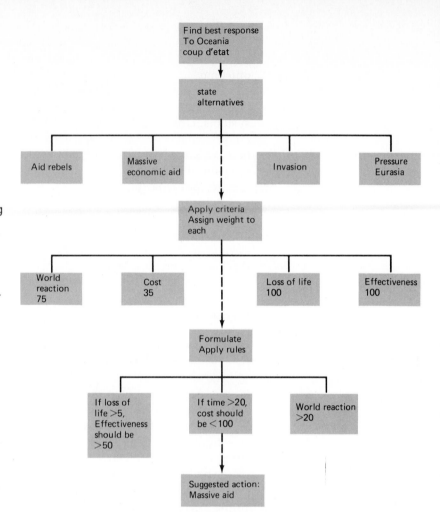

FIGURE 17.4
Example of decision-modeling software. Lightyear is not a true expert system but rather decision-modeling software designed to help make hard choices among similar or related alternatives. Lightyear forces decision makers to identify the alternatives, formulate and weight key decision criteria, apply the criteria to the alternatives, and then suggest a choice. The user may also invoke a number of constraints or rules regarding the possible outcomes. A true expert system would identify clearly the specific rules that lead to each alternative. (Adapted from *PC Magazine*, 1985.)

what is commonly thought of as an expert system in which most of the knowledge is embedded in the system.

The fundamental problem posed by expert systems is how to represent large amounts of knowledge in a manner that permits its effective use to solve problems. Not all human knowledge, perhaps not even most of it, can be captured in the form of "if-then" rules. Even the kind of knowledge that can be so expressed requires sensitive people to make it useful and understandable to others. Critical elements, then, in the usefulness of expert systems are the quality of the system's design and the ability of the project to modify itself over time as a deeper understanding of the problem is developed.

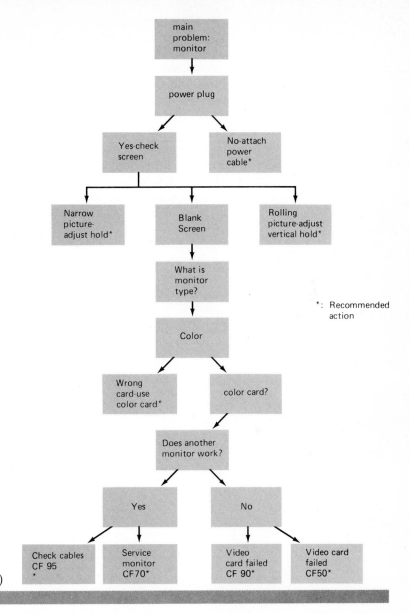

FIGURE 17.5
How M.1 solves a problem.
(Adapted from *PC Magazine*, 1985.)

A third approach is to have a "knowledge engineer" custom build an expert system. A knowledge engineer plays much the same role in developing an expert system that a systems analyst does in developing an application system. The knowledge engineer interviews the expert (or experts), develops the decision rules and knowledge frames, and builds the expert system. Large knowledge systems are created by knowledge engineers. These engineers acquire knowledge from a human expert and then seek to embed it in an expert system. Of necessity, knowledge engineers are specialists in getting information from experts, prototyping a system, and working with the experts to improve the system until a useful system has been created. This suggests a highly interactive and evolutionary approach to systems.

In building the system, the knowledge engineer may use a development tool such as an artificial intelligence shell. More commonly, however, a programming language such as LISP, Prolog, FORTRAN, or some other language that is useful in representing the knowledge will be used.

Knowledge engineers therefore need a highly developed ability to interview and understand experts in the knowledge domain. They must also have considerable knowledge of and experience with computer hardware and software. Generally, these projects involve one or a few knowledge engineers and a few experts. Only the largest corporations attempt to build extensive custom-developed systems.

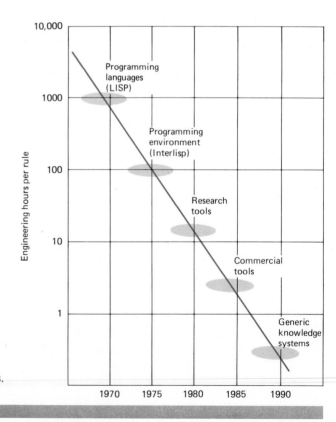

FIGURE 17.6
The efficiency of knowledge engineering tools, according to some experts, doubles every 2 years. (Adapted from Hayes-Roth, 1984.)

There is a very close parallel between knowledge engineers and traditional systems analysts. Systems analysts are typically concerned with actual and ideal business procedures. They spend most of their time identifying business procedures and specifying systems to automate them. To be sure, interactions with persons are an important part of their job, but not so important as for the knowledge engineer.

Knowledge engineers require a broader background than systems analysts in cognitive psychology, learning theory, and training in personal interviewing techniques.

Supporters of expert systems believe that with the development of better software, in a particular artificial intelligence shells, it will be feasible to codify more complex bodies of knowledge for use in expert systems. They argue that the efficiency of expert system tools has grown exponentially in recent years (see Figure 17.6).

17.3 An Expert System Life Cycle

An accepted systems development life cycle for expert systems has yet to be developed. One possibility suggested by some authors is a six-phase life cycle (see Figure 17.7). This cycle is not fixed; it may

Phase 1	Select appropriate problem	1–3 months, resulting in proposal
Phase 2	Development of prototype	6–9 months, resulting in prototype and design for complete system
Phase 3	Development of complete system	12–18 months, resulting in operational system
Phase 4	Evaluation/ calibration	12 months, resulting in adjustments to fit working environment
Phase 5	Integration of system	3 months, resulting in field-tested, fully operational system
Phase 6	Maintenance	Ongoing changes in rule base

FIGURE 17.7
A life cycle for expert systems. (Adapted from "The Engineers Behind Expert Systems," *Computerworld*, March 18, 1985, and updated by the authors.)

involve several iterations among the phases before a full system is developed. Each of these phases will now be described.

Phase 1: Selection of an Appropriate Problem

Phase 1 involves finding an appropriate problem for an expert system, identifying an expert to contribute the expertise, establishing a preliminary approach, analyzing the costs and benefits, and finally preparing a development plan.

Most expert systems focus on a narrow specialty. It is important to avoid problems that involve:

- Understanding English
- Complicated geometric or spatial models
- Complex causal or temporal models
- Understanding human intentions
- A knowledge of organizational history
- Common sense or background knowledge

The important point in the early design stage is to avoid complex problems that are beyond the provable expertise of the designers.

Generally, finding an appropriate problem will put the knowledge engineer in touch with experts throughout the company, who would like to develp systems based on their knowledge. Obviously, expert systems require an expert who can and will explain how he or she works. A tentative approach to a problem can then be formulated.

Once a task has been identified, the potential savings produced by such a system must be balanced against the cost. Table 17.3 shows

T A B L E 17.3
Resources Required to Develop an Expert System

Resources	Type of system		
	Small	Large	Very Large
Rules	50–450	500–3000	3000–10,000
Person–years needed for development	0.25–0.50	1–3	3–20
Project cost (including design and development staff, knowledge engineers, computing, and overhead).	$40,000–60,000	$200,000–1 million	$1–20 million

Source: Adapted from ''The Engineers Behind Expert Systems,'' *Computerworld*, March 18, 1985, and updated by the authors.

an estimate of tentative costs related to system size. As expert system software becomes more efficient, it should become less expensive. Currently, expert systems of any magnitude are very expensive.

Phase 2: Development of a Prototype System

A prototype system is a small version of an expert system designed to test assumptions about how to encode the facts, the relationships, and the knowledge of experts. The prototype permits the knowlege engineer to gain the expert's commitment and to develop a deeper understanding of the field of expertise. Other subtasks in this phase include the following:

- Learning about the domain and the task
- Specifying performance criteria
- Selecting an expert-system building tool
- Developing an implementation plan
- Developing a detailed design for a complete system.

Phase 3: Development of a Complete System

The development of a full-scale system is probably the most complex stage of the effort. The core structure of the complete system has to be identified; that is, the knowledge base has to be expanded to the full knowledge base appropriate to the real world, and the user interface has to be developed.

The main work in this phase is the addition of a very large number of rules. The complexity of the entire system grows with the number of rules, and the integrity of the system is threatened. A fundamental conflict develops in this period between faithfulness to the complexity of the real world and the comprehensibility of the system.

Generally, during this stage, the system is pruned to make it more realistic and suitable to the real world. Eliminating rules and achieving simplicity and power are important aspects of developing a complete system.

Phase 4: Evaluation of the System

When the expert and the knowledge engineer are satisfied that the system is complete, it can be tested against the performance criteria established in earlier stages. It is also time to unveil the system to the organization and to invite other experts to test the system and to present it with new cases.

Phase 5: Integration of the System

Once built, the expert system has to be integrated into the data flow and work patterns of the organization. New procedures usually have to be developed, along with new forms, new subunits in the organization, and new training procedures. In this stage, the expert system has to be interfaced with other databases, instruments, and hardware. The speed and friendliness of the system usually must be improved.

Phase 6: Maintenance of the System

As with any system, the environment in which an expert system operates is continually changing. This means that the expert system must also continually change. For example, the DEC system called R1 (EXCON) (described previously), which configures new VAX computers installations, must continually change as DEC adds new lines of computer equipment. A group of DEC experts constantly changes the rules of the system as new computer systems and equipment are manufactured. The highly modularized nature of the rule-based system makes modification feasible and ensures that the system is always current.

Very little is known about the long-term maintenance costs of expert systems. Some expert systems, especially large ones, are so complex that in a few years the maintenance costs will equal the development costs.

TABLE 17.4
Custom Development Life Span

Stage	System Components	Duration	Level of Effort	Cost
Proof of concept	Small, simple knowledge base; skeletal control logic; skeletal user interface; operable by developers; no documentation	4–6 months	1–2 man-years	$150,000 to $400,000
Demonstration	Medium-sized knowledge base of moderate complexity; skeletal control logic; rough user interface; operable by trained experts; internal documentation	4–6 months	1–2 man-years	$150,000 to $400,000
Prototype	Multiple, large knowledge bases; complete, complex control logic; complete user interface; operable by trained users; design documentation	12–18 months	8–12 man-years	$1.2 million to $2.4 million
TOTAL RESOURCE COMMITMENT		20–30 months	10–16 man-years	$1.5 million to $3.2 million

Figures are based on Arthur D. Little, Inc.'s, experience in developing more than 30 large, strategic, knowledge-based systems, typically for Fortune 500 companies.
Source: Adapted from Harvey P. Newquist III, "Expert Systems—the Promise of a Smart Machine," *Computerworld*, January 13, 1986.

In addition to the skills of a knowledge engineer, skillful project managers and outside consultants are generally required by expert system projects of any size. Few knowledge engineers today have enough experience to determine what problems a company should address. Much political work is needed in an organization to provide the funding for large-scale projects. The money and time required to develop expert systems are generally far greater than predicted by early advocates of expert systems.

Table 17.4 illustrates the costs and development time required for stages of systems, as determined by the management consulting firm Arthur D. Little, Inc. This company's interpretation of prototype is closer to what we have described as the full system. Nevertheless, large system projects require 10 to 16 person-years of development and cost $1.5 to $3.5 million.

17.4 Problems with Expert Systems

Expert Systems Are Limited to Certain Problems

A thorough understanding of expert systems also requires awareness of their current limitations and problems.

In answer to the question "Why do some expert systems work?", critics point out that virtually all successful expert systems deal with problems of classification in which a relatively few alternative outcomes are known in advance. Even in these comparatively simple situations, however, expert systems require large, lengthy, and expensive development efforts. For these kinds of problems, hiring or training more experts may be less expensive than building an expert system.

Some financial firms that were early investors in large expert systems, like the Metropolitan Life Insurance Company, have found them to be of dubious value.

Important Theoretical Problems Exist

There are significant theoretical problems in knowledge representation. "If-then" knowledge exists primarily in textbooks. There are no adequate representations for deep causal models or temporal trends. No expert system, for instance, can adequately employ deep causal models of interesting phenomena. No expert system can write a textbook on information systems or engage in other creative activities not explicitly foreseen by system designers.

Many experts cannot express their knowledge using an "if-then" format. Sometimes expert knowledge is intuitive, based on analogy, on a "sense of things" that expert systems cannot yet replicate.

Experts Beat Out Expert Systems at Financial Firms

Metropolitan Life Insurance Company built an expert system to perform the underwriting function on personal insurance policies. Underwriters typically evaluate a mass of information to determine the degree of risk to the company and the appropriate premium.

The giant insurance company found that it cost more to have someone transcribe 20–30 pages of medical information into the system than it did to have an underwriter evaluate the information. Insurance companies are now using wider pools of cases in determining actuarial figures, and the expert system could not easily be changed to reflect this situation.

Roger Jones, director of the project, said that the system was built as a technical proof and was never intended as a production model. It was simply a corporate objective to stay current in technology. After 2 years of effort, Jones concluded that nobody had written anything in 10 years that is new. All of the successful expert systems—Dendral, Prospector, Dipmeter—were developed 10–20 years ago. These early systems mapped a very broad base of knowledge with simple facts. The rules and knowledge at the core are very simple, much simpler than insurance underwriting, Jones argued. Most financial institutions are finding it cheaper to train their own human experts.

Adapted from "Experts Beat Out Expert Systems at Financial Firms," *Computerworld*, September 2, 1985.

There is little substantiation for the claim that expert systems' methods or tools are well suited to the emulation or support of human expertise in decision making. At best, this is a hypothesis. Labeling oneself a knowledge engineer does not necessarily confer any special skills in eliciting the human intelligence of an expert.

Many claim that the new profession of knowledge engineering is just another case of glamorizing the familiar with pretentious new terminology. There is no credible evidence, critics argue, that knowledge engineers have advanced our understanding or mastery of the problems of knowledge acquisition, representation, or use.

Expert Systems Are Not Applicable to Managerial Problems

The applicability of expert systems to managerial problems is currently highly limited. Managerial problems generally involve drawing facts and interpretations from divergent sources, evaluating the facts, and comparing one interpretation of the facts with another. Most managerial problems do not involve analysis or simple classification. Expert systems based on the prior knowledge of a few known alternatives are essentially unsuitable to the problems managers face on a daily basis.

Expertise Is Collective

For many problems there is no single expert. Expertise may be distributed throughout an organization. Coordinating this expertise to formulate policies and actions is a key focus of management efforts. Expert systems cannot help here because they cannot synthesize knowledge based on several different experts.

Expert Systems Are Expensive to Teach

The knowledge base of expert systems is fragile and brittle; it cannot learn or change over time. In fast-moving fields like medicine or the computer sciences, keeping the knowledge base up-to-date is a critical problem.

For applications of even modest complexity, expert systems code is generally hard to understand, debug, and maintain. For example, adding new rules to a large rule-based program nearly always requires revision of the control variables and conditions of earlier rules. Which of these entities must be changed to make the new rule work is often far from obvious.

A More Limited Role for Expert Systems

Even the critics point out, however, that research on artificial intelligence and expert systems is useful. It may be entirely appropriate that artificial intelligence researchers based in university laboratories continue contemplating toy problems and simplistic models of cognition to highlight certain themes and issues.

Morever, expert systems may be used as electronic checklists for lower-level employees in service bureaucracies like banking, insurance, sales, and welfare agencies. There is clearly a market for software products like Paradox that employ artificial intelligence-like features or simply for intelligent programs to help users. The market for these kinds of applications may be substantial.

But when it comes to more complex problems, many critics point out that it is a very long step from the classroom to the factory floor, to the battlefield, to the management of a Star Wars defense, or to the corporate boardroom.

17.5 Summary

Artificial intelligence involves the development of computer-based systems that behave like humans. Such systems would be able to use natural language, accomplish physical coordination, adjust

Expert Systems Are Oversold

The media blitz is on, and hype is coming from all sides. If you read the popular magazines, you get the message. AI, especially expert systems, is here, it's new, it's revolutionary, it's exciting. Jump now or get stuck on the sidelines with the also-rans.

But real-world experience to date finds that expert systems are costly, take a very long time to develop, and often involve trivial problems. The techniques of expert systems—production rules (if-then, so-called knowledge base), blackboards, the so-called inference engine—are not new. They are 20 or more years old.

Can AI techniques be applied successfully to real-world problems, like commanding the Strategic Defense Initiative (Star Wars) or making real management decisions? No. The commercial tools are largely irrelevant to serious problems of advanced computing. Current expert systems orthodoxy is a naive belief in a magical computing methodology for solving difficult problems.

Adapted from Gary Martins, "The Overselling of Expert Systems," *Datamation*, November 1, 1984. Martins is president of Intelligent Software, Inc., and former director of the Rand Corporation's R&D program, where he launched Rosie and Ross artificial intelligence language projects.

behavior in accordance with perceptions, and exhibit intelligent behavior. The field is controversial because of disagreements about the theory, practical worth, and social consequences of artificial intelligence.

Human intelligence is a way of reasoning, behaving, comparing, and conceptualizing that appears to be unique to the human species. No artificial intelligence systems even approximate these qualities. However, the work that has been done is profoundly interesting and may have significant commercial application, although not in the ways depicted in the popular media.

Artificial intelligence has gone through three stages. The first stage involved the search for general problem-solving systems. The second stage involved the use of high-powered machines to scan millions of alternatives. The third stage, knowledge-based or expert systems, involves the pursuit of more limited objectives. Expert systems focus on specific knowledge domains that can be expressed with a few rules and facts. Other areas of artificial intelligence, ranging from robots to vision systems, have also withdrawn from early, overly ambitious goals to pursue more modest goals such as assembly-line vision and assembly programs.

Most progress in artificial intelligence has been made in expert systems. Expert systems are knowledge-intensive computer programs that solve problems that heretofore required humans. Expert systems embody human knowledge, using either rules or frames or concepts. Because these systems actively use human knowledge in their programs, they differ from truly artificial intelligent systems like autopilots.

There are three kinds of expert systems: assistants, colleagues, and fully capable systems. These systems are either purchased already built for a specific area (e.g., finance), built using an artificial intelligence shell, or custom-built using one of several artificial intelligence languages.

There are many examples of successful systems, but there is little agreement about what constitutes success. Many of the most famous expert systems are not used on a day-to-day basis because they are too expensive to maintain or are not particularly good.

Expert systems, like other systems, have a typical development life cycle. This cycle has six stages and tends to be far more evolutionary than that of traditional systems because of the continual need to alter the system as it approaches real-world situations and uses.

There are clear-cut limitations to current expert systems. They apply only to limited classes of problems, are not well suited to managerial decision making, and are expensive to build and maintain. Yet expert systems can perform many lower-level tasks usefully and less expensively than humans can. And for many new applications there is no human counterpart because of the cost and convenience. The hostage advisor system described in the case study at the end of this chapter may be such an example.

Key Words

Artificial intelligence
Human intelligence
General problem solver
Expert system
Neural net computer
Knowledge-based system
Assistant system
Colleague system
Rule-based system
Rule base

Forward-chaining system
Backward-chaining system
Frame-based system
Blackboard
Inference engine
Frame
Artificial intelligence shell
Knowledge engineer
Expert system life cycle
Collective expertise

1. What are the five elements of artificial intelligence research?
2. What is the difference between artificial intelligence and natural or human intelligence? What devices use truly artificial intelligence?
3. Name four attributes of human intelligence. Can you think of four more?
4. What are the three periods in the development of artificial intelligence? Describe the key aspects of each period.
5. Give four reasons why business should be interested in artificial intelligence.
6. Give a good working definition of an expert system.
7. Describe three different roles for expert systems in their interactions with humans.
8. What is the difference between a rule-based system and a frame-based system?
9. What is meant by forward and backward-chaining expert systems?
10. Give three examples of successful expert systems. How many rules does each possess?
11. List important criteria used to gauge the success of expert systems.
12. Describe three approaches to the development of expert systems.
13. What is the difference between knowledge engineering and systems analysis?
14. Describe the six stages of the expert system life cycle.
15. Describe five tasks (or jobs) that are suitable for an expert system and five tasks that are not.

1. Find a task in an organization (near your university) that requires some intelligence to perform and that might be suitable for an expert system. Describe as many of the rules required to perform this task as possible. Interview and observe the person performing this task. Consider changing the task in order to simplify the system. What does this experience teach you about expert systems?
2. A famous person has declared that artificial intelligence will lead to a fundamental redistribution of knowledge because all persons will be able to have their own knowledge-based system, giving them access to knowledge that heretofore only experts have possessed. Comment.
3. The CEO, in an effort to cut middle management costs, has just announced a major effort to use artificial intelligence and expert systems to assist managers and if possible, through attrition, reduce the total cost of management. Comment.

A Hostage Negotiation Expert System

Expert systems are developed so that human knowledge and reasoning abilities can be brought to bear on organizational or social problems by computers. One promising area for expert systems development is crisis management. Expert systems might ameliorate tragic incidents such as the following:

On July 23, 1984, near Tucson, Arizona, a 41-year-old woman threatened to kill herself and her 7-year-old son. When Pima County police arrived, they tried to negotiate with her, but soon called a SWAT team and a psychiatrist. Before they could arrive, a shot was heard inside house. Then the woman came out and leveled a shotgun at the police. She was shot and killed after opening fire.

In these kinds of unstructured situations, the police have to make decisions rapidly. There is a coherent body of knowledge on hostage negotiation. The number of trained experts who can respond to these situations, however, is quite small. This is an ideal area for expert systems development and exploration.

We first had to chose an appropriate model for representing the knowledge and reasoning process of officers in the hostage-taking situation. We chose the production rule model; for example, if X, then Y, because early interviews and studies indicated that this was appropriate. Other alternatives were examined. Now that the system has been developed, the frame-based approach may provide a useful alternative.

We then needed to break down the hostage situation into its basic elements. There were six: (1) the hostage taking itself, (2) the data obtained from the incident, (3) the inferences and interpretations drawn from the data, (4) the values applied to those inferences and interpretations, (5) the choice of a response, and (6) the act of responding itself.

In the human situation, people gathered the data, made inferences, applied values and chose the response. In an expert system, some of these tasks are transferred to the computer. The expert system helps to gather facts and makes interpretations and inferences. Even values, like "deescalate situation," can be invoked by the system. The response, of course, is still in human hands.

After 6 months of reading and field work, the first test system was produced. Called the Hostage-taking Information and Tactics (HIT) expert system, the system works with screens and dialogue, as illustrated below.
Underlying this dialogue is a body of experiential knowledge gained from books, experts, and common sense. An expert from the Tucson Police Department critiqued early versions of HIT. His real-world knowledge was slowly built into the early textbook versions in a lengthy development process.

A number of new rules were added over time that are counterintuitive and that a rookie or untrained officer might not consider. For instance, the system recommends that male hostages be released before women and children because males put more pressure on hostage takers and threaten "macho" acts. Also, the system recommends that fast food not be sent to hostage takers, but rather uncooked food requiring preparation. Prior knowledge indicates that food preparation has a calming influence and creates a communal atmosphere.

The HIT system is by no means finished. It is a successful prototype that can be used as a training tool for police and for people who might become victims of hostage situations (e.g., airline crews, retail merchants). New versions must be developed before it can be used in the

Sample Dialogue From HIT

(Please answer the following questions with a Y (yes), N (no), U (unknown), or W (why) unless asked for a specific value, in which case you should respond with a W (why) or an appropriate value.

Are you the responding officer?   (Y)
Do you need help for an initial police response?   (N)
Has a containment perimeter been established?   (Y)
Has police dispatch been advised of the total situation?   (Y)
Has a command post been established?   (N)

The system responds:

Action: → Establish Command Post

1. Identify location for command post
2. Consider:
   a. Cover and concealment from incident point
   b. Ease of access by responding personnel
   c. Space or staging area.
3. Advise other personnel of location

field. A smaller, more powerful computer is needed that can be taken to the field. The unit must be battle hardened. Newer, more powerful software is needed to create interfaces with other police networks (e.g., the National Crime Information Center and local criminal history systems). Nevertheless, HIT is an important first step in bringing expert systems to a pressing social problem.

Adapted from Richard G. Vedder and Richard O. Mason, "An Expert System Application for Decision Support in Law Enforcement." Department of Business Computer Information Systems, North Texas State University, Denton, Texas, and the Department of Information Systems, Southern Methodist University, Dallas, Texas.

Case Study Questions

1. Do you think that a rule-based approach is better than a frame-based approach for a hostage negotiation system? Why?
2. What are some of the limitations that HIT might have in the field?
3. If you were taken hostage, would you feel comfortable or uncomfortable knowing that the police negotiating your release were using a system like HIT?

References

Bobrow, D.G., Mittal, S., and Stefik, M.J. "Expert Systems: Perils and Promise," *Communications of the ACM*, Vol. 29 (September 1986).

"The Engineers Behind Expert Systems," *Computerworld* (March 1985).

Feigenbaum, Edward A. "The Art of Artificial Intelligence: Themes and Case Studies in Knowledge Engineering," *Proceedings of the IJCAI* Vol. 5 (1977).

Feigenbaum, Edward A. and J.A. (eds.). *Computers and Thought*. New Tork: McGraw-Hill, 1963.

Feigenbaum, Edward A., and McCorduck, Pamela, *The Fifth Generation: Artificial Intelligence and Japan's Computer Challenge to the World*, Reading, Mass.: Addison-Wesley, 1985.

Firdman, Henry Eric. "Choice of Technology Guides Thrust of Expert System Effort," *Computerworld* (January 13, 1986).

Hayes-Roth, Frederick, "Knowledge-Based Expert Systems," *Spectrum IEEE*, October, 1987.

"Lightyear's Ahead of Paper," *PC Magazine* (April 16, 1985).

"M.1 Makes a Direct Hit," *PC Magazine* (April 16, 1985).

Michaelson, Robert and Michie, Donald, "Expert Systems in Business," *Datamation* (November, 1983).

Navquist, Harvey P., "Expert Systems: The Promise of a Smart Machine," *Computerworld* (January 13, 1986).

Rich, Elaine. *Artificial Intelligence*. New York: McGraw-Hill, 1983.

Simon, H.A., and Newell, A. "Heuristic Problem Solving: The Next Advance in Operations Research," *Operations Research*, Vol. 6 (January–February 1958).

Waltz, David L. "Artificial Intelligence," *Scientific American* (December 1982).

Weizenbaum, Joseph. *Computer Power and Human Reason—From Judgement to Calculation*. San Francisco: Freeman, 1976.

Weizenbaum, Joseph. "ELIZA—A Computer Program for the Study of Natural Language Communication Between Man and Machine," *Communications of the ACM* (January 1983).

Williamson, Mickey, "Expert System Shells," *Computerworld* (July 14, 1986).

CHAPTER 18

Controlling Information Systems

■ OUTLINE

Scientists at Bell Laboratories created a computer program with a "secret hole" that was installed at different sites around the country, including the National Security Agency, which runs the Pentagon's computer security center. This program caused computers to skip normal security procedures when fed a particular password to give access to key secrets. The program was used at the National Security Agency for 2 years before it was detected.

It is not known whether any security breach occurred because this particular program required activation by telecommunications contact with another computer using that program.

However, programs of this sort could be designed to be activated by a series of events such as the electronic warnings for a nuclear alert. According to an article in *Proceedings of the United States Naval Institute*, such programs could cripple national defenses.

Pentagon officials are also worried because top-secret information can no longer be isolated to restricted computers or heavily guarded file drawers. Data from early-warning satellites, for example, must be carried on computer networks that span the globe, with many points of vulnerability.

From "Computer Security Worries Military Experts," *The New York Times*, September 25, 1983.

Such dangers are on the rise because of the growing dependence of the military on complex computer programming and the concentration of highly sensitive information in computerized form. And such worries are not limited to the Defense Department.

Computer systems play such a critical role in business, government, churches, and schools that these organizations too must take special steps to ensure that their automated information is accurate, reliable, and secure. Automated information systems must be properly *controlled* if they are to serve the purposes for which they are intended.

In this chapter the student will learn:

- Why automated information systems are so vulnerable to destruction, error, and abuse.
- How to identify the most vulnerable points in information systems.
- The characteristics of controls.
- The difference between general controls and application controls.
- The most important techniques for controlling information systems.
- The role of controls in maintaining security.
- The importance of auditing information systems.

18.1 Introduction

One of the main functions of information systems is to enhance management's control over the operational, strategic, and decision-making activities of the organization. However, information systems themselves must be properly controlled to realize this objective. Without proper safeguards, systems are vulnerable to destruction, abuse, error, and loss, which can totally undermine the organizations that rely on them. Special measures must be taken during the design and operation of information systems to ensure they are properly *controlled*.

In the past, the control of information systems was treated as an afterthought, addressed only toward the end of implementation, just before the system was installed. Today, however, organizations are so critically dependent on information systems that vulnerabilities and control issues must be identified as early as possible. The control of an information system must be an integral part of its design. Users and builders of systems must pay close attention to controls throughout the system's life span.

18.2 System Vulnerability and Abuse

Before computer automation, data about individuals or organizations was maintained and secured as paper records dispersed in separate business or organizational units. Information systems concentrate data in computer files that can potentially be accessed more easily by large numbers of people and by groups outside the organization. Consequently, automated data are more susceptible to destruction, fraud, error, and misuse.

Why Systems Are Vulnerable

There are many advantages to information systems that are properly safeguarded. But when large amounts of data are stored in electronic form they are vulnerable to many more kinds of threats than when

TABLE 18.1
Threats to Computerized
Information Systems

Hardware Failure	Fire
Software Failure	Electrical Problems
Personnel Actions	User Errors
Terminal Access Penetration	Program Changes
Theft of Data, Services, Equipment	Telecommunications Problems

they exist in manual form. For example, an organization's entire recordkeeping system can be destroyed by a computer hardware malfunction. Table 18.1 lists the most common threats against computerized information. They can stem from technical, organizational, and environmental sources.

Computerized systems are especially vulnerable to such threats for the following reasons:

- A complex information system cannot be replicated manually. Most information can't be printed or is too voluminous to be handled manually.
- There is usually no visible trace of changes in computerized systems because computer records can be read only by the computer.
- Computerized procedures appear to be invisible and are not easily understood or audited.
- Changes in automated systems are more costly and often more complex than changes in manual systems.
- The development and operation of automated systems require specialized technical expertise, which cannot be easily communicated to end users. Systems are open to abuse by highly technical staff members who are not well integrated into the organization. (Programmers and computer operators can make unauthorized changes in software while information is being processed or use computer facilities for unauthorized purposes. Maintenance staff may make unauthorized copies of data files for illegal purposes.)
- Although the chances of disaster in automated systems are no greater than in manual systems, the effect of a disaster can be much more extensive. In some cases, all of the system's records can be destroyed and lost forever.
- There are fewer hard-copy documents to process and review when systems are automated. Less manual scrutiny is possible.
- Most automated systems are accessible by many individuals. Information is easier to gather but more difficult to control.
- Data in computer systems undergo many more processing steps than in manual systems, each of which is open to errors or abuse. Each of these functions—data origination, recording, transmission for processing, processing, storage, retrieval, and dissemination— requires a separate set of physical, administrative, and technical controls.
- On-line information systems are even more difficult to control because data files can be accessed immediately and directly through computer terminals. Legitimate users may gain easy access to computer data that were previously not available to them. They may be able to scan records or entire files that they are not authorized to view. By obtaining valid users' log-ons and passwords, unauthorized individuals can also gain access to such

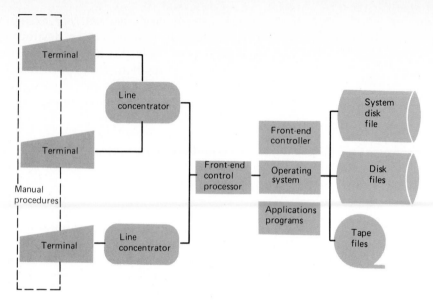

FIGURE 18.1

Vulnerabilities of on-line systems. This figure illustrates the various points where error, destruction, or unauthorized access can occur in on-line systems. The areas where on-line systems are vulnerable include manual procedures, computer terminal hardware, line concentrators, front-end control processors and software for on-line systems, the operating system, specific application programs, system files, application files on disk and tape, and central processing unit hardware.

Concerns Regarding On-Line Systems

1. Who is authorized to use this terminal?
2. Is the terminal being used only for the transactions specified for it?
3. Is the terminal operator authorized to access or update data?
4. Have all transactions been properly entered, tested, and recorded?
5. Are secret passwords required for individual operators to access and/or update data files for various applications?
6. What would happen if each of these points of vulnerability was tampered with or destroyed?

systems. The chances of unauthorized access to or manipulation of data are considerably higher than in the batch environment. Figure 18.1 illustrates the vulnerabilities of on-line systems.

New Vulnerabilities

Advances in telecommunications and computer software have magnified these vulnerabilities. Through telecommunications networks, information systems in different locations can be interconnected. The potential for unauthorized access, abuse, or fraud is not limited to a single location but can occur at any access point in the network. Figure 18.2 illustrates the points of potential penetration for only three dedicated telecommunications networks used by executive agencies of the federal government.

Additionally, more complex and diverse hardware, software, and organizational and personnel arrangements are required for telecommunications networks, creating new areas and opportunities for penetration and manipulation. The vulnerabilities of telecom-

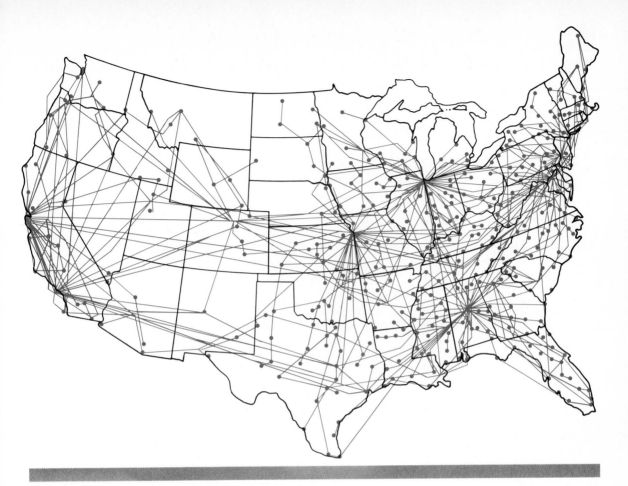

FIGURE 18.2
Telecommunication networks. This figure shows the geographic coverage of only three federal government agencies. Note the complexity of these networks. There are many points where unauthorized access could occur. (Adapted from the U.S. General Accounting Office, 1982.)

munications networks are illustrated in Figure 18.3. Developing a workable system of controls for telecommunications networks is a complex and troubling problem. Chase Manhattan Bank, discussed in the following account, is but one of many organizations with computer systems that have been penetrated by outsiders through telephone lines.

Advances in computer software have also increased the chances of misuse and abuse. Using fourth-generation languages, discussed in Chapter 15 end users can now perform programming functions

Youths Raid Chase Computer

At least 23 teenage computer users broke into a Chase Manhattan Bank computer installation by computer in July and August 1985, the FBI reported. Chase officials insisted that no money was stolen or transferred out of customer accounts, but at least one youth gained access to an account where funds could have been manipulated. This unauthorized access occurred when the youths dialed a toll-free telephone number connected to the computer of the Interactive Data Corporation (IDC) in Waltham, Mass. Chase uses IDC for much of its data processing and recordkeeping, including records of home mortgages and portfolios of major customers, and for maintaining its databases for economic forecasting. The unauthorized users had obtained or deduced the passwords for the computer system's first level of security. Once connected they changed at least two passwords, including one to the account of the Chase Home Mortgage Corporation, which prevented bank officials from gaining access.

Adapted from "Chase Computer Raided by Youths, Officials Say," *The New York Times*, October 23, 1985.

that were formerly reserved for technical specialists. They can produce programs that inadvertently create errors, and they can manipulate the organization's data for illegitimate purposes.

The growth of database systems, where data are shared by multiple application areas, has also created new vulnerabilities. All data are stored in one common location, but many users may have the right to access and modify them. It may not be easy to identify who is using or possibly misusing the data in such circumstances. Since the data are used by more than one organizational unit, the effect of an error may reverberate throughout the organization. There may also be less chance of discovering errors. Each functional unit has less individual control over the data and has less grounds for knowing whether the computer is right.

Concerns for System Builders and Users

The heightened vulnerability of automated data has created special concerns for the builders and users of information systems. These concerns include disaster, privacy, confidentiality, security, computer crime and abuse, and administrative error.

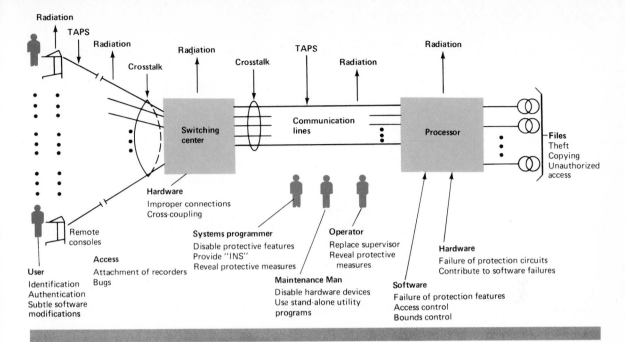

Radiation

TAPS

Radiation

Radiation

Crosstalk

Radiation

Crosstalk

TAPS

Radiation

Radiation

Switching center

Communication lines

Processor

Files
Theft
Copying
Unauthorized access

Hardware
Improper connections
Cross-coupling

Remote consoles

Systems programmer
Disable protective features
Provide "INS"
Reveal protective measures

Operator
Replace supervisor
Reveal protective measures

Hardware
Failure of protection circuits
Contribute to software failures

User
Identification
Authentication
Subtle software modifications

Access
Attachment of recorders
Bugs

Maintenance Man
Disable hardware devices
Use stand-alone utility programs

Software
Failure of protection features
Access control
Bounds control

FIGURE 18.3
Telecommunication network vulnerabilities. Telecommunication networks are highly vulnerable to natural failure of hardware and software and to misuse by programmers, computer operators, maintenance personnel, and users. (Adapted from the U.S. General Accounting Office, 1982.)

Disaster

Computer hardware, programs, data files, and other equipment can be destroyed by fires, power failures, or other disasters. Such disasters can disrupt normal operations and even bring an entire organization to a standstill. It may take many years and millions of dollars to reconstruct destroyed data files and computer programs. If an organization needs them to function on a day-to-day basis, it will no longer be able to operate. This is why Mastercard, for example, employs such elaborate emergency backup facilities.

Privacy, Security and Confidentiality

Privacy, security, and confidentiality are often confused. In fact, they refer to different but related aspects of information management.

In the United States, privacy is considered by many to be a basic constitutional right (much like freedom of speech). It is also protected by 15 major pieces of legislation in specific areas such as credit, banking records, tax records, and educational records (Laudon, 1986b).

Backing Up Mastercard

Processing billions of transactions from all over the world, MasterCard can't afford to have any part of its data center or communications network disrupted, even for a few minutes. Its World Data Center in St. Louis, which is the clearing center for all MasterCard credit transactions, must be fully protected against shutdowns from power failures. MasterCard employs multiple backup systems: It has two uninterruptable battery-operated power supply modules for short-term power supply and dual 750 kilowatt generators for long-term power supply. MasterCard's administration services manager notes that its backup systems are as important as its computers.

From "Backing Up MasterCard," *Infosystems*, November 1985.

The Privacy Act of 1974 protects the privacy of individuals vis-à-vis all civilian federal record systems. Most states have additional privacy protection laws covering state and local systems. Approximately 6723 personal data systems are operated by the federal government, with over 3.8 billion records on individuals (Privacy Protection Study Commission, 1977).

Privacy is a broad term that encompasses security and confidentiality. There are three elements of privacy:

- *Limits* on the collection of information and the existence of systems
- Specific *rights of individuals* to access, review, and challenge information about them
- *Management responsibility* for record systems

These principles evolved from a Code of Fair Information Practice conceived by a government advisory group in 1973. They constitute the core of all privacy legislation and regulation in the private and public sectors (HEW Advisory Committee on Automated Personal Data Systems, 1973). The code had eight principles:

1. *Openness.* There must be no secret systems.
2. *Individual access.* There must be a way for individuals to find out what information is on record, to determine how it is used, and to copy such information.
3. *Individual participation.* Individuals must be able to correct or amend data about themselves.

4. *Collection limitations*. There must be limits on what kinds of information are collected and the manner in which they are collected.
5. *Limits on use*. Data collected for one purpose cannot be used for a different purpose without the subject's prior consent or knowledge.
6. *Disclosure limitations*. There must be legally enforceable confidentiality limits on the disclosure of personal data to outside parties.
7. *Information management*. Information-gathering organizations are responsible for the currency, accuracy, and security of systems, as well as for compliance with privacy principles.
8. *Accountability*. Information-gathering organizations must be accountable for their personal recordkeeping policies, practices, and systems. Systems must be auditable so that the flow of information can be traced.

Security is a technical condition for achieving privacy. It refers to the policies, procedures, and technical measures used to prevent unauthorized access or alteration, theft, and physical damage to record systems. Security can be promoted with an array of techniques and tools to safeguard computer hardware, software, communications networks, and data. These tools and techniques will be described in subsequent sections.

Confidentiality refers to limits on the use of information collected from individuals. Personal data should be restricted to those in the organization who have a need to know and should not be disseminated outside the organization.

Computer Crime and Abuse

Through automation, valuable assets are increasingly being represented as information stored in computers. Computerized information has become an attractive target for crime. Illegal acts requiring special knowledge of computer technology for their perpetration, investigation, or prosecution have been termed *computer crime*.

Computers can provide the automated mechanism to modify and manipulate new forms of assets such as information representing money or computer programs. They can also serve as powerful symbols that intimidate or deceive. A stockbroker used a computer to produce forged investment statements, telling his clients that he had made huge profits on rapid stock option trading using a secret computer program from a Wall Street brokerage firm. Although he had no such program, he convinced hundreds of clients to invest a minimum of $100,000 each.

Experts also note that the magnitude of loss from computer crime is considerable because computerized assets are so concentrated and fragile. A $200 million Equity Insurance Company fraud, a $21 million bank embezzlement in Los Angeles, a $53 million securities fraud in Florida, and a $67 million inventory fraud in New York City were all

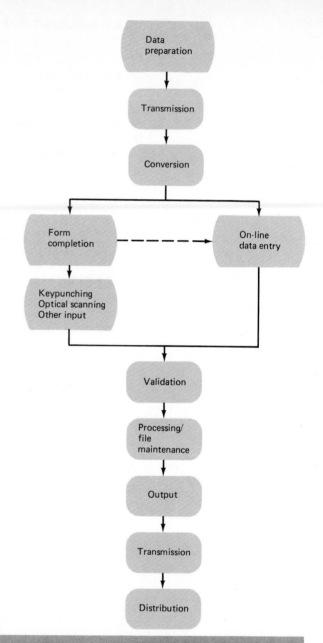

FIGURE 18.4
Points in the processing cycle where errors can
appear. Each of the points shown is a control point
where special automated and/or manual procedures
must be established to prevent errors from occurring.

record-breaking cases (Parker and Nycum, 1984). Because of the
growth of automated business activities, the incidence of such crimes
is expected to increase.

The term *computer abuse* has been defined as the use of a computer in ways that do not violate the law but that are still unethi-

cal. For example, at least 30 employees of the U.S. Department of Agriculture had unauthorized access to the department's automated files. Some of them used the computer facilities and the department's proprietary data for their own outside consulting work, making unauthorized and premature disclosure of information considered highly sensitive by the department. In another case, three clerk-typists at the Ford Motor Company allegedly used company word processors to run a $5000-a-week gambling operation (Buss and Salerno, 1984).

Error

Computers can also serve as instruments of error, severely disrupting or destroying an organization's recordkeeping and operations. Errors in automated systems can occur at many points: through data entry, program errors, computer operations, and hardware. Figure 18.4 illustrates all of the points in a typical processing cycle where errors can occur. Even minor mistakes in automated systems can have massive or even disastrous financial or operational repercussions, as illustrated by what happened to a medical institution when a computer operator mishandled a magnetic tape. (See vignette below.)

A Minneapolis bank had great difficulty in recovering $186,000 that was mistakenly deposited in a customer's account.

Errors have proved to be a greater threat to automated systems than computer crime. A 1984 study of computer crime by the American Bar Association concluded that 55% of the losses in information systems were due to errors, accidents, and omissions made by people inside the organization (Task Force on Computer Crime, 1984).

To minimize errors, disaster, computer crime, and breaches of privacy, confidentiality, and security, special techniques, policies, and procedures must be incorporated into the design and implementation of information systems. The combination of manual and automated measures that safeguard information systems and ensure that they perform according to management standards is termed *controls*. The major controls for information systems are discussed in the following section.

A medical institution lost its sole record of approximately $500,000 in cash receipts because a computer operator forgot to remove the protect ring on a magnetic tape where this information was stored. The tape was mounted on the wrong drive and erased. When records of past due receivables were finally reconstructed, the same accident happened again.

From Mair et al. (1978).

Bank Error Leads to Lawsuit

The Fidelity Bank Northeast of Minneapolis sued a customer after she spent $48,482 of the $186,392 it had erroneously credited to her account. The bank, which subsequently became an affiliate of Marquette Banks, based in Minneapolis, claimed that the woman "wrongfully converted" funds for her own use. The lawsuit acknowledged errors in the bank's accounting and data systems but would not elaborate on their cause. The customer believed the money had been deposited in her account by her father. Her attorney reported that as a result of the incident she was under psychiatric care.

Adapted from *The New York Times*, June 15, 1986.

18.3 Controls

Controls consist of all of the methods, policies, and organizational procedures that ensure the safety of the organization's assets, the accuracy and reliability of its accounting records, and operational adherence to management standards. Computer systems are controlled by a combination of *general controls* and *application controls*.

General controls are those that control the design, security, and use of computer programs and the security of data files in general throughout the organization. On the whole, general controls apply to all computerized applications and consist of a combination of system software and manual procedures that create an overall control environment.

Application controls are specific controls unique to each computerized application, such as payroll, accounts receivable, and order processing. They consist of both controls applied from the user functional area of a particular system and programmed procedures.

General Controls

General controls are overall controls that ensure the effective operation of programmed procedures. They apply to all application areas. General controls include:

- Controls over the system implementation process.
- Software controls.
- Physical hardware controls.
- Computer operations controls.

TABLE 18.2
Effect of Weakness
in General Controls

Weakness	Impact
Implementation controls	New systems or systems that have been modified will have errors or fail to function as required.
Software controls (program security)	Unauthorized changes can be made in processing. The organization may not be sure of which programs or systems have been changed.
Software controls (system software)	These controls may not have a direct effect on individual applications. Since other general controls depend heavily on system software, a weakness in this area may impair the other general controls.
Physical hardware controls	Hardware may have serious malfunctions or may break down altogether, introducing numerous errors or destroying computerized records.
Computer operations controls	Random errors may occur in a system. (Most processing will be correct, but occasionally it may not be.)
Data file security controls	Unauthorized changes can be made in data stored in computer systems or unauthorized individuals can access sensitive information.
Administrative controls	All of the other controls may not be properly executed or enforced.

- Data security controls.
- Administrative disciplines, standards, and procedures.

Weakness in each of these general controls can have a widespread effect on programmed procedures and data. Table 18.2 summarizes the effect of weaknesses in major general control areas.

Implementation Controls

The system development process can be audited at various points to ensure that it is properly controlled and managed. The system development audit should look for the presence of formal review points at various stages of development that enable users and management to approve or disapprove the implementation. (Examples of such review points are user and management sign-offs on the systems proposal, design specifications, conversion, testing, and the postimplementation audit described in Chapter 12.)

The system development audit should also examine the level of user involvement at each stage of implementation and check for the use of a formal cost/benefit methodology in establishing system feasibility. The audit should also look for the use of controls and quality assurance techniques for program development, conversion, and testing. (These issues are discussed in Chapters 11–13.)

An important though frequently neglected requirement of systems building is appropriate documentation. Without good documentation that shows how a system operates from both a technical and a user standpoint, an information system may be difficult, if not impossible, to operate, maintain, or use. Table 18.3 lists the various

TABLE 18.3

Essential User and Technical Documentation for an Information System. Many organizations require that such documentation be approved by a standards and controls group.

Technical Documentation	User Documentation
System flowchart	Sample reports/output layouts
File layouts	Sample input forms/screens
Record layouts	Data preparation instructions
List of programs/modules	Data input instructions
Program structure charts, flowcharts, or HIPOs	Instructions for using reports
Narrative program/module descriptions	Security profiles
Source program listings	Functional description of system
Module cross references	Work flows
Error conditions/actions	Error correction procedures
Abnormal termination	Accountabilities
Job setup requirements	Processing procedure narrative
Job run schedules	List/description of controls
Report/output distribution	
Responsible programmer contact	Responsible user contact
Job control language listings	
Backup/recovery procedures	
Run control procedures	
File access procedures	
Hardware/operating system requirements	

pieces of documentation that are normally required to run and maintain an information system. The system development audit should look for system, user, and operations documentation that conforms to formal standards.

Software Controls

Controls are essential for the various categories of software used in computer systems. These include controls over system software and computer programs.

System software controls govern the software for the operating system, which regulates and manages computer resources to facilitate execution of application programs. System software includes operating system compilers, utility programs, reporting of operations, file setup and handling, and library recordkeeping. It is an important control area because it performs overall control functions for the programs that directly process data and data files. *Program security controls* are designed to prevent unauthorized changes to programs in systems that are already in production.

Hardware Controls

Computer hardware should be physically secured so that it can be accessed only by authorized individuals. Access to rooms where computers operate should be restricted to computer operations personnel. Computer terminals in other areas or microcomputers can be kept in locked rooms. Computer equipment should be specially protected against fires and extremes of temperature and humidity. Organizations that are critically dependent on their computers must also make provisions for emergency backup in case of power failure.

Many kinds of computer hardware also contain mechanisms that check for equipment malfunction. *Parity checks* detect equipment malfunctions responsible for altering bits within bytes during processing. *Validity checks* monitor the structure of on-off bits within bytes to make sure that it is valid for the character set of a particular computer machine. *Echo checks* verify that a hardware device is performance ready. Chapter 6 discusses computer hardware in detail.

Computer Operations Controls

Computer operations controls apply to the work of the computer department and help ensure that programmed procedures are consistently and correctly applied to the storage and processing of data. They include controls over the setup of computer processing jobs, operations software and computer operations, and backup and recovery procedures for processing that ends abnormally.

Instructions for running computer jobs should be fully documented, reviewed, and approved by a responsible official. Controls over operations software include manual procedures designed to both prevent and detect error. These include specified operating instructions for system software, restart and recovery procedures, procedures for the labeling and disposition of input and output

Computer Error Triggers False Missile Attack

American defenses were triggered into a state of alert when a military computer erroneously indicated that the Soviet Union had launched nuclear missiles against the United States. A technician in North American Defense Command headquarters in Colorado had put into a computer a test tape simulating the firing of land-based and seaborne missiles. Through human error a connection was made between that computer and a "live" computer operating in the alert system. The simulation appeared as a real attack on monitors at the North American Defense Command and elsewhere.

Adapted from *The New York Times*, December 16, 1979.

magnetic tapes, and procedures for specific applications. A disturbing false missile alert in the North American Defense Command Computer in 1979, for example, could have been avoided by tighter operational safeguards.

System software can maintain a *system log* detailing all activity during processing. This log can be printed for review so that hardware malfunction, abnormal endings, and operator actions can be investigated. Specific instructions for backup and recovery can be developed so that in the event of a hardware or software failure, the recovery process for production programs, system software, and data files does not create erroneous changes in the system.

Data Security Controls

Data security controls ensure that data files on either disk or tape are not subject to unauthorized access, change, or destruction. Such controls are required for data files when they are in use and when they are being held for storage. It is easier to control data files in batch systems, since access is limited to operators who run the batch jobs. However, on-line and real-time systems are vulnerable at several points. They can be accessed through terminals as well as by operators during production runs.

When data can be input on-line through a terminal, entry of unauthorized input must be prevented. For example, a credit note could be altered to match a sales invoice on file. In such situations, security can be developed on several levels.

- Terminals can be physically restricted so that they are available only to authorized individuals.
- System software can include the use of passwords assigned only to authorized individuals. No one can log on to the system without a valid password.
- Additional sets of passwords and security restrictions can be developed for specific systems and applications. For example, data security software can limit access to specific files, such as the files for the accounts receivable system. It can restrict the type of access so that only individuals authorized to update these specific files will have the ability to do so. All others will only be able to read the files or will be denied access altogether.

Systems that allow on-line inquiry and reporting must also have data files secured. Figure 18.5 outlines the security allowed for two sets of users of an on-line personnel database with sensitive information such as employees' salaries, benefits, and medical history. A multilayered data security system such as the one just described is essential for ensuring that this information can be accessed only by authorized persons. The data security system suggested here even provides fine-grained security restrictions, such as allowing authorized personnel users to inquire about all employee information except confidential fields such as salary or medical history.

Although the security risk of files maintained off-line is smaller, such data files on disk or tape can be removed for unauthorized purposes. These can be secured in lockable storage areas, with tight procedures so that they are released only for authorized processing. Usage logs and library records can be maintained for each removable storage device if it is labeled and assigned a unique identity number.

Administrative Controls

Formalized standards, rules, procedures, and control disciplines are essential for ensuring that the organization's controls are properly executed and enforced. The most important administrative controls are (1) segregation of functions, (2) written policies and procedures, and (3) supervision.

Segregation of functions is a fundamental principle of internal control in any organization. In essence, it means that job functions should be designed to minimize the risk of errors or fraudulent manipulation of the organization's assets. The individuals responsible for operating systems should not be the same ones who can initiate transactions that change the assets held in these systems. Responsibilities for input, processing, and output are usually divided among different people to restrict what each one can do with the system. For example, the individuals who operate the system should not have the authority to initiate payments or to sign checks. A typical arrangement is to have the organization's information systems department responsible for data and program files and end users

FIGURE 18.5

Security profiles for a personnel system. These are examples of security profiles or data security patterns that might be found in a personnel system. Several individuals may have the same profile or type of access to the system. The first profile is for all employees who perform clerical functions such as inputing employee data into the system. All individuals with this profile can update the system but can neither read or update sensitive fields such as salary, medical history, or earnings data. The second profile applies to the divisional manager, who cannot update the system but who can read all employee data fields for his division, including medical history and salary. These profiles would be established and maintained by a data security system for this application.

responsible for initiating input transactions or correcting errors. Within the information systems department, the duties of programmers and analysts are segregated from those of computer equipment operators. (The organization of the information systems department is discussed in Chapter 4.)

Written policies and procedures establish formal standards for controlling information system operations. Procedures must be formalized in writing and authorized by the appropriate level of management. Accountabilities and responsibilities must be clearly specified.

Supervision of personnel involved in control procedures ensures that the controls for an information system are performing as intended. With supervision, weaknesses can be spotted, errors corrected, and deviations from standard procedures identified. Without adequate supervision, the best-designed set of controls may be bypassed, short-circuited, or neglected.

Application Controls

Application controls are specific controls within each separate computer application, such as payroll or accounts receivable. They include both automated and manual procedures that ensure that only authorized data are completely and accurately processed by that application. The controls for each application should take account of the whole sequence of processing, manual and computer, from the first steps taken to prepare transactions to the production and use of final output.

Not all of the application controls discussed here are used in every information system. Some systems require more of these controls than others, depending on the importance of the data and the nature of the application.

Application controls focus on the following objectives:

1. *Completeness of input and update.* All transactions must reach the computer and be recorded on computer files.
2. *Accuracy of input and update.* Data must be accurately captured by the computer and correctly recorded on computer files.
3. *Validity.* Data must be authorized or otherwise checked with regard to the appropriateness of the transaction. (In other words, the transaction must reflect the right event in the external world. The validity of an address change, for example, refers to whether a transaction actually captured the right address for a specific individual.)
4. *Maintenance.* Data on computer files must continue to remain correct and current.

Application controls can be classified as (1) *input controls*, (2) *processing controls*, and (3) *output controls*.

Input Controls

Input controls check data for accuracy and completeness when they enter the system. There are specific input controls for input authorization, data conversion, data editing, and error handling.

Input Authorization. Input must be properly authorized, recorded, and monitored as source documents flow to the computer. For example, formal procedures can be set up to authorize only selected members of the sales department to prepare sales transactions for an

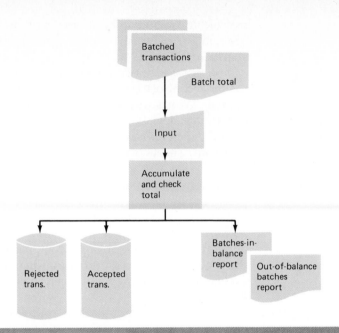

FIGURE 18.6

Batch totaling by computer. Transactions are manually grouped into batches, and a control total is established over each batch. The batch total can be a total document count, item count, or dollar amount. The batch total is calculated before processing and recorded on a special batch control record, which is input in addition to all of the transactions for that particular batch. The computer accumulates the batch total itself and compares it to the total input with the batch. If the totals do not agree, the computer rejects the batch and prints the details on the Out-of-Balance Batches Report. If the totals agree, the batch is accepted for further processing and is recorded in the Batches-in-Balance Report. Since the out-of-balance batches are held on a separate file, they can be corrected and reinput.

order entry system. Sales input forms might be serially numbered, grouped into *batches*, and logged so that they can be tracked as they pass from sales units to the unit responsible for inputing them into the computer. The batches may require authorization signatures before they can be entered into the computer.

Data Conversion. Input must be properly converted into computer transactions, with no errors as it is transcribed from one form to another. Transcription errors can be eliminated or reduced by keying input transactions directly into computer terminals from their source documents. (Point of sale systems can capture sales and inventory transactions directly by scanning product bar codes.)

Batch control totals are an extremely valuable technique in this area. They can be established beforehand for transactions grouped in batches. These totals can range from a simple document count to totals for quantity fields such as total sales amount (for the batch). Some applications write batch control totals on a separate batch control record. Computer programs then count the batch totals from transactions input and either compare them with the batch control record or print the totals. (If the totals are printed, they can be reconciled manually with the original batch totals.) Batches that do not balance are rejected. Figure 18.6 illustrates batch totaling.

On-line, real-time systems can also utilize batch controls by creating control totals to reconcile with hard copy documents that feed input or by assigning batch numbers to each on-line transaction that can be used for totaling automatically.

Edits. Various routines can be performed to edit input data for errors before they are processed. Transactions that do not meet edit criteria will be rejected. The edit routines can produce lists of errors to be corrected later. The most important types of edit techniques are summarized in Table 18.4.

An advantage of on-line, real-time systems is that editing can be performed up front. As each transaction is input and entered it can be edited, and the terminal operator can be notified immediately if an error is found. Alternatively, the operator may fail to correct the error on purpose or by accident. The system can be designed to reject additional input until the error is corrected or to print a hard-copy error list that can be reviewed by others.

Processing Controls

Processing controls establish that data are complete and accurate during updating. The major processing controls are run control totals, computer matching, and programmed edit checks.

Run Control Totals. Updating can be controlled by generating control totals during processing. These totals reconcile the input control totals with the totals of items that have updated the file. The totals, such as total transactions processed or totals for critical quantities, can be compared manually or by computer. Discrepancies are noted for investigation.

Computer Matching. Most matching occurs during input, but under some circumstances it may be required to ensure completeness of updating. Input data are matched with information held on master or suspense files, with unmatched items noted for investigation. For example, a matching program might match employee time cards with a payroll master file and report missing or duplicate time cards.

Programmed Edit Checks. Most edit checking occurs at the time data are input. However, certain applications require some type of reasonableness or dependency check during updating as well. For example, consistency checks might be utilized by a utility company to compare a customer's electric bill with previous bills. If the bill was

TABLE 18.4
Important Edit Techniques

Edit Technique	Description	Example
Reasonableness check	To be accepted, data must fall within certain limits set in advance, or they will be rejected.	If an order transaction is for 20,000 units and the largest order on record was 50 units, the transaction will be rejected
Format checks	Characteristics of the contents (letter/digit), length, and sign of individul data fields are checked by the system.	A nine-position Social Security number should not contain any alphabetic characters.
Existence checks	The computer compares input reference data to tables or master files to make sure that valid codes are being used.	An employee can have a Fair Labor Standards Act code of only 1, 2, 3, 4, or 5. All other values for this field will be rejected.
Dependency checks	The computer checks whether a *logical* relationship is maintained between data for the *same* transaction. When it is not, the transaction is rejected.	A car loan initiation transaction should show a logical relationship between the size of the loan, the number of loan repayments, and the size of each installment.
Check digit	An extra reference number called a *check digit* follows an identification code and bears a mathematical relationship to the other digits. This extra digit is input with the data, recomputed by the computer, and the result compared with the one input.	See the check digit in Figure 18.7 for a product code using the Modulus 11 check digit system.

500% higher this month compared to last month, the bill would not be processed until the meter was rechecked.

Output Controls

Output controls ensure that the results of computer processing are accurate, complete, and properly distributed. Typical output controls include:

- Balancing output totals with input and processing totals.
- Reviews of the computer processing logs to determine that all of the correct computer jobs executed properly for processing.

Product Code:		2	9	7	4	3
Weight:		6	5	4	3	2
Multiply each product code number by weight:		12	45	28	12	6
Sum results:		12 + 45 + 28 + 12 + 6 = 103				
Divide the sum by modulus:		103/11 = 9 with remainder of 2				
Subtract remainder from modulus number to obtain check digit:		11 − 2 = 9				
Add check digit to original product code to obtain new code:		297439				

FIGURE 18.7

Check digit for a product code. This is a product code with the last position as a check digit, as developed by the Modulus 11 check digit system, the most common check digit method. The check digit is 9 and is derived by the steps listed in the figure. Errors in the transcription or transposition of this product code can be detected by a computer program that replicates the same procedure for deriving the check digit. If a data entry person mistakenly keys in the product number as 29753, the program will read the first five digits and carry out the Modulus 11 process. It will derive a check digit of 4. When this is compared to the original check digit on the last position of the product code, the program will find that the check digits do not match and that an error has occurred.

- Audit of output reports to make sure that totals, formats, and critical details are correct and reconcilable with input.
- Formal procedures and documentation specifying authorized recipients of output reports, checks, or other critical documents.

Developing a Control Structure: Costs and Benefits

Information systems can make exhaustive use of all of the control mechanisms previously discussed. But they may be so expensive to build and so complicated to use that the system is economically or operationally unfeasible. Some cost/benefit analysis must be performed to determine which control mechanisms provide the most effective safeguards without sacrificing operational efficiency or cost.

One of the criteria that determine how much control is built into a system is the *importance of its data*. Major financial and accounting systems, for example, such as a payroll system or one that tracks purchases and sales on the stock exchange, must have higher standards of control than a system to inventory employee training and skills or a "tickler" system to track dental patients and remind them that their 6-month checkup is due.

Standing data, the data that are permanent and affect transactions flowing into and out of a system (e.g., codes for existing products or cost centers) require closer monitoring than individual order transactions. A single error in transaction data will affect only that transaction, while a standing data error may affect many or all transactions each time the file is processed.

The cost effectiveness of controls will also be influenced by the efficiency, complexity, and expense of each control technique. For example, complete one-for-one checking may be time-consuming and operationally impossible for a system that processes hundreds of thousands of utilities payments daily. But it might be possible to use this technique to verify only critical data such as dollar amounts and account numbers, while ignoring names and addresses.

A third consideration is the *level of risk* if a specific activity or process is not properly controlled. System builders can undertake a *risk assessment*, determining the likely frequency of a problem and the potential damage if it were to occur. For example, if an event is likely to occur no more than once a year, with a maximum of a $1000 loss to the organization, it would not be feasible to spend $20,000 on the design and maintenance of a control to protect against that event. However, if that same event could occur at least once a day, with a potential loss of over $300,000 a year, $100,000 spent on a control might be entirely appropriate.

Table 18.5 illustrates sample results of a risk assessment for an on-line order processing system that processes 30,000 orders per day.

TABLE 18.5
On-Line Order Processing Risk Assessment.

Exposure	Prob. of Occurr. (%)	Loss Range/ Average ($)	Expected Annual Loss ($)
Power failure	30	5000–200,000 (102,500)	30,750
Embezzlement	5	1000–50,000 (25,500)	1,275
User error	98	200–40,000 (20,100)	19,698

This chart shows the results of a risk assessment for three selected areas of an on-line order processing system. The likelihood of each exposure occurring over a 1-year period is expressed as a percentage. The next column shows the highest and lowest possible loss that could be expected each time the exposure occurred and an "average" loss calculated by adding the highest and lowest figures together and dividing by 2. The expected annual loss for each exposure can be determined by multiplying the "average" loss by its probability of occurrence.

The probability of a power failure occurring in a 1-year period is 30%. Loss of order transactions while power is down could range from $5000 to $200,000 for each occurrence, depending on how long processing was halted. The probability of embezzlement occurring over a yearly period is about 5%, with potential losses ranging from $1000 to $50,000 for each occurrence. User errors have a 98% chance of occurring over a yearly period, with losses ranging from $200 to $40,000 for each occurrence. The average loss for each event can be weighted by multiplying it by the probability of its occurrence annually to determine the expected annual loss. Once the risks have been assessed, system builders can concentrate on the control points with the greatest vulnerability and potential loss. In this case, controls should focus on ways to minimize the risk of power failures and user errors.

The U.S. federal government has mandated risk analysis at its computer centers. The purpose is to make sure that security measures are in place for the areas where there is a high risk of loss. The government does not want to lavish funds on too much security when risks are low or to develop the wrong kind of security for the risk profile (*EDP Analyzer*, 1986).

To decide which controls to use, information system builders must examine various control techniques in relation to each other and to their relative cost effectiveness. A control weakness at one point may be offset by a strong control at another. It may not be cost effective to build tight controls at every point in the processing cycle if the areas of greatest risk are secure or if compensating controls exist elsewhere. The combination of all of the controls developed for a particular application will determine its overall control structure.

18.4 Auditing Information Systems

Once controls have been established for an information system, how do we know that they are effective? To answer this question, organizations must conduct comprehensive and systematic *audits*. Large organizations have their own internal auditing group that is charged with this responsibility.

The Role of Auditing in the Control Process

An EDP audit identifies all of the controls that govern individual information systems and assesses their effectiveness. To accomplish this, the auditor must acquire a thorough understanding of operations, physical facilities, telecommunications, control systems, data security objectives, organizational structure, personnel, manual procedures, and individual applications.

The auditor should collect and analyze all of the material about a specific information system, such as user and system documentation,

Function: Personal Loans_____   Prepared by: ____ J. Ericson_____   Received by: _____ T. Barrow_____
Location: Peoria, Ill. _____   Preparation date:_ June 16, 1987 _____   Review date: _____ June 28, 1987 ____

Nature of Weakness and Impact	Chance for Substantial Error		Effect on Audit Procedures	Notification to Management	
	Yes/ No	Justification	Required Amendment	Date of Report	Management Response
Loan repayment records are not reconciled to borrower's records during processing.	Yes	Without a detection control, errors in individual client balances may remain undetected.	Confirm a sample of loans.	5/10/87	Interest Rate Compare Report provides this control.
There are no regular audits of computer-generated data (interest charges).	Yes	Without a regular audit or reasonableness check, widespread miscalculations could result before errors are detected.		5/10/87	Periodic audits of loans will be instituted.
Programs can be put into production libraries to meet target deadlines without final approval from the Standards and Controls group.	No	All programs require management authorization. The Standards and Controls group controls access to all production systems, and assigns such cases to a temporary production status.			

FIGURE 18.8
Sample auditor's list of control weaknesses. This chart is a sample
page from a list of control weaknesses that an auditor might find in a
loan system in a local commercial bank. This form helps auditors
record and evaluate control weaknesses and shows the results of
discussing those weaknesses with management. The form can record
corrective actions taken by management.

sample inputs and outputs, and relevant documentation about integrity controls. The auditor usually interviews key individuals who
use and operate the system concerning their activities and procedures. Application controls, overall integrity controls, and control
disciplines are examined. The auditor should trace the flow of sample
transactions through the system and perform tests, using, if appropriate, automated audit software.

The audit lists and ranks all control weaknesses and estimates
the probability of their occurrence. It then assesses the financial and
organizational impact of each threat. Figure 18.8 is a sample auditor's
listing of control weaknesses for a loan system. It includes a section
for notifying management of such weaknesses and for management's
response. Management is expected to devise a plan for countering
significant weaknesses in controls.

Data Quality Audits

An important aspect of information system auditing is an analysis of data quality. This can be accomplished by the following methods:

- Surveying end users for their perceptions of data quality
- Surveying entire files
- Surveying samples from files

Unless regular data quality audits are undertaken, organizations have no way of knowing to what extent their information systems contain inaccurate, incomplete, or ambiguous information. Some organizations, such as the Social Security Administration, have established data quality audit procedures. These procedures control payment and process quality by auditing a 20,000-case sample of beneficiary records each month. The FBI, on the other hand, did not conduct a comprehensive audit of its record systems until 1984. With few data quality controls, the FBI criminal record systems were found to have serious problems.

Table 18.6 shows the kinds of record quality problems uncovered in a recent study of the FBI's computerized criminal record systems. A total of 54.1% of the records in the National Crime Information Center System were found to be inaccurate, ambiguous, or incomplete, and 74.3% of the records in the FBI's semiautomated Identification Division system exhibited significant quality problems. A summary analysis of the FBI's automated Wanted-Persons File also found that 11.2% of the warrants were invalid. A study by the FBI itself found that 6% of the warrants in state files were invalid and that 12,000 invalid warrants are sent out nationally each day.

The low levels of data quality in these systems have disturbing implications.

- More than 14,000 persons are at risk of being falsely detained and perhaps arrested because of invalid warrants.
- In addition to their use in law enforcement, computerized criminal history records are increasingly being used to screen employees in both the public and private sectors. This is the fastest-growing use of these records in some states. Many of these records are incomplete and show arrests but no court disposition; that is, they show charges without proof of conviction or guilt. Many individuals may be denied employment unjustifiably because these records overstated their criminality.
- These criminal record systems are not limited to violent felons. They contain the records of 36 million people, about one-third of the labor force. Inaccurate and potentially damaging information is being maintained on many law-abiding citizens.

TABLE 18.6
Data Quality of FBI Criminal-History Systems: National Crime Information Center-Computerized Criminal History (NCIC-CCH) and Ident Criminal-History Records

	NCIC-CCH	Ident criminal-history records
Arrests in sample	400	400
Positive verification	256	235
Response rate	64.0%	58.5%
Arrests not verifiable because		
Pending or sealed	6	19
No record locatable*	54	37
No prosecution of arrest	10	7
Fugitive	1	1
No arrest data	24	—
	95 (37.1%)	64 (27.2%)
Total arrest cases verified	161	171
Characteristics of verified arrest case		
No disposition reported	27.9%(45)	40.9%(70)
Incomplete record	0.6%(1)	2.3%(4)
Inaccurate record	16.8%(27)	10.5%(18)
Ambiguous record	2.5%(4)	6.4%(11)
Combined problems	6.2%(10)	14.1%(24)
Complete, accurate, and unambiguous	45.9%(74)	25.7%(44)
Total	100.0%(161)	100.0%(171)

* In situations of "no record locatable," this generally reflected a police disposition of the arrest; for example, the person was released prior to presenting to a district attorney. This was removed from further analysis even though it might have been included as a "no disposition recorded"; hence, estimates of record characteristics are conservative.

1. If *no disposition* was reported ("record blank"), the data analysis exempted the record from further consideration even though it might have other problems of accuracy and ambiguity. Estimates of these features are therefore conservative.
2. A record was *incomplete* if it failed to record conviction or correctional data.
3. A record was *inaccurate* if it incorrectly reflected the court records of disposition, charges, or sentence.
4. A record was *ambiguous* if it indicated more charges than dispositions, but did not specify charges of conviction; or if a record indicated more dispositions than charges; *or* if for a number of reasons the record was not interpretable (see text).
5. A record had *combined problems* if it indicated more than one of the four logically possible permutations of incompleteness, inaccuracy or ambiguity.

(Adapted from Laudon, 1986a).

The level of data quality in these systems threatens citizens' constitutional right to due process and impairs the efficiency and effectiveness of any law enforcement programs in which these records are used (Laudon, 1986a).

18.5 Summary

Organizations have become so dependent on computerized information systems that they must take special measures to ensure that these systems are properly *controlled*. With data easily concentrated into electronic form and many procedures invisible through automation, systems are vulnerable to destruction, misuse, error, fraud, and hardware or software failures. The effect of disaster can be greater than in manual systems because all of the records for a particular function or organization can be destroyed and lost. On-line systems and those utilizing telecommunications are especially vulnerable because data and files can be immediately and directly accessed through computer terminals or at many points in the telecommunications network.

Controls consist of all of the methods, policies, and organizational procedures that ensure the safety of the organization's assets, the accuracy and reliability of its accounting records, and adherence to management standards. For computerized information systems, controls consist of both manual and programmed procedures. There are two main categories of controls: general controls and application controls.

General controls control the overall design, security, and use of computer programs and files for the organization as a whole. They include physical hardware controls; system software controls; data file security controls; computer operations controls; controls over the system implementation process; and administrative disciplines.

Application controls are controls unique to specific computerized applications. They focus on the completeness and accuracy of input, updating and maintenance, and the validity of the information in the system. Application controls consist of (1) input controls, (2) processing controls, and (3) output controls. Some of the principal application control techniques are programmed routines to edit data before they are input or updated; run control totals; and reconciliations of input source documents with output reports. To determine what controls are required, designers and users of systems must identify all of the control points and control weaknesses and perform risk assessment.

Comprehensive and systematic EDP auditing can help organizations to determine the effectiveness of the controls in their information systems. Regular data quality audits should be conducted to help organizations ensure a high level of completeness and accuracy of the data stored in their systems.

Key Words

System vulnerability
Privacy
Confidentiality
Computer crime
Computer abuse
Security
Controls
General controls
Application controls
Programmed procedures
Software controls
Segregation of functions

Edit checks
Reasonableness checks
Format checks
Check digit verification
Existence checks
Dependency checks
Run control totals
Risk assessment
EDP audit
Standing data
Data quality audit

Review Questions

1. Why are computer systems more vulnerable than manual systems to destruction, fraud, error, and misuse? Name some of the key areas where systems are most vulnerable.
2. Define privacy and confidentiality. Why have they become issues for computerized systems?
3. What is the difference between computer crime and computer abuse? Why have they become problems for computerized systems?
4. Name some features of on-line information systems that make them difficult to control.
5. What are controls? What distinguishes controls in computerized systems from controls in manual systems?
6. What is the difference between general controls and application controls?
7. Name and describe the principal general controls for computerized systems.
8. Describe how each of the following serve as application controls: batching, edits, computer matching, run control totals.
9. What kinds of edit techniques can be built into computer programs?
10. How does EDP auditing enhance the control process?
11. What is the function of risk assessment?
12. Why are data quality audits essential?
13. What is security? List and describe controls that promote security for computer hardware, computer networks, computer software, and computerized data.

Discussion Questions

1. It has been said that controls and security should be one of the first areas to be addressed by information system designers. Discuss.
2. The Young Professional Quarterly magazine publishing company receives thousands of subscription orders by mail each day. A document is created for each order. The order documents are batched in groups of 30 to 50, and a header form is completed

showing the total number of documents per batch. The documents are then keyed and verified by separate data entry clerks and processed each night. An edit/validation program rechecks the number of units in each batch. It prints valid and invalid batch reports and posts valid batches to a valid transaction file. The valid transaction file is fed to a series of programs that update Young Professional Quarterly's inventory, produce sales invoices, and feed the accounts receivable system. The Valid Batch Report is reconciled to the totals on the batch headers. Batches listed in the Invalid Batch Report are reviewed, corrected, and resubmitted.

List and discuss the control weaknesses in this system and their impact. What corrective measures would you suggest?

3. Suppose you were asked to help design the controls for an information system. What pieces of information would you need?

4. Many organizations, such as MasterCard, cited earlier in this chapter, take elaborate precautions for backing up their computer systems. Why is this essential? What considerations must be addressed by a backup plan?

5. Traditionally, organizations have devoted 75% of their security budgets to protect against penetration or damage by outsiders. Yet by far the largest source of losses has been errors, accidents, and omissions made by people inside the organization. Discuss.

Security Flaws in Treasury System

The Financial Management Service, with 2500 employees, is the part of the Treasury Department responsible for collecting and dispensing money for the federal government. It issues payments for most agencies that total about $1 trillion a year. It writes annually about 500 million checks for Social Security, veterans' benefits, government salaries, and other government payments. To assist the collection and disbursement of these funds, the Treasury Financial Communication System links the Treasury, the Federal Reserve System, and major banks in a nationwide electronic network. This network must be used when federal agencies make payments of $25,000 or more to government contractors.

Two confidential studies have found serious security flaws in this network, which transfers $1–2 billion a day. One study by the General Accounting Office concluded that the system's outdated technology left it open to forged payment vouchers submitted to disbursing centers. It found that passwords for accessing parts of the system were supplied to unauthorized users within the agency some time between October 1983 and February 1984. As of the writing of the study, the passwords were still not adequately secured. Furthermore, signatures of government officials authorizing huge payments were not always verified, nor were signature card files properly maintained.

The other study, by the Orkand Corporation, a private consultant for the Treasury Department, found numerous technical and administrative deficiencies in the system. It included a quantitative risk analysis of technical and procedural problems that estimated a loss of $15.4 million per year. At least $8.3 million of this loss could be attributed to improper uses of the system, security failures, personnel failures, and other performance problems. An annual loss of $7.3 million would result from interest that the government did not earn because it paid its bills too early.

The study found one middle-level Treasury Department computer expert who could independently modify the procedures of the entire system, working on a PC at home. Between $1 and $2 billion in transfers between various financial institutions could be affected. There was no evidence that this individual ever took advantage of his power. However, this person could have stolen billions of dollars or been forced by terrorists or criminals to transfer hundreds of millions of dollars out of the Treasury.

The study also found that the documentation for the system was inaccurate and inadequate. Poor documentation could lead to unauthorized payments, late payments, or misdirected disbursements or receipts. One inves-

tigator discovered that the locks had not been changed in 22 years on an important Financial Management Service safe outside of Washington. At least 38 current and former Treasury Department employees could have kept copies of the keys to open the safe without authorization.

In a statement to *The New York Times*, William E. Douglas, commissioner of the Financial Management Service, acknowledged that the Treasury network has hundreds of flaws. His report to Treasury Secretary James A. Baker 3rd noted that the Treasury computer network suffered from 450 different security problems, 195 of which were material. Douglas formally advised Baker that he could not guarantee the system's security.

Internal audits and reviews did not find any financial loss from security breakdowns in the Treasury Department's electronic payments system. Mr. Douglas stated that the Financial Management Service had corrected about 50% of the total weaknesses identified by early 1986 and that a schedule had been developed to fix the remainder.

Adapted from "Flaws Seen in Treasury Computers," *The New York Times*, February 13, 1986.

Case Study Questions

1. Other experts in risk analysis have stated that annual losses from the Treasury Department's financial communication system might be as high as $1.5 billion. Why?
2. What kinds of control weaknesses do the problems with this system exemplify?
3. Imagine yourself an auditor asked to recommend ways to tighten the controls for this system. What improvements would you suggest?
4. In addition to financial losses, what other problems could result from the vulnerabilities of this system?

References

Atkins, William, "Jesse James at the Terminal," *Harvard Business Review* (July–August 1985).

Bortnick, Jane. "Computer Crime and Security," Congressional Research Service, Library of Congress, September 1984.

Buss, Martin D.J., and Salerno, Lynn M. "Common Sense and Computer Security," *Harvard Business Review* (March–April 1984).

Chaum, David, "Security without Identification: Transaction Systems to Make Big Brother Obsolete," *Communications of the ACM*, Vol. 28 (October 1985).

Computer Services Executive Committee. *The Auditor's Study and Evaluation of Internal Control in EDP Systems*. New York: American Institute of Certified Public Accountants, 1977.

Fisher, Royal P. *Information Systems Security*. Englewood Cliffs, N.J.: Prentice-Hall, 1984.

Halper, Stanley D., Davis, Glenn C., P. O'Neill-Dunne, Jarlath, and Pfau, Pamela R. *Handbook of EDP Auditing*. Boston: Warren, Gorham and Lamont, 1985.

Hannan, James, ed. *A Practical Guide to EDP Auditing*. Pennsauken, N.J.: Auerbach, 1982.

"Information Security and Privacy," *EDP Analyzer* (February 1986).

Kneer, Dan C., and Lampe, James C. "Distributed Data Processing: Internal Control Issues and Safeguards," *EDPACS: The EDP Audit, Control and Security Newsletter*, Vol. 10 (June 1983).

Laudon, Kenneth C. "Data Quality and Due Process in Large Inter-organizational Record Systems," *Communications of the ACM*, Vol. 29 (January 1986a).

Laudon, Kenneth C. *Dossier Society: Value Choices in the Design of National Information Systems*. New York: Columbia University Press, 1986b.

Madnick, Stuart E. "Management Policies and Procedures Needed for Effective Computer Security," *Sloan Management Review*, Vol. 20 (Fall 1978).

Mair, W.C., Wood, D.W., and Davis, K.W. *Computer Control and Audit*. Wellesley, Mass.: Institute of Internal Auditors, 1978.

Parker, Donn B., and Nycum, Susan N. "Computer Abuse Assessment and Control Study." Stanford, Calif.: Stanford Research Institute, March 1979.

Parker, Donn B., and Nycum, Susan H. "Computer Crime," *Communications of the ACM*, Vol. 27 (April 1984).

Privacy Protection Study Commission. *Personal Privacy in an Information Society*. Washington, D.C.: Government Printing Office, 1977.

Task Force on Computer Crime, American Bar Association, Section of Criminal Justice. "Report on Computer Crime." Washington, D.C.: American Bar Association, 1984.

U.S. Department of Health, Education and Welfare Advisory Committee on Automated Personal Data Systems. "*Records, Computers, and the Rights of Citizens*." Cambridge, Mass: Massachusetts Institute of Technology Press, 1973.

U.S. General Accounting Office. "Federal Information Systems Remain Highly Vulnerable to Fraudulent, Wasteful, Abusive, and Illegal Practices," Washington, D.C.: U.S. General Accounting Office, April 21, 1982.

Ware, Willis. "Information Systems Security and Privacy," *Communications of the ACM*, Vol. 27 (April 1984).

Zimmerman, Joel S. "PC Security: So What's New?" *Datamation*, Vol. 31 (November 1985).

CHAPTER 19

System Success and Failure: Implementation

OUTLINE

Managers in a prominent commercial bank with branches throughout the United States and Europe find its batch loan account system virtually useless. Pages of reports are filled with zeroes, making it practically impossible to assess the status of a client's loan. The amount of the loan, the outstanding balance, and the repayment schedule must be tracked manually.

The bank is also highly dissatisfied with its on-line client reporting system. Although the bank maintains files on all areas for client accounts (loans, savings, Individual Retirement Accounts, checking), only checking and savings account data are available on-line. Therefore, managers and analysts cannot obtain complete client profiles when they need them.

This is a classic example of information system failure. Experiences such as these occur in nearly every organization. Because so many information systems are trouble-ridden, designers, builders, and users of information systems should understand how and why they succeed or fail.

In this chapter the student will learn:
- How to identify successful systems and system failures.
- Major problem areas in information systems.
- Criteria for determining whether a system is successful.
- The principal causes of information system failure.
- The relationship between implementation process and system outcome.
- How to minimize system failure by using appropriate strategies to manage the implementation process.

19.1 Introduction

A high percentage of information processing applications are failures. This does not usually mean that the information system is falling apart but rather that it is not used the way it was intended or is not used at all. Users may have to develop parallel manual systems to obtain the information they need or devise manual procedures to make the system work properly.

In some systems, nearly all of the reports put out for management are never read. They are considered useless, full of figures of no consequence for decision making or analysis (Lucas, 1981). Other automated systems go untouched because they are either too difficult to use or because their data can't be trusted. Users continue to maintain their records manually. Still other systems founder because of processing delays, excessive operational costs, or chronic production problems. In all of these cases, the information systems in

Washington County Hospital's DP Pains

Washington County Hospital in Hagerstown, Maryland, had relied entirely on a batch timesharing service for all of its data processing. Data processing, personnel and accounting departments had to time their activities around the timesharing service's operating schedule. The arrangement proved too inflexible: Payroll time cards had to be turned in on Monday, with no changes allowed after Tuesday evening to make the Thursday pay day. It was impossible for personnel administrators to change records conveniently, verify the revisions and run reports with the new data. Instead they had to wait 24 hours for the update. The resulting inflexibility limited human resources and personnel functions at the hospital and created problems such as the need to generate tapes. In March 1982 the hospital bought its own IBM 4331 mainframe and started converting to in-house systems.

Adapted from "Hospital Was in DP Pain Until In-House 'Rescue'," *MIS Week*, November 28, 1984.

question must be judged failures. Examples of all of these problems can be found in the vignettes in this section.

Information System Problem Areas

The problems causing information system failure fall into multiple categories, as illustrated by Figure 19.1. The major problem areas are design, data, cost, and operations. These problems can be attributed not only to technical features of information systems but to nontechnical sources as well. In fact, most of these problems stem from organizational factors.

Design

The actual design of the system fails to capture essential business requirements. Information may not be provided quickly enough to be helpful; it may be in a format that is impossible to digest and use; or it may represent the wrong pieces of data.

A system may be designed with a poor *user–system interface*. The way in which nontechnical business users must interact with the system is excessively complicated and discouraging. For example, an input form or on-line screen may be so poorly arranged that no one

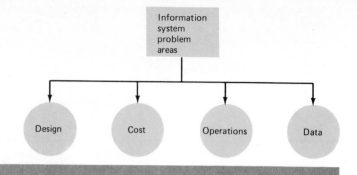

FIGURE 19.1

Information system problem areas. Problems with an information system's design, cost, operations, or data can be evidence of system failure.

wants to submit data. Or the procedures to request on-line information retrieval may be so unintelligible that users are too frustrated to make requests. As a result, a system may go unused and eventually may have to be discontinued.

Essential reports on search activity for a nationally known executive recruiting firm are routinely 3 months out of date. Statistics on the number of searches initiated in a given month must be developed manually. Recruiters have no way of tracking and coordinating searches among the company's branch offices in New York, Chicago, Houston, and Los Angeles.

For analysis of employee trends and strategic planning, the human resources department of a multidivisional manufacturing concern created an on-line "Employee History" system with a popular fourth-generation language. The file consisted of 5 consecutive years of year-end data from the main personnel database. The application was considered useless because the year-end data did not capture all of the discrete changes in employment status that had occurred throughout each year. Moreover, on-line response time was often over 15 minutes per query.

An information system will be judged a failure if its design is not compatible with the structure, culture, and goals of the organization. As pointed out in Chapter 4, management and organization theorists have viewed information system technology as closely interrelated with all of the other components of organizations—tasks, structure, people, and culture. Since all of these components are interdependent, a change in one will affect all of the others. Therefore, the organization's tasks, participants, structure, and culture are bound to be affected when an information system is changed. When we design a system, we are redesigning the organization.

Historically, information system design has been preoccupied with technical issues at the expense of organizational concerns. The result has been information systems that are often incompatible with their organization's structure, culture, and goals. Without a close organizational fit, such systems have created tensions, instability, and conflict.

Data

The data in the system have a high level of inaccuracy or inconsistency. The information in certain fields may be erroneous or ambiguous; or it may not be broken out properly (as illustrated by the following benefits system example) for business purposes. Information required for a specific business function may be inaccessible because the data have never been complete.

Cost

Some systems operate quite smoothly, but their cost to implement and run on a production basis is way over budget. These excessive expenditures cannot be justified by the demonstrated business value of the information they provide.

The employee benefits department of a multiunit manufacturing concern continues to maintain all of the benefits data for the company's 20,000 employees manually, despite the presence of an automated, on-line benefits system custom designed to meet Employee Retirement Income Security Act (ERISA) requirements. Users complain that the data in the system are unreliable because they do not capture the prior plan history for employees from acquisitions and because payroll earnings figures are out-of-date. All pension calculations, preretirement estimates, and benefits analysis must be handled manually.

An insurance company with over 5000 employees decides to convert its internally run company payroll system from batch to on-line. To save time and development costs, it opts for a highly touted on-line payroll package from a leading software vendor. Installation costs are almost twice what is budgeted and the project is completed a year late. Moreover, because of software design flaws, clock time for payroll undating is two to three times longer and operational costs are twice what is budgeted. Under instructions from management, costs are cut by converting the bulk of payroll processing back to batch mode. Only superficial editing and transaction processing can be performed on-line.

The accounts receivable system of a medium-sized consumer products manufacturer is constantly breaking down. Production runs have been aborting several times a month, and major month-end runs have been close to 3 weeks behind schedule. Because of excessive reruns, schedule delays, and time devoted to fixing antiquated programs, the data processing staff has no time to work out long-term solutions or convert to an on-line system.

Operations

The system does not run well. As illustrated by the preceding example, information is not provided in a timely and efficient manner because the computer operations that handle information processing break down. Jobs that abort too often lead to excessive reruns and delayed or missed schedules for delivery of information. An on-line system may be operationally inadequate because the response time is too long.

Measuring System Success and Failure

How can we tell whether a system is successful or not? This is not always an easy question to answer. Not everyone may agree about the value or effectiveness of a particular information system. Individuals with different decision-making styles or ways of approaching a problem may have totally different opinions about the same system. A system valued highly by an analytical, quantitatively oriented user may be totally dismissed by an intuitive thinker who is more

FIGURE 19.2

Measures of information system success and failure. MIS researchers have different criteria for measuring the success of an information system but these measures are considered the most important.

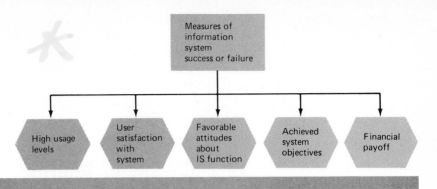

concerned with feelings and overall impressions. Likewise, a junior sales manager with a new MBA in marketing may be more appreciative of information system reports on the demographic characteristics of his territory than a veteran representative who has worked the same territory for 15 years and knows it thoroughly. The perception and use of information systems can be heavily conditioned by personal and situational variables (Lucas, 1981).

Nevertheless, MIS researchers have looked for a formal set of measures for rating systems. Various criteria have been developed, but the following measures of system success, illustrated in Figure 19.2, are considered the most important.

1. *High levels of system use*, as measured by polling users, employing questionnaires, or monitoring parameters such as the volume of on-line transactions.
2. *User satisfaction*, as measured by questionnaires or interviews. This might include users' opinions on the accuracy, timeliness, and relevance of information; on the quality of service; and perhaps on the schedule of operations. Especially critical are managers' attitudes on how well their information needs were satisfied (Ives et al., 1983; Wescott, 1985).
3. *Favorable attitudes* of users about information systems and the information systems staff.
4. *Achieved objectives*, the extent to which the system meets its specified goals, as reflected by the quality of decision making resulting from use of the system.
5. *Financial payoff* to the organization, either by reducing costs or by increasing sales or profits.

The fifth measure is considered to be of limited value even though cost/benefit analysis may have figured heavily in the decision to build a particular system. As discussed in Chapter 21, the benefits of an information system may not be totally quantifiable. Moreover, tangible benefits cannot be easily demonstrated for the more advanced DSS applications. And even though cost/benefit methodology has been rigorously pursued, the history of many systems development projects has shown that realistic estimates have always been difficult to formulate. MIS researchers have preferred to concentrate instead on the human and organizational measures of system success (Lucas, 1981).

19.2 Causes of Information System Success and Failure

As described in Chapter 4, systems are developed in the first place because of powerful external environmental forces and equally powerful internal or institutional forces. Many systems fail because of the opposition of either the environment or the internal setting.

As many MIS researchers have pointed out, the introduction or alteration of an information system has a powerful behavioral and organizational impact. It transforms the way various individuals and groups perform and interact. Changes in the way information is defined, accessed, and used to manage the resources of the organization often lead to new distributions of authority and power (Lucas, 1975). This internal organizational change breeds resistance amd opposition and can lead to the demise of an otherwise good system. An important characteristic of most information systems is that individuals are asked or required to change their behavior in order to make the system function.

But there are other reasons why a system may fail. Several studies have found that in organizations with similar environments and institutional features, the same innovation will be successful in some organizations but fail in others. Why? One explanation focuses on different patterns of implementation.

The Concept of Implementation

Implementation refers to all of the organizational activities involved in the adoption, management, and routinization of an innovation. Figure 19.3 illustrates the major stages of implementation described in the literature and the major approaches to the subject (see also Tornatsky et al., 1983; Westin and Laudon, 1988).

Some of the implementation research focuses on actors and roles. The belief is that organizations should select actors with appropriate social characteristics and systematically develop organizational roles, such as "product champions," in order to innovate successfully (see Figure 19.4). Generally, this literature focuses on early adoption and management of innovations.

A second school of thought in the implementation literature focuses on strategies of innovation. One extreme is top-down innova-

Implementation Stages

Approaches	Adoption	Management	Routinization
Actors, roles	XXXX	XX	
Strategy		XXXX	
Organizational factors		XXXX	XXXX

FIGURE 19.3
Approaches and stages in the implementation literature. The Xs indicate the stages of implementation on which the different approaches tend to focus. For instance, literature that uses an actor/role approach to implementation tends to focus on the early stages of adoption and management.

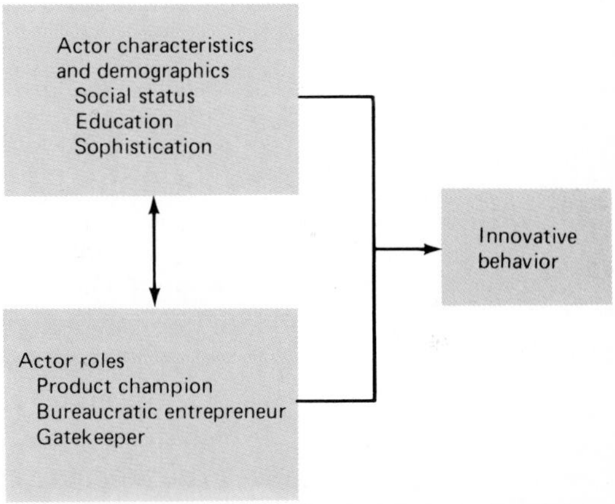

Actor characteristics and demographics
Social status
Education
Sophistication

Innovative behavior

Actor roles
Product champion
Bureaucratic entrepreneur
Gatekeeper

FIGURE 19.4
Actors in the innovation process.

tion and the other is grass-roots innovation. There are many examples of organizations in which the absence of senior management support for innovation dooms the project from the start. At the same time, without strong grass-roots, end-user participation, information system projects can also fail.

A third approach to implementation focuses on general organizational change factors as being decisive to the long-term routinization of innovations. Table 19.1 illustrates some of the key organizational actions required for long-term, successful implementation (Yin, 1981).

TABLE 19.1
Indicators of System Implementation

Support by local funds

New organizational arrangements

Stable supply and maintenance

New personnel classifications

Changes in organizational authority

Internalization of the training program

Continual updating of the system

Promotion of key personnel

Survival of the system after turnover of its originators

Attainment of widespread use

Source: Adapted from Yin (1981).

In the context of implementation, the systems analyst is a change agent. The analyst not only develops technical solutions but redefines the configurations, interactions, job activities, and power relationships of various organizational groups. The analyst is the catalyst for the entire change process and is responsible for ensuring that the changes created by a new system are accepted by all parties involved. The change agent communicates with users, mediates between competing interest groups, and ensures that the organizational adjustment to such changes is complete.

The Kolb/Frohman Model

One model of the implementation process is the Kolb/Frohman model of organizational change. This model divides the process of organizational change into a seven-stage relationship between an organizational *consultant* and his or her *client*. (The consultant corresponds to the information system designer and the client to the user.) The success of the change effort is determined by how well the consultant and client deal with the key issues at each stage. The Kolb/Frohman model, as applied to system implementation, is outlined in Table 19.2 (Kolb and Frohman, 1970).

Studies of the implementation process have examined the relationship between information system designers and users at different

	TABLE 19.2 Kolb/Frohman Model of Organizational Change for System Implementation	**Stage**	**Description**
		1. Scouting	The user and the designer assess each other's needs and abilities. An entry point for the project is selected.
		2. Entry	The user and the designer develop an initial statement of problems, goals, and objectives, resulting in mutual commitment, trust, and a "contract" for conducting the project.
		3. Diagnosis	The user and the designer gather the data to refine the definition of the problem. They assess the available resources for continuing the project.
		4. Planning	The user and the designer define specific operational objectives. They examine alternative ways of reaching these objectives and their organizational impact. They develop an action plan.
		5. Action	The user and designer implement the best alternative solution, modifying the action plan where appropriate.
		6. Evaluation	The user and the designer assess how well the original objectives were met, deciding whether to continue working on the project or to terminate it.
		7. Termination	The user and the designer confirm new patterns of behavior and complete the transfer of ownership and responsibility for the new system to the client.

stages of systems development, focusing on issues such as the following:

- Conflicts between the technical or machine orientation of information systems specialists and the organizational or business orientation of users.
- The impact of information systems on organizational structures, work groups, and behavior.
- The planning and management of systems development activities.
- The degree of user participation in the design and development process.

Causes of System Success and Failure

Implementation research to date has found no single explanation for system success or failure. Nor does it suggest a single formula for system success. However, it has found that implementation outcome can be largely determined by the following factors:

- The role of users in the implementation process.
- The degree of management support for the implementation effort.

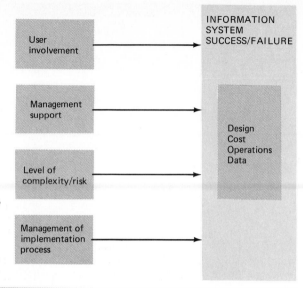

FIGURE 19.5
Causes of information system success and failure. The implementation outcome can be largely determined by the role of the users; the degree of management support; the level of risk and complexity in the implementation project; and quality of management of the implementation process itself.

- The level of risk and complexity of the implementation project.
- The quality of management of the implementation process.

These are largely behavioral and organizational issues and are illustrated in Figure 19.5.

User Involvement and Influence

User involvement in the design and operation of information systems has several positive results. First, if users are heavily involved in systems design, they have more opportunities to mold the system according to their priorities and business requirements. Second, they are more likely to react positively to the system because they have been active participants in the change process. Their participation in implementation fosters favorable attitudes toward the system and the changes it engenders (Lucas, 1974).

Experiments and field studies have shown that participation inspires favorable attitudes for the following reasons:

- The participation process is challenging and ego enhancing.
- Participation usually fosters more commitment to change.
- Participants in the process become more knowledgeable about the change itself and develop more skills and opportunities to control it.

Incorporating the user's knowlege and expertise leads to better solutions as well.

The User–Designer Communications Gap

The relationship between consultant and client has traditionally been a problem area for information system implementation efforts. Users and information system specialists tend to have different backgrounds, interests, and priorities. These differences lead to divergent organizational loyalties, approaches to problem solving, and vocabularies. Information system specialists, for example, often have a highly technical or machine orientation to problem solving. They look for elegant and sophisticated technical solutions in which hardware and software efficiency is optimized at the expense of ease of use or organizational effectiveness. Users, on the other hand, prefer systems that are oriented to solving business problems or facilitating organizational tasks. Often the orientations of both groups are so at odds that they appear to speak in different tongues. These differences are illustrated in Table 19.3.

Systems development projects run a very high risk of failure when there is a pronounced gap between users and technicians and when these groups continue to pursue different goals. Under such conditions, users are often driven out of the implementation process. Participation in the implementation effort is extremely time-consuming and takes them away from their daily activities and responsibilities. Since they cannot comprehend what the technicians are saying, the entire project is best left in the hands of the information specialists alone. With so many implementation efforts guided by purely technical considerations, it is no wonder that many systems fail to serve organizational needs.

TABLE 19.3

The User—Designer Communications Gap. The chart depicts the typical concerns of end users and technical specialists (information system designers) regarding the development of a new information system. One can see that they are markedly different. Communications problems between end users and designers are a major reason why user requirements are not properly incorporated into information systems and why users are driven out of the implementation process.

User Concerns	Technical Specialist Concerns
Will the system deliver the information I need for my work?	How much disk storage space will the master file consume?
How quickly can I access the data?	How many lines of program code will it take to perform this function?
How easily can I retrieve the data?	How can we cut down on CPU time when we run the system?
How much clerical support will I need to enter data into the system?	What is the most efficient way of storing this piece of data?
How will the operation of the system fit into my daily business schedule?	What database management system should we use?

Management Support

If an information systems project has the backing and approval of management at various levels, it is more likely to be perceived positively by both users and the technical information services staff. Both groups will feel that their participation in the development process will receive higher-level attention and priority. They will be recognized and rewarded for the time and effort they devote to implementation. Management backing also ensures that a systems project will receive sufficient funding and resources to be successful. Furthermore, all of the changes in work habits and procedures and any organizational realignments associated with a new system depend on management backing to be enforced effectively. If a manager considers a new system to be a priority, it will be more likely to be treated that way by his or her subordinates (Ein-Dor et al., 1978).

Level of Complexity and Risk

Systems differ dramatically in their size, scope, level of complexity, and organizational and technical components. Some systems development projects are more likely to fail because they carry a much higher level of risk than others. Researchers have identified three key dimensions that influence the level of project risk (McFarlan, 1981).

Project Size. The larger the project—as indicated by the dollars spent, the size of the implementation staff, the time allocated to implementation, and the number of organizational units affected—the greater the risk. Therefore, a $3 million project lasting for 4 years and affecting five departments in 20 operating units and 120 users will be much riskier than a $30,000 project for two users that can be completed in 2 months. Another risk factor is the company's experience with projects of given sizes. If a company is accustomed to implementing large, costly systems, the risk of implementing the $3 million project will be lowered. The risk may even be lower than that of another concern attempting a $200,000 project whose average project cost has been around $50,000.

Project Structure. Some projects are more highly structured than others. Their requirements are clear and straightforward, so that the outputs and processes can be easily defined. Users know exactly what they want and what the system should do; there is almost no possibility of their changing their minds. Such projects run a much lower risk than those whose requirements are relatively undefined, fluid, and constantly changing; where outputs cannot be easily fixed because they are subject to users' changing ideas or because users cannot agree on what they want.

Experience with Technology. The project risk will rise if the project team and the information system staff lack the required technical expertise. If the team is unfamiliar with the hardware, system software, application software, or database management system proposed for the project, it is highly likely that one or all of the

TABLE 19.4
Dimensions of Project
Risk

	Structure	Technology Level	Size	Risk
1.	High	Low	Large	Low
2.	High	Low	Small	Very low
3.	High	High	Large	Medium
4.	High	High	Small	Medium-low
5.	Low	Low	Large	Low
6.	Low	Low	Small	Very low
7.	Low	High	Large	Very high
8.	Low	High	Small	High

following will occur:

- Unanticipated time slippage because of the need to master new skills.
- A variety of technical problems if tools have not been thoroughly mastered.
- Excessive expenditures and extra time because of inexperience with the undocumented idiosyncracies of each new piece of hardware or software.

These dimensions of project risk will be present in different combinations for each implementation effort. Table 19.4 shows that eight different combinations are possible, each with a different degree of risk. The higher the level of risk, the more likely it is that the implementation effort will fail.

Management of the Implementation Process

The development of a new system must be carefully managed and orchestrated. Each project involves research and development. Requirements are hard to define at the level of detail for automation. The same piece of information may be interpreted and defined differently by different individuals. Multiple users have different sets of requirements and needs. Costs, benefits, and project schedules must be carefully assessed. The final design may not be easy to visualize. Since complex information systems involve so many interest groups, actors, and details, it is sometimes uncertain whether the initial plans for a system are truly feasible.

| Poor project management | → | Cost overruns
Time slippage
Technical shortfalls impairing performance
Failure to obtain anticipated benefits |

FIGURE 19.6
Consequences of poor project management. Without proper management, a systems development project will take longer to complete at excess cost, often lowering the quality of the end product. The resulting information system may not be able to demonstrate any benefits.

Often basic elements of success are forgotten. Training to ensure that end users are comfortable with the new system and fully understand its potential uses is often sacrificed or forgotten in system development projects. In part this is because the budget is already strained toward the end of a project, and at the very point of startup there are insufficient funds for training (Bikson et al., 1985).

The conflicts and uncertainties inherent in any implementation effort will be magnified when an implementation project is poorly managed and organized. As illustrated in Figure 19.6, a systems development project without proper management will most likely suffer these consequences:

- Cost overruns that vastly exceed budgets.
- Time slippage that is much greater than expected.
- Technical shortfalls resulting in performance that is significantly below the estimated level.
- Failure to obtain anticipated benefits.

The Implementation Process: What Can Go Wrong

The following problems are considered typical for each stage of the systems development life cycle when the implementation process is poorly managed.

Project Definition Phase

- Time, money, and resources have not been allocated to researching the problem. The problem remains poorly defined. Objectives of the implementation project will be vague and ambiguous; benefits will be difficult to measure.
- Little or no time is spent in preliminary planning. There are no standards to use in estimating preliminary costs or the duration of the project.
- The project team is not properly staffed. Personnel are assigned on an as-available basis and cannot dedicate themselves to the project.

User groups to be served by the system are not represented on the team.
- The information services staff promises results that are impossible to deliver.

Requirements Analysis ▬▬▬
- Requirements are derived from inadequate documentation of existing systems or incomplete findings from systems study activities.
- Users refuse to spend any time helping the project team gather the requisite information.
- Project analysts cannot interview users properly. They do not know how to ask the right questions. They cannot carry on an extended conversation with users because they lack good communications skills.

Design ▬▬▬
- Users, have no responsibility for or input to design activities. The design, therefore, reflects the biases of the technical staff. It does not mesh well with the structure, activities, and culture of the organization or the priorities of management.
- The system is designed only to serve current needs. No flexibility has been built in to anticipate the future needs of the organization.
- Drastic changes in clerical procedures or staffing are planned without any organizational impact analysis.
- Functional specifications are inadequately documented.

Programming ▬▬▬
- The amount of time and money required for software development is underestimated.
- Programmers are supplied with incomplete specifications.
- Not enough time is devoted to the development of program logic; too much time is wasted on writing code.
- Programmers do not take full advantage of structured design techniques. They write programs that are difficult to modify and maintain.
- Programs are not adequately documented.
- Requisite resources (such as computer time) are not scheduled.

Testing ▬▬▬
- The amount of time and money required for proper testing is underestimated.
- The project team does not develop an organized test plan.
- Users are not sufficiently involved in testing. They do not help to create sample test data or review test results. They refuse to devote much time to the testing effort.
- The implementation team does not develop appropriate acceptance tests for management review. Management does not review and sign off on test results.

Conversion ▬▬▬
- Insufficient time and money are budgeted for conversion activities, especially for data conversion.

- All of the individuals who will use the system are not involved until conversion begins. Training begins only when the system is about to be installed.
- The system is made operational before it is fully ready to compensate for cost overruns and delays.
- System and user documentation is inadequate.
- Performance evaluations are not conducted. No performance standards are established, and the results of the system are not weighed against the original objectives.
- Provisions for system maintenance are inadequate. Insufficient information systems personnel are trained to support the system and to make maintenance changes.

19.3 Managing Implementation

Not all aspects of the implementation process can be easily controlled or planned (Alter and Ginzberg, 1978). However, the chances for system success can be increased by anticipating potential implementation problems and applying appropriate corrective strategies. Various project management, requirements gathering, and planning methodologies have been developed for specific categories of problems. Strategies have also been devised for ensuring that users play an appropriate role throughout the implementation period and for managing the organizational change process.

Controlling Risk Factors

One way implementation can be improved is by adjusting the project management strategy to the level of risk inherent in each project. By placing a system development project in the proper risk category, levels of risk can be predicted in advance and strategies developed to counteract high-risk factors (McFarlan, 1981).

Implementers must adopt a contingency approach to project management, handling each project with the tools, project management methodologies, and organizational linkages geared to its level of risk. There are four basic project management techniques:

1. *External integration tools* link the work of the implementation team to that of users at all organizational levels.
2. *Internal integration* tools ensure that the implementation team operates as a cohesive unit.
3. *Formal planning tools* structure and sequence tasks, providing advance estimates of the time, money, and technical resources required to execute them.
4. *Formal control tools* help monitor the progress toward goals.

The risk profile of each project will determine the appropriate project management technique to apply, as illustrated in Table 19.5.

TABLE 19.5
Strategies to Control
Project Risk

Structure	Technology Level	Size	Risk	Project Management Tool
1. High	Low	Large	Low	High use of formal planning High use of formal control
2. High	Low	Small	Very Low	High use of formal control Medium use of formal planning
3. High	High	Large	Medium	Medium use of formal control Medium use of formal planning
4. High	High	Small	Medium-low	High internal integration
5. Low	Low	Large	Low	High external integration High use of formal planning High use of formal control
6. Low	Low	Small	Very low	High external integration High use of formal control
7. Low	High	Large	Very high	High external integration High internal integration
8. Low	High	Small	High	High external integration High internal integration

For example, projects with relatively *little structure* must involve users fully at all stages. Users must be mobilized to support one of many possible design options and to remain committed to a single design. Therefore, *external integration tools* must be applied.

- Users can be selected as project leaders or as the second-in-command on a project team.
- User steering committees can be created to evaluate the system's design.
- Users can become active members of the project team.
- The project can require formal user review and approval of specifications.
- Minutes of all key design meetings can be distributed widely among users.
- Users can prepare the status reports for higher management.
- Users can be put in charge of training and installation.
- Users can be responsible for change control, putting a brake on all nonessential changes to the system once final design specifications have been completed.

Projects with *high levels of technology* benefit from *internal integration* tools. The success of such projects depends on how well their technical complexity can be managed. Project leaders need both heavy technical and administrative experience. They must be able to anticipate problems and develop smooth working relationships among a predominantly technical team.

- Team members should be highly experienced.
- The team should be under the leadership of a manager with a strong technical and project management background.
- Team meetings should take place frequently, with routine distribution of meeting minutes concerning key design decisions.
- The team should hold regular technical status reviews.
- A high percentage of the team should have a history of good working relationships with each other.
- Team members should participate in setting goals and establishing target dates.
- Essential technical skills or expertise not available internally should be secured from outside the organization.

Projects with *high structure* and *low technology* present the lowest risk. The design is fixed and stable and the project does not pose any technical challenges. If such projects are large, they can be successfully managed by *formal planning and control tools*. With project management techniques such as PERT or CPM, a detailed plan can be developed. Tasks can be defined and resources budgeted.

- Milestone phases can be selected.
- Specifications can be developed from the feasibility study.
- Specification standards can be established.
- Processes for project approval can be developed.

Standard control techniques will successfully chart the progress of the project against budgets and target dates, so that the implementation team can make adjustments to meet their orginal schedule.

- Disciplines to control or freeze the design can be maintained.
- Deviations from the plan can be spotted.
- Periodic formal status reports against the plan will show the extent of progress.

Overcoming User Resistance

In addition to fine-tuning project management strategies, implementation risks can be reduced by securing management and user support of the implementation effort. Section 19.2 has shown how user participation in the design process builds commitment to the system. The final product is more likely to reflect users' requirements. Users are more likely to feel that they control and own the system.

However, MIS researchers have also noted that systems development is not an entirely rational process. Users leading design activities have used their position to further private interests and gain power rather than to promote organizational objectives.

Participation in implementation activities may not be enough to overcome the problem of user resistance. The implementation process is one of organizational change. Such change may be resisted because different users may be affected by the system in different ways. If the use of a system is voluntary, users may choose to avoid it; if use is mandatory, resistance will take the form of increased error rates, disruptions, turnover, and even sabotage. Therefore, the implementation strategy must not only encourage user participation and involvement, it must address the issue of *counterimplementation* (Keen, 1981).

Researchers have explained user resistance with one of three theories (Markus, 1983; Davis and Olson, 1985).

1. *People-oriented theory*. Factors internal to users as individuals or as a group produce resistance.
2. *System-oriented theory*. Factors inherent in the design create user resistance to a system.
3. *Interaction theory*. Resistance is caused by the interaction of people and systems factors.

Strategies have been suggested to overcome each form of user resistance.:

People oriented:	User education (training)
	Coercion (edicts, policies)
	Persuasion
	User participation to (elicit commitment)
System oriented:	User education
	Improved human factors
	User participation (for improved design)
	Package modification to conform to organizational procedures
Interaction:	Solve organizational problems before introducing new systems
	Restructure incentives for users
	Restructure the user–designer relationship
	Promote user participation when appropriate
	Sociotechnical approach to design/implementation

Strategies appropriate for the interaction theory incorporate elements of people-oriented and system-oriented strategies. There may be situations in which user participation is not appropriate. For example, some users may react negatively to a new design even though its overall benefits outweigh its drawbacks. Some individuals may stand to lose power as a result of design decisions (Robey and Markus, 1984). In this instance, participation in design may actually exacerbate resentment and resistance.

Designing for the Organization

The entire systems development process can be viewed as planned organizational change, since the purpose of a new system is to improve the organization's performance. Therefore, the development process must explicitly address the ways in which the organization will change when the new system is installed. In addition to procedural changes, transformations in job functions, organizational structure, power relationships, and behavior will all have to be carefully planned.

Although systems analysis and design activities are supposed to include impact evaluations, this area has traditionally been neglected. Much more attention needs to be paid to the way a proposed system will affect organizational structure, attitudes, decision making, and operations. To integrate information systems successfully with the organization, thorough and fully documented organizational impact assessments must be given more attention in the development effort.

Allowing for the Human Factor

The quality of information systems should be evaluated in terms of user criteria rather than the criteria of the information systems staff. In addition to targets such as memory size, access rates, and calculation times, systems objectives should include standards for user performance. For example, an objective might be that data entry clerks learn the procedures and codes for four new on-line data entry screens in a half-day training session.

Areas where users interface with the system should be carefully designed, with sensitivity to ergonomic issues. The impact of the application system on the work environment and job dimensions must be carefully assessed. One noteworthy study of 620 Social Security Administration claims representatives showed that the representatives with on-line access to claims data experienced greater stress than those with serial access to the data via teletype. Even though the on-line interface was more rapid and direct than teletype, it created much more frustration. Representatives with on-line access could interface with a larger number of clients per day. This changed the dimensions of the job for claims representatives. The restructuring of work—tasks, quality of working life, and performance—had a more profound impact than the nature of the technology itself (Turner, 1984).

Sociotechnical Design

Management and organizational researchers have suggested a *sociotechnical* approach to information system design and organizational change. Sociotechnical design aims to produce information systems that blend technical efficiency with sensitivity to organizational and human needs, leading to high job satisfaction (Mumford and Weir, 1979).

The sociotechnical design process emphasizes participation by the individuals most affected by the new system. The design plan establishes human objectives for the system that lead to increased job satisfaction. Designers set forth separate sets of technical and social design solutions. The social design plans explore different work group structures, allocation of tasks, and the design of individual jobs.

The proposed technical solutions are compared with the proposed social solutions. Social and technical solutions that can be combined are proposed as sociotechnical solutions. The alternative that best meets both social and technical objectives is selected for the final design. Systems with compatible technical and organizational elements are expected to raise productivity without sacrificing human and social goals.

19.4 Summary

A high percentage of systems are considered failures because they are not used the way they were intended or not used at all. System failure is evidenced by problems with design, data, operations, or costs. The sources of system success or failure are primarily behavioral and organizational.

Criteria for evaluating the success of an information system include (1) level of system use, (2) user satisfaction, (3) favorable user attitudes about the information systems staff, (4) achieved objectives, and (5) financial payoff to the organization.

Implementation is the entire process of organizational change surrounding the introduction of a new information system. One can better understand system success and failure by examining different patterns of implementation. The major causes of information system failure are (1) insufficient or improper user participation in the systems development process, (2) lack of management support, (3) poor management of the implementation process, and (4) high levels of complexity and risk in systems development projects.

Especially important is the relationship between participants in the implementation process, notably the interactions between system designers and users. The Kolb/Frohman model has been widely used to describe the organizational change associated with the implementation process. The success of organizational change can be determined by how well an organizational consultant and his or her client deal with key issues at various stages in their relationship.

The level of risk in a systems development project is determined by three key dimensions: (1) project size, (2) project structure, and

(3) experience with technology. Project risk factors can be brought under some control by a contingency approach to project management. The risk level of each project will determine the appropriate mix of external integration tools, internal integration tools, formal planning tools, and formal control tools to be applied.

Appropriate strategies can be applied to ensure the correct level of user participation in the systems development process and to minimize user resistance. Information system design and the entire implementation process should be managed as planned organizational change. Sociotechnical design emphasizes the participation of the individuals most affected by a new system and aims for an optimal blend of social and technical design solutions.

Key Words

System failure
Implementation
Change agent
Kolb/Frohman model
User–designer communications gap
Project risk
Project structure
External integration tools

Internal integration tools
Formal planning tools
Formal control tools
Counterimplementation
Organizational impact analysis
Sociotechnical design
People-oriented theory
System-oriented theory

Review Questions

1. What do we mean by information system failure?
2. What kinds of problems are evidence of information system failure?
3. How can we measure system success? Which measures of system success are the most important?
4. Define implementation. What are the major stages and approaches to implementation? Why is it necessary to understand the concept of implementation when examining system success and failure?
5. What are the major causes of system success or failure?
6. How does the Kolb/Frohman model help explain successful implementation?
7. What is the user–designer communications gap? What kinds of implementation problems can it create?
8. List some of the implementation problems that might occur at each stage of the systems life cycle.
9. What dimensions influence the level of risk in each systems development project?
10. What project management techniques can be used to control project risk?
11. What strategies can be used to overcome user resistance to systems development projects?

12. What organizational considerations should be addressed by information system design?

1. You are a member of your corporation's management committee, which oversees and approves systems development projects. What criteria would you consider in evaluating new project proposals? What would you look for to determine whether the project was proceeding successfully?
2. A prominent MIS researcher has observed that "The reason most information systems have failed is that we have ignored organizational behavior problems in the design and operation of computer-based information systems" (Lucas, 1974). Discuss.

CASE STUDY

Legislators Call SEC's Edgar Project a "Boondoggle"

At a hearing on March 15, 1985, U.S. legislators charged the Securities and Exchange Commission with making a "boondoggle" of its experimental electronic filing system. Representative John D. Dingell of Michigan, chairman of the House Committee on Energy and Commerce's Subcommittee on Oversight and Investigation, along with Representatives Gerry Sikorsky of Minnesota and Ron Wyden of Oregon, cited investigations by the subcommittee staff and the General Accounting Office (GAO).

The Securities and Exchange Commission awarded a $9.2 million contract to the accounting firm Arthur Andersen & Co. to set up a pilot project for an Electronic Data Gathering and Retrieval System (Edgar), with IBM and Dow Jones & Co. as subcontractors. The legislators noted that "Edgar" was a cost overrun project because the contract price was higher than the $6 million estimate given earlier to the House Appropriations Committee and that the SEC had rushed the contracting process to meet an early starting date. The legislators further claimed that the "Edgar" system was little more than a "glorified microfiche" system because it lacked "data-tagging" capabilities that would enable users to retrieve specific pieces of financial data from the database.

Since September 24, 1984, 144 companies had voluntarily submitted annual reports, proxy statements, and other securities documents to the SEC in electronic format. Although the documents are available for inspection at terminals and can be analyzed by the SEC enforcement staff, the SEC did not require corporate filers to submit the data in standard format. Special "data-tagging" software had to be developed to tag automatically important financial data, such as profit and loss figures, in nonstandard filings. The contractor, Arthur Andersen, had initially planned to develop the "data-tagging" software but dropped this feature from Edgar's pilot program.

SEC officials explained that the "data-tagging" facility had been postponed because of unexpected difficulty in developing the software, but the feature had not been eliminated. The SEC officials also claimed that "Edgar" was already much more than a "glorified micro-fiche" system, and featured electronic mail, access to external database services, word processing, and, in the near future, text-search capability. Kenneth A. Fogash, deputy execu-tive director of the SEC, also defended the project's starting date: The SEC wanted the "Edgar" pilot to start as scheduled to establish credibility with the securities industry and volunteer filers.

Adapted from "SEC's Edgar Project a 'Boondoggle,' Legislators Claim," *Computerworld*, March 25, 1985.

Case Study Questions

1. Would you consider the Edgar project a success or a failure? Discuss.
2. What mistakes were made in the management of the Edgar project?
3. If the SEC had the chance to redo the Edgar project, what recommendations would you make?

References

Alter, Steven, and Ginzberg, Michael. "Managing Uncertainty in MIS Implementation," *Sloan Management Review*, Vol. 20 (Fall 1978).

Best, James D. "The MIS Executive as Change Agent," *Journal of Information Systems Management* (Fall 1985).

Bikson, Tora K., Stasz, Cathleen, and Mankin, D.A. *Computer Mediated Work. Individual and Organizational Impact in One Corporate Headquarters*. Santa Monica, Calif.: Rand Corporation, 1985.

Davis, Gordon B. and Margrethe H. Olson "Developing and Implementing Application Systems," *Management Information Systems* 2nd ed. New York: McGraw Hill, 1985.

Ein-Dor, Philip, and Segev, Eli. "Organizational Context and the Success of Management Information Systems," *Management Science*, Vol. 24 (June 1978).

Franz, Charles, and Robey, Daniel. "An Investigation of User-Led System Design: Rational and Political Perspectives," *Communications of the ACM*, Vol. 27 (December 1984).

Ginzberg, M.J. "The Impact of Organizational Characteristics on MIS Design and Implementation." Working Paper CRIS 10, GBA 80-110. New York University Center for Research on Information Systems Area, Computer Applications and Information Systems Area, 1980.

Ginzberg, Michael J., "Early Diagnosis of MIS Implementation Failure: Promising Results and Unanswered Questions," *Management Science*, Vol. 27 (April 1981).

Gould, John D., and Lewis, Clayton. "Designing for Usability: Key Principles and What Designers Think," *Communications of the ACM*, Vol. 28 (March 1985).

Ives, Blake, Olson, Margrethe H., and Baroudi, Jack J. "The Measurement of User Information Satisfaction," *Communications of the ACM*, Vol. 26 (October 1983).

Keen, Peter W. "Information Systems and Organizational Change," *Communications of the ACM*, Vol. 24 (January 1981).

Kolb, D.A., and Frohman, A.L. "An Organization Development Approach to Consulting," *Sloan Management Review*, Vol. 12 (Fall 1970).

Lucas, Henry C., Jr. *Implementation: The Key to Successful Information Systems*. New York: Columbia University Press, 1981.

Lucas, Henry C., Jr. *Toward Creative Systems Design*. New York: Columbia University Press, 1974.

Lucas, Henry C., Jr. *Why Information Systems Fail*. New York: Columbia University Press, 1975.

Markus, M.L. "Power, Politics and MIS Implementation," *Communications of the ACM*, Vol. 26 (June 1983).

McFarlan, F. Warren. "Portfolio Approach to Information Systems," *Harvard Business Review* (September–October 1981).

Mumford, Enid, and Weir, Mary. *Computer Systems in Work Design: The ETHICS Method*. New York: Wiley, 1979.

Robey, Daniel, and Markus, M. Lynne. "Rituals in Information System Design," *MIS Quarterly* (March 1984).

Tornatsky, Louis G., Eveland, J.D., Boylan, M.G., Hetzner, W.A., Johnson, E.C., Roitman, D., and Schneider, J. *The Process of Technological Innovation: Reviewing the Literature*. Washington, D.C.: National Science Foundation, 1983.

Turner, Jon A. "Computer Mediated Work: The Interplay Between Technology and Structured Jobs," *Communications of the ACM*, Vol. 27 (December 1984).

Westcott, Russ. "Client Satisfaction: The Yardstick for Measuring MIS Success," *Journal of Information Systems Management* (Fall 1985).

Westin, Alan F., and Laudon, Kenneth C. *Information Technology at the Social Security Administration: 1935–1990*. forthcoming.

Yin, Robert K. "Life Histories of Innovations: How New Practices Become Routinized." *Public Administration Review*, (January/February 1981).

Using Critical Success Factors

This case study illustrates the use and benefits of the critical success factor (CSF) methodology. The methodology is used to identify corporate information needs and, subsequently, to develop a corporate information systems plan. The study was conducted at the Financial Institutions Assurance Corporation (FIAC), a pseudonym. The initial purpose of this study was to evaluate the firm's existing data processing system in light of intermediate-term corporate objectives. But as the firm became familiar with the CSF methodology, there was a fundamental rethinking of the nature of the corporation.

Introduction

FIAC is an insurance corporation that insures depositors at regulated financial institutions. FIAC works with state authorities and independent auditors. In the past, FIAC tended to react to situations developing in the field. As a result of the CSF study, however, FIAC has become much more proactive in its relationships with member institutions. Senior management has changed FIAC's use of information, created an MIS department, and begun to use information technology as a strategic weapon. The CSF methodology has been adopted as an ongoing tool to develop both MIS departmental goals and strategic plans for the firm.

Corporate History

FIAC is a private deposit insurer created in 1967 in North Carolina. The purpose of the corporation is to insure the deposits and liquidity of member financial institutions. FIAC protects depositors by seeing that institutions maintain an adequate net worth and cash flow. FIAC provides services similar to those provided by the Federal Deposit Insurance Corporation (FDIC). FIAC competes with the FDIC and other private firms for financial institutions' business.

At the end of 1983, FIAC insured 65 institutions with total deposits in excess of $2.8 billion. The rapid growth of the firm since 1967 had resulted in part from lack of competition. When FIAC was created, there was no national deposit insurance program for credit unions, and many savings and loan associations chose not to obtain insurance with the Federal Savings and Loan Insurance Corporation (FSLIC).

Competition heated up in the 1970s when the National Credit Union Administration (NCUA) was established as a federal agency to insure the deposits of credit unions. And as the savings and loan industry grew, more institutions became eligible for FSLIC. All of these developments put pressure on private insurers like FIAC.

However, FIAC had a number of operating advantages over the federal and state-run institutions. FIAC worked with state financial regulators and legislators to reform laws that restricted the operation of state-chartered financial institutions. These new laws and regulations allowed FIAC-insured, state-chartered financial institutions to better serve consumers. The federally insured institutions were restricted as to the types of loans they could make and the amount of interest they could pay on savings. To some extent, the state-chartered institutions operated in a riskier environment, as became clear in the mid-1980s when several state-chartered institutions failed. Nevertheless, the competitive advantage of the state-chartered, privately insured institutions was a contributing factor to federal deregulation of financial institutions in the early 1980s.

The rapid growth of FIAC business put increasing demands on its ability to monitor these institutions. Manual spread sheets gave way to programmable calculators, and finally to automated financial analysis systems run as a monthly batch job on minicomputers. The stability of the environment, the computerized information systems of FIAC's competitors, and the small scale of the operations monitored by FIAC allowed the original computer system to remain in place for several years.

In the turbulent period of the early 1980s, when interest rates skyrocketed, FIAC was able to withstand the fluctuations in interest rates without incurring any losses. Neither FIAC nor any of its insured institutions have ever had a loss from a deposit-related claim. Nevertheless, during this period, the pressures of maintaining a fiscally responsible position led FIAC to adopt a very defensive corporate posture.

Moreover, banking deregulation erased most of FIAC's competitive advantages. All institutions under deregulation could pay market interest rates. All institutions could enjoy broad asset and investment powers.

FIAC needed to regain its marketing edge and bolster its ability to maintain a record of safety.

In 1983, FIAC decided to pursue a strategy of geographic and institutional diversification in order to spread its risk and increase its market share. A change in enabling legislation allowed FIAC to offer deposit insurance to any institution eligible for FDIC, FSLIC, or NCUA membership, regardless of its geographic location. Prior to this change, FIAC could only insure credit unions and savings and loan associations in North Carolina. Now FIAC is the only private deposit insurer authorized to insure all types of financial institutions throughout the United States.

The Corporate Culture and Environment Prior to the CSF Study

FIAC was like many small businesses that had experienced rapid growth. Management deci-

sions were made by the chief executive officer and were centralized in a small group of individuals. All aspects of the corporation's operation were controlled centrally. Planning and operations were approached with a short time horizon. Staff members were hard-working "athletes" who maintained and actively fostered a corporate image of "lean and mean," which meant that there was very little management fat. Monitoring insured institutions generally meant the gathering of a large amount of data and a short analysis period. The corporate culture was characterized by informal and relatively infrequent communication between staff members. Higher-level managers were generalists with responsibilities in all areas.

The actual analysis of insured institutions required a great deal of work by a small group of individuals who gathered information from industry and regulatory sources, visited insured institutions, and analyzed the data. Individual analysts specialized in specific institutions because they were the only ones who maintained personal databases and personal information on those institutions. At times, the close, intimate client relations stood in the way of tough action by senior management against several insured institutions.

FIAC's original minicomputer system was purchased in the belief that customized, third-party software would be developed over several months and purchased for $10,000. The development actually took 18 months and the cost was over $40,000. Once installed, the system was maintained by a staff member in his spare time. This was a batch system that produced a standard set of reports on a monthly basis, using insured institutions' financial statements and statistical summaries as input. There was no corporate budget for data processing.

With the installation of this first computer system, data processing was viewed as a necessary evil to relieve tedious number crunching work. Staff analysts made extensive use of paper spread sheets and hand-held calculators both before and after the installation of this first system.

The maintenance of private databases by staff analysts based on their personal contact with the regulated institutions, as well as FIAC's entrepreneurial culture, did not make the efforts of the data processing staff easy. Information was viewed as a source of power by the professional analysts that could be used to influence decisions. It was not easy to get these individuals to give up control over information to a system. Other staff members argued that a central data processing staff might impair the corporation's flexibility.

The CSF Project

In 1983 FIAC was forced to review its data processing system. At first, senior management thought that this was merely a technical review of the system's capacity in light of the corporation's expansion plans. Management hoped to be able to improve the efficiency of the present system by simply increasing its size.

A consultant was hired to review the existing system's capacity and recommend a plan for enhancements. The consultant reported that senior management had underrated the potential impact that data processing could have in the corporation. He recommended use of a *critical success factor (CSF) method*. The CSF methodology was appealing to senior management and had their strong support.

The consultant also suggested that FIAC adopt an *information resources approach* to the project rather than the initial information function approach.

In an information resources approach, an organizationwide perspective is used in addressing MIS planning and the use of information in a firm. An information function planning approach deals mainly with the technical activities involved in establishing and managing a firm's information systems. The information resources approach is obviously much broader and emphasizes the relationship between the firm, on the one hand, and MIS on the other.

Methods

The consultant trained the corporate staff on the CSF concept. Each staff member was asked to make a list of personal CSFs and a list of corporate CSFs in preparation for meetings with the consultant.

A senior manager working with a consultant interviewed every member of the staff at all levels of the organization. The interviewee was asked to present his individual and corporate CSFs. The ultimate purpose of the CSF project (information resource planning) was not revealed to the interviewees. The interviewee was not asked to discuss sources of information until he had described all of his CSFs and related ideas. The consultant and the senior manager were careful not to bias or lead the discussion in any particular direction. Staff members were encouraged to be open and to express their own opinions, not simply to reflect their perception of management's opinion.

A chart of CSFs was developed by the consultant following the interviews. An aggregated list was made from this chart for the corporation as a whole. The list grouped trends, eliminated repetitive responses, and highlighted similarities and differences within departments. A list of corporate CSFs was then developed from this aggregated list.

Following the development of corporate CSFs, a staff retreat was held to examine and discuss the corporate, departmental, and individual CSFs. At this retreat, staff and management focused on required organizational changes that internal growth and external environmental change seemed to demand. By linking information resource planning, organizational design, and strategic planning through the CSF focus, information technology became a catalyst for discussions of organizational change.

FIAC hoped to leverage its staff through technology. In the retreat, it became clear that an information system directed toward the efficient processing of information would not be sufficient to meet all of FIAC's evolving information needs.

Unanticipated Benefits

The CSF process, as previously described, was very participative. A gap that had emerged between senior management and staff was to some extent overcome using this participative process. The process also led to the explicitly stated goals shared by both staff and management, and served to reduce conflict and increase cooperation among the various levels in the organization. A cross section of the staff reviewed and critiqued the final CSF list. A prioritized consensus list of CSFs was used to guide the development of a new organizational structure.

CSF List

The final CSF list included:

1. Prevent losses through risk management.
2. Increase diversification of the customer base.
3. Increase professional staff productivity.
4. Enhance the corporation's image with the firm's markets and the public.

With these corporate goals and objectives in mind, meetings were held with staff members to develop specific *organizational information needs*. These needs were then used as input into the design of the corporation's new computer based information system. Figure III.1 summarizes the process used in the study. Steps 1 through 9 are actual events and are highlighted by the accompanying interpretive remarks.

Corporate Impact

The CSF study had a profound impact on FIAC and how it used information. We will now describe four impact areas: the new information plan; a changing corporate attitude toward data processing; increases in staff productivity; and the adoption of the CSF methodology as a management tool.

The Information System Plan

The major planned result of the CSF was a redefinition of the corporation from an operations-driven deposit insurer to an information-driven risk manager. A three-stage approach to redesigning the corporation's information system reflects this new orientation.

Stage 1: Information Processing

First, the corporation's batch-oriented minicomputer will be replaced with a super mini to serve as a host to personal microcomputer work stations. The super mini will maintain a new database that will permit staff to access information that is currently stored off-line and is unavailable to analysts and managers.

The new system will also provide for the collection and retrieval of both hard and soft data. Information gathered by the analysts will now be stored centrally on-line. The host super mini will also provide access to external databases—something the staff wanted on a more systematic basis. Analysts will have the ability to download hard and soft data from the host to personal computers and to manipulate them using personally developed spread sheets, query, and word processing packages.

Time formerly spent using calculators and paper spread sheets to crunch numbers will be used for information analysis, problem solving, and direct contact with insured institutions.

Stage 2: Office Automation

In the second stage, data processing functions will be integrated with an office automation system containing word processing, graphics, electronic mail, electronic filing, calendar management, and project tracking software. Hopefully, this integration will enhance the efficiency and effectiveness of staff analysts. Such an integrated system will be accessed by field analysts using portable personal computers. This will enhance productivity outside of the office and increase communications. People will have access to information regardless of their proximity to the home office.

	STEP	OBSERVATIONS
1.	Develop a broad understanding of the firm and business, utilizing an external consultant.	
2.	The consultant develops a preliminary list of CSFs and suggests potential information system solutions.	Are the final CSFs biased by these preliminary findings?
3.	The consultant obtains senior management backing for the CSF concept.	The team of consultants and executives is coming closer to the organization's culture.
4.	Rockart's article on CSFs is used to educate the staff. People are asked to prepare CSFs for their interviews.	Corporate and personal CSFs are requested. Staff participation is critical.
5.	CSF interviews are held with each staff member.	The interview team should encourage each person to think creatively and independently.
6.	A chart of CSFs is developed from the interviews.	Representative CSFs and trends based on organizational level should be identified.
7.	The list of CSFs should be aggregated for the entire corporation.	
8.	CSFs should be used to promote redesign of the organization, strategic planning, and the organization's information system architecture.	This process is especially beneficial to smaller organizations and dynamic environments.
9.	The staff should be presented with the organization's CSFs and asked about specific information needs or information system products.	Prototyping may be useful for eliciting these information requirements. Problems often arise when linking organizational CSFs to individual information requirements.

FIGURE III.I
Processes in the Development of CSFs. (Adapted from "Critical Success Factor Analysis as a Methodology for MIS Planning," by Michael E. Shank, Andrew C. Boynton, and Robert W. Zmud. *MIS Quarterly*, Vol. 9, No. 2 (June 1985).)

Stage 3: Future Automation

The third stage of the information system plan involves developing direct access to the information maintained by insured institutions on their in-house or timesharing system. This involves building a communications bridge between FIAC and its clients. Management hopes that such an intimate client relationship will enhance the technological edge that the corporation now holds over its competitors.

Corporate Attitude Toward Data Processing

Senior management used to view data processing as a confining, costly, dysfunctional operation barely able to keep up with the changing environment. Now, however, management and staff view the information technology as a driving force that provides the corporation with a vital competitive edge. One senior manager expressed the change in his attitude as follows:

- "We don't need a computer."
- "What's wrong with the system we've got?"
- "When do I get my PC?"
- "When will the new database be operational?"

This changing management attitude from one of fear and distrust to one of active cooperation and understanding reflects the impact of the CSF process. FIAC has hired its first nonfinancial industry professional, a new MIS director. His position is closely tied to FIAC's planning process, and he is expected to influence the corporate strategy. Ten percent of the corporation's operating budget is now under the control of the MIS director. These expenditures are projected to be exceeded by increased revenues from expansion, new information-related customer services, and better risk management.

The changing corporate attitude toward information technology was captured in a recent presentation by the CEO to a state legislative commission. This CEO had been skeptical of the need for new information technology, but in his presentation he used the portable computer and a wide-screen television to present spread sheets, graphs, and an analysis of FIAC. The use of computers has added considerably to the effectiveness of presentations like these and has led to a changing perception in the marketplace of FIAC as a technological leader within the industry.

Staff Productivity

There is little doubt that the access to databases and decision support systems has increased information availability throughout FIAC. This has increased the productivity of established staff members, allowed new members to become productive far more rapidly, and contributed to the generation of new ideas at all levels of the corporation. The higher levels of communication and increased confidence in the system have increased the delegation of authority. Important management decisions have now been pushed further down in the hierarchy.

In its use of personal computers, FIAC has increased its ability to provide significant amounts of data to insured institutions. This is a new customer service. It has helped to rebuild the intimate relationship that existed prior to the early 1980s. Moreover, FIAC's ability to analyze information rapidly has increased its control over insured institutions. Staff analysts now

have more confidence and enjoy increased respect.

In the past, uncertainty and rapid change were viewed as threats by FIAC. Now FIAC has new confidence in its ability to use the CSF methodology and its enhanced information technology to cope with the uncertain environment. Now uncertainties are seen as opportunities that FIAC can exploit using its information resources.

Continued Use of the CSF Methodology

FIAC now uses the CSF methodology in a number of areas: information resource planning, strategic planning, and individual goal setting. As a result, staff members have a better idea of the goals and activities of the corporation. A common focus now exists throughout the organization and helps to align the goals of individuals and departments with the corporation's goals.

Why the CSF Project Succeeded

There are a number of factors that contributed to the success of the CSF methodology at FIAC.

First, the CSF methodology is a business-driven, rather than a technology-driven, method. FIAC was never a technically oriented corporation, nor was it experienced with computer systems. Its leaders and managers were business strategists and technicians first. Technological solutions were suggested by the CSF method only after business strategies and tactics were understood.

Second, the business strategies and tactics that emerged from the CSF project followed a top-down design process. Once all staff members understood and accepted the corporate CSFs, department and personal CSFs that were consistent with the corporation's CSFs could be developed. This resulted in a common organizational map that everyone understood.

A third factor is the strong senior management support of the CSF method. Without this strong individual championing of the project, it is unclear whether the method would have been successful.

Other MIS planning techniques might have produced similar results. The key was not the particular planning methodology but rather the planning behavior that resulted.

One of the problems with applying the CSF methodology was that not all levels of the corporation found it useful for defining information needs. It was only the firm's senior managers who found the methodology truly useful in defining their individual reporting and information needs. One reason why this may have been the case was the conceptual nature of CSFs. Lower-level managers had difficulty relating the broad corporate CSFs to their own information needs.

Guidelines and Cautions for Use of CSF Methodology in Other Organizations

In some ways, FIAC had a unique corporate environment caught at just the right moment to use CSF methodology successfully. There are a number of guidelines developed in this case that may be relevant to other organizations.

1. CSFs are flexible and easily understood, which may lead some users to be too casual in their application. Casual application without a thorough thinking through of the impiications of CSFs can lead to false results. CSFs have to be used with precision, as in a formal method.
2. The individual managing the CSF study should have a thorough understanding of the nature of the business. If MIS executives and senior management cannot speak the same language, the project will fail.
3. It is vital to have a senior manager champion the CSF project. One or more members of senior management must be available and active in the project to convince other senior managers to support it.
4. Other corporate members have to be educated in the CSF concept before they are interviewed. Otherwise, the interviews will produce useless information.
5. During the initial set of interviews, CSFs should not be linked explicitly to information requirements, computer applications, or other factors. CSFs should be identified in a broad corporate or personal sense first, and then information requirements should be deduced from them.

Conclusion

The CSF methodology was a major force in instituting corporatewide MIS planning at FIAC. It helped to focus the vital issues in both areas. CSF methodology was a practical and intuitive method that could be easily understood by senior management and MIS staff alike. The method provided assurance that critical information needs were explicitly addressed in the planning process by relating information resources to those areas of FIAC activity that must function well for the corporation to succeed. Perhaps most important, the CSF methodology developed a consensus and a core of information technology proponents throughout the organization. This enhanced the understanding of MIS by management. The CSF method continues to be used by FIAC to align its strategic MIS plans with those of top management.

Adapted from "Critical Success Factor Analysis as a Methodology for MIS Planning," by Michael E. Shank (Financial Institutions Assurance Corporation), Andrew C. Boynton, and Robert W. Zmud (The University of North Carolina, School of Business Administration). In *MIS Quarterly*, Vol. 9, No. 2 (June 1985).

Case Study Questions

1. How was the CSF method employed in this case different from a Business (or Enterprise) System Planning (BSP) method? Contrast both of these approaches to the other approaches identified in the chapters on systems analysis.

2. What difference would other approaches (previously identified) make for the kinds of systems developed at FIAC?

3. List the unique conditions at FIAC that contributed to the successful use of CSF methods.

4. According to the authors, the CSF method seemed to work best for the senior managers. Why might this be so? Why did the lower-level managers have a hard time connecting corporate CSFs and personal needs for information?

5. How might some personal CSFs contrary to corporate CSFs emerge in a study like this?

6. In this case, the aggregation of different CSFs proceeded smoothly. Can you expect this to happen in all cases? If not, why not? What impact will powerful underlying conflicts in the organization have on CSF methods?

P A R T   F O U R

Managing Information System Resources

Part Four concludes the text by pointing out the critical issues in information resource and technology management. Information systems are now so deeply embedded in organizations that their value is diminished unless information users fully understand and manage their data. Likewise, organizations must be able to adjust their information systems to changing technology, environmental pressures, and configurations of applications, intelligence, and data to take advantage of strategic opportunities. Important information systems management concepts are: data administration; strategic systems planning; management of information systems projects; establishing the worth of information systems; and effective utilization of information systems personnel.

Chapter 20 charts the emergence of a new organizational function to manage data resources called "data administration." As new applications, microcomputers, and end-user computing proliferate, organizations need to inventory their data and ensure that it is consistent, reliable, and compatible with the organization's information requirements. Data administration tools and methodologies include: strategic data planning; data dictionaries; data quality assurance techniques; and information management policies and procedures. This chapter also describes organizational obstacles to data administration and ingredients of effective information management.

Chapter 21 provides an overview of the major information technology management issues. This chapter discusses: strategic planning for systems; assessing system costs and benefits; management of information systems projects; management of information systems personnel; and designing the information architecture of the organization. The concept of "strategic transitions" dramatizes the need to understand and manage the changing relationship between information systems and the firm.

Part Four Case Study: "Systems Modernization at the Social Security Administration". The case describes one of the largest information system projects in history. In the early 1980s the Social Security Administration's information systems nearly collapsed. They were totally inadequate for its mission and operational needs. The SSA's solution was a massive Systems Modernization Plan. Its implementation and outcome illustrate many of the themes of this section: planning for systems; the need for data administration; management of large-scale information system projects; and organizational and management obstacles to "strategic transitions."

20

Managing Data Resources: Data Administration

■ OUTLINE

(Continued on next page.)

641

Before 1982 the Bank of America's 1000 branches managed information autonomously. They created their own standards and products, such as a cash management system for tracking accounts. Many of Bank of America's systems were developed to fulfill each unit's needs without an overall plan. In time the bank was faced with many incompatible systems that could not tie its products together. It was impossible to draw together all of the information the bank had on a particular customer. Separate searches had to be conducted to determine if the customer had a checking account, a securities account, an IRA account, or other relationships with the bank.

Decentralized information management increased both production costs and time to put new products on the market, making the bank less competitive. In 1982 Bank of America had to create a new Bank of America Systems Engineering Group (BASE) to improve coordination and utilization of its information resources.

Adapted from "BankAmerica Melds U.S., Foreign MIS Operations," *MIS Week*, February 6, 1985.

Like many organizations, Bank of America has found that mismanaged data can have important strategic and operational consequences. As information systems grow in number and sophistication, an organization's ability to use them successfully will depend increasingly on how well it can manage its data. A separate organizational function called *data administration* is required to manage the organization's data resources.

In this chapter the student will learn:
- Why data must be managed as a critical organizational resource.
- How to define data administration as a distinct organizational function.
- Major data administration functions.
- Data administration tools and methodologies: data planning, data quality assurance techniques, and data dictionaries.
- Data administration disciplines: information management policies and procedures.
- Organizational obstacles to data administration.
- Strategies for effective information management.

20.1 Introduction

In many organizations, the focus of information systems management has changed. In the past, the emphasis was primarily on managing computers and the technology to process information. In organizations where information system use is relatively advanced, the primary concern has shifted to the information in computer systems itself and the need to manage it as a strategic resource. (Nolan, 1979).

The Need for Managed Data

The growth of information systems as instruments of management control has led to the recognition of the critical value of data. It is through the information in these systems that managers control the organization's basic resources—financial, human, and physical. Information is also the wellspring for strategies and directions that bolster the organization's competitive edge. Therefore, information itself has become a strategic resource, requiring its own policies and procedures for management and control.

Fragmentation of Data Resources

As automated information systems proliferate throughout the organization, the need for managed data has become a critical issue. Computer applications can now be developed so rapidly and easily that many enterprises' data resources have become progressively decentralized and fragmented. Each group in the organization has its own systems and its own set of information. Enterprises typically implement major applications such as the general ledger or accounts payable one at a time and set up separate databases for each. Unless the organization has adopted a database development strategy, each system has its own files and stores its own version of data independently of other systems. (See the discussion of the traditional data processing environment in Chapter 8.)

Data Redundancy and Inconsistency

Much of the data stored in information systems are redundant. The same piece of information—for example, customer number—is stored in multiple files. Over time, as groups update these data according to their own timing standards and business requirements, inconsistencies develop. Data in one system become inconsistent and incompatible with the same data in another, as illustrated in Figure 20.1. Other parts of the organization that depend on the information from these systems may not have a reliable source to turn to.

In many organizations, for example, the payroll system and the personnel system may register different amounts for the piece of data "employee earnings" unless both share an integrated database. Actual employee earnings will be calculated and stored in the payroll system. The personnel system will not reflect this information until it is updated from payroll. If the personnel system is not updated frequently with payroll information, there will be periods of time

FIGURE 20.1
Data inconsistency. The same data element may appear in many different forms throughout an organization.

1. Homonyms

   Two or more data elements with identical names but different logical lengths.

customer-no	pic x(12)
customer-no	pic x(06)

2. Synonyms

   Two or more data elements with identical data names and logical lengths but with different formats.

customer-no	pic x(12) (alphanumeric)
customer-no	pic 9(12) (numeric)

3. Aliases

   Several data elements with the same logical length but with different names and perhaps different formats.

custom-no	pic x(12) (alphanumeric)
c-no	pic 9(12) (numeric)

FIGURE 20.2
How information can become inconsistent. (Adapted from Martin, 1983.)

Field definition: Different parts of the organization may have different interpretations for the meaning of the same field.

Field structure: The same field may have different sizes and formats in different files. It may have, for example, 6 bytes in one file and 5 bytes in another (size); may be represented alphanumerically in one and numerically in another (format); and may contain different coding structures.

Record structure: Records with the same key may have different structures in different files.

Timing: The same field may be processed monthly, weekly, daily, or interactively on-line in different systems. As illustrated by the preceding discussion of employee earnings, representations of this data in different systems will have different values because they have been updated at different times.

Update logic: Representations of the same piece of data may be processed and updated according to different rules in different systems.

when the employee earnings field in both systems will have different information because personnel has not been informed about the employee's most recent paycheck. Such incompatibilities have caused considerable confusion and have prevented companies from developing one reliable version of data for management decision making and analysis.

The sources of data inconsistency are summarized in Figure 20.2.

Problems Posed by Fourth-Generation Computing

The need for coordinated, controlled data resources has been dramatized further by the popularity of fourth-generation computing tools and personal computers (see Chapters 10 and 15). With these user-friendly tools it is even easier for various non-data-processing groups throughout the organization to build their own applications, adding to the vast sea of unsupervised files. Even though these fourth-generation technologies give users the power to access information directly from computer systems, users may not be able to use them effectively. Information will be stored on so many independent microcomputer diskettes and individual files that it will be exceedingly difficult, if not impossible, to determine systematically where it is located; what form it is stored in; and how it is related to other information in the organization. Information resource management will be even more essential to ensure that information is known and available to all of the business functions that need it.

The United Services Automobile Association

Prior to 1983, the United Services Automobile Association (USAA) had no central information management policy. Each department calculated claims by a different formula. No two claims databases contained the same assumptions. Departments could not agree even on the total number of USAA employees. For years, senior managers unknowingly based their monthly and long-range forecasts on inconsistent data. The cost per claim rose, while the number of total claims dropped. USAA had all the appropriate productivity measurement tools (such as spreadsheets) but they were neither consistent nor directly related to its business plan. To gain control over its data USAA had to get programmers, claims analysts, and financial and marketing managers to agree upon common definitions for claims databases using data dictionaries so that senior managers get information calculated the same way no matter whose telephone extension they dial. This management reorganization helped turn around USAA's claims experience. USAA realizes it must manage information as a resource, planning ahead for it, budgeting it, creating accountability and ensuring efficient use.

Adapted from "It's 1985. Do You Know What Your Information—Management Policy Is?" *Business Computer Systems*, March 1985.

The experience of the United Services Automobile Association typifies the operational and strategic problems created by uncontrolled data.

20.2 The Concept of Data Administration

The need to control and manage information in order to support the organization's operational and strategic goals has given rise to a separate organizational function for data resource management. This function is called *data administration*. It is responsible for policies and procedures through which data can be managed as a companywide resource. To treat data as a primary resource in its own right, such management activities must address the following areas:

- Planning for data
- Sources of data
- Uses of data
- Information flows
- Acquisition of data
- Maintenance of data
- Data quality
- Supplying of data to areas where needed
- Protection of data
- Inventorying of data
- Monitoring data usage
- Assessing the impact of data changes
- Consistent and systematic policies and procedures for data management

Data Administration versus Database Administration

Data administration has been used interchangeably with *database administration*, but the two concepts should be distinguished. *Database administration* refers to the more technical and operational aspects of managing data. Its functions generally entail physical database design; operation and maintenance of database management software systems; performance monitoring and security monitoring of database management systems; plus liaison with systems programming, applications development, and operational activities (Kahn and Garceau, 1985).

Data administration, on the other hand, is concerned with the planning, administrative, and control functions for managing information. Typically these consist of data planning, logical database design, information policy development, standards setting, data dictionary development, and monitoring the usage of data by applications development and end-user groups.

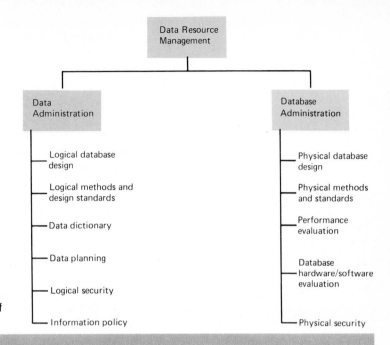

FIGURE 20.3
Data administration versus database administration. Both are components of data resource management.

Data administration is more organizationally or business oriented and less technically oriented than database administration. Effective management of information resources requires an in-depth understanding of the company's business functions, processes, organizational responsibilities, interactions, objectives, and priorities and their relationship to information architecture. Figure 20.3 illustrates the differences between data administration and database administration. Both data administration and database administration are required for successful data resource management.

The most fundamental principle of data administration is that all data are the property of the organization as a whole. They cannot belong exclusively to any one business area or organizational unit. All data are to be made available to any group that requires them to fulfill its mission. Specific data administration policies, procedures, and activities involve planning, organizing, and controlling the organization's data resources to realize this objective.

Information Policy

An effective data administration function requires changes in the way the organization treats its information. The organization must formalize its business rules to ensure that information is used and managed properly. These explicit rules governing information are called *information policy*.

Information policy establishes unified rules and guidelines for sharing, disseminating, acquiring, standardizing, classifying, and inventorying information throughout the organization. It lays out specific procedures and accountabilities by which organizational units share information; where information can be distributed; and who has responsibility for updating and maintaining it. Information policy also sets down standards for security—which individuals and groups can access information and the purposes for which the information can be used. Information policy may also encompass technical standards for software, computer hardware, telecommunications, and other devices that process and transmit information.

Some organizations have created an explicit data administration charter that defines the role of the data administration function in the organization so that it can be validated by all levels of management. A successful information policy will create the appropriate conditions for using information to fulfill organizational goals.

20.3 Data Planning

An organization must carefully plan for the development of its data resources so that they can effectively service strategic business requirements. *Strategic data planning* encompasses a formal database development methodology, policies, and procedures that ensure that the organization's data can meet this goal. Data planning methodology is a structured top-down approach that accomplishes the following (Martin, 1982):

- Defines the organization's business environment.
- Builds an inventory of data.
- Defines the organization's database environment.
- Supplies the framework for the development of applications, hardware, and software.

Data planning is based on the premise that the types of data used in an organization are relatively stable. Basic pieces of information, or *entities*, such as customers, parts, products, employees, or orders, do not change much over the lifetime of the organization. Once these entities and their interrelationships have been identified, stable models of the organization's data can be created. If properly designed, these models will meet both current and future information needs at all levels of the organization.

Creating an Organizational Model

The first step in strategic data planning is to create a model of the organization. This model has been referred to as either a *business model* or an *enterprise model*. (The latter term is more widely applicable because it encompasses organizations that are not strictly businesses such as government agencies or schools.)

The enterprise or business model details all of the *functions*, or major areas of activity, required to run the enterprise. For example, in a typical manufacturing concern, the major functional areas would include planning, finance, materials, production, marketing, sales, transportation/distribution, accounting, and personnel.

Each of these functional areas carries out a number or *processes*. For example, the sales function consists of processes such as territory management, selling, sales administration, customer relations, and plan management. Each process, in turn, can be further subdivided into specific *activities*. For example, customer relations might consist of customer calls/influence, customer service, and complaint resolution. (Additional detail on this topic can be found in Chapter 13, since enterprise analysis is an important methodology for defining information system requirements.)

By mapping these functions, processes, and activities, an organization can determine the basic categories for which it will require information. It can then develop a model of the classes or categories about which it needs to keep data and the relationships between those categories. These *data classes* are called *subject databases*. Subject databases are conceptual groupings of information that are independent of individual applications and systems. Figure 20.4 illustrates the data classes required to service all of the processes for the sales function.

FIGURE 20.4
Data classes for the sales function. By creating an enterprise or business model, the data classes and processes of each organizational function can be identified. Data classes for the sales functions are presented here.

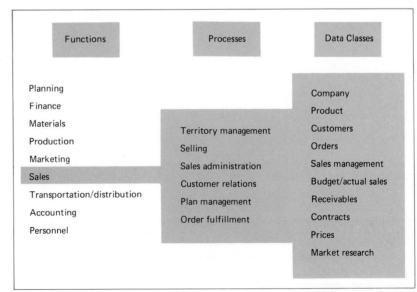

This business model of organization functions, processes, and data classes will produce data structures that are not likely to change over time. Even if the technology or applications change, these structures will remain stable. This high-level model of the data that the organization must maintain lays the foundation for actual database design.

Logical Database Design

Once the organization and its subject databases have been modeled, detailed data elements can be identified and documented. Entities can be defined and assigned standardized names and attributes.

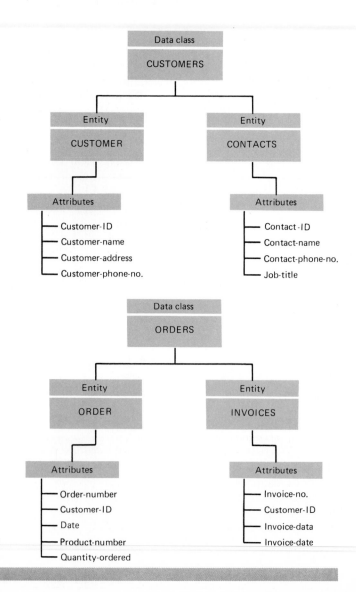

FIGURE 20.5
Entities and attributes of sales data classes. These charts depict some of the entities and attributes for the data classes identified for the sales function described in Figure 20.4.

Attributes are pieces of information about a given entity and represent all of the data items that one might want to store on a particular entity. For example, the attributes of the entity "employee" might include name, address, birth date, date of employment, and salary. Figure 20.5 depicts some of the entities and attributes defined for the data classes of the sales function.

Relationships between entities are then analyzed to determine the most efficient way to group data items together to meet information requirements. This view of data is called the *logical database* because it represents the data as perceived by users rather than the way they would actually be structured physically on computer storage units.

Physical Database Design

Database specialists can translate the logical database design into a *physical database*, the form in which the data are actually structured on computer storage media by database management software. The physical database design will take account of factors affecting ease of access and use: capabilities of database management software, data volumes and users' estimates of frequency of data usage, and data access requirements. Once the actual physical databases have been implemented, they can serve as the single managed source of data for multitudinous applications and systems. New applications can be developed from the databases that already exist. Database design issues are discussed in Chapter 8.

Figure 20.6 illustrates the sequence of steps in data planning and database development. Figure 20.7 relates the stages of data planning and database development to organizational functions and levels. Developing a business model and an information systems plan must be addressed at the strategic level, logical database design at the intermediate or management control level. However, both of these stages will incorporate requirements of the organization as a whole. Actual implementation of databases is project specific and more limited in scope.

Data-Managed Systems Development

Successful data planning involves a transformation in the methodology and the approach to systems design. Traditional systems development methodologies have centered on functions and processes. They treat data as a secondary component, a by-product of functional analysis and process design. Since traditional systems development methods replicate existing processes and data flows application by application, they tend to produce uncoordinated, incompatible files. Overall integration and planning of data across application boundaries are not properly addressed.

With data planning, the sequence of events in systems development is rearranged. Organizationwide planning for information precedes the development of local databases. The primary focus of

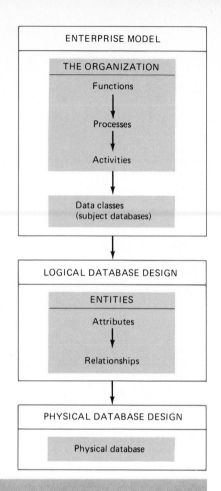

F I G U R E 20.6
Steps in data planning and database development. The enterprise model of organizational functions, processes, activities, and data classes lays the foundation for logical and physical database design.

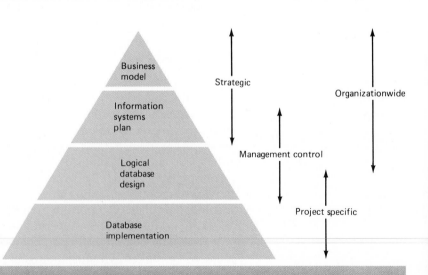

F I G U R E 20.7
The process of data planning and database development. The various stages are related to different organizational functions and levels.

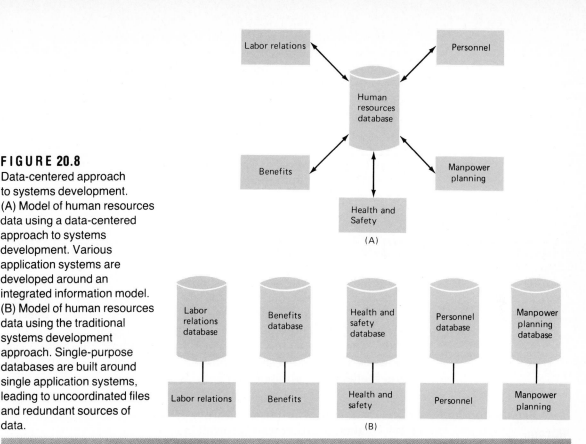

FIGURE 20.8
Data-centered approach
to systems development.
(A) Model of human resources
data using a data-centered
approach to systems
development. Various
application systems are
developed around an
integrated information model.
(B) Model of human resources
data using the traditional
systems development
approach. Single-purpose
databases are built around
single application systems,
leading to uncoordinated files
and redundant sources of
data.

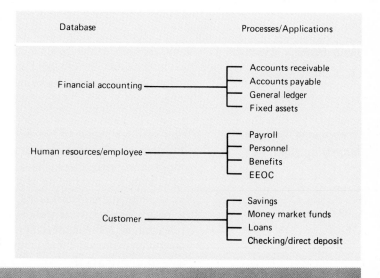

FIGURE 20.9
Integrated information model. This figure
illustrates how data-managed systems
development applies to a banking
organization. Instead of separate
applications and files, integrated
databases are built for the major
processes of the organization. The
processes and their applications are built
around a shared information model.

systems building shifts from a process orientation to a data orientation. This new data-centered approach, termed *information engineering*, views data as the foundation for systems design. Processes are subordinate to the creation of stable data models. Information engineering aims to create stable, nonredundant data structures that can be shared by multiple processes and applications. As illustrated in Figures 20.8 and 20.9, the focal point of systems development becomes an integrated information model with individual applications on the periphery. The various application programs and systems serve as input and output procedures for this centralized information hub.

20.4 Controlling the Data Resource

Information resources must be carefully supervised and controlled. The organization must clearly define the responsibilities associated with the use and maintenance of information through policies, standards, and procedures for collecting, accessing, and updating data. The policies and procedures for controlling information will now be discussed (Data Administration Function Project, GUIDE International Corporation, 1977).

Data Acquisition and Storage

The manner in which data are acquired and stored must support the information needs of the organization as a whole. Individual users of data cannot determine unilaterally what files a piece of information belongs on, how such files are organized, and how they are updated. Authority over acquisition and storage passes to the data administrators, who must consider all uses of data and select the storage medium and structure that provide the maximum benefit to all users.

Data Quality Assurance

Standards and procedures must be developed to ensure that information is accurate, timely, and easy to use and maintain. Data administration policies and procedures can control data quality in several ways.

Acceptance Tests for Modifying Data

They can set *standards for modification of files and databases* that will eliminate or minimize inaccurate, inconsistent, or redundant data. In cooperation with users, the data administrator can develop acceptability tests for modifying data elements, databases, or files. With formal acceptance standards, the data administrator can evaluate the need for each new data item to reduce or eliminate extraneous, irrelevant, or redundant data from the database. The organization can thereby ensure that there is one and only one source for a particular piece of information.

Coding Structure Reviews

The data administrator can review planned or existing *coding structures* to ensure that codes reflect their proper business purpose. Codes with irrelevant or confusing information can be streamlined or eliminated.

Audit and Control Procedures

The data administrator can establish standards and procedures for *audits and controls* to ensure the accuracy of automated data at all critical points of information flow. (This subject is explored in detail in Chapter 18.) The data administrator can also establish procedures to maintain and reproduce data in their latest correct version and to recover data lost by error or system failure.

Data Timing Standards

Data administrators, in conjunction with users, can establish *time standards* for updating information. Many inconsistencies in reports from different business areas are caused by differences in timing. Each application area will collect and update data with a time frame based on its own specific needs. With a broader perspective, data administrators can specify the source responsible for each data element; establish time standards for timely collection and updating; and develop policies and procedures for ensuring adherence to such time standards.

Data Security

If information is to be used to advantage, it must be readily available to authorized users while being protected from tampering and misuse. A major function of data administrators is to determine how to make data available for proper use while protecting them from unauthorized distribution or disclosure. Data administrators must develop security policies and procedures that consider legal requirements, such as federal privacy legislation, and the technical capabilities of current hardware and software. To control and monitor access to information, data administrators must address security at every point at which data can be accessed (see Chapter 18). In many companies, these may include the following:

- Physical hardware (computers, terminals, etc.)
- Log-ons and passwords
- Security software systems for individual applications
- Security software for database management systems
- Microcomputer files or data downloaded/uploaded between mainframe databases and micros
- Data flowing outside the organization

For each of these areas, data administrators can develop security policies and procedures that recognize the responsibilities of users, data processing specialists, and technical support staff. For example, users might be responsible for passwords and log-ons, physical security of terminals and microcomputers, and protection of hard copy reports with sensitive information. Data processing specialists might be responsible for protecting access to mainframes and automated files and for managing the software to control access to database management systems. The data administrator can also aid the establishment of security profiles, helping each business area determine which pieces of information it is responsible for; which pieces it can update or modify; and which ones it can access for inquiry only.

20.5 Organizing Information: The Data Dictionary

To be used efficiently, information must be systematically organized and inventoried. The principal tool for documenting and structuring the organization's information resources is the *data dictionary* (Kahn, 1985). The *data dictionary* stores information about information that is essential to its management as a business resource:

- What data are available
- Where the data are located
- Data attributes
- Who owns or is responsible for the data (either an individual or a business function such as production or marketing)
- How the data are used
- Who/what function is allowed to access the data for retrieval
- Who/what function is allowed to update/change the data
- Relationships to other pieces of data
- Security and privacy limitations

Data Dictionary Functions

The data dictionary contains a standard definition for each data element an organization wishes to catalog. The definition is an agreed upon standard for all systems that use that particular data element. A data element is defined only once, thereby eliminating any inconsistency or redundancy from different representations in different places and different definitions by various users. By cataloging data representations in a standardized, coordinated, and readily available format, the data dictionary becomes a multipurpose directory of the organization's data resources.

Although a data dictionary could be maintained manually with a card or index system, most organizations have far too many data items to make this feasible. Data dictionaries today are complex pieces of software, either custom written or packages. Major database management systems may have their own data dictionaries.

```
NAME:  AMT-PAY-BASE
FOCUS NAME :  BASEPAY
PC NAME        :  SALARY

DESCRIPTION :  EMPLOYEE'S ANNUAL SALARY

SIZE:  9 BYTES
TYPE:  N          (NUMERIC)
DATE CHANGED:  01/01/85
OWNERSHIP:  COMPENSATION
UPDATE SECURITY:  SITE PERSONNEL
ACCESS SECURITY:  MANAGER, COMPENSATION PLANNING AND RESEARCH
                           MANAGER, JOB EVALUATION SYSTEMS
                           MANAGER, HUMAN RESOURCES PLANNING
                           MANAGER, SITE EQUAL OPPORTUNITY AFFAIRS
                           MANAGER, SITE BENEFITS
                           MANAGER, CLAIMS PAYING SYSTEMS
                           MANAGER, QUALIFIED PLANS
                           MANAGER, SITE EMPLOYMENT/EEO
BUSINESS FUNCTIONS USED BY:  COMPENSATION
                           HR PLANNING
                           EMPLOYMENT
                           INSURANCE
                           PENSION
                           ISP


PROGRAMS USING:  PI01000
                           PI02000
                           PI03000
                           PI04000
                           PI04500

REPORTS USING      REPORT 124 (SALARY INCREASE TRACKING REPORT)
                           REPORT 448 (GROUP INSURANCE AUDIT REPORT)
                           REPORT 452 (SALARY REVIEW LISTING)
                           PENSION REFERENCE LISTING
```

FIGURE 20.10
Sample data dictionary report.

An automated data dictionary can maintain many different kinds of records and data relationships. It can document descriptive information about individual data elements and about an organization's system resources, such as records, files, reports, transactions, programs, and systems. The data dictionary can show which programs, files, systems, reports, and business functions use a particular data element and to what other data elements that piece of information is related.

The sample data dictionary reports in Figures 20.10 and 20.11 illustrate the kind of information about data resources that a data dictionary can maintain. Figure 20.10 is a sample data dictionary report showing the size, format, meaning, and uses of a particular data element. In addition to listing the standard name of the element (AMT-PAY-BASE), the dictionary lists the names that reference this element in specific systems. It also shows which individuals, business functions, programs, and reports use this data element.

LOGICAL DATA ELEMENTS	LEN DESCRIPTION	01	02	03	04	05	06	07	08	09	10	11	12	13	14	15
QTY-HOUR-OTHER	2 NUMBER OF HOURS PAID BUT NOT WORKED					R		R			A	R			
QTY-HOUR-PREM	2 NUMBER OF HOURS FOR PREMIUM PAY					R		R			A	R			
QTY-HOUR-WORK-NORM	5 NORMAL WORK HOURS					R		U			R	R	R		
QTY-HOUR-WORKD-CASUL	5 CASUAL EMPLOYEE HOURS WORKED	R									A	R			
QTY-HOUR-WORKD-EMPL	5 EMPLOYEE HOURS WORKED	R									A	R			
TAMT-EARN-PENS	5 TOTAL AMOUNT OF PENSIONABLE EARNINGS	R	R			R			R		R	A	R		R
TAMT-EARN-W2	5 TOTAL AMOUNT OF W2 EARNINGS		R			R			R		R	A	R		
TAMT-INCRS	5 TOTAL INCREASE AMOUNT							U			R	R	R		

LEGEND: 1-PENS 2-INSUR 3-EMPMT 4-EEO 5-LABOR 6-TRNG-DEVMT 7-PLAN-POSTN-CNTL 8-CMPSN 9-RELOC
         10-ISP 11-PAYR 12-CHRON 13-HOLD 14-XBENE 15-XPERS

FIGURE 20.11
Matrix report of data elements used by human resources business
functions. This report was produced using IBM's data dictionary.
R= read only; U= update and read; A = business area where the
data element originates. The report show each business function
that uses human resources data elements and the condition
of usage.

Figure 20.11 is an actual data dictionary report in matrix form that
supports business systems planning and enterprise analysis. For each
data element the report shows the definition, the business functions
where it is used, and the conditions of usage. For example, the field
QTY-HOUR-PREM originates in the payroll area but is used by the
labor relations and compensation functions and is maintained historically on the employee's record. With a data dictionary, documentation of an organization's data and system resources can be compre-
hensively consolidated into a single source.

Active versus Passive Data Dictionaries

Many data dictionaries contain facilities to enforce one standard
definition of the data as information systems are being used. The
dictionary can generate the views of data required by executable
programs (e.g., COBOL data division statements, PL/1 data descriptions, or the control blocks and parameters required by database
management systems). By automatically generating the data definitions used by programs, the dictionary forces diverse programs,
systems, and programming languages to adhere to the same definition of data. Programmers, analysts, and users who develop new
applications can use the same information standards.

Dictionaries with the facility to enforce a single representation of
data in all executable programs and other system activities are termed

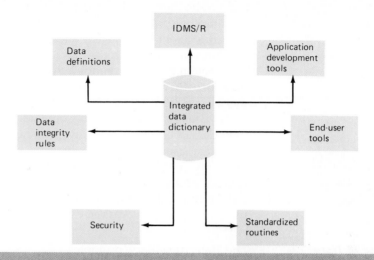

FIGURE 20.12

An active data dictionary. Cullinet's IDMS/R database management system and its languages are driven by an active data dictionary. By providing complete integration and active control of all data resources, the dictionary is the cornerstone of the IDMS/R relational database management system environment. All IDMS/R database structures are defined in the data dictionary. The dictionary contains information about the organization's data resources such as data definitions, physical characteristics, and users, as well as information about the database management system. All Cullinet data management tools populate and draw information from the data dictionary. By managing the use of all data definitions, greater control can be achieved over the organization's data resources and processing. The data dictionary enforces security measures to protect both dictionary data definitions and the database from unauthorized access. The dictionary can enforce naming conventions to guarantee that independently developed systems use the same data definitions for each category of information stored in the dictionary. Application developers can store standardized routines in the dictionary, allowing programs developed by different application areas to produce consistent results. The dictionary also enforces data integrity rules that regulate update functions against the database and protect data resources from inconsistencies and corruption. The data dictionary is also integrated with Cullinet's application development tools for information systems professionals and end users. (Adapted from IDMS/R Technical Summary with permission of Cullinet Software, Inc. Westwood, Mass.)

active data dictionaries. They tend to be closely integrated with a particular database management system. (Cullinet's integrated data dictionary, illustrated in Figure 20.12 is a good example.) All accesses to data flow through the dictionary. The dictionary drives the database management system's database language, assisting in processing information and retrieval.

Dictionaries that cannot automatically impose their data definitions on other systems and processes in the same machine environment are termed *passive data dictionaries.* They do not interact directly with database management software. They can't ensure whether their data definitions are always the ones used by executing programs and database management systems. Passive data dictionaries are primarily repositories of information about data. They can define, catalog, and describe data but require detailed manual procedures to ensure that their data definitions are consistent with those actually used by system processes.

Benefits of Data Dictionaries

The data dictionary promotes effective data resource management and control in several ways. (Ross, 1981).

Information Resource Directory

The data dictionary informs users of information systems about the data that are available. It inventories all of the pieces of data contained in the information systems it addresses. Users can employ the dictionary to find out what information is available, what it means, where it can be obtained, and whether or not it can be accessed without security restrictions. If the dictionary covers many systems, it can provide a comprehensive view of all of the information available for a particular business function, such as marketing, or all of the information maintained by the entire enterprise. It will supply users with the name, format, and specifications required to access data for reports. The data dictionary thus serves as a consolidated end-user information retrieval directory. It provides a central listing of all of the organization's data items.

Control of Data Definitions

The data dictionary controls the definition and representation of data. It consolidates multiple versions of the same data element into a single standardized description. By having all users of a particular data item accept a common definition, attributes, and naming convention, the dictionary helps to enforce common data standards. It promotes coordination, cooperation, and data sharing. To standardize and catalog a data item for the dictionary, different people with different interpretations of that data item must be brought together in a consensus. Discussing these standardized meanings helps to overcome semantic barriers among programmers, systems analysts, and different groups of business users. The dictionary enforces common naming standards.

The data dictionary also helps to ensure that the same data definitions are reflected in all of their computer representations. Powerful data dictionaries can generate the file descriptions used by various application programs. Some can also supply the edit and validation routines used by application programs.

Impact/Change Assessment

The data dictionary promotes better control of changes in information systems and data resources. Data dictionaries can store information such as all files, programs, transactions, reports, and systems where a specific data element is used. Therefore, the dictionary can generate reports showing exactly which files, programs, jobs, transactions, reports, and systems must be changed if there is any change in the size, format, or attributes of a data element. The dictionary can likewise show what data elements and files must be changed if a program is changed. This facility is called *impact/change assessment*. The impact of a proposed change can be assessed immediately without sifting through volumes of manual documentation or polling programmers. Failure to anticipate the full impact of data changes often results in lengthy delays in system modifications and extra reprogramming costs. The need for comprehensive impact/change assessment is even greater when systems are heavily integrated.

More Efficient Systems Development

The data dictionary can promote more efficient systems development. It provides a comprehensive list of existing data standards for systems analysts and programmers. With data elements already defined, applications developers have less need to create new files and fields. They do not have to spend as much time designing new files or establishing meanings for data. Dictionary facilities for automating file descriptions and editing requirements cut down on programmer coding time.

For example, the data dictionary developed by the database administration department of the Mobil Corporation has proved useful to all systems development projects, database and nondatabase alike. The dictionary captures information describing the attributes and interrelationships of data items. It also performs functional analysis based on its ability to define business activities in machine-readable form ("A New View of Data Dictionaries," 1981). If properly integrated into systems development methodology, an automated data dictionary can substantially reduce development costs, lead time, and duplication of effort.

Enhancing Security and Control

The data dictionary can promote security and control. It shows which individuals or business functions are authorized to access data and which ones have the authority to change data. The dictionary also

The Data Dictionary at the Mobil Corporation

At the Mobil Corporation, headquartered in New York City, the data dictionary is the principal tool for exerting control over the company's data resources. The dictionary shows what data are held; data item attributes, structure, and interrelationships; sources of data; and the different forms in which data appear for different purposes. Corporate policy requires that the dictionary be used for all database projects, although it is very valuable for non-database projects as well. Mobil's Database Administration Department monitors and edits data definitions to create standards for data that cross departmental boundaries. The dictionary helps it clarify and design data structures, eliminate unnecessary data redundancies, and assess the impact of proposed computer system changes. Editing key data definitions in all of the company's application systems is a large-scale undertaking. The Mobil DBA department must proceed step by step.

Adapted from "A New View of Data Dictionaries," *EDP Analyzer*, July 1981.)

shows which group or function owns or has primary responsibility for data. Data usage can be more easily monitored and controlled.

Audit Tool   *The data dictionary is an audit tool.* It can provide internal and external auditors with both an overview and details of systems to be audited. It contains standards with which audits can be performed.

20.6 Implementing the Data Administration Function

Implementation of an effective data administration function is ordinarily a long-term process. Extensive analysis and organizational coordination are required to establish priorities for information requirements, plan for strategic data needs, promote data sharing, and control redundant data items. Diverging needs and perspectives of numerous departments and functional areas must be reconciled (Goldstein and McCririck, 1980; Kahn, 1983).

Organizational Obstacles to Data Administration Disciplines

Resistance to formal data management disciplines has occurred primarily for the following reasons.

Improper Organizational Placement of the Data Administration Function

The data administration function has not been positioned properly in the organization to command sufficient resources and support. If it is part of the data processing department, it may be too far removed from business areas and too closely aligned with technical functions such as database management. Thus, it will have a very limited, narrow constituency and base of support. If data administration is positioned too low in the organization, it lacks the authority, resources, and backing from upper management to influence other groups.

Data administration standards and procedures are perceived as an added activity because they are not part of traditional business responsibilities. When implemented by the data processing department, data administration disciplines are resented even more, having been imposed by a nonbusiness area.

Resistance to Data Sharing

Many managers are reluctant to share "their" information with other areas of the organization. In organizations with heavy competition among departments, managers strive to protect their own domain. It is often advantageous to withhold information from other departments or higher management, especially when figures reveal poor performance or the size of departmental budgets (Keen, 1981). Managerial rivalry has been a major impediment to making information a companywide resource.

Problems in Standardizing Data Definitions

When a piece of information is used by more than one business area, or department, it is extremely difficult to standardize data definitions. Each group has its own needs and prefers to define data in its own way. For example, companies with diverse acquisitions have had trouble convincing production units to accept a common, companywide standard for the product code. Consequently, very few companywide data representations and coding structures have materialized.

Resistance from Application Developers

Application development teams have proven to be least responsive to data administration disciplines. They believe that using the data dictionary or data planning methodology will delay implementation of their systems development project. These groups have traditionally been rated by how quickly they can build new systems and how closely their projects conform to budgets and target dates. These groups are oriented toward short-term results, whereas effective data administration is a long-term goal.

Ingredients of Effective Information Management

Management of data resources has been successful in an environment that recognizes the following factors.

Management Support

The discipline to submit to data sharing and data administration policies and procedures is enforceable only with a strong and high level of management commitment. Data administration is also more likely to be allocated the requisite technical, organizational, and budgetary resources if it has management backing. It is recommended that data administration be positioned as high in the organization as possible, ideally under senior management.

User Involvement

Users have firsthand knowledge of the data, controls, and security required by their business functions. They promote management support because they are often either part of management or respected by management. They must be actively involved in data administration activities to understand the responsibilities surrounding the use and maintenance of information. Users should be heavily involved in data inventorying and planning; defining data items for the data dictionary; and identifying key business processes and functions.

Appropriate Tools and Techniques

Data resource management tools and techniques include data planning aids and methodologies (such as IBM's Business Systems Planning or enterprise analysis); database design methodologies; database management systems; and an automated data dictionary.

Education and Training

It is estimated that successful data administrators will spend 50% of their time educating the rest of the organization in data administration concepts and practices. Education helps build commitment to data administration disciplines and provides the training required to participate effectively in data management activities. Training topics include policies and procedures; data naming and definition standards; the data dictionary; and data security.

Service Orientation

Data administration is less likely to be perceived as a burdensome added activity if its concrete benefits can be immediately demonstrated. Even before the long-term benefits of information management have been realized, data administration can provide useful services that result in immediate productivity gains. For example, data administration specialists can help users find sources and formats of data required for reports; help application developers research and define data elements; and develop the file and record documentation for new applications.

Manageable Project Scope

Another way of quickly demonstrating the benefits of data administration is to start with a project of manageable scope. If data administration tries to capture all of the organization's data in the data dictionary at once, the effort will take many years and the costs will skyrocket. A more realistic approach is to use the data dictionary to inventory one or two small to medium-sized systems. Tangible end products and data dictionary benefits will be seen immediately.

20.7 Summary

In many organizations, information systems management focuses on the need to manage the information in computer systems as a strategic resource. Proliferation of information systems throughout the organization and end-user computing tools can create many versions of the same piece of information. Unless properly managed, data in one system become inconsistent and incompatible with the same piece of data in another system.

The organizational function responsible for management of data resources is data administration. This entails planning, administrative, and control functions: strategic data planning; establishing standards and procedures for data security and data quality assurance; and documenting and structuring the organization's data resources.

Data planning involves creating an enterprise model of the organization and identifying the data classes and individual data elements that should be captured on databases. Design can then follow for logical databases, or views of data as perceived by users and applications, and physical databases, the form in which data are actually structured on computer storage media. Data-managed systems development that subordinates processes to the creation of stable data models is called information engineering.

In addition to data planning, data administration disciplines include policies and procedures for data acquisition and storage; data quality assurance; acceptance tests for modifying data; coding structure reviews; audits and controls; data security; and establishment of data timing standards.

The data dictionary is the principal tool for documenting and structuring the organization's data resources. Active data dictionaries can enforce uniform data definitions in multiple applications because they are tightly integrated with database management systems. Passive data dictionaries cannot automatically enforce their data definitions across applications.

Organizational resistance can make data administration disciplines difficult to enforce. With user involvement, management support, and appropriate tools and techniques, an effective data administration function can be established.

Key Words

Data inconsistency	Entity
Data redundancy	Attribute
Data administration	Logical database
Database administration	Physical database
Data management	Information engineering
Information policy	Data dictionary
Data planning	Active data dictionary
Enterprise model	Passive data dictionary
Subject databases	Impact/change assessment
Data classes	

Review Questions

1. Explain the concepts of data redundancy and data inconsistency. Why are these undesirable?
2. What kinds of problems in corporate data resource management are caused by the phenomenal growth of PCs in organizations?
3. Distinguish between data administration, data management, and database administration. What are the functions of data administration?
4. What is information policy? What is its relationship to data administration?
5. What does strategic data planning encompass?
6. Explain the data-centered approach to systems development. How does it differ from traditional systems development methods?
7. Describe the major mechanisms for controlling data resources.
8. What is a data dictionary? What is its purpose? How can it help promote data administration?
9. Distinguish between active and passive data dictionaries.
10. What are some of the obstacles to implementing data administration in organizations? How can they be dealt with?

Discussion Questions

1. Distributed database technology (e.g., distributed data processing) is used in many organizations. A database is not stored in its entirety at a single location, but rather is spread across a network of computers that are geographically dispersed and connected via communications links. What issues does this approach raise for data administration?
2. The new use of end-user computing challenges the existing features of data resource management. End users are now provided with computer terminals or PCs with easy-to-use software for accessing databases, developing models, and performing information processing directly. What kinds of problems arise in controlling corporate data resources? Discuss.
3. Assume that you are put in charge of data administration for a nationwide chain of drug stores. You are supposed to reshape the

data administration function. What will be the steps in your data planning? What kinds of activities should be included in each step?

4. It has been said that without a powerful data dictionary an organization cannot have a fourth-generation environment. Discuss.

5. Create a data dictionary for a manual or automated information system with which you are familiar. (Your dictionary need not be automated.) List all of the data elements in the system and show their format, size, definition, and business usage. For a more complex system, you may wish to add more information to your dictionary, such as the relationship of each element to files, reports, transactions, programs, and various business functions.

Data Administration at the Upjohn Company

The Upjohn Company, headquartered at Kalamazoo, Michigan, is a worldwide manufacturer and marketer of pharmaceuticals, health services, chemicals, seeds and agricultural specialties. It has research, manufacturing, sales and distribution facilities in over 200 locations.

Upjohn's major operating divisions are fairly autonomous. Several divisions have their own data processing departments and their own computer centers. These independent divisional data processing departments range from large mainframe shops to small data processing groups with System 34's (an IBM minicomputer). Although Upjohn primarily uses IBM hardware, DEC (Digital Equipment Company) equipment is also prominent.

An Information Management Services division is a separate division reporting directly to the Vice President and Treasurer. Information Management Services serves as a support group for the corporation's other business units. On a chargeback basis it supplies services such as applications development, maintenance and use of its data center and computer facilities to any organization in the company that requests them.

There are four groups in Information Management Services: Customer Information Systems I and II are applications development groups roughly aligned with the divisions they serve. The Computer and Information Resources Services group operates Upjohn's Data Center and Information Center. Technical Information Services is responsible for software support, data administration and data security. Corporate Data Administration reports to the Group Manager, Technical Services.

Corporate Data Administration's major responsibilities are to provide training, internal technical consulting and administrative support for data planning, data base management, data base design and development, and data dictionaries. Corporate Data Administration does not adhere to one system development methodology and does not always use formal data modeling techniques.

Most of the staff is allocated to supporting applications development and the Data Dictionary. Corporate Data Administration staff design, implement and tune IMS (an IBM database management system) databases. Data base analysts are assigned to divisions to work closely with the applications development groups. Each data base analyst is responsible for logical data base design, physical data base design, backup, recovery, reorganization procedures, and data base tuning. Corporate Data Administration also provides general consulting on data base management systems throughout the company, suggesting design approaches and evaluating data base management software.

The Information Management Services division uses the Data Dictionary to store information about the systems it builds and maintains. It views the dictionary as an important productivity tool for programmers and analysts and as the major repository for documentation. The goal is to have the dictionary store all documentation generated from applications development (such as program code, job control instructions, file definitions, etc.). The only exceptions are operating instructions and a management summary of each system. Corporate Data Administration spends considerable time promoting and supporting the Data Dictionary. It has allocated two full-time programmers for dictionary enhancements and two technicians for quality assurance and user assistance. One full-time staff member is dedicated to training, selling and coordinating Data Dictionary activities.

Corporate Data Administration has set a goal of establishing data administration functions in each of the company's major divisions. It sees itself as a resource for specialized skills that cannot be provided by the divisions themselves and as a source of tools and training on techniques for which there is a company-wide need. This role reflects Upjohn's decentralized approach to information resource management.

Corporate Data Administration has found it must "sell" data administration and that data administration is very difficult to sell. Not all of the divisions are at the same level of sophistication in information resource management. Some feel the benefits of data administration are too long-range; others feel it is a solution to a problem they don't know they have. Programmers and analysts have proved especially resistant because they feel threatened once data administration gets beyond mere technical support for their projects.

Corporate Data Administration hopes to establish some type of formal information planning process in divisions where management is receptive. It reports success with a BSP (Business Systems Planning) approach but will experiment with others. One area is currently exploring data planning using entity-relationship diagrams.

Adapted from Mike Gottwald, "The Roles and Organizational Placement of DA. DBA and the Information Center at the Upjohn Company," Data Administration Users' Conference, Orlando, Florida, November 19–21, 1984.

Case Study Questions

1. Observers have noted that data administration at Upjohn is in its infancy. Discuss.
2. What characteristics at Upjohn have made data administration difficult to sell? What factors have helped to promote it?
3. What data administration tools and disciplines are being used at Upjohn? How are they being used? What kinds of data administration activities are most likely to be successful at this company?

References

"A New View of Data Dictionaries," *EDP Analyzer*, Vol. 19 (July 1981).

Data Administration Function Project, GUIDE International Corporation. "Establishing the Data Administration Function." GUIDE International Corporation, 1977.

Gillenson, Mark L. "Trends in Data Administration, 1981–1983," IBM Technical Report TR73-027. New York: IBM Systems Research Institute, January 1984.

Goldstein, R.C., and McCririck, I.B. "What Do Data Administrators Really Do?," *Datamation*, Vol. 26 (August 1980).

Kahn, Beverly K. "Some Realities of Data Administration," *Communications of the ACM*, Vol. 26 (October 1983).

Kahn, Beverly K. "An Environmentally Dependent Framework for Data Dictionary Systems." *MIS Quarterly*, Vol. 9 (September 1985).

Kahn, Beverly K., and Garceau, Linda. "The Database Administration Function," *Journal of Management Information Systems*, Vol. 1 (Spring 1985).

Keen, Peter W. "Information Systems and Organizational Change," *Communications of the ACM*, Vol. 24 (January 1981).

Martin, James. *Strategic Data Planning Methodologies*. Englewood Cliffs, N.J.: Prentice-Hall, 1982.

Martin, James. *Managing the Data-Base Environment*. Englewood Cliffs, N.J.: Prentice-Hall, 1983.

Nolan, Richard L. "Managing the Crises in Data Processing," *Harvard Business Review* (March–April 1979).

Ravindra, Palangala S. "Data Administration: An Old Function Adapts to Its New Role," *Journal of Information Systems Management* (Fall 1986).

Ross, Ronald G. *Data Dictionaries and Data Administration*. New York: American Management Association, 1981.

CHAPTER 21

21

Issues in the Management of Information Systems

▓ OUTLINE

(Continued on next page.)

670

In 1985 the board of directors of the GTE Service Corporation in Stamford, Connecticut, approved an unprecedented one-time investment of $10 million to purchase 1000 PC-XTs and ATs for office automation. To justify the expense, a Big Eight accounting firm, Peat Marwick, Mitchell and Co., was brought in to do a productivity analysis.

Prior to this effort, PC purchases were justified on an ad hoc, back-of-the-envelope basis. This resulted in micros being idle 90% of the time and not being used for business purposes. Before making a $10 million commitment, senior management wanted a detailed, focused plan on how specific jobs would use the PCs and how much productivity enhancement would result.

As a result of the analysis conducted by Peat Marwick, GTE discovered that marketing managers could save 8 hours a month, one day's work. Engineers could develop schematic drawings 10 times faster. Clerical workers also experienced large gains in productivity. Some senior managers used to doubt the productivity gains of office automation, according to Jonathan Brown, GTE productivity specialist. They've seen isolated instances of expensive executives doing simple programming on PCs. The way around that problem is detailed implementation, a business plan, proactive management, and lots of training.

Adapted from "Cost Justifying Information Systems," *Business Computer Systems*, February 1986.

Systems do not automatically lead to benefits or implement themselves. The GTE example illustrates the difficulties and opportunities created by new information systems based on distributed intelligence and data that serve professionals and managers. The benefits of these systems are often intangible and hence difficult to quantify; yet the cost of professionals and managers is high, and therefore gains in their productivity can lead to dramatic savings. Investments in new systems can also fail to produce expected benefits unless management has a clear-cut strategy and an implementation plan. The key to success is proper management of information technology.

In this chapter the student will learn:

- How the relationship between systems and organizations is changing.
- How to develop strategic systems.
- How to choose among alternative system projects.
- The pitfalls of project management.
- How to attract and keep high-quality systems personnel.
- How to recognize and manage strategic transitions.

21.1 Introduction

This chapter is concerned with the key information system management issues that organizations must address now and in the next few years. These issues face all managers, not just managers of information systems. Let us begin with an understanding of the factors that create management issues in the first place.

Changing Technology

One of the main factors creating an unstable management environment is the rapid rate of change in the capability of computing technology. For instance:

- Logic costs decline by a factor of 10 every 5 years.
- Main storage costs decline by a factor of 10 every 7 years.
- Secondary storage costs decline by a factor of 10 every 10 years (Phister, 1979).

There are several consequences of these rapid changes. First, old systems—some only a few years in operation—can become obsolete quickly and, relative to new equipment, very expensive. They may even put the organization at a competitive disadvantage. Hence continual review of existing systems is essential. Second, the systems staff must be continually retrained in order to remain competent in dealing with new applications. Third, there is a continuing stream of potential new applications.

Distribution of Intelligence and Data

With the declining cost of machinery and the growing ease of software use, information technology is no longer under centralized organizational control. In the 1970s minicomputers essentially fell under the control of divisions and functional areas; in the 1980s microcomputers fell largely under the control of local management and professional workers. The central data processing or MIS group still exists, of course, but its control over the evolution of computing and the distribution of machine intelligence and data has been weakened. This suggests new strategies for control of information systems and information technology, strategies that recognize the diversity of the interests involved.

Emerging Islands of Applications

Coupled with the distribution of intelligence and data is the growing range of applications. Up to the mid-1970s, the primary application of computing resources was in data processing—the operation of transaction processing and management information systems. Then in the 1970s a wave of office automation applications began, along with the building of impressive corporate telecommunications systems. By the 1980s these three islands of applications—*office automation*, *data processing*, and *telecommunications*—had been joined by a fourth, *microcomputing* (McKenney and McFarlan, 1982). Each of these islands of technology historically had a different form of management. Yet because they often share technology, data, and personnel, it is increasingly important that these islands be integrated or at least managed as a connected set of entities.

Shortage of Skilled Personnel

Systems personnel of all kinds—from programmers to managers—are among the fastest-growing occupational group in the American labor force. Unfortunately, as pointed out in previous chapters, the supply is not keeping up with the demand. Systems programmers and analysts are currently being imported from foreign countries at a record rate (McKenney and McFarlan, 1982; Canning, 1985). While these general shortages are severe, there is an even greater shortage of experienced, highly skilled, and perceptive systems analysts and managers. Moreover, as the mix of applications broadens, people who understand both the technology and the organization's problems are rare and in great demand.

The interaction between the shortage of personnel and the problems previously described above cannot be overemphasized. The changes in hardware, for instance, call for a labor force that can assimilate frequent changes. This requires very large training budgets or hiring policies that lead to high costs. New attitudes may be necessary to support new systems and new ways of doing business. The distinction between ordinary employees and systems personnel may decline in importance.

Environmental Change

The business and organizational climate in the United States and the world is one of uncertainty and rapid change. Among the more important changes are the following:

- Economic fluctuations.
- The changing role and scope of government (deregulation).
- The growth of international markets.
- Resource constraints.
- Growing employee claims for due process and fairness in employment.

- Demographic change in the labor force.
- The speed of technical change.

All of these changes put pressure on organizations to increase their efficiency. Since many corporations see information technology as a principal tool to ensure survival in this environmment, more and more pressure falls on information system departments to do more, do it faster, and spend less.

Strategic Role of Systems

Given the competitive pressures in the environment previously described, it is understandable that firms look to technology—including information technology—not just as a means of survival but as a tool to gain a permanent competitive advantage over other firms. As described in Chapter 3, there are now many examples of firms using information technology to establish new relations with customers, suppliers, and employees and to develop new products as well. For managers in all organizations, the question becomes "How can we use information technology to gain a competitive advantage? Where do we start?"

For instance, in a 1984 speech, the president of IBM predicted that by 1990 a PC work station will be available that has a 32-bit chip operating at 10 mips, with 16 megabytes of main storage and 400 megabytes of secondary storage (Canning, 1985). This machine will sell for about the same price as today's PC.

The principal problem raised by this development of powerful, inexpensive computing hardware will not involve technology, but rather people and organizations. The question is, how can organizations obtain a sizable payoff from the investment in such machinery? How can such investments make a strategic contribution to the firm? Last, given the new importance of systems, how should organizational behavior, attitudes, and structure change?

Having discussed the objective conditions that managers face, we now turn to the issues raised and some strategies for coping.

21.2 Organizational Control and Strategic Planning for Systems

In the current environment, managers of even small businesses who do not plan consciously for information technology run the clear risk of not surviving for more than a few years. One lesson of the recent past for large organizations—such as Bank of America, General Motors, and the Social Security Administration, described in previous chapters—is that large organizations that fail to control and plan for information systems will certainly be in trouble and may disappear.

A second lesson, equally harsh, is that simply engaging in and promulgating a strategic plan or a plan for systems is no guarantee of survival. Organizational control and strategic plans for systems are necessary but not sufficient conditions for survival and prosperity. The biggest difficulty with plans in general is *choosing the right plan* and *implementing it* effectively.

This section describes how to go about choosing a plan. A later section (on managing strategic transitions) describes how to implement plans.

The Problem

A *plan* is a connected and related set of actions. A *strategic plan* is a connected set of actions concerned with an organization's essential internal and external relationships and processes. By *essential* we mean relationships and processes that, if not performed well, lead to the extinction of the organization.

The real strategy pursued by a firm, the set of actions actually performed, may differ from the intended actions described in some formal document. Organizations often act, sometimes must act, in strategic ways not envisioned by formal documents. Nevertheless, in this chapter we will talk only about intended strategic plans (Mintzberg and McHugh, 1985).

The purpose of a strategic plan for systems is to establish the overall targets and goals of systems development. If the organization knows what it would like its systems to do, it selects new systems and eliminates others. The question, then, is, how do managers know what systems to develop? What are (should be) the goals of systems development?

Identifying the targets or goals of systems (the information systems plan) involves consideration of three elements—the *business strategic plan*, the *business organization*, and the *environment* (considered as a set of constraints, such as regulation, and opportunities such as new information technology) (Benson and Parker, 1985; Krcmar, 1985) (see Figure 21.1.)

This consideration process used to be simpler because prior to the 1980s information technology did not play a role in strategic planning for business. Figure 21.1 indicates that the information systems plan should consider changes in technology, existing business needs, and the strategic plan of the firm. That is, systems must align themselves with these three features.

A second aspect of Figure 21.1 is that key features of the environment—competitors' actions, new technology—must be included in strategic thinking about the firm as a whole. Information technology should be allowed to *influence strategic thinking* by suggesting new uses for the technology, new corporate products, and new relationships and activities.

In previous chapters on systems analysis, design, organizations,

FIGURE 21.1

The problem of planning
information systems. Planning
for systems must take into
account the environment
(especially new technology)
as well as the business
strategic plan and the existing
business organization.
(Adapted from Benson and
Parker 1985; Krcmar, 1985;
and authors.)

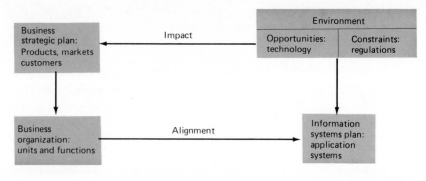

and decision making, we have described the importance of *aligning
systems with organizational needs and plans.* But how should or how can
a consideration of information technology and information systems
affect strategic planning?

Identifying Strategic Targets for Systems

One way to begin identifying strategic targets for systems is to
consider the broad strategy of firms. Four generic strategies have
been identified (Porter, 1980):

- Become the low-cost producer.
- Differentiate products and create niches.
- Develop new products.
- Change the organizational scope (i.e., shrink in size to reduce costs
  or grow in size to gain economies).

Consideration of these generic strategies is helpful for understanding when and where strategic opportunities exist. But it does
not help to define specific applications.

Identifying where information technology can be applied to
provide a strategic advantage requires a model of the firm and its
environment. Two such models are currently used: a value chain
model and a competitive forces model (Porter and Millar, 1985; Ives et
al., 1984). Each can be useful in identifying targets of opportunity for
strategic systems (Parsons, 1983).

The Value Chain Model

According to the *value chain* model of the firm, firms engage in several
interconnected *primary* and *support* activities that add value to inputs.
Information technology is important for the performance of each of
these activities. If the value added is greater than the cost, the firm
makes a profit (see Figure 21.2). Moreover, each firm is part of a series
of value chains that include suppliers and customers. At the boundaries between supplier and firm, and firm and customer, information
technology can be critically important.

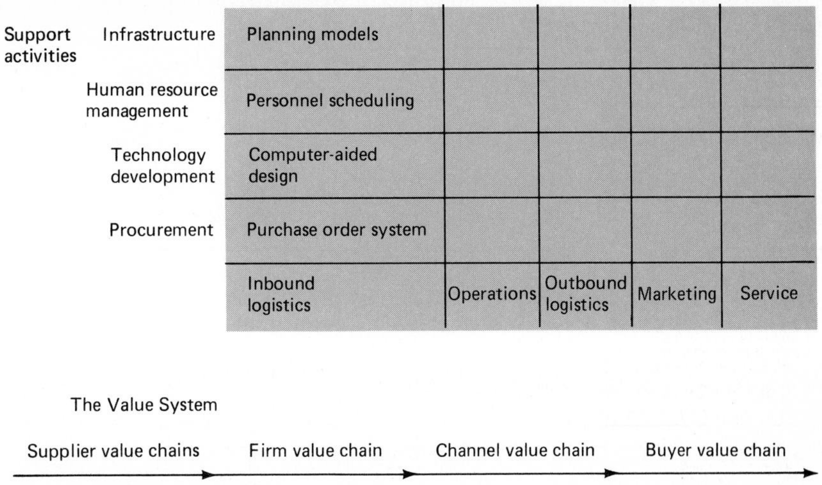

Support activities		Inbound logistics	Operations	Outbound logistics	Marketing	Service
	Infrastructure	Planning models				
	Human resource management	Personnel scheduling				
	Technology development	Computer-aided design				
	Procurement	Purchase order system				

The Value System

Supplier value chains → Firm value chain → Channel value chain → Buyer value chain →

FIGURE 21.2
This model illustrates where in the firm and where in the life cycle of a product value is created. Once this is identified, one can ask, "Where in the value chain can information systems be used, and with what effects on the competition?". (Adapted from Porter and Millar, 1985.)

There are several ways in which this model can be used. First, planners can establish where existing systems are located and where gaps exist. Second, planners can go through each cell of Figure 21.2 and ask if new technology or competitive developments suggest that new applications are needed. Third, planners can go up (or down) the value chain to seek mutual advantage.

For instance, suppliers might be able to save money if they deliver to the factory on a daily basis. This could lower their warehousing costs and the firm's inventory costs. A just-in-time inventory system could be installed, with terminals in the suppliers' shipping department indicating the firm's need for parts on a daily or hourly basis.

The Competitive Forces Model

A second model that is useful for strategic thinking about systems is the competitive forces model (Porter and Millar, 1985) (see Figure 21.3). In this model, a firm faces a number of threats and opportunities: the threat of new entrants, the strength of competitive forces, the pressure from substitute products, the power of buyers, and the power of suppliers.

With this view of the firm, a number of questions about systems follow (Ives and Learmonth, 1984). For instance, can systems:

- Be used to create barriers to entry?
- Alter the basis of competition?
- Build in switching costs for customers (locking them in to the firm)?
- Change the balance of power in relationships with suppliers?
- Generate new products?

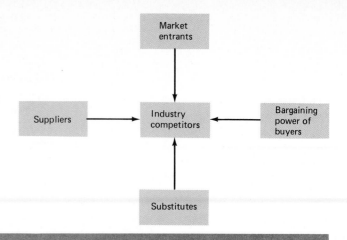

FIGURE 21.3
The competitive forces model. (Adapted from Porter and Millar, 1985.)

Several examples have been given in the text (Chapter 3 and elsewhere) of each of these uses of information technology. For instance, automatic teller machines help to create barriers to entry, alter the basis of competition, build in switching costs to customers (who wants to carry several bank cards?), and represent a new product. One way to use systems strategically is to spin off the systems division as a separate corporate entity, as described in the following account. In this way, software developed for one firm can

Banking on Innovation

In 1985 the Security Pacific Corporation, a $42.7 billion bank holding company, transformed its data processing group from an expense item growing at 28% per year to a new subsidiary that generates $19 million in revenues annually. Security Pacific Automation, Inc., was spun off from Security Pacific to bring electronic products to market faster and to lower the internal cost of systems by creating competition with other vendors.

Adapted from "Banking on Innovation," *Business Computer Systems*, February 1986.

be marketed to others and simultaneously can lower the costs of the original firm by creating a competitive internal market for systems.

The value chain and competitive forces models both involve *identifying critical leverage points* for the application of information technology and *estimating the power of information technology* to affect a specific leverage point. They help identify broad classes of systems for future development. A strategic analysis might identify the customer value chain as a target area in order to create barriers to entry. But many different projects, or a linked series of systems, may have this consequence. More refined criteria are needed to determine which specific projects to develop first and which ones to put off.

21.3 Establishing the Worth of Systems and Choosing Alternatives

Once a strategic analysis identifies the broad classes of systems likely to be of great importance to a firm, some mechanism must be established to choose among alternative systems, all of which achieve the same basic objective. Four methods are commonly used: cost/ benefit analysis, portfolio analysis, scoring models, and organizational models.

These methods are not mutually exclusive. In practice, large systems are built when they look good from a number of different perspectives.

Cost/Benefit Analysis

Cost/benefit analysis estimates and compares the costs and benefits of a system. It is used in a number of situations: to select prospectively among alternative systems, to justify a single system, as an auditing tool to evaluate post hoc existing systems, and as a means to develop quantitative support for a political decision, that is, a decision made for organizational reasons and having nothing to do with the costs and benefits of the system (King and Schrems, 1978).

Cost/benefit analysis assumes that all relevant and politically feasible alternatives have been examined; that their costs and benefits can be identified; and that these costs and benefits can be expressed in a common denominator (i.e., dollars).

There are several steps or stages in cost/benefit analysis (see Figure 21.4). First, the major alternative systems must be precisely specified in terms of labor and capital inputs, relationships with existing systems, and information requirements. Cost/benefit analysis does not generate new alternatives. One pitfall of this method is that some alternatives are not considered.

Second, the benefits and costs of all alternatives must be carefully specified. These include implementation, operational, and long-term

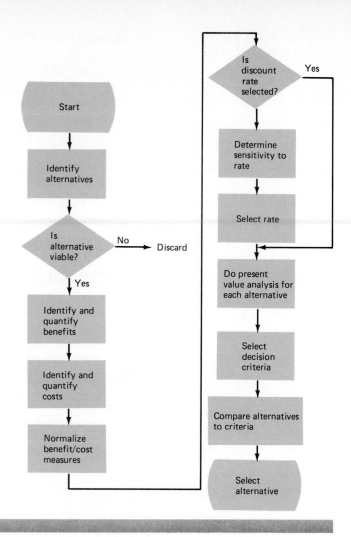

FIGURE 21.4
Stages in cost/benefit analysis. (Adapted from
King and Schrems, 1978.)

maintenance costs. On the other side, there are both tangible and intangible benefits (see Table 21.1).

Third, the alternatives are compared with one another using some financial dimension, usually net present value. Three steps are involved here. The costs and benefits are normalized and expressed in dollar terms. A discount rate is then established, which can be either the market cost of borrowing money or the internal cost of funds. Last, the net present value of the alternatives is calculated. Generally, in this stage, a sensitivity analysis is performed to see how critical the discount rate is to the final value of the alternatives.

Fourth, alternatives are chosen in accordance with the decision

TABLE 21.1
Costs and Benefits of Information Systems

Costs of Systems	Benefits of Systems
Implementation costs	Tangible
Computer time	Cost savings
Technical staff	Increased productivity
User time	Low operational costs
Cost of packages	Reduced work force
	Lower computer expenses
Operational costs	Lower outside vendor costs
Computer time	
Additional equipment	Cost avoidance
Software maintenance	Lower clerical and professional costs
Operating staff	Reduced rate of growth in expenses
User time	Reduced facility costs
Supplies	
Ongoing training costs	Intangible
Facility costs	Improved asset utilization
	Improved resource control
	Improved organizational planning
	Increased organizational flexibility
	More timely information
	More information
	Increased organizational learning
	Legal requirements attained
	Enhanced employee goodwill
	Increased job satisfaction
	Improved decision making
	Improved operations
	Higher client satisfaction
	Better corporate image

criteria of the firm. There are several common decision criteria:

- Maximize benefits for given costs.
- Minimize costs for given benefits.
- Maximize the benefit/cost ratio.
- Maximize net benefits (present value benefits minus present value costs).
- Accept the alternative if the net benefit greater than zero.
- Maximize the rate of return on the investment.

Some firms have a standing rule that projects are not acceptable unless they provide twice as many benefits as costs.

There are many well-known problems in applying cost/benefit analysis in the systems area. Cost/benefit analysis does not describe the risk and uncertainty of the benefits and costs of the entire project. Second, costs and benefits do not occur in the same time frame. Costs are tangible and up front, whereas benefits may be intangible and long-term, yet powerful. Third, inflation may affect costs and benefits differently. Fourth, technology can change in the course of the project, causing the estimated costs and benefits to be incorrect. Fifth, intangible benefits are hard to quantify. These factors may play havoc with cost/benefit analysis.

The most difficult problem with cost/benefit analysis is what might be called an *application bias*. Transaction and clerical systems may always produce more tangible benefits than MIS, DSS, or ESS. *As the sophistication of systems grows, they produce fewer tangible and more intangible benefits*. Moreover, there is no solid method for pricing intangibles. This is true by definition. Yet most observers would argue that MIS, DSS, and ESS systems are beneficial, indeed essential, to the company. They are capital expenses, like roofs on buildings. (See the essay at the end of this chapter, which describes a method for pricing intangibles.)

Like all techniques, cost/benefit analysis can be useful when used judiciously and in combination with other techniques.

Portfolio Analysis

A second way of selecting among alternative projects is to consider the firm as having a portfolio of applications. Each application carries risks and benefits. The portfolio can be described as having a certain profile of risk and benefit to the firm (Figure 21.5). While there is no ideal profile for all firms, information-intensive industries (e.g., finance) should have a few high risk–high benefit projects to ensure that they stay current with technology. Firms in non-information-intensive industries should focus on high-benefit–low risk projects.

The general risks are as follows:

- Benefits may not be obtained.
- Costs of implementation may exceed budgets.
- Implementation time frames are exceeded.
- Technical performance is less than expected.
- The system is incompatible with existing software/hardware.

Risks are not necessarily bad. They are tolerable as long as the benefits are commensurate.

In general, there are three factors that increase the risks of a project (Ein-dor and Segev, 1978; McFarlan, 1981):

- *Project size*. The larger the costs, staff involved, time of implementation, and scope of the project, the greater the risk.
- *Organizational experience*. Risks increase with decreases in staff familiarity with the software and hardware.

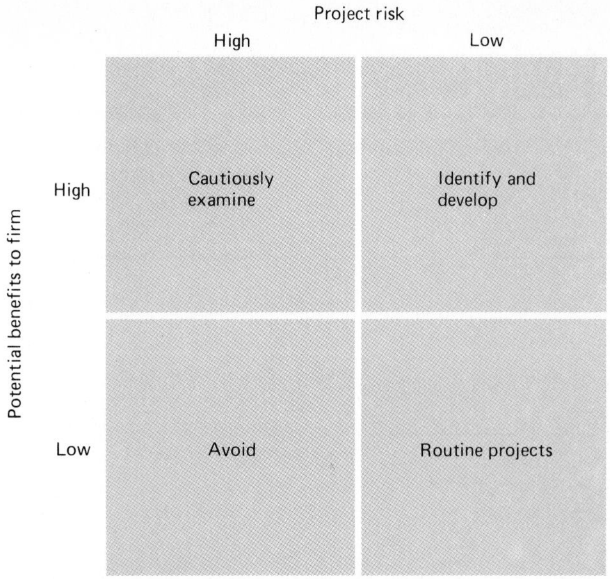

Project risk

	High	Low
High	Cautiously examine	Identify and develop
Low	Avoid	Routine projects

Potential benefits to firm

FIGURE 21.5
A system portfolio. Companies should examine their portfolio of projects in terms of political benefits and likely risks. Certain kinds of projects should be avoided altogether and others developed rapidly. There is no ideal mix. Companies in different industries have different profiles.

- *Project task complexity*. Risks increase as the complexity of the process to be automated increases. An order entry system whose outputs are clearly specified should be less risky than a personnel system whose outputs are not clearly determined.

Once strategic analyses have determined the overall direction of system development, a portfolio analysis can be used to select alternatives. Obviously, one can begin by focusing on systems of high benefit and low risk. These promise early returns and low risks. Second, high-benefit–high-risk systems should be examined. Low-benefit–high-risk systems should be totally avoided, and low-benefit–low-risk systems should be reexamined for the possibility of rebuilding and replacing them with more desirable systems having higher benefits.

Scoring Models

A quick, and sometimes compelling, method for arriving at a decision on alternative systems is a *scoring model*. Scoring models give alternative systems a single score based on the extent to which they meet selected objectives (the method is similar to the *objective attained* model) (Matlin, 1979).

In Table 21.2 the firm must decide among three alternative office automation systems (a mainframe system, a minicomputer system, and a microcomputer-based system).

TABLE 21.2
A Scoring Model Used to
Choose Among Alternative
Office Automation Systems*

Criterion	Weight	Central Mainframe		Department Minicomputer		Individual PCs	
Percentage of user needs met	0.40	2	0.8	3	1.2	4	1.6
Cost of the initial purchase	0.20	1	0.2	3	0.6	4	0.8
Financing	0.10	1	0.1	3	0.3	4	0.4
Ease of maintenance	0.10	2	0.2	3	0.3	4	0.4
Chances of success	0.20	3	0.6	4	0.8	4	0.8
			1.9		3.2		4.0

Key: 1 = low.
5 = high.
* One of the major uses of scoring models is in identifying the criteria of selection and their relative weights. In this instance, an office automation system based on PCs appears preferable.

Column 1 lists the criteria that decision makers may apply to the systems. These criteria are usually the result of lengthy discussions among the decision-making group. Often the most important outcome of a scoring model is not the score but simply agreement on the criteria used to judge a system (Ginzberg, 1979; Nolan, 1982).

Column 2 lists the weights that decision makers attach to the decision criterion. The scoring model helps to bring about agreement among participants concerning the rank of the criteria.

Columns three to five use a 1 to 5 scale (lowest to highest) to express the judgments of participants on the *relative* merits of each system. For example, concerning the percentage of user needs that each system meets, a score of 1 for a system argues that this system *when compared to others being considered* will be low in meeting user needs.

As with all "objective" techniques, there are many qualitative judgments involved in using the scoring model. This model requires experts who understand the issues and the technology. It is appropriate to cycle through the scoring model several times, changing the criteria and weights, to see how sensitive the outcome is to reasonable changes in criteria. Scoring models are used most commonly to confirm, to rationalize, and to support decisions, rather than being the final arbiters of system selection.

Organizational Models

It would be naive and incorrect to state that systems are chosen for development using purely objective models of selection. Even if the forms of objective methods such as cost/benefit analysis are used, they are quickly found to contain hidden assumptions and qualitative judgments that have organizational origins. While organizational politics plays a key role at the level of strategic decision making, it is also true that specific projects are chosen in part because of organizational considerations.

Some of the important organizational factors in choosing system projects are the following:

- What is the impact of the system on unionized and lower-level employees?
- How will the system affect the relative power of competing divisions and groups in the corporation?
- What major reorganizations are required by the system?
- What new corporate values are required to support the system?
- How will decision making change after the new system is installed?

Organizational, or even political, considerations in the selection of projects are not necessarily bad. Systems that look cost beneficial but threaten key interests in the firm would, if implemented, face the risk of great resistance and potential failure (Nolan, 1982).

A successful systems selection process is one that combines the virtues of several techniques. Ideally, systems should be selected that are cost beneficial, contribute to a balanced and appropriate portfolio of applications, and are organizationally compatible and supportable.

An Information Systems Plan

Once specific projects have been selected within the overall context of a strategic plan for the business and the systems area, an information systems plan can be developed. This plan serves as a *road map* indicating *the direction* of systems development, the *rationale*, the *current situation*, the *management strategy*, the *implementation plan*, and the *budget*.

The plan contains a statement of corporate goals and specifies how information technology supports the attainment of those goals. The report shows how general goals will be achieved by specific systems projects. It lays out specific target dates and milestones that can be used later to judge the progress of the plan in terms of how many objectives were actually attained in the time frame specified in the plan.

An important part of the plan is the management strategy for moving from the current situation to the future. Generally, this will indicate the key decisions made by managers concerning hardware acquisition; telecommunications; centralization/decentralization of authority, data, and hardware; and required organizational change.

The implementation plan generally outlines stages in the development of the plan, defining milestones and specifying dates. In this section organizational changes are usually described, including management and employee training requirements, recruiting efforts, and changes in authority, structure, or management practice.

TABLE 21.3
Information Systems Plan

1. Purpose of the Plan
   Overview of plan contents
   Changes in firm's current situation
   Firm's strategic plan
   Current business organization
   Management strategy

2. Strategic Business Plan
   Current situation
   Current business organization
   Changing environments
   Major goals of the business plan

3. Current Systems
   Major systems supporting business
       functions
   Major current capabilities
       Hardware
       Software
       Database
       Telecommunications
   Difficulties meeting business requirements
   Anticipated future demands

4. New Developments
   New system projects
       Project descriptions
       Business rationale
   New capabilities required
       Hardware
       Software
       Database
       Telecommunications

5. Management Strategy
   Acquisition plans
   Milestones and timing
   Organizational realignment
   Internal reorganization
   Management controls
   Major training initiatives
   Personnel strategy

6. Implementation Plan
   Detailed implementation plan
   Anticipated difficulties in
       implementation
   Progress reports

7. Budget Requirements
   Requirements
   Potential savings
   Financing
   Acquisition cycle

Table 21.3 outlines a sample information systems plan. Plans should, of course, be changed as conditions change. Most large organizations use *dynamic* or *rolling* 5-year plans. In this type of plan, the details of the plan are changed every year as projects are completed and as new projects are proposed and conditions change.

21.4 Management of Systems Projects

Once projects are selected, they must be properly managed so that delivery is on time and performance is up to expectations. Perhaps the greatest single cause of system failure is poor management of projects. Why are projects managed so poorly?

Optimism

The techniques for estimating the length of time required to analyze and design systems are poorly developed. There are no standards; there is little sharing of data within and across organizations; and most applications are "first time," i.e., there is no prior experience in the application area. One result is that estimates tend to be optimistic and "best case." It is assumed that all will go well when in fact it rarely does.

The Mythical Man-Month

The unit of measurement of systems project costs is the man-month. Projects are estimated in terms of how many man-months will be required. However, while costs may vary as a product of people and months, the progress of the project does not, as pointed out by Frederick P. Brooks (Brooks, 1974). As it turns out, people and months are not interchangeable in the short run on systems projects. (They may be interchangeable in the long run, but we live in the short run.) In other words, adding more workers to projects does not necessarily reduce the time needed to complete a systems project.

Unlike cotton picking, where tasks can be rigidly partitioned, communication between participants is not required, and training is not required, systems analysis and design involves *tasks that are sequentially linked, cannot be performed in isolation, and require extensive communications and training*. Software development is inherently a group effort, and hence communication costs rise exponentially as the number of participants increases. Moreover, when personnel turnover approaches 20–30%, many of the participants in software projects require a great deal of learning and communication.

Given these characteristics, adding labor to projects can often slow down delivery, as the communication, learning, and coordination costs rise much faster than the output of participants.

Falling Behind: Bad News Travels Slowly Upward

Slippage in projects, failure, and doubts are often not reported to senior management until it is too late. To some extent, this is characteristic of projects in all fields. The crash of the space shuttle Challenger in February 1986 is instructive.

The information that "O" ring seals on the space shuttle might not perform well in the cold February weather and that engineers strongly objected to launching the shuttle in cold weather did not reach the top National Aeronautics and Space Administration (NASA) management team, which ultimately decided to launch. The reasons, while not entirely clear, in part involve the well-understood principle that bearers of bad news are often not appreciated and that senior management wants schedules to be met.

Organizational hierarchy has a pathological and deadly side: Senior management is often kept in the dark (see Chapters 4 and 5).

For systems projects, this seems to be especially true. Systems workers know that management has promised a delivery date to important user groups, that millions of dollars have been spent, and

Communications Channels at NASA

Before the launch of the ill-fated space shuttle Challenger, two top NASA officials had battled with Thiokol engineers the night before. Thiokol [the maker of the solid fuel booster rockets] engineers argued that the O-ring seals might not work in cold weather. Despite this, these NASA officials never passed on the information to NASA's top leadership the next morning at launch. The problem with O-ring seals had been raised repeatedly by Thiokol engineers since the preceding summer. But memorandums from the engineers never were passed on to NASA.

Adapted from "Communications Channels at NASA: Warnings That Faded Along the Line," *The New York Times*, February 28, 1986.

that careers depend on timely delivery of the whole system. As the project falls behind, one day at a time, no one wants to bother senior management with minor slippage details. Eventually, days add up to months and then to years. By then it is too late to save the project no matter how many people are added to the team.

Solutions

A number of solutions to this problem are available. Given the uncertainties of estimating programming and analysis times, ranges should be estimated and final estimates inflated on the basis of management experience.

While men and months are not perfectly substitutable in the short term, in the long term they may be reasonably substitutable. A manager with information on daily or weekly performance might be able to respond with additional resources over long periods of time. It is useful, then, to hold weekly or even daily *status meetings* and utilize Gannt charts (or PERT charts) showing detailed tasks, planned and actual completion times, and dates (Figure 21.6).

Organizational policy changes may be necessary to convey bad news to the top so that management is not unprepared for calamitous events. Some strategies are suggestion boxes, open door policies, rewarding troubleshooters who bring attention to problem areas, and reducing the social distance between systems workers and project

HRIS COMBINED PLAN — HR

Task	Da	Who
DATA ADMINISTRATION SECURITY		
QMF security review/setup	20	EF TP
Security orientation	2	EF JV
QMF security maintenance	35	TP GL
Data entry sec. profiles	4	EF TP
Data entry sec views est.	12	EF TP
Data entry security profiles	65	EF TP
DATA DICTIONARY		
Orientation session	1	EF
Data dictionary design	32	EF WV
DD prod. coordn-query	20	GL
DD prodn. coord-live	40	EF GL
Data dictionary cleanup	35	EF GL
Data dictionary maint.	35	EF GL
PROCEDURES REVISIONS DESIGN PREP		
Work flows (old)	10	PK JL
Payroll data flows	31	JL PK
HRIS P/R model	11	PK JL
P/R interface orient. mtg.	6	PK JL
P/R interface coordn. I	15	PK
P/R interface coorn.	8	PK
Benefits interfaces (old)	5	JL
Ben. interfaces new flow	8	JL
Ben. communication strategy	3	PK JL
New work flow model	15	PK JL
Posn. data entry flows	14	WV JL

RESOURCE SUMMARY

Name		Who	1989 Oct	Nov	Dec	1990 Jan	Feb	Mar	Apr	May	Jun	Jul	Aug	Sep	Oct	Nov	Dec	1991 Jan	Feb	Mar	Apr
Edith Farrell	5.0	EF	2	21	24	24	23	22	22	27	34	34	29	26	28	19	14	4	3		
Woody Holand	5.0	WH	5	17	20	19	12	10	14	10	2										
Charles Pierce	5.0	CP			5	11	20	13	9	10	7	6	8	4	4	4	4				
Ted Leurs	5.0	TL		12	17	17	19	17	14	12	15	16	2	1	1	1	1				9
Toni Cox	5.0	TC	1	11	10	11	11	12	19	19	21	21	21	17	17	12	9	3	2		
Patricia Clark	5.0	PC	7	23	30	34	27	25	15	24	25	16	11	13	17	10	3				
Jane Lawton	5.0	JL	1	9	16	21	19	21	20	17	15	14	12	14	8	5					
David Holloway	5.0	DH	4	4	5	5	5	2	7	5	4	16	2								6
Diane O'Neill	5.0	DO	6	14	17	16	13	11	9	4	2	3									
Joan Albert	5.0	JA	5	6			7	6	2	1				5	5	1					
Marie Marcus	5.0	MM	15	7	2	1	1														
Don Stevens	5.0	DS	4	4	5	4	5	1													
Casual	5.0	CASL		3	4	3		4	7	9	5	3	2								
Kathy Manley	5.0	KM		1	5	16	20	19	22	19	20	18	20	11	2						
Anna Borden	5.0	AB					9	10	16	15	11	12	19	10	7	1					
Gail Loring	5.0	GL		3	6	5	9	10	17	18	17	10	13	10	10	7	17	14	13	3	1
UNASSIGNED	0.0	X												9	236	225	230	216	178	9	7
Co-op	5.0	CO		6	4			2	3	4	4	2	4	16							
casual	5.0	CAUL								3	3	3									
TOTAL DAYS			49	147	176	196	194	174	193	195	190	181	140	125	358	288	284	237	196	12	23

FIGURE 21.6

This is a Gantt chart produced by a commercial project management software package. It shows the task, man-days, and initials of responsible persons, as well as the start and finish dates for each task. The project described here is a data administration project. A good project manager should be able to summarize the total man-days, as in the lower panel. This summation table summarizes over many tasks.

managers. Close attention by the corporate data processing committee can also avert disaster (Nolan, 1982; Lucas and Turner, 1982). Failure to develop new communication channels and supportive values can lead to disaster, as described above.

21.5 Personnel: Attracting and Keeping Good Systems People

Industry surveys have found that the turnover of information systems personnel averages about 20% per year, and the demand for new systems personnel of all types grows at a rate of around 15% per year (Gray, 1982). Job satisfaction and organizational commitment surveys find that systems people are less committed to their organizations and more committed to their professions than other workers (Couger and Zawacki, 1978; Couger and Colter, 1983). Every 2 years, half of the information system staff in a typical organization changes. It takes 18 months for new employees in systems to become maximally effective (Bartol and Martin, 1982).

Clearly, organizations pay a high cost for 20% turnover rates simply in terms of lost productivity. On the other hand, high turnover has the positive result that new talent is continually being brought into the organization with new skills and backgrounds—assuming that the organization can recruit talented replacements. Still, most observers agree that turnover is too high and should be reduced.

The high turnover rates of information system personnel have been attributed to both market demand factors and internal organizational factors. With the growth in demand for systems personnel, market demand is high, salaries are lucrative, and offers to switch are frequent. Internal organizational factors include poor management of human resources, poor career pathing, and poor job design. We will now examine these factors.

Poor Management of Human Resources

There are unique problems in the management of systems work. A large part of systems work involves maintenance of existing programs. Among programmers this is considered low status drudgery. Professionally more exciting, and organizationally more rewarding, is the development of new systems. There is reason to believe that management faces a dilemma when allocating personnel to these two kinds of systems work.

On the one hand, management seeks to reward seasoned systems workers by assigning them to new development projects. On the other hand, new recruits with special talents (i.e., command of new technology and software) are often assigned to new projects, leaving loyal employees dissatisfied and feeling trapped in lower-level work. Sometimes the only way to attract skilled new employees is to promise interesting work on the latest equipment. For the experienced employee, often the only way to get interesting development work is to change jobs.

One possible solution to this problem is to have management carefully identify the professional expectations and motivational needs of systems workers. This requires both better personnel testing and attitudinal surveys of the organizational climate. Perhaps more important, management must actively seek out employees and discover their interests. A number of organizations have adopted flatter hierarchies in an attempt to put senior management on the work shop floor to better understand employees (Couger and Colter, 1983).

Career Pathing

In many organizations, the only way to advance is to become a manager in the systems area. Moreover, once an employee becomes a systems manager, it is difficult to move into higher-level senior management because of a bias against "technical operations types."

But many good programmers and analysts are not good managers. In order to reward these people, organizations should develop a *dual career path* or a *professional stage model* (Couger and Zawacki, 1978; Bartol and Martin, 1982; Cougar and Colter, 1983; Baroudi, 1985). In a dual career path model, a technical path is created that parallels the managerial path in rank and salary. For instance, a technical person would be promoted from programmer to programmer/analyst to systems specialist to senior technical specialist. In the professional stage model, an employee is assumed to progress from apprentice to colleague to mentor to project sponsor.

Both dual path and professional stage models provide important incentives to technical personnel to stay with their current organization.

Not all systems personnel want to remain in the systems area. Many would like to be considered for management positions elsewhere in the firm. Until recently, it was rare for systems personnel to move horizontally or vertically into senior management except in a staff position. This situation has changed.

Many organizations have opened up new career opportunities for systems personnel in user divisions. A new position in user departments has been created in many large financial institutions called the *business systems analyst*. Skilled systems personnel who understand systems analysis and design are hired by user departments (e.g., personnel, marketing) to act as liaison between user departments and the information systems department. These business systems analysts have a knowledge of systems but are primarily loyal to and understand the business of the unit that employs them.

Literature in the 1960s predicted that because information was so important to the organization, those who controlled information systems would rise to the top levels of organizations. This did not occur. Until the mid-1980s, it was rare for systems personnel to enter senior management, which was dominated by persons with finance, marketing, engineering, and legal backgrounds. This message was not lost on new MBAs, most of whom avoided tarrying in the systems department too long lest they become identified as a "technical" type.

In the 1980s this situation began to change slowly. Citibank, in 1984, was among the first companies to name a person with a systems background as its CEO. As systems take on strategic significance for organizations, more senior management positions will open for systems personnel.

Job Design

The design of jobs in the programming and analyst areas has changed little since the 1960s. Research has found that these jobs are characterized by growing role ambiguity and role conflict. In turn, these factors lead to declining job satisfaction and high turnover (Baroudi, 1985).

Role ambiguity refers to imprecise and unclear expectations of job performance and rewards; *role conflict* refers to conflicting job performance demands. Research literature shows that systems personnel frequently complain about continual reorganization in the systems area, uncertain job priorities, and no clear reward policies. Because systems personnel have to bridge the gap between users and the systems department, they are subject to conflicting demands.

They want to satisfy users but ultimately must work according to priorities set by information system management.

Both role ambiguity and role conflict are strongly influenced by management policy. Stabilizing the organization, buffering systems from reorganization, and making reward structures more precise and reliable are key management actions that can help.

21.6 The Management of Strategic Transitions

Changes in the objectives and role of information systems in the firm over the last decade indicate that managing systems development has taken on companywide significance. Systems is no longer a backroom operation; it is now part of the front office.

What Is a Strategic Transition?

Increasingly, the introduction of new information systems has brought about important changes in business goals, relationships with customers and suppliers, and internal operations. These systems are called *strategic systems*. While not all systems have such strategic consequences, they are increasingly common.

Creating a new system no longer means installing a new machine in the basement and retraining a few systems programmers. Today this process typically involves installing thousands of terminals or microcomputers on the desks of employees who have little experience with them; connecting the devices to powerful communications networks; rearranging social relations in the office; changing reporting patterns; physically rearranging work; and asking employees to achieve higher levels of productivity.

Briefly, new systems today often involve merging the separate islands of technology—data processing, telecommunications, office automation, and microcomputing—into single entities. These kinds of changes will increase in frequency and depth of impact as the underlying technology changes.

We will refer to these sociotechnical changes (affecting both social and technical elements of the organization) as *strategic transitions*—a movement from one level of a sociotechnical system to another.

The Management Problem

The management problem with strategic transitions can be succinctly stated: How can the organization obtain the maximal long-run benefit from the technology without destroying the positive features of the organization?

Figure 21.7 summarizes the factors that management must juggle when developing large system projects. Managers must adjust their

FIGURE 21.7
Factors in the management of strategic transitions. Important
changes in technology must be coordinated with the environment,
with management policies, and with the organization.

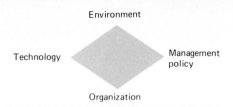

policies to the *technology*, the *environmental constraints and opportunities* (regulations, loyal customers), and the *organization*. These factors will now be discussed.

Organizational Issues

In bringing about change in organizations seeking to adopt new systems technology, four factors stand out as critical: the role of information systems in the firm; the internal organization of information systems; technology tracking; and changing organizational culture. Each of these is discussed briefly.

Role of Information Systems in the Firm

The most common difficulty in implementing strategic systems is the failure to recognize the new role of systems. Most organizations still isolate the systems function structurally and culturally and rigidly separate it from senior management. This is a vestige of the past, when the information systems department was simply a service function to line units. A sure candidate for the failure of strategic systems is the organization that isolates systems by putting the information system function two or three levels below senior management.

In order to implement strategic systems, the information system group should be raised to the level of senior management, with a fully independent senior vice-president or director in charge. In one case study used in this book—the Social Security Administration's Systems Modernization Plan—one of the first actions was to raise the systems director to the level of Deputy Commissioner, working with the Commissioner on a daily basis (Westin and Laudon, 1986).

Organization of Information System Departments

A common failing of many information system organizations is to combine operations and systems development into a single staff; at times on paper there is a separation, but in common practice development people and resources are used for maintenance whenever there is a crisis. In these kinds of information system organizations, crisis is the normal state of affairs, so that development work is interrupted and poorly planned.

It is wise to separate development and operations. Development groups should have their own machines on which to develop software, access to different software tools, and accelerated training programs. There are insufficient resources in most organizations to modernize thousands of line of existing code. The only leverage on future software exists in the development area. It is essential that only the most modern methods be used here and that sufficient resources and personnel be devoted to development.

Technology Tracking

Many corporations have created a new information system position, sometimes called *senior technology scientist*. In a world where information technology is spawning new business opportunities so rapidly, it is essential to keep track of major streams of development. It is necessary to have a systematic method for introducing new information technology into the firm.

To the question "Who is responsible for introducing new information technology and concepts into the firm?" most companies do not have an answer. One possible answer is a technology tracking senior manager who both understands the technology and has long experience in the business.

Figure 21.8 shows the stages of information technology assimilation: initiation, experimentation, control, and transfer (McKenney and McFarlan, 1982). These stages are no different than those for other technologies. One key difference, however, is that information technology must be experimented with in the field, using existing parts of the organization to demonstrate its worth. Once developed, new information technology applications can be passed on to the control of the information system group.

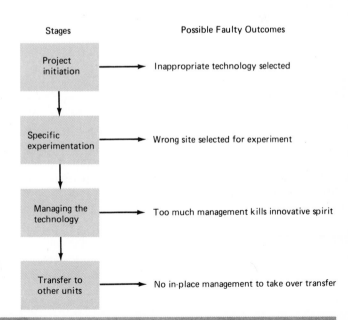

FIGURE 21.8
Implementing new information technology. Many things can go wrong between the adoption of a new technology and its final routinization in the organization. (Adapted from McKenney and McFarlan, 1982.)

Changing Organizational Culture

All of the changes discussed so far—the role of information systems in the organization, the proper organization of the group, and the development of technology tracking—all presuppose the following:

- The organization has supportive values that make these changes likely to occur.
- The groups with these values have power in the organization.
- The attitudes and behavior of employees (norms) are supportive.

Values, power, and norms are what define an *organizational culture*. Without a supportive culture, the changes previously discussed, and strategic transitions in general, are not possible. Stagnation and ultimate collapse are more likely.

How can cultures change? In general, changing the culture of an organization is a slow process that may take several years. That is precisely why organizations change more slowly than the technology and why there are so many organizations that do not have a supportive culture.

What kinds of supportive values are needed, and how can they be introduced? Some supportive values for strategic transitions include the following:

- Openness to new ideas of how to do business and what business to be in.
- A willingness to innovate, explore, and potentially change.
- Awareness of what other organizations are doing.
- An analytic approach that encourages systematic thinking through of problems.
- Sensitivity to employee issues.

Managements that have isolated themselves from competitors, other organizations, and their own employees are not likely to manage strategic transitions successfully.

Up to 1982, the Social Security Administration was acting in this way (see the case study "Systems Modernization at the Social Security Administration"). One solution to its problems was to bring in outside consultants to help generate ideas and plan for strategic change; to reeducate its senior managers by having them attend university-based seminars; to actively recruit new senior and middle management from outside the organization to bring in new ideas; and to initiate a massive retraining program for its employees.

On a smaller scale, these are all appropriate actions to take when beginning to change the organizational culture.

Bringing about changes in internal power alignments—ensuring that those with new values are in positions of influence—is more difficult. Internal power balances usually change as a result of some organizational crisis. Falling profits, threatened takeovers, inability to perform basic missions—these are the kinds of crisis needed to bring progressive groups to positions of leadership.

This kind of power change cannot be created by outside consultants; it usually requires a wrenching organizational experience. About the best that can be said is that organizations that fail to make strategic transitions in their information technology have a high probability of generating organizational crises. In 1981, for instance, the Social Security Administration almost failed to issue its 40 million monthly checks on a routine basis. The Systems Modernization Plan was a direct response to that crisis.

Once new supportive values have been adopted by management and progressive groups are in a position of leadership, it is possible to begin changing employee attitudes and expectations (norms). The resistance of employees to new information technology has in general been grossly exaggerated (Westin and Laudon, 1986). Employees are fundamentally interested in continued employment, a high-quality working life, and a pleasant organizational climate in which to work. Information technology generally does not lead to massive unemployment. But poor implementation of this technology can spoil otherwise satisfactory jobs.

A key complaint of unionized office workers at the Social Security Administration prior to systems modernization was that the old technology made their work difficult, slowed service to clients, introduced errors and delays, and frequently broke down. As systems modernization proceeds, the union wants to be made aware of planned changes, participate in their implementation, maintain job classifications and pay scales, and maintain the present level of employment or work toward slow attrition of the work force (Westin and Laudon, 1986).

In order to bring about new employee attitudes and ensure a smooth transition to modern systems, many organizations are devising new forums through which employees can participate in the design, implementation, and operation of advanced information technology.

General Motors and the United Automobile Workers union have agreed to a new quality of working life for the production of the Saturn car, in which union members play key roles in technology design, job design, job control, quality control, and employee evaluation. The Social Security Administration management and the American Federation of Government Employees (AFGE) have signed a similar agreement to implement the Systems Modernization Plan (Westin and Laudon, 1986). Several other unions have reached similar agreements with management, such as those at the Equitable Life Assurance Society.

Office Workers Gain a Landmark Pact

Office workers at the Syracuse office of the Equitable Life Assurance Society agreed to a labor contract—the first ever at Equitable—which the union believes sets new precedents for unions and office workers nationwide. The union is District 925 (9-to-5), which has successfully unionized women office workers in the Midwest. The contract includes provisions for medical vision care, installation of screens to prevent glare, detachable keyboards for flexibility, adjustable chairs, reductions in exposure of pregnant workers to terminals, and a provision that no worker is at a terminal for more than 2 consecutive hours.

Adapted from "Upstate Office Workers Gain a Landmark Pact," *The New York Times*, November 9, 1985.

Organizations without unions have developed quality control circles, participatory management, seminars, and other forums through which employees can be brought into the process of information technology change.

One part of the new organizational culture that is supportive of strategic information technology transitions is a strong belief that employees must be more closely integrated into the change process.

21.7 Summary

Changes in technology, the environment of organizations, and the growing role of information in the firm create challenges to contemporary management. Central information systems management is losing control of information and equipment. There are islands of emerging applications that are poorly integrated. There is also a shortage of skilled personnel who understand these developments. All of these environmental factors put a strain on contemporary organizations and management.

It is necessary for organizations to allow information technology to influence their strategic planning. Firms that fail to make this adjustment are likely to be outperformed by other firms. A value chain model and a competitive forces model can be helpful in identifying strategic targets for systems development.

Once strategic systems are identified, the right one must be chosen. There are several methods for choosing systems: cost/benefit, portfolio, scoring, and organizational. There is no one right method, and several of them can be used in combination.

Once systems are selected, they must be managed and staffed properly. Project plans usually underestimate the time and costs, sometimes by substantial amounts. High-quality systems workers must be properly tracked to ensure their commitment to the organization, and their jobs must be designed to reduce role ambiguity and role conflict.

New systems today often involve significant changes in organizational life. We have called these changes strategic transitions. Technology, environmental change, and internal organizational factors must be carefully balanced to bring about successful strategic transitions. In large-scale strategic transitions, employees must be more closely involved in system development.

Key Words

Emerging islands of applications
Environmental change
Strategic role of systems
Organizational plan
Strategic plan
Strategic targets
Strategies
Value chain model
Competitive forces model
Cost/benefit analysis
Tangible benefits

Intangible benefits
Portfolio analysis
Project risk
Scoring models
Organizational models
Information systems plan
Man-month
Career path
Job design
Strategic transition
Technology tracking

Review Questions

1. Describe the five major factors that confront managers in the information system area.
2. What is a plan, and what is a strategic plan? What is the purpose of a strategic plan for systems?
3. What is the difference between aligning systems with the business and permitting information technology to influence the business?
4. Describe four generic business strategies.
5. What are the value chain and competitive forces models, and how can they be used to develop a systems plan?
6. Describe the four methods used to establish the worth of systems.
7. Name some tangible and intangible benefits of systems. How can you quantify intangible benefits? Give some examples.
8. What are the major factors that create risk in systems projects?
9. What organizational factors should you consider when deciding about a system?

10. Name the major categories of an information systems plan.
11. What are the major factors that make management of systems development projects difficult?
12. What are three solutions to the difficulties of managing projects?
13. How much information system personnel turnover is there? What would you do to decrease turnover?
14. Define a strategic transition and give some examples in the systems world.
15. What are three actions you would take as a CEO to lead your organization to adopt new types of corporate systems?

Discussion Questions

1. Your CEO has just asked you as the head of the information systems department to come up with a strategic plan for systems that would lead in 5 years to state of the art computing at your firm. You have an appointment with the CEO tomorrow morning to discuss issues and the support you will need. What do you plan to ask the CEO?
2. A $3 million personnel benefits system will fall behind schedule unless something is done now. As manager of information systems, what can you recommend now to bring the project back on track?
3. Outline a management program for reducing information system turnover in your organization.
4. Outline a program of organizational change to make your organization more capable of implementing systems.

CASE STUDY

How to Measure the Benefits of Office Automation

Corporations used to be able to justify the costs of information systems in relatively straightforward ways. A $100,000 system might often save $100,000 in labor costs, or paper costs, or some other tangible cost item. This is not the case with management systems or office and professional systems. While systems have advanced, methods of determining their costs and benefits have not. In contemporary organizations, information systems costs beget more costs. Additional staff must be hired to maintain microcomputer hardware, procure software, train people, and so forth.

Because of the inability to account for benefits, much needed office and professional automation projects are put off by capital budget committees regardless of their intrinsic merit.

There are several methods for establishing the costs of office automation projects. *Activity analysis* is used by Booz Allen & Hamilton, a major accounting and consulting firm. In this method, managers estimate how much time they spend on various activities, (e.g., writing, reading, filing, traveling, meeting, speaking, telephoning). The activity profile is then examined and office systems are planned that attempt to shift executive time from low-value activities (e.g., traveling) to high-value activities (e.g., meeting or reading). The amount of money saved by an office automation system is made roughly equivalent to the hours of low-value activity avoided based on an hourly estimate of an executive's salary. If a manager is paid $40 per hour, saving 2 hours of travel time a week saves $80. A companywide system that similarly affects 1000 managers saves the company $80,000 per week.

A different method applicable in some situations is IBM's *common staffing system* (*CSS*). CSS compares productivity among similar business units. Activities are identified (billing, purchasing, maintenance, accounts receivable) and associated with quantifiable outputs (e.g., production volume, number of invoices, floor space, etc.). The total labor per unit of output is calculated. Office systems should reduce the labor per unit output ratio.

CSS works only where comparable production units are involved.

A third approach is used by General Electric. Called *Introspect*, this method focuses on the overall cost of managing an activity. By adjusting spans of control and redirecting efforts toward organizational objectives, Introspect measures a system's contribution. For instance, analysis of a manager's activities may find that some activities are not rationally connected to the goals of that manager's unit. These activities are either eliminated or a system is used to reduce these to a minimum. Office systems may be used to increase the span of control—increasing the number of people that one manager can supervise. This eliminates a management layer and is a cost saving.

A fourth approach was used in an extensive French national research project called *Kayak*. In this approach an in-depth analysis of office and managerial work is conducted using four instruments: an office support services questionnaire, a task force record form, a communication diary, and a detailed task analysis form. The questionnaire is used to gather attitudinal data about employee job satisfaction, unmet communication and information needs, and job design. Here the point of office automation is to develop jobs that are more fulfilling and satisfying to employees as well as cost effective for the organization.

The Kayak method is unique because it is the only method that directly takes into account job design and employee attitudes.

A fifth method can be called a *hedonic wage model*. Here management activities are recorded and divided into high value (managing, supervising, coordinating) and low value (data analysis, researching, filing, clerical). Office automation systems are expected to increase the hours of high-value work and decrease the hours of low-value work for managers. The amount of cost savings produced by a system is seen as a function of the implicit hourly cost of activities for the firm. If clerical workers are paid $20 per hour, for instance, and managers are paid $80 per hour, then an office automation system that increases managers' high-value work by 40 hours per month produces $3200 of value to the firm. Let's assume that this additional 40 hours of high-value time comes at the expense of reducing managers' clerical work by an equivalent 40 hours per month. This work is picked up by clerical workers at $20 per hour.

The hedonic model is interesting because it takes into account real costs of managers to the firm using current wages.

Adapted from Peter G. Sassone and A. Perry Schwartz, "Cost-Justifying OA," *Datamation*, February 15, 1986.

Case Study Questions

1. Which of the preceding models would you prefer to use in a medium-sized regional bank? Why?
2. Besides cost avoidance and savings, what other potential contributions do office systems make? Are these contributions measured by any of the models presented?
3. The preceding models rest, for the most part, on a distinction between managerial high-value and low-value work. Chatting at the water cooler might be considered low value, along with many other managerial activities not directly related to organizational goals. Review Chapter 5 and then ask if these distinctions make a great deal of sense.

References

Baroudi, Jack. "The Impact of Role Variables on IS Personnel Work Attitudes and Intentions," *MIS Quarterly*, Vol. 9, No. 4 (December 1985).

Bartol, K., and Martin, D. "Managing Information Systems Personnel: A Review of the Literature and Managerial Implications," *MIS Quarterly* (1982), pp. 49–70.

Benson, Robert J., and Parker, Marilyn M. "Enterprise-Wide Information Management: An Introduction to the Concepts." Los Angeles: IBM Los Angeles Scientific Center, May 1985.

Brooks, Frederick P. "The Mythical Man-Month," *Datamation* (December 1974).

Canning, Richard. "Six Top Information Systems Issues," *EDP Analyzer*, Vol. 23, No. 1 (January 1985).

Couger, J., and Colter, Mel A. *Motivation of the Maintenance Programmer*. Colorado Springs, Colo.: CYSCS, 1983.

Couger, J., and Zawacki, R. "What Motivates DP Professionals," *Datamation*, Vol. 24, No. 9 (September 1978).

Ein-dor, Phillip, and Segev, Eli. "Strategic Planning for Management Information Systems," *Management Science*, Vol. 24, No. 15 (1978).

Ginzberg, Michael J. "Improving MIS Project Selection," *Omega, International Journal of Management Science*, Vol. 6, No. 1 (1979).

Gray, S. "DP Salary Survey," *Datamation*, Vol. 28, No. 11 (October 1982).

Iacono, Suzanne, and Kling, Rob. "Changing Office Technologies and Transformations of Clerical Jobs: A Historical Perspective," Draft 5e. Irvine: University of California, 1985.

Ives, Blake, and Learmonth, Gerard P. "The Information System as a Competitive Weapon," *Communications of the ACM* (December 1984).

King, John Leslie, and Schrems, Edward L. "Cost Benefit Analysis in Information Systems Development and Operation," *Computing Surveys*, Vol. 10, No. 1 (March 1978).

Krcmar, Helmut A.O. "Expert Systems for Information Management," Draft. Los Angeles: IBM Los Angeles Computing Center, August 1985.

Lucas, Henry C., and Turner, Jon A. "A Corporate Strategy for the Control of Information Processing," *Sloan Management Review* (Spring 1982).

Matlin, Gerald. "What Is the Value of Investment in Information Systems?" *MIS Quarterly* (September 1979).

McFarlan, Warren. "A Portfolio Approach to Information Systems," *Harvard Business Review* (September–October 1981).

McKenney, James L., and McFarlan, F. Warren. "The Information Archipelago—Maps and Bridges," *Harvard Business Review* (September–October 1982).

Mintzberg, Henry, and McHugh, Alexandra. "Strategy Formation in an Adhocracy," *Administrative Science Quarterly*, Vol. 30, No. 2 (June 1985).

Nolan, Richard L. "Managing Information Systems by Committee," *Harvard Business Review* (July–August 1982).

Parsons, Gregory L. "Information Technology: A New Competitive Weapon," *Sloan Management Review* (Fall 1983).

Phister, M., Jr. *Data Processing and Economics*. Santa Monica Calif.: Santa Monica Publishing and Digital Press, 1979.

Porter, Michael E. *Competitive Strategy*, New York: Free Press, 1980.

Porter, Michael E., and Millar, Victor E. "How Information Gives You Competitive Advantage," *Harvard Business Review* (July–August 1985).

Rockart, John F. "The Changing Role of the Information Systems Executive," *Sloan Management Review* (Fall 1982).

Westin, Alan F., and Laudon, Kenneth C. "Information Processing at the Social Security Administration, 1935–1990." Prepared for the Office of Technology Assessment, United States Congress, 1986.

Systems Modernization at the Social Security Administration

Introduction

The Social Security Administration (SSA) consists of more than 88,000 employees located in 1300 field offices, 10 regional offices, 32 teleservice centers, 6 program service centers, 3 data operations centers, and the Baltimore headquarters. SSA administers the major social insurance programs of the United States and several other related programs, which include:

Income Support Programs
- Retirement and Survivors Insurance (RSI)
- Disability Insurance (DI)
- Supplemental Security Income (SSI)
- Aid to Families with Dependent Children (AFDC)

Other Social Service Programs
- Black Lung Disease (BL)
- Health Insurance (Medicare)
- Food Stamps
- Low Income House Energy Insurance
- Refugee Assistance
- Child Support Enforcement

In order to administer these programs, SSA maintains 260 million names in its account number file (enumeration file), 240 million earnings records, and 50 million names on its master beneficiary file. In addition to keeping these files current, SSA annually issues 10 million new Social Security cards, pays out $170 billion, posts 380 million wage items reported by employers, receives 7.5 million new claims, recomputes (because of changes in beneficiary sta-tus) 19 million accounts, and handles 120 million bills and queries from private health insurance companies, carriers, and intermediaries.

Virtually every living American has some relationship with SSA.

In the early 1980s, SSA approached the precipice of financial ruin and administrative collapse. The long-term funding for Social Security payments in the United States was in serious jeopardy, and SSA's computerized administrative systems were nearing collapse.

This was an unusual state of affairs for SSA. As the flagship institution of the New Deal, SSA had developed broad bipartisan support, and there was never any serious question about its long-term financial viability until the late 1970s. In addition, since its inception in 1935, SSA had been one of the leading innovators and implementors of advanced information technology in the United States. With a special long-term relationship with IBM from the mid-1930s to the late 1960s, SSA was a test site for many of the leading commercial hardware and software innovations of this period.

In 1982 the long-term funding for SSA was secured through a historic compromise between leading Democratic and Republican political figures. However, the administrative information systems of the SSA were still in jeopardy.

In 1982, SSA announced its Systems Modernization Plan (SMP)—a $500 million 5-year effort to completely rebuild its information systems and administrative processes. Since then, the SMP has been expanded to $1 billion and 10 years.

The SMP is one of the largest civilian information system rebuilding efforts in history.

SSA illustrates many central problems of management, information technology, and organization faced by private and public organizations in a period of rapid technical and social change. Although SSA operates in a unique federal government environment, many large private organizations have exhibited similar problems in this time period. The problems and solutions illustrated in this case are generic.

The case is organized into four sections. Section I describes the overall situation at SSA in the period before SMP, roughly 1972–1982. Section II describes the SMP plan and strategy. Section III describes the experience of SMP up to the time of this writing (Fall 1987). Section IV considers the long-term prospects of SMP.

Section I: Organization, Management, and Systems, 1972–1982

The overall system environment at SSA in 1982 could best be described as a hodgepodge of software programs developed over a 20-year period in four different machine environments. In the history of the agency, no one had ever conducted an information system requirements study to understand the overall requirements of the agency or the specific requirements of its subunits. There had been no planning of the information systems function for more than 20 years. Instead, as in many private organizations, systems drifted along from year to year, with only incremental changes.

Software

SSA software resulted from decades of programming techniques. The enumeration system—which supports the issuance of Social Security numbers—was designed in the late 1950s and had never been changed. The earning system was designed in 1975, the claims processing system was unchanged from the early 1960s, and other systems were also inherited from the late 1960s and 1970s. The software was a product of unplanned patchwork, with no regard given to its deterioration over time.

From the 1950s to the 1980s, there were four major equipment transitions. However, the software was not improved or redesigned at any of these transitions. All of SSA's files and programs were maintained on over 500,000 reels of magnetic tape, which was susceptible to aging, cracking, and deterioration. Because tape was the storage medium, all data processing was batch sequential.

In summary, there were 76 different software systems making up SSA's basic computer operations. These software systems were themselves congeries of programs that performed the primary business functions of SSA. There were more than 1300 computer programs encompassing over 12 million lines of COBOL and other code.

Most of the 12 million lines of code were undocumented. They worked, but few people in the organization knew how or why. This made maintenance extremely complex. Congress and the president in the 1960s and 1970s made continual changes in the benefit formulas, each of which required extensive maintenance and changes in the underlying software. A change in cost-of-living rates, for instance, required sorting through several large interwoven programs, which took months of work.

Because of the labor–intensive work needed to change undocumented software and the growing operations crisis, software development staff were commonly shifted to manage the operations crisis. The result was little development of new programs.

It did not help matters that few people in Congress, the Office of the President, the Office of Management and Budget, or other responsible parties understood the deleterious impact of program changes on SSA systems capabilities. Unfortunately, SSA did not inform Congress of its own limitations.

What is unusual about SSA is that in the late 1970s it had not begun to make the transition to newer storage technology, file management and database technology, or more modern software techniques. In this respect, SSA was about 5 years behind private industry in making important technological transitions.

Hardware

By 1982, SSA was operating outdated, unreliable, and inadequate hardware, given its mission. Of its 26 large-scale computers, 23 were supporting program-related operations, while the remaining 3 processed administrative workloads. There were no machines dedicated to the development of new systems. Many of the computers had not been manufactured or marketed for 10 years or more. Eleven IBM 360/65 systems were no longer manufactured or supported. Although more modern equipment might have required $1 million annually for maintenance and operations expenses, SSA was spending more than $4 million to keep these antiquated machines in service.

The antiquated hardware forced SSA to rely on third-party maintenance services. Because of frequent breakdowns, over 25% of the production jobs ended before completion (abended jobs) and 30% of the available computer processing power was idle.

As a result of hardware deficiencies, a number of specific program impacts became apparent in 1982:

- Earnings enforcement operations, which help detect overpayments, were more than 3 years behind schedule.
- The computation of benefit amounts to give credit for additional earnings after retirement was 3 years behind schedule.
- SSI claims and posteligibility redeterminations could only be processed three times a week rather than five times a week. This meant delays of several days or weeks for SSI beneficiaries.
- In order to process cost-of-living increases in 1982 for 42 million individuals, SSA had to suspend all other data processing for 1 week.
- In 1982, there was a 3-month backlog of data needed to notify employers about incorrectly reported employee earnings. This created a suspense file with more than 2 million entries of unposted earnings and required additional manual work to handle employer correspondence.

SSA estimated that its gross computing capacity was deficient by more than 2000 CPU hours per month. SSA estimated that it needed 5000 central processing hours per month, but its capacity was only 3000 CPU hours per month.

Telecommunications

SSA depends heavily on telecommunications to perform its mission. Its 1300 field offices need timely access to data stored at the central computer facility in Baltimore. In 1982, however, SSA's telecommunications was the result of an evolving system dating back to 1966. The primary telecommunications system was called the Social Security Administration Data Acquisition and Response System (SSADARS). It was designed to handle 100,000 transactions per day. One year after it was built in 1975, the system was totally saturated. Each year teleprocessing grows by 100%. By 1982 the SSADARS network was frequently breaking down, and was obsolete and highly inefficient.

One result of the saturated communications system was that senior SSA local executives working in field offices were forced to come in on the weekends in order to key in data to the SSADARS system, which was overloaded during the week. The total system downtime in 1982 was 385 hours, or about 11% of the total available hours. By 1982, there was little remaining CPU telecommunications capacity in the off-peak periods to handle the normal growth of current workloads. Entire streams of communications were frequently lost. At peak times, when most people wanted to use the system, it was simply unavailable. The result was telecommunication backlogs ranging from 10,000 to 100,000 messages at a time.

Database

The word *database* can be used only in a very loose sense to refer to SSA's 500,000 reels of magnetic tape on which it stored information on clients in major program areas. Each month SSA performed 30,000 production jobs, requiring more than 150,000 tapes to be loaded onto and off of machines. The tapes themselves were disintegrating, and errors in the tapes, along with their physical breakdown, caused very high error rates and forced a number of reruns. Many of the tapes had no internal labels. More than one-third of the operations staff (200 people) was required simply to handle the tapes.

As in many private sector organizations, data were organized at SSA by programs, and many of the data elements were repeated from one program to the next. SSA estimates that there were more than 1300 separate programs, each with its own data set. Because there was no data administration function, it was difficult to determine the total number of data elements, or the level of redundancy within the agency as a whole or even within program areas.

Management Information Systems

Management information systems (MIS) are designed to support middle- and senior-level management by providing routine reports on the operations of the organization, as well as responding to ad hoc inquiries. The data for these reports are generally derived from transaction processing systems at the operational level.

In 1982, SSA had a woefully inadequate capability in the MIS area. Because the data were stored on magnetic tape and were generally not available to end-user managers throughout the organization, all requests for reports had to be funneled through the information systems operations area.

But there was a crisis in operations, and this meant delays of up to several years in the production of reports crucial for management decision making. As long as all of the data were stored in a format that required professional computer and information systems experts to gain access to them, general management always had to deal with the Information Systems Department. This group had a stranglehold over the organization. Their attitude, as one commentator noted, was summed up in the statement "Don't bother us or the checks won't go out."

How Could This Happen?

There are two explanations for SSA's fall from a leading-edge systems position to near collapse in the early 1980s. First, there were internal institutional factors involving middle and senior management. Second, a sometimes hostile and rapidly changing environment in the 1970s added to SSA's woes.

The Environment

In the 1970s, Congress had made more than 15 major changes in the RSI program alone. These changes increasingly taxed SSA's systems to the point where systems personnel were working on weekends to make required program changes.

In 1972 Congress passed the Supplemental Security Income (SSI) program, which converted certain state funded and administered income maintenance programs into federal programs. SSA suddenly found itself in the welfare arena, which was far removed from that of a social insurance agency. Unprepared local staffs suddenly faced thousands of angry applicants standing in line. In some cities, riots occurred. Other programs, such as Medicaid and changes in disability insurance, as well as cost-of-living (COLA) escalators, all severely taxed SSA's systems and personnel capacity. The 1978 COLA required changes in over 880 SSA computer programs.

The number of clients served by SSA doubled in the 1970s. But because of a growing economic crisis combining low growth and high inflation (stagflation), Congress was unwilling to expand SSA's work force to meet the demands of new programs. There was growing public and political resistance to expanding federal government employment at the very time when new programs were coming on line and expectations of service were rising.

SSA management in this period consistently overstated its administrative capacity to Congress and failed to communicate the nature of the growing systems crisis. SSA pleas for additional manpower were consistently turned down or reduced by Congress and the White House. Workloads of employees dramatically increased, and morale and job satisfaction declined. Training was reduced, especially in the systems area, as all resources were diverted to the operations crisis.

Toward the end of the 1970s, the political environment changed as well. A growing conservative movement among Republicans and Democrats interested in reducing the size of all federal programs led to increasing pressure on SSA to reduce employment levels. In the long actuarial funding debate at the beginning of the 1980s, there was talk about "privatizing" Social Security and abolishing the agency altogether.

Complicating SSA's environment was the Brooks Act of 1965, which mandated competitive procurement of computing equipment and services. Up to 1965, SSA had had a long-standing and beneficial relationship with IBM. Virtually all of SSA's equipment was manufactured by IBM and purchased on a noncompetitive basis. IBM provided planning, technical support, software support, and consulting services to SSA as part of this relationship.

By the 1970s this close relationship had ended. IBM shifted its support and marketing efforts away from the federal arena because of the Brooks Act. SSA found itself in a new competitive environment, forced to do all of its own planning, development, and procurement work. As the workload rapidly expanded at SSA in the 1970s, the agency needed a well-planned, closely managed transition to new computing equipment and software. This transition never occurred.

Institutional Factors

A challenging environment might have been overcome by a focused and dedicated management group. Perhaps the most critical weakness of all in SSA's operation in the 1970s was its inability to gain management control over the information systems function and over the information resource on which the organization itself was based.

Senior management turnover was a critical problem. In its first 38 years, SSA had had six commissioners with an average tenure of 6.5 years. Two men led the agency for 27 of its 38 years. But from 1971 to 1981, SSA had seven commissioners or acting commissioners with an average tenure of 1.1 years. None of these commissioners had any experience at SSA. The senior staff of the agency was also repeatedly shaken up in this period. Compared to earlier senior managers, those of the 1970s failed to realize the critical importance of information systems to SSA's operation. Long-range planning of the agency or systems became impossible. Authority slowly but inevitably devolved to operations-level groups—the only ones that knew what was going on.

With new senior management came four major reorganizations of the agency. Major SSA programs were broken down into functional parts and redistributed to new functional divisions. Program coherence was lost. Performance measures and management control disappeared as managers and employees struggled to adapt to their new functions.

Efforts at Reform

SSA made several efforts in this period to regain control and direction in the systems area on which its entire operation critically depended.

In 1975, SSA created the Office of Advanced Systems (OAS) within the Office of the Commissioner. SSA hoped that this advanced, high-level planning group with direct access to senior management would develop a strategy for change. OAS developed such a plan called the *Green Book*, which laid out a total reformation of SSA's largely manual and batch processes. From client intake interview to final check dispersal, the Green Book promised virtually total automation at SSA.

Unfortunately, this effort failed. Systems operations management opposed the plan as unworkable, wild-eyed, and lacking any implementation plan. Given the day-to-day crisis of SSA, there were no resources to fund the program. The union was opposed to the plan. There was no White House support for it and no suggestion from Congress or the White House that needed funding would be forthcoming. In 1979 the OAS was abolished by a new management team.

A second effort at reform began in 1979. This time the idea originated with new senior management. Called *partitioning*, the new reform effort sought to break SSA's internal operations into major program lines—like product lines—so that each program could develop its own systems. This plan was quickly rejected. White House and congressional staffs believed that such a strategy was simply an effort by SSA to obtain new hardware without rethinking either the way in which SSA does business or the tremendous software and database problems of the agency. Outside professionals criticized the plan for going in the opposite direction from private industry, which was building integrated databases, distributed systems, and telecommunications networks. The partitioning strategy was never implemented.

A third reform effort also began in 1979. Here SSA sought to replace the aging SSADARS telecommunications network with new, high-speed communications terminals in the district offices and new telecommunications computers in the Baltimore headquarters. After a competitive procurement process, SSA contracted with the Paradyne Corporation for 2000 such terminals.

Unfortunately, the first 16 systems failed all operational tests on delivery in 1981. Investigations produced charges of bidding fraud (selling systems to SSA that did not exist, "black boxes with blinking lights"), securities fraud, bribery, bid rigging, perjury, and inadequate SSA systems requirements definition.

By 1983 SSA took delivery of all of the terminals, and they did perform for their expected life of 8 years. But the procurement scandal further reduced SSA's credibility in Congress and the White House.

Results of Management Chaos

Senior management turnover, lack of concern, and failed efforts at reform took a severe toll in the systems area. Planning of information systems was either not done or was done at such a low operational level that no major changes in operations could be accomplished.

The absence of planning meant that there was no program for replacing the many experienced programmers who were about to retire in the early 1980s. In 1981, for instance, SSA lost 112 of its 560 experienced programmers. These people took with them the knowledge of the patchwork software that actually ran the agency. Training recruits in this patchwork software required more than a year.

The absence of management planning also meant that the integrity of SSA programs was directly threatened. Privacy protection, physical security, prevention of program abuse, prevention of malicious damage, unauthorized access, program accountability, and systems backup and recovery—all of these areas of systems integrity suffered. Specific examples are as follows:

- There was no systematic method for communicating among various SSA programs, so that an individual could obtain multiple benefits under several programs, leading to overpayments.
- Duplicate payments were difficult to correct because there was no system to examine the output of checks.
- There were no mechanisms within the system to protect against the unreported deaths of beneficiaries.
- The existing SSADAR system lacked automated controls and audit trails to support the

determination of eligibility, payment of benefits, recovery of erroneous payments, or the tracing of fraudulent claims.

- There was a complete absence of adequate systems backup and recovery plans. For instance, there were so many hundreds of thousands of reels of computer tape that there were simply not enough resources to make backup copies of them. If certain critical tapes were destroyed—indeed, if the whole Baltimore data complex was destroyed—it would be impossible to recover the earnings records or beneficiary payments of millions of individuals.

Section II: The Systems Modernization Plan— 1982-1992

As the crisis at SSA became increasingly apparent to Congress, the General Accounting Office, and the President's Office, pressure was placed on SSA to develop a new strategy.

In 1981 a new commissioner, John Svahn, a recently appointed former insurance executive with systems experience, began work on a strategic plan to try to move SSA data processing from collapse to a modern system. The result was a 5-year plan called the Systems Modernization Plan (SMP). SMP was intended to bring about long-range, tightly integrated changes in software, hardware, telecommunications, and management systems.

The plan departed from previous SSA plans, which had sought to develop all of their own systems by SSA personnel. The SMP explicitly provided for the use of external experts and contractors.

At $500 million, the original cost estimate in 1982, the SMP was one of the most expensive single information systems projects in history.

SMP Goals
The goals of the SMP were as follows:

- Restore excellence to SSA systems and return the agency to its state-of-the-art position.

- Avoid disruption of service.
- Improve service immediately by purchasing modern hardware.
- Improve staff effectiveness and productivity.
- Restore public confidence by enhancing accountability, auditability, and detection of fraud.

SMP Strategy
As a bold effort to secure a total change at SSA, the SMP adopted a conservative strategy. This strategy called for SSA to do the following:

- Achieve modernization through incremental, evolutionary change, given the unacceptable risks of failure.
- Separate the modernization program from the operations and maintenance programs.
- Use an external system integration contractor to provide continuity to the 5-year project.
- Utilize industry-proven, state-of-the-art systems engineering technology.
- Build on the existing systems, selecting short-term, feasible approaches that minimize risks.
- Establish a single organizational body to plan, manage, and control SMP.
- Elevate systems development and operations to the highest levels of the agency.

SMP Implementation
The original plan foresaw a 5-year effort broken into three stages: survival, transition, and state-of-the-art. In the survival stage (18 months), SSA would focus on new hardware acquisition to solve immediate problems of capacity shortage. In the transition stage (18 months), SSA would begin rebuilding software, data files, and telecommunications systems. In the final state-of-the-art stage, SSA would finalize and integrate projects to achieve a contemporary level of systems.

Specific Projects
The SMP involved six interrelated programs.

1. The Capacity Upgrade Program (CUP)
In 1982, SSA was operating equipment that

could no longer meet the basic computing needs of the agency. The CUP program was developed to reconfigure and consolidate the physical computing sites around central headquarters in Baltimore; to acquire much higher-capacity and more modern computers; to eliminate sequentially organized magnetic tape files and switch over to direct access devices; and to develop a local computing network for high-speed data transfers.

2. The System Operation and Management Program (SOMP)

The SOMP program was intended to provide modern automated tools and procedures for managing and controlling SSA's main computer center operations in Baltimore. Included were automated job scheduling tools, job station monitoring and submission systems, operational job procedures, training, and a central integrated control facility to ensure that SSA would make a smooth transition to a modern data center environment.

3. The Data Communications Utility Program (DCUP)

The DCUP was designed to reengineer SSA's major telecommunications system (SSADARS). What SSA wanted was a transparent conduit for the transmission of data between and among processing units of different manufacture using a single integrated network.

Before 1982, terminals were dedicated to particular host processors and applications. Programmers developing interactive applications used terminals for program development that were different from the terminals used for the development of batch applications. Other terminals were connected to the tape library system, and still other terminals of a different manufacturer were used for performance monitoring and job submission. The DCUP was designed to integrate all of the machine and program environments within SSA.

More than 17,000 on-line terminals will be used in the 1300 field offices.

4. Software Engineering Program (SEP)

SEP will upgrade the existing software and retain as much of it as possible so that entirely new code does not have to be written.

A critical part of the SEP is a top-down functional analysis (using the enterprise system planning method) of the Social Security process—all of the business and organizational functions of SSA. Hopefully, this top-down planning effort will provide the framework for the redesign of SSA's total system by establishing the requirements for improvements in existing software.

A second key aspect of the software engineering effort is the implementation of new software engineering technology. This involves developing and enforcing programming standards, developing quality controls, and using modern computer-aided software development tools. Special emphasis is placed on the development of modern program documentation, standardization of programs, and conversion to higher-level languages whenever possible.

5. Database Integration

SSA has to maintain for a lifetime the identity, earnings, and benefit records for more than 250 million individuals. The ability to manage these data is absolutely critical to the agency's mission. The original database integration plan called for two major projects: data administration and database management.

The database integration project involved four objectives. As a survival tactic, SSA wanted to reduce the current labor-intensive, error-prone magnetic tape operation by converting all records to high-speed disk, direct access storage devices (DASD). A second goal was to establish a data administration function to control the definition of data elements and files. A third goal was to eliminate the data errors by establishing data controls, validating files, and developing modern storage disk technology. A fourth objective was to integrate the variety of databases, making communication among them transparent.

6. Administrative/Management Information Engineering Program (AMIE).

In 1984, 2 years after the original SMP was published, a major new program was added, one designed to develop an MIS capability within the agency. The original SMP plan focused almost entirely on SSA's programmatic systems environment and addressed the data processing needed to carry out the primary responsibilities. Little mention was made in the original plan of the systems required to manage the human, financial, and material resources of SSA or those systems that would be needed to provide executives, managers, and operations staff with the essential information for effective decision making.

SSA was fundamentally dependent on manual activities to conduct most of its administration. Requests for personnel actions, purchase requisitions, telephone service, travel orders, building modifications, training requests—all of these administrative matters were processed manually.

The AMIE program was designed to integrate MIS with other programmatic modernization activities: to automate and modernize labor-intensive administrative processes and to develop management MIS to improve the planning and administrative process.

Section III: Where the SMP Is Now

By 1987, the SMP had doubled in size to $1 billion, and the time required to reach state-of-the-art processing had been extended to 1992. Nevertheless, SSA had documented steady improvement in a number of measures of service to beneficiaries, many of which are due to the SMP:

- A 25% decrease in RSI claims processing time.
- A small decrease in DI claims processing time (2.2 days).
- A high and improving rate of RSI claims accuracy (95.7–97.2%).

- A 41% decrease in SSI processing time.
- A 7% decrease in SSI blind/disabled processing time.
- A 47% decrease in RSDI (Retired Survivors Disability Insurance) change of status processing time.
- Stable administrative costs in RSI since 1980 (1.1% of benefits).

The key changes brought about by the SMP will now be described.

Management Changes

SSA created a new deputy commissioner for systems development and raised the status of systems in the organization to the senior management level. Development of the SMP was separated from operations, and both functions were adequately funded.

A major new step for SSA was the hiring of an outside systems integration contractor, Electronic Data Systems (EDS). This company has played a key role in devising the SMP plan and providing the necessary integration within the agency for the plan.

To ensure union support, SSA senior management entered into a historic agreement with the American Federation of Government Employees (AFGE), permitting union participation in the implementation of SMP and promising union input to design decisions.

Although John Svahn left the agency in 1982 for the White House domestic policy staff, he was replaced by an acting commissioner, Martha McSteen, a skilled SSA administrator strongly committed to the SMP who gained public and congressional support for the plan. McSteen was replaced in 1986 by a permanent commissioner, Dorcas Hardy, a former Health and Human Services Department (HHS) administrator. She had no direct experience in SSA.

Capacity Upgrade

The capacity upgrade program is largely on time and completed. Programmatic systems computers were upgraded in 1984; a separate test and development facility for new software was created that same year; and the mainframe computers were upgraded to National Advanced System (NAS) mainframes. Currently, SSA has a considerable surplus of CPU processing power.

Systems Operation Management Plan (SOMP)

The SOMP plan has been implemented. The central processing facility in Baltimore has now developed efficient job scheduling standards and procedures for handling tapes and documents, and has centralized control of the data center.

Administrative/Management and Information Engineering (AMIE)

The AMIE program is essentially on schedule in the late 1980s. An MIS plan has been developed. A business systems plan for AMIE was completed to establish the information requirements of management.

Data Communications Utility (DCU)

The major trunk lines of the DCU are now operational. They connect the regional processors to the mainframe in Baltimore, using 56-kilobit per second lines running through either satellites or cable systems. The entire backbone of the data communications utility is now operational. Currently, SSA is purchasing 50,000 modems and terminals to be used in the 1300 local district offices; these will be operational shortly.

Database Integration

SSA successfully completed the transition from 500,000 reels of tape to more modern DASDs.

In this transition, the files had to be reorganized. SSA developed its own in-house software called the Master Data Access Method (MADAM). This is a data management system (not a true database) that handles all on-line and batch inquiry access to SSA master files. Through MADAM, it is now possible for local district offices to inquire directly on-line for client files.

A data administration function has been established and a complete data dictionary of all of the data elements of SSA's major functional programs is available. Enforcing the use of the dictionary for all new programming and maintenance efforts is now underway.

However, SSA has still failed to develop an integrated database for all or even some of its major programs. The data are still organized on disk according to major program areas. MADAM is a highly efficient file manager, acting as a traffic cop between users and physical data. A major difficulty that SSA faces is deciding on an overall database architecture and establishing the functional requirements for the exchange of information between the major program areas.

SSA has experienced considerable delays in making this key database architecture decision. Because of this delay, it has also put off choosing a vendor or group of vendors capable of providing the database hardware and software. The lack of a database decision will, in turn, stall software redevelopment at SSA and may lead to a large loss of time and money.

Software Engineering

SSA hoped that 75% of its existing code could be kept. Unfortunately, this hope was based on no empirical evidence. At best, 10–15% of the code was in fact salvaged. As SSA developed interactive systems for delivering its services to clients in district offices, it was required to write entirely new code.

It is now apparent that with new ways of doing business, the old software is simply inadequate. This old software is predicated on the old way of doing business—batch processing. Nevertheless, the software program has accomplished the following:

- Installed software engineering tools.
- Completed a business systems plan functional requirements analysis.
- Redesigned earnings and debt management systems.
- Documented much of the SSA's critical software for earning systems, disability, and claims processing.
- Began the software improvement process.

The SEP program has not enforced the use of new software engineering tools. New tools are being installed, but it has proved to be difficult to obtain programmers' compliance with them. While some systems have been redesigned, many others—like enumeration and calculation of benefits—are unchanged from the manual and batch processing days.

One success of the SMP software program is the Claims Modernization Project/Field Office Systems Enhancement (CMP/FOSE). This project developed an on-line, interactive system for both the initial claims interview and case control at the district level. The system became operational in 1988.

The CMP/FOSE is a modern, if not leading-edge, client management system. On entering the office, a client is preinterviewed by a secretary and sent to an appropriate claims representative, depending on the type of claim involved. The claims representative interviews the client, asking questions prompted by a desktop terminal. The desktop unit is connected through the data communications utility directly to the Baltimore mainframe. Following the interview, the client data is sent directly to a regional minicomputer and then over the data communications utility to Baltimore, where the claim is further processed for earnings information, search of the master beneficiary record, and vertification of the information given. At the same time, a local printer prints out the results of the interview; one copy is given to the client

and another is used for internal, local case control.

Section IV: Prospects

For most of the 1980s the environment was supportive and sympathetic to the SMP. Toward the end of this period, however, criticism was beginning to develop over the rising costs and seeming endless time frame.

Turmoil in senior management did not end. McSteen was never fully supported by the White House and remained an acting commissioner, as did the deputy commissioners. The White House increasingly pressed SSA to make plans for reducing its staff by one-quarter, or 20,000 positions. McSteen refused and was replaced. The new commisssioner, Hardy, is expected to pursue the goal of sharp staff reductions.

Under pressure from the White House, the new commissioner is abandoning the pact with the union. The union is preparing for a long, drawn-out battle, which will stall SMP implementation either by resistance on the shop floor or by political lobbying of Congress.

The General Accounting Office (GAO), responding to requests from the House Government Operations Committee [Rep. Jack Brooks (D.) of Texas, chairman], has issued several reports that are critical of SSA's procurement of terminals and telecommunications capacity; the GAO alleges that SSA has failed to redevelop software or to develop a true database architecture. It is calling for a halt to procurements.

A major report by the Office of Technology Assessment (OTA, a congressional research agency), issued in 1986, concluded that SSA, Congress, and the White House were all to blame for SSA's current situation.

The White House was blamed for prematurely seeking huge work force reductions before the new systems were in place. It was also blamed for continuing political interference in the agency and for failure to support senior management.

Congress was blamed for not understanding the complexity of SSA programs and for failing to understand the long-term nature of total systems change. In addition, OTA blamed new procurement laws for slowing down and complicating the purchase of new hardware.

OTA pointed to a number of faults at SSA. From the very beginning of SMP, SSA failed to rethink its method of doing business. SMP basically sought to automate an organizational structure and way of doing business established in the 1930s. SSA failed, for instance, to question the role of 1300 field offices—are they really needed in a day of packet switched networks and PCs? Should SSA's major data files be centralized in Baltimore? OTA also pointed to SSA's failure to develop new software on a timely basis and a new database architecture.

OTA concluded that, these faults notwithstanding, the SMP was a reasonable plan with attainable goals. However, it stated that superior management would be required to complete the program in a timely fashion. The principal danger, according to OTA, is that external forces—at the White House and Congress—might derail the SMP permanently and destroy the progress already made.

Adapted from Kenneth C. Laudon (with Alan F. Westin), *Information Technology At SSA, 1935–1990*, forthcoming; and Office of Technology Assessment, *The Social Security Administration and Information Technology, A Case Study*, Washington D.C.: U.S. Congress, 1986.

Part Four Case Study Questions

1. What were the major factors in SSA's past that made it a leading innovator in information systems technology? How did these supportive factors change in the 1970s?
2. Describe briefly the problems with SSA's hardware, software, data storage, and telecommunications systems prior to SMP.
3. What were the major environmental and institutional factors that created the crisis at SSA?
4. Why did SSA's reform efforts in the late 1970s fail?
5. What were the major elements of SSA's implementation strategy for SMP? Why was it called a conservative strategy? Compare SMP to an earlier reform plan.
6. Describe briefly the major projects within SMP.
7. What successful changes in management and organizational structure have been brought about by SMP? How secure are these changes (what environmental factors could destroy them)?
8. In what areas has SMP had the greatest success? In what areas has SMP not succeeded? Why?
9. In what ways has SSA failed to seriously rethink how it conducts its business? Do you have any suggestions for changing SSA's business operations in which systems might play a large role? What private sector analogies are useful?

Glossary

Active data dictionary One closely integrated with a database management system so that it can enforce the same definition of data in all executable programs that reference the DBMS.

Analog computer One that represents digits and symbols through a continuous physical dimension, such as a voltage level or thickness of material. A slide rule is an example.

Application The application of computer technology to create an information system to solve a specific business problem or to perform specific business functions. A payroll system is an application.

Application controls Specific controls unique to each computer application, such as payroll or order processing.

Application generator Software system with preprogrammed modules that can generate entire applications, based on functions specified by users for a particular application.

Application software Programs written for a specific business application in order to perform functions specified by end users.

Arithmetic-logic unit The part of a computer's central processing unit that performs computations and logical operations.

Artificial intelligence Field of research trying to use computers to solve problems that appear to require humanlike intelligence.

Assembly language A programming language developed in the 1950s that resembles machine language but substitutes mnemonics for numeric codes.

Assembler A special type of compiler that translates assembly language into machine language.

ASCII Stands for American National Standard Code for Information Interchange. One of the major binary codes for representing numbers, alphabetic characters, and symbols. Used in data transmission and for microcomputers.

Attribute Pieces of information about a particular entity that represent all of the data items one might want to store on that entity. For example, attributes of the entity "product" might be product number and product cost.

Backward-chaining system Type of expert system with a control mechanism that starts with a tentative solution and then searches the system's rule base and blackboard to find justification for the hypothesis.

Bandwidth The difference between the highest and lowest frequencies on a telecommunications transmission medium.

Batch processing A technique in which transactions are accumulated and stored in groups, or batches, over a period of time until it is efficient or necessary to process them.

Baud A binary event, in which a signal change sends one bit of information. Used as a measure of signaling speed.

Bit A binary digit, either 0 or 1, representing the smallest unit of data in a computer system.

Blackboard Collection of facts about the real world used in a rule-based expert system.

Business systems analyst A systems analyst tied to an end-user business area with specialized understanding of the business information requirements of that particular functional area. The business systems analyst is responsible for translating those specific business requirements into information systems for that functional area.

Byte A string of bits, usually 8, used to represent a number or character.

CBIS Abbreviation for computer-based information system, which is one relying on computer hardware and software.

Centralized system One in which the data and computer processing equipment for an application used by more than one location are centralized in one location rather than being distributed among multiple locations.

Check digit A extra digit in a key field, such as product number, determined as the result of some calculation on the key. Helps check the validity of the key by performing an arithmetic operation on the key field and comparing the result to the check digit.

COBOL Stands for Common Business Oriented Language and is a high-level programming language used primarily for business applications.

Competitive forces model One kind of model of a firm and its environment that can be used to identify strategic opportunities for information technology. The competitive forces model sees the firm as facing threats and opportunities from the power of buyers and suppliers, new market entrants, and competitive forces. The role of systems would be to alter the basis of competition or to recast the balance of power with buyers and suppliers.

Compiler Part of the operating system that translates a higher-level language into machine language that the computer can execute it.

Computer A device capable of solving problems by performing arithmetic or logical operations on data and supplying the results of such operations without the intervention of a human operator during the operations.

Computer abuse The use of a computer in ways that are not illegal but are unethical (e.g., using a corporation's computer for one's private consulting work).

Computer crime Illegal acts requiring special knowledge of computer technology for their perpetration, investigation, or prosecution.

Confidentiality Limits on the use and dissemination of information collected from individuals.

Control unit The portion of the computer's central processing unit that selects, interprets, and executes programmed instructions and directs other parts of the computer to perform the tasks required by program instructions.

Controls All of the methods, policies, and procedures that ensure protection of the organization's assets, accuracy and reliability of its accounting records, and operational adherence to management standards. There are both general controls for the firm's entire information systems environment and specific application controls for each business application.

Conversion The process of changing from an old system to a new one, entailing potential changes in hardware, software, and manual procedures.

Cost/benefit analysis Methodology for estimating and comparing the costs and benefits of developing and operating an information system. Used to establish the worth of systems or to choose among alternative systems.

Counterimplementation A deliberate strategy to thwart implementation of an information system or an innovation in an organization.

CPU Stands for central processing unit, the portion of the computer that contains the circuits controlling the interpretation and execution of instructions.

Critical success factors A new method of eliciting information requirements, especially useful for systems serving higher management. Managers are interviewed to determine the "critical success factors" for themselves and the organization as a whole.

Data administration A special organizational function for managing the organization's data resources, concerned with data planning, information policy, maintenance of data dictionaries, and data quality standards.

Data definition language A special language that is used with a database management system to describe the relationship between logical and physical views of the data.

Data dictionary An automated or manual tool for storing and organizing information about the data maintained by an individual information system or by all the information systems in an organization.

Data flow diagram The primary mechanism for graphically analyzing a system during Structured Analysis. Data flow diagrams depict all of the component processes of a system and the flow of data between them. (See Chapter 11 for illustrations.)

Data management The function of controlling the acquisition, analysis, storage, retrieval, and distribution of data in an organization.

Data manipulation language A language associated with a database management system that is employed by end users and programmers to manipulate data in the database.

Data modeling The process of defining logical relationships among data.

Database Collection of data organized to service many applications and different groups in the organization at the same time.

Database administration Refers to the more technical and operational aspects of managing data, including physical database design and operation, maintenance, and performance monitoring of DBMS software.

Database management system (DBMS) Special software programs to create and maintain a database and enable individual business applications to extract the data they need without having to create separate files or data definitions in their computer programs.

Decision support system (DSS) An interactive, highly "user-friendly" system that supports management decisions that are semistructured or that cannot be specified in advance. Compared to MIS, DSS use more analytical models and draw information from multiple sources.

Decision table A method of documenting decision rules in matrix or tabular form, showing a set of conditions and the actions that can be taken on these conditions.

Decision tree Method of documenting decision rules by graphically depicting decision paths based on conditions to be considered and the actions that must be taken for each contingency.

Digital computer One that operates by reducing all symbols, pictures, and words to a discrete, quantifiable string of binary digits.

Digital image A paper document or an image from a paper document that has been translated into bytes and bits to be stored on a computer file.

Direct access storage device (DASD) Another name for disk technology. This involves the ability to store information on magnetic disks and access individual records directly.

Distributed database A database that is partitioned, or distributed in more than one physical location. Parts of the database stored are physically in one location and other parts are stored and maintained in other locations.

Distributed data processing The dispersion and use of computers among multiple, geographically separated locations so that local computers handle local processing needs.

Downloading The process of extracting data from a mainframe or minicomputer file and transmitting it to a microcomputer file.

Edit checks Computerized routines to edit input data for errors before they are processed.

End user The individual or group of individuals who actually use an information system, as opposed to technical specialists who design and program. An example of an end user would be the accounting clerk.

End-user computing Refers to the creation of programs and entire information systems by end users with little or no professional programming assistance.

Enterprise analysis A new method of eliciting information requirements focusing on the data needs of the entire organization. The entire organization is analyzed in terms of organizational units, functions, processes, and classes of data. Requirements and databases are derived from data groups that can support related organizational processes.

Entity A person, place, or thing about which information must be kept.

Environmental factors Factors external to an organization to which the organization must adjust. Examples might be changes in governmental regulations or in the work force.

EPROM Stands for erasable programmable read-only memory and is a type of ROM chip. This is a kind of semiconductor chip that can be programmed and reprogrammed to make changes. Such chips are used in device control, as in robots, where the program may have to be frequently revised.

Executive support system (ESS) A system for senior managers that utilizes heavy graphic displays and draws together data from numerous internal and external sources.

Expert system A computer system programmed to use knowledge that has been supplied by a human expert to solve a problem that normally requires human expertise. This term is often used interchangeably with artifical intelligence, although the meanings are not identical.

Feasibility Assessment of whether a proposed system would be cost effective and technically and operationally possible within the budgetary, time, and organizational constraints established by management.

Fiber optics Telecommunications transmission medium of high capacity utilizing a bundle of thin glass filaments.

Flowchart Graphic representation of the types and sequences of operations in a program *or* the flow of data through a sequence of processes and procedures in an entire information system.

Formal system One that rests on accepted and fixed definitions of data and procedures for collecting, processing, storing, and disseminating the data.

Forward-chaining system Type of expert system that begins with a premise and searches the system's rule base and blackboard to find possible solutions.

"Fourth-generation" language A programming language with easy-to-use features that can be employed directly by end users or less skilled programmers. Such languages can develop computer applications more rapidly than conventional programming languages and promise dramatic boosts in productivity.

Frame-based system Type of expert system consisting of collections of knowledge (frames) that describe related concepts by listing each concept's features and showing the relationships to other concepts.

Front-end processor An auxiliary computer attached to a host computer that interfaces it with other elements in a telecommunications network.

General controls Overall controls that ensure the effective operation of programmed procedures and apply to all application areas. They establish a framework for controlling the design, security, and use of computer programs throughout an organization.

Gigabyte Stands for 1 billion bytes and is a measure of computer hardware capacity.

Graphics language A computer language that is used to retrieve data from files or databases and display it in graphic format.

Hardware Refers to the physical components of a computer system.

Hertz Cycles per second of a telecommunications signal, used as a measure of frequency.

Hierarchical DBMS One type of logical database structure that organizes data in a tree-like structure. A record is subdivided into segments that are connected to each other in one-to-many parent–child relationships.

High-level language A programming language that is closer to English than to machine language. When translated it generates multiple machine language instructions for each statement.

HIPO Stands for Hierarchical Input-Process-Output and is a methodology for documenting program and system design. Breaks a system down into component modules and describes the inputs and outputs for each.

Implementation Refers to all of the organizational activities involved in the adoption, management and routinization of an innovation. For an information system, implementation is the entire process of introducing, building, and installing the system and can be considered a complex process of deliberate organizational change.

Index A table or list that relates record keys to physical locations on direct access files.

Inference engine Set of procedures in a rule-based expert system that searches the rule base and blackboard of facts to solve a given problem.

Informal system One that does not have fixed definitions of data or fixed procedures for processing and distributing the data, resting on unstated agreements and behavior. An example would be an office gossip network.

Information architecture The particular form that organization technology takes in a specific organization, including the extent to which data and processing power are centralized or distributed.

Information center A special facility providing end users with direct access to computing tools and data so that end users can create their own information system applications.

Information engineering Data-centered approach to systems development whereby emphasis shifts from processes to the creation of stable models that can be shared by multiple applications.

Information policy Formal rules governing the maintenance, distribution, and use of information in an organization.

Information resource management The idea that information is a critical resource for the organization and must be managed accordingly.

Information system A set of procedures to collect, process, store, and disseminate information to support decision making and control.

Input device A device for entering data into a computer system. Includes keypunch machines and CRT terminals.

Installation The final steps to put a new system into operation—testing and conversion.

Institutional factors Factors internal to an organization to which the organization must be respond. Such factors include values, norms, and political interest groups within the organization.

Intangible benefits Benefits that cannot be immediately quantified (such as more efficient service) but that may lead to quantifiable gains in the long term.

Integrated circuit Electronic circuits that can be reproduced on miniaturized silicon chips and used for storing computerized data or instructions.

Interpreter A special translator of source code into machine code that translates each source code statement into machine code and executes it one at a time. Used for languages such as BASIC.

Inverted file A file that references entities by one or some of their attributes.

Knowledge engineering A methodology for eliciting the specifications for an expert system, used to build artificial intelligence applications. A human expert must be exhaustively interviewed to provide the decision rules and knowledge frames that can be embedded in an expert system.

Local area network (LAN) Interconnecting computers via telecommunications devices in a single building or complex of buildings to form a network of small geographic scope, using the firm's own telecommunications media.

Logical view Representation of data as it would appear to an applications programmer or end user.

Long-haul network Telecommunications network tying together cities and countries.

Maintenance The process of modifying an existing system, through changes to hardware, software, documentation, or procedures, to correct errors, meet new requirements, or improve processing efficiency.

Management information system (MIS) A term with several meanings. It can refer to one of the five different kinds of information systems described in this text. In this context a MIS is a kind of system that helps managers with their planning, controlling, and monitoring functions and supports primarily structured decisions. MIS provide routine summary and exception reports, often drawing on transaction level data. MIS is sometimes used to refer to all of the computing systems in the organization that support management. A third definition of MIS is the MIS or information systems field, which fuses computer technology with business applications.

Management-level system One that services the monitoring, controlling, decision-making, and administrative activities of an organization.

Master file A file containing relatively permanent data about a particular application. An example would be a payroll master file.

Memory Synonymous with primary storage.

Microcomputer A computer small in size but not in power. Can fit on a desktop. Sometimes called a personal computer, to be distinguished from larger computers, such as minicomputers or mainframe computers.

Microprocessor A one-chip central processing unit.

Modem A device that translates digital computer signals into analog form for transmission through a telecommunications medium.

Modularization A methodology for partitioning a computer program into component modules, each constituting a logical unit that performs one or a small number of functions.

Multiplexing Dividing up the bandwidth of a telecommunications medium into several discrete channels to increase transmission capacity.

Multiprocessing A method of executing two or more instructions simultaneously in a single computer system by using more than one central processing unit.

Multiprogramming A method of executing two or more computer programs concurrently in the same central processing unit. The CPU only executes one program at any given instant but can service the input/output needs of others at the same time.

Nanosecond One billionth of a second, used as a measure of processing speed.

Network DBMS A type of logical database structure that is useful for depicting many-to-many relationships.

Neural net computer Computer with an architecture that mimics the brain's fast web of interconnected neurons, using hundreds of thousands of processors that can respond to a problem simultaneously.

Object code Program instructions that have been translated into machine language so that they can be executed by the computer.

Office automation system (OAS) System that integrates computer and communication technology to automate traditional office processes, such as word processing, document transmission, etc.

On-line processing Processing transactions immediately as each is entered into a terminal or device in direct communication with the computer.

Operating system Software that assists and controls the operations and resources of the computer.

Operational-level system One that tracks the elementary activities and transactions of the organization, such as sales, receipts, cash deposits, or the flow of materials in a factory.

Optical storage Method of using laser technology to store data on compact disks at much greater density than magnetic materials.

Organization A stable formal social structure that takes resources from the environment and processes them to produce outputs. An alternative definition is a collection of rights, privileges, obligations, and responsibilities that are delicately balanced over time through conflict and conflict resolution.

Output device A device by which data processed by a computer system can be received. Includes printers, video display terminals, or microfiche.

Parallel processing Method of computer processing in which multiple processors handle one problem simultaneously, as opposed to serial processing.

Passive data dictionary A type of data dictionary that cannot automatically impose its data definitions on other systems and processes in the same machine environment.

PBX Stands for private branch exchange. Exchange serving an individual organization that is connected to the public switched network.

Physical view Representation of data as they would actually be stored and organized physically on computer storage media.

Pointer A special type of data element attached to a record that shows the absolute or relative address of another record.

Portfolio analysis A methodology for selecting among alternative systems projects whereby a firm chooses from among a "portfolio" of potential applications, each with a different mix of risks and benefits for the firm.

Postimplementation audit Formal review process after installation of a system whereby users and technical specialists evaluate a system to determine how well it has met its original objectives.

Primary storage Part of the computer in which data and program instructions are stored before processing.

Privacy A broad term that, when applied to information systems, sets limits on the collection of information about individuals; establishes specific rights of individuals to access, review, and challenge information about them; and stipulates management responsibility for record systems.

Procedural language A programming language that describes data processing or computational processes in terms of the sequence of algorithmic steps.

Program flowchart A detailed graphic way of depicting the logical steps that are taking place in a computer program.

Programmer Information system specialist who concentrates on the writing of instructions for the computer.

Programming The process of translating design specifications into software for a computer system.

Pseudocode Method of expressing the logic to be used in a computer program using plain English statements rather than a programming language.

PROM Stands for programmable read-only memory and is a form of memory that can be programmed only once. Used to store certain utility programs or frequently used routines.

Protocol Set of procedures or conventions that are used to formalize information transfer between two devices communicating with each other.

Prototyping An alternative method of building an information system in which requirements are determined by building an experimental model of the system for users to interact with. The prototype is revised over and over again until end users are satisfied that requirements are met. Instead of specifying requirements before building the system, end-users specify requirements as they use the prototype.

Query language A high-level computer language used to retrieve specific information from databases or files.

RAM Stands for random access memory, and is a semiconductor storage area. This form of memory can be either read from or written to under program control.

Real-time system A computer system that can immediately capture data about ongoing events or processes and provide information to affect the outcome of the process.

Relational DBMS A type of logical database structure that treats data as if they were stored in two-dimensional tables. It can relate any piece of information stored in one table to any piece in another as long as the two tables share a common data element.

Report generator A high-level language that can be used to produce reports in almost any format.

Requirements analysis Identification of the information requirements of a system, identifying who needs what information, where, when, and how. Details the functions a system must perform within specified economic, technical, time, and organizational constraints.

ROM Stands for read-only memory, which can only be read from and not written to under program control. It is used to store computer instructions that cannot be altered.

Rule-based system Type of expert system consisting of a rule base (decision rules supplied by an expert), blackboard (listing of facts), and a program to search the rules and facts and come up with a solution (inference engine).

Run control totals An application control technique whereby totals of items input into a computer job are reconciled with totals of items that have updated a file and/or totals of outputs.

Secondary storage A device for storing computerized data outside the CPU. Includes magnetic tape or magnetic disk.

Security Refers to all of the policies, procedures, and technical measures that can be applied to prevent unauthorized access, alteration, theft, or physical damage to information systems.

Sequential file One in which all of the records in the file must be read one by one in serial order, to access an individual record.

Sociotechnical design Approach to information system design that seeks an optimal design solution that can satisfy both technical and human/organizational requirements.

Sociotechnical system One that involves an arrangement of both technical and social elements to form a single entity. Information systems are "sociotechnical" systems because they combine human and organizational elements (jobs, procedures, power relationships) with technical elements (computer hardware and software).

Software Instructions that control the physical hardware of a computer system, consisting of computer programs, routines, and procedures.

Software package A set of standardized computer programs, procedures, and related documentation commercially marketed to serve as the basis of an information system application.

Source code Program instructions written in a high-level language that must be translated into machine language in order to be executed by the computer.

Spreadsheet Used by accountants for performing financial calculations and recording transactions. Automated spreadsheet software would be Lotus 1–2–3 or VisiCalc.

Standing data Data that are permanent and affect transactions flowing into and out of a system (e.g., a table of product codes).

Strategic information system One which gives the firm a competitive advantage by creating new products and services, changing relationships with customers and suppliers, or changing the way the firm operates internally.

Strategic-level system One that addresses strategic issues and long-term trends within an organization and in its external environment. Serves the decision-making needs of senior management.

Strategic transition Changes affecting both technical and social elements in an organization that entail movement from one level of a sociotechnical system to another.

Structured analysis A popular methodology for graphically modeling the flow of data throughout a system, illustrating the inputs, processes, and outputs of a system at different levels of abstraction. The primary tool of Structural Analysis is the Data Flow Diagram.

Structured decision Type of decision that is repetitive, routine, and involves a definite procedure that can be used each time the same decision problem is encountered.

Structured decision Type of decision that is repetitive, routine, and involves designed from the top down and in hierarchical fashion and refined to successive levels of detail. Also referred to as top-down design.

Structural programming A discipline for writing program code that insists on the use of three basic control structures and modules that have only one entry point and one exit point.

System design The blueprint of an information system showing the hardware, software, and procedural configurations for meeting information requirements. Whereas systems analysis determines *what* has to be done, systems design shows *how*.

System flowchart A general overall diagram that shows the data flow and operational sequence of a system.

Systems life cycle The traditional method for building an information system and still the principal methodology for large projects. The systems development process is partitioned into formal stages, each of which must be performed before subsequent stages. The methodology has been criticized for being too time consuming, expensive, and resistant to changes that naturally occur as a system is being implemented.

System software Special software to manage computer resources, such as processing time, storage, printers, and communications links.

Systems analysis A detailed step-by-step investigation of an organization and its systems for the purpose of determining what must be done in relation to information systems and the best way to do it.

Systems analyst Information system specialist responsible for the analysis and design of an information system and for eliciting information requirements from end-users.

System programmer A programmer who specializes in writing system software.

System testing Testing of the functioning of an information system as a whole, making sure program modules work together as planned.

Tangible benefit A benefit that is directly quantifiable, such as lower computer operating costs.

Telecommunications The movement of data and information from 1 point to another by means of electrical or optical transmission systems.

Transaction file A file containing relatively transient information, such as individual sales transactions occuring during one day.

Transaction processing system (TPS) These systems automate clerical and operational functions and track data at the most elementary level in the organization. An example of a TPS would be an order entry system that records orders for a specific product.

Unit testing Testing of individual program modules. Also called program testing.

Unstructured decision One in which the decision maker must provide judgment, evaluation, and insight because the decision problem is novel, nonroutine, and has no agreed-upon procedure for solving it.

Uploading Transferring data that has been stored and/or manipulated on a microcomputer back to a main corporate file that is stored on a mainframe or minicomputer.

Value-added network Telecommunications system that "adds value" to the common carrier's network services by adding computer control of communications.

Value chain model Model of the firm that can be used to identify opportunities for strategic information systems. Sees nine interconnected activities that add value to inputs. Information technology can help the firm add value, thereby enhancing profits, especially in activities concerning the firm and its suppliers and customers.

Company Index

Name Index

Subject Index

general, 63
history, 62–64
interpretation, 19–20
nonsystematic, 18
as resource, 235
strategic resource, 64
time decay, 20
understanding, 19–20
Information architecture, defined, 15
Information center, 95, 327, 482–486
defined, 482
example, 483–484
function, 482–483
hardware, 483
role, 485–486
software, 483
Information engineering, 651–654
Information Engineering Workbench, 342
Information for Motivation Reporting System, 74
Information management
decentralized, 642
policy, 645
Information Management Services, 667–668
Information Management System, 242, 248
Information policy
data administration, 647–648
defined, 648
Information processing
batch processing, 219, 220
immediate processing, 219–220
traditional approach, 236–240
types, 219–221
Information Quality Analysis, 433
Information resources
controlling, 654–656
directory, 660
manager, 407
Information resources management, 64
Information service, delivery methods, 98
Information services department, 485
Information specialist
external, 99
internal, 99
Information storage, 30–31
Information system, 4–24
abuse, 577–580
ad hoc, 130
application controls, 580, 586–591

auditing, 593–597
basic operations, 5
behavioral approach, 16–17
changing, 11–13, 20–21
changing technology, 21
characteristics, 34
competitive advantages, 75
complexity, 616–617
contemporary approaches, 15–17
controls, 570–597, 580–593
auditing role, 593–594
benefits, 591–593
costs, 591–593
weaknesses, 594
cost, 607
cost/benefit analysis, 679–682
data, 607
defined, 5
design, 605–607
development cost, 21
estimation, 687
evaluation, 679–686
failure, causes, 610–620
features, 28
formal, 5, 129
formal organizational unit, 99
as change agent, 99
size, 100
functional specialty, 9
general controls, 580–586
hierarchy, 6, 7
high expectations, 21
history, 11–13, 94–95
informal, 5
management support, 616
man-month, 687
measuring success, 608–610
operation, 608
operational-level, 7
organizational characteristics, 94–95
organizational, 5
organizational model, 684–685
organizational topology, 97
personnel positions, 694, 695
plan, 685–686
planning, 675–676
politics, 106–107
poor management factors, 686–688
portfolio analysis, 682–688
problem areas, 605–608
project management, 686–690
reasons for using, 102–103
environmental factors, 103
institutional factors, 103
risk, 616–617

scoring model, 683–684
selection, 679–686
slippage reporting, 687–688
sociotechnical systems perspective, 17, 18
status meeting, 688
strategic implications, 75–77
strategic level, 37
strategic plan, 675
strategic role, 64, 674
success
causes, 610–620
measurement, 608–610
symbols, 30
technical approach, 16
technical quality, 376–377
types, 6–8, 33, 37
vs. computers, 6
vulnerability, 570–577
new, 572–575
reasons for, 570–572
work quality, 107
work redistribution, 107
Information systems department, 99
Information systems manager, 123
Information technology
assimilation stages, 695
changing nature, 13
manager's role, 79–80
new applications, 13–14
organizational change agent, 62
INFORUM teleconference system, 45
INGRES, 252
Inheritance, 545
Initial Attack Management System, 51
In-line sequencing, 152, 153
advantages, 153
defined, 153
Innovation
actors, 610–611
implementation, 610–611
Input, 393
Input authorization, 587–588
Input control, 587–589
Input device, 161, 191–197
Installation
package, 455
systems development, 397–400
Institutional change. See Organizational change
Insurance, 267–268, 332, 630
prototyping, 444
Intangible benefit, 722
Integrated circuit, 170–171, 178
Integrated information model, 653

Integrated services digital network, 43
Integrated system, 4
Integration, 37–38
  software, 230–231
Integration contractor, 73
Intelligence, decision making, 132–133
Interactive data entry, 193–194
  advantages, 194
  disadvantages, 194
Interactive Financial Planning System, 8, 506
Interfacing, software, 230–231
Inference engine, 721
Interlisp, 550
Internal integration tool, 620–622
Interpreter, 221
Introspect, 701
Inventory control, 68, 69
  strategic, 74
Inverted file, 241, 242
Investment decision, 497–499
Invoice computation, 456
Iteration structure, 350

Job design, 692–693
Job satisfaction, 690
Join, 253
Josephson junction, 198
Journal of Management Information Systems, 16
Just-in-time delivery system, 69, 70–71
Just-in-time scheduling, 151, 152, 153

Kayak, 701
KEE, 550
Key indicator, 438
Key indicator approach, 428
Key-to-disk data entry, 192, 193
Key-to-tape data entry, 192, 193
Kilobyte, defined, 163
KL-Two, 550
Knowledge base, 543–544
Knowledge engineer, 14
Knowledge engineering tool, efficiency, 554, 555
Knowledge transfer, 533

Language. *See* Specific type
LANLink, 306

Laptop computer, 314
  portable, 195–196
Large-scale integrated chip, 178
Laser storage, 190
Layered documentation, 407
Leadership, organization, 89–90
Lightyear, 506, 551–552
Line printer, 196
Linkware: Information Server, 312
Lisa, 316
Local area network (LAN), 149, 282–283
  benefits, 283
  criteria, 283
  hardware, 283
  vs. PBX, 282–283
Local network, 275
Logic Theorist, 530
Logical application group, 432
Logical database, 651
Logical design, 392
Logical office, 313–314
Logician, 550
Long-haul network, 275, 283
Lotus, 210
Lotus 1-2-3, 305, 306, 330
Lotus spread sheet, 506

M.1 551–553
3-M machine, 550
Machine, 550
Machine language, 208–209
Magnetic core memory, 170–174, 175
Magnetic disk, 186–188
  advantages, 189
  disadvantages, 189
Magnetic tape, 184–186
  advantages, 185
  disadvantages, 185
Magneto-optic disk, 191
Mail, electronic, 9, 319
Mail system, electronic, 34
Mainframe computer, 13
  defined, 180
  evolution, 180–183
  microcomputer, 311–313, 316–317
  software, 212–213
Maintenance
  cost, 418–420
  expert system, 558
  package, 455
  Social Security Administration, 706
Maintenance programmer, 101

Management
  behavioral model, 121–123
  centralized, 152
  classical model, 120–121
  end-user systems development, 486–489
  implementation, 617–618, 620–625
  microcomputer, 321–326
  Social Security Administration, 709–710
  systems design, 128–130
  systems development, 377–378
  telecommunications, 291–294
  turnover, 708
Management control, 131
Management control system, strategic, 74
Management information system, 8, 16, 28, 35–36, 491–492
  centralized, 153
  characteristics, 47
  coordinating, 45
  decentralized multisystem, 334
  decision support system, 502–503
  history, 63
  integrated, 37–38, 72–73
  policy/planning, 45
  role, 45–46
  Social Security Administration, 707
  strategic business unit, 45, 46, 48
  strategic internal, 72–75
  total systems view, 37–38
  user interaction, 49
  vs. decision support system, 504–505
  vs. microcomputing, 504–505
Management information systems department, 99
Management level system, 8
Management science, 16
Management services group, 99
Manager, 100
  activity characterization, 121–123
  ad hoc information system, 130
  communication, 122
  critical success factor, 433–436
  decision making, 127–128
  decision support system, 508–509
  formal information system, 129
  functions, 120–121
  future, 126–127
  network building, 125
  personal agenda, 125
  personal support, 55
  policy making, 127–128

RISC computer, 203
Risk, 139
Risk, defined, 416
Risk assessment, 592–593
Risk level, 592
Robotics, 530, 538
Role ambiguity, 692–693
Role conflict, 692
ROMC, 512
Root, 248, 250
Rosie, 550
Rule base, 543–544
Run control total, 589

S.1, 550
SABRE system, 71–72, 81–82
Sacon, 548
Sales order entry, 33
Sales-Use Tax package, 456
SAS, 475
Satellite
   technology, 278, 279
   telecommunications, 297
   transmission, 285
Scoring model, 683–684
SDM/Structured, 368
Secondary storage, 183–190
   floppy disk, 187–188
   hard disk, 186–188
   magnetic disk, 186–188
   magnetic tape, 184–186
   types, 184
   vs. primary, 184
Secondary storage device, 161, 170
Security, 240, 569, 575, 577
   data, 655–656
   data dictionary, 661–662
   defined, 577
   fourth-generation language, 482
   microcomputer, 322, 324–325
   policy, 586–587
   procedure, 586–587
   supervision, 587
Security profile, 585, 586
Segment, 248
Segregation of function, 585–587
Select, 253
Selection construct, 362
Semi-Automated Business Research
      Environment, 81–82
Semiconductor, 178
Semiconductor memory, 170–171
   erasable programmable read-only
      memory, 174
   programmable read-only
      memory, 174

read-only memory, 174
   types, 174
Senior technology scientist, 694
Sequence construct, 360, 361
Sequence structure, 349–350
Service bureau, 423
Shipment tracking system, 470
SideKick, 306
Sidney, 197
Signal
   analog, 276, 277
   digital, 276, 277
Silicon chip, 171, 173, 178
Slot, 545
SMP/Macsyma, 550
Social Security Administration,
      704–715
   database, 706–707
   external environment, 707–708
   hardware, 706
   history, 704–710
   institutional factors, 708
   maintenance, 706
   management
      changes, 712
      chaos, 709–710
      weaknesses, 708
   management information system,
      707
   Office of Advanced Systems,
      708–709
   partitioning, 709
   planning, 709
   program pressures, 707–708
   reform efforts, 708
   reorganization, 708
   software, 705–706
   telecommunications, 706
Social Security Administration
      Data Acquisition and
      Response System, 706
Sociology, 16
Sociotechnical system, 375–377
Software, 6, 101
   anti-ballistic missile defense, 212
   appropriateness, 224
   artificial intelligence, 534
   changing nature, 13
   cost, ideal vs. real, 403
   ease of use, 102
   efficiency, 225–226
   end-user applications, 473–475
   end-user data access, 211–212
   evaluation, 206
   fourth generation, history, 210
   functions, 206
   generations, 208–210

information center, 483
integrated development tools,
      402
integration, 230–231
interfacing, 230–231
mainframe, 212–213
maintenance, 70
major trends, 210–212
manual development techniques,
      402
microcomputer, 304–306
organizational considerations, 224
overview, 207
recentralization, 335
selection, 224–226
Social Security Administration,
      705–706
sophistication, 224
space defense, 212
Star Wars, 212
support, 224–225
types, 207–208
user interface, 210–211
Software control, 583
Software engineering, 437
Software Engineering Program,
      711, 713–714
Software package. See Package
Source code, 221
Space defense, software, 212
Specialization, 88
Sperry Corporation 9080 computer,
      466
Sperry Univac software system, 470
Spread sheet, 319, 549
SPSS. See Statistical Package for
      the Social Sciences
Standing data, 592
Star Wars, software, 212
Statistical Package for the Social
      Sciences, 210
Statistical program, 214
Status meeting, 688
Steamer, 547
Storage technology, future trends,
      200
Strategem, 335
Strategic analysis, 433–436
Strategic business unit system, 45,
      46, 48
Strategic data planning, 648
Strategic decision making, 130–131
Strategic information system, 61,
      693
   change resistance, 79
   common industry practice, 77, 78
   competitive advantage, 75–77

benefits, 288
cost, 288
Vector processing, 199–200
Vehicle registration system, 389
Very large integrated circuit, 170–171
Very-high-level language, 178, 208, 226–227, 474, 491
advantages, 226–227
types, 227
Very-high-speed integrated circuit, 198
Very-large-scale integrated chip, 178
Vice president of information, 260
Video display terminal, 196
Video teleconferencing, 45
Virtual storage, 217–218
advantages, 218
page, 217–218

Virtual table, 254
Virtual Telecommunications Access Method (VTAM), 231
VisiCalc, 305, 507
Visual system, 538
Visual table of contents, 363, 364
VM, 548
Voice recognition software, 211
Voice recognition system, 195
Voice simulation, 530
Voice wire, 278
von Neuman computer, 539
Voyage estimating, 51–53

Wang VS 80 minicomputer, 334
Weld Scheduler, 546–547
Who and Referral System, 149
Wide area network (WAN), 275, 276

Wide area telephone service (WATS) line, 284
Wisard, 539
Wizard system, 72
Word processing, 34, 319
Word processing pool, 107–108
Word processing technician, 108
Work
computer systems, 109
quality, 107
redistribution, 107
social character, 107
Work group, 92, 94
types, 94
Write once, read many (WORM), 200

XCON, 547